Clothing through American History

Clothing through American History

THE BRITISH COLONIAL ERA

Kathleen A. Staples and Madelyn Shaw

 GREENWOOD

AN IMPRINT OF ABC-CLIO, LLC
Santa Barbara, California • Denver, Colorado • Oxford, England

Library of Congress Cataloging-in-Publication Data

Staples, Kathleen A.
 Clothing through American history : the British colonial era / Kathleen A. Staples and Madelyn Shaw.
     pages cm
 Includes bibliographical references and index.
   ISBN 978-0-313-33593-8 (hardcopy : alk. paper) — ISBN 978-0-313-08460-7 (ebook) 1. Clothing and dress—United States—History. 2. Clothing and dress—Social aspects—United States—History. 3. United States—Social life and customs—To 1775. 4. United States—Social conditions—To 1865. I. Shaw, Madelyn. II. Title.
   GT607.S78 2013
   391.00973—dc23   2013000307

ISBN: 978-0-313-33593-8
EISBN: 978-0-313-08460-7

17 16 15 14 13   1 2 3 4 5

This book is also available on the World Wide Web as an eBook.
Visit www.abc-clio.com for details.

Greenwood
An Imprint of ABC-CLIO, LLC

ABC-CLIO, LLC
130 Cremona Drive, P.O. Box 1911
Santa Barbara, California 93116-1911

This book is printed on acid-free paper ∞

Manufactured in the United States of America

Contents

Preface

Between the founding in 1607 of the first permanent settlement in British North America, in Jamestown, and the end of the American Revolution, in 1785, about 430,000 English, more than 260,000 Africans, 145,000 Scots, 100,000 Germans, and countless thousands of other continental Europeans had emigrated—forcibly or of their own free will—to settle in Britain's 13 colonies. By 1775, immigration and natural increase had expanded the population of these nonindigenous inhabitants to 2.5 million. In the process of colonization, European and African immigrants encountered Native People, whose numbers had already deeply declined due to diseases introduced by Spanish explorers in the late 15th and 16th centuries. The population of Native Americans continued to diminish throughout this period as those of the colonists swelled.

Regardless of the ethnic, racial, and/or economic status of the inhabitants of colonial America—and although legal and logistical challenges influenced the choices these people made about what they wore—fashion in dress was one of the primary agents that fueled colonial economies and ultimately helped shape the colonists' shared experience as consumers prior to the Revolutionary War. As fashion, dress was, to paraphrase one scholar, "socially digested" to some extent by all levels of colonial society, whether free or enslaved, indigenous or immigrant (Cumming 1984, 12–16). This volume, *Clothing through American History: The British Colonial Era*, explores the increasing importance of dress in the colonial setting in the contexts of settlement patterns, social pressures and preferences, fashion technology, the clothing trades, and the change of fashion through time.

Colonial North America was a colorful place. Not everyone dressed in sober colors or subdued patterns. Although portraits of the well-to-do often depict men in browns, blacks, and greens and the women in blue or brown satin or gold, brown, green, or ivory damask, in reality all social and economic ranks wore a range of colors and patterns.

Unlike probate inventories and merchants' advertisements, which do not necessarily need to describe clothing items by color or pattern, notices for stolen or lost goods usually do, as color and pattern could identify an item for recovery. In 1740, for example, a woman's light red riding hood and a boy's red great coat were lost in Boston (*Boston News-Letter*, July 31, 1740). A year later a green broadcloth suit—coat, jacket, and breeches—all lined with blue taffeta, a black broadcloth coat and jacket, and a dark cinnamon broadcloth coat were stolen from a Boston house (*Boston News-Letter*, July 9, 1741). In just a handful of lost-and-stolen advertisements from the *Pennsylvania Gazette*, run between 1735 and 1773, the following fabrics were described:

> *chintzes and calicoes:* sky-colored sprigged with red; green flowered with red and white; red and purple spotted; purple and white with bold red flowers; white with a black pattern like the ace of spades; black with white spots; white with a flower pattern "like a strawberry leaf and butterfly."
>
> *silks:* striped; flowered striped; yellow and white shot; blue and white shot; chestnut colored; light blue; red, yellow, and white striped.
>
> *linens:* red striped; purple striped; yellow striped; yellow and blue striped.

The cost of a fabric did not dictate how richly colored or patterned it would be. The upper ranks may have sported attire fashioned from luxury fabrics like brocaded silks and flowered chintzes, but the indentured and the enslaved got themselves noticed as well. A sampling of women's clothing from runaway advertisements documents red petticoats, cloaks, and shoes; striped gowns; a red gown with white spots; a brown and yellow gown with a blue petticoat; and a blue worsted damask striped petticoat. Men's jackets and waistcoats were black and white, "mingled" red, yellow, or green striped; and cinnamon, brown, blue, yellow, white, red, claret, and olive colored. Their coats could be colored pale or deep blue, cinnamon, reddish-brown, white and reddish, black and white, orange, yellowish, or pink. Breeches as well could be black and white, blue and white, or ticking striped, and colored red or blue.

In the colonial period it is perhaps a misnomer to talk about fashion as an industry. Clothing was not constructed in large factories, and the mechanisms of labor specialization, mass production, and distribution of goods that mark the Industrial Revolution were yet to be developed and perfected. Yet in Britain the manufacture of worsted and woolen fabrics for dress as well as the trades that produced ready-made clothing and the accessories of dress were of great commercial importance to the country. The products of these manufactures joined silks woven in France and Italy; innumerable types of linen fabrics produced in the Netherlands and what is now Germany; and plain, printed, painted, and embroidered cottons from India as imports to Britain's colonies in North America. At various times throughout this period the colonists engaged themselves in weaving cloth for clothing and engaged the indigenous populations in trade for furs and skins.

Clothing was not socially neutral, however. What people wore was influenced by many more factors other than their cultural and religious backgrounds and the kinds of fabrics that were available to them. Dress was an immediate form of communication used to convey information about social, economic, and legal status; ethnicity; and religious affiliation. Society was stratified and hierarchical: appearance, including dress, was an outward and visible sign of a person's place in that society. And appearance was expected to be supported by behaviors, activities, occupations, environments, education, carriage, and manners appropriate to status.

RESEARCHING THIS VOLUME

Finding sources for the study of dress practices in colonial America is challenging. Relatively few pieces of clothing with clear colonial provenance survive, and most extant examples were owned and worn by the economically privileged. Since clothing and cloth were expensive, reuse of old-fashioned but expensive fabrics and recycling of worn out garments to outfit smaller family members or servants were common; linen and cotton rags eventually found their way into paper manufactories. Conservative consumers or those whose primary need was durable clothing often chose not to keep up with the mode, and the poorer classes who could not afford to do so also maintained older styles. The old and the new usually overlapped for many years—countless probate inventories include at least a few pieces of clothing described as "old." Thus, dating clothing is an inexact art.

Pictorial evidence in the form of portraits, prints, and fashion plates is valuable because often the apparel and fashion accoutrements of a sitter are more accurately depicted than his or her visage. Portraits are not without bias, however, because they might, in fact, record the choice of dressed "self" that the sitter wished to present to the viewer rather than what the sitter actually owned and wore. In many instances, especially in women's portraiture of the 18th century, the clothing is not only not authentically the sitter's, but is also often invented or imagined.

Documentary evidence is also uneven. Typically, comments about clothing are scattered throughout writings whose subject matter concerns something other than dress. And because everyone wore clothing, few thought to comment on the subject in a sustained way. Members of the elite and well-to-do artisans and professionals have left us traces of how they viewed attire in diaries and journals, letters, and in their wills and probate inventories. It is more difficult to retrieve this information for the non- or partially literate—unskilled workers, the enslaved, Native Americans, and the poor. Written evidence is often incomplete as well. Probate inventories, for example, may not include garments given away to relatives and friends just before the owner's death. However, newspaper advertisements, sumptuary legislation, comments left by observers, and court records provide glimpses into this stratum of society.

WHAT IS INCLUDED

We have included in this volume a considerable amount of information on not only the clothing trades, but also the trades, terminology, and techniques related to the textiles and other materials used to construct clothing. This was a deliberate choice. Today most of us are far removed from the basics of how the clothes we wear are produced. In preindustrial times this was not the case. Cloth and clothing took far more time to make and consumed a far larger proportion of the wearer's available income than they do today, and many people below the most elite levels of society were involved intimately in some aspect of clothing production. So the finished goods were valued very differently than they are today. It is essential to understand this with regard to British colonial dress and fashion, the two of which are not necessarily the same thing.

In addition, we have tried to convey the complexity of trade and commerce with regard to textiles and clothing. Textiles linked the Baltic region, Britain, France, Italy, the Middle East, India, and China with Britain's North American colonies; economic or political upheaval in one region affected its partners in commerce. The global economy may have moved more slowly before the era of instant communications, but it did exist.

Clothing and textiles touch all of us and inform us in so many areas of study: agriculture, industry, commerce, human behavior, the environment, and politics. The colonial period is an especially rich and fruitful era for the study of dress; one can follow the evolution of a society from its initial contacts with indigenous communities to political independence and economic uncertainty, and to the eve of the Industrial Revolution. Accordingly, Chapter 1 introduces the settling of British North America between 1607 and 1785 and the makeup of the region's inhabitants. Chapter 2 provides an overview of the social and cultural uses of dress and fashion by the elite, middling sorts, servants, and the enslaved. Because the production of clothing was an essential component of trade on both sides of the Atlantic, we have devoted Chapter 3 to discussions of the raw materials of textiles, their processing, home production and imports, and the extensive kinds of textile trades. Chapters 4, 5, and 6 comprise surveys of men's, women's, and children's attire, respectively, and include sample wardrobes over time and across social, economic, and racial boundaries. Chapter 4, "Women's Fashion," and Chapter 5, "Men's Clothing," are divided into two eras, roughly corresponding to the nearly two centuries of American British colonial life: the early colonial period of 1608–1714, and the later period of 1715–1785.

Following Chapter 6 is a glossary that gives brief definitions of terms related to clothing, textiles, and fashion, many of which present-day readers may be unfamiliar. More than 200 words and phrases, ranging from *alamode*, a type of silk used for scarves and mourning clothes, to *wrapper*, a type of woman's gown, tied with a sash, are explained. After the glossary is a list of selected, recommended print resources and a descriptive list of museums, their locations, and websites. A comprehensive index concludes the volume.

Investigations of military dress and clerical garb are outside the scope of this study.

A NOTE ON LANGUAGE

Language can be a thorny issue when using primary sources. In order to preserve their original tone, all quotes from primary sources retain their archaic spellings, capitalization and punctuation, and use of italics. In this volume, the word "negro," whose use is an anathema today, is present only in period quotations; these describe either an enslaved runaway or an individual who is to be sold or describe fabrics and clothing for slaves. In the colonial period Native people did not have a single term for themselves. Today many Natives accept the terms "Indian," "American Indian," or "Native People." Despite questions about the possible political correctness of these words, all are used interchangeably in the text.

REFERENCE

Cumming, Valerie. 1984. *A Visual History of Costume: The Seventeenth Century.* London: B. T. Batsford.

Chronology, 1585–1785

1585	English colonists (91 men, 17 women, and 10 children), led by Sir Richard Grenville, attempt to establish the first English settlement, Roanoke Colony, in present-day North Carolina. The settlement is known as the "Lost Colony" because the fate of the colonists has never been determined.
1589	William Lee invents the knitting frame in England but is refused a patent by Elizabeth I, who fears the effects on England's hand-knitting industry. The machine is finally in use by 1663 when the London Company of Framework Knitters is granted a charter.
1600	The English East India Company is granted a charter and pursues trade with India mainly in cotton, silk, indigo, salt, tea, and opium.
1602	The Dutch East India Company is established to carry out colonial activities in Asia, including trade, the ability to wage war, negotiate treaties, and coin money.
1603	Elizabeth I (1533–1603; House of Tudor) dies.
	James I (1566–1625; House of Stuart) ascends the English throne and rules until his death.
1604	The English Parliament nullifies all penal laws concerning apparel.
1607	Supported by the London Company, 104 male settlers arrive at a site they name James Cittie (later Jamestown, Virginia), the first permanent English settlement in the New World. They build a fortification called James Fort.
1608	The first two women arrive at Jamestown.

1609   From September to May 1610, the "starving time" in James-
            town reduces the population from 500–600 to 60 wasted
            survivors.

            English explorer Henry Hudson, sponsored by the Dutch
            East India Company, explores the Delaware Bay and Hudson
            River, laying the foundation for colonization of the region by
            the Dutch and Swedes as New Netherland and New Sweden.

            Tea from China is shipped for the first time to Europe by the
            Dutch East India Company.

1611   The Authorized Version, or the King James Version, an En-
            glish translation of the Christian Bible from Hebrew, Greek,
            and Latin sources, is published. James I conceived of the proj-
            ect in 1604, in response to problems in earlier translations as
            perceived by the Puritan faction in the Church of England.

1612   John Rolfe plants orinoco tobacco (*Nicotiana tabacum*) as a com-
            mercial crop in Virginia. By 1616 it is a staple export commod-
            ity from the colony.

1614   Pocohantas (born Matoaka), a daughter of Chief Powhatan,
            marries John Rolfe.

            John Smith sails up the Atlantic coast to what is now Cape Cod
            and Penobscot Bay, mapping the coastline and giving English
            place names to native settlements.

1616   John Smith's *A Description of New England* is published, con-
            taining his map of New England, the first realistic treatment
            of the region by an Englishman.

            New England's Indian population is significantly reduced by
            a smallpox epidemic.

1618   The beginning of the Thirty Years' War (ends 1648), which
            eventually involves most European countries. One of the
            longest and most destructive conflicts—in population as well
            as land and property—in European history, the war is fought
            over religious conflicts, internal politics, and the balance of
            power among rival rulers.

1619   A Virginia census records the presence of 32 Africans. Twenty
            Africans are purchased from a passing Portuguese slave ship.

            The Virginia Assembly enacts sumptuary laws to regulate
            dress; an amendment is passed in 1621.

Ninety young women are transported to Virginia to make wives for former tenants; the Virginia Company prices them each at 150 pounds of "best leafe Tobacco."

1620 Led by Miles Standish and financed by the Merchant Adventurers, 101 English colonists sail from Plymouth, England, in the *Mayflower*; they land and establish Plymouth Colony.

James I charges the Virginia Company to establish silk works in the colony.

1622 Indian attacks by warriors of the Powhatan Confederacy kill a quarter of English settlers in Jamestown, then the capital of the Virginia colony, and set off a war that lasts a decade.

1623 The Dutch organize New Netherlands (now part of the mid-Atlantic states of New York, New Jersey, Delaware, and Connecticut, with small settlements in Pennsylvania and Rhode Island) as a province.

1624 English settlers establish a fishing village at Cape Ann (near present-day Gloucester), Massachusetts. Financial support from England is withdrawn and the site is abandoned about two years later.

1625 Charles I (1600–1649; House of Stuart) ascends the English throne and rules until his death, by beheading.

New Amsterdam, at the southern tip of the island of Manhattan, is established as the capital of New Netherland.

1626 The Dutch West India Company purchases the entire island of Manhattan from the Lenape Indians for 60 guilders.

1628 One hundred new Puritan settlers, led by John Endecott, join others already in Massachusetts to establish the Massachusetts Bay Colony.

1629 The Province of New Hampshire is established; it comes under the government of the Massachusetts Bay Colony in 1641.

The first tannery in the colonies begins operation in Lynn, Massachusetts.

1630 John Winthrop, English Puritan leader, founds Boston.

1631 Dutch West India Company establishes a settlement at the Delaware River.

1632 Charles I issues a charter for the colony of Maryland, named to honor his wife, Queen Henrietta Maria. It is a haven for

English Catholics although Anglicans, Puritans, and Quakers also settle.

1634   Massachusetts Bay Colony issues sumptuary legislation regulating dress; additional laws are enacted in 1636, 1639, 1651, 1652, and 1662.

1635   Saybrook Colony is founded in what is now part of Connecticut.

1636   Connecticut Colony (originally known as the River Colony) is organized as a haven for Puritans, who settle first in present-day Hartford.

Roger Williams is banished from Massachusetts for religious dissension and establishes Providence Plantations, a colony in the area now known as Providence, Rhode Island.

1637   New Haven Colony is established in what is today part of Connecticut, New Jersey, and Philadelphia.

1638   The first Swedish colonists settle in Delaware.

The first printing press is established in the colonies, in Cambridge, Massachusetts Bay Colony.

1641   Massachusetts becomes the first colony to recognize the legal status of slavery.

1642   The First English Civil War begins (ends in 1646).

1643   A fulling mill, the first such documented in the American colonies, is constructed in Rowley, Massachusetts.

1644   Saybrook Colony merges with Connecticut Colony.

The settlements of Providence, Portsmouth, and Newport unite to create the Colony of Rhode Island and Providence Plantations.

1648   Beginning of the Second English Civil War (ends in 1649).

Massachusetts Bay Colony orders that damages be awarded to owners of sheep that have been injured or killed by dogs.

The Massachusetts General Court allows the creation of a shoemakers' guild in Boston.

1649   Charles I is beheaded (January 29); England is declared a Commonwealth.

Oliver Cromwell (1599–1658) begins ruling England as head of state, then as Lord Protector in 1653, and rules until his death.

1650	The population of colonial America is about 50,000.
1651	Parliament adopts the First Navigation Act, which stipulates that trade with the colonies is to be conducted in only English or colonial ships; subsequent acts are passed in 1662, 1663, 1670, and 1672. These acts prohibit direct colonial trade with the Netherlands, France, and other European countries.
1652	Maine is joined to Massachusetts Bay Colony.
1655	Sephardi Jews establish a congregation in New Amsterdam (present-day New York City).
1658	Richard Cromwell (1626–1712), son of Oliver Cromwell, rules England as Lord Protector until 1660.
1660	Restoration of the monarchy: Charles II (1630–1685; House of Stuart) ascends the English throne and rules until his death.
1662	Colony of New Haven is annexed to Connecticut.
1663	Birth of Cotton Mather, Puritan minister who preaches against the wearing of fashionable dress, especially for women.
	Carolina Colony is established, covering much of present-day North and South Carolina and Georgia.
1664	The Dutch surrender New Netherland to the English; part of the area is established as New York Colony and part as New Jersey Colony.
1665	The Great Plague kills an estimated 100,000 people, or about 20 percent of London's population.
	New Haven Colony merges with Connecticut Colony.
1666	Great Fire of London.
1672	Charter of the Royal African Company in Britain for the purpose of trading in slaves. Between 1672 and 1689 the company transports an estimated 90,000 Africans as slaves.
1673	Parliament's Test Act excludes Roman Catholics and Dissenters from office in England.
1674	New Jersey Colony is divided into two political divisions: East and West.
1675	King Philip's War (ends 1678), the bloodiest conflict in colonial American history, fought between Indians and whites in the Connecticut River Valley, the Plymouth Colony, and Rhode Island.

1676	The Connecticut Court passes the colony's first sumptuary legislation and legislates the prices for locally made shoes.
	English dyers begin to experiment with block printing and mordant dyeing.
1677	William III of Orange marries Princess Mary, daughter of James II.
1680	New Hampshire separates from Massachusetts and becomes a colony.
1682	Given a land grant from Charles II, William Penn founds Pennsylvania as a refuge for Quakers; Penn then establishes Philadelphia.
	The Maryland General Assembly offers premiums for the home production of linen and woolen cloth.
1684	Immigrants from Krefeld, Germany, who settled in Germantown, Pennsylvania, begin to produce linen for sale in Philadelphia.
1685	James II (1633–1701; House of Stuart) ascends the English throne and rules until he is deposed, in 1688.
	James II decrees that Maine, New Hampshire, Massachusetts Bay Colony, Plymouth Colony, Rhode Island, Connecticut, Province of New York, East Jersey, and West Jersey are to be consolidated into one colony to be called the Dominion of New England.
	France's Louis XIV revokes the Edict of Nantes (1598), under which Henry IV had guaranteed religious freedom to French Protestants (Huguenots). A large number of Huguenots, many of whom are skilled in the textile trades, leave France for England.
1688	The Glorious Revolution leads to the overthrow of James II, who exiles himself in France. This sets the stage for the Jacobite rebellions of 1715 and 1745, which encourage subsequent migrations of large numbers of Scots to the colonies.
1689	William III (1650–1702) and Mary II (1662–1694; House of Stuart) ascend the English throne as king and queen; William rules until his death.
	The Dominion of New England is discontinued and the nine former colonies reestablish their separate political and geographic identities.

King William's War begins (ends 1697) between England and France. The fighting affects frontier settlements in the colonial northeast, where French Canadian colonies and their Indian allies are close to British settlements.

1690   Charleston, South Carolina, is the fifth largest city in the American colonies.

1691   Plymouth Colony and Massachusetts Bay Colony merge to form the Province of Massachusetts Bay.

1692   Witchcraft trials in Salem, Massachusetts; 19 people formally tried and hung as witches, one man pressed to death, and two accused die in prison.

1699   Williamsburg becomes the capitol of the Virginia colony.

Parliament passes the Wool Act, which forbids the export of wool, woolen yarn, or woolen cloth outside the colony in which it is produced.

1700   Population of colonial America is about 250,000. Boston, the largest city, has about 7,000 residents.

1702   Anne (1665–1714; House of Stuart) ascends the English throne and rules as Queen of England until 1707. In that year she begins her rule as Queen of Great Britain and continues until her death.

Queen Anne's War begins (ends 1713). England and her colonies fight the French and Spanish and their American Indian allies.

The colonies of East and West Jersey are united as New Jersey Colony.

1703   Birth of Methodist preacher John Wesley (d. 1791), whose sermons support the rights of the privileged to wear fine clothing but caution those of the middle and lower ranks.

1704   The first colonial newspaper, the *Boston News-Letter*, begins publication.

1707   Charleston merchants export 121,335 deerskins to England.

Parliament passes the Acts of Union, joining the Kingdom of England and the Kingdom of Scotland into a single Kingdom of Great Britain.

1710   The Act of Queen Anne, effective in 1711, establishes general post offices in the American colonies.

1712	Carolina Colony is divided into North and South Carolina. Both become royal colonies in 1729.
1714	George I (1660–1727; House of Hanover) ascends the British throne and rules until his death.
1715	Yamasee War begins (ends 1717). British settlers in South Carolina fight with warriors from over 14 Native Nations in one of the most disruptive conflicts of colonial America.
1718	Parliament passes a measure prohibiting the emigration of artisans or manufacturers to the colonies.
1721	Massachusetts passes sumptuary legislation to regulate apparel for funerals; a second law is passed in 1742. These laws are renewed in 1750 and 1760.
	Boston holds its first public spinning demonstration, on the city's common.
1722	Scots-Irish settlers in Londonderry, New Hampshire, begin selling locally made linen.
1727	George II (1683–1760; House of Hanover) ascends the British throne and rules until his death.
1729	In Philadelphia, Benjamin Franklin begins publishing the *Pennsylvania Gazette*.
1732	Parliament passes the Hat Act to control hat production and to restrict hiring and apprenticeship practices in the American colonies.
	Georgia Colony, named after England's George II, is established, carved out from land in South Carolina. Charter holder, James Oglethorpe, envisions the province as a place of resettlement for debtors and a buffer area against Spanish Florida.
	The *South-Carolina Gazette* begins publication in Charleston.
1733	In England, John Kay invents the flying shuttle, which allows for mechanized weaving at a faster rate.
1735	South Carolina passes sumptuary legislation to regulate the clothing of its enslaved population; a second law is passed in 1740.
1740	King George's War begins (ends 1748), with Spain and France allied against Britain. The war disrupts transatlantic commercial activities in South Carolina.

1741   Moravians establish the settlement of Bethlehem in Pennsylvania.

1750   Parliament passes an act prohibiting the exportation of tools or utensils used in the woolen and silk trades; the law is extended in 1781.

The population of colonial America is about 1,170,000. Philadelphia is the largest city and busiest port in the colonies.

Lynn, Massachusetts, is the colonial center for the production of readymade shoes.

Newport and Bristol, Rhode Island, are the major slave markets in the American colonies.

1751   Seeking to protect British merchants and creditors from being paid in depreciated American colonial currency, Parliament passes the Currency Act, which restricts the issuing and use of colonial paper money. A second act is passed in 1764.

1752   Hibernian Francis Nixon introduces the use of large engraved copper plates for printing textiles at the Drumcondra works, near Dublin. By 1754, the technology is transmitted to England.

1754   The French and Indian War begins (ends 1763), fought primarily between the British American colonies and their Native American allies on one side and French forces in America and their Indian allies on the other. Although Britain is the victor, the war nearly doubles its national debt, and the Crown attempts to pay off this debt by imposing new taxes on the colonies. For many Indian tribes, the victory means loss of lands, dispossession, and increased tribal tensions.

1755   South Carolina exports 500,000 pounds of indigo.

1758   Knitters in Germantown, Pennsylvania, produce 60,000 pairs of linen stockings for resale.

1760   George III (1738–1820; House of Hanover) ascends the British throne; he is the last monarch to rule the American colonies.

Dr. Nathan Aspinwall introduces Mansfield, Connecticut, to sericulture with the distribution of mulberrry cuttings and silk eggs from Long Island. In 1788 a group of Mansfield men form "The Director, Inspectors, and Company of Connecticut Silk Manufacturers."

1761	The Hand-in-Stocking Manufactory begins advertising in Philadelphia.
1764	In England, James Hargreaves invents the spinning jenny, which allows one spinner to supervise several spindles.
	To increase revenue in the aftermath of the French and Indian War, Parliament passes the Sugar Act, which increases import duties on goods such as sugar, textiles, coffee, wine, and indigo dye.
	In reaction to the Sugar Act, Boston merchants organize to boycott imported British luxury goods.
1765	Parliament passes the Stamp Act, the first direct tax on the American colonies. The act requires a stamp on all printed materials, such as newspapers and legal documents, payable to Parliament.
	Organized by the Sons of Liberty and colonial merchants, non-importation associations answer Parliament's Stamp Act and subsequent Townsend Acts in 1767 with agreements to boycott English goods. Because British merchants and manufacturers suffer curtailed trade with the colonies, they pressure Parliament to repeal the legislation. Non-importation agreements continue for ten years as the economic weapon colonists employ to win political rights through peaceful means.
	New York City hosts the first "Market for Home Manufactures" (October 24), which offers domestically produced textiles and clothing.
1766	Parliament repeals the Stamp Act but passes the Declaratory Act, which upholds its right to impose legislation on the colonies. The colonies briefly relax their boycott of British imports.
	In Philadelphia, Daniel Mause establishes the Hand-in-Hand Stocking Manufactory.
1767	Parliament passes a series of laws called the Townsend Acts, which place a tax on common British products; this leads to renewed boycotts of imported goods throughout the colonies.
	Lynn, Massachusetts, shoemakers produce 80,000 pairs of shoes for resale.
1769	In England, Richard Arkwright invents the spinning, or water, frame, a machine that spins cotton yarns strong enough to be used for warp threads for weaving.

Scottish inventor James Watt enhances the power and efficiency of the steam engine, improvements that significantly contribute to the development of the industrial revolution in Britain.

Following the passage of the Townsend Acts, the Daughters of Liberty organize spinning parties and contests to encourage the home production of textiles.

1770   The population of colonial America is over 2,000,000 people.

On March 5, British soldiers stationed in Boston to enforce parliamentary legislation kill five colonists. Amid the tension, a mob begins to harass a group of British soldiers, who fire into the crowd—without orders—killing three instantly and wounding others. Two more die later of their wounds. The incident is referred to as the Boston Massacre.

On April 12, Parliament repeals many of the duties of the Townshend Acts.

1772   On June 9, The HMS *Gaspée*, a British customs schooner, runs aground in Rhode Island's Narragansett Bay while chasing a colonial packet boat, the *Hannah*. Members of the Providence group of the Sons of Liberty board the ship, force its crew ashore, and then burn the vessel to the waterline. The incident is known as the *Gaspée* Affair.

Purrysburg, Georgia, exports 455 pounds of raw silk to England.

1773   On May 10, George III agrees to enact Parliament's Tea Act, the objective of which is to reduce the immense surplus of tea held by the British East India Company by allowing the Company to ship tea directly to North America without paying export duties. The tea tax imposed by the Townshend Acts, however, is to remain in force.

After Boston officials refuse to return three shiploads of taxed tea to Britain, a group of colonists organized by the Sons of Liberty boards the ships and throws the cargoes of tea into the Boston Harbor. Referred to at the time as "the destruction of the tea," in the 19th century the event is renamed the Boston Tea Party.

1774   Parliament passes the Intolerable, or Coercive, Acts in direct response to the Boston Tea Party. These punitive measures close down the port of Boston until the East India Company is repaid for the destroyed tea; bring the Massachusetts government under direct control of the British; allow trials of accused royal officials to move to another colony or to Britain; and allow British troops stationed in the colonies to be billeted in unoccupied buildings.

Called in response to the passage of the Coercive Acts, on September 5, the First Continental Congress convenes in Philadelphia. Attending are 56 delegates, representing all of the colonies but Georgia.

John Hewson establishes the first colonial manufactory for printing fabrics, outside of Philadelphia.

1775   In the early morning of April 19, seven hundred British troops prepare to capture and destroy military supplies in Concord, Massachusetts, and are surprised by colonial militia. In the first opened armed conflict between Great Britain and the colonies, battles ensue on Lexington Green and Concord Bridge. The American Revolutionary War will end in 1783.

On May 10, the Second Continental Congress is convened in Philadelphia to organize the defense of the colonies at the start of the American Revolution. All 13 colonies are represented. George Washington is appointed general and commander-in-chief of the new Continental Army.

On December 23, George III closes all American colonies to foreign trade, effective beginning March 1776.

1776   On January 5, New Hampshire adopts the first state constitution.

On April 6, the Continental Congress declares colonial shipping ports open to all except the British.

On May 4, Rhode Island is the first colony to declare independence from British rule.

On June 15, in anticipation of the Declaration of Independence, the Lower Counties of Delaware declare separation from rule by Pennsylvania and become the colony of Delaware.

On July 4, the Continental Congress adopts a declaration of independence from Great Britain, drafted by Thomas Jefferson, Benjamin Franklin, John Adams, Roger Livingston, and Roger Sherman.

France begins delivering covert economic, military, and tactical aid to America.

1777 The Continental Congress adopts the Articles of Confederation and Perpetual Union, legally establishing the United States of America as a confederation of sovereign states. Ratification by all 13 states is completed in early 1781.

1778 On February 6, France formally recognizes the United States.

1779 In England, Samuel Crompton invents the spinning mule, which spins a fine, even thread suitable for use in the manufacture of muslin.

1781 On October 19, the British, under the command of Lord Cornwallis, surrender at Yorktown, Virginia, after a long siege by the American army under the command of George Washington, and French forces led by the Comte de Rochambeau.

1783 On September 3, the Treaty of Paris is signed by the United States and Great Britain. Congress ratifies the treaty on January 14, 1784.

1784 The *Empress of China*, a three-masted square-rigged sailing ship, is the first American vessel to enter directly into the China trade. Arriving at Canton, China, from New York, the ship returns with a cargo of silks and tea.

1785 New York City serves as the capital of the United States until 1790.

1

Settling British Colonial America

The history of the settlement of British North America is a story of complex transformations—of people, of land, and of institutions. English and European settlers did not suddenly become Americans; nor did they immediately shed their homeland traditions in the face of novel situations. They brought with them the attitudes, values, and norms shaped by their experiences in their home villages, towns, and counties. Not all colonial settlements have been studied in depth; neither are records from some of these places currently easily accessible. So the discussions that follow are selective, based on studies of probate inventories and contemporary commentary as well as the work of other scholars of colonial America.

For the 17th and most of the 18th centuries, it is not possible to talk about colonial English society—only about *societies*. Although they were all linked to England by political, economic, social, and cultural ties and arguably most importantly by imported goods, the settlements of New England and the Chesapeake, and later New York, the mid-Atlantic colonies, Pennsylvania, the Carolinas, and Georgia established distinctly different societies with different economic bases, family patterns, religious affiliations, and ethnic and racial makeups. All social and economic groups were represented, but to differing extents. The least represented group was the aristocracy, but many of the ranks of gentry, merchant, professional, yeoman, and working poor were willing to take a risk to establish themselves in Britain's colonies.

THE PEOPLE

Indigenous Populations

Estimating the size of the populations of indigenous peoples—Native Americans—living in North America before all European contact has been a contentious issue with scholars for close to a century. The classic estimate for this region proposed in 1928 was 1,152,000. In 1983, Henry Dobyns asserted a population size for Indians living north of Mexico of 18 million. Many scholars currently agree on an estimate for the contiguous United States between those two extremes: 4 to 5 million people (Thornton 2005, 23–24). Whatever the precontact size, depopulations began to occur among Native communities almost immediately after European contact although not all Native communities suffered equally. Much of this reduction was due to diseases that Europeans—and later Africans—unintentionally introduced and that Native Americans had never experienced, including small pox, measles, bubonic plague, cholera, typhoid, diphtheria, scarlet fever, influenza, malaria, and yellow fever. For example, the first English settlers in Jamestown met with Algonquian speakers, members of a network of some 30 communities living in eastern Virginia who owed tribute to a paramount chief named Wahunsenacawh, also known as Powhatan. Although the estimated population of the Powhatan confederation was 24,000 in 1607, by 1669, disease and war reduced their numbers to about 2,000. The confederation had all but disappeared by 1715 (Taylor 2001, 136).

Other factors contributed to the Indians' population decline in the colonial period. As European wars spread to America, the British, French, Spanish, and in the 17th century the Dutch wooed various Indian polities as allies. Indian leaders attempted to use these alliances to weaken not only the threatening Europeans but also their Indian competition. These conflicts and other warfare with the colonists killed many and scattered the survivors. The defeated were driven from their lands and deprived of traditional resources. Relocation, dietary change, disruption of traditional social structures, and enslavement—all diminished Native communities' capacities to maintain their cultures and contributed to a decline in fertility and increases in mortality (Thornton 2005, 24). Some groups moved further into the interior; the remnants of many groups joined together to form new communities. Others attempted to hold their lands and coexist with the colonists. The frontier continually adjusted as settlers moved inland into the piedmont and foothills; so too the status of Indian communities constantly changed.

In the colonial period, American Indian communities are best understood as language groups rather than as tribes. The three most populous of these were Anglonquian, Iroquoian, and Siouan speakers. Before European contact, a shared linguistic heritage meant greater ease of communication and often created natural alliances, while linguistic differences could create tensions and hostility. Disputes over land and resources, however, sometimes led to warfare among groups despite their linguistic ties. These complex bonds, coupled with shrinking populations, often strained relationships with the English and Europeans, as the following examples illustrate.

Algonquian speakers inhabited New England and the Ohio Valley and could be found from New York to Virginia (including the Abnaki in Maine and New Hampshire; the Mahican, Narragansett, and Pequot in Rhode Island and Connecticut; and the Massachuset, Wampanoag, Mohegan, and Poktumtuk in Massachusetts). Although some Algonquian communities were friendly toward English settlers, others sided with the French whenever European wars spilled over into North America. But quarrels among Algonquian groups were not uncommon. One of the earliest set the Narragansett and Wampanoag against the Pequot. Hostilities spread from Plymouth down through Rhode Island and eventually grew into the King Philip's War (1675–1676). It ended with the near destruction of all the Indian groups involved, including the nearby—and neutral—Niantic.

The Wappinger, who spoke a form of Algonquian, were a loose confederacy of Native communities spread along the eastern bank of the Hudson River, Manhattan Island, and northward. These groups came into contact with the Dutch in the early 1600s and interacted with them primarily through the fur trade. Their population, which in 1600 was estimated at 3,000, was reduced by half in 1645 when they engaged in a war against the Dutch and Mohawk (Trelease 1997, 5). The Algonquian-speaking Delaware (or Lenni Lenape) lived along the Delaware River Valley. Threatened by the Iroquois to the north and west and pressured by Europeans to the east and south, the Delaware migrated into western Pennsylvania by 1720. By the 1750s, they had left their eastern homeland entirely to settle in Ohio and a generation later in Indiana.

The Iroquois Confederation consisted originally of five polities: Seneca, Cayuga, Onondaga, Oneida, and Mohawk, all of whom were settled in Pennsylvania, western New York, and Canada prior to European settlement along the Atlantic coast. The Tuscarora, Iroquoian speakers from the south, joined the Confederation after losing much of their population and their coastal North Carolina lands in a war (1711–1713) with British, Dutch, and German settlers. This new union became known as the Six Nations Confederacy or *Hau de no sau nee*. The Confederacy fought not only against Algonquian tribes but also against other Iroquois speakers. In the 17th century, it largely destroyed both the Huron and the Erie, forcing the few survivors (who would take on a new identity as the Wyandot) to join Algonquian groups in present-day Wisconsin, Indiana, and Michigan. The Susquehanna, Iroquoians living along the Susquehanna River from Pennsylvania south to the Chesapeake Bay, also suffered the assaults of the Confederacy. A remnant of the Susquehanna converted to Christianity, becoming known as the Conestoga, but endured attacks by the French and their Algonquian allies in 1755 and then again by English settlers in 1763. The survivors moved to Ohio before the Revolutionary War, allying themselves with the Algonquian Delaware.

During the French and Indian Wars, the Confederacy sided with the British against the French and their Algonquian allies. The Six Nations were divided, however, over support during the American Revolution; eventually the Tuscarora and Oneida chose to support the colonists' cause while the Mohawk, Seneca, Onondaga, and Cayuga upheld the Iroquois' alliance with Britain. In 1778 this latter faction joined British forces to raid settlements in New York and Pennsylvania, massacring hundreds of soldiers and civilians as well as Iroquois who were loyal to the patriot cause. A year later General Washington responded with a campaign of "total destruction and devastation of their [hostile tribes of the Six Nations] settlements, and the capture of as many prisoners of every age and sex as possible" (Washington 1779). The Sullivan Expedition, as it came to be known, devastated Iroquois villages and crops, leaving thousands of Iroquois refugees ill equipped to survive the winter of 1779–1780.

Also Iroquoian speakers, the Cherokee, whose mountainous territory extended from southwest Virginia through the Carolinas, into Tennessee and Georgia, were strong British allies for much of the 18th century. The Cherokee participated in over 18 treaties with the British; these documents covered everything from land cessions and trade to peace treaties. Their hunters were the primary source for South Carolina's lucrative deerskin trade for all of the colonial period. Although the Cherokee allied with the British at the start of the French and Indian War, tensions, often violent, led to an independent declaration of war against Britain in 1758 (the Anglo-Cherokee War); the fighting did not end until 1761. At the conclusion of the peace treaties, three Cherokee leaders, Ostenaco, Standing Turkey, and Wood Pigeon, voyaged to London with Henry Timberlake, emissary to the Overhill Cherokee. Arriving in June 1762, the trio drew considerable public attention, met with George III, and sat for the artist Sir Joshua Reynolds. They returned to America in August of that year.

British and European Settlement, 1607–1714

Between the founding of the first lasting settlement in British North America, in Jamestown, Virginia colony, in 1607, and 1700 approximately

The Three Cherokees, came over from the head of the River Savanna to London, engraving, produced by George Bickham the Younger, London, c. 1762. (Private Collection/Peter Newark American Pictures/The Bridgeman Art Library)

500,000 men, women, and children left England, Wales, and Scotland to work in the plantation economies of the American mainland, Bermuda, and the English West Indies (Horn 1994, 24). They were joined by emigrants from European polities who came as both free and indentured colonists. Contact among these groups could be inconvenient to antagonistic or relaxed to friendly, and the nature of these interactions is often difficult to reconstruct from primary source records. Although their individual reasons for emigrating differed, as groups all of these early settlers were tied to Great Britain's mercantile interests. Four distinct regions developed on the mainland: the colonies of the Chesapeake Bay, New England, the middle colonies, and the Lowcountry.

Chesapeake Region

The Chesapeake region encompassed the colonies of Virginia and Maryland. Until the final decades of the century the region was a society of immigrants: most of the settlers were born and raised in England. They either paid their own passage or bound themselves as indentured servants to repay the costs of transportation, food, and sometimes clothing. To alleviate England's criminal population, its courts also sent hundreds of convicts as bound labor. According to one estimate for this period, for every one free immigrant, three or four were bound by a labor contract (Horn 1994, 25). By the end of the century, however, enslaved Africans had replaced indentured servants as the primary source for labor.

Agriculture was the driving force in the Chesapeake. In 1616, Virginian John Rolfe (husband of Pocahontas) led successful efforts to cultivate the West Indies strain of tobacco so popular for smoking in England and Europe. For most of the century, tobacco was not only the sole staple commodity of the region, but it also served as the region's currency, paying for imported and locally produced goods, servants (and later slaves), and services. Toward the end of the century, planters began to cultivate other crops—wheat, barley, and oats—which were sold in periods when tobacco prices were low. The economic development of the two colonies differed primarily in that Virginia was a colony of large estates with few small holdings, while the small plantation was a feature of Maryland.

For most of this early period the demographic circumstances of the Chesapeake were unusual: a low ratio of females to males, a high death rate, and a relatively young population. For example, "for every female servant who left London for Virginia in 1635, there were six males"; for those leaving from Bristol between 1654 and 1686, the ratio was three men for every woman (Horn 1979, 62). One proposed reason for this disparity is that male servants were likely more desirable as agricultural workers than females because they could handle long hours of labor with no interruptions for pregnancy and child rearing. Although not precisely known, mortality rates in the 17th century were noteworthy enough to provoke contemporary comment. Mortality was highest during the first year, most likely due to disease and unhealthy environments; survival of this period was called "seasoning." Both of these circumstances help explain why the population of the Chesapeake was unable to reproduce itself until the last quarter of the century and required a persistent influx of new immigrants.

Two social groups were conspicuously absent from the Chesapeake: the aristocracy and skilled and specialist craftsmen. The former found little to attract them. For the latter, the lack of towns and a dispersed population could not support most trades full time until the last decades of the century. With the absence of a true nobility, the Chesapeake elite evolved from members of the gentry and successful merchants and professionals. Because of a more fluid social structure, many from the lower to middle ranks in England became successful planters and traders.

Although the official religion of Virginia was the Church of England, the lack of resident clergy meant that the church's hold on the colony was weak. Maryland's founder, Lord Baltimore, George Calvert—a Roman Catholic—established a government with inclusive religious tolerance. This combination of religious factors was attractive for those whose beliefs were marginalized in England. Roman Catholics settled in both Maryland and Virginia; Puritans could be found on the eastern shore of Virginia by midcentury; and Quakers put down roots throughout the region.

New England

Immigration to New England—Massachusetts, Rhode Island, Connecticut, and New Hampshire—contrasted sharply with that of the Chesapeake. Instead of single immigrants, settlers came mostly in family groups; those who had servants who were willing to make the journey paid for their passage. People who left from the same areas in England often initially relocated together in a region or town in New England. As free immigrants, they generally brought more resources to begin new lives. The ratio of men to women was more equal, facilitating population growth earlier in the century. Although disease was present, the cooler climate supported a healthier population whose members lived longer.

Although adventurers were among those who crossed the Atlantic from England in the 1620s and 1630s, the overwhelming majority of those who founded Plymouth Plantation (absorbed by Massachusetts in 1691) and Massachusetts Bay Colony did so for religious reasons. The Separatists (later called Pilgrims), who established the Plymouth settlement in 1621, wished to practice their Protestant beliefs without any restrictions from the Church of England. Puritans, who began arriving in the mid-1620s, left England because they were unable to change, or "purify," the Anglican church. The Puritan migration of roughly 20,000 people from various English counties to New England—settling generally near Boston—between 1630 and 1642 has been called the Great Migration of the 17th century. With the beginning of the English Civil Wars (1642–1651) and the end of religious restrictions there, fewer than 50 English immigrants arrived per year; an estimated 7–11 percent of New Englanders returned to the mother country after 1640 (Anderson and Thomas 1973, 647, 651; Moore 2007).

As might be expected, New England's forms of congregational worship varied from colony to colony. The Massachusetts Bay and New Haven colonies were the strictest in religious practices. The Massachusetts General Assembly, in particular, passed legislation designed to regulate church attendance and prohibit other religious groups, such as Quakers and Baptists, from settling in the colony. Plymouth colony was more lenient and did not enforce church attendance until 1651. Unlike Massachusetts and New Haven, Connecticut did not require freemen to be church members. Although the situation was not harmonious, Rhode Island had no established church and allowed the greatest religious tolerance——of all the New England colonies.

Immigrants who were discontented with established social, economic, political, or religious practices often moved to—or were forced to resettle in—another colony. Relocation to Connecticut and Long Island occurred because of a combination of economic and religious factors, the most common of which were insufficient or unproductive agricultural land; lack of occupational opportunities; and/or religious discontent. Between 1636 and 1638 Puritan harmony was challenged in Massachusetts by Bostonian Anne Hutchinson (1591–1643), the leader of a religious group called the Antinomians (who believed that certain religious laws were subject to personal interpretation). After weeks of debate in Boston's court over the group's challenge to Puritan theology, the General Court disenfranchised, disarmed and banished many of its members; the church excommunicated Hutchinson. In the spring of 1638 Hutchinson, members of her family, and others trekked south and settled on land that became part of Rhode Island. Sometime after her husband's death, in 1641, she moved to New Netherland and settled in an area that is now part of the Bronx. Hutchinson was killed in a raid by local Siwanoy.

Middle Colonies

The settlers of the middle colonies of New Jersey, New York, Delaware, and Pennsylvania were the most ethnically diverse among the colonial regions. Until 1664 much of the area was controlled by the Netherlands and organized in 1614 as the colony of New Netherland, its provincial capital, New Amsterdam, on the southern tip of Manhattan Island. In addition to Dutch, New Netherland was home to German, French, Scandinavian, English, Hebrew, Portuguese, and Spanish speakers. (New Sweden, located in parts of present-day Delaware, New Jersey, and Pennsylvania, had been a Swedish colony beginning in 1638; in 1655 it was incorporated into New Netherland.) Most of New Netherland's settlers were Calvinists, but Lutherans, Mennonites, and Quakers were represented and there was a small community of Jews in New Amsterdam. "Liberty of conscience," the cornerstone of religious tolerance in all Dutch provinces and colonies, was rooted in the Union of Utrecht of 1579, which stated "each Individual enjoys freedom of religion and no one is persecuted or questioned about his religion" (quoted in Haefeli 2012, 20).

New Netherland was surrendered to the English at the conclusion of the first Anglo-Dutch War, in 1664. England's Charles II gave the area between New England and Maryland to his brother, the Duke of York (later James II) as a colony, which was renamed New York. Although the legal system changed from Dutch to English, much of the Dutch personality of the region, multilingualism, and trade practices continued. In 1670, Daniel Denton noted that the population of New York was mostly English and Dutch, both of whom had considerable trade with local American Indians for furs: "Bevers, Otter, Raccoon skins, with other Furrs; As also for Bear, Deer, and Elke skins" (Denton 1902, 41). The land west of the Hudson River was renamed New Jersey. In 1681, a small tract was published in London outlining this colony's successes, the anonymous author relating that many families had transported themselves and servants to New Jersey and had already established themselves as husbandmen, millers, brewers, and tradesmen. "The Country also produces Flax and Hemp, which they already Spin and Manufacture into Linnen: They make several Stuffs and Cloath of Wool for Apparrel: They Tan Leather, Make Shooes and Hats" (quoted in Myers 1912, 191). Whatever the colonists did not use themselves, they "sell to their Neighbours, and Transport the Rest to the other American-Plantations" (192).

In 1681, William Penn received a large land grant, Pennsylvania, from Charles II and area of present-day Delaware from the Duke of York. (Delaware split from Pennsylvania in 1701.) Penn recruited settlers to Pennsylvania through a pamphlet, arguing that many in England could not even afford to marry, let alone live in any degree of comfort "and allow themselves Cloaths." In Pennsylvania, however, these same individuals not only could marry but also "bestow thrice more in all Necessaries and Conveniencies (and not a little in Ornamental things too) for themselves, their Wives and Children, both as to Apparel and Household-stuff," that is, the products of necessity and convenience exported from England (Penn 1912, 203–4). In a pitch to potential merchants and traders, Penn noted that "Cloaths and many sorts of Tools and Utensils from England" were imported for use by "many thousand Blacks and Indians" (204).

Himself a member of the Society of Friends, Penn had meant Pennsylvania as a colony of religious tolerance, his "Holy Experiment." The majority of Quakers who were persuaded to settle emigrated from England and

Wales and a considerable number from Ireland. Penn also invited 13 German families, Quakers and Mennonites from the Rhine Valley, to resettle. Emigrating in 1683, these latter families founded Germantown, outside of Philadelphia.

Lowcountry

The Carolina Lowcountry was the seaboard territory directly south of Virginia and north of Spanish-controlled Florida (North and South Carolina did not become separate colonies until 1729). It was initially settled in 1670, not by a company from England, but by colonists from Barbados, a group composed of planters, indentured servants, and African slaves—all already seasoned to the climate. To attract more colonists, the aristocratic absentee-owners of the Lowcountry region promised religious toleration—Roman Catholics were excluded—political representation in a local assembly, and large land grants. Although early in the period enslaved people accounted for about one in four, by 1710, South Carolina became the first colony in British North America with a black majority, a situation that persisted for most of the decades through 1860 (Taylor 2001, 224, 237, 238; Wood 1974, 143–66).

In contrast to the Chesapeake, the Lowcountry economy, which in the 17th century did not have a dominant staple, quickly developed two economies. One was centered on pioneering activities, especially cattle ranching. Slaves, both African and Native, and indentured servants worked together to clear land, cut wood, cultivate provisions, and experiment with staple crops. For example, John Smyth, who died in 1682, had an estate that included nine African slaves, four Indians, and three whites (Morgan 1998, 6). Some Africans apparently retained their native skills in tending livestock. In 1673, Virginian Edmund Lister transported a group of his slaves into South Carolina, sending them ahead to establish a cattle ranch (Morgan 1998, 5).

The other economy was the Indian trade. Planters purchased pelts and skins, which Native men hunted and Native women processed, but they also purchased so-called enemy Indians who had been taken captive in wars and conflicts by Britain's Indian allies. The planters sold these prisoners as slaves to other colonists. Between 1670 and 1715, Lowcountry English slavers sold an estimated 30,000–50,000 people, exporting more slaves than they imported (Gallay 2002, 49, 299). In 1708, the governor's and council's report on South Carolina noted the destinations of Indian slaves within the colonies: "We have also Commerce with Boston, Road Island, Pennsilvania, New York & Virginia to which we export Indian slaves" (quoted in Galley 2002, 301–2).

British and European Settlement, 1715–1785

The main beneficiaries of 18th-century immigration were the regions of the Chesapeake, the middle colonies, and the Lowcountry, which, from 1732 on, included Georgia. While English men and women participated in the new wave of immigrations, which was concentrated in the first half of the century, they were far outnumbered by Scots and Germans. Spurred by economic hardship and political strife, three distinct groups from the Scottish diasporas found their way to colonial America: Highlanders, Lowland Scots, and Scots whose forebears had settled in Ulster, Ireland, in the 1690s. Scots could be found among the merchants, professionals, and craftsmen in established coastal towns from New England to Georgia and as farmers and craftsmen in backcountry communities from New York into North Carolina. Highland Scots often settled in clusters in frontier communities, and their isolation led to subsequent generations maintaining some of that original culture and language. Lowlanders, who most often emigrated as individuals or single families, tended to assimilate into the dominant En-glish culture. Ulster Scots, or Scots-Irish, began emigrating in large numbers in about 1717, forced out by multiple seasons of poor harvests and rent increases, coupled with British-imposed trade and manufacturing restrictions. By 1720 they were settling in Pennsylvania in large numbers, but soon began to relocate south through the Piedmont region into Georgia.

Germans were second only to the Scots in the numbers who left the Old World for the New in the 18th century. Most of them had come from the German Palatinate in the Rhine Valley, where an increasingly poor economy coupled with internal wars, heavy taxes, and religious intolerance made the prospects of greater opportunity in America seem worth the risk of emigration. These were joined by emigrants from the polities of Württemberg, Silesia, Alsace, Bohemia, and Moravia. A variety of Protestant denominations were represented—Lutheran, Pietist, Reformed, Calvinist, Moravian, Mennonite, Amish, Baptist, and Schwenckfelder. These new colonists included farmers, laborers, and skilled craftsmen, both poor and prosperous, indentured and free.

Other ethnic groups from Europe sought new lives. These included French Huguenots, members of a Protestant minority group who fled France, especially after France's King Louis XIV made the practice of their faith illegal in 1685. By the time of the American Revolution, the colonies had absorbed appreciable numbers of Irish, Welsh, Dutch, and Swedes. Charleston, South Carolina, in particular, received numbers of Jews who had been expelled from Spain or Portugal or were Ashkenazi from central and Eastern Europe.

Many factors are responsible for the decline in English emigration in the 18th century. In the early 18th century English manufacturing was expanding and with it came the need for more cheap labor to compete in international markets. The many wars England engaged in during the first half of the century required a much-enlarged military. Religious controls had been loosened from the previous century, allowing dissidents greater freedom of worship. Of those English who did emigrate, more than half were convicts who had been offered transportation instead of execution—the punishment for even petty crimes against property—and were sold in the colonies as indentured servants. Their terms were twice as long as the normal indenture contract. Other English, both free and bound labor, left after the Seven Years' War (1756–1763) as economic problems caused a drop in English manufacturing and trades.

While in the early 17th century the sex ratio of male to female colonists was about three to two in New England, and about six to one in Virginia, these numbers evened out considerably by the mid-18th century, especially among the population of free white settlers. The ratio of men to women among the indentured servant and transported convict populations was still likely to be imbalanced in favor of males, by two or three to one. The middle colonies, which saw the most immigration in the 18th century, had slightly more males than females, New England, which saw little immigration, was more nearly balanced. By the third quarter of the 18th century, Rhode Island and Massachusetts had slightly more females than males.

African Immigration and Settlement

Tobacco planter John Rolfe penned the account of the landing of Africans in Jamestown in 1619 in a letter to the Virginia Company of London. He noted that a ship had arrived that "brought not any thing but 20 and odd Negroes, wch the Governor and Cape Marchant bought for victuale . . . at the best and easyest rate they could" (quoted in Rein 2006). These individuals appear to have been treated as indentured servants. New scholarship of the past decade has revealed that the vessel was a Portuguese slave ship that had been seized by British pirates. It is likely that these 20 and odd had been baptized as Christians in their homelands; this may be one reason why some of them were released from their indentures rather than sentenced to a life of bound labor.

More ships brought Africans to Virginia—and later to New England and Maryland. For most of the 17th century the racial relations between free and indentured whites and free, indentured, and enslaved Africans formed a complicated web that today is not easily unwoven. As historian Philip Morgan notes for Virginia, "the fluidity and unpredictability of race relations . . . gradually hardened into the Anglo-American mold more familiar to later generations" (Morgan 1998, 13). As late as 1670 Africans still numbered only about 5 percent of the population of the colony—perhaps 2,000 of about 40,000. Only after the supply of indentured servants declined in the 1660s did tobacco farmers begin to purchase Africans as field workers and legislation make hereditary slavery binding on Africans.

In the first decade of the 18th century, the cash crops of tobacco in Virginia, Maryland, and North Carolina and rice in South Carolina led to the encouragement and protection of the use of enslaved labor, both African and Native American. This transition has been called the change from a slave-owning society, in which enslaved labor is used but is never a high

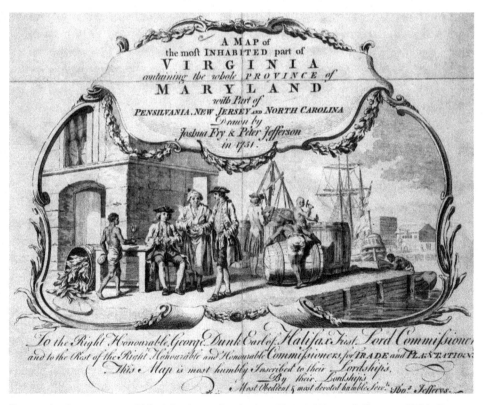

Cartouche from a map of Virginia drawn by Joshua Fry and Peter Jefferson, 1751. Enslaved workers ready hogsheads of tobacco for shipment to Britain. (Library of Congress)

proportion of the population, to a slave society, in which slavery becomes the basis for the economic functioning of society (Morgan 1991, 163).

Until about 1675, most Africans were brought to the mainland colonies from the West Indian plantations. In the last decades of the century, however, slave ships headed directly to colonial ports from Africa, and by the early 18th century this direct trade brought more than 90 percent of the slaves to the colonies (Kulikoff 1978, 230). The slavers traded along the coast of West Africa, from present-day Senegal south and east to the Congo, in West-Central Africa. This region included Senegambia, the Ivory (or Windward) Coast, the Gold Coast, Dahomey, Benin, Biafra, Nigeria, Cameroon, and Angola. Some slaves arrived all the way from Madagascar, off the southeast coast of Africa. As the market for slaves in the Americas grew larger, slavers enlarged their territories, reaching further inland from the African coast to assemble their human cargoes. As a result, the enslaved Africans who arrived in the colonies represented dozens of different kingdoms and linguistic groups. Surviving records from York County, Virginia, show that the origins of the slaves in that county were very mixed, although the largest number came from Biafra (Kulikoff 1978, 231–32). One study of the origins of South Carolina's slaves attributed 40 percent to Angola (Wax 1973, 390). Several of the regions in which Africans were captured for the slave trade by the 18th century held significant Muslim populations. The most likely points of origin for Muslim slaves were parts of Senegambia, the Gold Coast, and northern Nigeria. Evidence suggests that most of these slaves lived scattered through Georgia and the Carolinas, and vestiges of their religious practices may have survived through generations.

Purchasers of slaves overwhelmingly preferred adult men to women and children. As a result, slave ships carried more men than women by a ratio of two to one, and more than 80 percent of the total was adults. This gender imbalance was gradually equalized during the 18th century, as slave populations on the colonial mainland formed family groups and bore children born into slavery.

African slaves existed in relatively small numbers in northern colonies, where agricultural patterns did not support a plantation system. For the most part, northern slavery tended to isolate slaves as house servants or individual laborers on small farms, making it more difficult for enslaved individuals to create families and communities. New York, which did not have a cash crop that required enslaved labor, still had 2,383 black slaves in 1703, a number which grew to 8,941 in 1737 and to 19,883 in 1771 (cited in Lydon 1978, 388). Rhode Island's slave population was higher in proportion to its white population than the rest of New England, perhaps because of the intensive farming of the fertile Narragansett Plantations. Although Philadelphia merchant Anthony Benezet had begun publishing antislavery tracts in 1750 (and by the time of the Revolution was supported by a majority of Philadelphians and Quakers from New Jersey and Rhode Island as well many Presbyterians and Congregationalists), it was not until 1787 that the first states (New Jersey and Rhode Island) made importing slaves illegal.

The southern colonies varied greatly in the distribution of slaves, and patterns of slaveholding changed over the course of the colonial period. In the first decades of the 18th century, for example, Maryland consisted primarily of small farms, usually employing fewer than 20 slaves (Kulikoff 1978, 240). After 1740, however, plantations increased in size and required larger numbers of enslaved workers; then almost half of Maryland's slaves lived on plantations with at least 20 others (Kulikoff 1978, 246). Virginia's tobacco plantations were large, and the number of slaves working in those fields had increased from about 6,000 in 1700 to more than 170,000 by 1775—almost half the population of Virginia. North Carolina relied on the produce of its pine forests and its tobacco crops for cash; still, the numbers of enslaved grew there from about 6,000 (against 30,000 Europeans) to approximately 66,000 (just under a third of the total population) by 1775. Georgia, whose original charter under the Trustees had banned slavery from the colony as detrimental to the industry and morals of the white population, turned to enslaved labor as soon as the colony's governance reverted to the crown in 1751. By 1775 the population of the colony was approximately half enslaved.

Many South Carolina rice planters owned several plantations rather than a single large estate, and their slaves holdings were distributed among all of them. Rice was a labor-intensive crop requiring many field hands. By 1720 65 percent of approximately 18,000 people living in the colony were African or African American slaves (www.sciway.net/afam/slavery/population. html). This black majority continued for the rest of the colonial period. In Charleston, the site of the town homes of planter and merchant elites, enslaved workers had more access to a diversity of working conditions. House servants usually lived with their masters; however, laborers or skilled artisans might live independently. Others worked as self-hired labor, returning from none to most of the income from their employment to their owners. Charleston's slave population was greater than the population of European descent. In 1770, one estimate listed 5,030 white colonists, 5,833 black slaves, and 24 free blacks and mulattoes (Bridenbaugh 1955, 333).

Table 1.1
Population Changes in Colonial America

Colony	Year A/ Population	Year B/ Population	European % A/B	African % A/B	American Indian % A/B
Virginia	1624/1,275	1703/60,606	98.4%/ est. 87%	1.7%/ est.12.8%	
New York	1698/18,067	1771/168,007	88%/88.2%	12%/11.8%	
Maryland	1701/32,358	1762/164,007	87.2%/69.7%	12.8%/30.3%	
Rhode Island	1708/7,181	1774/59,607	94.1%/91.4%	5.9%/6.2%	?/2.3%
South Carolina	1708/9,580		42.6%	42.8%	14.6%
New Jersey	1726/32,442	1772/120,000–140,000	92%/92.5%	8%/7.5%	
Georgia	1738/1,110	1756/6,355	?/70.8%	?/29.2%	
Connecticut	1756/130,612	1774/197,842	97.2%/96.7%	2.3%/2.6%	0.5%/0.7%
New Hampshire	1767/52,700	1775/81,300	98.8%/99.2%	1.2%/0.8%	
Massachusetts	1764/245,698		?/97.2	?/2.1%	0.7%

Source: Table data taken from: Robert V. Wells, *The Population of the British Colonies in America before 1776: A Survey of Census Data* (Princeton, NJ: Princeton University, 1975), 260–73, tables VII-1, VII-2; Evarts B. Greene and Virginia D. Harrington, compilers, *American Population before the Federal Census of 1790* (New York: Columbia University Press, 1932); Alan Taylor, *American Colonies* (New York: Viking Penguin, 2001), chapters 8, 14; Herman R. Friis, "A Series of Population Maps of the Colonies and the United States, 1625–1790," *Geographical Review,* vol. 30, no. 3 (July 1940): 463–70; Russell R. Menard, "Was There a 'Middle Colonies Demographic Regime'?" *Proceedings of the American Philosophical Society,* vol. 133, no. 2 (June 1989): 215–18; Marc Egnal, "The Economic Development of the Thirteen Continental Colonies, 1720–1775," *William and Mary Quarterly,* 3rd ser., vol. 32, no. 2 (April 1975): 193–97.

THE INDIVIDUAL AND THE FAMILY

During the colonial period, the family structure generally followed an English model, which gave the male head-of-house ultimate authority over and responsibility for the family unit. Unlike the modern nuclear family, which consists of a pair of adults and their children, the colonial family comprised parents, children, and extended relations living in the household as well as servants, whether indentured or free, and, in the households of tradesmen, apprentices. Peter Laslett has pointed out that the colonial family was three societies "fused together; the society of man and wife, of parents and children, and of master and servants" (Laslett 1965, 2). The social order was dependent upon these interrelationships.

Gender Roles

In the pre-industrial age, the duties of adult males and females were defined by tradition as well as law (Main 1994). The husband provided food, shelter, and clothing or the means to acquire them; in 17th-century Puritan New England, the husband also was ultimately responsible for providing religious instruction (he may have been aided by his wife if she were literate) and upholding religious strictures concerning his family and servants. A married woman's role was defined by society's expectations for her as a child bearer and household manager. She owed obedience to her husband and, in turn, expected obedience from her children and servants. Giving birth and raising children occupied many women for decades of their married lives. Depending on the wealth and size of her household, a wife carried out or supervised the maintenance of her home, the care of infants and children, the preparation and storage of food—including care of the garden and dairy—and the making of clothing for family members. She also may have been given authority to purchase household necessities and clothing and hire servants.

The English common law doctrine of coverture was acknowledged throughout the colonies. Women and girls did not have a separate legal status as individuals; they were subsumed under the guardianship of their father or husband as a *feme covert*. A single woman without a father or husband, however, was legally a *feme sole*, and had rights equal in law to those of men (also see the discussion of coverture in Chapter 4). The children of a marriage were legally under the control of the husband, and mothers had no legal right to interfere in any arrangements made by the husband for their children. Female children rarely received real estate as bequests from their fathers, but were granted movable goods such as household furnishings or livestock and sometimes money. As one scholar has written, "Daughters were ultimately supported by their husbands, not by their paternal inheritance" (Norton 1984, 603).

It generally was believed (based on physical realities as well as culturally imposed stereotypes) that men were inherently superior to women in physical strength and intellect. Colonial society considered that it took the physical strength of males to cut timber, plow fields, grow field crops, work iron and shoe horses, and butcher animals. And because society then judged that males were more capable of intellectual development, generally only boys received the education that led to careers in commerce, law, religion, medicine, politics, and many other trades. Women's lesser physical strength was more appropriate for tending kitchen gardens, milking cows, making butter and cheese, keeping hens, preparing food, washing clothing and linens, maintaining the house, preparing and spinning fibers to make cloth, and constructing the clothing that did not require advanced arithmetical skills to cut and fit. Men and women collaborated, however, in many agricultural pursuits such as sowing and harvesting crops. Young children engaged in whatever household tasks were suited to their strength and skill, regardless of gender. As soon as they were old enough, boys and girls took on appropriately gendered tasks within the household, or outside it as apprentices or servants. Boys were apprenticed more often than girls, and girls were more likely to be sent out for household work than to learn a trade.

Many factors had an impact on gender roles, however, such as where a family lived and its social or economic status. In frontier communities, where neighbors were distant and help scarce, women often joined their husbands and sons in the hard labor of making a farm out of wilderness. Women in rural areas supplemented family incomes through selling or bartering foodstuffs they raised, goods they made, and services such as spinning or cleaning. For example, Nathaniel Chamberlin, a blacksmith living in Pembroke, Massachusetts, kept an account book between 1743 and 1806, which listed not only his own work but that of his first and second wives, four sons, and five daughters. Its entries indicate that the family practiced a traditional division of labor, with the females engaged in making textiles and clothing and cleaning, and the males in heavy agricultural labor (Cochrane 2000).

In areas with concentrated populations women ran taverns, shops, and schools, and often took over family businesses when a husband became incapacitated, was absent, or died. Sometimes married women conducted businesses in their own right, legally as a *feme sole*. For example, at the age of 16 and with her father absent from the family, Eliza Lucas (c. 1722–1793;

married Charles Pinckney 1744) managed three plantations in South Carolina. Today she is best known (while still single) for establishing indigo as a successful and profitable crop in that colony. Another South Carolinian, Martha Daniell Logan (1704–1799; married George Logan Jr., 1719), occasionally ran a boarding school for girls in Charleston and experimented with plant breeding. Her garden supplied plants and seeds to local gardeners as well as American botanist John Bartram (1699–1777), whom Logan met in 1760. In 1752, she wrote the first treatise on gardening published in America: a "Gardener's Calendar," which appeared in John Tobler's *South Carolina Almanack*.

In towns and cities, other free women and girls might work outside the home employed in domestic duties, agriculture, or in trades. One survey of classified notices in colonial newspapers shows that about half of those advertisements involved the offer of or search for domestic or personal services, such as wet-nurses, housekeepers, cooks, cleaners, and attendants. The other half included a wide range of trades and professions: shopkeeper, milliner, seamstress, or dressmaker; midwife; printer, or bookbinder; manager or keeper of a farm, inn, tavern, boardinghouse, or coffeehouse; teacher; and performing and literary artists (Schultz and Lantz 1988). In many parts of the country, girls went to work in a neighboring household through an informal apprenticeship to learn housekeeping and other skills; she might be treated more as a family member than as a servant. Although women entered outside employment in increasing numbers during the 18th century, they accounted for only about 10 percent of the free working population and could expect to earn less than half of what men earned for similar work.

Among members of the enslaved population, gender roles were often irrelevant for field work. House servants and skilled workers, however, were trained according to the same traditional division of labor that ruled the European community. Studies of slave populations in the Chesapeake suggest that only in the mid-18th century did stable family structures develop among the enslaved, aided by the drop in imports of new slaves and the rise in numbers of those who were native born. As the family unit strengthened, gender roles within the family were reinforced along European lines as well.

Marriage

Studies have shown that women in the mainland North American colonies generally married younger than they did in Europe. Marriage patterns were influenced by many factors: whether a region was originally settled by groups of families or by men on their own; whether the settlement consisted of villages or plantations; whether the climate and environment were harsh or mild; and whether eligible men and women were free to make decisions about their lives or emigrated as indentured servants.

There were significant regional differences in marriage practices between northern and southern colonies. For most of the 17th century, the Chesapeake was focused on the large-scale production of cash crops on plantations using indentured white male laborers. Women—whether settlers or servants—were relatively rare. Diseases such as typhoid, dysentery, and malaria were common, and mortality rates were high among adults as well as children. Fewer immigrants survived to create families, perpetuating the imbalance between males and females. The available women—apart from indentured servants—married young; if widowed, women found remarriage easy due to the surplus of men. In contrast, it was more difficult for a man to find a wife. Chesapeake families were small; most couples had only two or three children; unions were often broken by the death of at least one spouse as early as within seven years of the marriage. This situation did not change significantly in the region until late in the 17th century. All of these factors contributed to difficulties early immigrants faced in trying to recreate or continue the traditional ways of life they had experienced in England.

A different model operated in the north. New England's early settlers emigrated as family units, some of them complete with household servants and married adult children. The more even ratio of men to women gave New Englanders greater opportunity to marry. Their families grew faster and tended to be larger, and they outlived their counterparts in the Chesapeake. The decrease in immigration after the first decades of settlement (because of the English Civil Wars) also meant that a native-born population dominated New England society at an early date. New England's women also married younger than those in England, but in the northern colonies they also lived longer and bore more children. Although subject to illness and disease, northern settlers were less affected by the debilitating heat and humidity their fellow colonists endured further south. Quaker families in New York, New Jersey, and Pennsylvania, who also immigrated as families, followed similar patterns to New England colonists.

In the 18th century, except perhaps in the colony of Georgia until the 1750s, regional differences in gender ratios and marriage patterns were less significant although some holdover of the earlier patterns did remain. By the beginning of the 18th century, enslaved African men were replacing indentured white males as workers in Chesapeake's tobacco fields, and the ratio of white males to females was less skewed. For most of the 18th century, southern women followed their northern sisters, marrying two to six years earlier than their European counterparts, at an average age of 22. Colonial men generally married between the ages of 25 and 27, much the same as European men. In the third quarter of the century, young men in all regions began to move away in large numbers from the coastal settlements into newly opened sections of the interior. As a result, young single women began to outnumber young single men in coastal areas, and the average age of marriage partners in the long-settled areas began to rise, as did the number of women who never married. For most of the 18th century, however, the fact that colonial women married younger and lived longer than European women led to larger families in the colonies as well. On average, a woman could expect to have six to eight children during the course of her married life, although much larger and much smaller families are known.

Marriage patterns among enslaved Africans and African Americans varied by region and according to whether they were recent arrivals from Africa, the West Indies sugar plantations, or had been born in America. In the settled areas of the southern tidewater, for example, by the second quarter of the 18th century American-born slaves tended to live in family units, while the recent arrivals were housed in "sex-segregated barracks. Seasoned immigrants often lived in conjugal units without children" (Kulikoff 1978, 244).

HEALTH AND HYGIENE

Illnesses and Treatments

Colonists suffered from physical and mental illness, nutrition-related illnesses, and medical conditions related to accidents or complications from childbirth. They were constantly subject to infections, and parasites such as intestinal worms were a common problem. The causes of disease were not well understood, and there was no concept of the role of germs or bacteria in spreading infection. Many of these illnesses affected the appearance of the sufferer, whether in faces scarred by smallpox, distorted by the loss of teeth, or made pale and drawn by consumption or depression. In 1754, the *Pennsylvania Gazette* published a list of illnesses for which patients had been admitted into the Pennsylvania Hospital since the institution's founding

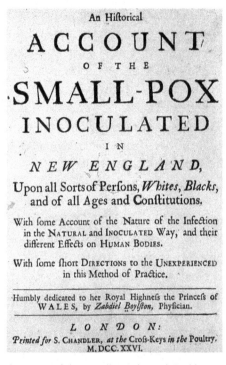

An Hiſtorical

ACCOUNT

OF THE

SMALL-POX

INOCULATED

I N

NEW ENGLAND,

Upon all Sorts of Perſons, *Whites, Blacks,* and of all Ages and Conſtitutions.

With ſome Account of the Nature of the Infection in the NATURAL and INOCULATED Way, and their different Effects on HUMAN BODIES.

With ſome ſhort DIRECTIONS to the UNEXPERIENCED in this Method of Practice.

Humbly dedicated to her Royal Highneſs the Princeſs of WALES, by *Zabdiel Boylſton*, Phyſician.

LONDON:

Printed for S. CHANDLER, *at the* Croſs-Keys *in the* Poultry. M.DCC.XXVI.

Account of the small pox inoculated in New England, pamphlet published in London, 1726. (MPI/Getty Images)

in 1752. Among the physical ailments were agues, cancer, consumption, cough, dropsy, falling sickness, fever, fistulas, palsy, rheumatism, sciatica, scurvy, ulcers, and vertigo (August 8, 1754). Melancholy and lunacy were recognized as mental disorders.

Small pox was a particularly destructive disease in colonial America. In towns and cities, isolation of victims was the first defense against its spread. Inoculation was introduced by Zabdiel Boylston and Cotton Mather in Boston in 1721; the procedure involved injecting the infection into a healthy patient, who generally came down with a milder form of the disease. This prophylactic was not without its critics, however. For those who had already contracted the disease, doctors offered a number of remedies, most of which read today as medieval. For example, in 1738 Dr. A. Garden offered subscribers of the *South-Carolina Gazette* a remedy that included blood-letting via leeches, poultices of cow's dung boiled with milk, and spoonfuls of syrup of poppies (June 1).

Options for formal and informal medical treatment in the 18th century included the housewife, the midwife, the apothecary, the surgeon, and the physician. None but the physician ever completed any kind of formal training, and only the physician was considered a gentleman, a member of the professional or upper ranks. Housewives were expected to have the knowledge and ability to nurse members of their family and often helped their neighbors. They dispensed remedies made from plants and other ingredients according to recipes passed down orally from mother to daughter or published in housewife and apothecary's manuals. Diarist Elizabeth Drinker, for example, wrote in 1764 and 1765 of family members bothered by worms and of the teas and powders with which she attempted to cure them (Drinker 1991, 1:111). Female midwives attended almost all births in the colonial period although beginning in the late 17th century a male physician might be called in to consult in difficult cases. In the 17th and early 18th centuries, some physicians viewed the female medical practitioner as an important practical assistant who would do the actual work while the physician removed himself from actual contact with the patient. In return, a female professional might seek the advice of the physician to support her own diagnosis or when she had no remedy to offer (Tannenbaum 1997, 279–80).

Apothecaries and "Chymists" sold all sorts of drugs and medicines for the trained and untrained medical practitioner. They imported many of these products not only from London but also procured locally found substances and prepared some concoctions themselves. The former included medicines of doubtful efficacy such as Godfrey's General Cordial; Greenough Tinctures for Toothache; Francis Female Elixir; and Turlington's Balsam, the latter, patented in Britain in 1744, which claimed to cure kidney and bladder stones, colic, and inward weakness (Drinker 1991, 1:121, n. 10). In Philadelphia, chemist William Shippen offered "all manner of Chemical Preparations, and Galenical [i.e., herbal] Medicines, also Squire's grand Elixir, Hungary Water, Daffy's Elixir, Stoughton's Bitter, Poyntz's Elixer, Oyl of Turpentine, Sweet Oyl, Barbadey Tar, Spices, Tea, Loaf Sugar, and all Sorts of Drugs" (*Pennsylvania Gazette*, March 24, 1737).

Men of uncertain character also advertised suspect remedies for assorted medical conditions. Along with his usual work of cleaning clothes, Henry Brabazon, a "wet and dry scowerer," advertised his own medicines for "the gravel of stone" and the flux (*Pennsylvania Gazette*, September 27, 1753). Patrick Willson claimed to be able to cure coughs, headaches, "megrims," "hysteric disorders caused by worms," and skin eruptions with a compound made of seven different roots and herbs, which would act as "detergent, discussive, and purgative" (*Pennsylvania Gazette*, April 27, 1774).

The surgeon, who also could be the local barber—Ferdinand Facundus was surgeon-barber in Philadelphia—specialized in blood-letting, setting bones, performing operations, and amputating limbs. Many colonial surgeons gained experience by serving in the army or navy where they honed their skills on the casualties of war. (In Britain, under pressure from the medical profession, surgeons split from barbers in 1745 to form their own guild.)

Most colonial physicians were formally trained in medicine at a British or European university; some of them also practiced surgery. Cadwallader Colden (1688–1776), the son of a minister, was trained in medicine at Edinburgh University and practiced first in Philadelphia (1708–1715) before moving to New York in 1718. Better known as a government official, he nevertheless published two medical works: *Account of Diseases Prevalent in*

America (1736), and *Essay on the Cause and Remedy of the Yellow Fever so Fatal at New York* (1743).

Many 18th-century colonists had trouble with their teeth, but dentistry was as rudimentary as the rest of the period's medical practices. One visitor to Philadelphia wrote in 1777 that although the women were "well-shaped," they had "very bad teeth" by the age of 25 (Cresswell 2007, 270). Relief from a toothache was most often achieved by pulling the affected tooth. Surgeon-dentists were practicing in the colonies by the second half of the 18th century, and toothbrushes and powders were available at apothecary shops. Michael Poree, a surgeon-dentist who had been practicing in New York, advertised in Philadelphia in 1771 that he made and sold artificial teeth and cleaned and whitened natural teeth (*Pennsylvania Gazette*, June 6). That same year, Mr. Baker, a surgeon-dentist, offered his services to Williamsburg's residents, noting that he could remove tarter from teeth and would fill up "with Lead or Gold, those but are hollow, so as to render them useful" (*Virginia Gazette*, December 26). In 1776, Katherine Greene Amory noted the visit of a Mr. Whitehord to treat her husband's teeth; she then invited him to stay for dinner (Amory 1923, 101).

African Americans suffered from the same illnesses and disorders as those of European descent; however, the death toll for certain diseases was generally higher among the former, whether slave or free, simply because they were more likely to be malnourished, suffer from exposure to cold, and unable to retreat from outbreaks of infection. Scholars believe, for example, that in Philadelphia, Africans had higher death rates in the winter from pulmonary infections while Europeans were more likely to die in hot weather from malaria and typhoid. Volumes have been written about the extreme toll taken on the population of American Indians from the introduction of European communicable diseases for which they lacked immunity. Particularly lethal were measles, smallpox, cholera, and yellow fever. English colonists also introduced alcohol—brandy, rum, and beer—for which American Indians had no counterpart in their own culture. Access to spirits was limited in the 17th century; however, as the fur and skin trade increased throughout the colonies in the 1700s, alcohol became a common trade good. Overconsumption led to health problems and early deaths and encouraged violent behavior; drunken individuals lashed out not only at their suppliers but also at their own people.

Personal Hygiene

By modern standards personal hygiene in the colonial period was minimal. A basin of water and a cloth or sponge to wash with were customary: the bather stood on a towel, rug, or in a flat pan and rubbed himself or herself down with a wet cloth or sponge. Soap was used in households primarily for washing clothes and textile furnishings and for shaving. Babies might be dunked in water, often cool or cold water, to "harden" them in their first year. Men and boys might swim or bathe in a local fresh or saltwater source—a stream, pond, or cove—but women and girls rarely had the same occasion, and soap was not a part of the process. For perhaps most people, daily washing consisted of rinsing the hands and face morning and evening. Studies of probate inventories have found that wash stands were not found in more than 10 percent of American households until the 1830s.

Not until the 1770s did immersing the body in water and scrubbing oneself with a sponge or brush become a behavioral norm in England and in her colonies. Public bathhouses and tubs for bathing in private homes then began to come into fashion, but not until the mid-19th century did they become common.

Those with pretensions to gentility washed their hands before meals and subscribed to other rules of polite conduct as laid down in manuals of polite behavior and manners (also see Chapter 2 for a discussion of colonial refinement). Part of the etiquette of refinement was in keeping oneself well groomed: clean fingernails, clean clothes, a clean handkerchief, and clean teeth.

Care of Clothing

Washing clothing was an important but labor-intensive task in a period when water had to be drawn by hand from wells or streams and heated on open fires (for which wood had to be gathered) and when soap was often homemade. Among the earliest laws passed in the colony of Virginia, in 1610, were proscriptions for launderers and laundresses concerning the disposal of wash-water, the use of soap from public stores, and the return of linens to their proper owners (Force 1963, 15, 18). Washable clothing included shirts, shifts, under-petticoats, drawers, stockings, caps, aprons, and suits of ruffles—all garments and accessories made of undyed linen or cotton, linen and wool or cotton and wool mixes. Because wool shrinks when subjected to hot water and the friction of rubbing, woolen garments had to be treated carefully and separately from the linens.

Laundry soap made at home was composed of lye and fat. Wood ashes were collected in a container to which water was added to leach out the alkali; the liquid drained off from the container was called lye. Fats saved from cooking and butchering were rendered by boiling and cooling. The lye and purified fat were boiled together to make a soft soap. Soap could also be obtained from local makers—some of the earliest settlers in both

Virginia and Massachusetts were soap boilers—or purchased as imported goods.

Laundering was usually an outdoor activity although in the 18th century some city and plantation houses had separate laundry rooms or washhouse outbuildings. Those who could afford the expense might send clothing out to be cleaned (also see Chapter 3 for laundress). Laundry was set to soak in tubs of hot soapy water; the load was worked with a large stirring stick or paddle to move the suds through the clothing. The worker also scrubbed heavily soiled areas with extra soap. The clothes were then rinsed, put in a fresh bath of hot soapy water, and agitated and rinsed again perhaps multiple times. Starch might be added to the final rinse water in preparation for ironing. Most laundry was hung or laid flat to dry outdoors. Whites were refreshed by the bleaching action of the sun. Ironing with flatirons and smoothing irons, which were heated by a fire, took place indoors after the pieces were fully dried.

Washable under-linen usually provided some protection to outer garments from body soil and perspiration; the latter were most subject to soiling from spills and contact with dirty surfaces. Brushing or beating the garment removed dried mud or dust. Any discoloration left behind was treated with nonwater-based solvents or absorbent materials such as fuller's earth or kaolin (soft white clay), both used to absorb oils; vinegar, a solvent; and lemon juice, a mild bleaching agent. (Petroleum solvents were not discovered until the 19th century.)

Serious stains on expensive clothing—especially silk fabrics—were best addressed by a professional clothier or dyer. Garments that could not be satisfactorily cleaned could be redyed and refinished for a second chance at usefulness. Fullers and clothiers, who dressed cloth off the loom, and specialist dyers often advertised that they would clean and redye soiled, stained, and damaged clothing (also see Chapter 3 for these trades). Damaged garments might also be cut down for wear by a child or smaller adult, working around the stains and spots to fashion a new article.

THE ECONOMY

Foreign Trade in the 18th Century

The different trading relationships that colonial regions developed with Britain and Europe depended on the economic circumstances of the region. Commerce in all regions was affected by wars that disrupted local production and made merchant ventures subject to capture by enemy naval or privateer vessels. Labor scarcities and unpredictable weather affected local agricultural output. Economic depressions in England affected the prices and quantities of colonial exports. Nevertheless, colonial seaports were the centers of communications and commerce and also centers of wealth (also see Chapter 2).

By the 18th century, merchants in many colonies had established commercial relationships with colleagues in Europe, the West Indies, and Canada. European cities with strong commercial ties to colonial ports included London, Liverpool, Bristol, Glasgow, Dublin, and Amsterdam. Merchants hired agents in other ports to conduct business matters such as the sale of cargo, the purchase of return shipments, solicitation of freight cargos from other merchants, filing of insurance and bills of exchange, and even the management of personal shopping commissions. These agents were sometimes, but not always, family members, and a colonial merchant's success depended in large part on the reliability of his agent.

New England's colonies never developed an agricultural staple product to provide the basis for an overseas trade with England. Instead, ships set sail from its many ports to create a network of maritime trade with Europe, Africa, and the West Indies. New England's greatest financial success was a triangular, cyclical trade in which its merchants purchased molasses from the West Indies, shipped the molasses to New England to distill it into rum, sold the rum in Africa for cargoes of slaves, and sold the slaves in the West Indies for molasses, which they then shipped back to New England.

Smaller trade networks contributed to this triangular trade. Naval stores and timber from New Hampshire and Massachusetts were sold in England. Fish from Newfoundland and New England and Rhode Island's Narragansett-bred horses were traded in the West Indies for West Indian sugar; the sugar was shipped to London in payment for textiles, spices, wines, and other luxury goods and necessary manufactures, which came back to Boston, Salem, Newport, and Portsmouth for local sale or for the coastal trade with the other colonies.

In the Middle Atlantic colonies grain quickly became the most important export to foster foreign trade. Philadelphia was the most important regional port, with the easiest access to local agricultural products. Its merchants sold wheat, flour, bread, and hard biscuit, as well as meats, butter, and timber to the West Indies, England, Scotland and Ireland, the Netherlands, and Portugal. New York City, the second largest port, grew to be more important than Boston during the 18th century; profits from its large coastal trade financed foreign ventures. New York merchants were also involved in the slave trade with Africa. Agricultural products from northern New Jersey and furs and skins from upstate New York purchased

Eighteenth-century label advertising "Best Virginia" tobacco with an image of London's Royal Exchange. (Virginia Historical Society, Richmond, Virginia, USA/ The Bridgeman Art Library)

textiles in the Netherlands and wines from the Portuguese-owned island of Madeira and the Spanish-controlled Canary Islands. Like New England, the middle colonies conducted over half their foreign trade with the Caribbean.

Among the southern colonies, Virginia, Maryland, and northern North Carolina counted on tobacco as the cash crop. South Carolina, Georgia, and the southern part of North Carolina exported a variety of agricultural products and natural resources; the most important of these were rice, indigo, deerskins from the Indian trade, and naval stores. Rice exports were stimulated by an Act of Parliament in 1730 that allowed these colonies to trade directly in rice with Portugal and the Mediterranean. For the most part, however, southern exports were shipped to Britain, both for home consumption and for trans-shipping to other markets. In return European consumer goods and useful tools and manufactures returned to southern towns for distribution among plantations and the backcountry. Southern merchants were also heavily involved in the slave trade. By far the wealthiest city in British colonial America, Charleston, South Carolina, was the most important southern port. It also was landfall for an estimated 40 percent of all enslaved Africans brought to the colonies in the 18th century.

Trade among the Colonies

Colonial merchants established intracolonial relationships in order to create smaller trading networks for raw materials and finished goods for sale. These networks consisted of coastal shipping trade, conveyance along navigable inland waterways, and transportation along roadways between towns and into the backcountry. Imported goods that arrived in quantity in the large port cities were divided into smaller lots and shipped up and down the coast. Those same ships brought back cargoes of cash crops and raw materials for sale to another colony or in London. These ports were also terminus points for wagons and small boats, which carried inland products to the coast and returned to the backcountry with small freights of manufactured goods. Established cities in the north—Boston, New York, Newport, and Philadelphia—sent a wide range of goods from their own manufactories to smaller towns and into the back-country.

New England's exports to other colonies largely involved the re-export of the molasses, sugar, and rum it purchased in the West Indies. The colonies' forest products, dried fish, whale oil and spermaceti candles, and finished shoes and iron goods were also important trade goods. It imported large quantities of grains and flours from the middle colonies. Colonial merchants were heavily engaged in the coastal transfer of local goods and brought back goods made in Amsterdam and London as part of the triangular trade in slaves and rum. Rhode Island exported hats (in violation of the many acts of Parliament passed to prevent colonial production) and several grades of furniture to South Carolina. New England's coastal trade was so important that one study of the total tonnage leaving Boston between 1768 and 1772 estimated that 54 percent of it was being shipped to other mainland ports (Egnal 1975, 218).

The middle colonies established direct trade with southern Europe to sell rice purchased from the southern colonies and purchase wines, which they traded in large quantities to New England and the Lowcountry. Their balance of trade also was kept stable by the large quantities of grain, flour, bread, dried and salted meats, fruit and vegetables, and dairy products exported to South Carolina, New York, and New England, and the iron shipped to blacksmiths and ironmongers up and down the coast. New York served as the center of trade for Long Island, parts of Connecticut, northern New Jersey, and its own backcountry, trading northern foodstuffs and local manufactures for Lowcountry rice, indigo, and skins to sell in Europe. By mid-century, grain and flour surpluses from the region had become the most important exports (Matson 1984, 398, 406). Philadelphia handled the trade for Delaware and much of New Jersey. About one third of the goods handled by New York and Philadelphia between 1768 and 1772 were destined for the coastal trade (Egnal 1975, 218).

Exports of deerskins and leathers from the Lowcountry fueled colonial leather goods industries and artisans such as Philadelphia's leather breech makers and shoemakers in Lynn, Massachusetts. The Chesapeake developed a coastal trade in corn during the 18th century. Savannah became Georgia's main port, and traded primarily up along the coast with Charleston.

Intra-colonial trade did not occur only along the coast. At least half the year, navigable waterways were ready trade routes into the interior of the colonies. Small cargo and passenger boats sailed or rowed up rivers in to deliver goods and search for trade opportunities. For those who preferred terra firma, the first stagecoach line between Boston and Newport began in 1736; less than 10 years later two competitors provided the route with weekly service. New Jersey had internal stage routes by the 1740s. Also by this decade, roads were so well established in the north that a map of the roads between New York and Philadelphia was published. Regular stage service was joined by scheduled boat services by the 1750s, and in many places travel times were shortened by the existence of connections between land and water routes. The stagecoach ride between New York and Phila-delphia, for example, was a two-day journey, but the New York terminus was really across the river in New Jersey.

The reduced threat of Indian attack at the end of the French and Indian War, in 1763, encouraged the establishment or expansion of towns in the interior, such as Lancaster, Pennsylvania; Albany and Schenectady, New York; Elizabeth Town in New Jersey; Pittsfield in western Massachusetts; and Augusta, Georgia. These communities became the trading posts for the backcountry; as new roads were built, regularly scheduled wagons and stagecoaches as well as jobbing carters brought foreign-made and colonial consumer goods to the inhabitants. The Savannah, Georgia, firm of Haber-sham and Harris, for example, had well-established overland trade routes to western Florida by the 1750s.

REFERENCES

Amory, Katherine Greene. 1923. *The Journal of Mrs. John Amory, 1775–1777*, edited by Martha C. Codman. Boston: Merrymount, 1923.

Anderson, Terry L., and Robert Paul Thomas. 1973. "White Population, Labor Force and Extensive Growth of the New England Economy in the Seventeenth Century." *Journal of Economic History* vol. 33, no. 3 (September): 634–67.

Bridenbaugh, Carl. 1955. *Cities in Revolt: Urban Life in America, 1743–1776*. New York: Alfred A. Knopf.

Cochrane, Laura. 2000. "From the Archives: Women's History in Baker Library's Business Manuscripts Collection." *Business History Review* 74 (Autumn): 465–76.

Cresswell, Nicholas. 2007. *The Journal of Nicholas Cresswell, 1774–1777*, re-print. Carlisle, MA: Applewood Books.

Denton, Daniel. 1902. *A Brief Description of New York, Formerly Called New Netherlands,* reprint of 1670 ed. Cleveland: Burrows Brothers, 1902.

Drinker, Elizabeth. 1991. *The Diary of Elizabeth Drinker,* edited by Elaine Forman Crane. Vol. 1, 1758–95. Boston: Northeastern University.

Egnal, Marc. 1975. "The Economic Development of the Thirteen Continental Colonies, 1720–1775." *William and Mary Quarterly* 3rd ser., vol. 32, no. 2 (April): 191–222.

Force, Peter, ed. 1963. "Articles, Laws, and Orders, Divine, Politique, and Martiall for the Colony of Virginia." In *Tracts and Other Papers, Relating Principally to the Origin, Settlement, and Progress of the Colonies in North America, from the Discovery of the Country to the Year 1776.* Vol. 3, 9–19, reprint of 1836 ed. Gloucester, MA: Peter Smith.

Gallay, Alan. 2002. *The Indian Slave Trade: The Rise of the English Empire in the American South, 1670–1717.* New Haven, CT: Yale University.

Haefeli, Evan. 2012. *New Netherland and the Dutch Origins of American Religious Liberty.* Philadelphia: University of Pennsylvania.

Horn, James. 1979. "Servant Emigration to the Chesapeake in the Seventeenth Century." In *The Chesapeake in the Seventeenth Century: Essays on Anglo-American Society,* edited by Thad W. Tate and David L. Ammerman. Chapel Hill: University of North Carolina.

Horn, James. 1994. *Adapting to a New World: English Society in the Seventeenth-Century Chesapeake.* Chapel Hill: University of North Carolina.

Kulikoff, Allan. 1978. "Origins of African-American Society in Tidewater Maryland and Virginia." *William and Mary Quarterly* 3rd ser., vol. 35, no. 2 (April): 226–59.

Laslett, Peter. 1965. *The World We Have Lost.* New York: Charles Scribner's Sons.

Lydon, James G. 1978. "New York and the Slave Trade, 1700–1774." *William and Mary Quarterly* 3rd ser., vol. 35, no. 2 (April): 357–94.

Main, Gloria L. 1994. "Gender, Work, and Wages in Colonial New England." *William and Mary Quarterly* 3rd ser., vol. 51, no. 1 (January): 39–66.

Matson, Cathy. 1984. " 'Damned Scoundrels' and 'Libertisme of Trade': Freedom and Regulation in Colonial New York's Fur and Grain Trades." *William and Mary Quarterly* 3rd ser., vol. 51, no. 3 (July): 389–418.

Moore, Susan Hardman. 2007. *Pilgrims: New World Settlers and the Call of Home.* New Haven, CT: Yale University.

Morgan, Philip D. 1991. "British Encounters with Africans and African-Americans, circa 1600–1780." In *Strangers within the Realm: Cultural*

Margins of the First British Empire, edited by Bernard Bailyn and Philip D. Morgan, 157–219. Chapel Hill: University of North Carolina.

Morgan, Philip D. 1998. *Slave Counterpoint: Black Culture in the Eighteenth-Century Chesapeake and Lowcountry.* Chapel Hill: University of North Carolina.

Myers, Albert Cook, ed. 1912. "The Present State of the Colony of West-Jersey, 1681." In *Narratives of Early Pennsylvania, West New Jersey and Delaware, 1630–1707.* New York: Charles Scribner's Sons.

Norton, Mary Beth. 1984. "The Evolution of White Women's Experience in Early America." *American Historical Review* vol. 89, no. 3 (June): 593–619.

Penn, William. 1912. "Some Account of the Province of Pennsilvania, by William Penn, 1681." In *Narratives of Early Pennsylvania, West New Jersey, and Delaware, 1630–1707,* edited by Albert Cook Myers, 197–215. New York: Charles Scribner's Sons.

Rein, Lisa. 2006. "Mystery of Va.'s First Slaves is Unlocked 400 Years Later." *Washington Post,* September 3.

Schultz, Martin, and Herman R. Lantz. 1988. "Occupational Pursuits of Free Women in Early America: An Examination of Eighteenth-Century Newspapers." *Sociological Forum* vol. 3, no. 1 (Winter): 89–109.

Tannenbaum, Rebecca J. 1997. " 'What is Best to Be Done for these Fevers': Elizabeth Davenport's Medical Practice in New Haven Colony." *New England Quarterly* vol. 70, no. 2 (June): 265–84.

Taylor, Alan. 2001. *American Colonies: The Settling of North America.* New York: Penguin Books.

Thornton, Russell. 2005. "Native American Demographic and Tribal Survival into the Twenty-First Century." *American Studies* vol. 46, no. 3–4 (Fall–Winter): 23–38.

Trelease, Allen. 1997. *Indian Affairs in Colonial New York: The Seventeenth Century,* 2nd ed. Lincoln: University of Nebraska.

Washington, George. 1779. George Washington to John Sullivan, May 31, 1779, with Instruction. *Writings of George Washington from the Original Manuscript Sources,* edited by John C. Fitzpatrick. memory.loc.gov/cgi-bin/ampage?collId=mgw3&fileName=mgw3b/gwpage009.db&recNum=27&tempFile=./temp/~ammem_8yVt&filecode=mgw&next_filecode=mgw&itemnum=1&ndocs=100

Wax, Darold D. 1973. "Preferences for Slaves in Colonial America." *The Journal of Negro History* vol. 58, no. 4 (October): 371–401.

Wood, Peter. 1974. *Black Majority: Negroes in Colonial South Carolina from 1670 through the Stono Rebellion.* New York: Norton.

2

Society, Culture, and Dress

London's Samuel Pepys (1633–1703) is an important diarist whose numerous reflections on sartorial matters in the 1660s attest to the central importance of dress both in his life and in the lives of many during his era. Pepys delighted in his dressed self and found it unsettling when he was inappropriately attired for a social occasion or uncomfortable when his fashionable apparel was too thin for inclement weather. He was also attuned to the latest fashion and conformed to trends as much as his purse could afford. For example, on October 8, 1666, Pepys recorded, "The King [Charles II] hath yesterday in Council declared his resolution of setting a fashion for clothes, which he will never alter. It will be a vest . . . but it is to teach the nobility thrift, and will do good" (Pepys 1895, 6:11). Within the week, members of the Houses of Lords and Commons took on this new look, trading in their doublets for vests and pairing them with new coats and fitted breeches. Within the month Pepys had ordered a vest and coat from his tailor and on November 4, donned his new clothes for a social occasion.

Although Pepys never lived in or visited British North America, his sartorial observations are a useful beginning for studies of dress in Britain's colonies. They reveal that far more than just meeting the practical necessities of protecting the body from the elements, dress and appearance in the colonial period were tangible expressions of a wearer's economic and social status. These expressions were shaped by a range of prescriptive and proscriptive forces fueled by commerce, manufacturing, and agriculture; art, novelty, and cultural interchange; health, occupation, and location; and political and religious discourse. For example, when Charles II (1630–1685) declared the new style for gentlemen's clothing, his motives ran deeper than to control the aesthetics of the clothing worn by male courtiers (and their less affluent imitators); he also needed to control the economic drain caused by extravagant expenditures for apparel. All of

Samuel Pepys, portrait by John Hayls, 1666. Samuel Pepys noted in his diary that he had "hired," or rented, the informal gown or banyan he wore when he sat for this portrait. (National Portrait Gallery, London, UK/The Bridgeman Art Library)

London was still in shock in the aftermath of the Great Fire, which had swept through the central part of London in early September 1666, just a month before the monarch announced his sumptuary resolution. In July of the year before, the plague had come to London; the death toll, in the scores of thousands, did not diminish significantly until February of the following year. Coming in such close succession, these two calamities crippled London's financial and commercial markets, compounding the economic challenges that Charles already faced in financing England's war against the Dutch Republic, which had been declared in March of 1665. The hard currency being shipped abroad to pay for the upper-class appetite for luxury goods translated to fewer warships and soldiers with which to prosecute the war.

Across the Atlantic, the inhabitants of England's colonies lacked up-to-the minute access to changing fashions at court. As long as the colonies remained a sparsely settled frontier, few had the financial means to acquire expensive fashionable attire. Colonists were neither unaware of nor ignored changing fashions, however. Increasingly in the colonial period consumers purchased and incorporated into their daily lives a flood of goods imported exclusively from Britain, including fabrics and ready-made clothing. In general, the same goods were available in all port cities. As newspaper advertisements of the 18th century confirm, Bostonians could purchase the same general range of India export cottons, Chinese export silks, and Norwich worsteds as folks in Philadelphia and Charleston. At the same time, the cultural practices of dress—how dress can define status, religion, age, gender, ethnicity, and race—at work in England informed and influenced the apparel choices colonists made. Clothing consumption in England's colonies was influenced in large part by three factors: the relationship of clothing to the notions of fashion and gentility, the communicative qualities of clothing, and the factors that affected access to apparel.

CLOTHING AS FASHION

Style and Fashion

There is a distinct difference between style and fashion in clothing. Style refers to the shape or form of a garment or personal accessory. Fashion refers to the most favored, or preferred, style of a garment or accessory at any particular time. Throughout the colonial period changes in fashion emphasized or even distorted different parts of the body at the expense of others. Fashion also exploited all the possibilities of a style; once all the variations had been exhausted, new styles developed. Fashion sometimes produced an entirely new garment—for example, the woman's one-piece gown replaced the separate bodice, skirt, and petticoat. But fashion also changed merely with a new hairdressing accessory or a different style of collar.

Well-to-do folks did not always keep up-to-date with European high fashion. What constituted the latest fashion may have been an upgrade in look rather than an entire ensemble of newly tailored garments of fashionable textiles. Perhaps a new stomacher, apron, petticoat, or waistcoat was sufficient to refresh an ensemble. Rather than order or make new apparel, older garments often were remade to conform to the latest fashion. In this case, the style of the remodeled attire was up-to-date; the fabric—the most costly part of any item of dress—was not. At the other end of the social and economic spectrum, working sorts and their families might add a less expensive variant of a fashionable accessory to generic pieces. Members of nonelite groups who adopted elements of fashionable apparel to emulate their betters raised fears that the social order might be subverted. They also followed hierarchies of fashion that did not conform to society at large.

Fashion, Refinement, and Gentility

Seventeenth-century settlers represented many different classes and backgrounds. The first colonists to Virginia were male, drawn heavily from the ranks of the gentry with some skilled artisans and laborers. In contrast, Plymouth colony's Protestant dissenters were mostly of the middling sort: farmers, artisans, and tradesmen with their families and some servants. All brought with them, however, the sense of social hierarchy bred into them in England. Although the colonial hierarchy lacked titled nobility and was more fluid than English society, it was organized on the bases of birth and wealth.

The colonial social structure differed in one significant way, however, from its English model. In England, gentlemen did not engage in trade, instead they lived on the profits received from their land, either as rents or the returns of their own agricultural pursuits, both usually managed by an agent. In contrast, wealthy colonial merchants were counted among the social elite. Members of governing councils or assemblies might also be considered gentry, since such positions depended on possessing some degree of education and fulfilling property requirements. Those colonial artisans and craftspeople who established themselves and acquired wealth often acquired culture; they too moved into the ranks of the gentry. Professional men—lawyers, physicians, clergymen, teachers at grammar schools and colleges—could be considered among the upper ranks, but positioned a rung or two below the merchant and ruling elites. Most of the middling sorts comprised farmers who owned their own land—they also may have plied a part-time trade such as weaving, blacksmithing, or shoemaking— and trades people, such as small shopkeepers, tavern keepers, printers, and tailors. Servants, unskilled laborers of all kinds, and tenant farmers made up the lower rungs of society, while the very lowest stratum was accorded to slaves. In the colonial period, standards of conduct tended to mean a set of accepted behaviors for the elite, and a prescription of "deference for everyone else" (Hemphill 1996, 319). Seventeenth-century efforts to regulate behavior also included sumptuary laws, attempts to restrict the consumption of certain goods to those at and above a certain economic level.

The concept and realization of fashion were inextricably tied to the notion of *refinement*, that is, a particular mode of speech, dress, body carriage, and manners that defined the gentry. Although retarded to some degree in the colonies by the rigors of establishing settlements, the refining process was well underway in colonial America by the 1690s, particularly in the oldest settlements and colonial capitals (Bushman 1992; Smith 2002). Botanist John Bartram (1699–1777), for example, was advised by a London friend to buy new clothes for a visit to some Virginia planters, "for though I should not esteem thee less, to come to me in what dress thou will,—yet these Virginians are a very gentle, well-dressed people—and look, perhaps, at a man's outside than his inside" (quoted in Breen 2004, 160). By the 18th century, the colonies were far from homogeneous in their social, economic, and racial makeup so the degree to which refinement was embraced or achieved varied considerably.

The idea of refinement was rooted in the courtesy literature that developed in Renaissance court culture in the 1500s and 1600s. This early courtesy literature prescribed a code of behavior for aristocratic males that included conversational skills, table manners, and rituals of courtesy (Bryson 1990, 140). The elite now sported apparel appropriate for the new rituals and used utensils and other paraphernalia intended for genteel dining.

Extending the trappings of courtesy, they procured and displayed exotic artifacts and foreign luxury items to distinguish themselves as persons of refined taste as well as affluence.

By the 17th century, the codification of manners was no longer just about ceremonial deference but about self-presentation at all times. Now, under the influence of courtesy literature, the gentry joined the aristocracy in adopting practices of self-restraint and self-control. The terms *civility* and *politeness* joined *courtesy* to prescribe the genteel practices to which gentle-born people were expected to conform: fashionable dress conveyed gentility. As a symbol of status, fashion was altered constantly: nonelite groups imitated fashionable dress, forcing the elite continually to adopt new styles.

By the early 1700s, colonists in the oldest settlements were taking stock of their situation. No longer at daily risk of losing life and property to hostile attack or famine, they began to look to British models of behavior and standards of living to mark their success. The concepts of refinement and gentility spread rapidly through New England after 1715 with the publication of *The School of Good Manners,* a conduct manual for children. The author, Boston schoolmaster Eleazar Moody, had borrowed the manners sections of his book from a London publication of the same name published in 1685. One segment of the text cautioned young readers about the conduct of their religious lives: another laid out rules of behavior for church, school, home, and play, "the observation whereof will deliver you from the disgraceful titles of sordid and clownish, and entail upon the mention of you, the honor of genteel and well bred children" (Moody, 1805, 23). In America, *The School of Good Manners* enjoyed 34 editions between 1715 and 1846.

The behavior of one quintessential American was probably molded by such conduct rules. By age 16, George Washington (1732–1799) copied, probably as school exercises, a series of 110 "Rules of Civility and Decent Behaviour in Company and Conversation." The list was based on tenets composed by French Jesuits in 1595 and translated into English and published in 1640 by 12-year-old Frances Hawkins under the title *Youth's Behaviour, or Decency in Conversation among Men.* The work went through at least 11 editions through 1672. Washington's exercises were copied from the work of an unidentified individual who "selected, simplified, and arranged" Hawkins's work (Moore, 1926). Several of the maxims concern dress and public appearance:

51st Wear not your Cloths, foul, unript or Dusty but See they be Brush'd once every day at least and take heed tha[t] you approach not to any Uncleaness.

52d In your Apparel be Modest and endeavour to accomodate Nature, rather than to procure Admiration keep to the Fashio[n] of your equals Such as are Civil and orderly with respect to Times and Places.

53d Run not in the Streets, neither go t[oo s]lowly nor wit[h] Mouth open go not Shaking yr Arms [kick not the earth with yr feet, go] not upon the Toes, nor in a Dancing [fashion].

54th Play not the Peacock, looking every where about you, to See if you be well Deck't, if your Shoes fit well if your Stokings sit neatly, and Cloths handsomely. (Washington, 1744)

In the 18th century, one of the most important markers of social class in Britain and her colonies was the degree to which one's manners, appearance, surroundings, and behavior agreed with accepted standards of gentility and refinement. These standards reached every aspect of daily life, both private and public. Gentility required outer clothing free of soil and food residue and clean linen underclothing that was changed regularly, if not daily. Food should be well prepared, served in the proper dishes, and eaten with the proper utensils—forks joined knives and spoons as tableware in the 18th century. Houses and furnishings should be kept clean and rooms or spaces within rooms set aside for genteel pursuits and entertainments. The adoption of this latter proscription can be seen in interior architecture and probate inventories over time from small rooms with multipurpose furnishings to larger rooms with a single function, furnished accordingly.

Wealth alone, and the ability to acquire material comforts and luxuries, did not guarantee gentility. The truly genteel demonstrated a refinement of taste and a knowledge of the arts as expressed in one's person, home, garden, and estate. Refined behavior was articulated in polite good manners, proper deportment, and graceful carriage. A cultured mind was expressed in the abilities to make conversation and display accomplishments such as drawing, languages, fancy needlework, or playing a musical instrument.

As long as they could read, colonists of every situation in life had access to information on how to behave in a genteel manner. Courtesy manuals guided readers with advice on proper greetings and farewells, acceptable table manners, and how to avoid awkwardness and maintain elegance in body movements and facial expressions. With the aid of books and pamphlets colonists could cultivate their minds: learn Latin and Greek, read the ancient classics and the modern philosophers, and delve into the natural sciences, literature, and the arts. "By the eighteenth century, 'genteel' was used to describe a host of objects, situations, persons, and habits. There were genteel wigs, genteel saddles, genteel speech and letters. Martha Washington (1731–1802) ordered a genteel nightgown from a genteel shop in London. . . . Strangers in taverns or boardinghouses were able to evaluate the gentility of the other guests, or of the host, the food, the furnishings. . . . The word had vast scope and energy" (Bushman 1992, 61).

Forces for Change

The forces that governed a person's preferences in attire were influenced by various factors. To some extent the fashions set at England's court and modified by its country gentry influenced its subjects on the other side of the Atlantic. For example, Charles II's previously mentioned sartorial resolution introduced the vest, coat, and breeches ensemble, a variation of which is still with us today as the three-piece suit. In England the ensemble was made up in silk fabrics for formal court wear and good English woolen textiles for almost every other occasion. In the colonies it also became fashionable to use fabrics like linen and cotton, more suited to a hotter summer climate. At the end of the 1600s, England's elite began to replace their heavy needle lace cravats and cuffs with accessories made of the fine India-export cotton fabric called muslin, which were sometimes lightly embroidered. This shift in fashion was important, not only because the muslin replaced lace for both everyday wear and more formal events among all classes of wearers, but also because the widespread use of muslin for all occasions influenced the designs and techniques workers used to develop laces in the 18th century.

Fashion hegemony was not exclusive to the court, however, and non-elite groups—sometimes unwittingly—established themselves as alternative sources for fashion. England's two Civil Wars, 1642–1646 and 1648–1649, profoundly affected dress. The religious controversy over doctrine and ostentatious display in church resulted in adoption by some religious groups of a plain style of dress that proclaimed the wearer's religious and political beliefs and affiliations. This practice continued in America, for example, among members of the Society of Friends (also known as Quakers) into the 19th century. In the colonies, where the landed well-to-do were often more active in managing their farms and plantations than in England, articles of practical attire sometimes moved up the social hierarchy and were accepted into fashion. In the early 18th century, breeches made of leather were considered mechanic's, or workman's, clothing—"fit to be worn only by the laborious," to quote one contemporary English observer. Landowners, however, found that the long-wearing skins protected their legs better than cloth when riding or walking through brush and high grass. By the 1750s the garment "is become fashionable, and universally worn from the tradesmen to those of the first rank in the kingdom" (Postlethwayt 1971). In the 1760s wearing leather clothing of colonial manufacture became a symbol of resistance against the increasing interference of the British government in the commercial affairs of the colonies in the 1760s. The *Boston Gazette* reported on a resolution of "a very great Number of the respectable Tradesmen of this Town . . . to wear Nothing but Leather for their Working Habits, for the future, and that to be only of the Manufacture of this Government" (September 24, 1764).

Not all colonists subscribed to the practices of gentility as they pertained to clothing; some were indifferent to public opinion and others were unwilling to expend the personal energy and money necessary to keeping up appearances. Susan Vincent has noted: "Before the mechanisms of mass production, consumers took a much more active part in the creation of their clothing, their choices determining the colour, cut, fabric and style of a new garment. Individuals thus 'made' their clothes; in turn the public response to this vestimentary project made or unmade the self" (Vincent 2003, 9). Alexander Hamilton (1712–1756), an Annapolis physician of Scottish birth, encountered one "unmade" self in 1744, at Perth Amboy, New Jersey, while on a roundtrip journey from Maryland to Maine. Breakfasting one morning, Hamilton observed "an antick figure pass by having an old plaid banyan, a pair of thick worsted stockings, ungartered, a greasy worsted nightcap, and no hat." When he inquired after the old man, his landlord explained, "Tho he makes but a pitifull appearance, yet is he proprietor of most of the houses in town. He is very rich" (Hamilton 1948, 38). Others were woefully aware of their inadequacies—especially in comparison to European fashion. Abigail Adams (1744–1818) had a suit of homespun ready for her husband, future president John Adams (1735–1826), when he arrived home after his long absence in Philadelphia during the debate over colonial independence in 1776 (Adams and Adams 2002, 136). Upon his arrival in France as minister in 1782, however, Adams confided to his diary, "The first thing to be done, in Paris, is always to send for a Taylor, Peruke maker and Shoemaker, for this nation has established such a domination over the Fashion, that neither Cloaths, Wigs, nor Shoes made in any other Place will do in Paris. . . . It is a great Branch of the Policy of the Court, to preserve and increase this national Influence over the Mode, because it occasions an immense Commerce between France and all the other Parts of Europe. Paris furnishes both the Materials and the manner, both to Men and Women, every where else" (John Adams 1782).

CLOTHING AS COMMUNICATION

People where they are not known, are generally honour'd according to their Cloaths and other Accoutrements they have about them; from the richness of them we judge of their Wealth, and by their ordering of them we guess at their Understanding. It is this which encourages every Body, who is conscious of his little Merit, if he is any ways able, to wear Cloaths above his Rank, especially in large and populous Cities, where obscure Men may hourly meet with fifty Strangers to one Acquaintance, and consequently have the Pleasure of being esteem'd by a vast Majority, not as what they are, but what they appear to be. (Mandeville 1729, 89–90)

What Bernard Mandeville (1670–1733) observed about the communicative qualities of dress in British society in 1717 aptly describes one nonpractical function of dress in colonial America. Most folks, whether residing in the largest population centers of the colonies—Boston, Philadelphia, New York, Newport, and Charleston—or inhabiting small communities like Deerfield, Massachusetts, St. Mary's City, Maryland, and Northampton, Virginia, presumed that apparel reflected one's station in life. In fact, dress and hierarchy were inextricably tied. James Habersham (c. 1712–1775), a prominent merchant, landowner, and politician in mid-18th-century Georgia, asserted, "I would not be quite in, neither would I be quite out of the fashion." He preferred to tread a middle ground in keeping with his status in the community: not conspicuous either because his appearance was ultrafashionable or out-of-date. His friend and agent William Knox, in London, oversaw an order of some new clothes for him in 1768. Habersham approved of the new coat, but wondered "how you send so gay a waistcoat," feeling that the colorful fabric might be out of keeping with his age and position (Habersham 1904, 61, 75). In contrast, Nicholas Boylston (1747–1828), who was among the wealthiest of Boston's merchant elite, had himself depicted in a dashing and sumptuous banyan, waistcoat, and turban, all of silk, by artist John Singleton Copley (1738–1813) in about 1769. He may indeed have owned and worn such garments—in fact, his brother, Thomas, was portrayed by Copley in similar clothing in his portrait of the same year. Boylston's choice of this informal apparel for his portrait speaks not only to the expensive silks he could afford, but also to the strength of his position in society. A less secure subject likely would have chosen more conservative and formal attire.

The wealthiest tier of society generally dressed in the most expensive textiles; the garments were tailored to fit well (the elite remarked on and

Nicholas Boylston, by John Singleton Copley, c. 1769. Bostonian Nicholas Boylston wore informal, but expensive, clothing for his portrait. (Harvard Art Museum/Art Resource, NY)

deplored poor workmanship and fit) and of the latest fashion that news from across the Atlantic could bring. Professionals and trades folk and their families might own articles of clothing that were made-to-order for them, but of harder-wearing and less ornamented fabrics. They likely bought imported ready-made apparel as well. In some circumstances clothes were the product of home labors. The fit was not always perfect. The working poor, who included laborers, farm workers, servants, sailors, and apprentices, wore indifferently made and loose-fitting clothing of cheap fabrics, whether made-to-order or ready-made. The poorest segment of colonial society wore whatever clothing its members could find or were given. In sum, the details of clothing construction, and the nature and kind of the textiles used in that construction distinguished the status of the wearer.

But appearances could be deceiving. In 1762, Thomas Ward experienced the theft of a horse hired by a person that Ward perceived "had the Appearance of a Gentleman; he is sometimes dressed with a blue Coat, a Scarlet Waistcoat, with Gold round the Button Holes, and a narrow Silver Lace, [or] blue Sattin Waistcoat, and a light coloured Coat; and sometimes appears in a Banyan" (*Pennsylvania Gazette*, September 2, 1762). The thief even had a decently dressed male servant with him.

Sumptuary Legislation

As Mandeville noted, status-conscious underlings could subvert the status quo by wearing clothing above their rank. That men and women, including enslaved individuals, did so in the colonies is confirmed by the sumptuary legislation passed in Massachusetts and Virginia in the 17th century and in South Carolina in the 18th. In England, sumptuary laws had been enacted by various monarchs, beginning with Edward III (reigned 1327–1377), designed to regulate aspects of personal conduct, including the cut of one's clothes, diet and drink, and personal lifestyle. Among the concerns that drove these regulations were the desire to preserve distinctions of status, "so that any stranger could tell by merely looking at a man's dress to what rank in society he belonged"; to control practices that were perceived as extravagances "harmful to the morals of the people"; and economic motives, including "attempt[s] on the part of the sovereign to induce his people to save their money, so that they might be able to help him out financially in time of need" (Baldwin 1926, 10). In 1604, parliament, under the new English king, James I (1566–1625), nullified all previous penal laws restraining excesses in apparel (Baldwin 1926, 249).

Fifteen years later, in 1619, the first Virginia Assembly enacted the earliest sumptuary law in British North America. The legislation tied the value of clothing to the amount of money a man would be assessed for the support of the church: "if he be unmarried according to his owne apparell, if he be married, according to his owne and his wives, or either of their apparell" ("Proceedings of the Virginia Assembly, 1619"). The ruling carried a practical message: the more modestly one dressed, the less one was assessed. A 1621 amendment established that only members of Virginia's Council of State and the owners of the large tracts of land called hundreds could "wear gold in their clothes, or to wear silk till they make it themselves" (Hening 1823, 1:114). Later in the century, garments of silk—except for hoods and scarves—as well as accessories of silver, gold, and linen lace and ribbons woven with gold or silver were considered contraband (Bruce 1935, 2:187–88). These articles were to be confiscated and sent back to England. Evidently, there was concern that colonists were funneling their resources into dress—and therefore unseemly display and careless expense—rather than into goods that would benefit the colony.

In the 1600s, the Massachusetts General Court peppered colonists with sumptuary legislation concerning dress. The earliest ruling was passed in 1634; successive laws were altered and expanded in—ultimately futile— attempts to control what the court viewed as the corrupting excesses of dress, especially among the nonelites. The first law forbade all ranks to wear for everyday "new fashions, or long hair, or anything of the like nature"; "slashed clothes, other than one slash in each sleeve, and another in the back"; "immoderate great sleeves . . . great rayles, long wings, etc." (quoted in Fischer 1989, 141, 143). Also prohibited were laces, girdles, and hatbands made of silver, gold, or silk. Two years later, a statute prohibited the manufacture and sale of any kind of lace as well as selling clothing decorated with lace (Fischer 1989, 143).

By 1638, Puritan leaders realized that legislation alone was not solving the problem of what then-governor John Winthrop (1588–1649) called "the great disorder general through the country." The General Court decided

New England's leaders railed against excesses in fashion among the non-elite such as the wearing of silk hoods by women and girls whose husbands or fathers were worth less than £200. *Woman Wearing a Dark Hood*, engraving by Wenceslaus Hollar, 1640s. (The Thomas Fisher Rare Book Library, University of Toronto)

that this was a matter for the colony's ministers to handle, but "little was done about it." Winthrop (1908, 1:279) blamed the women: "divers of the elders' wives, etc., were in some measure partners in this general disorder." Legislation passed in 1651 targeted, in particular, "people of mean condition" who "[took] upon them the garb of Gentlemen . . . or Women of the same rank" but were not entitled to do so because of the meager worth of their estates or lack of education. The court ordered selectmen in each town to "take notice of Apparel of any of the Inhabitants . . . and whosoever they shall judge to exceed their ranks and abilities, in the costliness or fashion of the Apparel in any respect . . . shall have power to assess such persons" if their real and personal estates did not exceed 200 pounds in value (Whitmore 1890, 5). The selectmen were to look for residents who wore gold or silver lace, gold or silver buttons, expensive linen lace and ribbons, silk hoods or scarves or "great Boots (Leather being so scarce a commodity in this Country)." Those found in violation were to be fined 10 shillings for each offense. The law exempted from prosecution magistrates and public officers and their families, settled military officers and soldiers, and "any other whose education and imployment have been above the ordinary degree, or whose estate have been considerable, though now decayed" (Whitmore 1890, 5). An addendum to this statute, passed in 1662, warned that the rising generation was "in danger to be Corrupted and Effeminated" by the excesses of fashion. It added the children of the meaner sorts as well as household servants to the list of those prohibited from wearing costly dress or accessories, upon penalty of increasing fines for offenses (Whitmore 1890, 5–6). These laws remained in force at least through the 1680s.

Inhabitants were brought to court for violations. The cases of Humphry Griffen and John Kemball, brought to court on April 28, 1659, are typical. Griffen was fined 10 shillings "for his daughter's presentment for wearing a silk scarf." A formal complaint was brought against John Kemball's wife for wearing a silk scarf, but he "proved that he was worth above 200 pounds and was discharged" (Dow 1912, 2:153).

Attempting to curb the wearing of apparel that "is unbecoming a wilderness condition and the profession of the gospell," in 1676 the Connecticut Court deemed that only those who paid the public rate based on an estate of £150 or more—plus members of their families—were entitled to wear "gold or siluer lace, or gold or siluer buttons, silk ribbons, or other superfluous trimings, or any bone lace aboue three shillings per yard, or silk scarfes" because this apparel was "suitable to their ranke." Exempted were magistrates and public officers of the colony, who were entitled to discretion about what they or their family members would wear, and settled military commissioned officers "whose quality and estate haue been aboue the ordinary degree though now decayed." Those who violated this order were fined 10 shillings for each offence. Further, "if any taylor shall fashion any garment for any child or servant contrary to the minde of the parent or master of such child or servant, he shall forfeitt for every such offence ten shillings" (Trumbull 1852, 283).

In 1735, Charleston, South Carolina, attempted to regulate the attire of its lowest social stratum: the enslaved—African, African American, and American Indian men and women. The legislation specifies that because sufficient numbers of its enslaved population were dressing above their social station, legal remedies were in order: "[M]any of the slaves in this Province wear clothes much above the condition of slaves." Known today as the Slave Act of 1735, the law enumerated both the imported fabrics acceptable for slave clothing and the maximum price to be paid for those fabrics. Included in the list were "negro cloth, duffelds, coarse kearsies, osnabrigs, blue linen, checked linen or coarse garlix or calicoes, checked cottons or scotch plaids" (McCord 1840, 7:396). Slave owners were not to pay above 10 shillings per yard for imported cottons and linens (these were woven in northern Europe and India), but prices for woolen goods— all products of English manufacture—were not specified. This act, reiterated in 1740, underscores that perhaps a sizable segment of Charleston's enslaved population wore fashionable clothing constructed of not-inexpensive materials. One owner declared of his runaway enslaved servant, Prince, "As he has a great many suits of cloaths, it's impossible to describe his dress" (*South-Carolina Gazette*, August 29, 1754). In 1744, Charleston's grand jury noted, "[I]t is apparent that Negro Women in particular do not restrain themselves in their cloathing as the Law requires, but dress in Apparel quite gay and beyond their Condition" (*South-Carolina Gazette*, November 5, 1744).

Reinforcement of Group Identity

As discussed above, colonial America's social hierarchy was defined and maintained visually by dress. England's Puritan leaders, however, delineated stricter sartorial boundaries for their female parishioners—regardless of their social status—in language that equated modest dress with piety, humility, and obedience. In 1702, Puritan minister Cotton Mather (1663–1728) warned New England's women against indulging in current fashion. This included the "laying out of hair, . . . naked necks and arms, or, which is more abominable, naked breasts" (Mather 1853, 2:324). In his view, such fashions incited men to the sin of lust and women to the sin of immodesty.

In contrast, Methodist preacher John Wesley (1703–1791), drawing on New Testament exhortations from 1 Peter, 1 Timothy, and Luke, supported the right of those of high rank and those in authority to wear "those beautiful things, with which God has so amply provided us" (Wesley 1829, 2:310). In his sermon "On Dress," Wesley argued that the mistake was in allowing "ordinary Christians, those in the lower or middle ranks of life, to be adorned with gold, or pearls, or costly apparel" (1829, 311). He reasoned that fine clothing had "a natural tendency to make a man sick of pride" and "tends to breed and to increase vanity" (1829, 312). Moreover, purchasing costly apparel left fewer resources for clothing, feeding, housing, and ministering to the poor, the sick, and the imprisoned (1829, 314). Wesley's attitudes resonated with colonial congregations. In 1735, he was extended an invitation by Georgia's governor, James Oglethorpe, to become the minister of the newly formed Savannah parish. Wesley later recalled that his sermons on the reform of dress had an effect: "All the time that I afterward, ministered at Savannah, I saw neither gold in the church, nor costly apparel. But the congregation, in general, was almost constantly clothing in plain, clean linen or woollen" (Wesley 1827, 2:159).

Theologian Jonathan Edwards (1703–1758), founder of the colonies' Great Awakening in the 1730s, saw the fabric of clothing—wool, silk, and linen—as symbols of more complex religious ideas that bound people together. Fleeces from sheep represented Jesus Christ "who is the Lamb of God"; silk, the product of the silk worm "that the worm yields up at his death," represented the "glorious clothing we have for our souls by the death of him who became a man." Flax represented the spiritual clothing of virtue and purity: the fiber "is exceedingly bruised and broken and beaten with many blows, and so yields us its coat to be our clothing. And Christ, through exceeding great suffering, yields us his righteousness, that is as fine linnen, clean and white" (quoted in Schmidt 1989, 50).

Colonial clergy often established their religious authority through the gowns, linen accessories, and other tangible symbols of their ministerial office. Rev. John Rodgers (1727–1811), a Presbyterian pastor in New York City, was of the mind that a clergyman attentive to and well ordered in his dress will inspire respect among all classes: "A clerical fop is, indeed, contemptible; but a clerical sloven, deserves no slight reprehension" (quoted in Miller 1813, 341). On his visit to Philadelphia, New York, and Newport between 1772 and 1773, world traveler Rabbi Haim Isaac Carigal (1733–1777) met Newport's Congregational minister the Reverend Ezra Stiles; the two became close friends. A keen observer, Stiles described Carigal as having a long beard but a shaven head. Attending the 1773 Purim service at the Newport synagogue, Stiles noted that the rabbi was "dressed in a red Garment with the usual Phylacteries and habiliments, the white silk Surplice; he wore a high brown furr cap," which resembled a woman's muff and was closed at the top with a green cloth (Stiles 1901, 1:363). (A phylactery, or tefillin, is a strip of parchment inscribed with passages from the Exodus 13 and Deuteronomy 6 enclosed in a black calf-skin case and fastened by thin straps to the forehead or left hand or arm.) Stiles commissioned a portrait of Carigal for Yale University. It shows the rabbi in a red robe or coat that appears to close down the front, with white cuffs showing at the wrists and the straight-sided fur hat described above. It is unclear whether Carigal wore this attire only when conducting services and for formal occasions or if it was his everyday garb.

Colonial hierarchy faced greater challenges from dissenter groups that identified plainness with godliness and advocated a more egalitarian religious society. William Penn (1644–1718), America's foremost Quaker and founder of Pennsylvania, urged fellow members of the Society of Friends to temper their style of dress regardless of their economic and social standing: "Chuse thy Cloaths by thine own Eyes, not another's. The more plain and simple they are, the better. Neither unshapely, nor fantastical; and for Use and Decency, and not for Pride" (Penn 1863, 18, no. 74). The ruling of the Philadelphia Yearly Meeting in 1695 reinforced the importance of simple dress in maintaining Quaker identity: "none [shall] wear long-lapped Sleeves, or coats gathered at the Sides, or Superfluous Buttons, or broad Ribbons about their Hats, or long curled Periwiggs, . . . or . . . dress their heads immodestly or wear their Garments indecently, . . . and that all be careful about making, buying or wearing (as much as they can) strip'd or flower'd Stuffs" (quoted in Schmidt 1989, 40–41). South Carolina Quaker Sophia Hume (1702–1774) echoed this central role of dress in guiding the pious life: *"For tho' Religion stands not simply in Clothes, yet true Religion stands in that which sets Bounds and Limits to the Mind with respect to Clothes, as well as other Things"* (Hume 1752, 30). In practice, Quakers usually kept up with the fashionable silhouette but chose plainer fabrics in more subdued colors and less ostentatious trimmings. Eighteenth-century well-to-do Quaker women wore silk but selected unpatterned silk satins in browns or grays rather than brightly colored brocaded floral patterns.

In 18th-century Pennsylvania, Moravians (a Protestant sect founded in Saxony) used plain clothing and subtle details to define themselves as a religious community. Members divided themselves by age and sex into groups called choirs: children of both sexes, older girls, single women, the married women and men, widows and widowers, and older boys and single men:

> The sisters wore a uniform costume of gray or brown, and white for special festivals. While the sisters' costume was uniform from the girls' choir to the widows' choir, all wore the *Schnebelhaube* or cornered cap, the color of the cap-ribbon, by which the cap was tied under the chin, designated to which choir the wearer belonged. Thus the children's caps had red ribbons; those of the older girls, light red; those of the single sisters, pink; those of the married sisters, blue; and the widows wore a white bow. (quoted in Yoder 1982, 309)

Clothing was also used to construct, determine, and mask gendered identities. The Virginia court case of Thomasine Hall (born c. 1605), a 17th-century indentured servant, demonstrates the role community could play in defining gender through clothing. Born at or near Newcastle upon Tyne, England, Hall was christened and raised as a girl. In 1627, at about age 22, Hall adopted a new gender identity: he "[c]ut of[f] his heire and Changed his apparel into the fashion of man and went over as a souldier in the *Isle of Ree* [Îsle de Ré] being in the habit of a man." Returning to Plymouth, England, after service in France, Hall resumed the identity of Thomasine and supported herself in the needlework trades, including making bobbin lace. By the beginning of 1628, Hall had once again swapped a feminine for a masculine identity and sailed to Virginia, probably as an indentured servant. Hall's first master purchased him as the man Thomas. Then Hall was legally declared to be a woman and was acquired by a second master as Thomasine. This suggests that once in Virginia, Hall was not consistent in wearing men's or women's clothing. Court records do not mention when Hall's neighbors began to raise questions about Hall's sex; four separate physical examinations of Hall yielded conflicting conclusions. Such ambiguity challenged not only norms about sexual identity but also about cultural practices in early Virginia society: how was Hall to behave and what was Hall's proper role in the community as an indentured servant? With gossip abounding, the matter was referred to Virginia's General Court in 1629. After hearing testimony, the judges declared Hall to be both a "man and a woman" and used clothing to define Hall's dual sexual status. "[A]ll the Inhabitants there may take notice thereof and that hee shall goe Clothed in mans apparel, only his head to bee attired in a Coyfe and Crosecloth wth an Apron before him" (quoted in Norton 1997, 40–66).

Gendered identities were masked in the 18th century as well. In 1785 a reward was offered for the apprehension of an African American who ran away from his master in Delaware. The runaway, named Simon but "formerly called Dick," was a large man who could "alter his voice on each extreme" and understood not only farm work but could "wash, spin, sew, knit, &c." He also masqueraded as a woman: "it is probably he may change his clothes and put on womens, in order for better concealment, as he did so once before" (*Pennsylvania Gazette,* January 26).

For women who wished to engage in activities considered the domain of men, dressing the part was essential. From the late 17th to the early 19th centuries, more than 20 English women are known to have dressed as men to serve as seamen in Britain's Royal Navy or Marines (Stark 1996, 82–122). Although it is not known how many colonial women donned men's garb to sail on colonial ships trading along the eastern seaboard or bound for international ports, newspaper advertisements of runaways confirm the practice. In 1752, Sarah Benfield, an English indentured servant living in Williamsburg, Virginia, ran away from her master wearing her own clothing but stole other garments, including "an old starr'd Man's Flannel Jacket, a Pair of bluegrey Mens Stockings, [and] check'd Trowsers . . . and 'tis suppose'd will endeavour to make her Escape on Board some Ship in a Sailors Dress" (*Virginia Gazette,* October 6, 1752).

Certainly, it was as easy to seek employment aboard a trading ship as a warship—there was no physical examination, no requirement for proof of identity, no need to demonstrate literacy in reading or writing. Once on board, sailors rarely undressed because they seldom bathed, and they slept in their work clothes. Even when sick or wounded, they were not thoroughly examined before treatment. Women seamen would have prepared for shipboard life by purchasing used or inexpensive ready-made clothing—a loose-fitting shirt, jacket, and trousers—called slops and perhaps by binding their breasts. They might have bought tobacco to smoke or chew, an activity that, along with drinking, would have helped them fit in with fellow sailors.

Although there are no published accounts of colonial women seaman, the contemporary accounts of the self-confessed pirate Anne Bonny—like

Colonial pirate Anne Bonny often donned men's clothing. In this engraving of her firing a pistol, she also wears a bandoleer with a hatchet. Engraving published in Amsterdam, 1725, from *General History of the Robberies and Murders of the Most Notorious Pyrates.* (Bettmann/Corbis)

the narrative of Thomasine/Thomas Hall—sheds light on how clothing was used to mask gender identities. Much of what is known about her was published by a Captain Charles Johnson (likely a pseudonym) in 1724 (Johnson 1998, 125–31). According to Johnson, Anne was born in Cork, Ireland, the daughter of a married attorney and his house servant. Her father wished to raise her in his household, but needed to disguise the matter from his wife and the town. So "he had it [i.e., Anne] put into breeches, as a boy, pretending it was a relation's child he was to breed up to be his clerk." This pretence evidently did not work; leaving his wife behind, Anne's father took both the servant and their daughter to South Carolina, where he became a successful planter/merchant. Johnson indicated that in her teens, Anne was fierce and independent: "once, when a young fellow would have lain with her, against her will, she beat him so, that he lay ill of it a considerable time." She turned her back on her father's fortune and married a sailor who "was not worth a groat." The couple headed for New Providence Island, in the Bahamas, where Anne caught the attention of the pirate Calico Jack Rackam. Abandoning her husband, Anne went to sea "in men's clothes" with Rackam, joining a gang of pirates that included another woman, Mary Reed.

In 1720, Rackam's vessel was captured near the island of Jamaica and the group was put on trial there. Printed testimony from the proceedings indicates that when the pirate vessel was engaged in attack or chase, Anne and Mary wore men's clothing—"Mens jackets, and long Trouzers, and Handkerchiefs tied about their Heads, and that each of them had a Machet[e] and Pistol in their Hands." At other times, however, witnesses observed them dressed in women's garb. One witness was not fooled by their masculine dress: "the Reason of her knowing and believing them to be Women was, by the largeness of their Breasts" (quoted in Rediker 1996, 7).

CLOTHING AND ORNAMENTATION
AS MEDIATING AGENTS

In general, enslaved individuals—from both Africa and indigenous populations—were expected to conform to European standards and styles of dress. Men wore shirts and loose trousers or more fitted breeches; women wore shifts, petticoats and jackets, or gowns. Advertisements for runaway slaves are a rich source for descriptions of clothing worn by these individuals. A survey of these notices reveals that male runaways were described as wearing combinations of the following: breeches or trousers, jackets, shirts, coats, waistcoats, hats, shoes, and stockings. The clothing of female runaways included gowns or short gowns, petticoats, aprons, shifts, shoes, and stockings. Enslaved male workers were less likely to wear shoes, stockings, and hats than the rest of the male population and were more likely to wear jackets and trousers rather than coats and breeches. What distinguished urban from rural slaves and house servants from field hands were the quality of the fabric and cut and ornamentation of the clothing they were given or acquired. And as noted earlier in this chapter, South Carolina legislated the kinds of fabrics and clothing suitable for slaves. Plantation owners attempted to control their slaves' appearance by giving out either a set of ready-made clothes or requisite lengths of cloth—often called "negro cloth"—to make approved clothing on a seasonal or annual basis.

Many slaves flouted these rules if they could find the resources and the time. House slaves and skilled enslaved artisans had perhaps the easiest access to information about fashionable dress and had more opportunity to either purchase or barter for better fabrics or acquire more up-to-date second-hand clothing. If allowed to market the produce from family garden plots or earn wages through the practice of self-hiring, even field hands could and did acquire finery. In notices for runaways, descriptions of colorful cloth—red, green, and blue—in fashionable fabrics such as moreen, plush, velvet, and sarsanet were used to identify the petticoats, breeches, handkerchiefs, and men's and women's cloaks, capes, and jackets worn or taken by individuals. Patterned clothing, such as striped jackets and petticoats and gowns of printed calico—purple or red-on-white—is also found in the notices. Sometimes elaborately worked or trimmed clothing is mentioned, such as the "blue sarsanet handkerchief, trim'd with gauze, and with white ribbon sew'd to it" listed among the many items taken by one Maryland runaway. Her male companion sported a "blue camblet jacket, with gold lace at the sleeves, down the breast, and around the collar" (*Annapolis Maryland Gazette*, August 16, 1777).

RUN away, the 23d of this Inftant *January*, from *Silas Crifpin* of *Burlington*, Taylor, a Servant Man named *Jofeph Morris*, by Trade a Taylor, aged about 22 Years, of a middle Stature, fwarthy Complexion, light gray Eyes, his Hair clipp'd off, mark'd with a large pit of the Small Pox on one Cheek near his Eye, had on when he went away a good Felt Hat, a yelowifh Drugget Coat with Pleits behind, an old Ozenbrigs Veft, two Ozenbrigs Shirts, a pair of Leather Breeches handfomely worm'd and flower'd up the Knees, yarn Stockings and good round toe'd Shoes Took with him a large pair of Sheers crack'd in one of the Bows, & mark'd with the Word [*Savoy*]. Whoever takes up the faid Servant, and fecures him fo that his Mafter may have him again, fhall have *Three Pounds* Reward befides reafonable Charges, paid by me *Silas Crifpin.*

In this Philadelphia newspaper advertisement for a runaway indentured servant, his master has carefully described not only his physical features but also the kind and quality of the clothing he wore when he absented himself. (MPI/Getty Images)

If a slave was prone to running away, the owner might brand the individual as both a punishment and for identification, as the following examples from the *South-Carolina Gazette* illustrate. Thomas Wright of Charleston offered a £10 reward for the capture of his slave Trampuse, who was branded on the right shoulder TW (January 31, 1736). Thomas Porter offered a £5 reward for the apprehension of two slaves, "branded TLP all in one" (October 7, 1740). A newly enslaved man and woman were brought to the Charleston work house, identified by "having the brand of a pipe-bowl on each of their shoulders" (September 19, 1753).

Numerous enslaved Africans, however, carried visible reminders of their own tribal identity—and perhaps social, political, and religious roles—in the form of ritual scars and other body modifications. It is not clear, however, whether the owners of these individuals recognized the significance of a particular mark. The following examples, all concerning males, were culled from the *South-Carolina Gazette*. A "new Negro [i.e. recently arrived from Africa] speaks very little English [and] has his Country marks on both

Cheeks" (April 26, 1735). An Ebo man named Primus had "Scars on each side of his Stomach down his Belly" (July 5, 1735). An Angola-born slave named Jamie had filed teeth (January 22, 1756). A young African boy from Guinea, "who calls himself Carolina, which is all the English he speaks," was described only by the "Holes in his Ears"; another slave from Guinea, called Boatswain, trained as a cooper, had "his fore teeth filed, but has none of his country marks" (October 13, 1757; July 17, 1762). Cysar, an elderly slave from Angola, had filed teeth and wore a blue indigo cloth about his middle (February 23, 1765). An unusual notice concerned a woman, newly arrived in Charleston, "named Mindo, aged about 19 Years, . . . has filed Teeth, with Plenty of her Country Marks about her Breast" (*South-Carolina Gazette; and Country Journal*, September, 1766).

Some slaves retained West African forms of dress and accessories. Recent archaeological excavations at the African Burial Ground, used between 1712 and1795, in New York City yielded a female skeleton around whose waist was a string of beads and shells associated with West African customs (*New York Times*, February 25, 2010). African and African American women also appropriated European neckwear for use as a head wrapping in a non-Western style. In the 18th century, a handkerchief was a large square of cloth worn by both men and women as a neck covering (our modern handkerchief would have been called a pocket handkerchief). Enslaved women folded the handkerchief into a rectilinear shape, wrapped it around the head and tied it somewhere on the crown of the head, either at the top or on the sides, completely covering the hair (Griebel). Philis, a young household slave employed by South Carolina governor Robert Johnson, ran away wearing "a Negro cloth Gown dyed yellowish, & a white handkerchief about her head (*South-Carolina Gazette*, February 1, 1735). In 1754, an enslaved house servant named Venus absented herself from her Charleston master wearing a white garlick gown with a handkerchief about her head (*South-Carolina Gazette*, April 2, 1754).

Almost from the beginning of English settlement the expanding consumer base for imported products included American Indians as well as Africans; by the early 18th century, many Indian towns were termini in a network of trade that stretched from the colonial frontier across the Atlantic to Britain and the East. Indians quickly developed a sensibility for European and British textiles and incorporated them into their own clothing traditions. Clothing and cloth were not only among the most important commodities for the pan-colonial trade in animal pelts and skins, but they also played an essential part in the diplomatic treaty negotiations between Native American communities and colonial officials. On the part of the colonial ruling elite, the fur and skin trade—also called the truck trade—was viewed as "the Way and Method the Government is now in for keeping Peace and Friendship with the Indians on our Frontiers. . . . [A]s interest sways mankind in general, so you may bore their Ears to your Door Posts, by still easing them all you can in the Truck Trade" (*Pennsylvania Gazette*, October 8, 1730). It is not known why indigenous people developed a preference for textiles over fur and hide, but scholars have speculated that depletion of animal resources may have prompted a greater dependence on woven goods and Indians may have found that wool cloth in particular had advantages over furs and hide. Trade goods also likely satisfied individual and tribal social and aesthetic values. Scholar James Axtell has argued that, in fact, American Indians who were trading with Europeans had been undergoing a consumer revolution of their own, which had started with the Spanish and French long before contact with the British:

> Sooner or later, some daring Creek or Cherokee individualist had the courage or temerity to adopt a new fashion first seen in cosmopolitan Charles Town or New Orleans or in the home or on the person of the native wife of a local trader. If he or she was a respected leader, a chief or warrior or clan mother, the change in fashion would probably spread more rapidly, just as it would in London or Paris if the queen or a noble took the first step. How else can we explain the Creeks' adoption late in the eighteenth century of items of Scottish dress or the wrap-around turban of brightly colored cloth that men affected for many years? (Axtell 1997, 63)

Indians dictated the quality and design of some of the trade textiles. In his 1677 history of Oxfordshire, England, Robert Plot observed that duffels, "otherwise called Shags, and by the Merchants, Trucking-cloth [trade or barter cloth]," was made "in pieces about 30 Yards long, and one Yard 3/4 broad, and [they] dye them Red or Blue, which are the Colours that best please the Indians of Virginia and New-England" (Plot 1705, 284). When Philadelphia merchant and Quaker James Logan ordered strouds and blankets for the Indian trade from his English factor in 1714, he emphasized that the style and fineness of the cloth must be considered. The stroud—a woolen cloth—should be "blue or red in purchasing wch a regard must be had not only to the Cloth & Colour but also to the list [selvage] about which the Indians are Curious [i.e., exacting]. This is of the common breadth viz. about 3 fingers with a Stripe or two of white generally. Sometimes in black in ye blue pcs. and always black in ye red." Striped blankets were to have broad stripes "only towards the ends as each 2 red and 2 blue or black near" (quoted in Montgomery 1984, 353). The Catawba, Siouan speakers living in South Carolina and Georgia Piedmont, were discriminating shoppers when it came to beads. Archaeological evidence suggests that those living west of the fall line preferred large blue and red glass trade beads while those in towns to the south would trade only for small black and white ones (Merrell 1989, 32).

Gifts of textiles were used to cement alliances. Catawba living at the Congaree Fort in South Carolina in 1752 received a shipment of dry goods probably sent by Governor Glen to prevent an "alienation of affections" from the English. Of the 30 categories of objects, 10 percent were textile goods: stroud, striped duffel, embossed serge, osnaburg, white and checked shirts, men's coats, gartering, caddice, sewing needles, thread, and scissors (McDowell 1958, 217–18). In November of 1751 Governor Glen received a group of Cherokee from towns east and north of the Hiwassee River who had come to negotiate new terms for the deerskin trade. Glenn presented them with gifts that included clothing. The headman, called the Raven, was given "a scarlet Coat, Wastcoat and Breches, ruffled Shirt, gold-laced Hat, Shoes, Buckles, Buttons, Stockins and Gartring, . . . a Piece of Stroud, 5 Yards of Callico, ten Yards of Em[bossed] Serge." Raven's nephew, Moitoy, received gifts of clothing which included "one of the best Coats out of the Publick Store, a white Shirt, . . . Shoes and Stockins, Buckles and garters, a laced Hat and 5 Yards of em[bossed]Serge." The remaining members of the delegation each received "a Coat, Gun, Shirt, Flaps, Hat, Boots each" (McDowell 1958, 161–62). As the gift of a coat "out of the Publick Store" indicates, some trade clothing was kept on hand in quantity for unannounced visits.

Wampum

Wampum, or wampanoag—from the Narragansett word for "white shell beads"—was a form of currency among Native Americans and used in trading for goods with European settlers. In the early colonial period, it was also used among settlers themselves for payments of small amounts. The cylindrical beads, made from shells that were drilled, rubbed, and polished, were of two types: white shell—six of these were equivalent to an English penny in 1643—and a black-blue shell, three of which equaled an English penny. Wampum beads were threaded onto leather strings; six feet of strung beads was called a fathom. Rows of beads were also woven together into wide patterned bands that were worn as belts, bracelets, and collars.

Besides furs and skins, Native land was sometimes traded for cloth and clothing. Tailor Thomas Stebbins (c. 1620–1683) immigrated as a boy with his family to Roxbury, Massachusetts, in 1634 and then resettled in Springfield in 1639. In Springfield, Stebbins opened an account with the successful merchant John Pynchon in August 1652. Six months later Stebbins's debt amounted to more than £14, but he worked this off by making clothing for Pynchon to sell: "12 waste-coats . . . 10 doz caps . . . 11 doz & 9 Wast-coats . . . 3 doz & 1 coates . . . one doz stockens [the stockings likely not knitted but made of cloth cut on the bias]" (Greenlee and Greenlee 1904, 1:65). In a subsequent transaction Pynchon delivered 54 yards of white shag (woolen fabric) for waistcoats and stockings, red tape, and another 30 yards of cloth in remnants, out of which Stebbins fashioned 17 dozen caps, and over one hundred waistcoats (1:65). Many of these items likely were for Pynchon's extensive trade with Native Americans. In fact, it is probable that Stebbins's handiwork was among the "two blue coats, the blue waist-coat, the red cotton and the breeches" that Pynchon gave to a local Indian headman, Umpanchela, in partial payment for land on which the town of Hadley was later established (Cooley 1941, 73).

Umpanchela was a sachem of the Nipmuc, a geographic classification for Algonquian Indian communities located in central Massachusetts and adjoining parts of New England. His sachem status indicated that he was able to take care of his people and that he could move comfortably in the world outside his community. Trade goods allowed him to accomplish this, whether he wore them, gave them to others, or traded them for other goods or services. Umpanchela's land-for-clothes deal with Pynchon was not the first time that he had engaged in transactions involving clothing. According to John Pynchon's account books, during a 15-month period from September 1659 to December 1660, Umpanchela assumed substantial debts for purchases that included red shag wool, lengths of blue and white cloth, a pair of stockings, blue waistcoat, two shirts, two pairs of breeches, and seventeen coats. Because he could not pay the 300 fathoms of wampum agreed upon for these goods, Umpanchela was forced to turn over several lands held by the Nipmuc (Nash 2009, 33–34).

In its first years of existence, the Society for the Propagation of the Gospel in Foreign Parts (SPGFP), organized in London in 1701, attempted to persuade Native Americans to accept Christianity with bribes of clothing and cloth. In 1702, the Society sent Rev. Samuel Thomas (died 1706), who was working in Charleston on behalf of the Society, "tenn pounds . . . to be layd out in stuffs [i.e., woolen cloth] for the use of the wild Indians of those parts of South Carolina where the said Mr Thomas is to reside" (Thomas 1904, 21–22). In March of 1704, Thomas penned a letter to his superiors in London concerning another gift: "You sent . . . me stuff to make match coats . . . I had no opportunity to dispose of the [fabric] to the end for which you designed it, and finding that it was like to decay, . . . I had it appraised and sold it" (Thomas 1903, 280). (The matchcoat was not a coat or jacket but a kind of mantle worn by Native Americans, originally made of furs and/or skins but later of woven woolen trade cloth.)

CLOTHING FOR SOCIAL RITUALS

Few life-cycle events required highly specialized clothing in the colonial period. Until the Industrial Revolution's firm hold on the textile industries in the 19th century made cloth inexpensive to purchase and easy to replace, most clothing was too costly—either in terms of the outlay of cash or of time—to be used only on special occasions for anyone below the social level of the elite. Still, in certain circumstances, additions to the wardrobe were expected, particularly of higher status individuals and family members. Most often these situations involved courtship and marriage, childbirth, and mourning.

Courtship

From the beginning to the end of the colonial period, courtship rituals changed profoundly. For example, in 17th- and early-18th-century New England, laws gave parents both the responsibility and power to dispose of their children in marriage: a father had the legal right to determine which men would be allowed to court a daughter and to give or withhold consent to a marriage. In most cases, Puritan parents played a small role in the actual selection of a spouse but they could influence the timing of a marriage by delaying the distribution of property. More control was exerted, however, on unions in which financial and property distribution were involved. A proper Puritan marriage was considered to be based not on love and affection, but rather on considerations of property, compatibility, and religious piety. By the mid-18th century, parental influence over the choice of a spouse declined as new romantic ideals of love came into fashion via advice books, magazines, and works of fiction.

A custom called bundling was practiced primarily in rural communities from Maine to Pennsylvania. The courting couple shared a bed for the night, perhaps fully clothed; when Abigail Adams described her voyage to France in 1784, she claimed that her cabin was so little separated from that of the men on board that "we only in part undress, about as much as the Yankee bundlers" (Abigail Adams 1841, 2:282). Primary sources are not explicit on the subject of bundling: did it consist of all-night conversation, a prolonged period of sexual play or perhaps sexual intercourse? An analysis of Abner Sanger's journal, which covered life in Keene, New Hampshire, between 1774 and 1782, suggests that five young women who had practiced bundling (Sanger called it "staying with") with Sanger or his friends were apparently not pregnant at marriage (Ulrich and Stabler 1987). Some accounts of bundling tell of a long board placed between the couple, but this practice could not be documented for the 18th century.

In 1759, Reverend Andrew Burnaby left Greenwich, England, to tour the colonies. Among the local customs he chose to record in his journal was bundling, which he called tarrying. His description of the practice deserves to be quoted in full:

A very extraordinary method of courtship, which is sometimes practised amongst the lower people of this province [i.e. New England], and is called Tarrying, has given occasion to this reflection. When a man is enamoured of a young woman, and wishes to marry her, he proposes the affair to her parents, (without whose consent no marriage in this colony can take place); if they have no objection, they allow him to tarry with her one night, in order to make his court to her. At the usual time the old couple retire to bed, leaving the young ones to settle matters as they can; who, after having sate up as long as they think proper, get into bed together also, but without pulling off their under-garments, in order to prevent scandal. If the parties agree, it is all very well; the banns are published, and they are married without delay. If not, they part, and possibly never see each other again; unless, which is an accident that seldom happens, the forsaken fair-one prove pregnant, and then the man is obliged to marry her, under pain of excommunication. (Burnaby 1775, 144–45)

Courtship included few customs that related to clothing, and none of these was prescribed. Museum collections contain hand-made accessories with oral traditions identifying them as betrothal gifts between engaged couples, for example, men's embroidered pocketbooks and carved wooden busks for stays, but a piece of furniture in which to store clothing, household linens, or personal treasures might also be given. For example, Rhode Islander Peleg Arnold (1762–1825) fashioned a wooden busk in March of 1785 for 16-year-old Lucy Hopkins, whom he married in October of that year (Kane 2006). A year after his marriage, Peleg made a Chippendale-style chest of drawers for Lucy and marked in black paint along the front of the top "PELEG: ARNOLD: LUCY:ARNOLD, HIR DRAWS & 1786" (Rhode Island Furniture Archive).

Although the period of getting to know a prospective spouse might last several years, formal engagements were usually short. The betrothed couple used the time to make and collect the goods required to "go to housekeeping" in their own home. If a bride's father could afford it, he was expected to supply a marriage portion of household goods, such as bed and table linens; quilts, coverlets, and featherbeds; and crockery, pewter plates and cups, knives and spoons, cooking utensils, and candlesticks. The three daughters of the Samuel and Mary Lane family of Stratham, New Hampshire, each received very similar, and extensive, marriage portions, including tables, chairs, and case furniture; a spinning wheel and other textile-working tools; and a cow, milk pails, and a churn (Nylander 1993, 61–62). Some couples waited for several weeks or even months after the wedding before moving into a house, either because they and their families were still completing the furnishings or they had traveled to visit friends and relatives before settling down.

Marriage

In 17th-century New England, marriages were civil ceremonies, which generally took place in the bride's home. In Plymouth Colony, the event might be marked by the entertainment of a few guests with cake, wine, and sometimes gifts for those guests. In neighboring Massachusetts, however, the event was often accompanied by festivities, including feasting. Southern colonies, in general, viewed marriage as a contract publicly entered into and preferably in a church. The greatest number of Roman Catholics lived in Maryland, where weddings were celebrated according to Catholic tradition with a nuptial mass, a ring for the bride blessed with holy water, and the crowning of the bride and groom. Marriages among members of the Society of Friends, or Quakers, were contracted by the couple with an exchange of vows at the Meeting, but usually with no further ceremony. Irregular marriages were unions that took place outside the church or without a proper minister or civic leader presiding. Such unions were accepted by the community. For example, in Maryland in 1684, Elesabeth Lockett and Thomas Bright broke "a peace of money . . . betwixt" them in front of witnesses. The intent of this ceremony would have been legally binding; unfortunately for the bride, Thomas was already married (quoted in O'Day 2007, 48).

Sarah Tyng Smith wore this dress of brocaded silk with interlacing serpentines of ribbon and flowers at her marriage to Richard Codman in Portland, Maine, on February 23, 1763. (Museum of Fine Arts, Boston, Massachusetts, USA/Gift of Miss Florence Codman and Dr. Charles Austin Eager Codman/The Bridgeman Art Library)

In the 18th century, marriages were once again considered religious ceremonies, although the event was celebrated differently along religious and socioeconomic lines. Most of the practices that characterize wedding ceremonies today, such as the bride wearing a veil and white dress, did not come into fashion until the 1840s. There is documentary evidence, however, that men and women occasionally had special garments made for their marriage ceremonies. A wedding dress was rarely white, and it certainly never was worn just once. After the wedding, it usually served the bride as her best dress for church or social occasions. Susannah Shepherd of Hartford, Connecticut, bequeathed her wedding gown to her daughter-in-law in 1698 (Manwaring 1904, 583). For her marriage to Charles Phelps on June 14, 1770, Elizabeth Porter (1747–1817) had a wedding gown made of dark brown ducape (Huntington 1891, 35). She had this gown altered 18 years later and again in 1812. Students of historic dress should be wary, however, of the women's gowns and men's waistcoats housed in museum and historical society collections that are accompanied by oral histories of wedding associations, including the assertion that the treasured items were remodeled and worn again by subsequent generations. (Examples include garments at Historic Deerfield, Museum of Fine Arts Boston, and the Museum at the Rhode Island School of Design.) The clothing must be examined carefully to determine whether the styling of the garments and the fabrics they are made from agree with genealogical evidence for the dates of the marriages recorded in the family stories.

In contrast to brides with specially made wedding gowns are the instances of "shift marriages" recorded in Rhode Island, Connecticut,

Maine, Vermont, and Pennsylvania. Marrying a woman dressed only in her shift signified that the new husband was not responsible for any debts the bride-to-be had incurred prior to the marriage; if the bride was a widow, the new groom would not be burdened by debts from the former marriage. The specifics of shift marriages varied by location. The bride might appear naked behind a large textile held by female family or friends; or the ceremony might take place on public property such as a roadway or common area rather than in a private home. In Narragansett, Rhode Island, the wife-to-be had to cross the road to the wedding clad only in her shift. According to the Connecticut court record for the April 1673 shift marriage of John and Abigail Betts, John "took her in clothes of his own providing to her, Shift and Stareless, being stript as aforesaid by the aforesaid women, and the sayd John Betts in Court renounced all claymss and Interest to her estate, both Debts and Credit" (Manwaring 1904, 183).

It is not known if the use of wedding rings was widespread. There is evidence that betrothal rings were customary in 17th-century Maryland; engagement rings did not become common until the end of the nineteenth century. In 1746, Philadelphian Mary Fenbey announced that she and her husband had parted by consent, but that he had not yet fully complied with their agreement to divide their goods in that he "detains her Bed and Wedding Ring" (*Pennsylvania Gazette*, August 7). Christopher Gadsden reported that one of his house slaves had found a plain wedding ring "Inscribed E.G. to R.W. May 1, 1759" and offered to return the item for the price of the advertisement (*South-Carolina Gazette*, January 28, 1773). Charleston jeweler John Paul Grimké advertised "diamond hoop wedding rings" and "Shagreen Boxes" in which to store them (*South-Carolina Gazette*, June 31, 1756; November 24, 1759). George Christopher Dowig, jeweler and goldsmith, offered "most curious Wedding rings of an entire new Invention," but offered no details about their construction (*Pennsylvania Gazette*, August 1, 1765).

Pregnancy and Childbirth

Most colonial women spent the better part of 20–25 of their menarcheal years either pregnant or nursing. Pregnancy required some modifications in dress for women who wanted to maintain a claim to gentility and, therefore, some semblance of the fashionable silhouette. These adjustments included adding laced openings to the side front seams of a corset to make it expandable and wearing a petticoat with extra long side ties or a drawstring waist.

Merchants, milliners, and shopkeepers advertised suits of ready-made imported child-bed linens, "childbed baskets," and "white sattin pincushions" (*Pennsylvania Gazette,* December 1, 1763). However, a woman might make bed clothing for herself and clothes and bedding for the new infant. These items were saved for subsequent births and loaned out. Many sets were considered valuable enough to hand down to a next generation. For example, Frederick Jones of North Carolina bequeathed to his eldest daughter "all her Mothers Child bede Linnen with white silk Damask Gown," and Mary Atkins of Charleston willed a kinswoman all her "childbed linen and all other Cloaths belongeing to a Child" (quoted in Spruill 1972, 50).

What constituted a set of child-bed linen likely varied according to the parents' social and economic standing. The anonymous author of *Instructions for Cutting Out Apparel for the Poor,* published in London in 1789, includes items for the lying-in mother and child-bed linen to lend to the poor; the list also suggests what well-to-do mothers might assemble: "2 Frocks, 2 Bedgowns [for the mother], 6 Shirts, 6 Caps, 6 Under caps, 24 Squares of double Diaper, 2 Robe blankets, 1–3/4 Yards of White Baize flannel, 2 Shifts, 2 Skirts, 1 Pair of sheets, 2 Pillow-cases" (Anonymous 1789, 85).

Babies were born at home and the event was generally a social one. Mothers-to-be in the middling to upper ranks of society were attended to and supported by female relatives and friends, who also took over some of the household tasks. Salem, Massachusetts, resident Mary Vial Holyoke (1737–1802) made dozens of entries that recorded the births of her own, her daughters' and her neighbors' children. For example, on March 3, 1763, Mary took to her chamber and called for a nurse. The next day she was "Brought to bed of [i.e., gave birth to]" a daughter, Peggy. Subsequent sitting-up visits from fourteen female friends and neighbors occupied some of her time between March 20 and 31. Another daughter, Polly, was born on January 9, 1765, and christened on the 13th. Sitting-up visits began a week later. Mary's first "getting out" was more than a month later, to visit a friend who had given birth three days previously. Mary's midwife did not leave until February 15. On September 9, 1771, Mary felt "very poorly" and "put up bed [i.e., arranged her birth bedding]." Three days later and "quite alone" in the house, she gave birth to a daughter, Elizabeth. Although she received four visitors the next day, her sitting-up week commenced on October 7. She did not leave the house until October 22 (Holyoke 1911, 58, 62–63, 77). The journal of Philadelphia Quaker Elizabeth Sandwith Drinker (1735–1807) contains numerous references to the activities of childbirth. For example, in 1758 Elizabeth "Help'd to make Baby Cloaths, for Betty Smith"; in 1759 she "help'd Sally to Iron Baby Cloaths" (Drinker 1991, 1:1, 10).

On February 17, 1759, Elizabeth "Call'd after Dinner to See Sally Wharton, who was lyeing-in, with her Son Samuel" (1:12).

Mourning

The types of material goods used in mourning the loss of a family member or revered member of the community reflected social status, religious affiliation, and location. The wealthy could afford special clothing; less affluent artisans and farmers may have had to dye clothing black. Among the poorer working sorts, their best, or Sunday, dress—usually of a drab or dark color—would have been worn to a funeral. The poorest ranks could not have afforded mourning clothes. Household servants and slaves, however, were sometimes provided with funereal clothing made from less expensive fabrics. In the 17th and early 18th centuries, mourning called for a plain style with no ruffles, no shiny buttons or buckles. However, as the 18th century progressed, the differences between mourning and non-mourning styles narrowed until both were cut according to the current fashion, the differences confined to color, fabric, and accessories.

In 17th-century New England, home of dissenting Protestants, funerals were prescribed to be simple—no sermons or readings at the graveside were allowed. In contrast, the New York service held on the death of Governor William Lovelace in 1671 was elaborate to an extreme. Before burial the body rested in a room draped with black cloth and hung with fam-

---

Mourning Fashions among Britain's Elite

Members of the colonial elite could emulate current mourning fashions in Britain by following funereal notices in the foreign section of colonial newspapers. For example, after Queen Caroline's death on November 20, 1738, *the South-Carolina Gazette* (January 19, 1738) and the *Pennsylvania Gazette* (February 28, 1738) carried details of the 6-month mourning to be followed by "all Peers, Peeresses, and Privy Counsellors" of the realm:

> The Gentlemen to wear black Cloth, without Buttons on the Sleeves or Pockets, Cambrick Cravats and Weepers broad hemm'd, Shammey Shoes and Gloves, Crape Hatbands, black Swords, Buckles and Buttons. The Ladies full Dress, black Bombazeens, broad hemm'd Cambrick Linnen, Crape Hoods, Shammey Shoes and Gloves, and Crape Fans. Their Undress dark Norwich Crape, and glaz'd Gloves.

ily crests, and the bier was decked with an embroidered pall and canopy, garlands and mourning ribbons in black and white. A description of those who walked in the funeral procession singled out eight girls "clothed in white silk" wearing scarves and gloves, and two of them with ribbons of black and white; six male pallbearers in mourning with scarves and gloves; various family members in mourning; and innumerable English and Dutch men and women, "the greatest part of them in black" ("Interment of William Lovelace, New York, 1671").

By the early 1700s funerals had become costly events; custom and fashion requiring the family of the deceased to wear black garments and to give scarves, gloves, and rings as gifts to mourners. European mourning goods were imported for those who could afford them. Among the *South-Carolina Gazette*'s notices, merchants Binford & Osmond offered mourning crapes; Richard Goodwin sold mourning fans; Watson & McKenzie imported "black & scarlet cloths, padusoys, bombazeens, and all other fashionable Mournings" (October 25, 1735; February 14, 1736; March 9, 1738). Sarah Packe, a Williamsburg shopkeeper, advertised "Bombazeens, Crapes, and other Sorts of Mourning, for Ladies; also Hatbands, and Gloves, for Gentlemen" (*Virginia Gazette*, March 1, 1738). Sometimes an entire community went into mourning for the death of a public figure. In 1732, for the death of South Carolina Governor Johnson's wife, the *South-Carolina Gazette* reported, "We hear that most People design, on this Occasion, to put themselves in Mourning" (July 15, 1732).

Perhaps the most common symbol of mourning was the mourning ring. In most regions, these rings were given by bequest to family members and close friends. New York City goldsmith and jeweler John Dawson made mourning lockets as well as rings (*New-York Mercury*, May 4, 1767). The partnership of Bennett & Dixon, also in New York, noted that they made "Mourning rings, plain or set, with any kind of stone with hair work'd in landskips" (*New-York Journal or General Advertiser*, August 6, 1772). Williamsburg, Virginia, resident Philip Ludwell advertised that he lost a gold mourning ring "having, on a Lozenge, a black enamel'd Cross, between 4 small Sparks; and round the Hoop these Words: H. Ladwell, 4 Aprilis, 1731, AEt. 52" (*Virginia Gazette*, November 5, 1736).

In 1721, Massachusetts, hoping to encourage thrift and reduce expenditures on luxuries, imposed a £20 fine on the givers of mourning scarves. Diarist Samuel Sewall noted for September 7, 1721, that the funeral of one Mrs. Frances Webb was perhaps the "first public funeral without scarves" (Sewall 1973, 2:982). The fact that a second, more comprehensive law was established in 1742 to regulate not only scarves, but all gift giving, as well as the consumption of wine and rum at funerals, suggests that that the earlier law had been rarely obeyed. According to the new law, a pair of gloves could be given only to the six pall-bearers and each minister at the deceased's church and increased the fine to £50 for scarves. Renewed in 1750 and 1760, the laws were no more observed than their predecessors. Account books show the purchase of black silk fabrics, women's gloves, fans, and neckerchiefs for mourning in 1741 in Salem, Massachusetts (Anderson 1977, 647). The funeral of a Boston minister in 1743 was paid for by his congregation and involved dressing his entire family of 10 in mourning clothing, distributing more than 40 rings and a gross of men's and women's gloves to attendees, and decking out the pallbearers and deacons in black gloves, with "weeds" (probably scarves) to hang from their hats (Anderson 1977, 648).

During the import tax crisis of the 1760s, some colonists adopted fewer signs of outward mourning to support both greater economy and American manufacture. In Boston, men who wished to express sorrow for a deceased friend or relation were urged to wear only a black crape hatband and "a Piece of Crape . . . to be tied upon the Arm, after the Manner of the military Gentlemen" (*New-York Gazette or the Weekly Post-Boy*, August 30, 1764). The Boston funeral of Ellis Callender in 1764 was conducted according to "an Agreement lately entered into by a great Number of the most respectable of its Inhabitants" in which no sort of mourning clothing was worn. The chief mourner "appeared in his usual Habit, with a Crape round his Arm; and his Wife . . . with no other Token of Mourning than a black Bonnet, Gloves, Ribbons and Handkerchief" (*Boston Gazette*, September 24). A New London, Connecticut, town meeting resolved that only gloves of American manufacture (black gloves excepted) and no new Garments but that were absolutely necessary would be worn to funerals (*New-York Journal or the General Advertiser*, February 11, 1768).

By the time George Washington's stepdaughter, Martha Parke Custis, died in 1773, however, nonimportation was no longer at the forefront of colonial politics. Washington, who habitually ordered clothing and household furnishings through his agent in Britain, ordered mourning clothes for himself and his wife from London. These garments included a "Black silk sacque and Coat prop'r for Second Mourning" with a "Suit of fashionable linen" to wear with it (probably sleeve ruffles, a neckerchief, and ruffles for the neckline of the dress). He also requested two caps, and a "handsome fan" for Martha, and a suit for himself (Washington 1773).

The death of a husband often forced some changes in lifestyle for the widow. At the least a wife received dower rights, or life interest, equal to one-third of her husband's estate if there were children of the marriage, and one half if there were not. Legally, everything a woman brought to the marriage belonged to her husband—even her clothing and personal effects. This situation is reflected in the language of a husband's will, in which he left his wife's wearing apparel to her. Most colonial courts, however, recognized the widow's "rights of paraphernalia," which meant that she was entitled to keep her clothing and personal possessions upon the death of her husband, even if those possessions were not specifically left to her in his will.

CLOTHING AND FABRICS AS CURRENCY

In the 1600s, colonies relied on a financial system based on exchange in its most basic form: a product or service was given for a product or service. Specie, or coin, circulated only in small quantities in North America, even at the end of the century. England forbade the establishment of a colonial mint and discouraged the issuance of paper money by colonial governments. With hard currency from any country in short supply, it was legal to pay bills in kind. Nehemiah Allen, a Philadelphia cooper, made bread barrels and flour casks for Samuel Carpenter and Isaac Norris, both of whom had export trade to the West Indies. Carpenter and Norris paid Allen "in rum, flour, cheese, flannel, stockings, and other sundries." Brewer Henry Badcock paid Allen partly in cash and partly in beer. Allen, in turn, paid his suppliers' invoices with some of the bartered goods received from his customers (Dunn and Dunn 1982, 21). In Virginia and Maryland, tobacco measured in pounds was the standard of value and the currency with which most supplies—domestic as well as imported—were purchased and fees, church tithes, wages, and debt were paid. In New England cattle, barrels of Indian corn, and skins substituted for tobacco.

Contemporary court documents reveal that from time to time apparel and cloth functioned as a standard in-kind substitute. In April of 1649, New Plymouth resident Robert Barlet purchased from Richard Church a house and land and some basic furnishings. Barlet agreed to pay Church £25 in the form of commodities, which included a red ox named Mouse, cattle and corn at current market prices, and if necessary, according to the rate merchants would pay, "linnen and woollen and shoos and stockens" (Shurtleff 1861, 1:165–66).

In St. Mary's, Maryland, a lawsuit charged that John Warwick had not paid Richard Ridgell and his wife for nursing Warwick and dressing his wounds over a four-month period in 1676. The agreed-upon price was in tobacco but the Ridgells took clothing as a security: "One silke suite mens wearing apparel of the price of One thousand pounds of tobacco, One serge suite of the price of One hundred and fifty pound of tobacco, One hatt and razor of the price of One hundred pounds of tobacco, One paire of stockins and golves to the value of sixty pounds of tobacco in the whole to the value of thirteene hundred & ten pounds of tobacco." Warwick refused to deliver the tobacco when he had recovered so Ridgell kept the clothing (Merritt 1954, 66:252).

Early county court records from Accomack-Northampton, on Virginia's eastern shore, are particularly rich in references to clothing and cloth being used to pay for goods and services. In 1639 the wife of Leven Denwood contracted with George Willis's wife that the latter would "wash for her one whole yeare in Consideration whe[reof] the said Denwoodes wife was to allowe the wife of the said Willis a hatt" (Ames 1973, 12). George Willis agreed to provide the wife of John Wilkins "one Heifer with Calfe a payre of shoes and stockings and a shirt Cloath" in 1643 for nursing services to his family (269). In that same year Rowland Vaughan hired himself out to Phillip Taylor for 12 months, in consideration of which Taylor was to pay Vaughan "one shute of Broad cloath one shute of Tradeing cloath [probably of duffels] two paire of shoes two paires of stockings a hatt a Cowe and a calfe" (289).

Debts could be satisfied with payments in clothing as well. Before setting out on a journey in 1640, Reynold Fleete and Thomas Hoult stayed with Jonathan Gilles for an unspecified length of time, enjoying their host's food as well as lodging. To compensate Gilles "in Case they did not retorne againe for the satisfaction of diet which they formerlie had att this deponents [Jonathan Gilles] house," the pair gave him "one Cloath sute one payer of Good Britches one waistcoat of painted Callico one payer of ould silke stockings Five yards and a quarter of Frise." Fleete and Hoult did not return and the Northampton Court found that Gilles could keep the clothing as payment for his hospitality (Ames 1973, 57). At James Perreen's death in 1643, his administrators were unable to satisfy the terms of a debt owed to John Major. In reaching an alternative for the original terms, the court ordered the administrators to pay Major cash money, spirits, and "the valew of the making of a shute of Cloathes" (269).

Throughout the colonies clothing was also part of the payment made at the expiration of their terms to voluntary servants, that is, apprentices and indentured servants. The position of both apprentice and indentured servant was established by a formal written agreement between the father or legal guardian of the son or daughter (or the apprentice if an adult) and the master. The agreement specified the obligations of each party.

Apprenticeship was the system of training by which an individual obtained specialized skills. The apprentice paid the master who trained him or her with labor and perhaps a small fee. Many masters contracted to ensure that their charges learned to read and perhaps write and cipher;

other contracts included money, books, and instruments of the trade. In Massachusetts, the most common end-payment, or freedom dues, consisted of clothing: two suits, one for Sunday—the Lord's Day—and one for work days. An agreement made in 1687 detailed that the apprentice was to have, upon expiration of his contract, "double clothes throughout as: Jackets, coats, Waistcoates, Briches, Drawers, trousers, Shirts, neck-clothes, Hatts, stockings shoes, gloves, Hankerchiefs" (quoted in Seybolt 1917, 68). Although bound out to a tradesman, it was rare that a female apprentice was taught a trade; most were used as household servants, but they often were taught to read and/or to do plain sewing work. In 1719, Susannah Maria Beyer, an orphan, was ordered by the Mayors Court of New York to be apprenticed to Obadiah and Susannah Hunt for nine years, "to Maintain with Apparell Meat Drink washing & Lodging & teach her Housewifery" (quoted in Towner 1998, 29).

Under indentured servitude, a master provided a servant with certain goods and services—transportation, food, clothing, lodging, and an endpayment of some kind—in exchange for labor. The position of indentured laborer developed in response to the labor shortage in England's New World colonies. As outlined in the contract, upon completion of the length of the indenture, the servant was to receive freedom dues, the nature of which was arbitrary and determined in the place of servitude. Because most of those who entered into such a contract were poor, the merchants, ships' captains, and others who invested in the servant trade paid for food and clothing as well as the passage for each servant immigrant. That sum, together with expenses in supporting the servant while he or she waited for passage across the Atlantic, was charged to the colonial master. Among the papers of the High Court of Admiralty Miscellany is the 1636 report of Thomas Anthony, an English servant trader. Anthony collected a cargo of Irish servants—men and women—who were to be indentured for four years' service in Virginia. Before leaving port, he delivered woolen and linen cloth and buttons to Hugh Neal, a tailor, whom he had hired to make clothing for the servants. Neal worked through the summer to make suits of clothing, blankets, and woven stockings. Although the number of servants is not known, the cost of the suits was seven or eight shillings each, the blankets were nine shillings per pair, and the stockings eight shillings and three pence per dozen pair (Smith 1947, 63).

While the practice of indentures was adopted to some extent in New England, Pennsylvania, New York, and New Jersey—with freedom dues usually including suits of clothes—most indentured servants arrived in southern colonial ports. George Alsop, who described his lot as an indentured servant in Baltimore County, Maryland, penned a pamphlet in 1666 probably for use as propaganda in England for the overseas trade in servants. Alsop reported to interested readers that according to Maryland's "Custom of the Country," a male indentured servant served for four years. At the expiration of he was considered a freeman and, by provincial law, his master was to give him "Fifty Acres of Land, Corn to serve him a whole year, three Sutes of Apparel, with things necessary to them, and Tools to work withal" (Alsop 1910, 358). In 1642, the monthly court of Northampton County, Virginia, ordered Alexander Williams to pay and deliver what was owed a former indentured servant, Edward Monnck, as his freedom dues: "one new Kersey shirte one paire mans new shoes and stock; one good Locrum shurt and three barrels of good Indian Corne." This was to be done "att the Comeing in of the first ship into this Colony," suggesting that Monnck's clothing payment was in the form of imported ready-made clothing (Ames 1973, 198).

The practice of including clothing as end-payment for apprentices and indentured servants continued through the 18th century. In Maryland men were to receive at the expiration of their indentures "one new hat, a good suit, one new shift of white linen; one new pair of bench-made shoes and stockings; two hoes, and one ax; and one gun of twenty shillings price." Women who had completed their indentures were to be given "a waist-coat and petticoat, a new shift of white linen, shoes and stockings; a bib apron; two caps of white linen; and three barrels of Indian corn" (quoted in Douglass 1921, 38–39, n. 6). South Carolina allowed only clothing as an end-payment for an indenture. New York followed New England's lead for apprentice contracts. In addition to "sufficient meat drinke Apparell Lodging and washing fitting for an Apprentice" and instruction in a trade, the master was to give to give the apprentice as his freedom dues "two new suits of Apparell the one for working days the other for Sundays and holy days" (quoted in Seybolt 1917, 89).

ACCESS TO CLOTHING

Many factors affected the kinds of clothing and textiles to which colonists had access. Arguably, the most important of these was the contradictory legislation enacted by Parliament and colonial assemblies, which both restricted and encouraged the production of textiles for clothing. The economic theory under which England had operated since the beginning of her settlement of the New World held that the colonies were possessions subject to the economic exploitation of the mother country and their activities should be limited where they encroached on her economic welfare. In 1651 Parliament passed the first of a series of laws—subsequent laws were enacted in 1660,

1662, 1663, 1670, and 1672. Collectively known as the Navigation Acts, they were intended to restrict and regulate trade with British colonies. As they pertained to textiles, the laws were, in effect, sumptuary legislation. Prior to 1651, colonists obtained most of their textile supplies directly from Holland as well as from Britain. The new laws prohibited the shipment of goods to and from Britain and her colonies in vessels other than those belonging to and built in England, Ireland, or her plantations. These proscriptions cut off, with a few exceptions, the colonies' direct trade with Europe. Textiles not made in England had to be imported first to England and then loaded onto English ships for the voyage to America. To reduce the colonial prices for imported goods, a system of drawbacks was developed, which exempted from duties, subsidies, and taxes all foreign merchandise destined for the colonial market. It was hoped that this would encourage the colonies to trade with England rather than to turn to home manufactures.

The effects of the navigation laws on colonial textiles varied according to the economic condition of the particular colony or region. For example, New England had been accustomed to trading with the Dutch, whose goods were cheaper than their English substitutions. Because of restrictions on the agricultural and staple commodities that the colonies were allowed to ship to England in payment for textiles, New Englanders— at least after 1660—found it more practical and cheaper to produce linen fabric at home. In contrast, those living in the colonies south of Pennsylvania produced commodities qualifying for export—naval stores, tobacco, rice, indigo, and deerskins—and could afford to purchase large quantities of imported linen and quantities of ready-made clothing for themselves as well as for their enslaved workers. Because of the system of drawbacks noted above, southern colonists were able to purchase linens from Germany and Holland less expensively than English consumers could buy linens of English and Irish manufacture.

In addition to the Navigation Acts, Parliament passed a series of laws restricting the establishment of certain manufactures in the colonies and "prohibiting the exportation of men with knowledge of, and implements used in, fabricating cotton, woolen, linen, and silk cloth" (Tryon 1966, 25). The acts of 1699 and 1732 attempted to restrict textile manufacturing that was already in operation; weaving for household use was exempted. By the end of the 17th century, New England's woolen manufactures had become successful enough to draw the attention of English manufacturers and merchants. The 1699 law enumerated 14 types of wool products, including worsted, bay, "says, frizes, druggets, cloth-serges, shalloons" that were forbidden to be produced for shipment either to another colonies or abroad (quoted in Tryon 1966, 25). Similar fears arose when German wool weavers from the Palatinate settled in New York in the early 18th century. The law of 1732 specifically addressed the flourishing colonial hat-making industry, stipulating that hats made in one colony could not be exported to another.

In the 18th century, Britain was so concerned with protecting her home industries that Parliament passed repeated measures aimed at prohibiting those with knowledge of, and any machines or implements used in, the manufacture of wool, linen, silk, and cotton cloth from immigrating or being imported to the colonies. The first of these laws, enacted in 1718, threatened fines and imprisonment for anyone caught enticing an artisan or manufacturer to the colonies. In 1750 the law was expanded to include the exportation of equipment used in the production of wool and silk. It was again extended in 1750 to include equipment used for cotton and linen cloth. The 1781 version of the law added penalties and prison time for the exportation of machinery, engines, presses and other paraphernalia used to prepare, work, or finish wool, silk, cotton, or linen textiles. The continual enhancement and reinforcement of these laws suggest the degree to which they were habitually ignored.

While Parliament was busy enacting legislation to restrict colonial production, beginning early in the 17th century, colonial governments actively passed legislation of encouragement, especially for raising of wool and flax for clothing. In October of 1648 the General Court of Massachusetts Bay Colony declared, "Whereas the keeping of sheepe tends much to the benefit of the country, & may make a good supply in short time towards the cloathing thereof if they were carefully preserved, and for as much as all places are not fit [or] convenient for that end, it is therefore ordered, that [hence]forth it shall be lawfull for any man to keepe sheepe in [any] com[m]on . . . belonging to the towne where he lives, or where at that time he may have right [to] com[m]on." The legislation also directed that damages be awarded to the owners of sheep that were molested or killed by dogs (Shurtleff 1853, 2:251–52). In 1682 the Maryland General Assembly, noting "the great quantys of Linnen and Woollen Cloath wch are brought from forreigne pts into and spent in this Province," wished to encourage provincial production of linen and woolen cloth. A premium of six pounds of tobacco was offered for the production of every yard of linen cloth at least three-quarters of a yard wide and 10 pounds for every yard of woolen cloth of the same width. The law was to run for three years (Browne 1889, 7:324–25).

Despite the legal prohibitions, northern colonies continued to foster the local manufacture of wool and linen in the 18th century. In contrast, until the 1760s, southern colonies resorted to local manufacture of textiles only when foreign wars obstructed overseas shipping. For example, for most of the 1740s, King George's War (the American phase of the larger War of the Austrian Succession) disrupted the profitable commercial activities of South Carolina merchants (Stumpf 1976). Spanish privateers based in St. Augustine, Florida, and Havana, Cuba, captured or harassed ships, which meant heavy financial losses. The losses, in turn, meant dramatic increases in insurance and freight rates, and the lucrative trade in human cargo was closed for most of the duration of the war. It was only during this period of economic downturn that advertisements for spinners and weavers were posted in Charleston's *South-Carolina Gazette.* In 1743 Thomas Webb announced that he would weave "either Woollen or Linnen," "done in the best Manner, and at very reasonable Prices" if patrons would deliver yarn to his house on Francis Gracia's plantation or Gracia's house in Charleston (March 7, 1743). In 1746 James Marions announced the sale of an enslaved sawyer and carpenter, "who from his Youth was brought up to weaving, can weave 11 Yards a Day, as his common Task, and make his own Loom" (September 22, 1746).

The passage of the Townsend Acts of 1767, which placed a tax on common products imported into the colonies such as lead, paper, paint, glass, and tea, brought about a general rethinking about British goods and about what kinds of goods colonists were willing to boycott. Among the items Bostonians were prepared to deny themselves, according to a list compiled in 1767, were "men and women's hats, men and women's apparel ready made, . . . gloves, men and women's shoes, sole leather, . . . gold and silver and thread lace of all sorts, gold and silver buttons, . . . broad cloths that cost above 10 shillings per yard, muffs, furs and tippets, and all sorts of millenery ware, starch, women's and children's stays, . . . silk and cotton velvets, gauze, . . . lawns, cambricks, silks of all kinds for garments" (quoted in Breen 2004, 236). South Carolina urged its citizens to avoid silks, woolens, and cottons, but because the colony's economy depended on slave labor, exempted fabrics used to construct slave clothing. By 1769 colonial newspapers up and down the eastern seaboard called for public displays of homespun clothing, and colonial governments encouraged spinning and weaving operations for linen and wool. Judging from the output for 1767 and 1768 on George Washington's plantation, the resulting fabric was far from crude or drab and included stripes and plaids (Tryon 1966, 110). Nor did the wearing of homespun necessarily blur the distinction between gentlemen and the middling sorts.

Economic factors also influenced access to textiles and clothing. Adequate transportation was crucial. Folks who lived along the eastern seaboard in population centers or near navigable rivers had greater and more constant access to goods through shops and markets and could more easily dispose of their own surplus staples and household manufactures than those families living in back country areas or on the frontier. The pack horses that served traders engaged in the deerskin trade with Native Americans since the mid-17th century could carry small loads of goods inland. Until adequate roads were created, however, there was no way to ship bulky commodities produced on back country farms to markets and exchange them for imported goods.

REFERENCES

Adams, Abigail. 1841. *Letters of Mrs. Adams, the Wife of John Adams*, 3rd ed. Vol. 2. Boston: Little, Brown.

Adams, Abigail and John Adams. 2002. *The Book of Abigail and John: Selected Letters of the Adams Family, 1762–1784*, edited by L.H. Butterfield, Marc Friedlaender, and Mary-Jo Kline. Boston: Northeastern University.

Adams, John. 1782. Diary of John Adams, 26 October. Adams Family Papers: An Electronic Archive. masshist.org/digitaladams/aea/diary/.

Alsop, George. 1910. "A Character of the Province of Maryland, by George Alsop, 1666." In *Narratives of Early Maryland, 1633–1684*. New York: Charles Scribner's Sons.

Ames, Susie M., ed. 1973. *County Court Records of Accomack-Northampton, Virginia, 1640–1645*. Charlottesville: University Press of Virginia.

Anderson, Gillian B. 1977. "The Funeral of Samuel Cooper," *The New England Quarterly* vol. 50, no. 4 (December): 644–59.

Anonymous. 1789. *Instructions for Cutting out Apparel for the Poor; Principally Intended for the Assistance of the Patronesses of Sunday Schools, and Other Charitable Institutions, but Useful in All Families*. London: J. Walter.

Axtell, James. 1997. *The Indians' New South: Cultural Change in the Colonial Southeast*. Baton Rouge: Louisiana State University.

Baldwin, Frances Elizabeth. 1926. *Sumptuary Legislation and Personal Regulation in England*. Baltimore: Johns Hopkins Press.

Breen, T.H. 2004. *The Marketplace of Revolution: How Consumer Politics Shaped American Independence*. Oxford: Oxford University Press.

Browne, William Hand, ed. 1889. *Archives of Maryland: Proceedings and Acts of the General Assembly, October 1678–November 1683*. Vol. 7. Baltimore: Maryland Historical Society.

Bruce, Philip Alexander. 1935. *Economic History of Virginia in the Seventeenth Century*, 2 Vols. New York: Peter Smith.

Bryson, Anna. 1990. "The Rhetoric of Status: Gesture, Demeanour and the Image of the Gentleman in Sixteenth- and Seventeenth-Century

England." In *Renaissance Bodies: The Human Figure in English Culture, c. 1540–1660,* edited by Lucy Gent and Nigel Llewellyn, 136–53. London: Reaktion Books.

Burnaby, Andrew. 1775. *Travels through the Middle Settlements in North-America in the Years 1759 and 1760.* Dublin: R. Marchbank.

Bushman, Richard. 1992. *The Refinement of America: Persons, Houses, Cities.* New York: Vintage Books.

Cooley, Mortimer Elwyn. 1941. *The Cooley Genealogy: The Descendants of Ensign Benjamin Cooley.* Rutland, VT: Tuttle.

Douglass, Paul Howard. 1921. "American Apprenticeship and Industrial Education," unpublished dissertation, Columbia University.

Dow, George F., ed. 1912. *Records and Files of the Quarterly Courts of Essex County, Massachusetts, 1636–1691.* Vol. 2, 1656–1662. Salem, MA: Essex Institute.

Drinker, Elizabeth. 1991. *The Diary of Elizabeth Drinker,* edited by Elaine Forman Crane. Vol. 1, 1758–1795. Boston: Northeastern University.

Dunn, Mary Maples and Richard S. Dunn. 1982. "The Founding, 1681–1701." In *Philadelphia, a 300-Year History,* edited by Russel F. Weigley. New York: W. W. Norton.

Fischer, David Hackett. 1989. *Albion's Seed: Four British Folkways in America.* New York: Oxford University.

Greenlee, Ralph Stebbins and Robert Lemuel Greenlee. 1904. *The Stebbens Genealogy.* Vol. 1. Chicago: privately printed.

Griebel, Helen Bradley. "The African American Woman's Headwrap: Unwinding the Symbols." char.txa.cornell.edu/Griebel.htm.

Habersham, James. 1904. "The Letters of Hon. James Habersham, 1756–1775." *Collections of the Georgia Historical Society.* Vol. 6. Savannah: Georgia Historical Society.

Hamilton, Alexander. 1948. *Gentleman's Progress: The Itinerarium of Dr. Alexander Hamilton, 1744,* edited by Carl Bridenbaugh. Chapel Hill: University of North Carolina.

Hemphill, C. Dallett. 1996. "Middle Class Rising in Revolutionary America: The Evidence from Manners." *Journal of Social History* vol. 30, no. 2 (Winter): 317–44.

Hening, William Waller, ed. 1823. *The Statutes at Large; Being a Collection of All the Laws of Virginia from the First Session of the Legislature, in the Year 1619,* 2nd ed. Vol. 1. New York: R. and W. and G. Bartow.

Holyoke, Mary Vial. 1911. "Diary of Mary Vial Holyoke." In *The Holyoke Diaries, 1709–1865,* edited by George Francis Dow, 47–138. Salem, MA: Essex Institute.

Hume, Sophia. 1752. *Exhortation to the Inhabitants of the Province of South-Carolina*. London: Luke Hinde.

Huntington, Arria Sargent. 1891. *Under a Colonial Roof-Tree: Fireside Chronicles of Early New England*. Boston : Houghton, Mifflin.

"Interment of William Lovelace, New York, 1671." *American Historical Review* vol. 9, no. 3 (April, 1904): 522–24.

Johnson, Charles. 1998. *A General History of the Robberies and Murders of the Most Notorious Pirates*, intro. David Cordingly, reprint of 1724 ed. Guilford, CT: Lyons Press.

Kane, Patricia E. 2006. "The Peleg and Lucy Arnold Chest of Drawers." *Magazine Antiques* Vol. 169, no. 5 (May): 126–27.

Mandeville, Bernard. 1729. *The Fable of the Bees: or Private Vices, Publick Benefits*, 6th ed. London: J. Tonson.

Manwaring, Charles William, ed. 1904. *A Digest of the Early Connecticut Probate Records*. Vol. 1. Hartford, CT: self-published.

Mather, Cotton. 1853. *Magnalia Christi Americana; or the Ecclesiastical History of New-England from its First Planting, in the Year 1620, unto the Year of our Lord 1698*. Vol. 2. Hartford, CT: Silas Andrus and Son.

McCord, David J., ed. 1840. "An Act for the Better Ordering and Governing Negroes and Other Slaves," *The Statutes at Large of South Carolina*. Vol. 7. Columbia, SC: A. S. Johnston.

McDowell, William L., Jr., ed. 1958. *Colonial Records of South Carolina: Documents Relating to Indian Affairs, May 21, 1750–August 7, 1754*. Columbia, SC: South Carolina Archives Department.

Merrell, James H. 1989. *The Indians' New World: Catawbas and Their Neighbors from European Contact through the Era of Removal*. Chapel Hill: University of North Carolina.

Merritt, Elizabeth, ed. 1954. *Archives of Maryland: Proceedings of the Provincial Court of Maryland, 1675–1677*. Vol. 66. Baltimore: Maryland Historical Society.

Miller, Samuel. 1813. *Memoirs of the Rev. John Rodgers, D.D.* New York: Whiting and Watson.

Montgomery, Florence. 1984. *Textiles in America, 1650–1870*. New York: W. W. Norton and Company.

Moody, Eleazar. 1805. *The School of Good Manners: Composed for the Help of Parents in Teaching Their Children How to Behave during their Minority*. Newburyport, MA: W. & J. Gilman.

Moore, Charles, 1926. "Origin of the Rules of Civility." In *George Washington's Rules of Civility and Decent Behaviour in Company and Conversation*.

Boston: Houghton Mifflin. gwpapers.virginia.edu/documents/civility/ index.html.

Nash, Alice. 2009. "Quanguan's Mortgage of 1663." In *Cultivating a Past: Essays on the History of Hadley, Massachusetts,* edited by Marla R. Miller. Boston: University of Massachusetts.

Norton, Mary Beth. 1997. "Communal Definitions of Gendered Identity in Seventeenth-Century English America." In *Through a Glass Darkly: Reflections on Personal Identity in Early America,* edited by Ronald Hoffman, Mechal Soibel, and Fredrika J. Teute, 40–66. Chapel Hill: University of North Carolina Press.

Nylander, Jane C. 1993. *Our Own Snug Fireside: Images of the New England Home, 1760–1860.* New York: Alfred A. Knopf.

O'Day, Rosemary. 2007. *Women's Agency in Early Modern Britain and the American Colonies.* Harlow, UK: Pearson, Longman.

Penn, William. 1863. *Fruits of Solitude, in Reflections and Maxims Relating to the Conduct of Human Life.* London: A. W. Bennett.

Pepys, Samuel. 1895. *The Diary of Samuel Pepys,* ed. Henry B. Wheatley, 8 vols. London: George Bell and Sons.

Plot, Robert. 1705. *The Natural History of Oxford-shire, Being an Esssay towards the Natural History of England,* 2nd ed. Oxford: Leo. Lichfield.

Postlethwayt, Malachy. 1971. *The Universal Dictionary of Trade and Commerce,* reprint of 1774, 4th ed., 2 vols. New York: Augustus Kelley.

"Proceedings of the Virginia Assembly, 1619." etext.lib.virginia.edu/etc bin/jamestown-browse?id=J1036.

Rediker, Marcus. 1996. "Liberty beneath the Jolly Roger: The Lives of Anne Bonny and Mary Reed, Pirates." In *Iron Men, Wooden Women: Gender and Seafaring in the Atlantic World, 1700–1920,* edited by Margaret S. Creighton and Lisa Norling, 1–33. Baltimore: Johns Hopkins University.

Rhode Island Furniture Archive at the Yale University Art Gallery, RIF1742. rifa.art.yale.edu/detail.htm?id=113130&type=0.

Schmidt, Leigh Eric. 1989. " 'A Church-going People are a Dress-loving People': Clothes, Communication, and Religious Culture in Early America." *Church History* vol. 58, no. 1 (March): 36–51.

Sewall, Samuel. 1973. *The Diary of Samuel Sewall, 1674–1729,* edited by M. Halsey Thomas, 2 vols. New York: Farrar, Straus and Giroux.

Seybolt, Robert Francis. 1917. *Apprenticeship and Apprenticeship Education in Colonial New England and New York.* New York: Teachers College, Columbia University.

Shurtleff, Nathaniel B., ed. 1853. *Records of the Governor and Company of the Massachusetts Bay in New England, 1642–1649.* Vol. 2. Boston: William White.

Shurtleff, Nathaniel B., ed. 1861. *Records of the Colony of New Plymouth in New England, Deeds, &c.* Vol. 1, 1620–1651. Boston: William White.

Smith, Abbot Emerson. 1947. *Colonists in Bondage: White Servitude and Convict Labor in America, 1607–1776.* Chapel Hill: University of North Carolina.

Smith, Woodruff D. 2002. *Consumption and the Making of Respectability, 1600–1800.* New York: Routledge.

Spruill, Julia Cherry. 1972. *Women's Life and Work in the Southern Colonies,* reprint of 1938 ed. New York: W. W. Norton.

Stark, Suzanne J. 1996. *Female Tars: Women aboard Ship in the Age of Sail.* Annapolis: Naval Institute Press.

Stiles, Ezra. 1901. *The Literary Diary of Ezra Stiles,* edited by Franklin Bowditch Dexter. Vol. 1. New York: Charles Scribner's Sons.

Stumpf, Stuart O. 1976. "Implications of King George's War for the Charleston Mercantile Community." *South Carolina Historical Magazine* vol. 77, no. 3: 169–71.

Thomas, Samuel. 1903. "Letters of Rev. Samuel Thomas, 1702–1706." *The South Carolina Historical and Genealogical Magazine* vol. 4, no. 4 (October): 278–85.

Thomas, Samuel. 1904. "Documents Concerning Rev. Samuel Thomas, 1702–1707." *The South Carolina Historical and Genealogical Magazine* vol. 5, no. 1 (January): 21–55.

Towner, Lawrence William. 1998. *A Good Master Well Served: Masters and Servants in Colonial Massachusetts, 1629–1750.* New York: Garland Publishers.

Trumbull, J. Hammond, ed. 1852. *The Public Records of the Colony of Connecticut from 1665 to 1678,* transcribed and edited by J. Hammond Trumbull. Hartford: F. A. Brown.

Tryon, Rolla Milton. 1966. *Household Manufactures in the United States, 1640–1860,* reprint of 1917 ed. New York: Augustus Kelley.

Ulrich, Laurel Thatcher and Louis K. Stabler. 1987. "'Girling of it' in Eighteenth-Century New Hampshire." In *Families and Children.* Vol. 10, 24–36. The Dublin Seminar for New England Folklife. Boston: Boston University.

Vincent, Susan. 2003. *Dressing the Elite: Clothes in Early Modern England.* Oxford: Berg.

Washington, George. 1744. "Rules of Civility and Decent Behaviour in Company and Conversation," manuscript. gwpapers.virginia.edu/documents/civility/transcript.html.

Washington, George. 1773. George Washington to Robert Cary & Company, July 10, Account Book 2. The George Washington Papers at the Library of Congress, 1741–1799. memory.loc.gov/ammem/mgwquery.html.

Wesley, John. 1827. "Advice to Methodists with Regard to Dress." In *Sermons on Several Occasions*. Vol. 2, 153–61. New York: J. J. Harper

Wesley, John. 1829. "On Dress." In *Sermons on Several Occasions*, 10th ed. Vol. 2, 310–19. London: Thomas Tegg.

Whitmore, Williams H. 1890. *The Colonial Laws of Massachusetts, Reprinted from the Edition of 1672.* Boston: Rockwell and Churchill.

Winthrop, John. 1908. *Winthrop's Journal, "History of New England," 1630–1649,* edited by James Kendall Hosmer, 2 vols. New York: Charles Scribner's Sons.

Yoder, Don. 1982. "Folk Costume," in *Folklore and Folklife: An Introduction,* intro. Richard M. Dorson, 295–324. Chicago: University of Chicago Press.

3

Clothing and Textile Technologies and Trades, 1607–1785

In 1776, Adam Smith reminded readers of his *Wealth of Nations* how many different trades and employments were needed to make even the most homely of garments: "The woolen coat, for example, which covers the day-laborer, as coarse and rough as it may appear, is the produce of the joint labour of a great multitude of workmen. The shepherd, the sorter of the wool, the wool-comber, or carder, the dyer, the scribbler, the spinner, the weaver, the fuller, the dresser, with many others, must all join their different arts" (Smith 1904, 11). Making cloth for clothing, whether in a workshop for the trade or in the home for domestic use, was time consuming. Regardless of where fibers were processed and fabrics woven, the techniques and procedures varied little from region to region until the Industrial Revolution of the later 18th century mechanized these processes.

CLOTHING TECHNOLOGY

From Raw Materials to Yarns

In the 17th and 18th centuries and indeed, until the early 20th century, most fabrics for clothing were woven from yarns or threads spun from just four fibers: wool from the fleece of sheep, silk from silkworm cocoons, linen from flax plants, and cotton from the cotton plant. Hemp and jute, also common plant fibers for textiles, were generally used for cordage and sailcloth or sacking, not clothing. A few other animal fibers, such as mohair from Angora goats and camel hair, were spun into yarns for weaving. But the most widely used fibers were wool, linen, silk, and cotton. In addition, clothing was made from animal skins and furs that colonists acquired through hunting and through trade with Native Americans.

The discussion of how fibers are processed into yarns and fabrics begins with the land. All textile workers, whether in workshops or at home, had either to raise the sheep or silkworms, grow the cotton or flax plants or acquire those raw materials from someone else who had. This first step was time consuming. Sheep, for example, are typically shorn only once a year, and silkworms need around-the-clock attention for weeks until they begin to spin cocoons. The following sections describe these processes in more detail.

Animal (Protein) Fibers: Wool and Silk

Shearing sheep was—and still is—a springtime event. Great skill was required to hold the sheep down while using hand clippers to clip the fleece close to the animal's skin without accidentally cutting the animal. In general, fleece was clipped off the belly, chest, face, and sides of the sheep first and then off the back. It was important not to mix fleece from these sections because the sections were sorted according to length (wool fibers grow to different lengths on different parts of the animal's body). Before the wool was spun into thread, it had to be cleaned of dirt and much of the fleece's natural lanolin. This washing process was called scouring.

Wool is a staple fiber, which means that the fiber's length can easily be determined. The relative length of the wool—its staple length—generally dictated how the fibers were prepared for spinning. Shorter lengths, called woolen fibers, were prepared for spinning by carding, a process that removed additional bits of debris and aligned the fibers for spinning. Using two handheld carding boards (resembling modern flat pet brushes) a worker brushed small amounts of fibers between the boards until all the fibers were transferred to one board. The wool was then formed into a roll called a sliver, from which the yarn was spun. Longer lengths, called worsted fibers, were prepared by running the fibers first through the cards, and then through a pair of combs to remove the shorter fibers and any remaining dirt and to align the fibers parallel to one another. After combing, the wool was rolled into a sliver. (A modern distinction in terminology is made between rolls made of woolen wool, called rolags, and rolls made of worsted wool, called slivers.)

Cultivating silkworms (*Bombyx mori*) in captivity to produce silk is called sericulture. Raised on large trays, silkworms, which are the caterpillar-stage of the silk moth, require constant attention and a fixed temperature as they grow from the egg stage to fully matured larvae. Eating ceaselessly, they must be supplied with fresh, chopped mulberry leaves and the trays must be cleaned at regular intervals for four to six weeks. In colonial America this work was accomplished by women and children, free, indentured, and enslaved.

A single mulberry tree could supply about 100 pounds of leaves per season. Two dozen trees yielded a half ton. This latter amount was considered adequate to feed an ounce of moth eggs over the course of the animals' growing cycle. One ounce of eggs hatched into 10,000 caterpillars, and 10,000 caterpillars spun between five and six pounds of raw silk (Billings 2004, 72–73).

When the larvae are about three inches long, they stop eating and are ready to pupate, or spin their cocoons, which in the colonial era also were called silk balls. Two specialized salivary glands produce the liquid silk, secreted as a long continuous filament through openings, called spinerettes, located in the head. The liquid silk hardens with exposure to the air. For three to five days the silkworm rotates its body in a figure-eight pattern to construct a cocoon made of as much as a half-mile of silk filament.

The highest-quality silk thread is composed of filament silk, the continuous strand created by the pupating caterpillars. To prevent them from metamorphosing into moths and eating their way through the cocoons, workers kill the larvae by exposing them to heat via steaming, boiling, or baking. Silk workers then soak the cocoons in a basin of near-boiling water to loosen the gummy substance called sericin, which binds the silk filament to itself as the cocoon is formed.

In the colonial era, workers used a small brush to whisk the water in the basin, teasing out the ends of the cocoons. These ends were pulled off together and twisted into a very fine thread that workers wound on a wheel. A consistent diameter of thread was maintained by adding new filaments as the thread thinned. This process, called reeling, was important because the reeled threads of raw silk had to be of a consistent diameter to be suitable for further processing into yarns for weaving or sewing. Skill at reeling required training, and most colonial reelers were recruited from England or France.

Some moths are allowed to emerge, breed, and lay the eggs that hatch into the next generation of silkworms. *Bombyx mori* moths breed shortly after emerging from their cocoons. After mating a female moth lays three to four hundred eggs and both sexes die soon after this event. The silk from these broken cocoons and cocoons damaged in the heating process and leftover ends of silk are processed like staple fibers. The fibers are first heated in water to remove the sericin and then combed in preparation for spinning. Staple, or spun, silk thread is not as strong as filament silk. In the 17th and 18th centuries, it was generally used for sewing and embroidery or as supplementary patterning yarns in certain woven fabrics, since the pattern yarns did not have to be as strong as the ground yarns.

Plant (Cellulose) Fibers: Flax and Cotton

Flax is a tall plant whose long stems contain two types of fibers: a fine fiber called linen and a somewhat coarser fiber called tow. In the colonial era it was a time-consuming and labor-intensive crop to grow and process and the work was accomplished by women as well as men. Flax plants cannot tolerate hot temperatures. For that reason, in many flax-producing areas, the date for planting flax seeds was determined by counting back 100 days—the amount of time needed between planting and harvesting the flax—from when the temperature usually began to warm excessively. The plants do not compete well with weeds and had to be carefully tended while still seedlings. When they turned brown and their leaves withered, the plants were ready to harvest. However, they had to be reaped immediately to avoid losing the sap, which affected the quality of the linen. Each plant was pulled, not cut, to preserve both the sap and the full length of the stem fibers.

The method for separating the linen and tow fibers from the plant's woody outer structure was strenuous. The harvested flax plants were tied into bundles and dried thoroughly. In a procedure called retting, workers then soaked the bundles in a stream or pond for a week or more—until the outer sheath of the plants had rotted and softened. After drying again, the flax was dressed in a three-step process to remove the outer bark, or sheath. Workers first broke up the decomposed stalks with a tool called a flax brake, or a beetle, so that the exterior bark could be separated from the interior fibers, called bast, which were used to make the linen thread. Workers followed breaking with scutching. Using long sword-like tools, they beat and scraped off the broken bits of the sheath to release the inner fibers. In the third step, heckling, workers pulled these inner fibers through a series of progressively finer comb-like implements called heckles, or hatchels, which separated the longer finer fibers, called linen, from coarser and shorter tow fibers. This also aligned the fibers to make them ready for spinning into yarn. The fibers were then rolled into slivers. The longer linen fibers were used to weave fine fabrics for clothing and household textiles. Coarser tow fibers produced rough sturdy fabrics suitable for work clothing, sacks, and wrapping material.

Cotton is a water- and nutrient-hungry plant that requires plenty of sunlight and a moderate rainfall. Before mechanization, mature cotton bolls were hand-picked at harvest time. In order to use the fibers, they had to be separated from the seeds, a laborious task when done by hand, before the widespread use of the cotton gin after 1793. Like wool, the cotton was either carded or combed and then formed into loose rope-like batts, called

"A Plate representing the common Method of Beetling, Scutching and Hackling the Flax," aquatint by William Hincks, 1783. The young woman at left beats the dried flax with a wooden mallet, or beetle to loosen the outer parts of the stem. The woman at center right strikes the stems with a long wooden blade to separate the fibers from the woody stems in a process called scutching. The hackler, the male worker at far right, combs the fine fibers. (Library of Congress)

rovings, ready for spinning. In some 17th- and 18th-century documents, cotton was referred to as cotton wool.

Spinning

Spinning, or twisting, fibers into yarns for use as weaving and sewing threads is an exacting task, requiring patience and skill. In preindustrial times spinning was most often allotted to women and girls, but young boys were also sometimes charged with the task. For linen and wool, the earliest technology required only the spindle and distaff, implements still employed in the colonial period. The spindle was a wooden shaft with a hook at one end and weighted at the other with a circular whorl. A starter yarn was wrapped from below the whorl up the length of the spindle and through the hook. A handful of wool or linen from the roving was then overlapped on the free end of the starter yarn. The worker then twisted the spindle in a clockwise direction with one hand while holding the overlapped yarn and fibers in the other. As the spindle turned, the yarn and fibers twisted together to form new yarn. The worker then drew out more fibers and continued the spinning process. When most of this fiber was spun, the worker added a new handful. As yarn accumulated, it was wound on a stick called a distaff. The evenness of both the twist and the yarn's diameter depended on the skill of the spinner. Some spinners rested the spindle on a surface, such as a thigh; others allowed the spindle to hang in the air. This latter technique was called drop spinning.

The spinning wheel, used throughout the colonial period, improved the hand-spinning method described above. Instead of the spinner turning the spindle, the spindle was rotated by a wheel. There were many types of spinning wheels. The great, or walking wheel, at which the spinner worked standing, was used to spin carded wool. As she walked backwards, away from the wheel, she pulled out wool fibers and turned the wheel to twist them into yarn. From time-to-time, the spinner walked forward toward the wheel, turning it in the opposite direction to wind the yarn on the spindle. Smaller than great wheels, flax wheels had a treadle, by which the spinner could rotate the wheel with her foot. This allowed her to have both hands free to spin the yarn, and the spinner could sit at the wheel to work. The addition of a flyer allowed the newly twisted yarn to wind automatically, saving the spinner time. Saxony and upright wheels were treadle-type machines powered by the spinner to spin worsted wool yarns.

In order to produce a fine, even thread the tension on the wheel and the quantity of fiber being fed into the thread had to be carefully controlled. Long staple fibers such as combed cotton and worsted wool produced smoother, stronger threads that were in demand for more expensive fabrics. In addition to the finely spun yarns, however, there were ample uses for coarser or thicker yarns, which might not require the same degree of skill to produce. In order to be usable as a weaving or sewing thread, reeled filament silk had to be made into a stronger yarn by twisting several reeled threads together by hand. This process was called throwing. The number of reeled threads used and the degree of twist related to how the resulting yarn was used. Staple silk was spun on a spinning wheel in the same way as other staple fibers. After throwing or spinning, the yarns could be washed to remove the last traces of sericin before they were dyed.

The 18th century saw improvements in spinning for English manufactories. The first machine to allow one spinner to supervise several spindles was invented in about 1764 by James Hargreaves, an Englishman who named the device after his daughter, Jenny. The spinning jenny was followed in 1769 by Richard Arkwright's spinning frame (later called the water frame), a machine that spun cotton yarns strong enough to be used for the warp threads stretched on a loom. In 1779, Samuel Crompton's spinning mule spun a fine, even thread. These machines also revolutionized weaving technology; by reducing the amount of time needed to produce yarn for weaving: a single spinner could provide enough yarn to keep a weaver busy at the loom, making the mass production of cotton fabrics a possibility. None of these machines, however, was imported to America before the end of the American Revolution.

From Yarns to Fabrics

Five techniques created the rich range of textiles that clothed and ornamented the inhabitants' colonial America: weaving, knitting, felting, plaiting, and looping. Weavers produced everything from narrow (as fine as one-quarter inch) tapes of worsted wool or silk for binding the top edges of shoes to wide (over five feet) fulled woolen broadcloths for men's suits, women's gowns, and matchcoats for the Indian trade. Woven cloth ranged from simple plain-weave linen shirtings to elaborate compound-weave brocades of silk and metal threads. Knitters made a textile that had inherent elasticity and was much used in the colonial period for stockings and caps, but the well-to-do donned knitted waistcoats, jackets, and breeches. Like woven fabrics, knitted goods could be constructed of silk, wool, linen, cotton, and even metallic threads. In contrast to weaving and knitting, felting does not rely on yarns for its production. Instead, a mass of fibers is treated with moisture, heat, and pressure to form a firm fabric. In the colonial period felt was most often associated with hat making. Plaiting, or braiding, could be used to make narrow tapes and cords from any kind of thread and hats from straw, thin wooden strips or horse hair. Using very fine linen or silk filament thread, however, it was also the technique used to make the type of lace called bobbin lace. Looping, which is related technically to knitting, was used to make a second type of lace, called needle lace.

Textiles were often enhanced by dyeing. The yarns of which the textiles were constructed could be dyed before they were manipulated. Or the fabrics themselves could be dyed, printed, or calendered. More color and texture could be created with embroidery, beads, sequins, buttons, or the fancy trims called *passementerie*. These could be added either before or after the textile was made into a garment.

Weaving

Two sets of yarns are required to weave cloth on a loom. The most basic loom consisted of two bars between which was stretched, under tension, the set of yarns called the warp. The back bar of the loom was called the warp beam; it was around this beam that the weaver wound the warp yarns. Each warp yarn was then individually drawn through heddles, devices that controlled the raising and lowering of the yarns for weaving, and then through the reed, located toward the front of the loom, which helped control the spacing of the yarns during weaving.

The weaver interlaced these warp yarns with the second set of yarns, called the weft (or filling), to create a textile. Weft yarns were wound onto bobbins, or quills, which fitted into a shuttle that the weaver passed back and forth through the warps. The weaver sat at the loom with the warp yarns stretched out horizontally in front of him or her and pressed foot

"Plate representing Winding, Warping with a new improved Warping Mill and Weaving," aquatint by William Hincks, 1783. (Library of Congress)

pedals to raise a heddle, making the opening called a shed, through which the weft yarns were passed alternately from left to right and right to left. As the warp filled to form the cloth, it was rolled onto the cloth beam, a cylinder at the front of the loom. When no more wefts could be added, the warp ends were cut from the loom. The length of fabric as it came from the loom was called a piece. In nonmechanized weaving, the maximum width of the cloth was the maximum span of a weaver's outstretched arms. This was because the shuttle, holding the weft yarn, had to pass back and forth from left hand to right hand. Wider fabrics, such as woolen broadcloth, required two weavers seated side-by-side passing the shuttle between them. In 1733 an English inventor, John Kay, devised the flying shuttle, which allowed the shuttle to be shot back and forth across a wider expanse of warp threads and allowed for weaving at a faster rate. This improvement was not available, however, in colonial America. While looms to weave fabric might be large enough to fill a small room, tabletop looms were used to weave narrow trims such as ribbons and tapes. Instead of pedals, the weaver manipulated sets of warp threads by hand to create the opening shed through which the weft passed.

Although in the colonial period most woven fabrics were made from a single fiber, there were common mixtures. For example, linen yarns were generally very strong and were often used as the warp threads. With the linen warp a weaver might use cotton for the weft to make a fabric called fustian or wool wefts to make linsey-woolsey. The most expensive silk fabrics were made from warps and wefts of filament silk. However, a less expensive silk could be produced by using filament silk for the warp and spun silk yarn for the weft or by mixing a silk warp with a cotton weft.

Weave Structures

Two weave structures were used either alone or in combination to create most of the plain and patterned textiles used for clothing in the colonial period. The first, and most basic, is called plain weave. To create a plain weave, the weft yarn was passed over and under successive warp yarns across the width of the cloth in one direction; working in the opposite direction, the weaver reversed the over–under sequence in passing the weft yarns through the warp.

When either the weft yarn or the warp yarn crosses over two or more of the opposite set of elements in an organized arrangement, the weaving structure is called a float weave. The most common float weave patterns are twill and satin. Twill-weave fabrics show diagonal ridges, created by a repeated, stepped arrangement of floats. Satin weave fabrics have a smooth, glossy surface created by long irregularly spaced floats.

These two simple weave structures—plain and float—were made to look more elaborate by introducing color. For example, the warp yarns could be dyed one color and the weft a completely different hue, creating what was called a changeable fabric. A plain weave fabric with a purple warp and a yellow weft looked yellow when viewed in one direction, purple in another, and appeared brown when viewed straight on. (This effect was best seen in a textile woven of silk.) Stripes, checks, and plaids were created by using bands of different colors in the warp and weft sets.

The addition of a color was not always necessary to create a pattern. Weavers also created patterns on the loom by changing weave structures. The weaver could interrupt his interlacing of warp and weft yarns at regular intervals by floating the weft yarns over the warp to make a geometric motif or small floral sprig (liseré patterning). A more elaborate form of patterning called damask was created by weaving contrasting areas of weft floats and warp floats, either as satin or twill weaves. In a damask the contrasting float-weave structures create a contrasting play of light on the fabric—matte against shiny. Silk produced the highest contrast, followed by linen and then wool.

Compound weaves are those in which the weaver combined two or more weave structures and/or introduced extra sets of warp and/or weft yarns. One of the most common compound weaves of the colonial period was brocade. The weaver began with a plain, twill, or satin weave construction, and added weft threads, called supplementary wefts, of different colors wherever he wished to create a floral or geometric pattern. These extra weft threads were introduced only where the specialized patterning was to be located; they were not carried across to the long finished edges, or selvages, of the fabric. Brocaded clothing fabrics usually were made of silk (the most expensive adding metallic threads) or worsted wool.

A second common compound weave was pile. Pile fabrics have a set of supplementary yarns that stand erect in loops—or when if the loops were cut, tufts—off the surface of a plain-weave fabric. Velvet referred to a cut-pile fabric made with an extra set of warp yarns; velveteen had an extra set of wefts. Corduroy was a cut pile-fabric made with an extra set of weft threads whose loops were vertically aligned so that when cut, they formed ribs parallel to the warp.

Knitting

Unlike weaving, which interlaces two sets of yarns—warp and weft—to produce a fabric, knitting uses one continuous yarn. Knitting requires the use of two or more needles to create loops of yarn that are drawn through other loops already formed. All of the loops on the working edge of a knitted fabric are held by one or more of these needles. The loops are then worked off one at a time to other needles as new loops are formed. Each worked loop is called a stitch. Knitting may be worked back and forth to create a flat fabric or around in a closed circle to form a tubular shape. By manipulating the loops, various knitted patterns can be devised. Colors may be added to form patterns, motifs, and horizontal stripes.

In the colonial period needles were also referred to as pricks, pins, sticks, or wires. Slender and pointed at both ends, needles were made of steel, wood, bone, and ivory. The size of the loop is determined by the diameter of the needle, and in general, knitting from the colonial period is quite fine, regardless of the quality of the knitting yarn. Knitting needles were commonly available from shops or itinerant peddlers; they were also produced domestically.

Another tool useful for hand knitting was the knitting sheath. This small implement played a supporting role for many knitters in the 17th and 18th century; by means of a narrow hole drilled into one end, the sheath could rigidly hold the end of one of the knitting needles. This allowed the knitter to sit, stand, or walk and continue her work. Made of a variety of materials—wood, bone, horn, ivory, brass, iron, and silver—some sheaths were elongated forms that hooked through the waistband. Others were carved or cut into shapes, most often a heart, shield, or fish, and sewn or pinned onto the knitter's skirt.

By the early 17th century, England's hand-knitting industry was already producing a variety of wearing apparel in all price ranges for both domestic consumption and export. The demand for stockings knit of wool, worsted, linen, and silk fueled this industry (cotton thread for knitting was introduced in the 1690s). Between 1697 and 1698, England's exports of knitted stockings to Europe and North America were estimated at 1.75 million pairs (Thirsk 1978, 168). Knitted caps were also popular, from plain skull caps to flat and round caps, caps with flat crowns, and caps with narrow brims. Wealthy patrons ordered waistcoats of worsted wool or silk, sometimes highlighted with metallic thread, and elegant knitted gloves. The knitting industry was so important to England's economy that all segments of English society participated: professionals in urban workshops, cottagers knitting as a by-employment, and the working poor.

The knitting frame, which mechanized hand knitting, was invented in about 1589 by Englishman William Lee, but it was not in use until the early 17th century. The machine featured a series of fixed hooked needles, one needle for each loop of yarn in a row of knitted loops. The frame initially was used to make silk stockings, but late in the century it was adapted to knit woolen and worsted yarns. Working the knitting frame was strenuous, requiring both hands and arms to move the heavy iron carriage and both feet to operate the treadles. Because of the physical effort involved, men usually operated the frame. The fabric created was flat, not tube shaped, and required finishing, usually by women. For example, a stocking required sewing a back seam and sewing the flap of the foot to the leg (Baumgarten 2002, 165). Both women and children also wound the yarn from hanks onto bobbins to ready it for the frame.

Further modifications were made to the knitting frame in the 18th century, allowing frame knitters to compete more successfully with hand-knitters. Previously, hand-knitting had been finer than that produced on the machine; hand knitters could make garments such as waistcoats, gloves, and stockings to fit an individual wearer; and they could knit with metallic threads. Moreover, hand-knitting was portable and less strenuous than framework, so hand-knitters could work for longer hours and earn higher wages under the piecework system.

During the 18th century, English hand- and frame-knitters produced an even wider assortment of garments for export and local consumption. These included knitted breeches, petticoats, jackets, waistcoats, stockings, gloves, caps, and purses. At the same time, knitting became a pastime for the wives and daughters of the more well-to-do, joining embroidery and needlework as suitable leisure activities for respectable folk.

Felt

In felting, animal fibers that have not been spun or twisted into yarn are arranged in a haphazard way in a single layer and treated with heat, pressure, moisture, and friction to form a firm textile. Only fibers with pronounced scales, such as sheep's wool and the undercoats of certain wild animals, can be felted. During the colonial period, probate inventories and newspaper advertisements attest to the popularity of felted hats, and they were the most important felted commodity. By the 18th century, they were so much in demand that the felt hat industry had become the driving force behind the North American fur trade. Malachy Postlethwayt (c. 1707–1767), a professional writer on trade and commerce, discussed hats and hat making in his magnum opus, *The Universal Dictionary of Trade and Commerce:* "Those most in esteem are made of the pure hair of the castor or beaver, which are plentifully taken in Canada, and other provinces of North America" (Postlethwayt 1971).

The manufacture of felted hats, regardless of the animal fiber used, was a complicated process, but the production of hats from pelt fur was injurious to the health of the hatters. One of the first steps in processing a pelt was to remove the long guard hairs, leaving only the softer undercoat or wool. When only the wool remained, the hatter brushed a solution of mercury nitrate on the pelt. This process was called carroting. The solution caused the minute scales—which are characteristic of all animal wool fibers—to swell up, increasing the fibers' ability to matt. It also turned the tips of the fibers orange, the side effect from which the process got its name. The hatter then removed the carrot-colored fur, now called fluff, from the skin with a knife.

Carroting produced serious side effects. The fumes from the carroting solution, especially when heated, were highly toxic to all who worked in the hat-making environment. Hatters suffered from nervous disorders, odd behavior, dementia, and various physical disorders. By the early 19th-century, the phrase "mad as a hatter" was already well understood.

Postlethwayt outlined the elaborate steps required to produce a felted hat. The fluff was first carded and weighed, with the amount of fluff adjusted to the size and thickness of the hat to be made. The fluff was then cleaned, matted, and shaped into two triangular pieces in a process called bowing. In the second step, basoning, the two pieces were joined together, using pressure, moisture, and heat, over a mold. At the end of this step the hat, now called a capade, met "in an angle at top, forming one conical cap." The last step of the matting process was called planking. The capade was dipped in a hot solution of water, sulfuric acid, beer grounds, and wine sediments. Then it was placed on a sloping plank and worked by hand and with a wooden roller to further shrink and thicken the fibers. The process of dipping and rolling was repeated for up to four or five hours or until the capade shrunk to the required dimensions.

To give the hat its final form, the capade was put over a wooden mold of the proper crown size and tied around the mold with a string called a commander. The hatter then beat the commander downward with an iron rod. When completed, the top of the hat was tightly stretched over the mold to form the crown; the excess felted edge at the bottom became the brim. The hat was then set aside to dry, after which the hatter removed the rough hairy surface of the felt and then smoothed the nap. The final step was to cut the brim to the desired width.

The finished hat was sent to the dyer. Depending upon the color desired, the hat might be boiled in dye "for about three quarters of an hour, then taken out to cool, and returned to the dye, for ten or twelve times successively." When dry, the hat was sent back to the hatter for waterproofing, final shaping, and lining. To waterproof it, the inside was coated with a solution of gum Arabic or gum Senegal (treating the outside of the hat would ruin its surface). In the final steaming, the hat was shaped according to the current fashion and any seam marks were removed. Again dry, the hat was brushed and smoothed and fitted for a lining. External ornamentation such as a hat band or ribbon might be added by the hatter or a haberdasher.

Plaiting and Looping: Bobbin and Needle Laces

In the colonial period both men and women wore lace accessories. In the 17th century two kinds of lace vied for popularity: needle and bobbin. Needle lace is the older of the two. It evolved from various whitework embroidery techniques practiced in Europe in the 15th and early 16th centuries. These techniques, all of which depend on a woven ground, include cutwork, drawn-thread work, and pulled thread. True needle lace has no woven foundation. It is constructed of successive rows of detached buttonhole stitches, made with a needle and thread. These stitches are built

Stomacher of bobbin lace worked in silver thread, silver strip, silver covered parchment, and silver spangles, England, 1740–1750. (Victoria and Albert Museum, London)

up as filling patterns attached to outlines of thick threads that have been tacked down along the design lines drawn on either parchment or heavy paper. Variations in the filling patterns depend on how the buttonhole stitches are grouped and whether the stitches are open, twisted, or knotted. After all the patterns are completed, the lace maker links the outlined shapes together with small bars of detached buttonhole stitches or creates a background of net mesh to hold all of the patterns together. When both the pattern and ground are complete, she cuts the tacking stitches to release the lace from the drawn design.

Developed in the 16th century in Europe, bobbin lace, also known as pillow or bone lace in the period, completely different in execution than needle lace. Rather than a line drawing, the design for a bobbin lace pattern is marked by a series of pricked holes on parchment or paper. This pricking is then attached to a hard rounded or cylindrical pillow. Following the pricked pattern, the worker plaits, twists, and/or weaves together a number of threads wound on small bobbins. Each completed interworking is called a stitch. She keeps the stitches in place as she works by pinning them in place through the pattern prickings. Pins are removed as the work progresses.

Bib collar with needle lace fronts, linen fabric and lace, Venice, 1660–1680. (Victoria and Albert Museum, London)

Lace bobbins were slender, cylindrical tubes of mammal bone, wood, bamboo or, rarely, ivory. Their length, about three to five inches, was dependent on the kind of bobbin lace being made. Surviving bobbins from the colonies are of plain bamboo.

There are two kinds of bobbin lace, part and straight. Part lace consists of small sections of pattern that are made separately and then joined together by bars or a net mesh ground. Straight lace is made all in one piece, both the pattern shapes and the linking bars or net ground. Straight lace can be made with as few as three pairs of bobbins or more than 300 pairs.

In the early 18th century a third form of lace, Dresden work, entered the vocabulary of the fashion conscious. As it is an embroidered lace, it is discussed in the following section.

Embellishments: Passementerie, Needlework, and Embroidery

The French term *passementerie* refers to a wide range of narrow trimmings used to strengthen or to ornament clothing and upholstery. The trimmings could be woven, braided, or twisted. Types of colonial-era *passementerie* included coach lace (a narrow patterned tape used to cover seams in upholstery), livery lace (similar to coach lace but used to decorate specialized clothing worn by male household servants), fringes, gimp, ribbon, tape, and galloon. The final use of the trimmings depended on their weight, the materials from which they were constructed, and the elaborateness of their design. Simple cords and flat-woven trimmings were useful to stitch into seams or around buttonholes or to fold over the edges of garments to protect those edges from dirt and abrasion. More dimensional trims were purely ornamental, adding an impression of wealth and status to the wearer's clothing. Although trimmings were produced in professional English and European workshops and exported for sale in the colonies, surviving looms and trimmings attest that plain and ornate versions were made in colonial households as well.

All of the weave structures used to create broad-width textiles—plain, twill, satin, pile, and compound—are represented in historical trimmings. Flat tapes and ribbons as well as more complex dimensional *passementerie*, such as fringes, gimps, and galloons, were woven on narrow looms. The weaving materials could be as simple as linen, wool, or silk thread; skilled weavers incorporated silk cords, very narrow tapes, wire or thin strips of metal. The designs were limited only by the ability and imagination of the weaver, the availability of materials, and their cost.

Some narrow fabrics, such as braids and cords, could be made by plaiting, or braiding, yarns together on the diagonal, a fabric structure known today as oblique interlacing. Making small quantities of these braids did not require a special frame or equipment because the set of threads could be tied to the back of a chair and worked from that point of tension. Commercial quantities, however, were made using a frame.

Additionally, many common 18th-century trimmings were made by cutting broad-width fabric into narrow strips. Strips, cut on the diagonal, or bias, of the fabric and then folded lengthwise to encase a thin cord or string, were stitched into seams, both for decoration and for reinforcement. For fashionable silk dresses, trimmings called robings were made by cutting extra dress fabric into straight strips. The edges of some strips were cut with a special tool to create a scallop or zigzag. The strips were then drawn up into ruffles by gathering stitches worked down the center of each strip and stitched down the front of the dress. Other strips were gathered along each edge and drawn up into little puffs, or ruchings. These, too were stitched down the front of the dress. Ruffles and ruchings were also used to ornament stomachers, hats, and bonnets.

The terms sewing, needlework, and embroidery are often used interchangeably today to describe a variety of practical and ornamental techniques executed with a needle and thread. These terms had more specific meanings in the colonial period. Sewing was practical work that included the construction of garments and accessories; darning and mending; hemming; the attachment of hooks, eyes and buttons; and marking. Marking involved working small, discrete initials, usually in some variation of cross stitch, on a garment in order to designate ownership. Common in Europe from at least the 1500s, marking can be found on surviving shirts and smocks, collars, and cuffs, petticoats, stomachers, pockets, pocketbooks, and handkerchiefs. Stitched initials were essential to the maintenance of the household. They helped distinguish ownership when inventories of personal and domestic effects were taken. They made sorting the laundry much easier, both by the staff in large families and by professional laundresses in their own shops. And they ensured that linens sent out to be worked on were returned to their proper owners. Young girls were introduced to marking by stitching alphabets on an embroidered sampler. Of course, all the fabric trimmings discussed above, as well as decorative bits—glass beads, metal sequins, and feathers—were attached to the surfaces of clothes, hats, gloves, and shoes using plain sewing techniques.

Allied with sewing was needlework, which referred to ornamental stitching executed on a moderately priced background fabric, such as linen and wool—and by the second half of the 18th century also on fine cotton fabric. The thread could be silk, linen, or worsted (crewel) wool. Examples of colonial needlework include crewelwork petticoats, tamboured baby caps, and Dresden work neck handkerchiefs. In contrast, embroidery described ornamental stitching executed on more expensive fabric, most often satin-weave silk. The threads also were more expensive: sewing silk and silk floss, silk chenille, and silver and gilt-silver threads. Embroidery also made use of beads, pearls, sequins, and other applied materials.

The stitches of needlework and embroidery fell into two categories in the colonial period: surface stitching and counted work. Surface stitching disregards the woven grid or knitted structure of the textile being embroidered. The embroidery threads are worked over and through the surface of the cloth in any direction to complete the desired pattern. Examples of stitches common to surface work include running, stem, satin, chain, and buttonhole. Counted work, however, relies on the grid structure of the woven fabric or the loops of a knitted textile: the embroiderer counts warp and weft threads or knitted loops to place the stitches. Cross, tent, and Irish stitches are commonly used in this type of embellishment.

Quilting is a practical sewing technique used to join together two layers of fabric (often a third filling layer is added, usually for warmth), typically in a decorative pattern. Quilting consists of single rows of running or back stitch, the stitches worked closely together. The patterns made by these rows were as simple as an allover grid or lattice, but more complicated repeat rectilinear and curvilinear patterns and individual motifs were also executed. Surviving quilted clothing includes petticoats, waistcoats, and caps.

As noted in the discussion of bobbin and needle laces, the early 18th century saw the introduction of an embroidered lace known as Dresden work. It successfully competed with the two other lace forms because it complemented the plain fabric accessories that had become fashionable with the importation of sheer cotton muslin and linen from India. Flemish bobbin lace makers were the first to produce this densely decorated but delicate fabric. It combined pulled thread embroidery, a technique that had been practiced in Europe since the 16th century, with counted geometric patterns and surface stitches, all worked on very fine muslin. The best examples were produced in the German-speaking region of Saxony. It reached the rest of Europe, Great Britain, and America through merchant wholesalers in the town of Dresden. This led to its being called Dresden work or Dresden point (Staples 2003, 36–44). In the 18th century, Dresden work was classified as a lace and sold by lace dealers (Levey 1983, 72). It was so successful that by the second quarter of the 18th century European lace makers were imitating Dresden's look in bobbin lace. By the mid-18th century, Dresden work had entered the repertoire of the amateur embroiderer, and colonial schoolmistresses began to include Dresden work in their embroidery curricula. For example, in 1754, Sarah Moffit, an itinerant teacher who had held

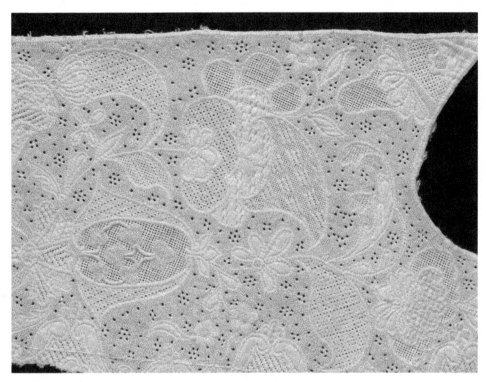

Detail of a Dresden work panel for a bodice, Germany, 1700–1729. Bodice panels like these were imported ready-made to the colonies through Britain. (Victoria and Albert Museum, London)

classes in "Philadelphia, Baltimore, and lately at Portsmouth," advertised in Norfolk, Virginia, that she would offer instruction in several branches of needlework, including "true Dresden and Catgut, either coarse of fine, in a direct imitation of lace" (*Norfolk and Portsmouth Journal*, July 23, 1754).

Finishing the Cloth

A textile was not finished when it came off the loom, the knitter's needles or the lace-maker's pillow or lap. At the very least, fresh cloth had to be washed to remove everyday grime before it could be used to make clothing or furnishings. If the yarns themselves had not been dyed to add color or pattern to the fabric, the fabric could be dyed. Woven fabric also could be printed with one or more colors to add pattern. Other finishing processes existed to further ornament the fabrics' surface, to make fabrics whiter or softer, to make them more effective protection against inclement weather or to tighten the weave to make them less likely to fray. The most common of these processes in the colonial period were dyeing, printing, bleaching, fulling, napping, and calendering.

Bleaching

Bleaching made use of soap, acids, and alkalis to whiten fabrics, especially linen. Postlethwayt described different methods for bleaching "silks, linen cloth, and woolen stuffs." Both alkalis and acids were used in the process. The traditional alkali was a mixture of ashes and soft soap, the acid sour or butter milk.

Treated in the skein before it was woven, silk was boiled twice in a solution of river water and a little soap. The solution of the second boiling had an added ingredient, "a little indigo, which gives it that bluish cast, that is commonly observed in white silk." To dry them, the skeins were put in a stove in which sulfur was burned, the vapor of which also whitened the silk.

Postlethwayt described three ways to bleach wool. The first he called the "natural method." After the fabric was fulled, it was again washed, in warm water with the addition of soap, and "worked with the hands" over a wooden bench. A second method was to expose stretched, half-dry, fabrics to "vapour of sulfur." Postlethwayt noted, however, that woolens that had been exposed to these vapors were difficult to dye "unless it be a black or blue." In the third method, the fabric was "well stirred and agitated" in a solution of cold water, chalk (to soften the water), and a little indigo. After rinsing, the fabric was stretched and exposed to sulfurous vapors.

Bleaching linens and cottons to a fine white might take months to achieve. Before the discovery of chlorine bleaches, the most common way to make linen or cotton white was to soak it in lye or bran, and then dry it in the sun. Large parcels of flat, grassy ground were set aside near streams or ponds as bleaching grounds for linen manufacturing. In the 17th and early 18th centuries, this complex and time-consuming process was most successfully executed in Holland and Flanders, and British linen producers sent their fabrics to those countries to be bleached. The first step in the process was to wash the linen fabric several times in a solution of wood ashes and water (lye), rinsing it in clear water. After each rinse, the fabric was spread out flat in a meadow "where they are now and again watered with clear water out of small canals." When a desired degree of whiteness was achieved, the fabric was rubbed with soap to remove any remaining grease and clean the selvages of the fabric. After a thorough rinsing the fabric was then soaked in cow's milk, the cream being first removed. "This perfects their bleaching, gives them all their softness, and makes them cast a little nap [i.e., have a slightly napped surface]." The fabric was rinsed in cold water for a last time and dipped in a solution of water and starch mixed with just enough pale smalt—powdered glass colored blue with cobalt—to impart a crisp white color to the fabric without turning it blue. After the linens dried, they were delivered to merchants for further processing. This included beating the fabric "on marble blocks with very smooth wooden mallets" to beat down the grain of the fabric and impart a smooth finish. All bleached fabrics were then carefully folded and put in a press before wrapping them for shipment.

Fulling

Fulling is a process in which woolen woven or knitted fabric was subjected to heat, moisture, pressure, and friction to shrink, thereby tightening and thickening the interlocked yarns. This process produced a fabric that was "thick, compact, and durable" (Postlethwayt 1971). The fuller employed a claylike soil, called fuller's earth, kneading the substance along with water into the fabric to absorb oils, grease, and other impurities used in dressing and finishing the wool. An example of a fulled fabric used for clothing in the colonial period was broadcloth, a carded plainweave.

When a fabric shrinks, it is often difficult to see the interworked elements of the warp and weft threads because the surface resembles felt. Fulling should not be confused with felt, however: fulling is a process to which a woven cloth is subjected while felt is a nonwoven fabric (see Felt above).

Napping

Nap refers to raised surface fibers on a fabric. Nap occurs naturally in woven and knitted fabrics because the yarn itself is fuzzy; the process of making felt also produces a fuzzy or rough surface. A finished fabric can be given a napped surface by undergoing a process that raises the surface fibers. Napped fabrics were useful for cold weather wear since the raised fibers trapped air and provided insulation.

In the colonial period, nap was produced, or raised, by combing the surface of the cloth with the dried pine-cone shaped flower heads of teasels. The heads had curved spines, or burrs, to "tease" the fibers gently up from the surface. Once raised, the fibers could be brushed to increase and lengthen the nap—worsted shag and woolen duffel, both used for coats, are two examples. Or the nap could be shorn close to the surface of the fabric. Woolen baize, or bays, and flannel are examples of short-napped fabrics.

Calendering

A calender was a machine composed of two rollers "of very hard and polished wood" through which woolen, silk, and linen fabrics were run "to make them smooth, even, and glossy, or to give them waves, or water them" (Postlethwayt 1971). The rollers were set between two thick smooth boards; the bottom board was fixed but the top board was moveable and weighted down with large stones. A combination of rolling, pressure, and movement of the upper board produced either a smooth glossy finish or a distinctive wavy pattern called watering (now commonly known as *moiré*) pressed into the fabric. The pattern disappeared if the fabric was washed. Tightly woven solid-color fabrics with a slight rib, such as worsted calamanco and silk taffeta, often were given this treatment.

Dyeing and Dyes

Adding color(s) to yarns and fabrics through dyeing and printing was the province of skilled artisans. Seventeenth-century Europeans were adept at dyeing silk and wool in bright, fast colors, and they brought these skills to the colonies. While there was certainly home dyeing of fabrics and yarns in the colonies, there were many skilled artisans who called dyeing their trade. Professional finishing of even homemade cloth surely enhanced its look and feel. Imported new fabrics, of course, would arrive in the colonies dyed and finished, ready for cutting up into garments. Sometimes, however, fabrics would be damaged by moisture or mildew during the sea voyage. These fabrics were brought to local dyers for redyeing and finishing.

To ensure a consistent color throughout a textile, sometimes the fibers were dyed before they were spun—this was referred to as "dyed in the wool"—or the yarns were dyed before they were made into fabric, referred to as "dyed in the grain." But fabrics were also dyed after they were woven, knitted, or plaited—"dyed in the piece." Well-dyed fibers, yarns, and textiles depended on the cleanliness of the materials, the purity of the dyestuffs, and the dyer's skill in preparing the solutions properly and using them correctly.

Fabrics to be dyed were first washed to remove any grime that settled during production. This helped the fibers more readily accept the mordant and the dye. Wools and linens were scoured to remove excess oil and wax; silk was washed to remove excess gummy sericin. While soap was commonly used as a cleansing agent, cotton was washed in a weak solution of water and vitriol (sulfuric acid); fermented urine (ammonia) was an ingredient in washing wool.

Some dyes could be made fast—fixed permanently to the fibers of the cloth so the color would not wash out—by using mordants (from the Latin "to bite"). These fixed dyes were known as "great" or "dyes in grain." The "lesser," or fugitive, dyes ran when the textile was washed. In the dyeing process, the dye was dissolved in a liquid, usually water; the mordant was dissolved with the dye or prepared as a separate solution to apply to the fabric before or after dyeing. This procedure was determined both by the nature of the fabric and the color desired.

The most common mordents were alum, crude tartar (potassium tartrate), and cream of tartar (potassium hydrogen tartrate); copperas; vegetable ashes (potash and barilla); gall nuts, such as oak gall; the leaves of the sumac; and lime. Other organic substances were useful as mordants because of their chemical properties. Vinegar, bad wine and beer, and lemon juice had natural acids. Wheat, rye, meal, hay, and potatoes were fermented to produce an acidic "sour water" (Fairlie 1965, 492–93). Fermented human urine was useful for mixing and dissolving dyes. Animal dung was also used.

Dyestuffs were an important trade commodity the world over. While preferred, good quality dyes—which produced strong colors, were fast to washing, and did not readily fade when exposed to sunlight—were expensive. The colonial landscape produced a bounty of native dye-bearing plants for domestic use and a few for export. One hope of the English textile industries was that the colonies could and would cultivate the indigo plant, the best and most lasting source of blue dye, in enough quantity to make imports of indigo from Asia unnecessary. Indigo began to be imported from Asia into Europe in quantity in the 17th century and rapidly replaced woad, a plant native to Europe that produced an inferior dye. Indigo became a cash crop for South Carolina plantation owners in the second half of the 18th century. Eliza Lucas (1722–1793) first experimented with indigo cultivation on her father's plantation in the early 1740s. The plant soon became an important export staple. In 1747, she and other South Carolina planters produced more than 135,000 pounds of the plant for export; more than a million pounds were shipped in succeeding years (Pinckney 1997, xxix–xx). Eighteenth-century merchants' advertisements in the *Pennsylvania Gazette* indicate that dyestuffs such as indigo, madder, logwood, oak galls, and fustic as well as common mordants such as alum and copperas were being sold by a variety of merchants and shopkeepers, including those who sold dry goods, drugs, and paints and pigments.

Whether native or imported, dye stuffs were extracted from plants, chemical compounds, and, in one case, an animal. (Mineral dyes were not available until the 1820s; synthetic dyes, by-products of the Industrial Revolution, were not introduced until 1856.) These yielded blues, reds, yellows, fawns, oranges, greens, and gray and black. Fast reds came from the dried bodies of cochineal insects and madder root. In the colonial period cochineal was so costly that it was used primarily to dye silk and worsted wool. Lesser reds were obtained from orchilla—a lichen—and brazilwood and other redwoods. If treated with acid, logwood produced a fugitive red.

Weld, a flowering plant, and the fustic tree were the most common sources of a fast yellow, although these yellows did tend to fade out of printed textiles. A lesser yellow was produced from turmeric, a rhizome of the ginger family, saffron, and safflowers. Walnut hulls, alder and oak bark, logwood, and sumac produced fast beiges if processed with alum, copperas, and oak galls. There were no fast natural oranges or greens. A fugitive orange could be produced from fustic. Lesser greens were obtained from verdigris—the patina formed on weathered copper, brass, or bronze—and blue copperas, a form of iron sulfate. Nonfast grays and black generally were produced from soot. Fast black and brown-black were obtained from madder mixed with iron oxide or by treating brown dyes such as alder and sumac with iron, copperas, or galls.

Most of the fast blues came from indigo (*Indigofera tinctoria*). Because the colorant in the indigo plant is not water soluble, the leaves must be soaked and fermented; then the resulting solution is treated with an alkaline chemical to precipitate out the dye. Unlike other dyestuffs, indigo does not need a mordant to become fixed in the cloth. Fabric dipped into a vat of indigo dye does not turn blue in the vat. The fabric must be removed from the dye and exposed to air: the blue color appears through oxidation. The dyer controlled the shade of blue by the number of times the process of dipping and drying the cloth was repeated. Indigo was processed with a variety of substances, including lime, potash, or urine, to make the dye bath.

Not all fabrics took dyes in the same way. Wool was the easiest to color with vegetable dyes. Because of their surface properties, silk, linen, and cotton were progressively more difficult to color. The amount of dye used depended on the fiber. For example, one pound of wool required only one ounce of cochineal while one pound of silk needed twice that amount (Fairlie 1965, 491). While cochineal worked well on protein fibers, like wool and silk, it was not compatible with linen and cotton, so madder was used to dye these cellulosics. The only dye that worked equally well on all four fibers, allowing for slight differences in the processing, was indigo.

Application of different mordants to a single fabric by painting or printing produced different colors on the cloth from just a single dyebath. For example, madder treated with an acidic mordant produced a yellowish red while an alkali mordant made the red more crimson, and iron oxide produced a brownish-black. The range of colors produced by these mordants was extended by treating the cloth with additional substances, such as oils or minerals, to create different shades. Dyes and mordants also reacted with the metal of the dye vat, so vessels of pewter, lead, copper, and iron were used with different dyes to keep the colors true.

Finally, many colors that could not be achieved with a single dye or a dye-and-mordant combination were created by overdyeing one color with another. For example, blue cloth dyed yellow made green, and red dyed yellow made orange, at least until the yellow began to fade away. Blue over red gave shades of purple. A dyer's skill was marked by how many dyestuffs he knew to use and how many shades he could produce from them.

Printing and Painting

The same dyes discussed above were used to imprint textiles by stamping or painting. Patterning was introduced in the dye vat by applying a substance to the cloth that would either resist the take-up of dye in certain areas or discharge (bleach out) the dye. Mordants, resists, and discharges could be hand painted onto the surface of the cloth, applied by carved wooden blocks or, by the mid-18th century, applied by engraved copper plates. In the 18th century, "clouded" fabrics, usually silk, were made by setting up the warp yarns on a frame and then printing or painting a pattern on them before they were woven. The French called this type of design a *chine à la branche*.

For most of the 17th century the best quality of printed and mordant-dyed cotton fabrics, boasting colorful floral or exotic designs, were produced in and imported from India. By the fourth quarter of the century, however, Europeans had discovered some of the secrets of dyeing with mordants. The first English venture into block printing and mordant dyeing opened at around 1676 (Pettit 1976, 34). Shortly thereafter, importing Indian chintzes to England was prohibited in order to support this new English industry. Indian-made chintzes were, however, still fashionable and desirable. Although fabric printing as an industry was officially discouraged in the British colonies, fabric printers and stampers appear in newspaper advertisements in several of the northern colonies soon after the turn of the 18th century. Printing sometimes was offered as an extra service by dyers.

Until the 1760s, European and Indian textile printers either hand-painted designs or used carved wooden blocks. A design would be drawn and colored on paper and then divided into segments whose size was governed by how big a block of wood a printer could lift up and down dozens—if not hundreds—of times a day. Each segment required a different block of wood to be carved in relief for each color in the design. In a simple floral design, for example, one block would have the relief carving for black or brown stems, petal outlines, and veins in leaves; another for solid areas of red flowers, and a third for solid areas of pink flowers. The dyes were not printed directly onto the cloth; instead, mordants were printed that would combine with a single dyestuff (usually madder) to create different colors. The cloth was then submerged in a single dye bath. When it was removed from the bath and washed clear of dye from the unmordanted areas, the pattern remained. The methods for printing indigo on textiles were limited because the indigo produced color only after the dyestuff oxidized on the cloth. Indigo could be "penciled," that is, a dye solution that had been mixed with a chemical to retard oxidation was applied to the cloth with a fine brush. A resist (starch or wax) was printed onto the cloth after which the cloth was dyed in indigo to the desired depth of color. After about 1750, an indigo solution could be printed directly on the fabric, after which the fabric was treated with different chemicals to achieve the desired strength of blue. This latter process was referred to as China Blue (Montgomery 1970, 194–211).

Certain colors could not be obtained with a single printed dyestuff. Instead, overprinting one color with another created the desired shade. Blue on top of red made purple. Yellow dye applied by hand or block over blue areas made green for leaves. Prints with colorful floral designs against a dark ground (often a shade of brown) were popular imports in the colonies, and required yet another set of blocks to print the mordant for the background color.

Colonial printers used only the block-printing technique. In 1752, however, Francis Nixon of Drumcondra, Ireland, introduced in Europe the use of large plates of copper, as large as a yard, engraved with complex floral or landscape patterns. This technique spread to England and France by the late 1760s, and copperplate prints became a coveted fabric among the colonial upper classes. Such prints were usually a single color; if additional colors were required they were applied by brush or with wooden blocks.

Animal Skins

Shoes, boots, gloves, workmen's aprons, jerkins, and breeches were the most common garments and accessories constructed from processed animal skins, or hides. These leather products were important complements to clothing made of woven goods. Leather production was focused primarily on skins from oxen, cows, and calves; deer; sheep and lambs; and goat. In addition to the cows, oxen, and sheep raised locally, England relied on unprocessed and half-dressed skins imported from Spain, Portugal, and Ireland. The late-17th- and 18th-century trade in deer skins was carried on almost exclusively between colonial middlemen and various Native American tribes. Native and colonial trappers also supplied smaller quantities of skins from indigenous animals such as beaver, otter, marten, fox, raccoon, muskrat, elk, moose, and buffalo.

Postlethwyt opined, "the skins of our own production, and those imported from our North American Colonies, when dressed in this kingdom, make the best leather in the world, and therefore is an article of very great importance to the trade of the nation." He outlined the three principal procedures for preparing animal skins: tanning, dressing in oil, and dressing in alum, noting, "the order and number of these operations vary in different places, but the material part is always the same." Skins arrived at the tanner or dresser either raw as they came off the animals, with or stripped of their hair or salted to preserve them if they were being shipped long distances.

The tanner's business was to soak skins in water to which was added the ground-up bark of young oak trees, which contain an astringent chemical called tannin. Tannin draws out the protein in the animal skins, preserving the skins and making them waterproof. After soaking, the skins were referred to as leather. Some leather was sent directly from the tan-yard to shoemakers and others "who employ hard leather." Other processed skins were sent to the currier, whose job was to soften them. These leathers were especially appropriate for the upper sections of shoes and the legs of boots. Because the processed skins from the tanner's yard still had "many fleshy fibers on them," the currier soaked the skins a second time and scraped off the flesh. After a third soaking, the currier "tramples them with his heels, 'till they begin to become soft and pliant." This was followed by a soak in train oil, harvested from whales. The final operation involved folding, squeezing, and moving the skins back and forth under an instrument called a pummel. A thick piece of wood, "the underside whereof is full of furrows crossing each other," the pummel broke any stiffness left in the leather. At this stage, the currier might rub the skin with chalk or white lead and then with a pumice stone to whiten it. To blacken the skin, the currier painted the skin with water impregnated with iron, followed by a second painting with a mixture of water, soot, vinegar, and gum Arabic. These processes were repeated until the skin "is of a shining black."

The leather dresser processed oil- and alum-dressed skins. These skins were generally thinner than those used by the tanner. Both processes included the necessary soakings in water, scraping, and beating. Instead of being treated with tannin, however, the skins were put in a lime pit, in order to loosen the hair for scraping. Oil-dressed skins were treated with fish oil—often from cod—before the final drying. Alum-dressed skins, also called tawed skins, were soaked in a mixture of water, salt, and alum (a double salt compound) before drying. Alum-dressed skins were usually reserved for fine leather goods such as gloves.

Other ways of treating leather produced Hungary leather, Morocco leather, and shamoy, or chamois. Workers of Hungarian leather—supplied to harness, saddle, and belt makers—used tallow or suet instead of tannin to treat the hides. Dressers of Morocco leather used crushed sumac leaves and a solution of water and animal dung to create a wrinkled or furrowed grain in the skins and also added dyes to color the leather. Shamoyed leather was treated with oil or grease; deer skins were usually shamoyed.

PROBLEMS IN TERMINOLOGY

Contemporary distinctions among terms are important in discussing the history of textile production for clothing. For example, although the words fabric, textile, and cloth are now used interchangeably, in the colonial period "cloth" almost always referred to a fabric made of wool; "stuff" also referred to fabric. Linen, cotton, silk, and wool are terms that describe only the raw fiber that a textile was made from, not the structure of that fabric. Conversely, a generic name like satin or damask did not always indicate the fiber of which the textile was made. Velvet, for instance, describes a particular pile-weave structure that, in the colonial period, could have been made of wool, linen, silk or cotton. When velvet appears by itself in an inventory or advertisement, it might have been made of any of these fibers.

Seventeenth- and 18th century men and women knew dozens of different woven fabrics by name. Generic terms such as serge, broadcloth, and velvet covered a variety of weave structures, weights, and finishes. Other names became generic over time. Osnaburg, for example (also spelled oznabrig or oxenbrig), was a coarse, unbleached plain-weave linen that in the 17th century was made in Osnabruck, Germany. It had many uses from wrappings and sacks to servant and slave clothing. In the early 1740s, Scottish linen weavers began to imitate this type of linen. By the 1760s, colonial shopkeepers advertised "oznabrigs" from Scotland, Germany, and Lancashire, England (*Pennsylvania Gazette*, September 7, 1767).

Serge was another fabric with international connections. It is unclear whether the French or the English first developed this good-quality, light-weight, woolen twill-weave fabric. Both countries, however, were manufacturing serge in the 17th century. The French called their version *serge de Nimes*, to designate its place of manufacture, Nimes, in southern France. The English picked up this appellation and produced a woolen textile called "sergedenim," giving rise to a shorter name, denim. In the 18th century, German and Italian weavers produced their own versions, called by the English German serge and *serge de Rome,* respectively. Serge of all sorts (and by different names) as well as denim were advertised in colonial newspapers. Commercial correspondence reveals that even merchants were sometimes confused by these names. By the end of the 18th century denim was also made of wool and cotton (Montgomery 1984, 216, 344–45). Colonial denim should not be confused with jeans, which were twill-weave fustians (linen warp/cotton weft). Jean cloth was first made in the Italian city-state of Genoa, in the 16th century. (Today denim commonly refers to a blue warp, white weft cotton twill fabric, and jeans are used to describe trousers, often made of denim, which are a form of casual dress.)

To further complicate matters, a particular type of fabric might be known by different names in different places, and those names might change over time. For example, the plain, unbleached cotton cloth known today in the United States as muslin is called calico in Great Britain. In the 17th and 18th centuries, however, muslin was a diaphanous, white cotton fabric, while calico was one of the names used for a light-weight, but not sheer, cotton fabric; both were imported from India. When printed with colorful patterns, calicos were also known as pintados, chintz, or chints, and *toiles peintes.* (In 19th-century America, calico referred to a cotton cloth printed with small repeating patterns in two or three colors, a meaning it retains today particularly among quilters.)

In addition, a word known to have one meaning might also be found in a different context with a different meaning: thread stockings and thread lace, for example, refer to textiles made from linen yarns. The term "cloth-colored," often found in inventories and advertisements, may be confusing since cloth refers to woolen fabric, but cloth-colored means a shade of beige or light brown (Rothstein 1976, 26). Spelling was also rather individual. Camlet is found as camlett and camblet; tamy as tamie and tammy; serge was also searge and sarge; perpetuana is also found as perpcheana. In rare instances fabrics were described in detail, or labeled samples were attached to documents or letters; this information gives modern researchers clues about what at least one individual thought was meant by a particular term. Unless information can be confirmed from several sources, however, it is still difficult to be confident about anything more than a general description of any given fabric.

In reading colonial inventories and 18th-century advertisements, there can be much confusion about the following five terms: pieces, patterns, suits, gowns, and shapes. For example, how did colonial readers interpret James Wallace's advertisement for "flower'd silk in shapes for waistcoats, . . . scarlet and saxon green worsted pieces, in patterns for waistcoats and breeches" (*Pennsylvania Gazette,* May 24, 1750)?

"Pieces" referred to finished lengths of textiles as they came off the loom or knitting frame. For example, in 1752, Green and Whitlock offered "linen worsted and cotton wove [i.e., woven] pieces for breeches and waistcoats," and Charles Willing sold "crimson and green silk pieces" for the same (*Pennsylvania Gazette*, March 3, April 2, 1752). From the 16th century, the lengths of at least some fabrics were locally legislated, and a lead seal was often affixed to finished cloths as evidence that they had been examined. In Norwich, England, the broad version of russel had to be woven 15 and a half yards long and half an English ell (45 inches) and one nail (two and a half inches) wide (Kerridge 1985, 70–1). Another form of legislation dictated the length of the warp threads; this was the case with baizes (100). Other fabrics were of a particular length because of tradition. For example, English mockado was usually 14 yards long and half a yard wide (68). (In notices, fabrics that were not full lengths were advertised as remnants, or patches.) In the 18th century, knitted fabrics, also, were manufactured in lengths on knitting frames and referred to as pieces. Frame knitters produced not only shaped stockings but also piece goods that were cut up "for caps, waistcoats, scarves, gloves, and shirts" (Perris 1914, 94).

"Patterns" referred to designs woven into or printed or painted onto fabric or worked into a knitted fabric, not to the paper patterns used today to construct clothing. (The paper pattern for sale to home sewers was not invented until the 1860s.) For example, Robert and Amos Strettell advertised "scarlet and black, and silk and worsted, knit patterns for waistcoats and breeches" and "narrow striped cherryderries in patterns for gowns" (*Pennsylvania Gazette*, October 4, 1744; May 30, 1745). James Wallace imported "great choice of light and dark ground calicoes and chints, of the newest fashioned patterns" (*Pennsylvania Gazette*, May 24, 1750). Hugh Donaldson and John Troy sold "patterns for aprons and handkerchiefs" (*Pennsylvania Gazette*, February 12, 1751). Isaac Jones offered "wove worsted patterns for breeches . . . cotton and linnen patterns for gowns, linnen patterns for petticoats" among a long list of fabrics he imported from London and Bristol in 1739 (*Pennsylvania Gazette*, June 28, 1739).

The term "suit" must be read carefully in context; its meaning changes depending on whether the source document is a probate inventory, account book or newspaper advertisement. The term can denote apparel. For example, a notice for a runaway stipulated that "he has two Suits of Clothes with him" (*Pennsylvania Gazette*, October 20, 1763). Joseph Stides sold "Ready-made cloaths in Suits, both broadcloth and drugget" (*Pennsylvania Gazette*, April 8, 1742). For one of his enslaved servants, George Washington ordered from his London tailor in 1764 a "livery suit to be made of worsted Shagg . . . The Coat and Breeches alike . . . the waistcoat made of red Shagg" (Washington 1764). In all of the above examples, suit refers to an ensemble of coat, waistcoat, and breeches.

A suit also denoted a set of finished textiles to complete an ensemble, such as "Suits of Aprons, Ruffles, and Handkerchers" and "suits of the newest fashion'd gauze trimmed with satin" (*South-Carolina Gazette*, November 2, 1769). In 1772, Martha Parke Custis received a "Suit of Fash'e [fashionable] lace, Includ'g a Cap with Lappits, Ruffles, Tippet (or handkerchief &ca)" (Washington 1773). Other suits of personal and apparel trimmings were described as: "Complete Suits of Tambour worked and Feather stitched Muslins"; "elegant Suits of Dresden Linen"; and "LADIES Suits of Muslins and Lawns, full trimm'd" (*Pennsylvania Gazette*, December 12, 1749; *South-Carolina Gazette*, January 7, 1773; October 29, 1772; July 16, 1772).

Most commonly in advertisements, however, a suit was a requisite length of matching or complementary fabrics for an ensemble. It was almost always for men's wear and made of broadcloth. Suits were sometimes advertised with trimmings, such as "Superfine Spanish broadcloth in suits, with alopeen linings and trimmings" and "broad cloths and trimmings in suit" (*Pennsylvania Gazette*, December 12, 1749; November 10, 1737).

Advertisements for dry goods often include phrases like "silk and cotton gowns." Unless preceding or following the phrase "ready-made" or referring to the clothing of a runaway, it cannot be assumed that the term "gown" meant a finished woman's garment. References almost always meant a length of fabric suitable to make a gown. Examples include "holland and cotton gowns" and "Striped cotton gowns" (*South-Carolina Gazette*, November 5, 1753). In 1677, the inventory of the ship *Ruth*, from London and bound for Maryland, was seized for nonpayment of the hire of the ship and seamen's wages. In addition to yardage of osnabrig, fustian, jeans, dowlas, serge, and broadcloth packed in bales and trunks, there was a listing for 19 painted calico gowns (Merritt 1956, 67:33–36). This was not clothing, but lengths of decorated India export cottons suitable for women's apparel.

"Shape" referred to the various elements of a garment embroidered onto or woven into a length of fabric that a tailor would cut out and fit to a customer. For example, waistcoat shapes are the fronts of waistcoats with the collars, pocket flaps, or stands, and even button covers, all embroidered on one piece of fabric, often silk. Knitted fabric was also imported as actual shapes that could be sewn together to make a garment. William Grant offered "worsted pieces and shapes for waistcoats and breeches" (*Pennsylvania Gazette*, September 28, 1752). Hall and Smith imported into Charleston "Mens Gold and Silver embroidered Waistcoat Shapes" (*South-Carolina Gazette*, October 29, 1772). Bremar and Neyle sold "best Genoa Velvet, fine cut Velvet, and cotton Shapes for Vests" (*South-Carolina Gazette*, November 16, 1753). "Silver spangled shapes for shoes" were part of Thomas Fitzsimmons's imported wares in 1755, and Davies and Flanagan sold "gold and silver shoe shapes for women's shoes" in 1761 (*Pennsylvania Gazette*, November 27, 1755; October 29, 1761).

BESPOKE AND READY-MADE CLOTHING

Three mechanisms coexisted to provide clothing for colonists: (1) bespoke and ready-made clothing, imported from Britain and made by tailors and others in the apparel trades or made by colonial tradesmen and tradeswomen; (2) imported cloth from British, European, East Indian, and Asian looms; and (3) textiles of domestic production. The use of either imported or domestically produced textiles presupposed either dress-making skills within the home or the existence of a class of artisans who were paid for turning flat textiles into three-dimensional garments. Most colonists put their wardrobes together using some combination of these mechanisms and trades; the percentages varied according to wealth, station, location in the colonies, and in the 1760s and 1770s, political principles.

Early on in the settlements all three sources were exploited. John Winthrop wrote to his wife Margaret from Boston in 1631, requesting that she bring with her to New England not only the "strongest welt leather shoes and stockings for children, and hats of all sizes," but also shoemaker's thread and hobnails for making or repairing shoes on the spot (quoted in Earle 1895, 158–59). Once in Boston, Margaret continued to order clothing from the same London tailor, a Mr. John Smith, who had served her in England. The fact that John Winthrop sent to England for a flax brake in 1634 suggests that the flax crops were plentiful enough by then for Bostonians to begin making their own linen yarn, at the least for knitting and possibly for weaving (Earle 1895, 188). In 1696, the estate inventory of John Corse of Deerfield, in western Massachusetts, listed £5 worth of homemade kersey among his effects. Certainly by then, in what was still a frontier town, colonists had many choices available in regard to dress.

An analysis of expenditures for clothing listed in the plantation accounts of Maryland planter Robert Cole offers a general introduction to how these systems operated in a cash crop economy, where homespun found no place (Carr, Menard, and Walsh 1991, 21). Robert Cole and his wife, Rebecca, arrived in Maryland in June of 1652, together with four children and two indentured servants. They purchased a three-hundred-acre free hold in St. Clement's Manor, St. Mary's County, on the western shore of the colony.

In 1662, Robert Cole decided to return to England. Mindful of the hazards of again crossing the Atlantic, he inventoried his possessions in March and made his will in April. Sometime during these two months Rebecca died, but her passing did not deter Cole from his plans. He arranged for executors to carry out his will in the event of his death and sailed in the spring. By September of 1663 Cole himself was dead. He left two step-children (Rebecca's by a previous marriage) and five of his own. For over 11 years the executor, and Maryland neighbor, Luke Gardiner, kept detailed accounts of the income and expenditures on the Cole plantation. The household consisted of five children and four indentured servants: Francis Knott, Robert Cole, William Cole, Edward Cole, Betty Cole, Isabel Jones (indentured and working as the housekeeper), John Elton, Robert Gates, and John Johnson. The oldest girl, Ann Knott, had married by 1662, and Gardiner sent Mary Cole to live with her grandmother in England (169–207).

The pattern of expenditures revealed in these plantation accounts indicates that more than 55 percent went to imported goods and services, most importantly cloth, clothing, and shoes (81). Payments made in pounds of tobacco show that an unnamed tailor came each year from 1662 to 1672 to make clothes for the children and servants. Luke Gardiner regularly purchased shoes and stockings for the household's inhabitants. No spinning wheels or looms were listed in the inventory, so all of the fabric needs were met with textiles imported from England: woolen and linen fabrics manufactured in England; linen from Scotland; and a finer linen called holland. Knitted stockings, caps, and hats were ready-made accessories also brought on English ships. Cole possessed tailor's shears and lasts and awls for shoe -making. The tailor who came once or twice a year to make and mend clothing for the household may have used these shears, but a female household servant may have used them as well. Gardiner also purchased tanned hides to repair the family's shoes.

Although the tailor was paid for making and mending the children's apparel and making clothing for the male servants, it is possible that Isabel Jones was responsible for making aprons and neck cloths and doing simple mending. These latter articles of clothing are not shaped and would have involved stitching straight seams and hemming. Isabel rather than the tailor may have also been responsible for making her own clothing and such items as shirts for the men and boys and shifts for the girls. Because she was an indentured servant, Gardiner would not have accounted for her labor.

The Systems of Bespoke and Ready-Made

Fashionable apparel at all price ranges and clothes for working men and women were available to Britain's colonists through two systems:

bespoke and ready-made. These systems employed hundreds of men and women to cut, sew, and knit in urban centers like London and Bristol and in counties scattered throughout Britain. By the late 17th century this clothing was a staple commodity in Britain's transatlantic trade network. Early in 17th-century colonial America, bespoke clothing of local production was the subject of court disputes and appeared as line items in ledger books. The term bespoke means "spoken for," referring to garments that were individually made for a customer, per order, according to his or her particular body measurements. In the ensuing century, individuals and small manufactories in some northern colonies began to produce on speculation for resale whole garments and other items of apparel. Thus, both bespoke and ready-made are essential parts of the story of clothing in colonial America.

Bespoke Clothing

Wealthy colonists often placed custom orders for their bespoke clothing from tradesmen in Britain. Located mostly in London, these high-end tailors and milliners, who were joined in the 18th century by mantua makers, worked with the latest fashions and fabrics to fulfill the sartorial requests of their well-to-do patrons. Other artisans, such as seamstresses, lace and tape makers, hosiers, shoe and boot makers, and hatters, were also involved to create complete wardrobes. The following examples give a sense of the complexity of some of these custom-made "mail orders."

The first recorded bespoke wardrobe in British colonial America was made for George Percy (1580–1632), the highest-born gentleman among Jamestown's first settlers, who had arrived just a year after the colony was founded. It is not known what apparel Percy brought with him from England in 1606. He received several gifts of clothing, however, from his brother, the ninth Earl of Northumberland, beginning in 1608 with apparel assembled by the Earl's "Gentleman of Apparrell," William Lucas (Shirley 1949, 233). When Percy was elected President of the Virginia colony in 1609, Lucas was commissioned to organize five new suits and other apparel to befit Percy's elevated political status. For the suits, Lucas ordered yardage of "Chamlette," a worsted fabric; "Philizella," or filoselle, which at this date could have been made of wool or silk; "Perpetuano," a light-weight serge; "silke Mocado," a warp-pile fabric; fustian; and silk taffeta for facings. Six yards of broadcloth were transformed into a cloak, jerkin, and pair of breeches. To wear next to the skin to protect the new garments from body oils and sweat were 18 shirts of holland, a dozen of them fitted with cambric bands and cuffs. Footwear was supplied for formal, working, and leisure occasions: a dozen pairs of shoes, six pairs of boots, and a pair of slippers. To complete the wardrobe, Lucas procured a dozen pairs of worsted stockings, six pairs of boot hose, six pairs of garters, nine pairs of gloves, two hats "with silke and gould bandes"; "a Colored dutch hatt edged with gould"; a "Munimouth [Monmouth] Cappe"; six night caps, and a dozen handkerchiefs (237–38). A Monmouth cap was a round, flat cap of knitted wool that was fulled, shaped, shorn, and sometimes fitted with tassels. In 1611, Percy was no longer president, but he received a parcel of luxury goods from Lucas that included a pair each of silk stockings and silk garters, 23 ounces of gold lace, four dozen gold buttons, and "a dutch beauer hatt with a Cypres band and a Rose" (240). It is arguable just how practical all of this garb was for Virginia's climate and the living conditions at Fort James in the first years of settlement.

Like many of his contemporaries, 18th-century Charleston, South Carolina, merchant and factor Robert Pringle (1702–1776) had his clothing needs met by bespoke garments. His relationship with London tailor, David Glen, was long standing and his correspondence with Glen was frank. The letters reveal something of the process and pitfalls that accompanied doing sartorial business long distance. For example, in January 1739, Pringle placed an order for a new wardrobe, "which I am to Desire may be made in the best manner you can & am in a particular manner to take notice to you they may not be made Scanty but every way Large & full & if too Large may be Remedied, but if too Little or too Scanty can never be made Large. All the Cloaths you have hitherto sent me having been too Little & Scanty for me" (Pringle 1972, 1:63). The order, which demonstrates Pringle's considerable understanding of fabrics and their impact as a fashion statement and clothing construction, is as follows:

1. a Horseman's Riding Coat of the Best superfine Drabb of a fashionable Middling Colour, not Light & the Cape not of Velvet, but of the same Drabb with good neat strong Buttons of Horse hair & send some spare Buttons. 2. a Best superfine Scarlett Broad Cloath Jackett or Waist Coat, full trimm'd & pretty Deep or Long with gold Buttons & a full Lace with Best Gold Lace or gold arras & fashionable, & lined with Scarlett Alepine, & am to desire you'll please send me what Remains of the Lineing to mend same. 3. a Banyan morning gown and made in the same manner as the last you sent me, to weave both sides alike of a very fashionable worsted Damask of the finest & best sort, of a middling Colour not Light, or a gown of any other handsome stuff fashionable & full for a gown butt the two sides be of Different Colours & send me some spare Buttons & Stuff that Remains. 4. A superfine

fashionable broad Cloth Fly Coat & Breeches of a Dark Colour Lin'd
with deep Bleue Alepine & neat Buttons & please send some spare
Button's & the Lineing that remains. 5. Two finest India Dimitty Jack-
etts Larger & Longer than the two sent me. (1:63–64)

Drabb may have been a kind of worsted drugget, hot pressed to acquire
a smooth finish. Alapeen was a mixed cloth of wool and silk, used primarily for men's clothing. India dimity, imported from India, was a cotton
cloth with patterns like stripes, flowers, or diamonds woven into the fabric.
Pringle's request that Glen send whatever fabric ends remained after the
garments were cut out is significant. If a garment were too snug or short,
in some cases fabric could be added to widen or extend the problem area.
The excess lining materials were important to Pringle because garment linings wore out before the garment itself did and were patched or replaced
as necessary.

Glen shipped Pringle's order in August of 1739; it arrived in Charleston
the following April. Pringle was conditionally pleased: "Every thing fitts me
very well but you put too much wadding in the [fly] Coat for this Hot Climate
which makes it very heavy." Pringle thought the breeches fabric was too heavy
for the same reasons and questioned the high price of the banyan (1:188).

In 1744, Pringle was once again in need of new clothing, and according
to a letter he wrote to his brother, Andrew, in London, "there is no good
Cloth or Furniture [trimmings, buttons, etc.] to be had here [in Charleston],
& the workmanship very bad" (2:709). So in June he wrote to Glen. To ensure that the clothing would "be full made & fashionable," he sent along
his measurements. This order was equally detailed: "Coat, Jackett and two
pair of Breeches, the Cloath to be of the best super fine Broad Cloth of a
Grave Fashionable Colour, not a heavey thick Cloth, & Mounted with the
best plain Mohair or Hair Buttons of the same Colour full made & full
trimm'd, & lin'd with the best & strongest Mazarine Blue Alapine" (2:706).
Pringle specified garlick, a hard-wearing linen, for the lining of the body
of the jacket, two jacket pockets, and the breeches. A fob pocket was to be
added to each of the breeches.

The order was ready to ship by August of that year and, again, Pringle
received his package in April of the next. His pleasure was tempered; "My
Suit of Cloaths . . . are Very much to my likeing & fitt me Exactly excepting
that the Coat Sleeves are an Inch or an Inch & a half Two Long" (2:824).
This did not deter him, however, from ordering, in the same letter, a suit
of black: "a Coat of Best Super fine Black Broad Cloath, of a Good Black
Colour, full Trimm'd & Lined with Black Allepine & a Jackett for Same, &
two Pair Breeches of Figur'd or Rais'd or Cut Velvett. I mean the Jackett of

Cut Velvett & the Two Pair Breeches of Plain Black Velvett." He added, "& pray dont make the Coat Sleeves so Long as the last" (2:824).

George Washington had experiences similar to Pringle's when he ordered clothing from London for himself, his wife Martha, and his two stepchildren, John and Martha (Patsy) Custis. In 1762, he reported to his English tailor, Charles Lawrence, that goods purchased for Patsy arrived in good order, but were accompanied by a black calimanco petticoat and "full trimmed night-gown of a straw coloured lustring" that were sized for an adult woman. He concluded, "they must be packed up by mistake and as some expence and risque would accompany a return of them Mrs. Washington will keep them herself, and the cost please to place to my account" (Washington 1763). Two years later, dissatisfied with the cost and quality of an order, Washington threatened to conclude further business with Lawrence. "I shall only refer you generally to the Bills you have sent me for a Pompadour Suit forwarded last July amounting to £16.3.6 without Embroidery, Lace, or Binding, not a fine close cloth neither; and only a gold button that would not stand the least wear"

(Washington 1764). Washington must have received some satisfaction, however, for in 1768 he wrote again to Lawrence for tailor-made clothes. He asked Lawrence to pay more attention to his measurements, which he had sent to Lawrence more than once, because his clothing generally arrived too short and occasionally too tight (Washington 1768). In the tailor's defense, the following are the instructions he had been asked to follow in fashioning "a genteel suit of Cloaths" for Washington in April of 1763: "I should have Inclosed you my Measure, but in a general way they are so badly taken here that I am convinced it woud be of very little Service. I woud have you . . . take measure of a Gentleman who Wares well made Cloaths of the following size: to wit, 6 feet high and proportionably made; if any thing rather slender than thick for a person of that highth with pretty long Arms and thighs" (Washington 1763).

George Washington at Princeton, by Charles Willson Peale, 1779. Peale captured Washington's height (6 feet, 4 inches), narrow shoulders, wide hips, long arms and legs, and very large hands and feet. The general was a tailor's nightmare. (U.S. Senate Collection)

By 1771 Washington had a new London tailor, Thomas Gibson, but in 1772 he was again complaining of the fit: "The Coat and Waistcoat which you sent me last year . . . fitted very well, except . . . being too long in the Skirts (for I was obliged to cut off near three Inches from the length) and being at the same time a little too tight in the Sleeves." In the same correspondence he ordered clothing for John, now 19, with the caveat that the apparel "may be made larger than those you sent him last year as the Breeches were too small for him every way especially in the Seat, and the Coats too narrow across the shoulders over and above these alteration's you are to make a proper allowance for his growth since as he is not only Taller, but lustier in ev' other resp't" (Washington 1772). This selection of correspondence calls into question whether *any* clothing tailored at long distance and sent from abroad came close to fitting the recipient.

The quality of bespoke clothing of colonial craftsmanship depended upon the availability of materials and the competency of tailors and others to carry out the work. Seventeenth-century court records from Accomack-Northampton, Virginia, reveal how difficult this could be, at least in the early years of colonization. In 1641, Richard Young, of Accomack County, Virginia, supplied a neighbor, George Dawe with three and a half yards of Spanish cloth (a fabric of English and Spanish wool), which Dawe made into a "sute of Cloathes and a payre of Britches" (Ames 1973, 24–35). Unfortunately for Young, Dawe then disposed of the clothing to third parties. In 1642, John Stockley, a tailor, was sued for "spoyleing a Frize shute of cloathes" that he had made for William Stevens, a boatwright. Stockley was ordered to pay Stevens in pounds of tobacco for all costs involved with the clothing, but Stevens was ordered to pay Stockley for making the suit (200).

According to his bill to Jonathan Corwin of Salem, Massachusetts, William Sweatland seems to have been an accomplished tailor. In 1679, he did work for the entire family. For Mrs. Corwin he "plaited a gown"; made two new petticoats, including one of scarlet trimmed with silver lace; "new plaited" an old petticoat; made a plush somar (a kind of knee-length overdress, also spelled samare and somaire); altered and fitted a pair of stays; and made gowns of white sarsenett, silk with lace, and black broadcloth. Mr. Corwin received a broadcloth hat, a "haire Camcottcoat", and a black broadcloth coat. For the children Sweatland made two hats and jackets for boys and two children's coats. In addition, he made a somar and a gown for the maid (Earle 1894, 20–22). The children's hats may have been fashioned from felted shapes, formed into a kind of rounded crown and imported from Britain (in the 19th century these were called felt bodies). These conical shapes were steamed, pressed, and pulled to conform to the current fashion and to fit the wearer. In the process, usually the top portion of the crown was cut off and the resulting doughnut-shaped piece was reshaped and sewn onto the edge of the hat to make the brim.

Philadelphia merchant and loyalist-turned-patriot, Tenche Coxe (1755–1824) employed the services of several local members of the apparel trades for his bespoke clothing. In May of 1779, during the British occupation of Philadelphia, Coxe paid: (1) John Reedle to make three dimity waistcoats and breeches with trimmings, a camlet surtout, a silk waistcoat and breeches, and a green coat and breeches; (2) Mrs. Duncan to make two pairs of lace ruffles; and (3) Mrs. Stewart to tambour and make two waistcoats, one crimson and the other blue. From other vendors he also purchased buckles, a pair each of boots and pumps, a white hat, and four pairs of silk hose (Coxe).

The Development of England's Ready-Made Trade

In contrast to bespoke clothing, ready-made garments were made in volume and, in the early 17th century, generally were imported for working men. Ready-mades appear in early records of ships that carried settlers to the colonies. In 1620, for example, the ship *Supply*, out of London, carried 56 passengers and provisions to settle the plantation Berkeley's Hundred, located about 20 miles upstream from Jamestown, Virginia. Among the supplies onboard was men's clothing that had been made up just prior to departure. Although women were among the passengers, no clothing for women was enumerated, possibly because duties were assessed on women's clothing; exports to the colonies of women's hosiery, but not men's and children's, were taxed. The accounting included 30 suits of men's apparel: 20 cassocks (a coat-like man's garment) and breeches of broad cloth; 20 doublets of dyed "holmes" (i.e., from Ulm, Germany) fustian, the doublets faced with blue linen; and 10 doublets and breeches of russet-colored leather with leather linings (Kingsbury 1933, 3:385). Additional apparel-related supplies had been purchased for the settlers at the Bristol fair. These included buttons; yards of gartering; points; "one dozen of weomens sheares" and "4 payre of Taylors sheares of 2 sorte"; yardage of dowlas and canvas that were made, prior to embarkation, into 51 shirts; nine dozen falling bands; 10 dozen handkerchiefs; and 105 pairs of Irish stockings. Completing the apparel list were "200 payre of shoes of 4 sizes" and "100 of monmoth caps and bands" (3:386–89).

The Massachusetts Bay Colony's "company store" stocked considerable quantities of men's clothing, over and above what settlers were advised to bring for themselves. The goods brought from England to sell to the colonists included 300 suits of clothes, 400 shirts, 400 pairs of shoes, 200 suits of leather doublet and hose with hook and eye fastenings, 100 Hampshire kersey suits—the doublets lined with linen and the hose with skins—100 green cotton waistcoats bound with red tape, 100 Monmouth caps, 500 red knit caps, 100 black hats, 400 pairs of knitted stockings, 10 dozen pairs of Norwich garters (probably of woven wool), 300 plain falling bands, and 200 handkerchiefs (Dow 1935, 5). This same storehouse also supplied goods to the Reverend Samuel Skelton, whose "accompte" of 1629–1630 lists men's, women's, and children's stockings and men's shoes among a long list of fabrics (239–41).

Ready-made manufactures were given a boost in 1623 when the English Navy established the first official sailors' wear. Varying slightly in fabrics and colors from the generic laborer's dress worn on both sides of the Atlantic during this period, it consisted of loose-fitting breeches of ticking (a linen twill), a blue and white checked shirt, gray wool stockings, red cap, and blue neck cloth (Lemire 1997, 12). Called slop clothes, this uniform comprised the first utilitarian garments produced in bulk. (It would be incorrect to call these items "mass-produced." Mass production of garments is factory rather than workshop or cottage-industry work and involves the use of machinery to cut out fabrics and sew garments; in the colonial period, all of this work was done by hand.) The uniform was expanded in 1663 to include a knitted Monmouth cap, blue shirts and white shirts, a cotton waistcoat and cotton drawers (cotton here refers to a kind of woolen cloth with a napped finish), a suit of canvas, and "neat Leatherd flat heald Shoes" (14). In 1705, a full set of slop clothes included "a lined kersey jacket, a kersey waistcoat and breeches, a linen shirt and drawers, shoes, wool stockings, leather caps and buckles" (18). Slops were sold to the sailors when they entered service and were available for the seamen to purchase from the purser onboard ship.

In the colonies, variations of the loose-fitting slop clothing were purchased and worn by watermen, tradesmen, and those who worked on the land— free, indentured, and enslaved. For the first generation of settlement in all the colonies, fiber cultivation and textile production were too labor intensive for colonists to pursue, given the demands of finding and producing food and building adequate housing. Ready-made garments solved the problem of clothing oneself and a family. For example, Massachusetts colonist Edward Johnson noted in 1641 that hemp, flax, and cattle grew so well there, "the Farmers deem it better for their profit to put away their cattel and corn for cloathing, then to set upon making of cloth . . . assuredly the plenty of cloathing hath caused much excess of late in those persons, who have clambered with excess in wages for their work" (Johnson 1910, 174). Of the fiber crops just mentioned, the flax was probably destined to be sold for oil or seed in England, while the hemp was sold in England for making rope and canvas.

Virginia and Maryland planters preferred to purchase clothing for indentured servants (and later slaves) rather than to hire a tailor or seamstress to fashion garments from imported cloth. The inventory of planter Justinian Snowe of St. Mary's, Maryland, dated 1639, records quantities of men's garments, most of them to clothe an unknown number of male indentured servants (Browne 1887, 4:79–85). Items include 18 pairs of shoes, 10 pairs of coarse and three pairs of canvas drawers, five jackets, seven waistcoats, 16 shirts, 23 pairs of stockings, and six Monmouth caps. As Robert Beverley observed of Virginia in 1703, by the early 18th century, even the ranks of artisans, professional, and gentry "have their Cloathing of all sorts from England, as Linnen, Woolen, Silk, Hats, and Leather" (quoted in Tryon 1966, 95).

Most of the first imported ready-mades were neither fashionable nor long wearing; the materials were inexpensive and easily accessible. The labor force consisted of low-paid women and girls rather than guild-controlled workshops. Demand for goods and an increased base of customers on both sides of the Atlantic resulted in more variety in the quality of fabrics and construction and a wider selection of garments. These would have appealed to the middling sorts, such as artisans and tradesmen and their families.

By the mid-1600s, England's ready-made trades were producing women's clothing—especially stays, waistcoats, petticoats, stockings, and shoes. In 1679, three ships from Bristol arrived in Virginia with 17 dozen bodices [likely stays] (Lemire 1997, 33). The probate inventory of merchant Edward Wharton, of Salem, Massachusetts, lists a woman's yellow waistcoat; a jerkin; light colored silk say, perpetuana, and silk barratine under-petticoats; black serge upper-petticoats and linsey-woolsey petticoats; shifts; and wool, red worsted, and thread (linen) stockings (quoted in Dow 1935, 262–69). The probate account of merchant Captain George Corwin, also of Salem, includes "13 pr. [i.e., pairs] Bodys," "4 pr. Paragon bodys & Stomachers." and "11 pr. Small Bodys" (Dow 1910, 7). In 1686, New York merchant Francis Richardson ordered from London "Ready made womens Gownds of worsted & silk Crape." Richardson specified that if each gown could be made using less than eight yards of material, he wanted them lined in the bodice, "mantua fashion" (Richardson).

At about this time children's ready-made clothing, especially shoes and stockings, appears for the first time in colonial documents. The previously mentioned Edward Wharton carried cloaks and coats for boys and girls made of worsted, stuff, camlet, or tammy. Also listed in his probate inventory were children's stockings, waistcoats, gloves, shifts, boys' cotton drawers, a girl's petticoat, and a boy's castor hat (Dow 1935, 262–69). On his death in 1651, Boston shopkeeper Henry Landis left some unsold children's clothing—a pair of girl's bodies, or stays, and two child's waist-coats (Dow 1935, 83).

The probate records of some London manufacturers of ready-mades provide rich details of clothing that would have appealed even to wealthier colonists. The stock of London "Indian gown maker," Edward Gunn, who died in 1672, included gowns or banyans for men and women in silks of European and (East) Indian manufacture, women's waistcoats, mantles, and quilted petticoats. Among the gowns were "one stript lemon collourd Sattin gowne," "one pinck water tabby gown," "one hand colloured Indian satin gowne," and "one morning gowne of band silk stript with lemon" (quoted in Lemire 1997, 63). All of this merchandise was available in a variety of sizes to better fit the customer. The workforce of 17th-century London dealer Tomas Walker made apparel out of luxury textiles such as lustring, Bengal silk, mohair, Norwich crape, "Silk Stripe," and "Red Perragon." At his death, his inventory included 458 silk petticoats. In contrast, a London contemporary, John Broadhurst, used more utilitarian materials, such as fustian, kersey, stuff, serge, damask, and crape. Broadhurst's inventory included 160 mantuas with matching petticoats and hoods (Lemire 1997, 64).

Merchants did not have a monopoly on importing ready-made clothing to the colonies. Many immigrants were urged to bring apparel to sell for profit or barter for the goods they would need to sustain them in a new place. One of the earliest mentions of this practice is contained in a letter Henry Brigg wrote to his brother Thomas, a London merchant, in 1623 to complain about his sad condition in Virginia as an indentured servant and to beg provisions for himself. He added his willingness to venture commodities in Virginia for his brother "to make two for one cleare and pay all charges" for goods that included "Apparrell for men or women, Shoes & Stockings, points, gloues, Garters" (Kingsbury 1935, 4:236).

The first immigrants to Pennsylvania were urged to bring goods not only for personal use but also to sell for profit. Documents relating to 23 ships that sailed for Pennsylvania carrying settlers and provisions between late 1681 and 1682, the initial year of colonization there by the English, record exports of astounding quantities of wearing apparel and related goods (Balderston 1963). Seventy-four men on those ships took with them, with the intention to barter or sell in Pennsylvania and New Jersey, a total of 2,967 pounds, in weight, of shoes. Some quantities were designated as "new," a suggestion that at least some shoes were secondhand. Woolen stockings for men—3,306 pairs—1,350 pairs for children, and 704 pairs of men's worsted stockings were registered. Women's stockings are absent from the records, but likely not from the actual parcels and boxes shipped. Labeling goods as men's or children's was a way for exporters to get around the tax on women's hosiery. Shipments of hats totaled about 94 dozen felts,

English made; about 14 dozen castors; two demi-castors; and four dozen of woven straw. Gloves of plain sheepskin numbered 318 pairs; there were 28 handkerchiefs, 10 neck cloths, and four dozen Monmouth caps. The only female garment enumerated was the bodice; these totaled 310. Nonspecified garments, which could have been secondhand as well as ready-made can be described as follows: 199 individual garments, 120 suits of apparel, 14 parcels of apparel, one chest of wearing apparel, and 400 pounds of apparel. Trims, buttons, lace, and other goods belonging to the category of haberdashery amounted to 2,060 pounds in weight.

Imported Ready-Made Clothing in the 18th Century

By the 18th century the colonial customer base had diversified to the point that ready-mades might appeal to the gentle ranks as well as their servants with advertisements like "a large variety of ready made cloaths of the newest fashion" (*South-Carolina Gazette*, December 26, 1741). It is impossible to estimate for the 1700s how much ready-made clothing was being worn in contrast to home-tailored or professional bespoke work. But the phrases "ready made" or "London-made" are ubiquitous in advertising records. For instance, the *Boston Gazette* carried a notice for the public sale of men's clothing: "20 Suits London-made Claret & other Coloured Cloth Coats, Vests & Breeches" (December 5, 1763). In addition to expanding selections of clothing, manufacturers also offered a range of sizes and shifted with the pressures of fashion and consumer demand.

Whether stocked at a shop in town or a backcountry market, offered wholesale by a merchant or auctioned on a port city dock, goods for every taste and pocketbook could be found in colonial America. Merchants' and shopkeepers' advertisements from Philadelphia, Pennsylvania, and Charleston, South Carolina detail this wide range of goods. As the largest port in British North America, and one of the wealthier cities, Philadelphia naturally saw the most comprehensive selection of imported goods. Charleston seems to have been a town whose apparel trade, including main garments, for most of the 18th century was fueled by ready-mades rather than fabric yardage. Charleston merchant and factor Robert Pringle explained in a letter to a Boston merchant who had shipped to Charleston apparel fabrics that were not selling: "Womens wear comes all from London Ready made" (Pringle 1972, 1:317). A year later Pringle was explaining the same situation to London merchants whose goods had not sold: "as there are large Quantitys of ready made Cloaths imported from London, [this] hinders much the Sale of such Cloths [e.g., bays and broadcloths] here" (2:524). Pringle suggested that he ship the fabrics to Boston or Philadelphia, where they would sell better.

As port cities, Philadelphia and Charleston were temporary land bases for the hundreds of seamen whose ships crowded the wharfs. Merchants and shopkeepers inventoried quantities of slops for these men, whose ranks—judging by the number of references in the advertisements—included mere boys. Slops were also the uniform of the watermen who ferried goods up river to shops in smaller towns and drop-off points for overland transportation. Advertisements suggest that slops were also sold to servants and the working poor: "ready made Clothes of all Sorts for Sailors and others" and "ready made waistcoats for sailors or servants" (*Pennsylvania Gazette,* April 12, 1745; October 1, 1747). That sailors' clothing made a distinctive impression is seen in a notice for a runaway servant, Joseph Thornton, "dressed as a sailor, which he pretends to be but is not" (*Pennsylvania Gazette,* April 8, 1756). Most newspaper notices gave a general listing of "sailors clothes:" nondescript waistcoats, great coats, pea coats, jackets, breeches, and trousers. Others, however, present a more precise image of the apparel, sometimes in the kinds of fabrics used or in the color. Charlestonian James Reid imported shirts of checked material (whose colored warp and weft stripes intersected to form squares) from London, and Philadelphian Alexander Leith imported the same from Scotland (*South-Carolina Gazette,* January 8, 1741; *Pennsylvania Gazette,* April 23, 1747). In 1751, Benjamin Dart and Company of Charleston had on hand 21 dozens checked trousers as well as shirts. The company also carried jackets of flannel, a woolen that was often white, but could be dyed; witney, a woolen with a shaggy surface; and boys' beaver coats. Beaver was a woolen fabric with a raised nap that resembled beaver fur; the fabric was dyed gray, rust, brown or black (An Inventory . . . belonging to Benjamin Dart). Thomas Lloyd's business in Philadelphia catered to the sea trade. His advertisements are filled with ship chandlery merchandise that included "blue serge jackets and trowsers" (*Pennsylvania Gazette,* January 3, 1749). In Charleston, James Reid offered "buntin frocks and trowsers" (*South-Carolina Gazette,* January 8, 1741). Bunting was an open, plain weave woolen fabric also used for ships' flags. An anonymous Charleston merchant paid attention to seamen's head and feet as well, with "mill'd, strip'd, worsted, and cotton Caps of all Prices, Men and Boys plain and ribb'd knit and wove worseted Hose of all sizes and Colours" (*South-Carolina Gazette,* October 23, 1755).

As with notices for sailors' slops, most Philadelphia and Charleston advertisers used general terms to describe the men's ready-made garments for sale. Listings for surtout and great coats could refer to outerwear for tradesmen, professionals or gentlemen; besides price, the difference for the customer was the construction of the garment and the fabric(s) used in its construction. In Charleston, one merchant sold "Horse-mens Great coats of different Prices, . . . Mens and Boys Bear-skin Coats, . . . fear-nothing Great coats" (*South-Carolina Gazette*, October 23, 1755). Bearskin and fearnothing were thick woolen fabrics with a shaggy nap and often associated with servants' clothing. Another sold woolen duffel coats, —generally for working men, —and broadcloth coats and breeches, suitable as everyday wear for men from the middling ranks or working men who could afford them.

Likewise, jackets, waistcoats, breeches, and ready-made suits of clothes were seldom identified in the advertisements by fabric, other than to note that they were made "in patterns," that is, of patterned fabrics or of woven worsted or silk, such as "black worsted jackets and breeches" (*South-Carolina Gazette*, August 27, 1750). There are exceptions, however. Charleston notices include a "Broleau [probably broglio, a silk and wool mix] Jacket"; "scarlet and black Everlasting Breeches, Shagg ditto"; and "hairshag and honey-comb breeches" (October 23, 1755; January 8, 1741). Hair shag referred to either a heavy worsted fabric with a long nap or a worsted velvet weave; honeycomb was a cotton patterned velvet. These breeches were not working men's garb but respectable everyday wear. Archibald and Richard Park Stobo's notice of 1756, one of the most detailed of the period for men's ready-made wear, would have appealed to a broad range of clientele: "Portuguese camblet cloaks with bays, blue Spanish roquello's, cloth riding coats with capes; fearnought, duffel, rug, and coarse cloth great coats, whitney and beaver surtout coats, fearnought pea jackets and trowsers, check'd shirts, mens shag, cloth, everlasting, honeycomb, and other ready made breeches, mens and boys beaver fly[coats]; mens fine suits of broad cloth, German serge, and drugget; buck and doe skin breeches" (October 7, 1756).

For leisure wear at home, men of means wore a banyan and cap to keep shaved heads warm. Charleston merchants placed notices for banyans only in the 1730s; however, silk caps for men were advertised throughout the 18th century. No ready-made banyans were advertised in Philadelphia, although notices for stolen goods in that city included banyans. For example, school master William Sorsby had the theft of "a grey flower'd Damask Banyan lin'd with Tammy, made to wear either Side outwards" (*Pennsylvania Gazette*, December 1, 1737).Banyans were also called men's gowns or night gowns; there are a small number of notices for these, as "silk night Gowns of Banjans" advertised by James Crokatt (*South-Carolina Gazette*, May 26, 1733). The fabric choices for Charleston gentlemen included satin, plaid, and worsted. "Gentlemen's gowns, made of the very best worsted Damasks, and lined with the finest Callimanco, also Gowns Damask both Sides" likely were for cold weather (*South-Carolina Gazette*, January 18, 1748). Philadelphia advertisements refer only to "gentlemen's morning gowns."

Beginning in the 1740s, knitted waistcoats and breeches made of either worsted yarn or silk thread appear in merchants' notices in both Philadelphia and Charleston. This may have been due to surplus stock created by the increasing number of knitting frames in use in England. By this time, with improvements to the equipment, English frame-work knitters in London, Leicester, and Nottingham had triumphed over the hand-knitting industries, producing not only stockings (still seamed by hand) but also finer knitting in flat shapes that were seamed together to make garments and rectangular lengths, or pieces, of knitted fabric that were cut into shapes for seaming. Charleston merchants imported knitted garments, although their notices provide no details. In Philadelphia, John Wallace imported knitted waistcoats and breeches of worsted and marbled yarns (*Pennsylvania Gazette*, September 25, 1755). Benjamin Kendall offered knitted breeches and waistcoats "in patterns," that is, there was a pattern in the knitted fabric (*Pennsylvania Gazette*, May 26, 1757). By the 1750s, Philadelphia merchants were importing silk and worsted knitted breeches in an assortment of colors: black, blue, scarlet, and cloth-colored.

The first colonial notice for ready-made leather breeches—made of buckskin—appeared in the *South-Carolina Gazette* in 1733 and were offered by Peter Horry. In 1737, Charleston merchants Hutchinson and Grimké offered leather breeches in sizes for both men and boys (August 27). A year later Thomas Blondell noted that he had a "great count" of leather breeches (March 16, 1738). And in 1764, an anonymous jeweler brought home "some fine dressed English skin breeches" for resale from a trip to London (February 18). With the exception of this last notice, it is not known whether these were made locally of leather from Charleston's lucrative deerskin trade with Indian communities or imported from England. In Philadelphia, notices for ready-made leather breeches began in the 1740s and were intended to appeal to artisans, professionals, and the gentry. This can be inferred from the advertisements in the *Pennsylvania Gazette* of scourers who offered to clean leather breeches. For example, John Hickey offered to scour and dye leather breeches for two shillings a pair (May 1, 1755). Some of these breeches were imported from London; others were manufactured in Scotland and exported from Glasgow. Philadelphia leather workers, however, had begun making leather breeches in the 1730s. This manufacture is discussed below.

Although Robert Pringle noted that in Charleston much women's wear was sold ready-made, the evidence for women's gowns is elusive in newspaper advertisements. James Crokatt sold ready-made clothes for women "of cloth, plain and silk camblet, drugget, whitney &c." but did not specify items of apparel (*South-Carolina Gazette*, November 22, 1735). There are

many references to, for example, dimity, cotton, checked, striped, and figured gowns, but it is unclear whether these are lengths of fabrics suitable
for gowns or finished apparel. Peter Horry advertised "worked Gowns
of brown Holland," but again, it is unclear whether "worked" refers to a
printed or embroidered pattern on a holland fabric suitable for gowns or
to holland that was worked up into a gown (*South-Carolina Gazette*, February 9, 1734). It is the same case in Philadelphia, where newspapers carried
notices of gowns, but not with the term "ready-made." Joseph Beddome
of Philadelphia carried "worked linnen gowns," but the meaning of these
goods is today unclear (*Pennsylvania Gazette*, September 30, 1742).

Two articles of women's wear—cloaks and petticoats—were staples in
merchants' and shopkeepers' inventories in the 18th century. Long and
short cloaks for women and girls were most often dyed a scarlet color,
but in Philadelphia cloth-colored versions were also offered. By the 1760s,
fashionable milliners carried a wide selection of cloaks including "black
and coloured silk cardinals and white duffil ditto, [and] fashionable silk
shades or cloaks of all colours in the newest taste" (*Pennsylvania Gazette*,
May 5, 1768). Beginning in 1750, Charleston merchants offered black velvet
cloaks with hoods.

The petticoat, or "coat," or sometimes "quilt," was the most frequently
listed article of women's clothing in Philadelphia and Charleston newspapers. As with other ready-mades, many of the listings are general, either "petticoats," "silk petticoats," or "quilted petticoats." Pennsylvania
merchants and shopkeepers also carried Persian, cotton, calimanco, and
flannel petticoats; "womens calimancoe and Durant quilts," figured and
wrought petticoats; Portobello petticoats; Marseilles petticoats and quilts,
and Turkey (i.e., red) quilt petticoats (*Pennsylvania Gazette*, November 11,
1772). In Charleston, milliners and merchants offered silk, flannel, worsted, calimanco, Persian (a thin plain weave silk), russel (a worsted damask
similar to calimanco that was available in a single color, two colors, and
brocaded), satin, tammy (a plain weave worsted that was often glazed),
sarcenet (a thin plain or twill weave silk that was figured, striped, checked,
or plain), and durance (a thin highly glazed worsted).

A number of quilted petticoats survive in the collections of museums
and historical societies. Not all of these were made in the colonies. Specialized petticoat manufacturers were located in London and in the region of
Manchester, in the northwest corner of England (Lemire 1997, 67). Petticoats were ideal ready-made commodities because they did not need to be
fitted; the waistband tapes could be tied to fit and hooks and eyes or buttons could be added or moved as needed. The only dimension that really
mattered was the width of the fabric, which became the length—from waist

This 18th-century silk satin petticoat is likely English and made for the ready-made market. The bottom third of the petticoat was stitched in open, fluid floral motifs without much detail. Such a design could have been stitched free-form, without first drawing the pattern onto the fabric. (Museum of Fine Arts, Boston, Massachusetts, USA/Gift of the children of Mrs. M. A. DeWolfe Howe (Fanny Huntington Quincy), Miss Helen H. Howe, Quincy Howe, and Mark DeWolfe Howe/The Bridgeman Art Library)

to ankle—of the petticoat. In contrast to custom-made and homemade petticoats, the ready-made variety can be identified today by standardized elements of construction and composition.

In her study of over three dozen petticoats which ranged "from the economical to the extravagant," scholar Beverly Lemire found uniformity among many of them: "The top fabric was usually dyed silk or satin, the backing was either a linen or wool fabric, frequently a glazed worsted wool, with a wool batting for insulation. Linings occasionally matched the top fabric in colour, while the pocket and back openings were bound in matching tape or ribbon, as was the bottom hem of the petticoat" (1997, 66). The quilting, however, was the most telling aspect of the ready-made examples. The top two-thirds section of each of these petticoats was quilted, using a running stitch, in a simple repeated pattern of a lozenge, diamond or scallop. The bottom third of the petticoat featured various floral motifs "executed in fluid stitchery, leaving much of the ground unquilted. These goods were valued for the fabric and for the novelty, if not the perfection, of the quilting" (1997, 66–67).

As the above newspaper advertisements indicate, ready-made petticoats made of woolen fabrics such as calimanco were also available. These would have been less expensive than their silk counterparts. For the customer who demanded the finest goods, the silk fabric could be embroidered with silk thread—sometimes with the addition of gold or silver metal thread and spangles—before it was quilted. Two British sources from 1747 indicate that the quilting of petticoats and bedcovers was a workshop trade, rather than performed as outwork; the quilters took on apprentices and journeywomen at variable rates of pay (Campbell 1969, 213; Lemire 1997, 68). This was likely the case when expensive fabrics and threads were involved, but the quilting of cheaper fabrics may have been undertaken without direct supervision.

Imported Ready-Mades for Enslaved Workers

Slave clothing and related goods were among the first ready-mades advertised by Charleston merchants, and the first notices appeared in 1735. This garb, consisting of a jacket and breeches or loose-fitting trousers, was intended for men—enslaved Native Americans as well as Africans and their descendants—who worked in plantation fields and labored at other outdoor activities. The fabric most often used was Welsh plains, an inexpensive, loosely woven, woolen cloth first produced in Wales. Notices for pieces of plains suitable for slave clothing indicate that the fabric, and by extension the clothing, was available in white, blue, brown, green, and red. Clothing of cotton fabric was also imported; specific colors were white and gray.

James Crokatt imported "Negro cloathing of all the usual kinds and colours . . . [and] a great choice of all other kinds of cloaths," which suggests that slave clothing was distinctive and not like other forms of working dress (*South-Carolina Gazette*, October 11, 1735). He also imported "livery & common cloaths for negro men & boys" (October 2, 1736). Ready-made clothing for enslaved females does not appear in notices; however, fabrics for "negro wenches gowns" were advertised in the 1760s. In addition to apparel, advertisements note inventories of "large strong shoes for negroes"; coarse "negro" stockings, and "negro" caps (*South-Carolina Gazette*, January 5, 1767).

Imported Ready-Mades in the Colonial Backcountry

The lure of ready-made goods invaded the colonial Backcountry as market towns grew and settlers were exposed to "foreign finery." Families who had made their own fabrics and clothing were now able to trade homespun for ready-made goods. In 1787, an anonymous contributor, "A FARMER," wrote the *American Museum* complaining about the loss of his family's self-sufficiency (*American Museum* 1787, 11–12). The author described his life as a young man, outfitted at the end of his apprenticeship to a farmer with "two stout suits of homespun, four pair of stockings, four woolen shirts, and two pair of shoes." After his marriage, he first rented farm land and then accumulated enough capital to purchase 60 acres. This estate provided them with everything they needed to survive—fiber for clothing, food, and drink. When the time came for him to settle on marriage clothing for his eldest daughter, Molly, he considered her merit as "a dutiful working girl," and outfitted her well, at least to his mind: "Take the best of my wool and flax . . . to spin [yourself] gowns, coats, stockings, and shifts."

Two years later his second daughter, Sarah, was courted. The farmer's wife urged him to reconsider homespun clothing for the girl: "She ought to fare as well as neighbour N—'s Betty." So, with the farmer's purse in hand, the wife went to town. She returned a few days later with "a calico gown, a calamanco petticoat, a set of stone tea cups, half a dozen pewter tea-spoons, and a tea-kettle."

A further three years brought the third daughter to the altar. The farmer's wife once again asked for the purse and went to town. She returned, this time with an empty purse, and "a silken gown, silk for a cloak, a looking-glass, china tea-geer, and a hundred other things." The farmer noted that this was not the worst intrusion into his previous way of life. That first trip taken to town became a habit with the wife. Besides new household furnishings, "clothing of every sort is bought—and the wheel goes only for the purpose of exchanging our substantial cloth of flax and wool, for gauze, ribands, silk, tea, sugar, &c."

Ready-Mades of Colonial Production

Four notable exceptions to the general practice of importing ready-made clothing were hats, stockings, shoes, and leather breeches. Shoes were the first of the colonial ready-mades, constructed of imported or local leather. As early as 1662, Colonel Scarburgh, of Northampton County, Virginia, ran a shoe manufactory and employed nine shoemakers. His competition was a currier, Nathaniel Bradford, who owned a tannery as well as a shoe shop. At the time of his death, Bradford possessed 318 hides and 46 shoe lasts (Wise 1911, 302–03). Both men likely were supplying footwear for indentured servants and enslaved workers. Although small operations did exist in the South, in general the manufacture of shoes for resale—in contrast to use on plantations—was centered primarily in the North. In 1648, nine Boston shoemakers petitioned the General Court to form a guild in response to the shoddy workmanship of some of their contemporaries. The Court's response an act that allowed for the creation of a company, or guild, to assemble and meet "to make orders for the well-governing of their company, in the managing of their trade, and to annex reasonable penalties for the breach of the same" (quoted in Davis 1895, 197). In 1676, Connecticut legislated prices for locally made shoes: "five pence halfe penny a size for all playne and wooden heeld shoes, for all sizes above the men's sevens, three soled shoes well made and wrought, nor above seven pence halfe penny a size for well wrought French falls" (quoted in Weeden 1894, 1:308). Both Massachusetts and Connecticut were exporting shoes to other colonies by midcentury.

In the 18th century, Massachusetts continued to produce footwear for local consumption and for export to New York and Philadelphia. The town of Lynn became the center for the colonial production of the best quality shoes in the 1750s, when a Welsh immigrant, John Adam Dagyr, brought his shoemaking skills to the town. He was said to have been particularly accomplished in fashioning women's shoes: "The finer qualities were made with 'white and russet rands, closely stitched with white waxed thread. The toes are very sharp and the heels were of wood, covered with leather. These seem to have been important in defining the fashion of the shoe; they were half and inch to two inches high, and were called 'crosscut, common, court, and Wurtemburgh.' The wooden heels were manufactured separately, like lasts" (Weeden 1894, 2:682–83). In the 1760s, the *Boston Gazette*—not an unbiased observer—proclaimed, "It is certain that women's shoes, made at Lynn, do exceed those usually imported, in strength and beauty, but not in price" (October 21, 1764). New England newspapers reported that Lynn's output for 1767 was 80,000 pairs, of which about 40,000 pairs were women's (Bridenbaugh 1950, 49; *Pennsylvania Gazette*, November 12, 1767).

As discussed in Chapter 2, leather breeches were workmen's and tradesmen's apparel throughout the 18th century. For example, in 1729, Samuel Wright and Richard Kirby of Burlington County, Pennsylvania, reported two runaway servants, both Irishmen, who were wearing leather breeches (*Pennsylvania Gazette*, March 13, 1729). But planters and others began to realize that the leather protected the skin when riding through thick brush on horseback and walking through tall grass. Eventually, leather breeches were popular among all ranks. As noted above, leather breeches were manufactured in Britain and exported. But the wide-spread demand inspired colonial tradesmen in many colonies to manufacture leather breeches for resale. Of varying quality as well as fit, these products were sold throughout the colonies.

The first mention in the *Pennsylvania Gazette* of a leather breeches maker appears in 1731, in a notice for an absented servant. About 19 years old, the runaway, James Fitzgerald, was acknowledged as a "leather dresser breeches maker and glover by trade" (September 23, 1731). By the 1760s, several Philadelphia breeches makers advertised their skills on their own accounts; others appear in notices not related to the trade. Griffith Jones and his son, John, ran separate businesses where they dressed leather skins, buck, sheep as well as cow, and made breeches; John also cleaned breeches (January 15, 1761; June 11, 1761; February 4, 1762). Abel Gibbon advertised that he and others in his workshop dressed deer and sheep skins for shoemakers and for linings for tailors as well as made breeches and gloves (January 29, 1767). In business since at least 1750 as a skinner, John Correy was specializing in breeches in the 1760s and advertised in 1768 for the return of a servant born in England and by trade a breeches maker (December 15, 1768).

Philadelphia-made leather breeches were known and valued throughout the colonies before the Revolution. Breeches makers in other towns such as Newport, Rhode Island, and Hartford, Connecticut, advertised that their products were made in "the best Philadelphia manner" (Morgan 1962, 117; Bridenbaugh 1950, 48). At least one breeches maker was female. Mary Robinson, who carried on the trade of her deceased husband in Charleston, advertised making, mending, and washing buck and doeskin breeches, "either natural or black, purple and Cloth Colours, likewise white Leather" (*South-Carolina Gazette*, August 10, 1738).

In 1772, the proprietors of the province of Pennsylvania and the Assembly enacted a law to regulate leather working in the colony: how to skin an animal, how long the hides could lie in lime for softening, the temperature of the tanning vats, and when to curry the leather. Leather workers were required to mark their wares, everything from skins to shoes, with their initials or name. It is perhaps a testament to the quality of Philadelphia's breeches makers, however, that the only regulations on sewing and stitching were applied to shoemakers and cordwainers (*Pennsylvania Gazette*, April 9, 1772).

The manufacture of hats was carried on in the colonies with much success, in spite of the displeasure of a Parliament pressured by Britain's hatters. In 1724, Newport, Rhode Islander, William Pinniger was known to be selling his hats throughout New England, and his trade did not seem to be affected by the Hat Act of 1734, which made his commercial actions illegal. Bostonian Daniel Jones made and sold beaver, beaveret, and castor hats "at the Hat and Helmit," his shop sign in South Boston, while offering at the same time an assortment of imported castor, beaveret, and felt hats along with linings and trimmings (*Boston Gazette*, December 10, 1759). Boston, New York, Philadelphia, and Charleston—all could boast of numerous hatters by the 1770s.

The first large-scale production of knitted stockings was located in Germantown, Pennsylvania. When Andrew Burnaby visited the town in 1759 he discovered a considerable trade: "The German-town thread-stockings [i.e., stockings knitted of linen yarn] are in high estimation; and the year before last, I have been credibly informed, there were manufactured in that town alone, above 60,000 dozen pair. Their common retail price is a dollar per pair" (Burnaby 1775, 102–03). The success of the town's enterprise rested on the knitting frame.

Philadelphia was home to many stocking manufactories, which took advantage of knitting frame technology and the abundance of locally produced linen and woolen yarns. The first of these endeavors advertised in 1758. Run by Joseph Job, the business purchased both clean wool fiber and homespun yarn, which workers turned into "brown, blue and white Thread for Men; strong white Cotton and Thread for Women and Girls; Hemp Ditto for Men and Boys; and coarse cheap Stockings for Servants" (*Pennsylvania Gazette*, April 20, 1758). In 1761, the Hand-in-Stocking Manufactory produced for wholesale and retail a variety of worsted, linen and cotton stockings, mill yarn gloves, and lengths of knitted fabrics for waistcoats and breeches. The proprietors also handled Germantown linen and woolen stockings at wholesale prices.

Resistance to the Stamp Act of 1765 and the Townshend Acts of 1767–1768 is reflected in the increase of advertisements for colonial production of clothing-related goods including knitting. In 1766, hosier Daniel Mause established the Hand-in-Hand Manufactory in Philadelphia, advertising that he had a number of looms for making linen, cotton, and worsted stockings and offered hand-knit caps, gloves, and mitts. He claimed to use yarns only of American manufacture and sold his products at his manufactory and at the shop of Thomas Bond, Jr. (*Pennsylvania Gazette*, May 1, 1766; January 29, 1767). In 1768, Bond opened his own manufactory for hand-knit stockings and caps and advertised for spinners and knitters to work at the manufactory. He noted that he purchased local wool, flax, and cotton fibers and spun yarns "green or bleached." Bond was still in business four years later (*Pennsylvania Gazette*, September 22, 1768; September 30, 1772). An attempt was made to entice northern stocking makers to extend the trade south. An advertisement in the *Pennsylvania Gazette* asked for a "Sober industrious Family" to travel to Wilmington, North Carolina. Supplied with two looms and yarn, they would be assured of "constant Employ" (August 9, 1770). In Newcastle County, Delaware, James Popham sought financial backers for a scheme to process locally produced wool for fabrics. In addition, he was prepared to spin, dye, and mix wools and worsteds "according to the English Method of stocking making." He proposed importing Irish tradesmen to work initially, but "this need not last long, as Boys, young Girls, and Negroes, would soon learn to supply their Places," and create work for the local populace (*Pennsylvania Gazette*, January 25, 1770). The *New Jersey Journal* carried a notice in 1775 by James Wallace, who made and sold knitted silk and linen gloves, mitts, and stockings, "the silk of which is American produce" (quoted in Gottesman 1938, 249). Frederick

Wolber's inventory of machinery from his manufactory, which he put up for sale when he retired, is a unique window on this business: "four iron and one coarse stocking frame . . . and the coarse one, to manufacture all sorts of stockings; . . . with all that is necessary to carry on the work, viz. two thread-mills, two wheels, fulling machine, reels and reel-sticks, [and] a quantity of stocking forms of all sorts" (*Pennsylvania Gazette*, December 22, 1784).

An editorial in the *Pennsylvania Gazette*, published in June of 1788, sums up the condition of the hosiery industry in this state at the end of the colonial period:

> Several gentlemen have made a careful and impartial examination of the stockings manufactured in this city [i.e., Philadelphia], in Germantown, in the town and county of Lancaster, Bethlehem, and Reading, and they find that the thread stockings made in Pennsylvania . . . are the same fineness with imported stockings. . . . It is a well known fact that three pair of Pennsylvania made stockings will wear longer than four pair of those imported. There are now about 250 stocking looms in the different parts of the city and state, each of which makes, on a medium, one pair and a half of stockings every day. These, deducting Sundays, will amount to 117,375 pair per annum.

From time to time garments of colonial manufacture appear in the records. During the French and Indian Wars (1754–1763), for example, Pennsylvania produced ready-made clothing of homespun fabric and yarn for ordinary soldiers. George Bryan and Abraham and Robert Usher advertised "soldiers shirts made up" and shirts suitable for soldiers (*Pennsylvania Gazette*, July 21, 1757; March 23, 1758). In 1755, the Pennsylvania Assembly sent to Albany, "1339 warm Waistcoats, 1000 Pair of milled Stockings, and 332 Pair of knit Mittens for the Comfort of New England Troops, and others, that might remain in Garrison in that cold Country the ensuing Winter" (*Pennsylvania Gazette*, February 26, 1756). Boston tailor Samuel Blodgett targeted the officers and soldiers "engaged in the present expedition against Canada" in his 1759 advertisement for ready-made clothing, perhaps hoping to entice those who could not wait for custom tailored garments to be finished (Bridenbaugh 1950, 71).

Secondhand Clothing

Evidence for sales of used clothing is slim in the colonial record, although Britain did a brisk secondhand business at this time (Lemire 1988).

In both the 1600s and 1700s, colonists could acquire used clothing at estate sales. One such event, which took place in Accomack, Virginia, in 1641, included sales of a cloak for 34 pounds of tobacco; "a suite of Clothes" for 66 pounds; an old shirt for four pounds; "a stitch taffety gowne" for 220 pounds; "a paire of thred stockings and lace" for 30 pounds; and a hat for 31. As a point of comparison on the relative worth of this used apparel, a livery cupboard was sold for 32 pounds of tobacco and "1 Fetherbed and 1 boulster one Tapestry Covering, 1 bedstead and one paire of Curtaines and Vallance" brought 320 pounds (Ames 1973, 109–14). In 1644, Joanna Cummings, of Salem, Massachusetts, stipulated in her will, "I will haue all my best Apparel bed & bedding & my housould goods sould: & out of that a heafer of tow yere ould to be bought for Johanah Bourne [Joanna's granddaughter]" (Dow 1916, 1:34).

In the 18th century, a few advertisements for runaways and goods for sale verify this all but invisible trade. In 1734, Anthony Lea absented himself from his master wearing "a dark colour'd fine broadcloth second hand Coat fashionably made" (*Pennsylvania Gazette*, September 12, 1734). Runaway Henry Schoup owned a secondhand beaver hat (*Pennsylvania Gazette*, May 28, 1772). William Nichols held a "Publick Vendue [i.e., auction]" at the Royal Exchange Tavern in Boston in May 1738, at which among quantities of clothing fabrics and fabric furnishings, hose, mittens, shoes, and boots, "sundry suits of men's apparel new and second hand" were sold (*Boston News-Letter*, May 18, 1738). Zuriel Waterman of Rhode Island, a doctor serving as a privateerman during the American Revolution, wrote of selling at auction the clothing left behind by a runaway from the ship, but it is unclear whether the sale was made on land or to the other sailors aboard ship (Humphrey and Waterman 1984, 75–77).

IMPORTED FABRICS

Colonists who could afford to shop looked to every ship that docked and every new notice from a merchant or shopkeeper for fabrics that would meet their clothing needs. Before the Navigation Acts, vessels from Europe as well as Britain brought goods. After about 1660, except for smuggled goods, it was British ships that bore woolens from England and Scotland; linens from England, Scotland, Ireland, the Netherlands, Germany, the Baltic countries, and Russia; cottons from India and later England; and silks from England, Europe, the Middle East, India, and China. Throughout the colonial period hundreds of fabric names appear in inventories, account books, invoices, and newspaper advertisements. It is now almost impossible to determine the characteristics that distinguished Colchester serge from Irish serge and Turkey grogram from Turkey mohair. Names were assigned based on fiber content, weight, weave, finish, and—very often—place of manufacture. However, fabric names indicative of their origins, like holland and osnaburg, were often copied by weavers and clothiers in other cities and countries. It is clear, however, as evinced by shipping and merchants' records, that cloth became the single most valuable class of imports into the American colonies.

Why so many names? Seventeenth-century worthy Thomas Fuller quipped, "Expect not that I should reckon up their several names, because daily increasing, and many of them binominous, as which, when they begin to tire in sale, are quickened with a new name. . . . A pretty, pleasing name, complying with the buyers fancy, much befriendeth a stuff in the sale thereof" (quoted in Kerridge 1985, 86). Although the invention of new names for textiles often had something to do with capturing consumers' interest, the deliberate alteration of names likely had a legal basis. For example, to avoid problems of competition with local English weavers, Flemish weavers who immigrated to England made kerseys, but sold them as stammets, and camlets that were sold as grograins (Kerridge 1985, 86). Sometimes newly invented fabrics were innovations that deserved new names. In the 17th century, weavers of the thin worsted twill-weave fabric referred to as say developed many different varieties of the fabric, all with different names. Instead of weaving stripes of color or checks, worsted weavers twisted "one thridd of one coulour with another colour" before weaving and called the result pyramids. Cameleons were a kind of say that featured contrasting colors in the warp and weft. Each weft was a pair of threads, each thread of a different color. Prunella differed from standard say only in its twill structure (Kerridge 1985, 56–57).

As discussed in Chapter 2, in addition to its practical functions, colonial clothing conveyed the aesthetic, economic, and social preferences or other preoccupations of the wearer. These communications worked not only because of the "cut of the clothes" but also because of the fibers and materials of which the articles were made. Today we are removed from this more technical knowledge, but in the preindustrial past, people living at almost every social and economic level understood the importance not only of where the materials came from but also value of raw materials and the means of production. It is the reason that so many qualities of cloth were available to consumers and why men and women of the colonial era knew dozens of different fabrics by name. As researcher Florence Montgomery expressed it, "The names of high-priced fashionable clothing materials had to be distinguished from common, coarse goods worn by laborers in various agricultural and craft occupations; and among woolen goods, heavy fishermen's clothing and Indian blankets from fine-quality worsted for bed furniture or a gentleman's coat. Which linen and cotton textiles were for the house and which were used for grain bags, sieves, sails, or horse coverings" (Montgomery 1970, xi–xii).

Archaeological Evidence for Imported Fabrics

The earliest tangible pieces of evidence of imported fabrics in the period are the leaden cloth seals that have been recovered from early colonial sites near Chesapeake's shores. Cloth seals were part of the system of regulation of textiles intended for commercial sale in Europe and England, which was in use as early as the 14th century (Egan 1994). Originally attached to the outside corner section of lengths of cloth, the seals served several purposes. An alnage seal indicated, at least in theory, that an examination of the fabric had taken place—including measuring the length and width and establishing the weight—to insure that the fabric met standards of quality for the market and that a subsidy tax, a few pence per textile, had been paid to the Crown. Weavers, clothiers, dyers, and packers might also add seals, which meant that a single cloth might have several seals by the time it reached a shopkeeper's shelves.

The most common form of cloth seal consisted of two disks connected with a strip, all cast in lead as one piece. One disk had a cone-shaped rivet and the other a central hole. When the seal was folded, at the connecting strip, over a corner of the textile, the rivet pushed through both the fabric and the hole in the other disk. The seal was then stamped with a die or dies on one or both faces to secure it to the fabric and register the appropriate information. Sometimes this stamping also left impressions of the fabric weave structures on the underside of the lead disks.

Between 1994 and 1998 a number of cloth seals were excavated from various cellar holes and pits at the early 17th-century-settlement site of Fort James on Jamestown Island in Virginia (Interim Field Reports). All date to between the late Tudor period (about 1598–1603) and 1625, the termination of the Virginia Company's charter (Straube 2009). Analyses of the seals has brought to light, in several cases, what type of fabric these early colonists were using and where the fabrics were made. One early seal, with markings for the reigns of both Elizabeth I and James I, appears to be from the English county of Kent (Mallios and Staube 2000, 19). Kent produced primarily broadcloth, "rather coarse, heavy, woollen . . . well dyed in the wool by the clothiers themselves and sold by them ready dressed, finished and dyed or double-dyed in almost every conceivable colour or medley of colours" (Kerridge 1985, 17). Because of its nap, broadcloth was suitable for a wide range of clothing applications, including cloaks, jerkins, and breeches.

A seal with markings indicating that it was validated during the reign of James I (1604–1625), bears the legend "P. DO:CARSEY" (Mallios and Staube 2000, 20). Carsey refers to kersey, a less expensive twill-weave alternative to broadcloth with a napped surface that kept out wet and cold. The Jamestown archaeologists suggest that "DO" may refer to Dorset, an English county in which some kersies were woven. Another seal was crimped with the word "SEARCHED", meaning that the fabric had been inspected for quality. Additional letters "W (?) AD" may stand for "WOAD," the blue dyestuff used (and grown) in England before the introduction of indigo (Mallios and Staube 2000, 20).

Six seals from Fort James were once attached to fabrics woven in Germany, exported to London, and then shipped to Virginia. Five of these objects were crimped with the letter A and the heraldic badge of the city of Augsburg. Augsburg was known for the production of fustian, a large category of textiles that in the 17th century could have been woven with a linen warp and cotton and/or woolen weft (Montgomery 1970, 224). Among the English-made suits that George Percy received was a doublet of fustian with a "Joanes [i.e., jeans, a twilled weave] fustian" lining (Shirley 1949, 237).

Archaeological sites in Anne Arundel County, Maryland, also have yielded cloth seals, dating from the second half of the 17th century (Luckenbach and Cox 2003). Some of these were once attached to kerseys. A seal impressed "SOMERSET" likely may have qualified for sale a length of serge, which was produced in that county from midcentury (Egan 1994, 50–51). A twilled fabric with a worsted warp, a woolen weft, and a smooth surface, serge was judged to be of better quality than kersey. An alnage seal stamped "SUFFOLK 1674" was likely the tax subsidy mark for a broadcloth or aforementioned say (Egan 1994, 51). The weft was one or two untwisted threads while the warp was twisted from two or three threads. These threads could be of different colors (Kerridge 1985, 56–57).

Instead of seals, archaeological excavations of a 17th-century privy in Boston, Massachusetts, recovered a variety of textile fragments, the largest group of which consisted of silk fabrics and ribbons (Ordoñez and Welters 1998, 81–90). Most of the silks were identified as lustrings and taffetas, glossy silk fabrics with a thick weft that produces a horizontal rib in the fabric. Lustrings were popular for women's gowns and petticoats. Other fragments include tiffany, a silk gauze-weave popular in the century for women's hoods; thickly fulled woolens suitable for outdoor wear; wool–silk mixtures; knitted silk, probably from a stocking; and silk ribbons of various constructions, used to "decorate shoulders, tie sleeves, close shoes, encircle hats, or join collars" (Ordoñez and Welters 1998, 86). The fabrics and trims represented by these fragments are indicative of a family of fairly high standing.

Imported Fabrics in the 17th Century

What researchers lack in actual examples from the 17th century can be discerned from inventory records. By the midcentury, colonial merchants and shopkeepers were offering customers a wide selection of fabrics for apparel in silk and cotton as well as linen and wool. For example, a survey of shop and warehouse inventories from Massachusetts, taken between 1647 and 1660, reveals over 50 different fabrics, most of which were quite suitable for clothing (Dow 1935; 83, 242, 244, 258). Some of the names are exotic—for example, hair cameleon and Humanes—while others may have appealed to the notion of the latest fashion. The majority of the listings are woolens and worsteds of various qualities, all woven in England (e.g., frieze, pennyston, flannel, tammy, kersey, serge, broadcloth, cheny, perpetuano, and mohair). Linens, which may have been produced in Northern Europe as well as England, include more expensive lawn and holland and moderately priced dowlas, kenting, and lockrum. There are mixed fabrics that contained silk—Italiano, castilliano, and satinesco—as well as pure silks like grogram, mohair, Bengal taffeta, and satin. Some of these silks were produced in England while others may have been woven in Italy and France. Other mixed fabrics mentioned are fustian and linsey-woolsey. Least represented at this time are cotton fabrics, listed as plain and colored cottons and dimity. Calicoes from India are included as well but these were not used for clothing in Britain and her colonies until the 1680s.

Also listed in these inventories are trimmings and sewing supplies. Together with the large quantities of fabrics, these indicate that some colonists were either making or remodeling their own clothing or relying on tailors and seamstresses. Tapes, binding, silver and gold lace, ribbon, fringe, looped lace, loom lace, galloon, and laces (cords or braids) were available to trim garments, as was buckram, used by tailors to stiffen the foreparts of doublets and coats, and collars and belly pieces, the padded inner front parts of doublets.

Even in these early decades of settlement, shopkeepers kept assortments of goods to appeal to every level of local society. For example, Salem, Massachusetts, ship builder and owner George Corwin also engaged in retailing. At his death, in 1685, his shop contained—in addition to a variety of fabrics of wool, linen, some silk, and a cotton calico—yards of flowered, ferret, and cotton ribbon; linen, silk, and metal lace; various sorts of buttons; and several red feathers (Dow 1910, 6–11). This list reflects luxury as well as necessity. The inventory of Jonathan Newell, a merchant in York County, Virginia, who died in 1671, echoes the kinds of fabrics and trimmings that sold well to small planters in the third quarter of the 17th century. The limited selection and lower quality are in contrast to Corwin's goods. Among the woolens were red and white kerseys, broadcloth, pennystone, drugget, and generic woolen stuff. Linens were represented by osnaburg, lockeram, dowlas, and blue linen. Mixed fabrics were confined to linsey-woolsey. Although no silk yardage was listed, Newell sold trimmings of silk: ferret silk ribbon, silk galloon braid, and silk lace, perhaps for planters and their wives to use in retrimming and freshening older clothing (Billings 1975).

Between 1660 and about 1715, inventories, letters, accounts, and invoices again provide the evidence for fabrics that were common for clothing. All the fairly plain and modest fabrics mentioned above were still imported. By the 1680s, however, an even greater variety, including more luxury fabrics, was available to colonial consumers, although in small quantities. For example, simple camlet was joined by striped camlett, hair camlet, and worsted double camlet. Variations of serge included Irish serge and padaway serge. Silk fabrics such as silk say, striped tamarene, flowered silk draft, and silk barratine could be found. Scotch tabby, paduasoy, French stuff, crape, Bengal, velvet, and grosgrain also entered the colonies.

These woolens, linens, and silks were joined by colorful cotton fabrics imported through Britain from India. Collectively known as calicoes (calico was available also as a white fabric), the fabrics had been available earlier in the century, but were used primarily for household furnishings. In the early 1680s, chintz, a category of specially designed painted or printed calicoes, became fashionable for women's dress in England and was quickly adopted by colonial women of means (Gittinger 1982, 180). These cottons were lightweight, colorful, and, most importantly, washable because their brilliant dyes were colorfast. They were available in a wide variety of patterning, a testament to the skill of India's craftsmen: "This technology ranged from simply dyeing yarns for weaving to methods involving complex orchestration of a range of processes such as bleaching, pattern design, resist processes, application of mordants, the coordination of multiple carved stamps, mixing of complex dyes prepared for predictable effects, dyeing and painting of fine details, and finally, careful dyeing, washing, and occasionally, even the addition of tinsel" (Gittinger 1982, 16).

Numerous entries for calicoes and chintzes can be found in the personal and shop inventories of New York resident Margreta van Varick, taken in 1696. Her shop inventory included yardage of plain, flowered, and striped calico (Krohn and Miller 2009). Bequests of clothing to family members that were identified as made of calico included neckcloths, night gowns, aprons, quilted waistcoats, petticoats, baby's bibs, and clouts (diapers). Items identified as chintz included mantles, a petticoat, and a waistcoat.

Imported Fabrics in the 18th Century

The 18th century has an important documentary advantage: newspapers. Newspaper advertisements placed by merchants and shopkeepers detail fabrics available for purchase; personal advertisements call for the return of lost or stolen cloth-

Petticoat of fine cotton with a wide panel of hand-painted and dyed flowers and foliage, c. 1725. Chintz fabrics like this one were imported to Britain from India's Coromandel Coast. (Victoria and Albert Museum, London)

ing; masters describe the appearance and dress of runaway servants, apprentices, and slaves. It is important to note that merchants' notices tell us what was available while those placed by private individuals tell us what was actually owned and worn. This evidence, combined with information from inventories and wills, letters, and diaries, gives us a much clearer picture of the wardrobes of much of the colonial population at different economic levels.

The estates of two Providence merchants and kinsmen, Captain John Crawford, who owned three ships and died in 1718, and Major William Crawford, who kept a shop and died in 1720, included many luxury goods for resale. At least twice as many fabric names are mentioned in these inventories than in shopkeepers' inventories of the previous decade. Some fabrics, such as ticking and diaper, were probably most often used as furnishing fabrics; however, the vast majority—striped holland, calico, muslin, Bengal, cherryderry, alamode, Persian silk, crape, calimanco, camblet, bays, broadcloth, poplin, silk crape, shalloon, duroy, drugget, cambric, and kersey—were for clothing. William Crawford's inventory also mentioned 40 shillings worth of homespun flannel, probably goods that he had accepted in a barter arrangement, as he possessed no spinning wheels or looms (Rogers and Field 1901, 16:103–07; 148–59).

A 1729 advertisement in the *Pennsylvania Gazette* listed the items "lately imported from London, by John Le." Forty-six of the sixty-three items mentioned were textile or clothing related. A few of the fabrics named (callicoes, sheeting linen, diapers, cambricks, dowlasses, druggets, and chequered linnen) were qualified by the phrase "several sorts," indicating that either different colors or different qualities of these fabrics—and probably both—could be purchased (October 2, 1729). Apparel fabrics in this ad included Mantua silks, callimanco, fine kerseys, superfine double milled drab broad cloths, duroys, flannels, and London shalloons. Although goods were generally imported via London, not all goods were manufactured in Britain. Boston merchant A. Faneuil offered Venetian flowered silks (probably brocades) for women's gowns and matching petticoats in 1720 (*Boston Gazette*, February 8, 1720). Within a decade merchants were also offering fabrics imported from India and China, such as the exotic sounding (and exotically spelled) "Carridaries [cherryderries], . . . Cherconna [Cherconall?] Romalls, Bandannoes, Silk Lungee Romalls, Persians and China Taffaties" offered by Robert Strettell in 1738 (*Pennsylvania Gazette*, May 25, 1738).

By 1745 the numbers of fabrics available to colonists had again increased significantly. New silk and printed fabrics appeared among the favorite linens in a long advertisement by James Benezet, whose goods came in two different ships from London in the fall of 1745. Benezet knew his cloth: he carried not just lawn but "holland and German whited, long lawns, broad lawns, pistol lawns, narrow lawns, fine and coarse 7 eights wide clear lawns." Also in the shop were a large assortment of chintzes and calicoes, stamped linens, paduasoys, Persians, alamodes, veil silks, black and colored taffetas, Bengals, and "French prize black silks," the latter probably taken off a French merchant vessel by a British or colonial privateer. In addition to these fabrics, and others either commonly found on import lists or known through extant samples, there were unknowns such as "ellaches, singles and double tepoys, . . . peniascoes single and double, plain and masqueraded ditto, [and] chiloes" (*Pennsylvania Gazette*, September 26, 1745). Peniascoes may be an aberrant spelling for a fabric called peniskees; the rest, however, are a mystery. By the 1770s imported cloth from England, Ireland, Scotland, Holland, Italy, Russia, Germany, Switzerland, Flanders, India, China, and Turkey were routinely offered to the colonists.

Although settlers kept cattle and sheep whose skins were used to make shoes and gloves, leather also was imported from England. In the 18th century, Philadelphian Samuel Keimer, for example, who set up "The Friendly Office," advertised imported neats leather, that is, leather from the hide of an ox (*Pennsylvania Gazette*, March 27, 1729; December 30, 1735). Red and yellow leathers were advertised for shoes as well as for upholstery for chairs. Leather soles "fit for Shoes, Boots, and Double Channel Pumps" were imported from London (*Pennsylvania Gazette*, November 14, 1745). Morocco leather for shoes was often advertised.

Imported Fabrics in Southern Colonies

Attentive to the business of his British suppliers, Charleston merchant and factor Robert Pringle advised them about the kinds of fabrics "proper for So Carolina." For clothing, these included "Course Cloths & Heavies, Camblets of all sorts & Colours & Silk Camblets, Linnen & Cotton Checks . . . Gulix & Holland Cambricks . . . Garlix low pric'd. Brown Osnaburggs, Dowlas, & Russia Linnen . . . White, Bleue, & Green plains for Negro Clothing, Sagathy & Duroys & worsted Damask . . . Painted Callicoes . . . Scarlett, blue, & Superfine Broad Cloth" (Pringle 1972, 1:31). Coarse cloth, checks, garlick, osnaburg, dowlas, Russia linen, and plains were cheap linen and woolen fabrics for working men and women and the enslaved. Camlet, cambric, sagathy, duroy, damask, callico, and broadcloth appealed to the more genteel of the population. Pringle obviously had his finger on the pulse of fashion for a warm, humid climate because he shipped to Antigua three pieces of Italian silk "very fitt for mens Ware (but which are unsaleable here, Silk Cloaths for men being very Little in use here)." He also advised the Antigua merchant that unless the latter were prepared to have other silk inventory disposed of by "publick vendue," or auction, he should allow Pringle to ship the fabrics to Philadelphia "where very probably they may Sell much sooner & better than here" (1:267). He advised a new client about the timing of shipments of fabric: "The proper Season for Importing Woolen Goods is to have them arrive here in the Month of August of September & for Summer Goods to be here in the Months of February & March" (1:30). He cautioned another supplier that woolen goods remaining unsold by the early spring should be forwarded to northern cities for sale, "Woolens especially being a Very perishable Commodity in the Warm Climate & very lyable to be spoilt by the Moth, & are Wore only one half of the year" (2:525). These comments shed light on the practice of shipping imported fabrics within the colonies to find the most advantageous venues for their sale.

During the American Revolution and the British occupation of Charleston, South Carolina, women sympathetic to the patriot cause smuggled imported cloth out of the city to be made into uniforms: "These fair ladies, in consequence of their relation to the tories, could, at pleasure, pass into Charleston; which they never left without bringing off quantities of *broad cloth* cut and jumped into petticoots, and artfully hid under their gowns. The broad cloth, thus brought off, was regimentals for our officers" (Horry 1840, 224).

However, by far the largest volume of fabrics imported into the southern colonies of Maryland, Virginia, North and South Carolina, and Georgia during the 18th century was intended to clothe enslaved individuals working on plantations as field workers, as bound apprentice labor to artisans, and in the houses of the wealthy in both rural and urban settings. Robert Pringle advised British merchants to send white, blue, and green plains, a loosely woven woolen fabric, and osnaburg, a coarse linen; both were made into clothing for field hands. British ships carried hundreds of yards of these fabrics on every transatlantic voyage, and they are mentioned in almost every merchant and shopkeeper notice placed in southern newspapers. Planters and others with large holdings often ordered fabrics directly from Britain. In 1767, for example, the vestry of Petsworth Parish in Gloucester County, Virginia ordered the purchase, on the best terms, of "Green or Blue plains Or half thick & Canvis to Cloth the poor Children, & Cottin for the Negro Woman at the Work house" (Chamberlayne 1933, 332).

COLONIAL PRODUCTION OF TEXTILES: HOMESPUN

All fabric of colonial production, whether made by an amateur at home for domestic use or by someone in the trades for resale, was considered homespun. The term did not necessarily connote a fabric of lesser quality than imports; skilled workers on both sides of the Atlantic were essentially using the same equipment to produce cloth.

Homespun in the 17th Century

As discussed in the introduction to this volume, the most important economic role of the American colonies, in the eyes of the mother country, was to raise or locate, process, and export raw materials to feed English industries and then consume the imported products of those industries. In the earliest years of colonial settlement this economic activity, coupled with meeting the needs of shelter and food and maintaining relationships with Native Americans left little time or inclination for cultivating fibers and producing fabrics. As long as English ships docked at colonial ports on a regular basis, colonists could purchase articles of clothing and cloth produced in the mother country or exported by her. Raising flax and hemp, for example, was encouraged in most of the colonies, but more often to feed the raw material needs of the mother country than to clothe the colonists.

In New England this situation changed after 1640 with the great decline in immigration caused by the reforms begun by the Long Parliament in 1641. Fewer Puritan immigrants sought a new life in the New World, fewer ships sailed to New England, and the regular supply of commodities that had been flowing into northern ports ceased. With fewer newcomers, there were fewer new customers to purchase colonial resources, especially cattle, and little money or credit with which colonists could buy clothing and other necessities. Writing in his diary in 1641, John Winthrop explained the conditions:

> The parliament of England setting upon a general reformation of both church and state . . . this caused all men to stay in England in expecta-tion of a new world, so as few coming to us, all foreign commodities grew scarce, and our own of no price. Corn would buy nothing: a cow which cost last year £20 might now be bought for 4 or £5, etc. . . . no man could pay his debts, nor the merchants make return into England for their commodities. . . . These straits set our people on work . . . to sow hemp and flax (which prospered very well) and to look out to the West Indies for a trade for cotton. (Winthrop 1908, 2:31)

There was no shortage of skilled labor; among the early settlers were those knowledgeable in processing wool and flax as well as spinners and weavers. Equipment was also at hand; both the small linen spinning wheel and the great woolen wheel appeared in New England household invento-ries by 1640. Documentary sources tell us that before this crisis, there was some small-scale processing and weaving of locally grown and imported wool and linen, and cotton imported from the West Indies. For example, weavers from Yorkshire who settled in Rowley, Massachusetts, were ply-ing their old trade in new surroundings before 1642. Thus, the colonies' leaders hoped in 1640 that the enactment of laws to promote the cultivation of flax for linen, raising of sheep for wool, and processing cotton from the West Indies would be successful.

The Massachusetts General Court further encouraged household manu-facture in 1642 by authorizing the selectmen to apprentice children of par-ents found "not to able & fitt to imploy and bring them up" to "be set to some . . . imploymt wthall, as spinning upon the rock, knitting, weaving tape, &c." The selectmen were also directed "to pvide that a sufficient quantity of ma-terialls, as hump, flaxe, &cra, may be raised in their severall townes, & tooles & implements provided for working out the same" (Shurtleff 1853, 2:7).

Many individual farmers who heeded the laws resembled Hartford, Connecticut's John Willcock, who in 1651 willed to his wife "all my hempe and flaxe, both spun into yarn and unspun, and all that I have growing this year" (Manwaring 1904, 164). Probate inventories and other records indicate that spinning wheels outnumbered looms by a considerable margin, but the numbers of both increased during the 18th century. For example, of 300 estates settled in Essex County, Massachusetts, between 1665 and 1675, nine inventories listed looms, while 83 listed spinning wheels; fewer than one in three households at this date (Dow 1935, 151). A survey of 685 probate inventories from Massachusetts and Connecticut between 1632 and 1674 found that on average one in four households had spinning wheels in 1632, but twice that percentage owned them in 1674. Only six percent of Essex county households, however, owned looms by 1700 (Main 1994, 53, 60). The fact that spinning wheels vastly outnumbered looms hints that most of the weaving must have been done by professional weavers. The disparity is not unusual: it takes longer to spin thread than to weave cloth, and a weaver in a small community could easily keep up with the demand for cloth from several families that made their own yarn. Of course, homespun yarn was also used for knitting, a task performed in almost all households.

Inventories reveal other tools of the trade. For example, historians evaluating 17th-century probate inventories from Suffolk County, Massachusetts, discovered that in the 1670s "rural householders owned flax brakes, tow combs, and 'linnen wheels' as well as supplies of raw flax and 'yarn at weaving' " (Coons and Koob 1980, 8). Rural Suffolk County, Massachusetts, households possessed flax brakes, tow combs, and linen wheels, as well as raw flax and finished yarn put out to a local weaver in the 1670s (Dow 1935, 151). Probate inventories from coastal Plymouth Colony as well as Deerfield, on Massachusetts' western frontier, tell the same story beginning in the 1680s; they list great and little spinning wheels, tape looms, flax brakes, sheep shears, pairs of cards, combs and combing hooks, smoothing irons, hatchels, unprocessed wool and flax, and quantities of tow, linen, and woolen yarns (Doubleday).

It truly can be said of New England that the 17th century was the age of homespun industries. Not only did many households produce their own cloth and tailor it for clothing, some workers also exchanged their excess production at shops for imported Indian printed and painted calicoes and silks. For example, between 1685 and 1689 Mary Avery produced surplus yardage of wool—bunting, kersey, druggett, serge—cotton, and linen, which she bartered for goods at a Boston shop (Abbot 1910, 24). Edward Wharton, a Salem merchant, sold "home made wool hose" for men, women, and children (Dow 1935, 262).

During the 1600s, the provincial governments of other northern colonies continually enacted legislation to encourage the production of wool, silk, linen, and cotton and offered bounties, or bonus payments, for quantity as well as quality. Although some cloth production was accomplished by the trades for resale, most of the colonists' efforts, as well as the colonial legislation that encouraged such activity, was aimed at household or plantation use. This encouragement was prompted either because a colony lacked sufficient raw materials to use in trade for imported goods or in response to taxes or trade laws imposed by the British. In New Netherlands, inventories indicate that spinning wheels and looms were numerous. When the colony passed from Dutch to English hands in 1664, there was no negative effect on household output of textiles and no legislation prohibiting production. Writing in 1670, Daniel Denton noted that those who wish to settle in New York should "carry with them . . . Clothing" to trade for cattle "at an easie rate." In addition to cattle raising, the local population "sowe store of Flax, which they make every one Cloth of for their own wearing, as also woollen Cloth, and Linsey-woolsey, and had they more Tradesmen amongst them, they would in a little time live without the help of any other Countrey for their Clothing" (Denton 1902, 58). By 1681, Quakers who settled in New Jersey were weaving woolen cloth for apparel and tanning leather to make shoes and hats (Tryon 1966, 69–70). In the 1680s, Germantown, Pennsylvania, boasted of supporting a flock of sheep and a shepherd to provide wool for its three local woolen weavers (Little 1931, 48–49). Between 1684 and 1730, Pennsylvania's Council offered bounties for wool and linen cloth and for flax fiber by the pound (Tryon 1966, 37–38, n. 1).

In contrast, the colonies south of Pennsylvania had fewer occasions to revert to local production of cloth to supply their needs than their northern counterparts. In the 17th century, the colonial governments of Virginia, Maryland, and Carolina passed various acts encouraging the production of homespun wool and linen, but only when their other staple goods either did not make decent returns for importation or when the surplus was too great for the market. This legislation and the colonists' activities are discussed below, in the sections "Development of homespun: wool and linen" and "Development of homespun: cotton and silk."

Homespun in the 18th Century

For the better part of the 18th century—except in specific areas where Quakers, Germans, or Scotch-Irish settled—southern colonies (Maryland, Virginia, North and South Carolina, and Georgia) had no appreciable household manufacturing of textiles before the boycott of British goods brought on by the Townsend Acts of 1767. Their staple crops found steady markets in Britain and Europe, and in return well-to-do southerners could purchase necessities and luxuries either locally as imported goods or from abroad. After the boycott, however, southern newspapers ran accounts of home production of clothing like the one that appeared in the *South-Carolina Gazette* on August 24, 1769:

> As a proof, that we can manufacture for ourselves, if we should be reduced to that Necessity, we can assure our Readers, that a Gentleman who was in Town the Week before last, and resides near 100 Miles distant, was completely clad in the Produce and Manufacture of his own Plantation, except a Hat, which was made in his Neighbourhood. His shirt was fine Linen, his Coat Fustian, his Jacket Dimity, his Breeches Buck-Skin, his Stockings Thread; the Flax and Cotton grow on his own Place, and was spun, wove and knit by his own People [i.e., enslaved labor], the Buck-Skin was dressed there, and even the Leather of which his Shoes were made, tanned at Home.

Some southern plantation households came to depend on homespun to clothe their enslaved populations. In 1782, Eliza Yonge Wilkinson was living at her country house near Charleston, both of which—house and town—were controlled by British troops. While trying to thwart the advances of a Captain Sanford and at the same attempting to save her possessions from confiscation, Eliza recalled that she and the Captain "were interrupted by a little girl of mine, who came to tell me that the soldiers had cut my homespun out of the loom, and were bundling it up. 'Why, Capt. Sanford,' said I, 'you command a gang of them. Pray make them deliver the cloth. Your countrymen will not let us have Negro cloth from town, for fear the *rebels* be supplied; so we are obliged to weave' " (Wilkinson 1839, 105).

Between about 1700 and the mid-1760s, interest in and the amount of household cloth produced depended on geographic location. The northern region, which encompassed the colonies north of Maryland, and the whole of the southern Backcountry—culturally an extension of Pennsylvania—comprised an area in which working people usually produced the fabrics that they wore. This gave Britain cause for concern as an economic competitor. The Lowcountry, on the other hand, was not an economic threat to Britain's textile industries.

Of the northern colonies, New England was the acknowledged leader. Reports from the king's officers from the first two decades of the 18th century noted not only the increase in imports of textile-related tools to those colonies but also the increase in the numbers of country people and planters who clothed themselves in wool of their own manufacture. It is impossible to determine the extent to which New England's inhabitants wore the products of home manufacture, but the practice likely was due more to necessity than inclination. In 1709, Governor Dudley, of Massachusetts, expressed as much; his people would be "proud enough to wear the best cloths from England, if chopping, sawing, and building ships would pay for them" (Tryon 1966, 79). The legislation related to textile production that the Massachusetts Assembly passed between 1700 and 1766, newspaper advertisements for textile tools, and probate inventories all attest to the continued interest throughout New England in producing fabric of wool and linen. The economic conditions that had existed after the implementation of the Navigation Acts continued: New England had an abundant supply of raw materials but no staple that England would exchange for goods.

Eighteenth-century newspaper advertisements indicate the kinds of textile-related tools and utensils being imported or made in the colonies. Philadelphian Jacob Shoemaker made and sold spinning wheels from his shop in Market Street at least as early as 1738 (*Pennsylvania Gazette*, January 31, 1738). A common import throughout the period, sheep shears are listed in many trade notices. Wool cards, used to align the fibers before spinning, were also frequent imports. G. Burson, a maker of wool cards in Southwark, London, advertised widely in 1748 and 1749 that his maker's mark—G.B.—had been copied by makers of inferior cards. The notice lists New England, New York, and Philadelphia among the recipients of these poorly made tools, suggesting that by midcentury colonial woolen manufacturing was well under way (*Pennsylvania Gazette*, July 20, 1749). "Best GB wool cards" were still being imported and sold as late as 1771 (*Pennsylvania Gazette*, September 19, 1771). Cotton cards are found in merchant's notices in greater quantity after midcentury. Certainly by the time George Lachlar, a Philadelphia weaver who also made reeds—the part of the loom that keeps the warp threads separate and aligned—advertised his services in 1765, he was addressing a community of professional weavers, making his reeds available through middlemen in Lancaster, Reading, Allentown, and Chestnut Hill (*Pennsylvania Gazette*, July 18, 1765). The 12 fulling mills that existed in Philadelphia in 1770 probably supported these same weavers (Walton 1937, 213). Another reedmaker, Nathaniel Pike, opened his business in 1774, in Woodbridge, New Jersey, advertising in *Rivington's New York Gazette* as a way to encourage American manufacturing (Gottesman 1938, 254).

Account books and diaries from the New England colonies indicate that it was not uncommon for women and girls to spin for their neighbors, either working at home or at the neighbor's house or shop. Mary Wright

(Molly) Cooper, a farmer's wife in Oyster Bay, Long Island, confided to her diary between 1768 and 1773 some of the many textile and clothing related tasks undertaken by herself, her children, and her servants: "heshling flacks," combing wool, and carrying yarn to the weaver, for example (Sprigg 1984, 74). Nanny Green Winslow, another female diarist, wrote at the age of 12 of spinning enough yarn to make a 10-knot skein while visiting her aunt in Boston in 1772. A knot was composed of 20 threads; each thread was 74 inches in length (Tryon 1966, 118, n. 3). Nanny likely was not an expert at her task; her aunt told her, "it will do for the filling"—the weft of the cloth—but the yarn was apparently not even or strong enough to serve for the warp (Sprigg 1984, 75). In the mid-18th century, several Wampanoag Indian women living on Martha's Vineyard were noted in a shopkeeper's account book as having received store credit in return for spun yarn. Further studies of the probate inventories revealed that some Wampanoag families owned spinning wheels (Silverman 2005, 211). It is not known if they were paid in currency or in goods.

To sustain emotional interest in home production of textiles as well as provide employment for the poor, New England periodically experienced public spinning demonstrations. The first of these took place in Boston in 1721, where a year earlier a building was erected to house a spinning school to instruct the poor children of the town. At the school's opening women from all economic strata brought their wheels to the Common and competed with each other to test their skills. Although the school continued only three or four years, in 1731 a house was converted for use as a spinning school, again to instruct the poor. In 1751, to celebrate the second anniversary of the Boston Society for Promoting Industry and Employing the Poor, about 300 women gathered with their spinning wheels. Weavers were also present, dressed in apparel of their own weaving, and a demonstration loom was set up. Two years later Massachusetts appropriated £1500 to establish a spinning school, but the school's operation was short lived. A brief revival was tried in 1762, but the building was sold in 1767 (Tryon 1966, 85–88).

A "spinning craze" of a different kind started up in New England with Parliament's enactment of taxing measures in the 1760s. Stories abound in histories of the period of women and girls getting together for patriotic spinning parties. The Providence, Rhode Island, Daughters of Liberty began meeting in 1766 with 18 young women in the house of Dr. Ephraim Bowen, but moved their meetings to the courthouse as their numbers grew (Lippincott 1961, 139). Dr. Ezra Stiles, then pastor of the Congregational church in Newport, Rhode Island, hosted his own spinning parties in 1769 and 1770, again for the Daughters of Liberty. One of his 1769 events boasted 92 spinsters working at 70 wheels, finishing 170 skeins of wool and linen yarn in one day (Morgan 1962, 256; Woodward 1971, 133). Harvard College's 1768 commencement ceremonies presented an entire graduating class dressed in garments made from Rhode Island wool; in 1769, Rhode Island College's first graduates (seven scholars) also donned homespun for their ceremony, held in the town of Warren.

In August 1766, a report was demanded from all the colonial governors on the manufactures undertaken in their respective colonies since 1734. Their responses clearly indicate that household manufacturing of textiles, especially for clothing, was common practice among the laboring poor and country folk long before the crises produced by the Stamp and Townsend Acts. Governor Bradford's account of 1763 generally mirrors the responses given by many governors of northern colonies: "The inhabitants of the trading towns, men, women, children, have their whole supply of clothing from Great Britain. Most of the women in all other towns have the principal part of their clothing of British manufacture; the men have more or less. The poor laboring people in the country towns wear their own common clothes principally of coarse homespun linens and woolens" (quoted in Tryon 1966, 100).

The Development of Homespun: Wool and Linen

In the 17th century, fabrics made of wool and flax were important colonial commodities because of various factors that hampered efforts to acquire adequate supplies of clothing. Wool, whether in the form of livestock or fleeces, was brought to New England quite early, and legislation regarding the pasturing, protecting, and sale of sheep indicates the animal's importance. Colonial sheep were generally of an indifferent breed, and it was not until the 18th century that specialized breeds were developed. For example, Englishman Robert Bakewell selectively bred sheep that would provide substantial amounts of both meat and wool. Known by various names at the time—New Leicester, Bakewell Leicester, Dishley Leicester, and Leicester Longwool—the breed was familiar to colonial farmers; George Washington kept Leicester sheep at Mount Vernon. Merino sheep were not imported into America until after the American Revolution.

Sheep were brought to Plymouth Colony by 1628. As early as 1633, the colony took steps to encourage wool production within its borders by prohibiting sale of sheep out of the colony (Shurtleff 1855a, 1:13). In 1641, the Court clarified the act by ordering that anyone having sheep and departing the colony "shall bringe his sheepe to the towne of Plymouth . . . and shall sell them to any pson or psons that is disposed to buy them"; "for the rest that are not bought, he to be pmitted to carry them wth him whither he goes to dwell" (Shurtleff 1855b, 2:17–18).

For the next 20 years, the General Court of Massachusetts enacted many measures relating to wool and linen. Anticipating shortages in clothing, the Court offered bounties for "the manufacture of linnen, woollen, and cotton clothe" "as shall bee made wth in this iurisdiction, & the yarne heare spun also, & of materials as shalbee raised also wth in the same, or else of cotton" (quoted in Tryon 1966, 29–30). By 1645, European wars had begun to take their toll on imports of woolen cloth and ready-made clothing into the colonies: "destroying, in a great measure, ye flocks of sheepe amongst ym, & also ye trade & meanes it selfe of making woollen cloath & stuffs, by ye killing & othrwise hindring of such p sons whose skill & labors tended to yt end" (quoted in Tryon 1966, 31). New Englanders had access to cotton through the colonies' trade with the West Indies; however, cotton clothing did not provide enough insulation against the cold, especially for children: "childrn cloathing of cotton cloth (not being able to get othr) have, by yt meanes, had some of yir childrn much scorched wth fire, yea, divers burt to death" (quoted in Tryon 1966, 32). Thus, the Massachusetts Court urged inhabitants to protect and increase the current flocks of sheep. Further legislation, in 1648, provided for pasturing sheep on town commons and ordered fines to be paid by owners of dogs who "molest such sheope by driving them from their feeding"; "kill any sheope"; or "bene seene to course or bite any sheope" (Shurtleff 1855, 2:252). In the latter two cases, the offending dogs were also to be destroyed. Subsequent laws provided bounties for killing wolves.

Perhaps the most important piece of Massachusetts Court legislation enacted during the years of England's Civil Wars and the Interregnum was passed in 1656. With wearing apparel in short supply, the Court ordered "all hands not necessarily employd on other occasions, as woemen, girles, & boyes, shall, & hereby are, enjoyned to spin according to their skill & abilitie." The towns' selectmen were to ensure that every household "spin, for 30 weekes euery yeare. 3 pound p weeke of lining, cotton, or wooling" (quoted in Tryon 1966, 33).

With the restoration of Britain's monarch, Charles II, to the throne in 1660, New England turned its collective attention to the activities of fishing and shipbuilding. The Navigation Acts encouraged New England merchants to trade along the coast and to the island colonies, and ships brought back cargoes of textiles and other goods. Likely because of this increased trade, there was a decline in legislation promoting wool and flax production although not a decline in actual production. This situation is borne out by proscriptive legislation passed by Parliament. With the level of colonial production causing the home country considerable unease, a 1654 law made it illegal for the colonies to ship raw wool and woolen yarns for weaving to England. In 1660, the prohibition was extended to the exportation of sheep. By 1698 New England was exporting woolen goods. Fearing competition with home industries, in 1699 Parliament outlawed the exportation of wool, woolen cloth, and woolen clothing from its American colonies:

> No wool, woolfells, shortlings, mortlings, woolflocks, worsted, bay, or woollen yarn, cloth serge, bays, says, frizes, druggets, cloth-serges, shalloons, or any other drapery stuffs or woollen manufactures whatsoever, made or mixed with wool or woolflocks, being a product or manufacture of any of the English plantations in America, shall be loaden on board any ship or vessel, in any place or parts within any of the said English plantations, upon any pretence whatsoever. (quoted in Tryon 1966, 25)

In contrast, historical records indicate that during the first few years of settlement, the colonists at Jamestown were not to waste their time laboring in agriculture or any trade, hunting excepted. It was projected that most of their needs would be met either by supply ships from England or trade, especially in foodstuffs, with local Indian groups. The colonists were not expected—nor would it have been tolerated—to produce cloth. There were no sheep in the first group of domestic animals, and cultivation of flax was not mentioned in the settlement's earliest records. A writer for the eighth Federal Census declared that sheep were first introduced in Jamestown in 1609, but a tract printed in 1609 noted that there was no wool in the colony. No sheep were enumerated in the "Muster of the Inhabitants of Virginia," taken in 1625. By 1649, however, the colony could boast about three thousand head ("A Perfect Description of Virginia").

In spite of attempts to introduce flax growing in the first decade of settlement (Sir Thomas Dale initiated attempts in the spring of 1614), the Virginia General Assembly did not legislate flax production until August of 1633. During the English Civil Wars and the Interregnum, the Assembly continued to urge production because of the dearth of imported goods. In October of 1646, each county commissioner was ordered to choose two children, male or female, at least seven or eight years old, "from such parents who by reason of their poverty are disabled to maintaine and educate them" to be sent to James City "to be imployed in the public flax houses vnder such master and mistresse as shall be there appointed, In carding, knitting and spinning, &c." The children would be provided with food and utensils, bed and bedding, and "convenient apparel both linen and woolen, with hose and shooes" (Hening 1823, 1:336–37).

In the third quarter of the century, while a number of laws intended to stimulate the production of wool and prevent its export were enacted, more important legislation addressed the spinning and weaving of wool and linen cloth. The impetus for these latter acts was the low price of tobacco and a glut of the product on the market; the Virginia Assembly hoped to turn planters' attention to diversifying staple commodities. Legislation began in 1662 with a mandated purchase by the Assembly of flax seed from England. Thereafter, a premium of three pounds of tobacco would be offered to "whoever will spin the fflax and cause the yarne to be weaved into cloath of a yard wide." Five pounds of tobacco was to be awarded for "every yard of woollen cloath made of yarne here spun in the country" (Hening 1810, 2:120–21). Evidently there were an insufficient number of skilled weavers in the colony, so to provide for weaving homegrown wool and flax, in 1666 "An Act for Weavers and Loomes" was passed. Recognizing "the present obstruction of trade and the nakednes of the country," the Assembly charged each county to "provide and sett up a loome and weaver" at its own expense. It was estimated that "five women or children of 12 or 13 yeares of age may with much ease provide sufficient cloathing for thirty persons, if they would betake themselves to spinning" and looms and weavers were provided (Hening 1810, 2:238–39). Further legislation in 1668 required the construction of houses "for the educating and instructing poore children in the knowledge of spinning, weaving, and other useful occupations and trades" (Hening 1810, 2:267).

By the end of the century, however, the Virginia Assembly ceased encouraging home production of fabrics. In the 18th century, small planters would continue to provide some homespun for their enslaved workers and the family; but planters with large tracts of land purchased for their enslaved help either ready-made clothing or yard goods from which clothing would be constructed. Fancier fabrics for the family and household servants were purchased from local merchants or ordered from English factors.

The production of homespun cloth, especially of wool, both for household use and trade burgeoned in the north in the 18th century. As early as 1705, English observer and governor of New York, Lord Cornbury, warned that both Connecticut and Long Island were engaged in making woolen fabrics, and that Long Island serge was good enough to be worn by anyone, not just the lower classes (Little 1931, 53). Manasseh Minor, in Connecticut, wove "Blankuts, Cloath, Coverlids, Drugit, Rugs, and Lining (linen) and Coten Cloth" as well as "carsy [kersey]" (quoted in Adrosko 1976, 107). In

1720, the collector of customs in New Hampshire, a Mr. Armstrong, noted that thousands of pounds worth of New England stuffs and druggets—woolen fabrics—were sold in Boston shops (Lord 1896, 136). At this time more than 30,000 sheep were pastured on islands off the Massachusetts coast, the wool from which was exported to several northern colonies for processing. A serious industry developed in New Hampshire beginning in 1722, when 16 Scots-Irish families who had settled in the town of Nutfield renamed it Londonderry and began to ply their trade as linen weavers. By midcentury Londonderry's shirting linens were considered equal to fine imports.

The natural environment of Rhode Island's Narragansett plantations was particularly favorable for sheep farming, and wool and mutton were important agricultural products in the colony. One small farm of about a hundred acres, owned by the pastor of St. Paul's Anglican church, kept only a few sheep, but the Reverend MacSparran's diary indicates that he also bought wool fiber (50 pounds in May 1745) and his wife was given 12 pounds of wool by another farmer in return for her work during his sheep shearing. Along with hired help, MacSparran's wife, Hannah, processed the wool into yarns and cloth (Woodward 1971, 110–11).

A survey of probate inventories in Cumberland County, Pennsylvania, from 1750 to 1800 found that while wool production was more common in the early years of settlement, flax production caught up as population grew. The same survey also showed that more raw fiber was raised and processed in rural communities than in towns; this is consistent with land use and plot size in urban versus rural areas (Hersh and Hersh 1995, 30–32, 38–39). In general, domestic textile production grew as settlements became safer and larger. By the 1770s, nearly 60 percent of inventoried households in Pennsylvania's Cumberland County had spinning wheels, while additional records indicate that only about five percent of the county actually wove cloth (Hersh and Hersh 1995, 30–32, 38–39). The Philadelphia area, which had a high concentration of professional weavers of fabrics such as calamanco, camlet, kersey, plain linen, serge, and russels, boasted in 1743 of its own maker of worsted plush fabrics, a type of cloth that was difficult to weave and more often found in import lists (*Pennsylvania Gazette*, April 21, 1743; September 1, 1743). In the 1750s, Philadelphian Abraham Shelly bought unbroken flax and hemp and linen yarn from country spinners; he also put processed flax out to "good spinners" for cash wages. His products included white, brown, and colored threads for sewing clothing and shoes and knitting stockings, and he made cording for many household and farm uses. In an 18th-century example of branding a product by personal association with the maker, Shelly's name appeared on each ounce-skein of thread he sold (*Pennsylvania Gazette*, July 23, 1752; June 3, 1756; August 25, 1768).

During the second quarter of the 18th century, western Pennsylvania and the backcountry region of the southern colonies were being settled by Germans and Scotch-Irish, all of whom were small farmers. Their home production of fabrics is in contrast to the situation of the north, with its development of consistent production, and the more coastal south, whose production was sporadic. Because of their remoteness from the coast, the lack of markets and adequate cross-country transportation, and the Old-World practices they maintained, settlers in the Backcountry sustained themselves with the products of household manufacture from initial settlement.

As discussed in Chapter 2, home production of both linen and wool became symbols of resistance to the taxes imposed by the British government on the American colonies in the 1760s, particularly the Townshend Acts of 1767. One traveler explained the prevalence of homespun woolens and linens in Philadelphia during his visit in 1765 as "the natural consequence of restraining that branch of Trade, by which alone they got Specie, enabling them to make remittances for British Manufactories" (Gordon 1916, 41). One of the earliest manufactories was New York's linen factory—run by Obadiah Wells and in operation by 1766—which not only hired spinners to prepare yarn, but also sold "country" made cloth and stockings (Gottesman 1938, 249). German settlers living in the southern Backcountry may have been contributing to colonial production in the early 1760s when they brought flax "down to Charlestown [Charleston, South Carolina] in Waggons, drawn with four Horses, two abreast—perhaps at the distance of three hundred Miles" (Gordon 1916, 399).

Enterprising artisans came to the colonies to ply their crafts in the 1760s, hoping that patriotic fervor would make the locals support their efforts. The newcomers worked in many textile fields: George Williamson operated a flax and hemp dressing (processing the fibers to get them ready for spinning) business in Philadelphia in 1768; two English broadcloth weavers moved to Pottstown, Pennsylvania, in 1769 and were still advertising in 1773; and Christopher Leffingwell established a fulling mill and dyehouse in 1770 in Norwich, Connecticut (*Pennsylvania Gazette*, December 15, 1768; July 20, 1769; Bridenbaugh 1950, 47).

The Non-Importation agreements adopted in protest against taxation of imports in 1769 by all the colonies except New Hampshire encouraged the establishment of workshops, spurred household and plantation production, and supported the wearing of homespun apparel. By about 1772 wool manufactories were established in Hempstead, Long Island, and in New

York City. They were joined in 1775 by the United Company of Philadelphia for Promoting American Manufactures, which prepared to weave cloth of hemp, linen, and wool; employ women to spin yarn from fiber provided by the manufactory; and encourage country dwelling spinners to bring their own yarns to the factory to sell. A joint-stock company, the mission of the United Company was "to support the freedom, and promote the welfare, of our country . . . exciting a general laudable spirit of industry among the poor, and putting the means of supporting themselves into the hands of . . . [those] who at present are a public expence, and also to convince the public that our country is not unfavourable to . . . establishing manufactories" (*Pennsylvania Gazette*, February 22, 1775). (The United Company opened a linen bleachery, run by Daniel Burrell, outside the city the same year.) Soon the factory was advertising for weavers, either to work in the factory or to be provided with looms and yarns for outwork. Taking advantage of the great numbers of poor and unemployed in the area, the company was able, by September of 1775, to employ almost 400 people in a building it rented for 40 pounds a year (*Pennsylvania Gazette*, September 20, 1775). Weavers were allowed to work either in the manufactory building or elsewhere, and were "supplied with Looms to put up in their own Cellars, or any Part of the City" (*Pennsylvania Gazette*, June 5, 1776). Women were allowed to spin at home and bring their production to the manufactory for payment (Nash 1986, 216).

Commenting on all this activity in 1777, John Adams noted, "the Spirit of Manufacturing grows . . . Spinning, Knitting, Weaving, every trades-man is as full as possible. Wool and flax in great demand" (Adams, J. 1777). The United Company's manufactory closed during the British army's occupation of the city. Samuel Wetherill, one of the partners in this firm, wove fabrics to supply the Continental army for a time; in 1782, he advertised the manufacture of jeans, fustians, everlastings, and coatings in his shop (Walton 1937, 139–40). Lancaster, Pennsylvania, a backcountry town by 1770, had 15 master weavers, although about a third of the city's households were also producing linen and woolen cloth (Bridenbaugh 1950, 116).

In the south, plantation owners organized spinning and weaving operations to clothe the enslaved as well as members of the household. George Washington built a house expressly for this purpose at Mount Vernon. A surviving account book of 1767 and 1768 indicates that in the former year weaving was performed for plantation use, for Mrs. Washington, and 28 of their neighbors. The surprising variety of fabrics consisted of striped, plaided, birdeye, and plain woolens; plain linen; striped, birdeye, jump stripe, twilled, and plain cotton, India-cotton dimity; linsey-woolsey, both plain and plaid; "cotton stripd w' Silk"; "cotton & Silk"; and "Huccabac." The yardage totaled 1,059 for the plantation and 499 for neighbors (Commons 1910a, 2:320–21). The following year Washington summarized what his operations produced for his use: 815 3/4 yards of linen; 355 1/4 yards of wool; 144 1/2 yards of linsey-woolsey; and 40 yards of cotton. He noted that to spin all of this thread, he had expenses of the hire of a white woman and five enslaved girls, plus their clothing, food, and textile equipment (Commons 1910b, 2:324–25).

The zeal with which newspaper editorials, markets, and family operations embraced the call to resist buying imported goods is reflected in a poem that appeared in the *Massachusetts Gazette* in 1767:

Young ladies in town and those that live round,
Let a friend, at this season, advise you,
Since money's so scarce, and times growing worse,
Strange things may soon hap and surprise you.
First then, throw aside your high top-knots of pride,
Wear none but your own country linen.
Of economy boast, let your pride be the most
To show cloaths of your own make and spinning.
What if homespun, they say, is not quite so gay
As brocades, yet be not in a passion;
For when once it is known this is much wore in town,
One and all will cry out, "T is the fashion.'
And, as one and all, agree that you'll not married be
To such as will wear London Factory;
But, at first sight, refuse; tell 'em such you do chuse
As encourage our own manufactory. (quoted in Bagnall 1971, 57)

Home production during the American Revolution continued wherever and whenever possible, and patriots were called upon to furnish clothing and other supplies to the Continental Army. In June of 1776, each state was asked to furnish, "a suit of cloaths, of which the waistcoat and breeches may be made of deer leather . . . a blanket, felt hat, two shirts, two pair of hose, and two pair of shoes, to be manufactured, or otherwise procured . . . in their respective colonies, for each soldier of the American Army" (Ford 1906, 5:466–67). The manner of gathering the supplies was left to each state. In northern states spinning parties, or bees, were held in private homes; these were similar to the events Rhode Islander Jonathan Hazard coordinated during the winter of 1777–78 to supply soldiers at Valley Forge (Woodward 1971, 133). In 1781, Dover and North Brookfield,

Massachusetts, residents furnished socks, stockings, shoes, shirts, and blankets to soldiers from their home state (Tryon 1966, 115–16).

At the same time, home production had to supply at least some of the clothing needs of the roughly 2.5 million people living in the states at the war's commencement. The Marquis of Chastellux, a French officer who traveled in Connecticut during the war, came across professional weaving and finishing establishments, and commented on the fitness of their products to serve the populations of "any other town than Boston, New York, and Philadelphia" (quoted in Little 1931, 84). He seems to have discounted the willingness of the more cosmopolitan inhabitants to dress in anything but fine imported cloth. In more populated areas yarns, cloth, and ready-made articles could reach those in need by established roads and waterways. Those living on frontier areas, however, were practically economically independent.

Abigail Adams, writing to her husband John, away in Philadelphia with the Continental Congress, apprised him of the status of her household as affected by the Revolution:

> I seek wool and flax and can work willingly with my Hands, and tho my Household are not cloathed with fine linnen nor scarlet, they are cloathed with what is perhaps full as Honorary, the plain and decent manufactory of my own family, and tho I do not abound, I am not in want. I have neither poverty nor Riches but food which is convenient for me and a Heart to be thankfull and content that in such perilous times so large a share of the comforts of life are allotted to me. (Adams, A. 1777)

These many facets of colonial American homespun would become, after independence was achieved, important industries that would contribute greatly to the country's economic growth in the 19th century.

The Development of Homespun: Cotton and Silk

There is no evidence for the cultivation of cotton in the colonies in the 17th century. But beginning as early as 1636, cotton fiber was imported in small quantities from Britain's West Indian islands to her North American colonies (Walton 1937, 123). In 1641, the Massachusetts General Court organized a commission to be sent to England, part of whose mission was, "to seek out some way, by procuring cotton from the West Indies . . . for our present supply of clothing" (Winthrop 1908, 2:25). In 1648, the ship *Welcome* brought about 141 pounds of cotton from Barbados for John Pease of Boston (Aspinwall 1903, 141–42). Domestically carded and spun, it was usually used only for the weft yarns of cloth whose warps were of wool or linen. But occasionally, all-cotton cloth was produced. The fulling mill in Rowley, Massachusetts, which opened in 1643, was built to process both cotton cloth woven from West Indian cotton as well as the woolen cloth manufactured from the fleece of the colony's sheep.

Given the difficulties of processing cotton before the introduction of the cotton gin in the late 18th century, it is surprising how often references to raw and homespun cotton appear in early records. For example, at his death early in 1695, Thomas Angell of Providence, Rhode Island, owned "2 Cotten shirts" as well as a pair of "Cotton & linnen sheetes, & one pr. of all linnen sheetes" (Rogers, Carpenter, and Field 1894, 7:85). Thomas's son, James, a weaver, left at his death, in 1711, 15 pounds of cotton, 12 pounds of wool, and seven pounds of flax (Rogers, Carpenter, and Field 1894, 7:30). Another inhabitant of the town, William Whipple, who died a year later, possessed "Cotton & wooll Cloath," and "Cotten & linnen Cloath" (Rogers, Carpenter, and Field 1894, 7:96). By the end of the 17th century, cotton fiber was a common import for merchants in the New England/West Indies trade. In 1721, the Lords Commissioners of Trade and Plantations noted that Massachusetts inhabitants made use of cotton from the Indies in weaving a homespun linen that was "generally half cotton, serv[ing] only for the use of the meanest sort of people" (quoted in Tryon 1966, 78).

The southern colonies began growing two kinds of cotton early in the 18th century. Sea Island cotton, a long-staple fiber grown on southern coasts and the islands that skirt them, could be processed by the roller gin, a centuries-old device that effectively removed the loosely attached seeds from long staple. But the gin was ineffective in removing seeds from the inland-grown, short-staple cotton, whose seeds were tightly attached to the fibers and required removal by hand. Widespread cultivation of the short-staple plant for commercial manufacture did not begin until the 1790s, after the perfection in 1793 of the cotton gin, which quickly and efficiently separated the cotton seeds from the fibers. In 1728, while surveying the dividing line between Virginia and North Carolina, William Byrd II observed: "There is but little wool in that Province [North Carolina], tho' Cotton grows very kindly. . . . The Good Women mix this with their Wool for their outer Garments; tho', for want of Fulling, that kind of Manufacture is Open and Sleazy" (Byrd II 1901, 56).

Writing from Paris at the end of the American Revolution, Thomas Jefferson (1904, 5:408–09) argued, "If any manufactures can succeed there [America], it will be that of cotton." Although at that date no specialized equipment for processing cotton existed and no locally made cotton cloth was for sale, "in almost every family some is manufactured for the use of the family, which is always good in quality, & often tolerably fine. In the same way they make excellent knit stockings of cotton, weaving is in like manner carried on principally in the family way: among the poor, the wife weaves generally & the rich either have a weaver among their servants [i.e., enslaved labor] or employ their poor neighbors" (5:409). Jefferson observed of the southern region in general at war's end:

> The four Southernmost states make a great deal of cotton. Their poor are almost entirely clothed in it in winter & summer. In winter they wear shirts of it, & outer clothing of cotton & wool mixed. In Summer their shirts are linnen but the outer clothing cotton. The dress of the women is almost entirely of cotton manufactured by themselves, except the richer class, and even many of these wear a good deal of homespun cotton. It is as well manufactured as the calicoes of Europe. These 4 states furnish a great deal of cotton to the states north of them. (5:166)

Homespun has a different meaning when applied to the colonies' involvement in the manufacture of silk. At the beginning of the 17th century European sericulture and the silk-weaving industries were concentrated in France and Italy. At the same time, London's smaller-scale production of silk threads, fabrics, and trimmings, using raw silk imported from the eastern Mediterranean and Italy, was given a boost by an influx of skilled French Protestants (another wave of craftsmen arrived after the Revocation of the Edict of Nantes in 1685). In England, all of this production, whether cloth, silk stockings, embroidered caps, or silk fringe, was eagerly consumed by the middling sorts as well as the wealthy. Determined to support this luxury consumption while minimizing imported goods, James I laid the groundwork to create a domestic silk industry. In 1607, the king granted a license to William Stallenge to print a book of instructions on the cultivation of mulberry trees and the raising of silkworms. Stallenge published a translation, with woodcut illustrations, of a French work by Olivier de Serres: *Instructions for the Increasing and Planting of Mulberrie Trees and the Breeding of Silke-wormes, for the making of Silke in this Kingdome.* He was also given a monopoly on supplying mulberry plants and seeds, by the thousands, to counties in England. In 1609, James had ground enclosed near Westminster Palace to plant mulberry trees; by 1618 the monarch provided financial support for raising silkworms at both Oatlands Palace, in Surrey, and the royal palace at Theobalds, in Hertfordshire.

Reports of mature red mulberry trees growing wild in Virginia stimulated interest in producing raw silk in the colony and exporting it to England for weaving. (Ultimately, it would be understood that red was the wrong variety of mulberry for the optimum growth of silkworms; larvae fed on the white mulberry, which had to be imported before sericulture could become a serious business in the colonies, produced a better filament.) Silkmen, equipment, and silkworm eggs were in Jamestown by the fall of 1608; a building to cultivate the silk was erected in the first months of 1609 (Hatch 1957, 5–6). A servant of John Bonoeil—the latter raised the king's silkworms—traveled to Virginia to provide additional guidance in about 1615 and remained in the colony for at least six years. These efforts bore fruit; samples of reeled silk were sent back to England during the first decade of settlement.

In 1620, Bonoeil himself penned a treatise on sericulture, *Observations to be followed for making of fit roomes for silk wormes*, copies of which were shipped to Virginia for the colonists. The work included a letter from the king to the Virginia Company, recommending the establishment of silk works in the colony. Instructions from the Virginia Company to Governor Francis Wyatt, drawn up on July 24, 1621, charged the colonial government to ensure that settlers, "plant mulbury trees, and make silk, and take care of the French men and others sent about that work . . . and not let them forsake their trades for planting tobacco, or any such useless commodity" (Hening 1823, 1:115). The Virginia Company's instructions point out the ambivalence with which many in England viewed tobacco farming. In some circles, it was reckoned that the activity encouraged laziness and vice rather than careful husbandry. In 1655, Samuel Hartlib penned *Reformed Virginia Silk-Worm*, in which he argued that sericulture would keep planters and their servants active and industrious all year, with the additional benefit of setting an example for local Indians:

> [W]hen the Indians shall behold and see you begin the business [of sericulture], they will with all alacrity set upon it likewise, and imitate you. . . . And thus by the blessing of Almighty God, there may be good hope of their civilizing and conversion; so that they might be great gainers both in body and soul by this thing. (quoted in Braddick 2002, 101)

As an alternative to tobacco farming, in 1645 Virginian William Berkeley began sericulture efforts by planting a stand of mulberry trees. Three years later the trees were sufficiently established to provide an adequate quantity of leaves for the first batch of silkworms. He reported the results to John Ferrar, one of his correspondents in England: "Excellently well and to Evidence to all the world booth the fittnes of Clymate and the goodness of the Mulbery leafe: [Berkeley] to his greate Renowne Sent home this yeare 1649 May last a good parsell of Silke worme Bottomes to show the goodness of the Silke and the assured thriving of them" (quoted in Billings 2004, 73–74).

Governor Edward Digges followed Berkeley's example. Claiming that "silke will be the most profitable comoditie for the countrey," in 1656 he persuaded the General Assembly to enact a law requiring every land owner to plant 10 mulberry trees for every 100 acres held. A penalty of 10 pounds of tobacco would be levied on planters who either did not plant the trees or did not sufficiently tend them (Hening 1823, 1:420).

Despite the frequency with which the mother country and the governing bodies of Virginia urged planters to take up sericulture, in general the endeavor thrived only when supported by bounties or when the price of tobacco was low. In the 1650s alone, the Assembly passed three pieces of legislation awarding premiums in thousands of pounds of tobacco to planters who could produce for export in a single year a number of pounds of wound silk "all of his owne makeing." No records indicate that these bounties were ever earned.

Beginning in the 1670s and for the next 30 years, multiple attempts were made by South Carolina settlers and Englishmen alike to establish silk production in the Charleston area. In 1680, the vessel the *Richmond* transported French Protestants and silkworm eggs to Charleston. Unfortunately for the investors, "the [silkworm] Eggs which they [the Huguenots] brought with them hatch'd at Sea, before we could reach the Land, the Worms for want of Provision were untimely lost and destroyed" (quoted in Van Ruymbeke 2006, 206). Three years after the arrival of the *Richmond* settlers and the successful introduction of silkworms to Carolina, however, one of Huguenots produced 30 pounds of silk (Van Ruymbeke 2006, 206). Governor Sir Nathaniel Johnson successfully introduced sericulture in a small way on his plantation, Silk Hope, in 1693, but failed to produce enough silk to make a profit.

In the 18th century individual colonies took over their own promotional measures to develop and maintain sericulture; enterprises were continued in South Carolina and begun in Maryland, Connecticut, Rhode Island, Pennsylvania, and Georgia. Documents concerning Maryland's experiments with silk production are spotty. In 1777, George Thompson and W. Wilson placed an advertisement in the *Maryland Gazette* to announce their intention to "carry on a silk manufacture, near the Patowmack and Patuxent" and sought lands near these rivers with "good numbers of mulberry trees on them" (January 9, 1777). Whether this venture was started is un-known. The 1775 inventory of Baltimore County resident Colonel William Young, however, included two yards of "America Manufactured Silk" val-ued at £2. This yardage was likely manufactured in Maryland (Maryland Prerogative Court 1775).

In 1734, Connecticut's General Assembly offered bounties for sewing silk, silk stockings, and silk fabric produced in the colony. In 1766, a new law sent one-half ounce of mulberry seed to every Connecticut parish and offered a bounty on the raising of mulberry trees as well as reeled silk. This followed hard upon the sericulture efforts of Nathaniel Aspinwall, who planted mulberry trees in and around the Connecticut town of Mansfield. Silk production on a small scale thrived in the Mansfield area; in 1785, it evolved into the first of several silk manufacturing companies in the town: The Directors, Inspectors, and Company of Connecticut Silk Manufactures. Connecticut's sericulture industry continued through the early 19th cen-tury, and its practitioners eventually found several important American silk thread and fabric manufacturing concerns.

The domestic experiments of Reverend Ezra Stiles, minister of the First Congregational Church in Newport, Rhode Island, began in 1763 when Stiles received silkworm eggs from a Connecticut friend. Stiles, who had planted several mulberry trees in his garden in the 1750s, raised this first crop of silkworms with the help of neighbors who allowed him to harvest the leaves of their mulberry trees when Stiles's own were bare. The result of his work was about one pound of raw silk as it was reeled from the co-coons. It took him until 1771 to accumulate enough silk to have the thread woven into the fabric for a dress for his wife. Even then he had to buy 11 shillings worth of reeled silk to add to his own production (Morgan 1962, 147). Stiles's interest—but apparently not the practice—in sericulture con-tinued after he moved to New Haven in 1778 to become the President of Yale College.

Pennsylvania, too, had moderate success for a short time. To interest his fellow Pennsylvanians in developing a local silk industry, Benjamin Frank-lin reported in his 1749 *Almanac* the successes of the Derby silk factory in England: "there are 26,586 wheels, 97,746 movements; 73,728 yards of silk wound every time the water-wheel goes round, which is three times every minute; 318,504,960 yards of silk in one day and night; and consequently 99,373,547,550 yards of silk in a year" (Franklin 1749). At Franklin's urging, Philadelphia's American Philosophical Society promoted a subscription for a filature, which was opened in Philadelphia in 1769, to reel cocoons raised in New Jersey, Delaware, and Pennsylvania. In 1771, over two thou-sand pounds of cocoons were bought and reeled by the Society for Promoting the Silk Manufactory, which also sold mulberry tree seedlings for two and a half pence each (*Pennsylvania Gazette*, March 21, 1771).

John Fanning Watson (1779–1860) recorded the efforts of some female Pennsylvanian sericulturists and attached fragments of fabrics made of their local silk to his manuscript notes. He noted a woman in Chester County who raised 30,000 silkworms: "A parcel of it was sent to the Queen & she had it woven into a court dress" (Watson, 72). He included two fragments of dress silk, which he dated to 1770, from Susan Wright, of Columbia, Pennsylvania; she "had at one time 60 yards & mantua of her own raising. She used to manufacture herself excellent sewing silk which she dyed of different colours" (165). Germantown also raised silk worms and sent the thread to England to be woven (230). Watson also recorded that Deborah Logan provided silk of local manufacture for "Garments to our Ladies" during the American Revolution (230). Unfortunately, nowhere in the records does it mention how long it took for these silk entrepreneurs to accumulate the quantities of silk they were reported to have raised, and none of these enterprises seems to have survived the war.

Although silk production was still experimental, by the first decade of the 18th century, South Carolina was producing some silk thread and fabric for local consumption. In 1708, the Charleston goldsmith Nicolas de Longuemare ordered unworked and homespun silk, two handkerchiefs, and a nightcap from "Monsieur [Pierre] DuTartre." He also sold silkworm eggs to Benjamin Simons and purchased three bushels of eggs, at 15 shillings per bushel, from a Madame Poulain (Van Ruymbeke 2006, 207). Later the colony could boast of a small network of colonists who voluntarily participated in silk production as well as a significant number of French and English settlers who had been paid by the English government to instruct in the proper cultivation of silk. In the early 1730s, Jean Pierre Purry of Neufchatel, Switzerland, arranged for the transportation of about 450 of his countrymen to the colony to raise silk and other crops.

John Lewis Poyas, an Italian, was persuaded to immigrate to South Carolina, and arrived in the community of Purrysburg (established by Swiss immigrants) in 1734. Poyas and his wife understood "perfectly the manufacture of Silk in all its Process from the very planting of the white Mulberry to the spinning of the Superfine Organzine Raw Silk after the manner used in Turin and Italy" (quoted in Meriwether 1940, 37). In 1766, Purrysburg produced 6,000 pounds of silk cocoons, which were purchased by the Georgia government and wound in Savannah to make 300 pounds of raw silk (Meriwether 1940, 37). In spite of economic hardships and the revocation of cash bounties for production, the venture provided raw silk for decades. In 1772, Purrysburg exported through Charleston to England

455 pounds of "exceeding fine Raw Silk" (*South-Carolina Gazette; and Country Journal*, January 14, 1772).

Other sericulture ventures in South Carolina appear in the newspapers of the day. Eliza Lucas Pinckney (c. 1722–1793) produced enough silk at her Belmont Plantation in 1753 to have the thread made into fabric for at least one gown; the fabric was woven in England. A newspaper article of 1766 noted that Pinckney's plantation had produced nearly 50 bushels of cocoons that year (*South-Carolina Gazette*, June 30, 1766). In 1765, Gabriel Manigault sponsored the efforts of French immigrant Reverend Jean Louis Gibert, who raised 630 pounds of cocoons at Silk Hope Plantation (Meriwether 1940, 254). Apparently a tireless promoter, Gibert taught those interested how to wind silk and "has now a considerable Number of Silk Worms in the Old School-House near the New-Barracks, where Gentlemen . . . may at one Time see them in the various Stages of Life, some young, some full grown, and some spinning their Balls or Cocoons." He also oversaw the building of ovens for curing the cocoons and construction of a winding machines and a filature (*South-Carolina Gazette; and Country Journal*, May 12, 1767). All of this activity suggests that there was enough silk production in the colony to invest heavily in the venture. Not everyone who undertook sericulture in South Carolina did so for financial gain. Some experimented with silk production as a novelty, as indicated by the editor of the *South-Carolina Gazette and Country Journal* in 1767: "several Gentlemen and Ladies near Charles Town will make the private Amusement of raising Silk Worms tend to the Public Benefit by shewing how easily the Knowledge thereof is to be required."

Britain's hope for a sustainable and lasting silk-producing industry began with the founding of Georgia in 1733, an experiment well documented in letters written by the first settlers and trustees of the colonies. Among the first immigrants sent to the colony at the expense of the Trustees to "introduce silk in Georgia" were Paul Amatis, who "understands the Nature & Production of Raw Silk"; Joseph Stanly, "Stocking maker & can draw & reel Silk aged 45"; and Samuel Grey, "Silk Throwster aged 30 & his Apprentices Chetwin Furzer aged 16 & Cornelius Jones aged 15" (Egmont, A List of the Persons). An agreement had been negotiated between the trustees of the colony and Paul Amatis and his brother, Nicholas, to bring "2 Men and 4 Women who understand the whole of the Silk Business; and he is to have after the rate of £10 p Head in Discharge of all Expences whatsoever from Turin to London and £10 more to be paid to him for 4 lb. Silkworms Eggs and a Copper for boiling and a Machine for Winding" (Egmont 1732, 4). Amatis's brother, Nicholas, and Nicholas's indentured servant Jacques

Camuse, Camuse's wife, and three sons arrived in Savannah in late January of 1733 (Egmont 1733a, 21; 1733b, 24).

By May of 1735, Paul Amatis had sent to the trustees of the colony, at Westminster, the first box of wound silk from Savannah (Egmont 1735, 174–76). Most of the cocoons from which this silk had been reeled, however, came from South Carolina, as Savannah's mulberry trees were not mature enough to support silkworms. The Amatis brothers argued in the summer of 1735, and Nicholas left the colony. Paul left a few months after his brother, having lost the confidence of General Oglethorpe, the head of Georgia's Trustees. The Camuse family took over the jobs of encouraging the settlers to raise silkworms and teaching them to reel silk, but the Camuses were temperamental. They left Georgia in 1750, but were asked to return a year later to supervise work at the filature that had been built in 1750 by the newly appointed commissioner for silk, Pickering Robinson, with the support and guidance of the Trustees' Secretary in the Colony, William Stephens, and local merchant James Habersham. The trustees offered bounties to encourage mulberry plantations, raising silkworms, and reeling the silk from the cocoons. When Robinson became ill and returned to England, in 1753, his place was taken by Joseph Ottolenghe. All efforts were halted in 1769 when a killing frost destroyed many mulberry trees and Parliament discontinued the bounty on Georgia silk. In 1770, Ottolenghe moved to Philadelphia to run that city's filature (Shaw 2006, 68).

A second Georgia community, composed of German Protestants, also settled in 1734 and established silk production near Savannah, in Ebenezer. They had been given land grants on the condition that they plan 100 white mulberry trees on every 10 acres of land. The Salzburgers, as they were known, were so successful that by 1751 the trustees voted funds to enable them to build their own filature. Pickering Robinson and Joseph Ottolenghe, however, preferred to reel the Ebenezer-grown silk in Savannah, where they could keep a closer eye on quality and ensure their own control over the colony's silk industry.

Lord Adam Gordon described Georgia's production as having averaged 1,000 pounds of reeled silk exported to London per year in the mid-1760s, at the peak of its production. He added shrewdly, however, that silk "will stand in need of the aiding hand of Parliament" (Gordon 1916, 395) By 1771 the filature was no longer in use, but the equipment was given to the Salzburgers, who kept up production until the American Revolution interfered (Chambliss 1959). There is some evidence that the Salzburgers revived their sericulture efforts in a small way after the war, but it never contributed greatly to the state's economy (Shaw 2006, 69).

Home Processing of Leather

By the second half of the 17th century, New England had cattle in abundance. Husbandry was so successful in the colonies' Backcountry that beginning in 1648 surplus stock brought to Boston for sale required two fairs a year, the second exclusively "for Cattle to make provisions both for our selves and shipping" (quoted in Rutman 1965, 188–89). The hides salvaged from butchering operations there provided the raw material for tanners, glovers, and shoemakers. Finished leather goods were sold locally and exported to other New England colonies and colonies in the Caribbean.

Cattle raising was also among the earliest businesses in Carolina. Daniel Axtell, who emigrated from Massachusetts to near present-day Summerville sometime in the late 1690s, set up a tannery to process cowhide and occasionally deerskins from the trade with Native Americans. In 1705, he made large shipments to England of leather for shoes: sole leather and upper leather, a finer grade used for the uppers of shoes. Much of his business also supplied local shoemakers like John Branford. Branford, a cattle raiser as well as a shoemaker, frequently sold hides to Axtell. He was also one of Axtell's biggest purchasers of sole and upper leather. In return, Axtell— and the master of a large plantation Axtell managed—purchased most of their shoes from Branford, both for family members and the plantation's enslaved workers (Moore 1994; 285, 287, 289).

Articles describing how to tan, dress, and prepare skins for several uses appeared periodically in 18th-century colonial newspapers. These detailed informational pieces were intended primarily for plantation owners and others who might be interested in the trade. One such article, appearing in the *South-Carolina Gazette,* February 12, 1732, offered information on "preparing Buffelo, Deer, Sheep, Goat or Kid-Skins in Oil, in Imitation of Chamois" and covered in excess of two pages of the newspaper.

Perhaps the largest quantity of home production of leather was generated by the deerskin trade with American Indians. The overwhelming majority of these skins was processed, as dictated by custom, by Native American women. In the 17th century deerskins from northern and southern colonies were processed and exported to Bristol and London for England's leather working trades. By 1720, however, South Carolina emerged as the leader in this export commodity and remained so throughout the century. In 1750 alone Charleston's merchants, factors, and ship captains exported 150,000 skins, or 20 percent of the value of the colony's exports for that year. At one time or another, the Carolina Indian trade involved most of the major communities from the southern Appalachian Mountains to the lower Mississippi Valley. Not all deerskins were destined for export, however. Northern cities, especially Philadelphia and Boston, dressed skins for shoemakers, glovers, and breeches makers.

FABRIC QUANTITIES FOR CLOTHING

Surviving account books, whether tailor's records or personal and household accounts, show clearly that the most expensive part of a new garment was the cost of the fabric. Labor was cheap in comparison. For example, in 1768 a shoemaker in western Massachusetts had a coat and trousers made for him that required six yards of cloth at six shillings per yard. He paid the tailor only seven shillings to make the suit (Arms).

How much fabric did it take to clothe the average colonist? That depended in part on the prevailing silhouettes and in part on the type of fabric used to make the clothing. Fabric widths were not standardized. Plain fabrics such as linen holland, cambric, and lawn; woolen kersey and worsted calamanco; and silk taffeta were usually woven between about 24 and 36 inches wide. Eighteenth-century merchants' advertisements also noted width measurements like "three fourths," "seven eighths," and "yard wide." An even larger measure was the ell, which in England equaled five-fourths, or 45 inches. In Scotland an ell was about 37 1/2 inches and in Flanders 27. These local variations caused endless economic disputes. The ell was not commonly used and most often applied to widths of linen. Plain wool broadcloths were so named because they ranged 54 to 63 inches wide. Patterned fabrics, including brocades and damasks made of wool or silk, tended to be narrower, about 19 to 22 inches (Montgomery 1984; Rothstein 1987).

In 1650, a white male colonial of the middling sort wore a doublet or jerkin and full-cut breeches or hose, a shirt, collar, or band, stockings, shoes, and had a cloak or perhaps a surtout coat as outerwear. Linen fabrics made up the man's shirt and collar, requiring between three and four yards of 28- to 30-inch-wide fabric. The man's doublet and breeches required four to five yards of plain cloth, 36 inches wide or more, but between six and seven yards of 22-inch-wide patterned cloth. A semicircular short cloak used about three or four yards, depending on the width; less for fabric 36 inches or more wide; and more if the fabric was narrower.

His female companion wore a shift, stays (corset), at least one underpetticoat, a gown over a separate, but visible petticoat—or a jacket or doublet instead of a mantua—plus a cap and neck handkerchief. A woman's shift used between three and five yards of linen fabric. Her sleeved doublet or jacket required between two and three yards of 22-inch width. A skirt and petticoat each took about five widths of cloth cut to the proper length—about four and a quarter yards of 22-inch-wide cloth for a petticoat 29 inches long. A full gown or mantua used 10 to 12 yards of a 20-inch-wide cloth.

A century later, most men wore a shirt, waistcoat, coat, close fitting knee-length breeches or somewhat longer, looser-fitting trousers, stockings, shoes, and a hat or cap. Women still wore a shift, stays, an under-petticoat, and either a mantua or a short gown over an outer petticoat, with a neck handkerchief, cap, hat, shoes, and stockings. The amount of fabric consumed by male clothing rose sharply in the late 17th and first half of the 18th centuries because coat skirts were cut with many pleats and waistcoats were almost as long as coats and were sleeved in cold weather. Although shirts gradually became somewhat shorter and narrower by the end of the 18th century, they generally consumed about three and three quarters yards (or three ells) of linen. One analysis of an Englishman's accounts between the 1740s and 1770s records that the shirt sleeves were sometimes made of more finely woven linen than the body, and shirt ruffles, if attached at the wrists and front opening, were finer yet (Rothstein 1987, 152–53). Narrow knee breeches required about two yards, with a similar amount for either a stitched-in lining or separate drawers; a sleeveless waistcoat about a yard of a 30-inch-wide face fabric, less than a yard of a plain fabric for the back, and additional fabric for lining the front; a long sleeved coat with pleated skirts and deep cuffs might take seven yards, plus the same again for lining. A man's overcoat with a short shoulder cape, a high collar, and wide cuffs would use a yard or two more.

Woman's clothing took much the same yardage in the 1750s. Although style details changed, the fundamental silhouette of a tight fitting bodice and wide gathered skirt remained the essentially the same. The knee-length shift, or chemise, was rather less full than those of a century before, and one with elbow-length sleeves took about three yards of 30-inch-wide linen. A simply cut short gown took between two and one-half and three yards depending on the width of the cloth, and an outer petticoat for wear with the short gown used at least another three yards. Among main garments, the most voluminous was the style of gown called a sack back, or robe à la Française, with the bodice front fitted to the body, but the back falling from wide loose pleats stitched down at the neck. This style made up in 19-inch-wide silk used about 15 yards.

From 1746 to 1823 Englishwoman Barbara Johnson (1738–1825) kept a scrapbook of fabrics annotated with quantity, price, and use (this book is now in the collection of the Victoria and Albert Museum in London, England; Rothstein 1987). The album is invaluable for comparing quantities of different types of fabrics needed for specific garments during this period. For example, a brocaded silk gown from 1755 used 16 yards, while 22 yards of half-ell-wide figured silk ducape made up a formal "negligee" in 1767. In 1780 and 1781, Johnson recorded using six yards of ell-wide calico printed with a floral stripe pattern for a gown, and 10 yards of yard-wide red and white printed chintz for a gown and matching petticoat.

Smaller items such as caps and aprons used comparatively little cloth. Half a yard of 30-inch-wide linen was enough for a simple cap. A pair of pockets also took about half a yard although pockets were sometimes pieced in patchwork fashion from several different fabrics. Depending on the length a woman preferred for her apron, and how tall she was, a yard or so would suffice. Neck handkerchiefs (sometimes called a neckerchief, or for women a kerchief or fichu, but most often called simply a handkerchief) ranged from about 25 to 36 inches square. Women's fancy neck handkerchiefs might also be cut in half on the diagonal and embellished with embroidery.

COLONIAL CLOTHING TRADES AND CRAFTS

Wages for the Clothing Trades in Early Philadelphia

The evidence of the clothing trades in colonial America is scattered for the 17th century. Fortunately, we have the published report of Gabriel Thomas. Thomas, a member of the Society of Friends in London, had traveled to Philadelphia to gather information for a book intended to induce settlement in Pennsylvania and New Jersey. In his report, *An Historical and Geographical Account of Pennsylvania and of West-New-Jersey,* published in 1698, he listed textile trades currently active in Pennsylvania; these included bodice makers, skinners, furriers, glovers, and patten makers. Of the Germantown linen weavers, he noted that the quality of the fabric was "such as no Person of Quality need be asham'd to wear" and that in other areas woolen weavers produced "very good Druggets, Crapes, Camblets, and Serges." Thomas included an account of wages for certain trades practiced in Philadelphia. For example, a journeyman tailor received 12 shillings per week plus food. A journeyman shoemaker received two shillings per pair for men's and women's shoes. Weavers received 10–12 pence per yard for cloth that was about a half-yard wide. Wool combers were paid 12 pence per pound for processing fleece. "Tanners may buy their Hides green for Three Half Pence per Pound, and sell their Leather for Twelve Pence per Pound. And Curriers have Three Shillings and Four Pence per Hide for Dressing it; they buy their Oyl at Twenty Pence for Gallon." Felt makers could expect to sell hats for seven shillings a piece when a comparable hat in England would have cost two shillings "yet they buy their wooll commonly for Twelve or Fifteen Pence per Pound."

As discussed earlier in this chapter, craftsmen and women in the textile and clothing trades were well established in the colonies by the late 17th century. In Britain, many of these trades had been incorporated into highly regulated companies or guilds—by 1747 there were 91 companies—each holding a monopoly on its crafts. For example, the Company of Cloth-Workers, or clothiers, chartered by the Crown in 1482, included weavers, fullers, and other cloth-dressing occupations. Cloth dyeing, however, was the province of members of the Company of Dyers, chartered in 1472. Knitted textiles were made under the supervision of the Company of Frame-Work Knitters, chartered in 1663. While common tailors were not incorporated, in practice, there was a strict division of labor. The guilds also firmly controlled instruction in the trades, from apprentice to craftsman, to journeyman, and finally to master. In Britain's colonies, however, such strict control over labor and production did not exist. The apprentice/journeyman system was fluid, and many in the trades diversified their practices.

The first groups to settle in southern colonies included craftsmen in the textile-producing trades and allied trades, such as tailor, shoemaker, and hatter; however, there was little immediate use for their services in those capacities. Once plantations were established on land no longer occupied by native inhabitants, most craftsmen turned to farming because there was little full-time call for their trades. Some artisans did succeed, however, especially shoemakers who prepared leather for other purposes and tailors and weavers who practiced their crafts as itinerants. Legal documents indicate that, for example, between 1650 and 1700, Virginia supported at least 46 male and two female weavers across 11 counties; there are records for 15 male weavers in Maryland in six counties; and South Carolina could boast of 11 male weavers, six of whom were French Huguenots (MESDA).

In contrast to the early experiences of craftsmen in southern colonies, William Penn argued that among those emigrants most fit to settle in Pennsylvania were "Weavers, Taylors, Tanners, Shoemakers . . . where they may be spared or are low in the World: And as they shall want no encouragement, so their Labour is worth more there than here, and there provision cheaper" (Penn 1912b, 209). In 1685, Penn reported that among the tradesmen practicing in Philadelphia were tailors, shoemakers, glovers, tanners, and fellmongers (Penn 1912a, 261). These latter were craftsmen who prepared animal skins for tanning. Germans who settled in the colony—in Germantown—manufactured linen fabrics that in the 1680s were valued for their fineness.

Puritan Edward Johnson (1598–1672) noted that in the first half of the century of settlement in Massachusetts, "Farmers deem it better for their profit to put away [i.e., sell] their cattel and corn for cloathing, then to set upon making of cloth" (Johnson 1910, 211). Observing in 1642 that although flax and hemp could be grown easily and sheep flocks were on the increase, Johnson opined that cattle and corn sales (to English emigrants) were more profitable and less labor intensive. This situation changed before the end of the decade. Immigration slowed to a trickle as religious dissenters found reasons to stay in Puritan-controlled England. With fewer new customers, the price of cattle plummeted, and farmers and merchants alike lacked the revenue needed to purchase consumer goods. Pastoral pursuits became more profitable and acreage further inland had been cleared for cultivation and pasturing. Wolf populations, which had been a major threat to sheep, had succumbed to bounties.

In New England, once clothing trades had been established, it was common for some trades to receive town aid. For example, in 1656, Chelmsford (the present city of Lowell, Massachusetts), granted 12 acres of meadow and an equal plot of upland to William How, "provided he set up his trade of weaving and perform the town's work." In 1643, the town of Reading, Massachusetts, allotted land to a shoemaker; in 1699, Newbury gave land to a tanner (Clark 1916, 41).

Northern towns also gave assistance to new undertakings in the form of loans. For example, in 1685, Salem, Massachusetts, loaned John Wareing £5 to pay his spinners. In 1722, Boston loaned £300 for seven years to carry on spinning activities (Clark 1916, 42). Later in the 18th century, Pennsylvania gave aid in the form of loans or subscriptions to manufacturing societies and companies. In contrast, little of this kind of aid was given to tradesmen in the southern colonies because land was not held in the same kind of local control as in the north and the sparse settlement could not support small tradesmen. An exception was an act passed by Maryland in 1694 providing freemen's rights to tradesmen in the port town of Annapolis and sites in the town pasture to tradesmen, including tanners and dyers, who followed their trades (Clark 1916, 42).

By the mid-18th century, most population centers of even modest size could meet the apparel needs of many of their inhabitants. For example, Chester County, in southwestern Pennsylvania, was an essentially rural and agricultural region. It boasted many farmers who also possessed trade- or craft-related tools and equipment that went beyond the quantity necessary to create or repair farming equipment or personal goods. These farmers were invested in their crafts, serving local needs if not producing for more distant markets. Between 1750 and 1800 the county's towns included leather workers, cordwainers, heel makers, and leather breeches makers; textile artisans including weavers, spinners, lace makers, blue dyers, calico printers, fullers, wool combers, and bleacher; makers of spinning wheels, looms, and reeds; and clothing specialists such as tailors, milliners, mantua makers, staymakers, cap makers, hatters, stocking weavers, and hosiers (Hersh and Hersh 1995, 12–13). Some trades coalesced around a single town, but at least in the northern colonies weavers, tailors, and cordwainers were at work in small communities as well as in the largest urban centers.

Apprentices trained in the colonies were augmented by immigration, both free and forced. Indentured servants and convicts who had experience in the clothing trades—not only English, Scottish, and Irish but also German, Dutch, Welsh, and Swedish—arrived in colonial ports; sometimes their indentures were purchased by a tradesman in a related craft. For example, in February of 1741 a group of indentured servants—"all are young men and not convicts"—from Cork landed in Charleston; among them were a shoe maker, two weavers, and a tailor (*South-Carolina Gazette*, February 19). In 1752, the ship *Burwell*, from Ireland, delivered indentured seamstresses, stay makers, and mantua makers to West Point, on the York River (*Virginia Gazette*, May 8). A "parcel of likely men and women servants" who arrived in Philadelphia from Ireland in 1751 included shoemakers, tailors, weavers, woolcombers, peruke makers, skinners, breeches makers, and stay makers (*Pennsylvania Gazette*, August 8).

Not all Africans who were forcibly removed to the colonies worked as enslaved field hands or general house servants. Runaway and sale advertisements and legal documents attest to the high level of skills that some enslaved workers acquired. In Philadelphia, for example, Thomas Rodgers advertised for sale a young black man, "about 18 or 19 Years of Age, can make six or seven pair of Shoes a Week" (*Pennsylvania Gazette*, December 3, 1741). Another Philadelphia notice offered for sale a young enslaved man who was "a taylor by trade" (*Pennsylvania Gazette*, July 25, 1751). The *South-Carolina Gazette* included a number of notices for enslaved females for sale or hire that mention needlework skills; a 1745 notice reads, "TO BE HIRED OUT, a Home-born Negro Girl, about 13 or 14 Years of Age, who has been for some Years past kept employ'd at her Needle" (December 16). An enslaved woman named Patt, a weaver by trade, was part of an inheritance battle in Gloucester County, Virginia, in 1763 (*Virginia Gazette*, November 4).

While some artisans and mechanics clearly practiced one trade, many others diversified, probably to ensure a broader client base and earn a more comfortable living. Other workers drifted in and out of the trades or took work on a part-time basis if their other work was slow. This was particularly true of schoolmistresses who not only taught but also did seamstress work.

Elisha Clapp, of Little Compton, Rhode Island, owned both wig-making equipment and shoemaking tools and a workbench, which he left to his daughters at his death in 1777 (Wilbour 1945, 93). John Higgins, a barber and peruke maker in Maryland, maintained his business after his marriage to the widow of a tavern keeper—perhaps leaving the majority of the tavern work to his new wife (*Pennsylvania Gazette*, April 3, 1766). In 18th-century Georgia, a young and less wealthy colony, Thomas Mills made wigs but also sold imported jewelry and luxury foodstuffs, while John Doors combined wig making with the role of planter (Davis 1976, 110).

The following sections, while not an exhaustive list, discuss the most common colonial clothing-related trades.

Bleacher

The process of bleaching fabrics has been discussed earlier in this chapter. For most of the colonial period, whitening clothing was either a household task or the specialty of a laundress or scourer in the trade. Whitening of homespun fabrics certainly was attempted in the home, and scattered newspaper notices reference commercial ventures.

Eastern Pennsylvanians who engaged in home production of fabrics had access to several Philadelphians who offered bleaching services. James Rogers advertised his services as a linen bleacher, in 1747 (*Pennsylvania Gazette*, April 23); 10 years later Thomas Bury noted that he had a bleaching green where linen and cotton fabric would be whitened (*Pennsylvania Gazette*, May 5, 1757). This latter business was still thriving in 1765. The United Company of Philadelphia for Promoting American Manufactures, established in 1775 operated a bleachery outside of Philadelphia. Customers were requested to cut their lengths, or pieces, of cloth to about 25 yards each and "to mark their names at one end, and the number of yards at the other, with thread [i.e., linen thread], as silk or worsted, will wear out in the bleaching" (*Pennsylvania Gazette*, November 22, 1775).

Cleaner

As reflected in newspaper advertisements, cleaning clothes was often undertaken as a service by dyers or tailors. Petersburg, Virginia, tailor Robert Hitchings did not himself clean garments but offered to send gentlemen's or ladies' attire, "either Woolen or Silk," to "a complete Workman" in London who would do the task (*Virginia Gazette*, July 4, 1751). See also Dyer, Fuller, Lace Maker, and Laundress.

Clothier

In 16th- and 17th-century Britain, clothiers were weavers who were successful enough in business to have become masters, with several looms at work and employing apprentices, journeymen, and women. Some clothiers also employed their own carders, spinners, warpers, and even fullers and dyers (Kerridge 1985, 176–213). This is likely the sense in which the term was used in 17th-century colonial America. Judging from colonial newspaper notices, however, early in the 18th century the business of the clothier had evolved from overseer to a textile jack-of-all trades for the finishing aspects of textile production. For example, James Baird, self-identified as a clothier from Europe, advertised his services to Philadelphians, noting that he was engaged in "Fulling, dying and dressing of all Manner of Country made Woollen Cloth, Camblets, Worsteds, and Blanketing. Also scowering, and taking out Stains, and restoring the Colours of all Manner of Broadcloths, Silks, Plush, Cotton Velvets, &c." He also offered to clean fabrics for merchants and shopkeepers that were damaged in transit or were mildewed and to clean "made up Garments" (*Pennsylvania Gazette*, October 7, 1762).

In northern colonies the clothier became more important as the production of homespun fabrics expanded, especially in response to Britain's tariff laws of the late 1760s. For example, a notice from Boston reported, "A clergyman from the country lately appeared in town with a black cloak, made of fine cloth, manufactured in his family and finely dyed and dressed by a clothier in his town" (*Pennsylvania Gazette*, December 10, 1767). In 1767, Captain Walter, a Connecticut clothier, dressed "5915 yards of Wollen and linen cloth besides 300 yards manufactured in his own family" (*Pennsylvania Gazette*, April 25, 1768). Elijah Hollister, from Scotland, and Thomas-Smith Sterne, from Europe, formed a clothier trade partnership in Hartford, Connecticut, in the 1760s. Although they cleaned wool and silk garments and watered silk gowns, their specialty seems to have been dyeing, in "all colours, such as Blue, Green, Pompedore, Portabellow, Claret, Bloom Claret, Snuffs, and a great variety besides." They also dyed "any colour in the skain for Plads" (*Connecticut Courant*, August 25, 1772). See also Dyer and Fuller.

Dyer and Fabric Printer

In the colonies as well as in Britain, the business of the dyer usually included finishing, or dressing, the fabric as well as coloring it. While there is no evidence that fabric dyers were practicing their trade in southern colonies in the 17th century, a few dyers had established themselves in New England to meet the increasing wants of those who produced homespun. Benjamin Franklin's father, Josiah, was born into a dyer's family and was apprenticed as a dyer himself. He and his family settled in Boston in 1683, but Josiah found that the demand for his trade was low and turned to the trades of tallow chandler and soap boiler.

By the end of the 1600s, however, the trade of dyer was well established in Boston. Silk dyer Ambrose Vincent was in business before the end of the century. In 1711, his business was destroyed in the disastrous fire that took much of the area on and around Cornhill Street. In an advertisement announcing his move to another location, he identified himself as "Silk Dyer and Scowrer . . . who dyes all manner of Silks, Cloth and Stuff; and Scowres Mens Coats" (*Boston News-Letter*, November 5, 1711). The 1695 inventory of John Cornish, also of Boston, reveals the scope of one such business. Cornish had two furnaces in which he dyed wool; supplies of galls, red wood, potash, madder, and fustic to dye ranges of reds, yellows, and browns; copperas, a mordant used with indigo to produce blue; and pounds of worsted (long fiber) and noil (short fiber) wool undyed, mixed colored, blue, and white. Cornish owned combing cards and four looms but no spinning wheels, an indication that his raw wool went to others to be spun into thread for warps and wefts. In addition to dyeing and weaving, Cornish was able to full fabrics for his customers because his real estate holdings included a fulling mill (quoted in Weeden 1894, 390).

In the first three decades of the 18th century, Boston was home to at least nine self-described dyers, who also provided finishing services such as scouring, calendering, and fulling. In 1712, the aforementioned Ambrose Vincent faced competitors George Leason and Thomas Webber, who set up a dye house and calendering mill and offered to dye and scower "all sorts of silks" (*Boston News-Letter*, April 28, 1712). In 1722, Webber had a new partner, Samuel Hall, with whom he advertised the additional services of watering and scouring plus making linen cloth into buckram by finishing it with starch or other stiffeners (*Boston News-Letter*, June 25, 1722). The advertisement of Edward Carter, whose shop appropriately was named the Rainbow and Blew Hand, illustrates the range of fabrics and apparel that the trade handled for shops as well as individuals. Carter "Dy'd and Scower'd all Sorts of Brocades, Velvets, Damasks, Sattins, Lystrings, Tabbies, Burdets, Mohairs, Poplins, Sasnets, Persions, Cloths, Camblets, Stuffs, Linnins, Needlework and embroydery, Black Silks, White Sasnet-Hoods, Fine Chince and Callacoes, Men's and Women's Silk & Worsted Hose, . . . New Clothes Scower'd Wet & Dry, all Sorts of Shop Goods Callendard, Prest and Pack'd for Sale" (*Boston Gazette*, April 22, 1728).

When Alexander Fleming announced the opening of his dye business in Boston in 1754, he made it clear that not only was he a competent dyer of all shades on wool and silk, but he could also handle a few colors on linen yarn, and would undertake the processes of shearing, dressing, watering, and cleaning of fabrics and clothing as well (*Boston Gazette*, May 14, 1754). A competitor, Irish printer and dyer John Hickey, advertised in 1759 that he alone would guarantee his work to compare favorably with European goods, "as there has been several who have imposed upon this country in telling that they were printers" (*Boston Gazette*, May 7, 1759). Like Fleming, Hickey offered all manner of colors on silk and wool but only blue and "London red" on linen or cotton. This is probably the same John Hickey who briefly had been in business in Philadelphia as a linen stamper and dyer in 1754–1755 and who moved to Portsmouth, New Hampshire, in 1761, working there into the 1770s (*Pennsylvania Gazette*, June 6, 1754; October 2, 1755; *New-Hampshire Gazette*, March 27, 1761; *New-Hampshire Gazette, and Historical Chronicle*, November 15, 1771).

There was enough custom in the silk-dying trade to support a number of tradesmen in Philadelphia. The first to advertise was Michael Brown, who operated as a silk dyer and dry or wet scourer from at least 1737 until his death before 1758 (*Pennsylvania Gazette*, July 7, 1737; May 2, 1751). Brown also dyed cotton and linen clothing. He addressed the problems of shipping merchandize by sea by offering to take mildew and stains out of silk and wool fabrics thus affected. After his death his wife continued the business, sometimes with a male partner and sometimes on her own, until her death in 1764 (*Pennsylvania Gazette*, July 20, 1758; May 21, 1761; March 22, 1764).

Over 20 tradesmen advertised themselves as dyers in Philadelphia after 1750. Among them were blue dyers, experts in handling indigo. Frederick Pohlman and Jacob Beck may have used indigo to produce resist dye patterns as well as dyeing whole pieces of cloth (Eaton 2009). London-trained James Clark opened his business in 1774, offering a broad range of colors; he noted that he dyed black every Friday (*Pennsylvania Gazette*, September 28, 1774). In 1775, Clark solicited the custom of manufacturers, touting his years of experience in indigo dyeing on cotton and linen yarns to manufacturers' satisfaction (*Pennsylvania Gazette*, June 21, 1775). Clark's business survived the Revolution, and he was still advertising in 1784.

Notices for dyeing operations did not appear in southern colonies until late in the period. In 1771, South Carolinians Levi Manning and Andrew Lee purchased a saw, fulling, and grist mill with the intent of converting it to a dyeing and fulling operation (*South Carolina Gazette*, November 14, 1771). John Brown began advertising in South Carolina in 1773, noting that his dye house took silk and woolen clothing; he also scoured clothing (*South Carolina Gazette*, June 14, 1773).

In addition to dyeing, skilled tradesmen engaged in printing patterns on silk and wool and mordant dyeing patterns on cotton and linen. One early anonymous advertisement from the *Boston Gazette* reads: "The Printer hereof Prints Linens, Callicoes, Silks, &c. in good Figures, very lively and durable Colours, and without the offensive smell which commonly attends the Linens Printed here" (April 18, 1720). Clearly the craft had been established for a time, although not, perhaps, very competently practiced. Fourteen calico printers are reported to have advertised in New England newspapers between 1712 and 1776; there were undoubtedly more who had no need to advertise (Pettit 1976, 34). Michael Brown, discussed above, added linen stamping in three shades—blue, purple, and black—to his services in 1743 (*Pennsylvania Gazette*, December 1). French dyer Christian Rudolph offered linen and cotton stamping along with dyeing on silk, worsted, and cotton at his Philadelphia workshop in 1767 (*Pennsylvania Gazette*, March 12).

Some mordant printing was practiced in Virginia. At his death in 1762, Lazerus Coppedge, of Northumberland County, left one set of stamping instruments, oil for stamping, "sundry Stamping Coulers," indigo dye, alum, and a copper boiling pot (MESDA). In 1779, in Accomack County, Edward Taylor paid Hannah Emerson, a widow, 24 pence a yard "for Stamping 87 yards of Linen," for a total of £8.14 (MESDA).

The only colonial printer whose work is extant, however, is John Hewson, a self-described calico printer. In 1774, with encouragement from Benjamin Franklin, and in open defiance of the law against importing fabric printing tools and equipment from Britain and the Continent, Hewson opened a business that included a printworks in Philadelphia and a bleachery in Kensington, about a mile outside of the city. He advertised that his patterns, which could be printed in a variety of colors, consisted of designs for printing "calicoes and linens for gowns, &c. coverlids, handkerchiefs, nankeens, janes and velverets, for waistcoats and breeches, &c" (*Pennsylvania Gazette*, July 20, 1774). He also printed homespun. In 1778, during the British occupation of Philadelphia, loyalists destroyed Hewson's equipment and a number of prints (*Pennsylvania Gazette*, October 15, 1778). Serving for a time in the patriot cause, he reopened the printworks in 1781.

Likely one of Hewson's early works is a handkerchief whose subject is George Washington on horseback, surrounded by eight cannons and four flags, and all within a frame of flower sprays and gatherings of munitions. Evidence suggests that Martha Washington ordered the textile print from Hewson during her visit to Philadelphia in 1775 (Monsky 2002, 239–64).

Printed cotton handkerchief with likeness of George Washington on horseback, attributed to John Hewson, 1775–1800. (Collection of the New York Historical Society, USA/The Bridgeman Art Library)

She is known to have received, while in the city, a copy of an English engraving of Washington by C. Shepherd. This engraving is the source of the printed textile image of the commander-in-chief. (Perhaps encouraged by Hewson's success, two printworks opened in Providence, Rhode Island, in about 1780. The first was run by Zachariah Allen and Herman VanDausen, the second by Jeremiah Eddy. Neither seems to have been long lived.)

Textile dyes were readily available. In addition to dry goods and food stuffs, Joseph Saunders of Philadelphia sold "madder, ground red wood, fustick, galls, log wood, and brazilletto, indigo, allom, copperas, brimstone" (*Pennsylvania Gazette*, October 25, 1753). Solomon Fussell, also of Philadelphia, imported and advertised "ground redwood, ground fustick, umber, madder, venetian red, yellow oker, Spanish brown, &c. brimstone" (*Pennsylvania Gazette*, March 23, 1758). In the 1770s, Hartford, Connecticut, tradesman Samuel Marsh offered "For Clothier's Use, Redwood, Logwood, Fustic, Allum, Copperas, Oil Vitriol, Press and Catridge Paper, and Indico" (*The Connecticut Courant and Hartford Weekly Intelligencer*, October 23, 1775).

In South Carolina, planters and merchants seem not to have been as interested in importing dyes as they were in manufacturing them for export. In 1739, a two-part article on the "Description of Cocheneal, and the Manner of raising and curing it" ran in the *South Carolina Gazette* (March 17 and 24, 1739). Cochineal is an insect that thrives on the prickly pear cactus and produces a fast, bright red. Harvested as a dyestuff in pre-European contact times by Native groups especially in what is now Central and South America, cochineal was introduced into Europe by the Spanish. In the 18th century, the dye was an expensive but superior alternative to madder. There is no record, however, that production of cochineal was ever attempted in the colony. In the early 1740s, raising and processing indigo came to interest South Carolina planters, who were aided by helpful how-to articles in the *Gazette* and James de la Chappelle's printed instructions for making the dye, which were translated and published in the colony. De la Chappelle was in South Carolina by November of 1746 to work with planters and train overseers (*South-Carolina Gazette*, November 10, 1746). By the end of the decade, the price of indigo was listed in every issue of the newspaper and considered a staple product of the colony.

Embroiderer

Both the activities of amateur embroiderers and embroidery instruction for young girls by schoolmistresses have been documented for colonial North America in numerous volumes and are beyond the scope of this work. However, a number of women who ran schools and/or millinery establishments also offered to do professional embroidery work. Philadelphia's Madame Bontamps advertised millinery skills that included mending lace and doing tambour embroidery in metal threads, silk, or linen (*Pennsylvania Gazette*, December 29, 1768). Charleston's Frances Swallow carried "a variety of gold and silver thread and spangles for tambour work" and offered to make bespoke pieces (*South-Carolina and American General Gazette*, October 9, 1769). In 1773, a Mrs. Hughes of Norfolk, Virginia, announced that her daughter would begin teaching young ladies Tambour Work and that "Gentlemens Tambour Jackets" may be made up to order (*Virginia Gazette*, December 16). In New York, a Mrs. Cole worked with the needle and the tambour hook. She drew and worked needlework designs on shoes for one dollar per pair or on fabric yardage for making up into ladies gowns at two dollars per yard. She also worked "suits of linen," men's waistcoats ranging in price from 24 to 40 shillings, or in gold metal threads from three to five pounds sterling (Gottesman 1938, 280).

Embroidery work was not limited to females. New York's Levy Simons, a professional embroiderer from London, ornamented clothing and accessory items for men and women in silk, metal threads, and worsted wool (Gottesman 1938, 277).

Fuller

In his *The London Tradesman* (1747), Robert Campbell (1969, 201) explained that the business of the fuller was "to mill and thicken Cloth, lay the Wool one Way, cut it off equal with the Sheers, and smooth it with Tazels and then press it." Advertisements by or about colonial fullers (many of whom adopted the title clothier) list the same kinds of processes for woolen and worsted fabrics: fulling, finishing or dressing, carding, shearing, tentering, calendering, glazing, and pressing. Some fullers offered wet and dry scowering (cleaning) and dyeing services for silk and linen fabrics or garments, and a few dyed leather and reglazed printed cottons. The mills were located at the edge of a stream or river, which supplied the constant source of clear, running water required in textile finishing. In many advertisements, fullers and clothiers list the days of the week when they would be in town to pick up goods for processing or bring back the finished work.

The fuller's trade prospered in all areas of the colonies where homespun was produced in some quantity. Domestically produced cloth looked better when professionally finished: a 1748 notice describing the physical appearance of a runaway listed a waistcoat "made of country cloth, but as it has been dressed at the fulling mill it appears something like plains" (*Pennsylvania Gazette*, June 16, 1748). Fabrics of all kinds were subject to spotting, staining, and mildewing from damp conditions during sea voyages from Britain or the intercoastal trade. Since fabrics were expensive, refinishing or redyeing damaged goods made economic sense, and the process might also make old garments look new or at least suitable for handing down to a servant or cutting up for younger members of a household.

Perhaps the earliest colonial textile mill was the fulling mill that opened in 1643, in Rowley, Massachusetts. The subsequent opening of fulling mills throughout northern colonies—New London in 1693; Bissell's Mills, a village in Rhode Island's Narragansett plantation country, in 1720; Christopher Leffingwell's fulling mill and dyehouse in 1770, in Norwich, Connecticut; and the 12 that existed in Philadelphia in 1770—are evidence that communities of weavers were large enough to support these businesses (Woodward 1971, 111; Bridenbaugh 1950, 47; Walton 1937, 213). The mills usually supported a number of workmen. Boston clothier Samuel Foster hired indentured servants to work for him in the 1730s, including a young Irish man whose trade was worsted combing (*Boston News-Letter*, April 28, 1737). Even in smaller population centers the fuller's trade was important to the community. Norwich, Connecticut's clothier, John Brown, asked for and received financial support from the colony's Council in early 1714, after a long illness kept him from work and medical bills had eaten up all his savings (Hoadly 1870, 420).

Advertisements in Boston, New York, and Philadelphia newspapers indicate that in the 1700s fulling mills started up regularly. They were sold or rented regularly as well, sometimes as going concerns when artisans retired or died or sometimes as failed, but potentially lucrative, businesses. A fulling mill advertised for sale in the *New-York Weekly Journal* in 1738 counted among its equipment two dyeing furnaces, two pair of shears and a separate press house with a "press plate, screw, and other necessary tools" (February 6, 1738). Fuller Samuel Kitchen of Amwell, West Jersey, advertised in the *Pennsylvania Gazette* for another craftsman as a partner or lessee, stating "there is always plenty of work" (November 21, 1771). The fuller's trade was not practiced to any extent in southern colonies until the 1770s.

Goldsmith and Jeweler

Britain's guild system distinguished between the goldsmith, who also worked in silver, and the jeweler. The former concerned himself with constructing larger objects for use or ornament, the latter "only in Toys [i.e., trinkets] and Jewels" (Campbell 1969, 143). In the colonies this distinction was blurred, and goldsmiths and jewelers sold imported as well as bespoke items. Craftsmen who worked in larger population centers had sufficient patronage to make bespoke items, and they employed apprentices, indentured servants, and enslaved help who were trained in the trade.

Besides objects for household use and ornament—plates and cans, bowls and trays, candlesticks and clocks—these craftsmen carried the many accessory items that were indispensable to dressing to one's station. While evidence for colonial production in the 17th century is fragmentary, accessories like lockets, seals, buttons, buckles, rings, and necklaces were imported from Britain by the 1650s. By the 1730s all manner of personal luxuries were either imported into or made in the colonies: snuffboxes; étuis; toothpick and patch boxes; seals; cane heads; watches and watch chains; stay hooks; sword hangers; lockets, brooches, necklaces, mourning and fancy rings, and earrings; hair pins and sprigs. Lost and found and theft notices illustrate the range of jewelry and other personal accessories possessed and worn by colonists of all ranks.

Boston supported goldsmiths by the second half of the 17th century, but James Boyer was perhaps that city's first jeweler. In January 1723, Boyer, newly arrived from London, advertised in the *New England Courant* that he "setts all manner of Stones in Rings, &c. and performes every thing belonging to that Trade" (Dow 1935, 132–33). Mr. Boyer may have been incompetent or profligate or Boston may have preferred imported goods, because he died in 1741 "intestate and insolvent" (Dow 1927, 82). Boyer had local competition from at least two other jewelers, William Cario and Stephen Winter, as well as from goldsmiths who offered imported jewelry.

Between 1759 and 1771, Boston goldsmith Daniel Parker advertised his latest imports from London as well as thefts from his shop. An enterprising merchant, Parker supplied tools and wares to other craftsmen in the trade as well as offered imported finished goods and loose gem stones. In 1761, his shop was robbed of "Silver Shoe and Knee Buckles, large and small Spoons, Gold Necklaces and Earings, Stone Buttons set in Silver, &c. to the value of several Hundred Pounds" (quoted in Dow 1927, 70).

Edmund Milne of Philadelphia, who variously referred to himself as a silversmith, goldsmith, and jeweler, carried an extensive stock of imported accessories and jewelry. His advertised inventory included gilt, silvered, plated, "sanguined," garnet, paste and stone shoe and knee buckles; metal, silver, and gold seals; mochoa (mocha stone, or moss agate) sleeve buttons in gold, brown and white crystal, and topaz; gold, silver and silver gilt Mason's medals, gold and silver watches in engine-turned cases with gold, silver, and silk watch chains and strings. Women's accessories included diamond, false stone, green paste, garnet, and fancy rings; bracelets; gold and gilt brooches; and for children he had chased and plain gold lockets to wear around the neck (*Pennsylvania Gazette*, October 18, 1764). Competitor Charles Dutens, a London jeweler who had settled in Philadelphia, made and sold diamond rings, earrings, solitaires, stone lockets, and seals set in gold; and he engraved and enameled mourning rings. In 1752, he had loose stones—diamonds, rubies, opal, emeralds, amethysts, garnets, and all kinds of crystals—for rings, earrings, and lockets (*Pennsylvania Gazette*, November 30).

Jeweler John Paul Grimké (1713–1791), grandfather of the abolitionist sisters Sarah and Angelina Grimké, began his business in Charleston in July 1740 making and mending "all sorts of Jeweller's Work (*South-Carolina Gazette*, July 25). In November of that year a fire destroyed more than 300 houses and commercial buildings, including Grimké's shop. Less than a year later he was back in business in Charleston, advertising "a fresh assortment of Brilliant and Rose Diamonds, Rubies, Emeralds, Saphirs, Jacints, Topaz's, Amethists, Turky Stones, Garnett, and some ready made Rings" (*South-Carolina Gazette*, September 19, 1741). By 1743, he offered Charleston's residents, in addition to household silver, a wide assortment of men's and women's shoe buckles, some set with stones; waistband breeches buckles; spurs and sword belts; watch chains; fashionable fans; "necklaces and Lockets set with divers sorts of stones . . . silver framed spectacles . . . ear rings with single drops and three drops"—all imported from London (*South-Carolina Gazette*, May 23). About a decade later he was lending money on plate and jewelry (*South-Carolina Gazette*, November 20, 1755). Illustrating the extraordinary depth and breadth of his imported inventory, Grimké's advertisement of 1759 now included silver accessories for the Indian trade (*South-Carolina Gazette*, November 24).

With his gradual change in fortune, Grimké must have begun work on bespoke pieces because in 1752 he employed an enslaved silversmith (*South-Carolina Gazette*, August 10). The next year he offered for sale two enslaved boys brought up in the jeweler's trade "who can make gold rings and buttons, [and] engrave them very neatly" (*South-Carolina Gazette*, January 8, 1753). In July 1771, Grimké hired out a 16-year-old slave named Joe to another Charleston jeweler, James Oliphant. One month later the boy had disappeared, together with the money for his hire. According to runaway notices, Joe was well known in town, having worked for Grimké at the jeweler's trade (*South-Carolina Gazette; and Country Journal*, September 3, 1771; *South-Carolina and American General Gazette*, January 6, 1772).

By the 1760s even Georgia could boast of more than one local silversmith and goldsmith. Wigmaker Thomas Mills sold imported jewelry in his shop; William Sime, a goldsmith, did the same, while making some of his own products as well. Adrian Loyer, a Savannah silversmith, was so successful that he brought not only jewelry but also a skilled assistant over from London—perhaps the assistant was the runaway apprentice Loyer advertised about in 1774 (Davis 1976, 96, 107–08).

Hatter

In the 17th and 18th centuries, hatters were responsible for the construction of head coverings made of felted fur—from beaver, raccoon, fox, rabbit, and the like—and wool. A hatter was among the first 104 colonists to arrive in Plymouth in 1620, but it is unlikely that in his new wilderness home he had any call or opportunity to practice his trade in the initial years of settlement. By midcentury, however, in spite of England's desire to use the American colonies only as a source of raw materials and a market for finished goods, colonial hatters enjoyed a brisk business. These manufactures developed in competition with English goods, for both colonial consumption and export abroad. For example, in 1662 the Virginia Assembly offered 10 pounds of tobacco for every felt hat of good quality, made from the then-abundant fur of indigenous mammals.

Recognizing the strength of colonial hat manufacturing efforts, in 1732 Parliament passed the Hat Act, which attempted to prevent the export of finished hats from the American colonies and to restrict colonial manufacture by limiting the number of apprentices that colonial hat makers could train. Legal documents and the number and frequency of advertisements in northern and southern newspapers attest to the ineffectiveness of these proscriptions. The colonial port of Newport, Rhode Island, had at least one hatter, William Pinniger. In business by 1724, Pinniger sold his wares throughout New England for decades (Bridenbaugh 1950, 73). Little Compton, a relatively rural Rhode Island town in the colonial period, supported at least two generations of hatters in the first half of the 18th century. At his death in 1745, the town's hatter, Job Briggs, left a shop that had been bequeathed to him by his father. The inventory included hatter's tools, 77 musquash (muskrat) skins, 88 raccoon skins, and seven musk (beaver?) skins, along with a number of partially finished felt and beaver hats (Wilbour 1945, 42). Daniel Jones of Boston made his own beaver, beaveret, and castor hats and carried English-made castor and beaveret hats, felt hats, and hat linings and trims for sale (*Boston Gazette*, December 10, 1759). Nesbett Deane, an émigé from Dublin, made a similar line of goods in New York in 1765. Still active in 1771, he also made riding hats for men, women, and children (Gottesman 1938, 330).

A particularly rich source for the colonial hat-making trade, the advertisements of the *Pennsylvania Gazette* reveal facets of the trade from manufacture to wholesaling and business diversification. Few hatters advertised in the early years of the publication, whose inaugural issue appeared in 1728. The earliest mention, in 1730, was Jeremiah Clement's offer of an £8 reward for the return of his indentured servant. Clement was a hatter working in Chester, about 16 miles west of Philadelphia. Lawrence Murphy, the runaway in question, was skilled in both hat making and woolen weaving (May 21, 1730). More than ten hatters plied their trade in Philadelphia from the 1740s to the end of the colonial period. Charles Moore carried on his hatmaking business from at least 1740 to 1761, employing both indentured servants and apprentices to help him with his workload (March 27, 1740; March 11, 1756; December 3, 1761). In 1765, Richard Swan retailed gentlemen's and ladies' hats and offered them wholesale by the dozen to country storekeepers (February 21, 1765). This same year two competitors, Samuel Davis and Job Bacon, joined forces to establish a wholesale/retail "Manufactory for making Wool [felt] Hats" for men, women, and boys (February 28, 1765). In 1771, Caleb Hewes added a manufactory for wool hats to his regular business of making castor and beaver hats. Hewes, too, solicited wholesale and retail business (April 18). David Richardson sold hatter's trimmings and oiled cloth covers to protect hats from rain and snow and covered old hats to make them look new (November 23, 1774). Caleb Attmore was a successful hatter who survived the economic vagaries of the Revolution. In 1786, he wholesaled a good assortment of hat trimmings, including linings, hat bands, binding, cord, looping, and hatter's brushes as well as "country made felt hats by the dozen" (May 24, 1786).

Further south, William Dubberley set up a hat-making trade in Williamsburg, Virginia, in 1737 to produce men's and women's beaver hats "of any fashion or size." He also purchased "Beaver, Furr, Raccoon, Fox, Muskrat, and Hare Skins," cleaned old hats, and dyed silks, wools, and woollens (*Virginia Gazette,* July 8, 1737). Two years later Dubberley advertised, noting that his dyeing would "hold a reasonable Time, as well as any European Hats whatever" (*Virginia Gazette,* September 21, 1739).

Charleston, South Carolina, residents supported a number of hatters in the 18th century; the situations of these craftsmen compare with those of their northern counterparts. Hatter William Glen advertised in 1734 that he would pay "any person white Man or Negro" 2 shillings 6 pence for every fox or raccoon skin brought to him at his business on Broad Street (*South-Carolina Gazette,* October 26). He was still practicing his trade in the 1760s. John Gissentanner apprenticed with Glen and then established his own hat-making business in 1769 (*South-Carolina Gazette; and Country Journal,* August 1). Nathaniel Shephard had sufficient business in 1772 that he advertised for an apprentice (*South-Carolina Gazette; and Country Journal,* March 31).

Knitter, Stocking Weaver, Hosier

Although the bulk of the knitted goods—both hand-knit and loomed—sold in colonial America were imports, there are scattered references to colonial manufacture in the north. Germantown, Pennsylvania, was well established as a hand-knitting center by the 1750s. A British minister traveling in the region noted that in 1759, "the women of Germantown sold 60,000 pair of stockings of their own make" (quoted in Macdonald 1988, 6). Stocking frames had been introduced in the colonies before the 1740s;

Robert and Amos Strettell offered two such looms for sale in their Philadelphia dry goods shop in 1745 (*Pennsylvania Gazette*, June 13). In 1746, John George Cook, of New York, owned three looms and was knitting silk, cotton, worsted, and "country yarn" (i.e., linen) stockings (Gottesman 1938, 257). Philadelphia's The Hand-in-Stocking Manufactory was in operation by June of 1761 and possibly utilized looms. The business offered locally made three-thread worsted, linen and cotton stockings as well as knitted waistcoat and breeches patterns. Germantown- and Philadelphia-made stockings and gloves also were available wholesale, by the dozen (*Pennsylvania Gazette*, June 11).

Others in the trades specialized in repairing knitted goods. In 1748, Elizabeth Boyd of New York advertised that she repaired stockings and knit new items from old ones: "All sorts of Stockings new grafted and run at the Heels, and footed; also Gloves, mittens and Children's Stockings made out of Stockings." A notice appearing three years later indicates some success in this business: "Elizabeth . . . will continue, as usual, to graft Pieces in Knit Jackets and Breeches, not to be discern'd, also to graft and foot Stockings, and Gentlemen's Gloves, Mittens or Muffatees made out of old Stockings, or runs them in the Heels. She likewise makes Children's Stockings out of old ones."

Lace Maker, Lace Cleaner

England's lace industry was well established by 1600, but the country still received—and its wealthier wearers demanded—imports from Flanders and Italy. Although some laces—especially those made of gold, silver, and gilt silver metallic threads—were made by skilled craftspeople in the trades and some laces were made by the middling ranks for their own use, the craft was primarily an occupation for poor women. Because the use of lace was tied inextricably to mercurial changes in fashion, the livelihood of the lace maker was precarious. The work itself could cause severe eye strain and postural defects and in the case of lace created with linen thread, which was worked in damp conditions, lung problems.

In the 1600s, the decision to wear needle- or bobbin-made lace was determined by both clothing fashion and fabric design. Lace produced with a needle and thread was much heavier than that produced with bobbins and was seen to best effect when lying flat against the body or only gently gathered. Because of its visual—as well as actual—weight, needle lace was more appropriate for garments made of heavier textiles or those having a highly textured surface, such as velvets and napped fabrics. Bobbin lace gradually emerged as fashion's favorite before the end of the century because of its opacity and softness (Levey 1983, 24). Its delicate look enhanced satin-weave silks in single colors and the lighter weight cottons exported from India in the second half of the century. Equally important, lace designers could adapt bobbin lace designs to match whatever fabric designs were in fashion; needle lace was much less versatile in this regard.

Lacemaking in the colonies was primarily the work of individual women and girls, who produced lace trimmings of linen thread for consumption within the family and sometimes for local sale. Very few period records survive to document this activity. One of the earliest is a court case involving Elizabeth Dew (also Due), a young woman trained as a lace maker who was employed as a domestic servant in the household of Massachusetts Governor John Endicott. In June of 1654, as the

The lace-maker, by Wenceslaus Hollar, 1630. The young worker is making bobbin lace as evinced by the thread-wound bobbins draped off the sides of the pillow frame. (The Thomas Fisher Rare Book Library, University of Toronto)

defendant in a fornication case, Elizabeth claimed that the father of her unborn child was Endicott's son. She "complained of Zerubbabel Endicott's unseemly words and actions when she was at her work of lace making, pulling her cushion from before her" (Dow 1911, 1:361). The 1678 inventory of merchant Michaell Rochford, of Maryland, included eight parchment patterns on which to work needle lace (Maryland Prerogative Court 1679, 6:28). The 1742 inventory of Charleston resident John Sheppard included five pairs of bobbins, a parcel of linen thread, and a box in which to keep them (Inventory . . . of John Sheppard, 123). In 1770, Mary (Cary) Ambler (1733–1781), of Jamestown, Virginia, noted in her diary to order "a Groce of the smallest neat bobbins for Weaving Lace" for Sally, who was likely a household slave (Ambler 1937, 164). Late in the colonial period, Clara Trotti proposed to make "Thread [i.e., linen] lace of all Breaths, and to any Pattern" for Charleston residents (*South-Carolina; and American General Gazette*, September 4, 1777).

The one documented cottage industry for bobbin lace making was located in Ipswich, Massachusetts. Although this industry was at its height after the period under discussion, by the 1760s several Ipswich families were paying for goods with lace. For example, Mary Pitman, a widow, exchanged yards of linen lace for flour, molasses, sugar, and other necessities from dry goods merchant Ezekiel Dodge. Dodge's account book also shows payment in lace for imported chintz fabric (Raffel 2003, 17, 99). The laces produced in Ipswich were not on a par with the best European laces, the latter of which had complicated floral and arabesque patterns and were made in shapes for stomachers, caps, flounces, and sleeve ruffles. Examples from Ipswich that survive from the close of the century are narrow with fairly simple patterning and were likely used as edgings and trimmings.

Artisans in other textile-related trades sometimes noted that they cleaned lace. In 1739, Catherine Kay, of Charleston, advertised that she would wash and dress imported Brussels and Mechlin laces (*South-Carolina Gazette*, May 19, 1739). Robert Miller, a tailor, noted that he could remove stains from gold and silver lace and restore tarnished lace to its proper color (*Virginia Gazette*, December 22, 1752). In Philadelphia, Thomas Davies, a dry scourer from Dublin, specialized in cleaning gold and silver lace as well as embroidered and brocaded work (*Pennsylvania Gazette*, July 6, 1749). Also in Philadelphia, Mary Richardson announced that she performed clear starching on gauze and blond lace "done to appear as new, Dresden and sprigged work raised, and baby linen pinched" (*Pennsylvania Gazette*, July 25, 1771).

Laundress

In 1623, Jamestown, Virginia, resident Thomas Niccolls wrote an English correspondent that washing and soap for his clothing cost him £3 per annum and he wished that more women would be sent over (Kingsbury 1935, 4:231). Eventually more women did immigrate to southern ports as indentured servants to perform manual household labor. Later enslaved workers took over the task of washing shirts, shifts, stockings, neckwear, handkerchiefs, and diapers for their households. Advertisements for the sale of female slaves and the indentures of European servants are similar to the one placed by Margaret Warden for the sale of three slaves: "a venerable mustee wench that is a good seamstress, washes and irons very well, and . . . her daughter, a young wench grown, a very good washer and ironer. Likewise a girl about 11 years old, that works very well at her needle" (*South-Carolina Gazette*, August 27, 1750).

Washing was one facet of a range of services that a woman in the trades might advertise, but this cleaning was limited to fine accessories. For example, Elizabeth Prior, a clear starcher, advertised that she "WASHES Muslins, Lace, Gauze, Blown [blond?] worked Catgut, Silk Stockings,

&c" (*Pennsylvania Gazette*, May 9, 1765). The paucity of notices addressing washing in general is undoubtedly due to the fact that laundresses were among the working poor; they earned too little to afford advertisements and probably had a steady supply of customers for their services. Their activities can best be glimpsed in wills of the period, in which a male decedent provided the financial means for the upkeep of his surviving family in language similar to Charlestonian Henry Peronneau's: "Executors to sell &c. and while they board minor children with wife Elizabeth to allow £200 yearly . . . for dieting, washing, lodging, and mending of cloathes &c." ("South Carolina Gleanings in England" 1904, 219). Men in the cleaning trades, scourers, likely also took in washing and may have employed women for this service.

The soap most often used in washing linen apparel was composed of lime, animal fat in the form of tallow or oil (tallow for hard soap and oil for soft), salt, and ashes—all strained and boiled together. Many colonial households were equipped with a pot in which to make soap, but soap was also advertised in dry goods shops.

Leather Worker

Although hides and leather were among the most important colonial export products, not all hides were prepared for export. Leather working crafts abounded in the colonies, a dealer in hides arriving in Massachusetts as early as 1635 (Dow 1935, 129). The hides salvaged from butchering operations provided the raw material for tanners, glovers, and shoemakers.

Tanning was one of the earliest crafts to emerge in the colonies. In Massachusetts and Connecticut, tanneries operated before 1650 in Boston, Salem, Lynn, Charlestown, Watertown, Roxbury, and Newbury. Legislation controlling Connecticut's tanning trade was passed as early as 1640. New Haven traded its leather to Virginia by 1653. By the late 17th century tanning was an important industry in Pennsylvania, New York, New Jersey, and Delaware; the middle colonies had an abundance of trees from which to harvest tanning bark as well as easy access to a supply of hides from the Backcountry. Tanners were numerous enough in Boston in the 1740s to call general meetings of their trade to protest against the rising cost of raw hides (*Boston Weekly Post-Boy*, February 23, 1741; *Boston Gazette, or Weekly Journal*, December 29, 1747; January 5, 1748; January 19, 1748). Twenty-five tanners there agreed on a top purchase price for "green hides" as well as for sole leather of nine shillings per pound (Seybolt 1929, 307–9). One study of 18th-century probate inventories of tanners in New Hampshire, Massachusetts, and Delaware "show[s] that as artisans, they all amassed respectable quantities of plate, fine furniture, valuable land, and hard cash" (Welsh 1963, 300).

Because of the mess and the smell, tanners usually set up shop on the outskirts of a town, and many located their workshops on plantations. When William Reed decided to "decline the Business of Tanning," on Thomas Chalkley's plantation, he advertised the sale of his lease along with a parcel of newly tanned leather and tanning and currying tools (*Pennsylvania Gazette*, January 11, 1744).

Colonial glovers and breeches makers, who were often one-in-the-same craftsman, dealt with a different kind of leather than shoe makers. Leather for apparel and handwear was not tanned but alumed. Gloves were usually of sheep, kid or doe skin. Breeches were made of shammy (specially dressed sheep skin) or buck skin. Glovers made lined as well as unlined gloves, the former lined with fur or rabbit skin. Some produced fur muffs and tippets. Philip Freeman advertised in the *Boston Gazette* that he imported Norway doe gloves, sold winter gloves of his own manufacture, and relined old gloves with new fur. In a 1743 advertisement Freeman invited customers to purchase his black leather breeches and jackets, opining that they were "not to be discerned from the best superfine cloth." He also made a few other colors, and in 1754 advertised black, cloth-colored, and yellow leather stockings for sale (Dow 1935, 70, 131).

Buckskin breeches makers were located throughout the colonies. Although Philadelphia was well-known throughout the colonies for the quality of its product, Charleston supported several breeches makers in the 18th century, including Thomas Robinson, who advertised that he dressed buck skins, prepared alum leather, and washed and dyed buckskin breeches in several colors (*South-Carolina Gazette*, November 5, 1737). North Carolina merchant John Williams advertised a stock of imported white sewing silk for breeches makers and glovers, an indication that there must have been custom (*North Carolina Magazine; or Universal Intelligencer*, October 19, 1764).

Women as well as men appear to have been trained in the craft. In 1748, an indentured servant known as "hopping Peg," a breeches maker by trade, ran away from her master in Norfolk, Virginia (*Pennsylvania Gazette*, January 5, 1748). A convict servant named Sarah Rogers, a glover and breeches maker, ran away from her Maryland master in 1766 (*Pennsylvania Gazette*, May 22, 1766). Matthew Patten of Bedford, New Hampshire, recorded in his diary taking a trip to a neighboring town to pick up a pair of leather breeches made for him by a Mrs. Voce (Main 1994, 60).

Many of the leather trades employed skilled enslaved workers as well as white apprentices. In 1740, *Zenger's New York Weekly Journal* reported that an enslaved Native American leather dresser named Golloway had absented himself from his master, John Breese, of New York City (Scott 2000, 22). In 1734, a Mrs. Collins announced the sale of a slave who was a leather dresser by trade (*South-Carolina Gazette*, May 11). George Harding, a leather dresser on Market Street in Philadelphia, advertised the sale of Boss, about 20 years old, who "can work at the skinning business very well" (*Pennsylvania Gazette*, October 20, 1748).

Mantua Maker

In the 17th century, tailors were responsible for the construction of women's as well as men's garments. By the late 1600s, however, women entered the trade as the mantua, a one-piece robe, became the more comfortable alternative to the boned bodice and separate skirt then worn. By the 1700s, the mantua maker was responsible for making gowns, petticoats, and other garb for females. According to Campbell, to be a success in this trade, "she must learn to flatter all Complexions, praise all Shapes, and, in a word, ought to be compleat Mistress of the Art of Dissimulation" (Campbell 1969, 227). Colonial mantua makers took on female apprentices; in the southern colonies, these workers likely were enslaved help.

Newspaper notices concerning mantua makers are infrequent, but it cannot be assumed that the trade was uncommon. A 1729 advertisement by Philadelphia merchant Christopher Smith for his runaway servant maid, Mary Wilson, a mantua maker from London, is one of the earliest mentions of this craft in colonial advertisements (*Pennsylvania Gazette*, March 27, 1729). Several years later another mantua maker arrived in Philadelphia, her business announced by her husband, John Hunter, in a notice touting his own business of teaching mathematics and keeping accounts (*Pennsylvania Gazette*, March 11, 1735). A 30-year gap separates Mrs. Hunter from the next advertiser, a woman with the resounding name Mrs. Elphiston Rollo, a mantua maker from London (*Pennsylvania Gazette*, July 11 1765). Ten years later, Elizabeth Fox, having "served a regular apprenticeship to the mantua making business . . . in as capital a house as most in England" advertised her new business, and her willingness to take on a few apprentices "of good character" (*Pennsylvania Gazette*, March 22, 1775). Two women advertised boldly on their own account in 1780: Hannah Matlock and Betsey Collins were partners in a mantua-making establishment on Front Street (*Pennsylvania Gazette*, October 25, 1780). Lucy McCormick, mantua maker and milliner, advertised her skills and her apprenticeship with "the most eminent of her profession in Ireland" in 1784 (*Pennsylvania Gazette*, October 27, 1784).

George Francis Dow, in his analysis of the trades and occupations advertised in Boston newspapers between 1704 and 1775, does not list mantua makers (Dow 1927). However, in a letter to his soon-to-be wife, Abigail Smith, John Adams bemoaned the fact that a likely prospect for a maid for their new household told him that she had decided instead to go to Boston to be a mantua maker (Adams, J. 1764).

The earliest mantua maker to advertise in Charleston was a Mrs. Proctor, in 1742 (*South-Carolina Gazette,* February 13). Most mantua makers were women, but John Duvall was active in Charleston, advertising as a mantua and stay maker in the mid-1760s (*South-Carolina Gazette,* March 2, 1765). Margaret Fechtman was a mantua maker who ran her business with her husband, Christian, and one Joseph Tyrell; both of the latter were stay makers (*South-Carolina Gazette,* November 17, 1766). John Bulline owned a female slave who was advertised as a good seamstress and mantua maker (*South-Carolina Gazette,* April 9, 1763). Savannah, Georgia, supported milliners and mantua makers by the 1760s (Davis 1976, 161).

Merchant, Shopkeeper, Trader

Goods were distributed to most colonists through extensive networks of trade and commerce. At the top of this commercial hierarchy were the merchants, who imported goods directly from overseas and sold them in the colonies on a wholesale basis. They may have owned or leased the ships that carried their merchandise or paid for freight costs on ships owned by others. Some merchants also conducted a retail shop, a practice reflected in newspaper notices that indicate, "wholesale and retail." Records of businesses such as the Brown family of Providence, Rhode Island, include day books for the retail shop, where they sold a few yards of cloth or ounces of tea to local customers, and account books and invoices for the sale of large quantities of goods shipped to other wholesale and retail customers in outlying towns and in other colonies (Brown Family Business Papers). It is difficult to estimate from newspaper records alone how many merchants were active in the colonies; some never advertised their wares, but depended on the patronage of regular customers.

Second in the tier were shopkeepers. As retailers, they were dependent upon merchants for inventory or they might travel to London to purchase stock. Shopkeepers in the same city might advertise that their goods were imported on the same ship—and probably purchased from the same merchant. It was not uncommon for a shopkeeper also to be engaged in a craft trade. Notices occasionally glimpse at details of shop interiors. Robert

Lewis of Wilmington, Delaware, advertised property in the township of Kennett, in Chester County, Pennsylvania "on a great road from Lancaster to Wilmington and on a good stream for water, and well furnished for merchant work . . . [including] a store house, with shelves, drawers, and counter for a shopkeeper, having for many years been kept for that use" (*Pennsylvania Gazette*, February 20, 1750). In the areas of the Backcountry, goods also might be purchased from taverns as well as from stand-alone shops. One study of western North Carolina for the third quarter of the 18th century revealed at least 20 shops and 125 taverns doing business in a single county; business records have survived for at least two of these enterprises (Thorp 1991, 289–90). Supplies of goods came from local sources for fresh foodstuffs, whiskey, and beer and from imports shipped directly from the port cities or carried into the country by peddlers.

Traders—packmen, peddlers, chapmen, hawkers, and truckers—comprised the lowest tier. They purchased small quantities of goods; loaded them on a horse, in a wagon or on their backs; and trucked them into the interior to sell. In many colonies they were required to purchase a license from the colonial government. By facilitating the exchange of goods, packmen opened even the most remote areas to the currents of fashion, patterns of consumption, and the acquisition of status through ownership of goods.

Merchants and shopkeepers were active in the New England colonies soon after settlements were established. The inventory of the shop and warehouse contents belonging to George Corwin (1610–1685) of Salem illustrates the range of necessary and luxury clothing goods already available in the north in the 1600s. Besides a variety of woolen, worsted, silk, and linen fabrics, Corwin offered sewing thread, needles, and scissors; stockings; bodices and stomachers; bobbin lace, tapes, and flowered and plain silk ribbon; knitting needles; gloves; crowned hats and hat bands; black silk caps; buttons; buckles; cloak bags; and pattens (Dow 1910).

In the late 17th century, Charleston's merchants had established trade not only with European settlers but also with the Lower Towns of the Cherokee, exchanging muskets and shot, textiles, jewelry and beads, and tools for buck and doe skins. By 1720, the Indian trade consisted of three tiers: Charleston's merchants, who imported goods for the trade and exported skins; shopkeepers who set up stores in frontier outposts; and traders who lived in the Cherokee towns, many of whom allied themselves through marriage with female relatives of the local headmen.

In general, the only goods sold at large town markets were fresh foodstuffs: meats, fish, dairy products, fruits, and vegetables. In response to the import duties levied by Parliament in the 1760s, however, at least one market was founded in which domestically produced textiles and clothing could be sold. The *Pennsylvania Gazette* announced that the first "Market for Home Manufactures" had been held in New York City on October 24, 1765. The short article bemoaned the fact that there were many more buyers than sellers, and that at the next market day, on November 7, it was hoped that many more manufacturers of shoes, stockings, linen and woolen cloths, caps, gloves, and mittens would attend (October 31, 1765).

Milliner

In Britain the milliner's trade was the province of women, who produced and sold apparel goods for women. According to Robert Campbell, the milliners "furnish every thing to the Ladies, that contribute to set off their Beauty, increase their Vanity, or render them ridiculous" (207). More specifically, the milliner stocked fabrics appropriate for women's wear and also made up " smocks, Aprons, Tippits, Handerchiefs, Neckaties, Ruffles, Mobs, Caps, Dressed-Heads . . . Cloaks, Manteels, Mantelets, Cheens and Capucheens . . . Hats, Hoods . . . [they sell] Gloves, Muffs, and Ribbons . . . quilted Petticoats, and Hoops of all Sizes, &c. and lastly, some of them deal in Habits for Riding, and Dresses for the Masquerade" (207).

In the colonies, as in Britain, milliners were not confined to women's hat-making. They might indeed make modish caps and bonnets trimmed with silk flowers, ribbons or feathers—or employ workers to do so for their clients—but primarily they carried fashionable fabrics, trimmings, and accessories for women and girls. Advertising in Boston in 1743, Henrieta Maria East noted that she made head dresses, hoods, mantelets, pillerens, French cloaks, and bonnets (Dow 1927, 156). In Williamsburg, Virginia, Frances Webb carried lace, fine linens, calicoes and chintzes, velvet caps and hoods, women's gloves, and silk shoes (*Virginia Gazette*, June 20, 1745). In 1771, Margaret Hunter advertised that she made ladies' hats, bonnets, cloaks, and cardinals, and mounted fans; she later expanded her business to include the sale of silk fabrics, jewelry, gloves, and children's apparel (*Virginia Gazette*, May 2, 1771; October 31, 1771). Mary and Ann Pearson ran a shop in Philadelphia that carried imported luxury fabrics and fashionable accessories such as Brussels and Buckinghamshire lace; silk handkerchiefs and cravats; ribbons and flower trimmings; silk mitts and hose; hats, caps, and bonnets; finished cloaks; stays, petticoats, and shoes; threads for sewing and embroidery; and muffs, tippets, fans, stomachers, and paste jewelry (*Pennsylvania Gazette*, November 18, 1762). In Charleston, Ann Dalrymple, a milliner and children's coat maker, advertised a wide assortment of wares including fabrics, powder, gloves, masks, patches, embroidered aprons and handkerchiefs, petticoats, and "children's caps, stays, shoes & stockings . . . [and] leading strings." She also carried goods to vend at the Ashley-Ferry and Strawberry Fairs, both held outside of town (*South-Carolina Gazette*, May 7, 1737).

Colonial advertisements suggest that milliners who boasted of recent European training or employment, or perhaps a French surname, might attract a greater clientele. For example, Eliza Braithwaite, engaged solely in "making up" millinery work in 1769 was London trained (*Pennsylvania Gazette*, October 19, 1769); Philadelphia's Mrs. Bontamps called herself a "French Millener" (*Pennsylvania Gazette*, December 29, 1768); Charleston milliner Mary Scouvemont announced that she was from Paris (*South-Carolina Gazette; and County Journal*, April 1, 1766).

Peruke and Periwig Maker, Hair Dresser, and Barber

Personal appearance was an indicator of social status, and the proper dressing of hair was an important aspect of appearance. From the mid-17th century until the end of the 18th, wearing a periwig or peruke was a distinguishing badge of gentility. Robert Campbell noted of the London trades in 1747 that the trade of peruke maker (many of whom also practiced the barber's trade) was "but of short date." The introduction of "false curls" to English heads occurred at the restoration of Charles II to the throne in 1660 (the term "wig" is short for periwig, the latter term first appeared in the English language in the late 16th century). Campbell offered that originally, the fashion was to wear wigs that closely resembled one's natural hair color and "shaped in such manner as to make the artificial Locks appear like a natural Production." The natural look was relatively short lived, and Campbell's description of the change is worth quoting in full:

> In Process of Time full-bottomed Wiggs became the Mode; and the heads of our Beaus and Men of Fashion were loaded with Hair: To these the Tie-Wigg succeeded, and the Natural Colour was laid aside for Silver Locks. The Bobb, the Pig-tail, Tupee, Ramilie, and a Number of Shapes, that bear no Relation to the Human Head, are now become the Mode. Sometimes the Beaus appear plaistered all over with Powder and Pomantum, and their Curls frizzled out with laborious Nicety; at other Times the Powder Puff is laid aside, and they affect to dress in Wanton Ringlets. (Campbell 1969, 203)

Campbell noted that lately ladies had begun to don wigs: "The Black, the Brown, the Fair and Carroty, appear now all in one Livery; and you can no more judge of your Mistress's natural Complexion by the Colour of her Hair, than by that of her Ribbons" (203).

The most expensive wigs were made of human hair. Less expensive versions were of horse or goat. The tricks to creating a good peruke and periwig were to sort and mix the hair according to color and fineness; dye or bleach it as necessary; and then sew it in the right proportions and densities to a net foundation using "barber's raw silk" thread. Hair could be curled before making up into a wig by rolling sections around ceramic cylinders called rolls and baking the hair in an oven to set the curl (Campbell 1969, 206).

In 1734, Philadelphian peruke maker, William Crosthwaite, reported the theft of four wigs, two of which were of flax fibers, and one of these for a child, noting that he paid well for human hair, and "fine Horsehair" (*Pennsylvania Gazette*, December 12, 1734). The partnership of Matthews and Charlton advertised bespoke perukes of English hair made in any style, "Tyes, Bobs, Majors, Spencers, Foxtails, or Twists" and could match London's fashion and price. The pair also made "Curls or Tates" for all ranks of women of their own or English hair (*Pennsylvania Gazette*, July 26, 1744). London-trained Mr. Mathews worked with Jacob Mayer to make gentlemen's wigs, hairpieces, "tupees," curls, and "brains and cushions" for ladies who wished to imitate the latest English and French fashions (*Pennsylvania Gazette*, August 30, 1764; October 3, 1765; December 15, 1773). Peruke makers and others also sold boxes to store wigs, silk ribbons of various kinds to tie the hair back away from the face, and net bags, which were worn to hold long hair in place down the neck. For example, John Seymour offered "wig caols, wig ribbands, and barber's raw silk for weaving" (*Pennsylvania Gazette*, April 24, 1746).

Wig makers emigrated from Britain to Charleston before 1730 and advertised in the *South-Carolina Gazette*. Londoner Richard Herbert brought "all sorts of Human Hair" with him to Charleston in 1736 to custom-make fashionable perukes for gentlemen (August 7, 1736). George Hitchcock not only fashioned perukes at his establishment in Elliot's Street in Charleston but also attended the Ashley Ferry, Dorchester, and Childsberry Fairs either to take and deliver bespoke orders or to sell finished wigs. He noted that he imported English gray and grizzle-colored hair, but may have purchased hair in the countryside (September 18, 1736). Mungo Graham and Alexander Macaulay worked together as peruke makers and offered hair dressing and shaving services to gentlemen, hair dressing supplies such as wig cauls, wig ribbons, and razors (July 30, 1741; Mary 5, 1746). Edward Charlton, from St. James's, London, brought an assortment of English hair with him to make wigs that "shall never shrink, or the fore-tops part or come down." Charlton also advertised for the hiring of an enslaved barber and weaver to help in the business (January 28, 1751). Peter Butler was perhaps the most diversified wig maker of his day. In addition to wigs, he sold a variety of personal care products: eye water, "double-distilled lavender-water, honey and Hungary waters, fine pomatum, sticking-plaiter, and lipsalve for the ladies, perfumed wash-balls, a liquid for colouring the hair, teeth-powders and brushes" (January 23, 1762).

The trades of peruke and periwig maker, barber, and ladies' and gentlemen's hair dressers could overlap considerably. The 1729 sale of the contents of a Boston barber shop included inventory of wigs and hair (*Boston Gazette*, October 20, 1729). In Hartford, Connecticut, Samuel Mattocks advertised in 1765 that he "makes all sorts of wigs that are worn on the Continent; but also a new Fashion lately introduced in Boston, in Imitation of Hair" (*Connecticut Courant*, May 27, 1765). He cut and dressed hair as well, "for such as still continue to wear their Hair, notwithstanding it is so much out of Fashion, both in Europe and the fashionable Parts of America." He may have hoped that some of these latter customers would surrender to fashion and allow their heads to be shaved, because he noted that he also purchased hair to make wigs. Richard Wagstaff, who arrived in Philadelphia from London in 1760, called himself a peruke maker, tate and tatete maker, and hair cutter. The wigmaking business must have been a lucrative one as Wagstaff also imported hair to sell wholesale to his competitors (*Pennsylvania Gazette*, August 2, 1750; July 4, 1754).

Hairdressers were often, but not always, also peruke makers. John Prior of Philadelphia confined his business to hair dressing for ladies and gentlemen, and shaving for his male clients (*Pennsylvania Gazette*, August 23, 1764). Mantua maker Mrs. E. Atkinson of Boston combined the occupations of millinery work, schoolmistress, and "dressing of Heads and cutting of Hair" (Bridenbaugh 1950, 106).

Jewelers and goldsmiths often sold accoutrements for hair care. Boston Jewelers Roberts and Lee carried "hair powder scented & plain, powder knives, dressing and tail combs, tortoise shell pole combs, [and] black hair pins" (Dow 1927, 85).

Quilter

The trade in imported ready-made quilt petticoats was discussed earlier in this chapter. Although women quilted for home use in the colonies, documentation on quilting as a trade is scant. In Philadelphia, Dennis Flood advertised the sale of an enslaved woman who had been trained to "spin, sew, make gowns, quilt, &c." but it is not known whether her work was for home use only or for the trades (*Pennsylvania Gazette*, July 30, 1747). In Charleston, a Mrs. Grenier gave notice that "she perform's all sorts of quilted Work, Petticoats, coverlets &c." (*South Carolina Gazette*, May 24, 1735). When it appears in newspaper notices, quilting is among the activities undertaken by seamstresses, who often also advertised themselves as schoolmistresses.

Scourer

In the colonies scouring, dyeing and fulling were usually combined activities carried on by a single tradesman or at one mill. Scourers cleaned both cloth and leather. Henry Brabazon advertised in Philadelphia that "he wet and dry scowers men and womens apparel, and dies silk, cloth or leather, cleans leather breeches, and takes out mildew, lime juice, cat or dog piss, pitch, paint, tar or turpentine, &c." (*Pennsylvania Gazette*, September 27, 1753). Abraham Shelley, overseer of the Philadelphia's work house for the indigent poor, probably put his charges to work to provide the diverse services he advertised, which included scouring: "He takes in Linnen Yarn, to die blue, and fine Linnen, to dye, stiffen, and glaze, for the Lineing of Gentlemen's Cloaths, or Hat Lineings, printed Linnen and Callico, new or old to scower or glaze; Cloth Cloaths to scower and clean; Logwood, Redwood, and Fustick, to cut for Dyers and Hatters" (*Pennsylvania Gazette*, January 7, 1746).

Seamstress and Plain Sewer

In the days before sewing machines (invented in the mid-19th century) all clothing—and all textile furnishings—were constructed by hand. At a very early age, all females learned the basic stitches for making shirts, shifts, petticoats, and other garments. The 1668 will of Thomas Brooks of Hartford, Connecticut, requesting that his wife make sure their daughters are taught to read and sew and their sons to read and write illustrates this practical approach to girls' education (Manwaring 1904, 186). In Georgia's Bethesda orphanage, established in the early years of the colony to house and educate those children whose parents died while emigrating to or settling in the colony, girls were taught the essential female skills of sewing, knitting, and spinning (Davis 1976, 159). By the time they were 10–12 years old, girls were expected to sew well enough to contribute to making household necessities.

The most common apparel items made at home were men's and boys' shirts; women's and girls' shifts, and quilted petticoats; and smaller items such as aprons, pockets, and collars. For example, young Mary Downing, who resided in Boston, was berated in a 1635 letter from her parents, living in England, for neglecting to work on her brother's collars (Earle 1895, 232–33). In contrast, 12-year-old Nanny Green Winslow congratulated herself in her diary entry on March 9, 1772, for the quantity of chores she had done that day. Her work included sewing on "the bosom" of her uncle's shirt, mending two pair of gloves and two handkerchiefs, and sewing on half of an apron border for her aunt. Just over a week later she wrote that she had finished nine of the ten shifts her aunt had cut for her from a piece of linen, and would have finished the last "if my fingers had not been sore" (Sprigg 1984, 75–76). By the age of 12, Nanny probably had been doing plain sewing of increasing difficulty

The young seamstress wears a gown with frills at the elbows, a neck handkerchief, and a frilled cap; a ribbon box and pin cushion sit on a table to her right. Her posture indicates that she is wearing stays. (Lewis Walpole Library, Yale University)

for five or six years. Not all girls learned to sew with the same degree of skill. The time remaining—six years and eight months—of an 18-year-old Dutch indentured servant girl's contract was advertised for sale in 1773, for the reason that "she was purchased as a compleat Sempstress, which was what she was wanted for in the family she lives with, and does not turn out [to be] one" (*Pennsylvania Gazette*, February 17, 1773).

Plain sewing, however, had an important role outside the household in colonial communities. Hiring out as a professional seamstress was one way for girls and women to make money on their own. Rhode Island clergyman James MacSparran hired a tailor to make his jackets and breeches, his diary also recorded visits to the house by two women, Mary Chappel and Mrs. Heath, for sewing or mending (Woodward 1971, 111). An examination of Elizabeth Porter Phelps's diary, kept from 1768 to 1783, reveals that 12 women worked in the Phelps's home over the years to help keep the family clothed, making new stays, gowns, overcoats, and breeches, and altering old garments (Ward 1985, 385). In the mid-1700s, Merchant Ebenezer Hinsdale of Hinsdale, New Hampshire, paid two local women, Lucy Mun and Abigail French, to "make up" gowns that he sold to customers (Hinsdale).

In southern colonies, seamstresses were less common in advertisements, likely because plantation owners kept highly skilled enslaved help to perform these essential functions for the household and perhaps for the larger enslaved community. Advertisements for the sale of female slaves often refer to the sewing skills of these individuals. For example, George Saxby offered a household servant "that can wash and iron, and sew exceeding well" (*South-Carolina Gazette*, January 14, 1745). Thomas Porter wanted to hire out a young slave "very fit for a Nurse, and can sew, knit, and tend house" (*South-Carolina Gazette*, November 21, 1754).

Some seamstresses earned additional money by teaching sewing. Isabel Hewet, in 1768, and M. Webster and E. Hodgson, working together in 1774, took in needlework on commission and also ran classes to teach young girls a variety of needlework skills. Webster and Hodgson enumerated the types of work they would undertake: embroidering ladies' shoes, aprons, and ruffles, tambour embroidery and quilting of men's waistcoats, and making mantuas and children's slips. They did not, however, call themselves mantua-makers (*Pennsylvania Gazette*, September 29, 1768; December 21, 1774). In Charleston, a Mrs. Adams, wife of the writing master William Adams, advertised that she "will teach young ladies to sew and mark [i.e., mark household linens for identification] and as soon as possible will furnish herself with a compleat assortment of millinary; she will also clear starch, &c." (*South-Carolina Gazette*, June 15, 1767).

Sewing was such a common activity that most colonial advertisements for dry goods shops offered quantities of pins and needles imported from England. By 1742, however, Simon Smith was established in Boston making "white Chapple Needles . . . round and square" for stitching everything from linen to leather (Dow 1935, 137).

Shoemaker, Cordwainer, and Cobbler

Making and repairing shoes, boots, and other footwear was the province of three types of craftsmen: shoemakers, cordwainers, and cobblers. Shoemakers made all types of shoes and boots, including work shoes and clogs, of fabric and of leather. Cordwainers dealt not only with footwear, but also with other leather goods such as belts and harnesses. Cobblers repaired footwear and other leather goods.

Shoemakers relied on the skills of last makers to fashion in wood the foot shapes, or lasts, over which pieces of leather or fabric were stretched to form the upper part of the shoe. Last makers also supplied the shoe maker with wooden heels for men's and women's shoes. Colonial craftsmen may have turned to local wood workers to make lasts and heels, but many of these items were imported. Robert Campbell noted that making a woman's shoe with fabric uppers required more skill than making a man's, because "the Woman's Shoe-Maker requires much neater Seams, as the Materials are much finer. [In London] they employ Women to bind their shoes and sew the Quarters together, when they are made of silk, Damask, or Callimanco" (Campbell 1969, 218).

As discussed in the section on ready-mades of colonial production above, 17th-century documents testify to the importance of shoemakers. They had settled in Salem and Lynn, Massachusetts, in 1635 and were working in Boston in 1640. Shoemaker Francis Dorse was "in the employ" of Bostonian George Burden in 1640, which may have meant he had come to the colony as an indentured servant (Dow 1935, 140). When John Winthrop wrote to his wife in England in 1631, asking her to send dry goods to him that he could either use or sell, shoemaker's thread and hobnails were on his list (Earle 1895, 157–58).

In the 18th century, Philadelphia boasted a large shoemaking industry. While there are only a handful of trade advertisements the *Pennsylvania Gazette* for shoemakers or cordwainers, notices by those tradesmen for runaway apprentices, indentured servants, and enslaved artisans as well as merchants' offerings of shoemaker's tools abounded after 1730. Very occasionally, an artisan styled himself a shoemaker at one time and a cordwainer at another. In the main, shoemakers who advertised their services appear to have catered to the high-class trade. Some specialized in women's shoes of silk and wool fabrics, while others made both fabric and leather shoes for men, women, and children, plus leather boots and spatterdashes for their male clients. In 1774, 334 master shoemakers were at work in Philadelphia (Bridenbaugh 1950, 74).

Smaller communities could also rely on local shoemakers. Reverend MacSparran, who in the mid-18th century ministered to Rhode Island's Narragansett planters and farmers, recorded in his diary that he purchased leather tanned for both the soles and uppers from a local tanner, and dropped the pieces off with a local shoemaker, Benjamin Mumford, to be made into shoes for his slaves. MacSparran hired itinerant shoemakers from time-to-time who worked at the farm with leather purchased locally by the Reverend (Woodward 1971, 112). Three account books from the Pocumtuck Valley Memorial Association Library in Deerfield, Massachusetts, also shed light on rural shoemaking in the northern colonies during the 1750s and 1760s. Ebenezer Arms made and mended men's, women's, and children's shoes, pumps, hightop shoes, and boots, and men's and boy's "sandells"; and resoled shoes throughout the 1750s. His output for January 1751 included making 24 pairs of shoes and boots, mending 19 pairs, and soling 15 pairs (Arms). Moses Field made, mended, and soled shoes and boots as well, but his business was smaller than Arms's. In 1753, Field charged one customer 18 shillings to make a new pair of cloth shoes. A decade later he was charging from 3 to 5 pence to mend shoes, and from 2 shillings 2 pence up to 4 shillings to make most shoes and boots (Field). Ebenezer Hinsdale, a merchant from Hinsdale, New Hampshire, had shoes and pumps made locally for himself, his wife, and his children, as recorded in his account book between 1747 and 1751 (Hinsdale).

Advertisements for "Run away" and "To be sold" indicate that in addition to apprentices, many indentured servants and slaves had shoemaking skills. Shoemaker Thomas Powell advertised the remaining time for sale of one of his indentured servants, "by Trade a Shoemaker" (*Pennsylvania Gazette*, February 10, 1742). A slave shoemaker was offered for sale in Philadelphia in 1747 (*Pennsylvania Gazette*, December 3). In 1766, the ship *Jenny* carried English indentured servants to Virginia; among them were weavers, tailors, and shoemakers (*Virginia Gazette*, April 18, 1766).

Shoemaking in the southern colonies was largely restricted to leather shoes of a quality suitable for ordinary folk, servants, and slaves. One indentured servant working in Virginia in 1737 made 250 pairs of slave shoes to earn his release (Bridenbaugh 1950, 14). By the 1750s Georgia's towns were well supplied with shoemakers. In Charleston one enterprising shoemaker, John Lewis, took it upon himself to make a quantity of winter boots on speculation so that "country gentlemen who won't have time to stay to have them made purposely may nevertheless fit themselves" (*South Carolina Gazette*, September 23, 1756).

South Carolina leather workers also produced sole leather, which Charleston merchants shipped to both the West Indies and to Philadelphia. The 1743–1763 shipping returns for Gabriel Manigault's (1704–1781) business show that an average of 10,111 pounds of sole leather was shipped annually to the abovementioned destinations. In 1757, when 12,732 pounds of sole leather was shipped from Charleston, Manigault's share alone was 7,212 pounds (Crouse 1967, 226).

Starch Maker

Starch was used in the cleaning process to stiffen collars, sleeves, and ruffles of fine linen and cotton and linen lace as they were being ironed. In the 18th century, the finest starch was made in Europe; however, colonial manufacture was common. In 1731, Nathaniel Palmer advertised that he made starch and starch powder "after the English Manner, the Powder scented or unscented, and neatly put up in Pound, Half and Quarter Pound Papers, fit for Shopkeepers to retail out" (*Pennsylvania Gazette*, July 22). In Ansonborough, a suburb of Charleston, Robert Stringer established a starch manufactory and advertised "POLAND and Common Starch; fine Hair-Powder, plain and scented" (*South-Carolina Gazette*, September 15, 1773). He noted that although this was not the first manufactory of its kind to be tried in Charleston, his product had been perfected by using rice, one of South Carolina's staple commodities, as the principal ingredient.

Stay Maker

In London stay makers were men. Although they made ladies' stays, jumps, and bodices, according to Campbell, their real talents lay in creating foundation garments that would create "the delicate easy Shape we so much admire." To accomplish this, the stay maker must "mend a crooked Shape, . . . bolster up a fallen Hip, or distorted Shoulder" (224). The materials of stay-making were tabby, canvas, and thin slices of whale bone—actually baleen, the keratin plates from the mouths of baleen whales. The fabrics were cut in pieces to the woman's measured shape and sewn together. Rows of stitches were then added across the breadth of the fabric to create channels through which the whale bone was inserted to provide the stiffening for the stays. If the stays were bespoke, they were at first loosely sewn together so that they could be fitted to the wearer. If satisfactory, the stays were then bound, the seams covered with braid, and laced (226).

In the early 18th century, tailors sometimes made stays for women and children in addition to cutting clothing for men and boys and making "coats" (probably long dresses) for children. New York had at least one stay maker by 1735. Several in the trade advertised during the 1730s and 1740s in Philadelphia. Thomas Carter was in business from at least 1734 until his death in 1744 and left his apprentice, Michael Connor, to continue in the same location (*Pennsylvania Gazette*, February 2, 1744; August 13, 1747). Thomas Catringer, who plied his trade at the "sign of the green stays" was in business before 1748 and remained so until his death in 1759 (*Pennsylvania Gazette*, March 1, 1748; April 19, 1759). Philadelphia supported at least six stay makers in the 1750s, including Jacob Carver, who took the business run by his master, William Bromwich, when the latter returned to England in 1751. Bromwich returned a year later and reestablished himself in the trade (*Pennsylvania Gazette*, November 28 and December 7, 1751; May 7, 1761; May 31, 1764).

By the 1750s, however, stay makers no longer claimed to be tailors, concentrating instead on women's and children's stays and women's jumps. In New York in the 1770s, tailor Edward Griffiths employed stay maker William Warden, broadening the range of services he could offer his female clients (Bridenbaugh 1950, 111). Staymaker Henry Hineman, who arrived in Philadelphia in 1778, tried to appease both patriots and loyalists by offering English and French styles to potential customers (*Pennsylvania Gazette*, August 22, 1778). After the Revolution, Sebastian Finlass made stays in French and English styles, including riding stays, and also "turned stays and jumps, half-bone and whole-bone, very neat" (*Pennsylvania Gazette*, June 6, 1787). In 1737, Thomas Crawford challenged any resident in South Carolina to make a pair of stays equal to his in work and shape (*South-Carolina Gazette*, April 16, 1737). Judging from the advertisements, the 1760s saw a greater number of active stay makers in Charleston, some advertising that they had just arrived from London.

Although most stay makers were men, some women did advertise. Elizabeth Harvery of Charleston noted that she made stays and slips and sold bone to stiffen ladies' jackets (*South-Carolina Gazette*, August 28, 1762).

Tailor

No Man is ignorant that a Taylor is the Person that makes our Cloaths; to some he not only makes their Dress, but, in some measure, may be said to make themselves. The skilled tailor ought to have a quick Eye to steal the Cut of a Sleeve, the Pattern of a Flap, or the Shape of a good Trimming at a Glance. . . . He must be able, not only to cut for the Handsome and Well-shaped, but to bestow a good Shape where Nature has not designed it; the Hump-back, the Wry-shoulder, must be buried in Flannel and Wadding. . . . He must study not only the Shape, but the common Gait of the Subject he is working upon, and make the Cloaths fit easy in spite of a stiff Gait, or awkward Air. (Campbell 1969, 191)

Tailoring was one of the earliest established clothing trades in the colonies. In 1618, Virginia's Governor Argall emphasized the need for tailors to come to the colony in June in order to help settlers "get their cloathes [ready in] time enough for winter" (Kingsbury, 1933, 3:78). Several tailors are mentioned in Massachusetts records of the 1640s and 1650s, including Luke Potter of Concord, John Annable of Ipswich, and John Burne of Gloucester. In 1649, Potter took on 11-year-old Daniel Gaines as an apprentice for eight years, in order to teach him "the skill and mastery of a tailor" (Dow 1935, 141). Thomas Smith of Pawtuxet in the Providence Plantations (i.e., Rhode Island) colony took on two apprentices in the 1660s: William Knowles bound himself in 1661 for a term of five years and Joseph Stafford signed on for eight years beginning in 1665 (Chapin 1926, 265–66, 273–74).

The trade was overwhelmingly a male occupation. A few scattered instances exist from the 18th century of women training or working as tailors, or tailoresses, but generally the work was gender specific: cutting, stitching, and fitting of men's clothing and certain types of women's clothes, notably riding habits and stays, was performed by men, while cutting and sewing that required little or no skill in arithmetic was left to women. Exceptions include the daughter of a Hingham, Massachusetts, man, who in 1708 was given 40 weeks of training as a tailor, funded by her father's estate, and a woman from neighboring Milton, who was listed as a tailoress in the 1709 probate records for her estate (Main 1994, 59–60, n. 76). Although most tailors were one-man operations, by the 18th century, larger workshops were organized by a division of labor. The cutter was the most skilled and finished the garment as well as cut the patterns from the cloth. Less skilled workers and apprentices were employed to sew seams, make buttonholes, and prepare the garment for the cutter. It was customary for tailors, while sewing, to sit "cross-legged, always in one Posture" (Campbell 1969, 193).

The western Massachusetts town of Deerfield retains several account books from colonial merchants and artisans (Pocomtuck Valley Memorial Association Library). One of these, John Russell was a storekeeper and tailor, who cut and stitched coats, vests, breeches, banyans, and great coats (overcoats) for many of the town's male citizens during the third quarter of the 18th century. His accounts enumerate the items made, but do not detail the fabrics used (Maeder 2001). In contrast, surviving records from Cumberland County, Pennsylvania, list the quantities and types of fabrics and supplies used by local tailors for their clients' clothing. At least one tailor was established there by 1745, and many others joined him in the ensuing decades (Hersh and Hersh, 1995, 163–69).

Prices for bespoke clothing were subject to a number of variables. Tailors who had trained in Britain could command higher prices than those who apprenticed in the colonies (Bridenbaugh 1950, 111). William Thorne, a tailor and shopkeeper in New York in the 1770s, listed prices in his newspaper advertisement, but cautioned potential clients that the figures were only for "middle sized" men. Presumably those smaller or larger than average could expect adjustments depending on the quantity of fabric and trimmings their suits required (Gottesman 1938, 333). Prices ranged from £2 for a pair of silk breeches to £38 for a satin-lined suit of velvet. A "plain suit of second best cloth" cost only £7. In smaller towns prices for goods were lower. James Leech, of Sadsbury in Lancaster County, Pennsylvania, advertised in December 1770 for the young man who had commissioned a coat and jacket the previous January but had never returned to collect and pay for them. Leech had fronted the money for the materials, accompanying the young man to a local store to pick them out, and reminded his customer that the total debt including labor was £3.5.7 (*Pennsylvania Gazette,* December 20, 1770).

Tailors sometimes branched out into other trades. In Philadelphia, John Galloway set himself apart from his competitors, advertising that he could create any kind of fancy worked buttons, using metal threads, spangles, or silk embroidery on the customer's fabric so the buttons would match the clothes (*Pennsylvania Gazette,* October 18, 1775). Samuel Blodgett in Boston, in 1759, and Jacob Reed of New York, in about 1754, offered ready-made suits of clothes. Reed's selection included many sizes, colors, and qualities of cloth; Blodgett targeted the military officer or common soldier heading off to service in the French and Indian war (Bridenbaugh 1950, 70–71). Philadelphia tailors Nicholas Bowser and James Steward imported apparel fabrics, accessories, and trimmings from London (*Pennsylvania Gazette,* May 2, 1734; November 10, 1748; January 17, 1749).

Innumerable runaway servants or slaves were tailors by trade, and masters offered for sale full or partial indentures of trained tailors. A Philadelphia tailor offered for sale the indenture ("having one Year and Ten Months to serve") of "A VERY good Taylor" (*Pennsylvania Gazette,* July 27, 1737). In 1770, tailor Thomas Fell was in need of "two NEGRO MEN TAYLORS" and was willing to pay the owner(s) good wages for their hire (*South-Carolina Gazette; and Country Journal,* December 18, 1770). That same year another enslaved tailor was for sale, who "can cut and make Negro Clothes well" (*South-Carolina Gazette; and Country Journal,* September 24).

James Habersham, a prominent Georgia landowner and politician, apparently tried the services of more than one Savannah tailor in the 1760s, finally declaring them all "bunglers"; he then sent to London for new clothes (quoted in Davis 1976, 109). For those with less money or fashion sense, however, there were at least seven tailoring establishments active in Savannah in the 1760s and 1770s, including Robert Pattison, who came from London just before the outbreak of the Revolution (Davis 1976, 109).

Weaver

As Robert Campbell observed in 1747, the weaving business was extensive and divided into a number of branches. In the colonies weavers worked on room-sized looms to create woolens of broad widths and on smaller looms to weave linens whose width spanned the length of a man's arms, as well as weavers of narrow tapes, ribbons, and laces for trimmings, who worked on portable looms.

Textile scholar Rita Adrosko distinguished several types of weavers in colonial America. First were the public weavers, encompassing professional weavers, who worked either with family help or with a journeyman or apprentice in their homes or a small workshop, and semiprofessional weavers, who might weave for their neighbors or local community but only part time, perhaps also looking after a farm or another business. There were also enslaved weavers in plantation workshops and home weavers—women and men who worked at home, for themselves or others, regularly but not as a profession (Adrosko 1976, 111–13). She discounted the idea that itinerant weavers traveled the colonial landscape, carrying looms with them from town to town, arguing that looms consisted of four six-foot posts and additional lumber and harness, all of which was neither lightweight nor easily set up. It is likely that some weavers did travel about, but used looms belonging to those for whom they worked, either in a workshop or domestic situation. Two- and four-harness looms were probably most common in the colonies; there is no documentation of drawloom weavers until about 1800 (109).

A category that Adrosko did not address was the indentured servant. Among the advertisements for runaway servants are listings for weavers—usually males. These runaways may have been apprentices, indentured weavers working under a master weaver, or indentured servants for whom weaving was merely part of a series of household duties. A Philadelphia weaver in 1736 described his runaway servant weaver as about 30 years of age, old for an apprentice but about right for an indentured servant (*Pennsylvania Gazette*, April 1, 1736).

Some professional weavers engaged in several activities to make a living. Adrosko (1976, 107) cited the 1696–1720 diary of a Connecticut weaver, Manasseh Minor, who allowed neighbors to use his loom when he was not weaving himself. One of the most unusual combinations of trades was that of John Hanson, a Philadelphia weaver who, in 1743, claimed also to let blood and draw teeth "greatly to the satisfaction of the patient" (*Pennsylvania Gazette*, September 1, 1743). Most commonly, weavers were also farmers. Francis Plummer of Newbury, Massachusetts, gave his occupation upon his arrival in 1653 as a linen weaver. At his death, in 1672, he owned 36 acres of farm and grazing land in addition to his loom and tackle. William Ward Sr., of Middletown, Connecticut, divided up his estate in 1690 so that his two sons each received a half interest in William's fulling mill; but one son also received half the land around the mill and the other was left a loom (Manwaring 1904, 515). The three men may have run the weaving shop, the fulling mill, and the farm together; perhaps the division of the estate recognized greater skill or interest in certain areas on the part of each son. Ebenezer Smead of Deerfield, Massachusetts, was a weaver who also sold dry goods. His account book contains entries from 1723 into the 1760s, but after about 1732 weaving was no longer mentioned (Smead). Perhaps the most common were weavers like William Erwin, a Pennsylvania farmer who owned and operated two looms and was paid both in cash and in foodstuffs for his weaving (Hersh and Hersh 1995, 37).

In 1748, Moravians in Bethlehem, Pennsylvania, sent for four Moravian woolen cloth weavers then living in Yorkshire, England, to establish a cloth-making manufactory. In 1751, the enterprise was enlarged with the addition of a fulling mill, a stamp mill, and a larger dye house, to accommodate a fuller and blue dyer. Among the finished products of this enterprise, which continued into the second decade of the 19th century, were handkerchiefs, neck cloths, garters, stockings, and gloves (Bagnall 1971, 26–27).

In the northern colonies, professional female weavers were not uncommon in the 18th century. A probate inventory from 1754 in Cumberland County, Pennsylvania, listed the loom and weaving equipment owned by Elisabeth Douglas. Several examples of each type of tool (reeds, heddles, brushes, temples, warping bars, warping frame, quill wheel, and shuttles) were listed, suggesting that she was prepared to weave several different weights and types of fabric (Hersh and Hersh 1995). Another female weaver, Jemima Condict, a 17-year-old from a rural New Jersey community, recorded her weaving in the diary that she began in 1772 (Sprigg 1984, 73).

Skilled enslaved weavers were also common. Sometime between 1710 and 1715, Virginian William Byrd II (1674–1744) employed a weaver on his plantation "to weave course cloaths for my servants . . . [and] I charged him strictly to weave for nobody without my express orders." While Byrd was away, a house guest appropriated the weaver's time to weave a length of cloth for her and a second servant was ordered to make a beam for the warp threads. From the description of physical violence with which the poor weaver was threatened by both Byrd and his guest, it is likely that the weaver was a slave, who had no recourse but abject obedience (Woodfin 1942, 293). Among a group of slaves to be sold at the plantation of James Marion, outside of Charleston, was "an exceeding good Weaver" (*South-Carolina Gazette*, April 17, 1749). In 1765, Virginian John Wily wrote an instruction manual for raising sheep and flax and manufacturing wool and linen. He offered his services in North Carolina to "instruct Negroes in any branch of the woolen or linen manufactory on easy terms" (*Pennsylvania Ga-*

zette, September 5, 1765). In 1777, a planter south of Charleston "who three Months ago had not a Negro that culd either spin or weave, has now 30 Hands constantly employed, from whom he gets 120 Yards of good wearable Stuff, made of Woollen and cotton, every Week. He only requires one white woman to instruct the Negroes in Spinning, and one Man to instruct in weaving. He expects to have it in his Power not only to clothe his own negroes, but soon to supply his Neighbours" (*South-Carolina; and American General Gazette,* January 30, 1777). Examples of enslaved Native American employed as weavers can be found in New England: "An Indian lad . . . [who] can work at the weaver's trade" (*Boston Post-Boy,* May 2, 1743).

A specialty weaving activity was the creation of narrow tapes, tie laces, and braids on small portable looms. These were used as bindings for the edges of shoes, stays, and skirt hems; as drawstrings or ties for petticoats and pairs of pockets, and the necklines of shifts; as laces for bodices, the inner fitted linings of sack-backed gowns, and the backs of waistcoats; and as ties for petticoats and aprons. Wider tapes were used as garters to hold up stockings. Many of these narrow looms survive and fall into two main types: the table loom and the paddle. Tape looms occasionally appear in probate inventories, usually in inventories that also contain equipment such as spinning wheels, wool cards, or flax brakes.

Although making narrow fabrics fell into the category of household weaving, professionals plied the trade. As early as 1739, Philadelphia supported a professional tape weaver, Abraham Shelly, who also made and sold tailor's thread from linen yarns he purchased from local spinners (*Pennsylvania Gazette,* October 4, 1739). Shelly's *Gazette* advertisements suggest that after a few years he abandoned tape weaving and made thread and cords, wove some wider linen and hemp fabrics, and added dyeing and cleaning to his accomplishments, only reviving the tape weaving part of his business in 1775 (August 26, 1742; February 1, 1775). Jonas Osborn, an Irish lace weaver, advertised in 1743 his skills at making buttons, frog closures, cloak loops, watch strings, fringes, reins, tassels, garters, livery lace (a type of fancy woven trim), and shoulder knots, whether of linen, worsted wool, silk, mohair, or metal threads (*Pennsylvania Gazette,* May 5, 1743). In Charleston, Mary Perrey, who ran a boarding house and took in laundry, advertised that she wove garters for gentlemen and ladies, "with their names, or any posy on them" (*South-Carolina* Gazette, January 22, 1763). James Butland wove fringe and trims of all kinds for coaches, furnishings, and clothing in Philadelphia in the 1770s. His 1777 notice stated that "whole battalions" could have their hats and uniforms trimmed from his supplies, in gold, silver, or worsted yarns. Butland may have had a small manufactory and a few employees, since he promised to produce custom work in "any pattern

Portrait of Mr. and Mrs. Thomas Mifflin, 1773, by John Singleton Copley. Copley has painted Sarah Mifflin at work weaving on a tape loom. (The Philadelphia Museum of Art/Art Resource, NY)

or colour at short notice." That this required skilled labor is evidenced by Butland's call for workmen who understood 12 or 24 shuttle looms (*Pennsylvania Gazette*, August 27, 1777).

The probate inventories of Ezekial Bascom (1747) and Asa Childs (1756) from Deerfield, Massachusetts, both included tape looms (Inventory of Ezekiel Bascom; Inventory of Asa Childs). Bascom was undoubtedly a weaver by trade; his inventory listed a loom and tackle, spinning wheels, cards, combing hooks, hatchels, sheep shears, and a quantity of wool and flax. Childs's family may have assisted him in some of his work; his tools were limited to spinning wheels, a reel, shears, a flax brake, five pairs of knitting needles, and a set of shoemaker's tools, as well as raw wool, cotton, and flax. The tape looms may have been professional equipment or tools used by the women of the house for making personal items.

John Singleton Copley (1738–1815) painted Mrs. Sarah Morris Miflin (1747–1790), wife of Philadelphia legislator Thomas Miflin, at work on her tape loom in 1773, in a joint portrait with her husband. Having her portrait painted with this symbol of industriousness may have been a political statement as well as a personal one. Thomas Miflin's political leanings made him a member of the Continental Congress shortly after the portrait was finished, and Mrs. Miflin's fancy work may also have been her genteel contribution to domestic necessities—weaving silk tapes for trims, drawstrings, or stay laces in accordance with the ideals of the nonimportation agreements.

REFERENCES

Abbott, Edith. 1910. *Women in Industry: A Study in American Economic History*. New York: D. Appleton and Company.

Adams, Abigail. 1777. Letter from Abigail Adams to John Adams, April 17. Adams Family Papers: An Electronic Archive. www.masshist.org/digitaladams.

Adams, John. 1764. Letter from John Adams to Abigail Smith, September 30. Adams Family Papers: An Electronic Archive. masshist.org/digital-adams.

Adams, John. 1777. Letter from John Adams to Abigail Smith, May 28. Adams Family Papers: An Electronic Archive. masshist.org/digitaladams.

Adrosko, Rita. 1976. "Eighteenth-Century American Weavers, Their Looms and Their Products." In *Irene Emery Roundtable on Museum Textiles, 1975 Proceedings: Imported and Domestic Textiles in Eighteenth-Century America.* 105–25. Washington, D.C.: The Textile Museum.

Ambler, Mary. 1937. "Diary of M. Ambler, 1770." *Virginia Magazine of History and Biography* vol. 45 (April): 152–70.

Ames, Susie M., ed. 1973. *County Court Records of Accomack-Northampton, Virginia, 1640–1645.* Charlottesville: University Press of Virginia.

The American Museum or Repository of Ancient and Modern Fugitive Pieces, &c. 1787. Vol. 1, no. 1, 11–12. January, 2nd ed. Philadelphia: Mathew Carey.

Arms, Ebenezer, account book 14087, December 10, 1750–November 22, 1768. Pocumtuck Valley Memorial Association (PVMA), Deerfield, Massachusetts.

Aspinwall, William. 1903. *A Volume Relating to the Early History of Boston Containing the Aspinall Notarial Records from 1644 to 1651.* Boston: Municipal Printing Office.

Bagnall, William R. 1971. *The Textile Industries of the United States, Including Sketches and Notices of Cotton, Woolen, Silk, and Linen Manufactures in the Colonial Period,* reprint of 1893 ed. New York: A. M. Kelley.

Balderston, Marion. 1963. "William Penn's Twenty-Three Ships." *The Pennsylvania Genealogical Magazine* vol. 23, no. 2: 27–67.

Baumgarten, Linda. 2002. *What Clothes Reveal: The Language of Clothing in Colonial and Federal America.* New Haven, CT: Yale University.

Billings, Warren M., ed. 1975. "Inventory of Jonathan Newell, February 29, 1672." In *The Old Dominion in the Seventeenth Century: A Documentary History of Virginia, 1609–1689.* 192–94. Chapel Hill: University of North Carolina.

Billings, Warren M. 2004. *Sir William Berkeley and the Forging of Colonial Virginia.* Baton Rouge: Louisiana State University.

Braddick, Michael J. 2002. "Civility and Authority." In *The British Atlantic World, 1500–1800,* edited by David Armitage and Michael J. Braddick, 93–112. New York: Macmillan.

Bridenbaugh, Carl. 1950. *The Colonial Craftsman.* New York: New York University.

Brown Family Business Papers (BFBP). Providence, RI: John Carter Brown Library.

Browne, William Hand, ed. 1887. *Archives of Maryland: Judicial and Testamentary Business of the Provincial Court, 1637–1650.* Vol. 4. Baltimore: Maryland Historical Society, 1887.

Burnaby, Andrew. 1775. *Travels through the Middle Settlements in North-America in the Years 1759 and 1760.* Dublin: R. Marchbank.

Byrd, William II. 1901. *The Writings of Colonel William Byrd of Westover in Virginia, Esquire,* edited by John Spencer Bassett. New York: Doubleday, Page.

Campbell, Robert. 1969. *The London Tradesman,* facsimile copy of 1747 ed. Newton Abbot, Devon: David and Charles.

Carr, Lois Green, Russel R. Menard, and Lorena S. Walsh. 1991. *Robert Cole's World: Agriculture and Society in Early Maryland.* Chapel Hill: University of North Carolina.

Chamberlayne, C. G., ed. 1933. *The Vestry Book of Petsworth Parish, Gloucester County, Virginia, 1677–1793.* Richmond: Virginia State Library.

Chambliss, Amy C. 1959. "Silk Days in Georgia." *Georgia Magazine* (April–May): 19–20, 36.

Chapin, Howard M., ed. 1926. *The Early Records of the Town of Warwick.* Warwick, RI: Rhode Island Historical Society.

Clark, Victor Selden. 1916. *History of Manufactures in the United States, 1607–1860.* Washington, D.C.: Carnegie Institution of Washington.

Commons, John R. et al., eds. 1910a. "Record of Operations in George Washington's Weaving Establishment for the Year 1767." In *A Documentary History of American Industrial Society: Plantation and Frontier.* Vol. 2, 318–20. Cleveland: Arthur H. Clark.

Commons, John R., et al., eds. 1910b. "Summary by Washington of the operations of his weavers in the year 1768, and estimate of earnings." In *A Documentary History of American Industrial Society: Plantation and Frontier.* Vol. 2, 324–25. Cleveland: Arthur H. Clark.

Coons, Martha and Katherine Koob. 1980. *All Sorts of Good Sufficient Cloth: Linen Making in New England, 1640–1860.* North Andover, MA: Merrimack Valley Textile Museum.

Coxe, Tench. Journal of Tench Coxe, Coxe family papers, Collection 2049, Volume 15, Journal, Oct. 1777–Mar. 1783; Historical Society of Pennsylvania.

Crouse, Maurice. 1967. "Gabriel Manigault: Charleston Merchant." *South Carolina Historical and Genealogical Magazine* vol. 68, no. 4 (October): 220–31.

Davis, Andrew McFarland. 1895. "Corporations in the Days of the Colony" in *Publications of the Colonial Society of Massachusetts*. Vol. 1, 188–214. Boston: The Society.

Davis, Harold E. 1976. *The Fledgling Province: Social and Cultural Life in Colonial Georgia, 1733–1776*. Chapel Hill: University of North Carolina.

Denton, Daniel. 1902. *A Brief Description of New York, Formerly Called New Netherlands*, reprint of 1670 ed. Cleveland: Burrows Brothers.

Doubleday, William A., comp. Deerfield Probate Inventories Prior to the Year 1740, typescript mss. compiled and transcribed by William A. Doubleday, Memorial Libraries, Deerfield, MA.

Dow, George Francis, ed. 1910. *An Inventory of the Contents of the Shop and House of Captain George Corwin*. Salem, MA: private printing.

Dow, George Francis, ed. 1911. *Records and Files of the Quarterly Courts of Essex County, Massachusetts, 1636–1691*. Vol. 1, 1636–1656. Salem, MA: Essex Institute.

Dow, George Francis, ed. 1916. *The Probate Records of Essex County, Massachusetts, 1635–1664*. Vol. 1. Salem, MA: Essex Institute.

Dow, George Francis, ed. 1927. *The Arts and Crafts in New England, 1704–1775: Gleanings from Boston Newspapers*. Topsfield, MA: Wayside.

Dow George, Francis. 1935. *Everyday Life in the Massachusetts Bay Colony*. New York: Benjamin Blom.

Earle, Alice Morse. 1894. *Costume of Colonial Times*. New York: Charles Scribner's Sons.

Earle, Alice Morse. 1895. *Margaret Winthrop*. New York: Charles Scribner's Sons.

Eaton, Linda. 2009. Personal communication, March 10.

Egan, Geoff. 1994. "Lead Cloth Seals and Related Items in the British Museum." British Museum Occasional Paper 93. London: The British Museum.

Egmont, John Percival. 1732. Letter from James Oglethorpe to the Trustees on board the ship *Anne*, Nov 18. Egmont Papers, typescript of vol. 14207, letters to Georgia, June 1732–June 1735. Hargrett Rare Book Collection, University of Georgia. fax.libs.uga.edu/egmont/epmenu.html.

Egmont, John Percival. 1733a. Letter from Benjamin Martyn to James Oglethorpe, Feb 21. Egmont Papers, typescript of vol. 14207, letters to Georgia, June 1732–June 1735. Hargrett Rare Book Collection, University of Georgia. fax.libs.uga.edu/egmont/epmenu.html.

Egmont, John Percival. 1733b. Letter from Benjamin Martyn to James Oglethorpe, April 4. Egmont Papers, typescript of vol. 14207, letters to

Georgia, June 1732–June 1735. Hargrett Rare Book Collection, University of Georgia. fax.libs.uga.edu/egmont/epmenu.html.

Egmont, John Percival. 1735. Letter from Benjamin Martyn to Paul Amatis, May 15. Egmont Papers, typescript of vol. 14207, letters to Georgia, June 1732–June 1735. Hargrett Rare Book Collection, University of Georgia. fax.libs.uga.edu/egmont/epmenu.html.

Egmont, John Percival. 1732. A List of the Persons sent to Georgia on the Charity by the Trustees for Establishing the Colony there, 14a, 14d, 14e; Egmont Papers, typescript of vol. 14207, letters to Georgia, June 1732–June 1735. Hargrett Rare Book Collection, University of Georgia. http://fax.libs.uga.edu/egmont/epmenu.html.

Fairlie, Susan. 1965. "Dyestuffs in the Eighteenth Century." *The Economic History Review,* new series, vol. 17, no. 3: 488–510.

Field, Moses, account book, 5437, 1750–95, Pocumtuck Valley Memorial Association (PVMA), Deerfield, Massachusetts.

Ford, Worthington Chauncey, ed. 1906. *Journals of the Continental Congress, 1774–1789,* vol. 5. Washington, D.C.: Government Printing Office.

Franklin, Benjamin. 1749. "Poor Richard Improved: Being an Almanack and Ephemeris . . . for the Year of our Lord 1749." In *The Papers of Benjamin Franklin.* Vol. 3. franklinpapers.org.

Gittinger, Mattiebelle. 1982. *Master Dyers to the World: Technique and Trade in Early Indian Dyed Cotton Textiles.* Washington, D.C.: The Textile Museum.

Gordon, Adam. 1916. "Journal of an Officer Who Travelled in America and the West Indies in 1764 and 1765." In *Travels in the American Colonies,* edited by Newton D. Mereness, 369–453. New York: Macmillan Company.

Gottesman, Rita Suswein, ed. 1938. *The Arts and Crafts of New York: Advertisements and News Items from New York City Newspapers.* New York: Printed for the New York Historical Society.

Hatch, Charles E., Jr. 1957. "Mulberry Trees and Silkworms: Sericulture in Early Virginia." *The Virginia Magazine of History and Biography* vol. 65, no. 1 (January): 3–61.

Hening, William Waller, ed. 1810. *The Statutes at Large; Being a Collection of All the Laws of Virginia from the First Session of the Legislature, in the Year 1619.* Vol. 2. Richmond, VA: Samuel Pleasants.

Hening, William Waller, ed. 1823. *The Statutes at Large; Being a Collection of All the Laws of Virginia from the First Session of the Legislature, in the Year 1619,* 2nd ed. Vol. 1. New York: R. and W. and G. Bartow.

Hersh, Tandy and Charles Hersh. 1995. *Cloth and Costume, 1750–1800, Cumberland County, Pennsylvania.* Carlisle, PA: Cumberland County Historical Society.

Hinsdale, Ebenezer, account book, 1747–51, Pocumtuck Valley Memorial Association (PVMA), Deerfield, MA.

Hoadly, Charles J., ed. 1870. *The Public Records of the Colony of Connecticut from October 1706–October 1716.* Hartford, CT: Case, Lockwood and Brainard.

Horry, Peter. 1840. *The Life of General Francis Marion.* Philadelphia: J. B. Lippencott.

Humphrey, William and Zuriel Waterman. 1984. *Rhode Islanders Record the Revolution: The Journals of William Humphrey and Zuriel Waterman,* edited by Nathaniel N. Shipton and David Swain. Providence: Rhode Island Publications Society.

Interim Field Reports, 1994–98, Jamestown Rediscovery. www.preservationvirginia.org/rediscovery/page.php?page_id = 9.

An Inventory . . . belonging to Benjamin Dart and Company. *Inventories, Charleston, South Carolina, 1753–1756,* vol. 82B, typescript: 501–13.

Inventory of Asa Childs. www.historic-deerfield.org/files/hd/docs/childs_asa_1715–1756.pdf.

Inventory of Ezekiel Bascom. www.historic-deerfield.org/files/hd/docs/EZEKIEL-BASCOM-1700–1746.pdf.

Inventory . . . of John Sheppard, Deceas'd January the Nineteenth 1741/2. *Inventories, Charleston County, 1741–1743,* vol. 73, typescript: 122–24.

Jefferson, Thomas. 1904. *The Works of Thomas Jefferson,* Federal Edition, edited by Paul Leicester Ford. Vol. 5. New York: G. P. Putnam's Sons.

Johnson, Edward. 1910. *Wonder-Working Providence of Sions Saviour in New England,* reprint of 1654 ed. New York: Scribner's Sons.

Kerridge, Eric. 1985. *Textile Manufactures in Early Modern England.* Manchester: Manchester University.

Kingsbury, Susan Myra, ed. 1933. *The Records of the Virginia Company of London.* Vol. 3. Washington, D.C.: United States Government Printing Office.

Kingsbury, Susan Myra, ed. 1935. *The Records of the Virginia Company of London.* Vol. 4. Washington, D.C.: United States Government Printing Office.

Krohn, Deborah H. and Peter N. Miller, eds. 2009. "The Inventory of Margrieta van Varick." In *Dutch New York between East and West: The World of Margrieta van Varick.* 342–62. New Haven, CT: Yale University.

Lemire, Beverly. 1988. "Consumerism in Preindustrial and Early Industrial England: The Trade in Secondhand Clothes." *Journal of British Studies* vol. 27, no. 1 (January): 1–24.

Lemire, Beverly. 1997. *Dress, Culture and Commerce: The English Clothing Trade before the Factory, 1660–1680.* Basingstoke: Palgrave.

Levey, Santina M. 1983. *Lace: A History.* Leeds: W.S. Maney and Son.

Lippincott, Bertram. 1961. *Indians, Privateers, and High Society: A Rhode Island Sampler.* Philadelphia: Lippincott.

Little, Frances. 1931. *Early American Textiles.* New York: Century Company.

Lord, Eleanor Louisa. 1896. *Industrial Experiments in the British Colonies of North America.* Baltimore: Johns Hopkins.

Luckenbach, Al and C. Jane Cox. 2003. "Seventeenth-Century Lead Cloth Seals from Anne Arundel County, Maryland." *Maryland Archaeology* vol. 39, nos. 1 and 2 (March/September): 17–26.

Macdonald, Anne. 1988. *No Idle Hands: The Social History of American Knitting.* New York: Ballantine.

Maeder, Edward F. 2001. "A Man's Banyan: High Fashion in Rural Massachusetts." *Historic Deerfield Magazine* (Winter).

Main, Gloria L. 1994. "Gender, Work, and Wages in Colonial New England." *William and Mary Quarterly* 3rd ser., vol. 51, no. 1 (January): 39–66.

Mallios, Seth and Beverly Staube. 2000. "1999 Interim Report on the APVA Excavations at Jamestown, Virginia." Richmond: Association for the Preservation of Virginia Antiquities.

Manwaring, Charles William, ed. 1904. *A Digest of the Early Connecticut Probate Records: Hartford District.* Hartford, CT: self-published.

Maryland Prerogative Court. 1679. *Inventories and Accounts, 1679.* Vol. 6. Microfilm.

Maryland Prerogative Court. 1775. *Inventories, 1775.* Vol. 119. Microfilm.

Meriwether, Robert L. 1940. *The Expansion of South Carolina, 1729–1765.* Kingsport, TN: Southern Publishers.

Merritt, Elizabeth, ed. 1956. *Archives of Maryland: Proceedings of the Provincial Court of Maryland, 1677–1678.* Vol. 67. Baltimore: Maryland Historical Society.

MESDA (Museum of Early Southern Decorative Arts) craftsman database.

Monsky, John R. 2002. "Finding America in Its First Political Textile." *Winterthur Portfolio* vol. 37, no. 4 (Winter): 239–64.

Montgomery, Florence. 1970. *Printed Textiles: English and American Cottons and Linens, 1700–1850.* New York: Viking.

Montgomery, Florence. 1984. *Textiles in America, 1650–1870.* New York: W.W. Norton.

Moore, Alexander. 1994. "Daniel Axtell's Account Book and the Economy of Early South Carolina." *South Carolina Historical Magazine* vol. 95, no. 4 (October): 280–301.

Morgan, Edmund S. 1962. *The Gentle Puritan: A Life of Ezra Stiles, 1727–1795.* New Haven: Yale University.

Nash, Gary. 1986. *The Urban Crucible: The Northern Seaports and the Origins of the American Revolution,* abridged ed. Cambridge, MA: Harvard University.

Ordoñez, Margaret T. and Linda Welters. 1998. "Textiles from the Seventeenth-Century Privy at the Cross Street Back Lot Site." *Historical Archaeology* vol. 32, no. 3: 81–90.

Penn, William. 1912a. "A Further Account of Pennsylvania, by William Penn, 1685." In *Narratives of Early Pennsylvania, West New Jersey, and Delaware, 1630–1707,* edited by Albert Cook Myers, 255–78. New York: Charles Scribner's Sons.

Penn, William. 1912b. "Some Account of the Province of Pennsilvania, by William Penn, 1681." In *Narratives of Early Pennsylvania, West New Jersey, and Delaware, 1630–1707,* edited by Albert Cook Myers, 197–215. New York: Charles Scribner's Sons.

"A Perfect Description of Virginia 1649." etext.lib.virginia.edu/etcbin/jamestown-browse?id = J1080.

Perris, George Herbert. 1914. *The Industrial History of Modern England.* New York: Henry Holt.

Pettit, Florence. 1976. "The Printed Textiles of Eighteenth-Century America." In *Irene Emery Roundtable on Museum Textiles, 1975 Proceedings: Imported and Domestic Textiles in Eighteenth-Century America,* edited by Patricia L. Fiske, 33–57. Washington, DC: The Textile Museum.

Pinckney, Eliza Lucas. 1997. *The Letterbook of Eliza Lucas Pinckney, 1739–1762,* edited and introduction by Elise Pinckney. Columbia: University of South Carolina.

Postlethwayt, Malachy. 1971. *The Universal Dictionary of Trade and Commerce,* reprint of 1774, 4th ed., 2 vols. New York: Augustus Kelley.

Pringle, Robert. 1972. *The Letterbook of Robert Pringle,* ed. Walter Edgar, 2 vols. Columbia: University of South Carolina.

Raffel, Marta Cotterell. 2003. *The Laces of Ipswich: The Art and Economics of an Early American Industry, 1750–1840.* Hanover, NH: University Press of New England.

Richardson, Francis. Letterbook of Francis Richardson, 1681–1688. Historical Society of Pennsylvania.

Rogers, Horatio, and Edward Field, eds. 1901. *The Early Records of the Town of Providence.* Vol. 16. Providence: City Council of Providence.

Rogers, Horatio, George Moulton Carpenter, and Edward Field, eds. 1894. *The Early Records of the Town of Providence.* Vol. 7. Providence: City Council of Providence.

Rothstein, Natalie. 1976. "Silks Imported into America in the Eighteenth Century: An Historical Survey." In *Irene Emery Roundtable on Museum Textiles, 1975 Proceedings: Imported and Domestic Textiles in Eighteenth-Century America.* 21–30. Washington, D.C.: The Textile Museum.

Rothstein, Natalie, ed. 1987. *Lady of Fashion: Barbara Johnson's Album of Styles and Fabrics.* London: Thames and Hudson.

Rutman, Darrett B. 1965. *Winthrop's Boston: Portrait of a Puritan Town, 1630–1649.* Chapel Hill: University of North Carolina.

Scott, Kenneth, comp. 2000. *Genealogical Data from Colonial New York Newspapers,* reprint. Baltimore: Genealogical Publishing.

Seybolt, Robert Francis, ed. 1929. "Trade Agreements in Colonial Boston." *New England Quarterly* vol. 2, no. 2 (April): 307–09.

Shaw, Madelyn. 2006. "Georgia Silk: From Sericulture to Status Symbol." In *Decorative Arts in Georgia: Historic Sites, Historic Contexts.* Athens: Georgia Museum of Art.

Shirley, John W. 1949. "George Percy at Jamestown, 1607–1612." *Virginia Magazine of History and Biography* vol. 57, no. 3 (July): 227–43.

Shurtleff, Nathaniel B., ed. 1853. *Records of the Governor and Company of the Massachusetts Bay in New England, 1642–1649.* Vol. 2. Boston: William White.

Shurtleff, Nathaniel B., ed. 1855a. *Records of the Colony of New Plymouth in New England, Court Orders: Vol. 1. 1633–1640.* Boston: William White.

Shurtleff, Nathaniel B., ed. 1855b. *Records of the Colony of New Plymouth in New England, Court Orders: Vol. 2. 1641–1651.* Boston: William White.

Silverman, David J. 2005. *Faith and Boundaries: Colonists, Christianity, and Community among the Wampanoag Indians of Martha's Vineyard, 1600–1871.* Cambridge, MA: Cambridge University.

Smead, Ebenezer, account book. Pocumtuck Valley Memorial Association (PVMA), Deerfield, Massachusetts.

Smith, Adam. 1904. *An Inquiry into the Nature and Causes of the Wealth of Nations,* edited by Edwin Cannan, 5th ed. London: Methuen.

"South Carolina Gleanings in England." 1904. *South Carolina Historical and Genealogical Magazine* vol. 5, no. 4 (October): 218–28.

Sprigg, June. 1984. *Domestick Beings.* New York: Alfred A. Knopf.

Staples, Kathleen. 2003. "Dresden Embroidered Lace." *Sampler and Antique Needlework Quarterly* vol. 32, no. 3 (fall): 36–44.

Straube, Beverly, personal communication, February 13, 2009.

Thirsk, Joan. 1978. *Economic Policy and Projects: The Development of a Consumer Society in Early Modern England.* Oxford: Clarendon.

Thorp, Daniel B. 1991. "Doing Business in the Backcountry: Retail Trade in Colonial Rowan County, North Carolina." *William and Mary Quarterly* 3rd ser., vol. 48, no. 3 (July): 387–408.

Tryon, Rolla Milton. 1966. *Household Manufactures in the United States, 1640–1860,* reprint of 1917 ed. New York: Augustus Kelley.

Van Ruymbeke, Bertrand. 2006. *From New Babylon to Eden: The Huguenots and Their Migration to Colonial South Carolina.* Columbia: University of South Carolina.

Walton, Perry. 1937 *The Story of Textiles.* New York: Tudor Publishing.

Ward, Gerald W. R. 1985. *The Great River: Art and Society of the Connecticut Valley, 1635–1820.* Hartford, CT: Wadsworth Atheneum.

Washington, George. 1763. George Washington to Charles Lawrence, April 26; Series 5, Financial Papers, Account Book 1. The George Washington Papers at the Library of Congress, 1741–1799. memory.loc.gov/ammem/mgwquery.html.

Washington, George. 1764. George Washington to Charles Lawrence, August 10, Series 5, Financial Papers, Account Book 1. The George Washington Papers at the Library of Congress, 1741–1799. memory.loc.gov/ammem/mgwquery.html.

Washington, George. 1768. George Washington to Charles Lawrence, June 20, Series 5, Financial Papers, Account Book 1. The George Washington Papers at the Library of Congress, 1741–1799. memory.loc.gov/ammem/mgwquery.html.

Washington, George. 1772. George Washington to Thomas Gibson, July 15, Series 5, Financial Papers, Account Book 2. The George Washington Papers at the Library of Congress, 1741–1799. memory.loc.gov/ammem/mgwquery.html.

Washington, George. 1773. George Washington to Robert Cary & Company, July 10, Account Book 2. The George Washington Papers at the Library of Congress, 1741–1799. memory.loc.gov/ammem/mgwquery.html.

Watson, John Fanning. Watson's Annals, manuscript, 1069.F, 69–72; 163–166; 219–230. The Library Company, Philadelphia.

Weeden, William Babcock. 1894. *Economic and Social History of New England, 1620–1789*, 2 vols. Boston: Houghton, Mifflin.

Welsh, Peter C. 1964. *Tanning in the United States to 1850: A Brief History.* Washington, DC: Smithsonian Institution.

Wilbour, Benjamin Franklin, ed. 1945. *Little Compton, Rhode Island, Wills.* Little Compton, RI: privately published.

Wilkinson, Eliza Yonge. 1839. *Letters of Eliza Wilkinson during the Invasion and Possession of Charleston, S.C. by the British in the Revolutionary War.* New York: S. Colman.

Winthrop, John. 1908. *Winthrop's Journal, "History of New England," 1630–1649*, edited by James Kendall Hosmer, 2 vols. New York: Charles Scribner's Sons.

Wise, Jennings Cropper. 1911. *Ye Kingdome of Accawmacke or the Eastern Shore of Virginia in the Seventeenth Century.* Richmond: Bell Book and Stationery Company.

Woodfin, Maude H. ed. 1942. *Another Secret Diary of William Byrd of Westover, 1739–1741, with Letters and Literary Exercises, 1696–1726.* Richmond: Dietz.

Woodward, Carl R. 1971. *Plantation in Yankeeland: The Story of Cocumscussoc, Mirror of Colonial Rhode Island.* Chester, CT: Pequot.

Women's Fashion

In a newe plantation it is not knowen whether man or woman be more necessary.

—"Proceedings of the Virginia Assembly, 1619"

Determining the wardrobes of colonial women is a challenge for modern researchers, in part, because of the nature of women's legal and economic status in the colonial period. The underpinning of that status was the English common law tradition of coverture. Under coverture, when a woman married, her legal and economic identity became covered by that of her husband. A married couple was legally a single person with a single will. Because a husband and wife had a single will, they could not testify against each other. All property possessed by the wife was vested in her husband to use and dispose of as he saw fit and without her permission. Her protection in the event of her husband's predeceasing her was her dower right: the free use and improvement of one-third part of all real and personal property of her husband during her remaining life. The opposite of coverture, or *feme covert,* was *feme sole,* the unmarried woman. The *feme sole* clearly had property rights and could take legal measures to protect them.

The status of a woman as *feme covert* or *feme sole* had implications in probate records. Under coverture a woman who predeceased her husband had neither a will nor an inventory unless a prenuptial agreement had been executed or she had received outside gifts of property during her marriage. A woman who survived her husband was already entitled by law to one-third of his estate for use during her lifetime only. Thus, unless: (1) her husband bequeathed additional objects of value to her in his will; (2) she had a prenuptial agreement; or (3) she obtained goods of value on her own as a widow, there were no possessions to be inventoried after her death because her husband's will would be the only recognized legal instrument. If she had possessions of meager value, an inventory would not be taken. Both married and single women often gave away articles of clothing before they died, and bequests in women's wills often were carried out before an inventory was taken. For example, when the estate of widow Elizabeth Spooner was taken, in 1677, the assessors noted that her "waring Clothes with a hat [were] all giuen away" (Dow 1920, 3:142).

Thus, while inventories are among the most fruitful documents, they are not always a snapshot of a complete wardrobe and seldom include the belongings of impoverished or young women. Information concerning the sartorial possessions of the poorer sorts and the enslaved, however, can be gleaned from records of court proceedings, diary entries, letters, proscriptive statements by colonial courts and the clergy, and, in the 18th century, newspaper advertisements for runaways.

1608–1714

THE EVOLUTION OF CUT, CONSTRUCTION, AND SILHOUETTE, 1608–1714

What British clothing historian Janet Arnold observed about the clothing of England's Elizabeth I is true for the wardrobes of those women who settled in the colonies of Virginia, Plymouth, and Massachusetts during the earliest decades of the 17th century. "Each costume . . . was composed of a large number of detachable pieces"—ruff, sleeves, bodice, petticoat, stomacher, gown, and cap—"were all separate items, and interchangeable" (Arnold 1988, 14). But by the end of the second decade, women's clothing had undergone great changes because of the whims of fashion at the English Court. The kirtle, popular during the reign of Elizabeth I (died 1603), continued to be worn during the first decade of the reign of James I and Anne of Denmark (1604–1625), but eventually was replaced by the bodice and overskirt, or petticoat. Beginning in 1625, with the court of Charles I and Henriette Maria, women's clothing underwent a complete transformation. Farthingales, ruffs, and tightly laced and long-waisted bodices were replaced by simpler, and likely more comfortable, clothing. Most female colonists were unable to emulate the sartorial luxury of the courts; however, within the bounds of their purses and the availability of goods, both bespoke and ready-made, women in centers of larger population had the opportunity to keep up with changes in style. The third transition in women's clothing came in the late 1670s, when the separate boned bodice and skirt was replaced by the one-piece mantua.

Main Garments, 1608–1630

Very few records survive to document what early female colonists wore and those records begin in the 1630s. Women who immigrated to Virginia, beginning in 1608, were a mixture of indentured servants, orphans of an age to be indentured, and women of a more elevated social status. Some of the latter were married; they either were meeting husbands who had already immigrated or they accompanied their spouses. As noted in Chapter 2, the first suggestion that women as well as men were wearing "excesse in apparell" was the Virginia law of 1619 that assessed men—and if married, their wives—for the support of the church according to the value of their clothing. In contrast, the 18 adult women on board the *Mayflower* in 1621 were the wives of working men, who might have been called "Master" but not "Gentleman." Their clothing, while colorful, was serviceable. The Puritan women who accompanied their husbands to establish the Massachusetts Bay Colony in 1629 were married to educated, well-to-do middling sorts—skilled craftsmen, tradesmen, and those in professions; their wardrobes likely reflected their husbands' status. There were very few servants, and those who did emigrate were already employed by a family before leaving England.

Kirtle

A garment whose use dates back to at least the 14th century and always worn over a shift, or smock, the kirtle consisted of a fitted bodice with an attached floor-length skirt. The bodice was usually stiffened or lined. The kirtle had detachable fitted, wrist-length sleeves that tied to the top of the armholes of the bodice with ribbons or metal-tipped points, which laced through small eyelets. Kirtles intended to be worn with an overgown were constructed to lace up the back or sometimes at the side. If meant to be worn alone over the smock, it was laced up the center front. The skirt portion was made of rectangular panels that were wide enough to give fullness. Wealthier and more fashionable women wore a petticoat under the kirtle. Although the kirtle was obsolete in England by about 1620, the style continued to be worn in New England by older women into the mid-century. For example, the 1633 inventory of Separatist Mary Ring lists a kirtle of black say, a thin woolen twill weave (Inventory of . . . Mary Ring).

Gown or Overgown

A full-length overdress, the gown had either a fitted bodice or a loose top pleated into the shoulders; it was open down the front and worn over a kirtle, a bodice and petticoat, or waistcoat and petticoat. The gown either was sleeveless with crescent-shaped shoulder wings, or epaulets, or had short round attached sleeves. It could fasten with buttons and loops or a clasp at the throat and sometimes closed with a sash at the waist.

Bodice

An alternative to and eventual replacement for the kirtle was the separate bodice and overskirt. Opening down the front, the bodice was a tight-fitting garment, lined and usually stiffened, that covered the torso and flattened the bust. Tailors' patterns from 1618 show that the bodice was cut with the straight grain of the fabric down the center front. The front section was pointed or rounded and ended well below the waist; it extended around the body to the side back. The side back and center back seams were only slightly curved, creating the desired shape of a truncated cone. The neckline could be rounded and low or, for modesty, cut higher. The front opening was laced close with points or a triangular stomacher could be attached to the V-shaped opening with laces or hooks and eyes. To be more comfortable when pregnant, a woman loosened the lacings of her bodice and pinned a piece of cloth under the two fronts. For the poorer sorts, an apron tied higher up around the bodice likely substituted for this insertion.

Bodice sleeves were cut in two pieces, with a shallow curve at the front and a steeper curve from elbow to wrist down the back seam. The sleeves were either gathered or pleated into the bodice or detached and tied in place with points or laces. Flat crescent-shaped wings sometimes covered the join of the sleeve to the bodice. The wrist end of the sleeve fitted snugly. Bodice and sleeve seams were sometimes covered with braids or narrow lace of silk or metal threads. By the 1620s sleeve heads often had an additional row of flaps (tabs) or loops sewn into the sleeve cap, as in men's doublets.

Waistcoat or Jacket

Although a padded or quilted waistcoat might have been worn for warmth as an undergarment, a woman's waistcoat or jacket was for work, everyday, or informal wear. It was constructed of two front pieces that extended around the body to the side back; a back piece; and triangular gussets or gores, which were inserted into the seams to allow expansion over the hips into a short skirt called a *basque*. Opening down the front, jackets commonly reached several inches below the waist, and the necklines were higher than for bodices. Early in the period sleeves were cut into two pieces, shaped to curve with the bend of the elbow, and fit snugly. They were wrist length and sometimes cuffed; at the shoulder seam, narrow flat bands or tabs might be inserted. Sleeves became wider and more barrel shaped in the 1620s; their rectangular shape was gathered into the armseye and a wristband.

This loose-fitting, informal linen jacket was not meant to be seen in public. It was meant to be worn at home over a petticoat and stays. (Victoria and Albert Museum, London)

In England, between about 1600 and 1620, lavish versions of jackets were constructed of fine linen or silk and embellished with silk and metallic embroidery and/or lace; they likely were at-home attire for the well-to-do. The more ornate versions also may have been worn to be partly visible. There is no documentation, however, that highly ornamented waistcoats were worn in the colonies. Margaret Winthrop asked a Boston friend to buy her "five yards of flowered holland for a wastcott and tape to bind it" (Earle 1895, 237). The use of flowered holland suggests that the garment was for informal wear.

Petticoat/Overskirt

For much of the 17th century the petticoat referred to two different garments: one an outer garment, the other an undergarment. The outer garment, or overskirt, was cut from several full width-lengths of cloth, seamed into a tube, and gathered or pleated onto a waistband or headed with a drawstring casing. Many overskirts had an inverted V-shaped opening in front to expose an under-petticoat of a contrasting material. Petticoats for outer wear might match or harmonize with a bodice or other outer clothing. The over-petticoat attached to the bodice with points or with hooks and eyes. Early in this period, when the overskirt was worn with a farthingale, the skirt might expose the toes of the shoes. With the disappearance of the farthingale, however, the skirt became extremely full and reached the ground.

Stomacher

An essential piece in women's clothing of the colonial period, the stomacher was a panel that filled the V-shaped opening at the center front of a bodice. The stomacher added decoration and provided structure. It was pinned to the bodice—or stays if they were worn—and the bodice might then be laced close over it. Stomachers were generally decorative and might match a gown or contrast or harmonize with it both in fabric and trimmings.

In the early 17th century the stomacher was lined with pasteboard or heavy canvas and stiffened with strips of baleen or wood, it extended from the neckline to past the waist and onto the top of the skirt. In the late 1620s, as clothing became less restrictive, the stomacher was constructed to be less rigid.

Outer Garments, 1608–1630

Unfitted circular or semicircular cloaks, or capes, were important and common forms of outerwear for both women and men throughout this period. Ranging from waist to ankle length, they generally were based on a circular cut that required little tailoring even if there were seamed segments. Short, half-circle cloaks might be stiffened. Longer cloaks were more likely to be full circles and were less likely to have elaborate trimmings and stiffening. Both types usually had some sort of collar, either standing or flat, although an attached hood might also be found on occasion. Length depended on season and status. Fabric choice depended on season, degree of formality, and as always, the owner's ability to pay for quality goods.

An alternative to the cloak, the shawl wrapped around the shoulders and came down to points in the front. In 17th-century probate records from New England, shawls were called whittles. (Whittle was a local term for a kind of shawl worn by women living in the western counties of England.)

Vndergarments, 1608–1630

Shift or Smock

All white and most enslaved women owned at least one shift or smock (also called a chemise). The quality of the fabric generally suited the status of the wearer. The shape was similar to the man's shirt: it was cut from rectangles, squares, and triangles of fabric with the pattern laid out on the cloth to waste as little fabric as possible. Triangular gores may also have been added at the sides to add width at the hem without adding bulk around the waist. The shift reached to just below the knees.

Most often the body of the woman's shift was gathered to a straight band at front and back although some surviving English examples have the high neckline of a man's shirt. Large sleeves reached from just below the elbow to the wrist and were gathered into a narrow band. Women of status might have the neckline and sleeve bands finished with a ruffle, edged with lace, or embroidered. Surviving English and European examples also have embroidery, cutwork, or lace insertions on the body of the smock and/or the sleeves (Arnold 2008, 54–64).

No 17th-century colonial records exist concerning bed clothing for colonial women; however, in England women of any consequence wore a night shift or smock, which was also called a night rail. The garment likely had some form of fine lace trimming and for the more affluent, embroidery in silk and metal threads.

Drawers

In addition to a smock, some women wore drawers. Surviving English examples from the late 16th and early 17th centuries are of linen and decorated with silk embroidery. Some styles have a waistband and closure; others were tied to the stays with points. The legs, which extended to above the knees, were either cut straight to fit the upper leg or cut full and gathered into a narrow band with tying strings. Drawers were sometimes lined (Arnold 2008, 50–51).

Stays

In the 17th and 18th centuries the term "stays" referred to a stiffened underbodice that supported and molded the figure into the fashionable shape of the moment (the 16th-century term "pair of bodies" also referred to stays in this period). Stays were constructed of two layers of cloth sewn together with closely spaced vertical channels to carry either bundles of thin reeds—called bents—or baleen (erroneously called whalebone in the records) to stiffen the garment. Some versions left the breast area unstiffened. A wider channel may have been constructed at the front center to hold a busk—a wide piece of wood, bone, or ivory that extended the length of the center front to kept the stays straight. The busk was tied in position with a busk point through a pair of eyelet holes. The garment laced close through eyelets placed along the center back.

During this period, stays usually had attached shoulder straps and a pointed front that extended below the waistline. In the back, the bottom was finished straight across the waistline; stiffened skirt tabs were sewn to the sides and fell over the hips. The waist edge accommodated pairs of eyelet holes for the attachment of a farthingale or under-petticoat. The obverse side of the stays sometimes was covered with a finer fabric, either linen or more costly silk.

Petticoat

Women wore one or more under-petticoats over the shift to support the petticoat and gown skirts and give them the fashionable fullness. The petticoat appears to have joined the woman's wardrobe in England by 1585 although there is little documentation about its construction. It was probably cut, as it was in later years, from two or more breadths of fabric—not shaped—that were seamed together along the selvages. The resulting tube was either gathered at the front and back into a split waistband that tied or buttoned at the side seams or it was finished at the waist with a casing and drawstring and tied on around the waist. It was likely tied onto the stays to keep it in place.

Skirt Supports

Until about 1620, formal fashion at the English court dictated that the skirt of a woman's gown was held out over the hips. This was accomplished in one of two ways. The first was the farthingale, an under-petticoat reinforced with hoops of cane, baleen, or wire. The result was a drum-shaped underskirt that stood out horizontally at waist level.

An alternative to the farthingale was the hip, or bum, roll, also known as a French farthingale. Tightly stuffed, this tubular or crescent-shaped bolster was tied on around the upper hip. To accentuate this shape, the overskirt was pulled up at the waist and pleated all around like a great ruff. This ruff of material rested on the bolster and was held in place with pins and accented with ribbons. Women wore versions of the bum roll to achieve whatever silhouette was in fashion almost until the end of the 17th century.

Small Linen and Hats, 1608–1630

"Small linen" and "wearing linen" are period terms for fabric accessories women wore at the neck, wrist and on the head.

To complete an ensemble, all but the poorest women wore some kind of detachable collar, also called a band. High-ranking women wore a closed or open standing band, which could be made of sheer linen, linen with a lace edging, or completely of lace. Darted to fit and highly starched, the standing band spread out flat in a fan shape around the head. The closed version fit closely around the neck, the two straight ends of the collar meeting to form a horizontal line in front and fastening under the chin with strings. The open band framed just the back or the back and sides of the head.

Both styles were pinned to a rigid frame of shaped pasteboard or wire stiffened with paper or baleen variously called a *supportasse*, pickadil, or underpropper. Tied to the back of the gown with ribbon points, the supporter was covered in a fabric whose color would show through the diaphanous linen or lace. In England the popularity of standing collar lasted into the 1630s.

An elite alternative to the standing collar was the ruff. Ruffs were strips of lightweight linen, gathered into cartridge pleats and attached to a neckband, which closed either with buttons and buttonholes or eyelets and bandstrings. Heavily starched, the pleats were set in place by the laundress, who used a hot steel poking stick. The laundress might also use pins or wax to ensure that the pleats kept their shape (Mikhaila and Malcom-Davies 2006, 30). Colored starch was sometimes used, yellow being the most popular hue. Variations in style depended upon the type and amount of fabric used, the width of the strips, the number of layers, and the shape of the pleats. Seven surviving European and English ruffs were constructed of joined strips of linen that vary in length from one and a half to over 19 yards (Arnold 2008, 10, 28–31). Wider versions might be closed or open and were supported by an underpropper. The most expensive ruffs were ornamented with embroidery or spangles or edged with lace.

In the 1620 falling ruffs, made of several layers of pleated linen, with or without lace, and unstarched, became fashionable. In the colonies the use of lace and ruffs in any form depended on social and economic status. For everyday wear the falling band, a starched collar with one layer of cloth, was common. Shaped with darts to fit the neck, it was usually tied at the center front with cords called bandstrings, which might be tipped with tassels.

Instead of the heavier standing collar or ruff, a woman might have worn a partlet to fill the open neckline of a gown or bodice. A yoke-like fitted garment, the partlet closed with pins or loops and buttons and sometimes had an attached neckband. A surviving example shows that the two front panels were longer than that for the back. It was worn tucked into the bodice or stays and may have been pinned in place (Arnold 2008, 43, 101). Partlets for working women were made of plain linen. More expensive versions, made of fine, lightweight linen, had lace or embroidered embellishments. As an alternative to the partlet, a woman might wear a pinner to help fill the open neckline. The pinner was a wide linen or lace edging, flat or ruffled, that was pinned around the neck edge of a gown or bodice.

For those who could afford it, the wrists of the long, close-fitting bodice sleeves were covered with cuffs of fine linen and/or lace that were pinned in place. The lace might match that of the standing collar or pinner. Until the end of the 17th century, cuffs were darted, pleated, or gathered into the desired shape (Arnold 2008, 11).

The most common piece of headwear worn by women, the coif was a close-fitting cap constructed of one shaped rectangular piece of linen. The shape was folded in half and a seam stitched across one end, within small pleats for the back of the crown of the head. The other end had a narrow casing or loops for a drawstring, which usually tied at the nape of the neck, but could also be wound around that portion of the cap that covered the hair bun at back. The sides of the coif curved forward near the jaw line. Coifs with embroidered decoration were worn by the more fashionable and well-to-do.

The crosscloth, also called a forehead cloth, was a triangular piece of linen fabric worn under a coif (contemporary Dutch paintings sometimes show the forehead cloth on top of the coif). The bias edge usually was laid across the top of the forehead with the triangular point toward the back of the head (Mikhaila and Malcolm-Davies 2006, 30). Crosscloths worn by working women generally were not embroidered, but some English examples are embroidered to match the coif. Dutch pictorial works show women in bed or after childbirth wearing a crosscloth with a coif.

Over the crosscloth and coif a woman might wear one or more of the following: a hood, a scarf, or a hat. Constructed of a triangle of fabric with a curved V-shape cut into one corner to make a seam for the top of the head, the hood fitted closely on the head and fell softly onto or over the shoulders; side gussets increased the fullness (Arnold 2008, 104). Hoods could be made of linen, wool, or silk and might be lined for warmth. A scarf was a square of fabric folded into a triangle, worn with the folded bias edge framing the face; the two ends tied under the chin. Like hoods, scarves could be made of linen, wool, or expensive silk.

In the early 17th century women adopted the masculine, high-crowned, and wide-brimmed hat. Two styles were popular. The first, called a capotain, featured a tall crown, slightly conical, and a narrow brim. (Contrary to popular myth, the capotain never had a buckle at the front brim.) This style was worn into the 1620s. The second, today referred to as a sugar-loaf hat, resembled the capotain but had a stiff, wide brim that could be worn flat, turned up in front or turned down in both front and back. The sugar-loaf hat remained popular through most of the 17th century. The most costly of these would have been made of felted beaver; less expensive versions were of felted wool. The hat was often decorated with a band of fabric or a wide tape. Women of status might add a feather.

Footwear, 1608–1630

Stockings or Hose

In England, wealthy women wore stockings of knitted silk or fine linen; working women wore coarse linen or woolen knitted stockings. The poorest sorts probably went bare legged. Six of the 57 women who sailed from the Isle of Wight to Jamestown in 1621 as potential wives for Virginia planters were provided by Virginia Company investors with two pairs of stockings as well as worsted and yarn for stockings, presumably for the women to knit themselves—one of women, Susan Binx, was noted to be skilled in the craft (Ransome 1991, 15–16). Stockings were held up with tapes or ribbons called garters. These were tied just above or just below the knee.

Shoes

Until the mid-19th century, shoes for men as well as women were not differentiated for the left and right foot, but rather cut to a straight pattern.

Constructed using a last, the shoe had a long tongue that could extend over the top of the foot to the ankle. The vamp, or top of the shoe, was cut low to the instep. Attached to or made in one with the quarter—the rear and sides—were two straps called latchets, which were tied together with a cord or ribbon on top of the foot.

During this period, latchet shoes had rounded toes and small, hand-carved wooden heels that curved in from the sole to the base. Elegant versions had thinner latchets and smaller quarters and vamps. Most women's shoes were made of sturdy leather; however, more luxurious versions were of thin kid leather or had vamps, latchets, and quarters covered in a patterned silk or wool. Women's shoes were usually hidden by their skirts although the toes of the shoes were sometimes seen.

For protection in inclement weather or on impassible streets, women wore protective overshoes—clogs and pattens—that elevated the feet above the mud. Clogs, made of wood or cork, generally had a low, flat sole. Held in place by leather or fabric bands, pattens were platforms that elevated the wearer by several inches. Although sometimes made completely of wood, common 17th-century pattens were of metal: a metal plate was nailed onto a flat wooden sole and elevated by metal strips attached to a flat metal ring. Only the ring touched the ground.

Hairstyles and Grooming, 1608–1630

Working women pulled back their hair into a large bun or roll at the nape of the neck and covered the head with a coif. In contrast, fashionable women tended to leave off hoods and caps in order to show their hair. The hair was drawn back from the forehead and over the ears, and dressed high on the head, supported from under the hair with a roll. In the 1620s, fashion dictated that the hair at the sides curl or wave loosely around the face, at about chin level. The hair at the back might also fall to about shoulder length or be tied up high on the back of the head in a knot. A small fringe or fine curls sometimes was seen on the forehead.

Accessories, 1608–1630

Aprons had dual functions: as a practical garment to protect the skirt from dirt and cooking liquids and as a fashionable accessory. In later colonial records, aprons for work were most often of a woolen fabric. Decorative aprons were of fine linen and might be embellished with embroidery or lace.

An accessory that women had worn for centuries, the girdle was a woven belt or decorative cord that went around the waist. It was hung with small tools and accessories, such as keys, a small devotional book, a pin ball, a knife, scissors, and a needle and thimble case. Plain girdles might be made of wool or linen, but more fashionable and more expensive versions were made of silk and metallic threads; some European examples were not woven but constructed of fine, intertwining metal links.

Sometime in the 17th century, many women adopted the pocket or a pair of pockets. Bag-shaped and with a center slit, the pocket tied around the waist with a tape or string, under the overskirt; when two pockets were worn, one was carried on each hip. They were accessed through openings in the side seams

German or Dutch woman wearing a long linen apron, ruffled collar, and wide-brimmed hat, engraving by Wenceslas Hollar, c. 1640. (Library of Congress)

of the skirt. Pockets either replaced or supplemented the girdle as a carrier for sewing tools, a diminutive book, keys, letters, and other small personal items. Researchers have noted that during an era in which a woman had few private spaces and few objects to call her own, the pocket was one of the few spaces she had for storing small possessions. Many pockets were made out of plain durable fabrics, but surviving examples also exhibit embroidery.

Affluent English women might wear a small drawstring bag looped over the sash or belt at the waist or carried in the hand. Made of a luxury fabric or elaborately embroidered, these tiny bags held sweetmeats, a handkerchief, or a few coins.

Like fashionable men, well-dressed women sometimes wore gloves with long gauntlets, the latter often decorated with lace or embroidery.

Gloves that reached only the wrist or covered it were of lambskin, knitted wool, or plain linen. The less affluent might wear knitted mittens or mitts, the latter lacking covers for the fingers.

In England, the most popular forms of women's jewelry were clasps, pins, gold earrings with drops of pearls or small colored stones, gold chains with lockets or gemstones in gold settings. Rings were worn on any finger, including the thumb. English portraits show gold rings with a thin band and single colored stone, or a seal of carved stone or metal. Mourning rings, or the money to have one made, were left as legacies. Jewelry for the common sorts was made of base metal with paste stones.

Trimmings and Ornaments

According to English portraits of the period, fashionable women might wear a rosette of ribbons at the breast or a sash of ribbon or fabric around the waistline of the bodice. Among the most popular of fashionable trimmings was robings, which had just come into use in the early 17th century. Robings was a straight strip of fabric, the long edges of which usually were cut to create a scallop or zigzag. Strips were joined together and stitched to the back neck of the bodice and down the front. Robings usually ended at the waist although they sometimes were carried down to the hem of the overskirt. They could be of the same material as the bodice or of a contrasting material or color. Later robings were embellished with embroidery.

Main Garments, 1631–1670

"The upstart impudence and innovation of naked breasts, and cutting or hallowing downe the neck of womens garments below their shoulders, an exorbitant and shamefull enormity and habit . . . is another mere piece of refined Barbarisme" (Bulwer 1650). On both sides of the Atlantic, women's fashions were a point of contention among the clergy. In colonies where sumptuary legislation was enacted—Virginia, Massachusetts, and Connecticut—in spite of whatever influence female colonists felt, legal attempts to curb excesses in dress were never effectively enforced (see Chapter 2). Probate evidence also suggests that during this period, while both information on new fashions and the latest bespoke and ready-made garments were available from England, old styles persisted—whether for religious reasons, from force of habit or out of economic concern.

Bodice

Formal dress adopted a fitted bodice with a short skirt, or peplum. The skirt was either cut in one with the bodice, with triangular inserts at the waist to create width over the hip (*basque*) or made of tabs of shaped pieces that were stitched to the bodice waist. The neckline was low-cut and could be square, rounded, or V-shaped. The bodice laced close either down the front or the back. As with the gown, the bodice sat above the natural waistline in the 1630s. An unboned bodice dated about 1635 was cut with a wide square neckline. It has a front opening, which does not meet at center front but laces close from short extensions, and full, attached two-piece sleeves with cuffs and shoulder wings or epaulets (Waugh 1968, 39, diag. iv).

In the 1640s the waist was again at the natural level; the separate tabs narrowed and shortened. At about midcentury the tabs disappeared. Now the bodice fitted snugly with a long waist that descended to a long point in the front; the back of the waist was rounded. In the 1630s, the attached sleeves were puffed; by midcentury they were elbow-length and either barrel-shaped or a loose-fitting two-piece curved shape.

Waistcoat or Jacket

Still for everyday and informal wear, the sleeved waistcoat was made to resemble the fashionable bodice style but without the boning. In contrast to the plain woolen or worsted waistcoats, some with trimming, worn by many New England women in this period, in the early 1640s, an unnamed woman in Maryland owned a "wrought" dimity waistcoat (Browne 1887, 4:95). The dimity fabric, which may have been of cotton and woven in India or of linen and woven in England, was patterned in the loom and possibly was ribbed or tufted. In the 17th century, the term "wrought" referred to any sort of added decoration, such as embroidery or cutwork, lace insertions, or paint.

Petticoat or Skirt

Until about midcentury the skirt generally was cut to form an inverted V-shaped opening at the front, exposing the under-petticoat. After about

1650, the skirt was worn more frequently closed. Instead of soft gathers, the material was pleated over the hips where the skirt met the pointed waistline of the bodice. In 17th-century New England, petticoats were most often made of woolen or worsted fabrics. Inventories of prosperous widows from Maryland, New York, and Virginia mention silk, sometimes embellished with lace. Probate inventories in this time period often refer to petticoats as "coats."

The will of Joanna Cummins of Salem, Massachusetts, dated May 11, 1644, mentions a petticoat for outer wear—a stamell (red) kersey petticoat "mitered about the scirts with vellvit." Three other petticoats—a green kersey petticoat, a blue petticoat, and a woolen petticoat—might have functioned as skirts or under-petticoats (Dow 1911, 1:65, 66). The 1666 inventory of Jane Hartry, of Northampton County, Virginia, lists 10 petticoats, all stored in an "iron bound trunk." Five of them were likely skirts, embellished with silver lace: one shag, a gray serge, a red wool, one of watered tammy, and one mohair. The remaining five included a yellow tammy, a "satinisco," and three white, the latter were likely under-petticoats (Northampton County, 13). The 1662 inventory of the unnamed wife of Jacob de Lange of New Amsterdam (later New York) includes woolen petticoats with black lace, one red and one of striped fabric; five of drugget, two with gray linings two with white linings, and one with pointed lace; one of black silk with an ash gray silk lining; and two of "potto-soo [paduasoy?]," one with a black silk lining, the other with a lining of taffeta (Earle 1903, 1:100).

Gown

By 1630 the word gown (or nightgown) was used in a way that suggests it now referred, not to an overgown, but to an informal dress with a bodice and attached skirt. The bodice opening allowed for a stomacher or decorative stays and the skirt opening showed off the petticoat. The gown was confined at the waist with a ribbon or sash. Gown sleeves were short puffs that were paned, or slashed, in the front to show off the puffed sleeve of the shift. The waistline rested above the actual waist during the 1630s, but descended again to the actual waistline in the 1640s and remained there through the rest of this period. The neckline was wide and low in the front, but it came above the shoulder blades in the back. In 1644, Joanna Cummins bequeathed to family members a sad-colored kersey gown and matching hood and a black grogram gown (Dow 1911, 1:65, 66). Jacob de Lange's wife owned three calico nightgowns, one of resist-dyed and painted flowers and two red (Earle 1903, 1:100).

Somaire

The somaire, or samair, was a knee-length overgown worn with an over-petticoat. According to the English antiquarian Randle Holme (1627–1699), the garment's skirt had four side tabs. The somaire is uncommonly found in records and inventories and then generally of well-to-do women in northern colonies. For example, in New Amsterdam, Mrs. de Lange owned a "potoso-a [paduasoy?] samare" with lace; one "tartanel [possibly tiritaine, a linsey-woolsey or all-wool fabric] samare" with a tucker (similar to a pinner); one of black silk crape with a tucker; and three of flowered calico. In 1679, Salem, Massachusetts, tailor William Sweatland charged a woman six shillings to make over her plush somaire and ten shillings to make a new somaire for the woman's maid (Earle 1903, 1:100, 103–04).

Stomacher

The shape of stomacher changed through time with the changing position of the bodice waistline. It might match or contrast with the fabric of the petticoat or the gown and/or be embellished with embroidery, tapes, or lace. The inventory of Salem resident, Margery Wathin includes six white stomachers, three of wool—likely for warmth—and three that were "wrought," that is, embellished with embroidery, lace, or ribbons (Dow 1911, 1:71).

Kirtle and Overgown

Although out-of-date as a fashionable garment in this period, kirtles were recorded in New England inventories. The 1633 probate inventory of Godbert and Zarah Godbertson lists a waistcoat and kirtle (Inventory of . . . Godbert Godbertson). Mr. John Lowle's inventory of 1647 includes old styles of clothing, such as "one grogram kertle and gowne" and "one popus gown and kertle" (Dow 1916, 5:329). The 1654 inventory of George Burrill of Lynn, Massachusetts, includes his wife's "stuff kirtle" (Dow 1911, 1:353).

Outer Garments, 1631–1670

Cloaks with or without hoods and of varying lengths and mantles provided protection against the elements. Elizabeth Lowle's inventory, taken in 1651, includes a white cloak and a mantle (Dow 1913, 3:380). The 1663 inventory of the estate of John Antrum of Salem, lists a cloak and hood for a woman (Dow 1913, 3:72, 73). The shawl, or whittle, was popular with New England women; a 1659 Massachusetts inventory lists a woolen whittle of mixed colors (Dow 1912, 2:165).

A safeguard was a heavy petticoat worn as an overskirt while riding to protect a woman's petticoats from dust and mud. In 1644, Joanna Cummins of Salem, Massachusetts, bequeathed to her friend, Goody (i.e., Goodwoman) Beacham a green safeguard (Dow 1911, 1:65, 66).

Undergarments, 1631–1670

Shift or Smock

While the cut and construction of women's shifts were universal; the quality and whiteness of the linen depended on the wealth and/or status of the wearer. Working women and indentured servants might own one or two shifts, but those of higher status owned enough to change their garments daily without daily laundering. By the 1630s, the practice of embroidering the neckline and sleeve hems of a shift had faded, but the neckline might still be edged with lace. The shift was visible above the neckline of the bodice until the 1650s, when, with a change in the cut of the bodice, it either showed only as a narrow white edge or was completely hidden. In the 1660s, the shift edge was allowed to show again; the practice remained fashionable through the end of the century.

Beginning in the 1630s, the stiff lace ruffles at the end of the shift sleeves were replaced with tapered sewn-on or detached turn-up cuffs. These cuffs were barely visible below the long dress sleeves. In the 1660s, shorter dress sleeves once again exposed the sleeves of the shift; now sleeve cuffs were replaced by dropping frills that fell from the narrow sleeve band. The band was constructed with buttonholes through which ribbon ties occasionally were fastened. If the frills were omitted, the sleeves might be puffed and held by a length of ribbon tied around the arm.

In New England, it was not seemly for a woman to be seen in public wearing only her shift as an upper garment. In 1662, the wife of Robert Wilson was sentenced for "her barbarous & unhuman goeing naked [i.e., wearing only her shift] through the Towne." She was sentenced, along with her mother and sister who helped her, to be tied to the tail-end of a cart, "naked to their shifts to ye wast," and whipped "from

Mr. Gidneyes Gat till she come to her owne house, not exceeding 30 stripes" (Dow 1913, 3:17).

Stays

Extant gowns from this period in English museum collections tend to have heavily boned bodices, which may indicate that stays were not worn frequently. Stays, or bodies, are found in colonial inventories, however; and they followed the cut of fashionable bodice styles, which dictated how high the neckline was, whether the pieces had straight or curved vertical seams, and whether the front ended in a point, was rounded or stopped at the waist. Salem Widow Margery Wathin owned a pair of whalebone bodies (Dow 1911, 1:71–72). In 1660, the estate of Boston merchant William Paine included five pairs of ready-made "bodeys" (Dow 1912, 2:271). The inventory of Mrs. Jane Hartry of Northampton County, Virginia, listed two pairs of "bodys" and "1 serge jump" (Northampton County). Fitting more loosely than stays, jumps were padded or quilted and laced in front. They were generally worn at home but might be worn instead of a bodice.

Under-Waistcoat

Evidence from Massachusetts inventories suggests that in colder climates, women sometimes wore an under-waistcoat made of wool flannel for warmth. These were variously described as white cloth, white cotton, and flannel. For example, the 1655 inventory of Elinor Tresler of Salem listed a "white Cotten wascoate & a short Coate [i.e. short petticoat]," which were likely undergarments (Dow 1911, 1:397).

Petticoat and Skirt Supports

In this period the fashionable silhouette maintained a relatively flat front so the fullness at the waist of the under-petticoat was drawn to the sides and back. It is of note that, according to 17th-century colonial inventories from this period, the color of many under-petticoats was red. This is likely because the red could be dyed quite cheaply using madder.

In England a stuffed tubular hip roll or bum roll, or a pair of stuffed pads worn over the hips, maintained the fashionable skirt shape for formal dress throughout this period. These supports do not, however, appear in the inventories surveyed for this project. They may not have been worn, they may have been given away as bequests, or they may have been considered too insignificant to be inventoried.

Small Linen and Hats, 1631–1670

Beginning in the 1630s, women's neckwear reflected the more relaxed fashions of their outerwear. Linen and silk pinners, with or without lace, were still fashionable, but now wider pinners with darts were seen, some of which fell over the shoulders (Arnold 2008, 44). The front edges, which were pinned at the neck, had either rounded or V-shaped points. In the colonies, a pinner might have been referred to as a band; versions that were tucked into the neckline rather than pinned were called tuckers. In 1652, Arthur Kippin was fined because his wife, Abigail, wore an especially broad-width bobbin lace—which may have been a pinner—in public in defiance of sumptuary legislation (Dow 1911, 1:273). A more expensive alternative was the falling band or whisk, a wide-shaped collar of linen and lace or of lace alone that encircled the neck and fell to or slightly over the shoulders. The front edges met along their entirety or formed a curved inverted V-shape.

A neck handkerchief might be worn over the bodice and neck linen, especially when the wearer was out-of-doors. Neck handkerchiefs were large squares of linen folded to make a triangle and wrapped around the neck and shoulders. In front, the linen was pinned under the chin, and the folded front corners fell over the breast. The finest were white, diaphanous, and edged with lace, but working women and the poor used coarser fabrics that might be plain, striped, or checked.

When the bodice sleeves were long, women wore funnel-shaped cuffs that turned back from the wrist. As the sleeve length shortened through time, a woman might pin wide cylindrical cuffs to the edges of the bodice or allow the sleeves of her shift to show in puffs tied with ribbons. A 1642 Maryland inventory included a extensive collection of small linen, including nine shadows, or head veils, two plain and seven decorated with lace; five plain and eight laced neck handkerchiefs; a pair of holland sleeves; two pairs of cuffs; and two laced gorgets. The latter may have been falling bands (Browne 1887, 4:95). For women who could afford it, a suit of small linen—band, cuffs, and neck handkerchief—might be edged in matching lace.

The coif had gone out of fashion in England by 1630. According to legal records from the *Records and Files of the Quarterly Courts of Essex County*, however, it persisted in New England for most of this period. For example, Joanna Cummins owned a coif of white cutwork, one of black fabric with lace—each worth one shilling and three pence—and one of grogram (silk and worsted) (Dow 1911, 1:65, 66). Jane Gaines of Lynn owned 12 coifs and crosscloths and three headcloths (1:80). In 1649, Susan Archer was brought to the Salem, Massachusetts, court for "hauinge a nedle worke napkin founde in her hands and Converted into Coives." Appearing in court to bring the claim, a Mrs. Gedney offered proof that the napkin was hers and that she had "wrought," or embroidered, it with her own hands. Susan Archer's husband, Samuel, was ordered to pay Mrs. Gedney three shillings (Dow 1911, 1:185).

Hoods and scarves remained popular through the end of the 17th century, and capotain- and sugarloaf-style hats were worn by New England women. The inventory of widow Mary Williams of Salem, Massachusetts, records four hoods, two of which were white and one of silk; a taffeta scarf; and two hats, one a demicaster and the other of felted wool (Dow 1911, 1: 377–78). At her death in 1666, Jane Hartry, of Virginia, owned two hoods of sarcenet—a thin, translucent silk—one of them white, a "black curld" hood, and a love-hood (possibly for mourning) and scarf (Northampton County, 13). The wife of Jacob de Lange owned four love-hoods, three black and one white (Earle 1903, 1:100–01).

At the quarterly court held in Ipswich, Massachusetts, on September 27, 1653, a number of husbands and wives were summoned for presentment before the court because the wives had worn silk scarves or hoods in public in defiance of the 1651 Massachusetts General Assembly order against excessive dress (see Chapter 2 for a discussion of sumptuary legislation). The spouses of Joseph Swett and William Chandlour were fined 10 shillings for wearing silk hoods because their husbands' estates were worth less than £200; however, because of coverture the husbands were expected to pay the fine. The wives of Nicolas Noice, Richard Knight, John Whipple, and Anthony Potter were discharged because each of the husbands' estates was proven to be worth at least £200. The wife of John Hutchings was discharged because she testified that she had been "brought up above the ordinary rank." Thomas Harris, Thomas Wayte, and Edward Browne appeared in court to argue in favor their spouses' wearing silk scarves on account of their "wives' education and upbringing." One of the three contended that because his wife was brought up wearing "silke and silluer" and continued to do so to honor her parents' status, he was "bound by coushens [conscience] and loue" to maintain her no "worss then i found her." Furthermore, "i conceiue my [wife's] wearing of a scarfe is not guillty of prid . . . becaus when she doth weare a scarfe it is not because she would be in the fashion or that she would be as fine as another becaus it is for nessesity and presseruing of health . . . becaus she ordinarily weares a scarfe but at two seasons the first is in winter when it is very colde the other ssesson is when it is very wett weather" (Dow 1911, 1:303–04).

Footwear, 1631–1670

As the population of the colonies grew and its wealth diversified, merchants and shopkeepers could afford to offer a greater range of sartorial accessories, including footwear. For example, in 1644 John Bland, a Virginia planter and merchant, prepared a shipment of goods from London to Virginia that included 14 dozen pairs of women's stockings, most of them worsted and likely all of them knitted (Williams 1964, 38). In addition to woolen and worsted, merchants stocked silk and fine linen hose for the wives and daughters of the affluent and those in positions of government. Some of these high-quality knitted stockings were ornamented with knitted patterns or ribbing or they were embroidered up both sides of the leg beginning at the ankle with elaborate designs, called clocks. Worked in polychrome silk and/or metallic threads, clocks designs ranged from simple arrows, scrolls, and medallion motifs to elaborate floral ornaments.

In general women's as well as men's latchet shoes followed the same construction and shape. By the 1640s, women's shoes had squared toes and slightly higher wooden heels with curved backs. In New England, fashionable shoes were subject to the same sumptuary restrictions as other articles of clothing. John Kindrick was fined in 1663 because his wife was seen in public in an excess of apparel, "wearing a silk hood, scarf, and French fall shoes" (Dow 1913, 3:66).

An alternative to the latchet shoe for indoor wear was the slipper: a heeled shoe with a vamp but without a quarter or latchets. Various contemporary names for this style were pantoffle, pantacle, and pantable. Pattens and clogs continued to be worn to protect shoes when outdoors. Jane Gaines of Lynn, Massachusetts, owned a pair of pattens, which at her death in 1645 was assessed at one shilling (Dow 1911, 1:79, 80).

Hairstyles and Grooming, 1631–1670

At the beginning of this period, fashion-conscious women continued to wear their hair as before, with the side hair full and framing the face in soft curls. Elite women might allow one curl to grow longer and bring it forward over the shoulder. This curl was called a lovelock. By the end of the 1630s, hairdressing dictated longer hair at the sides of the head, with the back of the hair arranged in a knot and ornamented with ribbons. Instead of a fringe or curls on the forehead, the hair might be smooth at the temples. In the 1650s and to the end of this period, the side hair was allowed to grow to shoulder length or longer and was artificially arranged in cascading ringlets; the knot of hair at the back of the head was dropped down from the back of the crown. For informal occasions, the side hair was allowed to fall around the face naturally.

Accessories, 1631–1670

Inventories of this period record work and formal aprons, pockets, purses, gloves, pocket handkerchiefs, girdles, rings, and masks. The latter were worn out-of-doors to protect the complexion from sun and wind. At her death in 1644, Joanna Cummins owned one "tauney seay [i.e., say, a thin woolen twill weave]" and one "green say" apron, a blue apron, and two calico aprons trimmed with lace (Dow 1911, 1:65, 66, 67). The fabrics and colors suggest that the woolen aprons and the blue apron were for work while the calico aprons were for show. The 1642 inventory of Richard Lusthead of Mattapanien, Maryland, included a woman's taffeta purse—likely a drawstring bag—which contained a parcel of silk, some linen thread, and buttons (Browne 1887, 4:95). In 1667, a Miss Perkings, who ran a boarding house in Boston, was given "sundry gifts" by gentlemen boarders, among them was a "bangle purse" (Dow 1913, 3:471). At her death in 1666, Virginian Jane Hartry owned a pair of woven linen gloves and "1 paire Leather gloues Embroydred" (Northampton County, 13). In 1665, servant Sarah Roper was accused of stealing a number of items from Patience Denison during her employ, including a taffeta stomacher, some silk lace, a scalloped cap of fine holland, a coif, and a busk (Dow 1913, 3:245). Hannah Smith was brought to court for stealing a silk girdle, two crosscloths, and a pair of knitted wool gloves (Dow 1911, 1:110). The inventory of Lynn, Massachusetts, resident George Burrill Senior in 1654, included his deceased wife's two masks and a pair of gloves (Dow 1911, 1:352, 353).

Main Garments, 1671–1714

Gown or Mantua

In the late 1670s, the mantua, a one-piece gown that had evolved from the loose and informal gown, or nightgown, replaced the separate bodice and skirt. Now appropriate for all occasions, the mantua was the main garment of the wives and daughters of successful artisans, the wealthy, and those in prominent positions. Open in the front from neckline to bottom hem and with a square or round neckline, it was worn with stays and a petticoat and sashed or belted at the waist. The fabric was pleated to fit smoothly over the body. The set-in, relaxed sleeves reached the just below the elbow and were turned back to form a soft cuff.

In the 1680s, mantua skirts were often looped up to the back of the waist to reveal most of the petticoat underneath. In England, fashionable women wore a bustle or small hoop under the mantua skirts to support them, but it is not known if bustles were worn in the colonies.

The silhouette of the first 15 years of the 18th century was a continuation of the previous decades: open mantua skirts were pulled back over the petticoat, creating a full effect at the hips and back. Beginning in the early 1700s, a hooped petticoat (see below) was worn under the petticoat, giving it a modified A-shape. The set-in sleeves of the manuta reached to below the elbow, and were shaped but not tightly fitted. Some extant examples have vertical pleats to control fullness down the back of the sleeve. Wide, shaped cuffs were pleated horizontally at the inner elbow.

Waistcoat, Jacket, Bodice, and Petticoat

Although the mantua became fashionable late in the decade, period documents reveal that many planters' wives and others of the middling ranks were more conservative in their dress and continued to don a waistcoat or jacket with a separate petticoat. Elite women might wear a loose, one-piece overgown or nightgown over this ensemble. At her death in 1679, Margarett Jackson, a South Carolina spinster who owned a slave, had a plush petticoat, a sad-colored satin waistcoat, a red serge petticoat and bays waistcoat, a quilted waistcoat, an old purple gored petticoat and waistcoat, and a purple morning gown (Bates and Leland 2005, 1:37–38).

Indentured servants and the enslaved generally were provided with an unboned bodice or jacket and a petticoat to wear over their shift. In 1707, a Boston indentured servant, a "Carolina Indian Woman named Sarah," ran away from her master wearing two jackets—one striped red, blue, and white homespun, the other solid red—over a "black and white silk crape petticoat" (*Boston News-Letter*, September 8, 1707).

Outer Garments, 1671–1714

An ensemble of clothes that was especially designed for ladies to wear when riding on horseback had appeared in England in the second half of the 17th century. It generally consisted of a close-bodied coat with masculine lines worn over a waistcoat and a flared skirt over a petticoat—all of which might have been constructed of the same fabric—and a hat. Judging from probate inventories, the outfit was only slowly adopted in the colonies in this period. One early record is the inventory of Elizabeth Lowle, presented to the Ipswich, Massachusetts, court in 1651, which listed a woman's "rydeing sute," worth two pounds (Dow 1914, 4:380).

Undergarments, 1671–1714

In the late 17th and early 18th centuries, the neckline of the shift followed the shape of the bodice neckline and was very low on the shoulders. Gathered into the armseye, the full sleeves were elbow-length and gathered into a band. An attached frill or detachable lace showed below the sleeve of the gown.

In this period, some stays appear to have been made in two parts, to lace up both the front as well as the back. As well as confining the waist and chest, the stays also lifted the breasts. A more comfortable substitute for stays was the unboned bodice known as jumps.

New England inventories from the second half of the 17th century occasionally list women's drawers. For example, the 1676 inventory of Hilliard Veren included "3 pair of women drawrs, 7s" (Dow 1917, 6:174).

The hooped petticoat was introduced in the early 18th century. Made of a fabric, it was stiffened with six to eight graduated hoops of cane or baleen that increased in circumference from the waist down. Until about 1720, this shape resembled an inverted funnel or bell.

Small Linen and Hats, 1671–1714

For the wives and daughters of the colonial well-to-do, this was an era of wearing layers of fine silk, linen, and lace accessories. Rebecca Howlett of Newbury, Massachusetts, owned two silk scarves, three hoods (two of them silk), nine neck-handkerchiefs (one of them calico), five whisks, four coifs, eight laced caps, and four pairs of sleeves (Dow 1920, 3:416–17). The unnamed wife of Stephen Harding Jr., of Providence, Rhode Island, owned at her death a silk hood and scarf and a tiffany whisk (Rogers, Carpenter, and Field 1894, 6:23).

From about 1690 through about 1710 the most fashionable hairstyles incorporated a tall head-dress called a fontange, an accessory that was imported from France into England. It consisted of a tall wire frame, or commode, shaped like a half-opened fan, which was fitted with layers of lace or linen frills and attached to a starched linen cap. It was worn tilted slightly forward, but the height and angle varied according to the wearer's whim. The hair was curled and pinned up into and around the commode and cap; small ringlets might frame the face. False curls could be added to increase the effect. Usually two long linen or lace lappets, called cornets, hung from behind the fontange; these could be worn down across the front of the shoulders of the gown or turned and pinned up. Elaborate and expensive examples of this head-dress included ribbons, or knots, and diamond-headed (likely paste, or faceted glass) pins. The vertical line of the fontange elongated and emphasized the vertical line then popular in the female silhouette and accentuated the layered look of the mantua and petticoat. In England, by the end of the first decade of the 18th century, the height of the head-dress had become unwieldy and its use was discontinued.

Colonial inventories do not reflect the prevalence of the fontange, but it likely was worn only in areas of concentrated populations. An alternative head-dress was the simpler linen cap, often edged with lace. The inventory of Thomas Newhall Sr. of Lynn, in 1674, included a black coif (Dow 1916, 5:365). In 1711, a 10-year-old indentured servant from Switzerland, Anna Maria Barbarie Collier, ran away from her master wearing a wool gown, a petticoat with white and "sad coloured stripes"; "she commonly us'd to wear on her head a black velvet Cap, after the Dutch mode" (*Boston News-Letter*, January 28).

Footwear, 1671–1714

From the last quarter of the 17th until about the first quarter of the 18th century, fashionable women's shoes were still made with squared toes and higher wooden heels. For most of the 17th century, women's shoes were generally imported—both for working women and the well-to-do. For example, in 1677, a ship from London to Maryland carried two dozen pairs of women's shoes with wooden heels (Merritt 1956, 67:47). However, by the end of the century, as the population of female indentured servants and slaves increased, New England's shoe makers likely made leather shoes for working women as well as men.

Hairstyles and Grooming, 1671–1714

The fashionable ringlets of the 1650s and 1660s gave way in the 1670s to masses of tight curls and ringlets that stood out from the sides of the face. This hairdressing was assisted by false hair. In 1679, Cotton Mather railed against such vanities: "What shall we say when men are seen in the Streets

Pair of leather shoes with wooden pattens, English, c. 1700. The shoe at right has been fitted with a patten. (Victoria and Albert Museum, London)

with monstrous and horrid *Perriwigs*, and Women with their *Borders and False Locks* and such like whorish Fashions" (Mather 1676, 9). In the 1680s, the masses of curls were still in vogue, but the hair was now smoothed back from the forehead. Beginning in about 1690, a fashionable hairstyle was enhanced by a fancy laced cap or tall head-dress (see above). By the end of this period, simpler, low hairstyles were in vogue. Most of the hair was pulled to the back of the head in a braided bun, with curls around the face.

Accessories, 1671–1714

Inventories taken in the late 17th and early 18th centuries record aprons of fine linen as well as wool; girdles or chains with attachments; plain and lace-edged pocket handkerchiefs; fans; gloves of kid leather and knitted silk or wool; and a wide range of jewelry, which included rings, pearl or coral necklaces, and pendant earrings. A 1682 New York City inventory included "one embroidered purse with silver bugle" with a chain to attach it to a girdle, a pair of pendants, each with ten diamonds, two diamond rings, a gold ring, and a gold ring "bound round with diamonds" (quoted in Cornelius 1926). Executing part of her husband's estate in 1689, a Madam Pepin, widow of a Charleston merchant, gave her daughter goods and money valued at over £24. Among the objects were three gold rings, a necklace "of fine pearle," a gold heart, a silver hat band, and a silver chain "with the furniture" (Bates and Leland 2005, 1:117). This latter was likely a girdle of fine silver links hung with small sewing tools, such as a scissors, thimble and needle cases, and round pincushion, and/or other small accessories such as a folding knife and keys.

In 1704, 38-year-old Sarah Kemble Knight (1666–1727) traveled alone on horseback from her hometown of Boston to New York City. In her diary of the journey, she observed how differently the women of Dutch descent living in New York dressed from their English counterparts: "The English go very fashionable in their dress. But the Dutch, especially the middling sort, differ from our women, in their habit go loose [i.e., wear no stays], were French muches, wch are like a Capp and a head band [i.e., forehead cloth] in one, leaving their ears bare, which are sett out wth Jewells of a large size and many in number. And their fingers hoop'd with Rings, some with large stones in them of many Coullers as were their pendants in their ears, which You should see very old women wear as well as Young" (Knight 1992, 54–55).

CLOTHING FOR THE ENSLAVED, 1620–1714

According to surviving records from late in this period, servants and slaves—American Indian as well as African—generally were treated similarly in terms of clothing, shelter, and diet. Descriptions reveal few differences in the amount or styles of clothing worn by either group, and masters could be generous or tightfisted. For example, in 1681, an unnamed female slave ran away from her master at "hott waters in Chicahominy," Virginia, wearing "a sad Colord wastcoate, a red trading cloth peticoat & a Canvas under peticoate" (*York County Deeds, Orders, and Wills Book 6*: 57). In New York City an 18-year-old mulatto woman was brought to court for stealing from her mistress "as much Bristol Stuff as would make her a Gown and Pettycoat and also a Silk Muslin handkerchief and a Small piece of Callico." She took the fabric to a tailor to make up the garments, explaining that she stole the goods because "She was almost Naked & her Mistriss would give her no Clothes" (quoted in Goodfriend 1992, 122).

A number of runaway notices for "Carolina Indian" enslaved female servants appeared in the *Boston News-Letter* before 1715. These unfortunates, primarily from the Southern Piedmont and Lowcountry, had been either captured directly by the British during raids or sold to the British by other Indians. Men as well as women were transported from Charleston and sold to masters in Boston, Rhode Island, Pennsylvania, New York, and Virginia (Gallay 2002, 299, 301–02). Three examples from 1711 illustrate the clothing transformation that took place as Carolina Indian women were forced to adapt to the ways of British New England. Moll ran away from her Boston master carrying a bundle of clothing: "a Pladd Stuff Jacket broad Check'd, a Peticoat small Check'd; an old dark Home-spun Jacket, a dark colour'd Kersey Peticoat, & a strip'd Home-spun Peticoat Cotton & Wool; several Cotton & Linnen Shifts . . . several pair of Stockings, & several Lace Caps; blue Gloves, and Shooes about half wore out" (August 6). As the notice did not indicate that these were stolen goods, the garments likely belonged to Moll. Jenny left her owner wearing a "flower'd Callico Jacket, blue and white chequer'd plad pettycoat and a lac'd night Cap" (September 10). Phillis stole herself away clad in a "white Linnen Jacket, a speckled callico Pettycoat, and a flowered searge one, a lac'd night Cap, red and white Stockings" (September 10).

CLOTHING OF AMERICAN INDIANS, 1607–1714

Main Garments

Seventeenth-century chroniclers and others provided a wealth of information concerning the dress of indigenous peoples. Although it is beyond the scope of this discussion to examine the dress of all the Indian tribes encountered by the first English settlers, writers noted two basic garments for women: the apron and the mantle. Before European contact, these items were made of animal skins or furs. With burgeoning trade between the Old and New Worlds, however, Western cloth, clothing, and accessories gradually became integrated with traditional materials and styles. In 1607, John Smith observed that the women of the Powhatan confederation of tribes in Virginia were "always covered at the waist with a skin" (Smith 1907, 100). Writing in 1612 of the same group, William Strachey noted that upon reaching puberty, a young woman began to wear a skin apron, which might be "shapped and fringed at the skyrt" (Strachey 1849, 65). New Englander William Wood, who wrote in 1634 about Indian tribes living to the north of the Massachusetts Bay Colony (he called them collectively Aberginians), described the Indian women's lower garment as a petticoat "of cloath [i.e., trade cloth] or skinnes wrapt like a blanket about their loynes, reaching downe to their hammes which they never put off in company" (Wood 1865, 108).

Hung from the shoulders, the mantle might be wrapped around the body or crossed under one arm. "The better sort of women" of the Powhatan had finely dressed mantles "carved and couloured with some pretty work, or the proporion of beasts, fowle, tortayses, or other such like imagry, as shall best please or express the fancy of the wearer" (Strachey 1849, 65).

Thomas Morton, who traded for furs with various Algonquian-speaking tribes in Plymouth Colony, recorded in about 1634 that the Indian women he saw wore a long mantle made of deer or bear skin "to cover their nakedness." This mantle was longer than that worn by the men, made of two skins sown together, "and it so lardge that it trailes after them like a great Ladies trane" (Morton 1883, 144). An anonymous chronicler of Maryland tribes observed that both the women and men wore large mantles, which either reached to the middle of the leg or to just above the ground. Mantles for summer were fashioned from skins; those for winter were of fur. If the women were working or the weather was hot, the mantle was put aside ("A Relation of Maryland" 1910, 87).

Footwear

Women went barefooted unless they ventured into the woods. Then, to protect their legs and feet, they wore skin moccasins and leggings; the latter could extend up to the loin area and were wrapped around the legs with leather cords. Roger Williams, who studied Rhode Island's Narragansett Indians and learned their language, noted that women and men wore deerskin moccasins and leggings when they traveled, especially in the wet and snow: "the water cleane wrings out; and being hang'd up in their chimney [the central hearth of the Indian house structure], they presently drie without hurt as myselfe hath often proved" (Williams 1827, 107).

Hairstyles and Adornments

Adult women generally wore their hair long and might ornament it with ocher and grease, feathers, beads, shells, and bones. Some of these hairstyles matched the artistry of Indian men (see Chapter 5).

Body adornments among American Indian women took the forms of jewelry, paint, and body modifications. John Smith noted that Indian women in Virginia commonly had three "great holes" in each ear, through which they hung "chaines, bracelets, copper" (Smith 1907, 100). Women of Maryland's coastal tribes wore beaded chains and bracelets, but "some of the better sort of them" wore "ropes of Pearle about their necks, and some hanging in their eares, which are of a large sort." These latter, however, were often spoiled because the Indians roasted the oysters for food before they harvested the pearls ("A Relation of Maryland" 1910, 87–88). Narragansett women prized the looking glasses they received as trade goods and consulted them when painting their faces (Williams 1827, 136).

Women as well as men practiced scarification and tattooing. According to Smith, "Their women some have their legs, hands, brests and face cunningly imbrodered [i.e., tattooed] with diverse workes, as beasts, serpentes, artificially wrought into their flesh with blacke spots" (1907, 100). Strachey also noted the elaborate tattoos of the women: "flowers and fruits of sondery lively kinds, as also snakes, serpents . . . and this they doe by dropping uppon the seared flesh sondry coulers, which rub'd into the stampe, will never be taken awaye agayne, because yt will not only be dryed into the flesh, but growe therein" (1849, 66).

As noted above, enslaved Indians were provided with European-style dress. However, body modifications were permanent reminders of their tribal affiliations. In 1707, Sarah, who tied up her "long straight black Hair" with a red hair-lace, ran away from her Boston master wearing "a striped red blue and white Homespun Jacket, & a red one, a black and white silk Crape Petticoat, a white Shift, as also a blue one with her, and a mixed blue and white Linsey Woolsey Apron" (*Boston News-Letter*, September 8). The owner noted that she was "very much mark'd or cut in the hands and face." These marks may have been ritual scars or tattoos rather than evidence of corporal punishment. In 1711, an Indian woman named Rose, about 40 years old, ran away from her mistress in Marblehead, Massachusetts. Her dress was typical for any female slave or indentured servant from a northern colony—"a red Jacket, bound with edging, and a white Flannel Petticoat." Her mistress, however, also described Rose's tattoos: "her Neck, Arms, and Leggs Marked with Flowers, after the Indian manner, and some stroaks in her cheeks" (*Boston News-Letter*, October 1711).

CLOTHING IN PORTRAITURE, 1616–1714

Pocahontas (c. 1595–1617), a daughter of Powhatan, the paramount chief, or *mamanatowick*, of a large alliance of Algonquian-speaking communities living in the tidewater area of Virginia, married planter John Rolfe in 1614. Two years later the couple traveled to England, during which time she had her likeness painted as the wife of a prosperous Englishman. The engraving, taken from the portrait, reflects the sartorial goods an English woman of social and economic standing might have brought to America in the early years of colonization. For her sitting, Pocahontas (this was her childhood name; she was also called Matoaka or Amonute and took the name Rebecca when she was baptized into the Anglican faith) donned a buttoned and sleeved jacket of patterned fabric; the sleeves extend to the wrist and are ornamented with funnel-shaped linen cuffs edged with lace. Over this she wore a richly patterned overgown with wings and short barrel-shaped

Pocahontas (1595–1617), after an engraving published in London, 1618. (Library of Congress)

sleeves, which have buttoned seams. Her head is set off by a stiffly starched, supported lace standing collar. The stylish beaver capotain, dyed white, has a wide braided hat band and a feather. Pocahontas holds an ostrich-feather fan and wears a pearl earring in her left ear. Not seen are her shift and stays as well as tattoos that she likely would have received upon reaching puberty.

Boston merchant and mariner John Wensley was wealthy enough to afford the elite-style clothing that his wife, Elizabeth (1641–1711), donned for her portrait without concerning himself with the colony's sumptuary proscriptions. Painted by an anonymous artist the 1670s, the portrait shows a woman, aged 30 to 35, in rich, formal attire. Over stays and a low-necked and full-sleeved shift, Elizabeth wears a wide-necked silk gown of patterned stripes, lined or faced with a red fabric. The elbow-length gown sleeves have been turned back, revealing the lining, and kept in place with loops and buttons, two of which can be seen on the proper left sleeve. The full sleeves of her shift puff out below the gown sleeves and are tied just above the elbows with bows. Full cuffs of fine lace are attached on top of the shift ruffles, and the neckline is finished with a pinner of wide lace. The gown is drawn back at the skirts, revealing both the lining and a petticoat likely of patterned fabric, possibly brocade. Elizabeth wears a stiff embellished stomacher that extends below the natural waistline. The gown is closed below the waistline with a striped sash that is knotted on the proper left side. Her hair has been parted in the center of the crown and smoothed over her temples; some side hair falls in soft waves. Most of the hair, however, is covered by a lace-edged cap and scarf or hood. Her jewelry consists of ear drops, a close-fitting necklace, and one or more rings on the ring finger of her left hand, which holds a folded fan.

In 1679, Bostonian Martha Woody Patteshall (1651–1718) sat with her child for a portrait wearing a fashionable black gown with short sleeves, open at the skirt to reveal a red petticoat. The gown's bodice is closed, its low, wide neckline covered with a fine white lace whisk that lies over her shoulders ties at center front. Below the gown's proper right sleeve, which ends well above the elbow in a black lace frill or ruffle, the full shift sleeve is puffed up and held with a wide black bow. The wrist end of the shift sleeve is tied up as well to create a second puff; attached to it is a diaphanous, patterned falling ruff, likely of embroidered lawn. Martha's hair is conservatively dressed: most of the hair has been smoothed back to create a bun or knot at the back of the head, and her face is framed in small curls. Pearl drop earrings and a necklace complete her outfit. Martha was the second wife of Richard Patteshall, a Boston merchant with landholdings in Maine. Because the family was well-to-do, she well may have owned the lace collar and jewelry shown in the portrait. Of note, Martha was the great-grandmother of Paul Revere.

COMPOSITION OF A WARDROBE, 1608–1714

Initial Settlements

While no records survive to document what the first female colonists wore, it is certain that they were not "the veriest beggers in the worlde." In a 1619 letter, Secretary of Virginia John Pory (c. 1570–1636) observed that in Jamestown even the wife of a Croydon collier wore "her rough bever hatt with a faire perle hatband, and a silken suit thereto correspondent" (Pory 1907, 285). The first English females to settle in Jamestown were Anne Forrest, wife of Jamestown gentleman financier Thomas Forrest, and her maid, Anne Burras. The two women landed in 1608. Because Anne was the wife of a gentleman, she was accustomed to life in England in the circles of the well-to-do. This status suggests that her wardrobe might have included bodices and skirts, at least one set each of silk and wool, with a farthingale under-skirt; under-petticoats; a stomacher; several shifts; stays; a ruff or standing collar with supporter and possibly wrist cuffs; a fashionable linen apron; embellished or laced coifs and crosscloths; a hood and/or scarf; a beaver hat, fine knitted stockings; and one or more pairs of shoes. Her maid likely owned a bodice and overskirt of wool with an under-petticoat, one or two shifts, woolen work aprons, a plain coif, and perhaps a felted wool hat.

In contrast, each of six women who left England in 1621 to find husbands in Jamestown were provided by the financial backers of the Virginia Company with a petticoat and waistcoat, two smocks, two pairs of stockings, a pair of garters, two pairs of shoes, a pair of white lamb gloves, one round band (a collar), an apron, a hat and bands, two coifs, and two cross cloths (Ransome 1991, 16). These women were part of a larger group of 57, all daughters of the gentry, artisans, or tradesmen.

Sample Wardrobes through Time

When Mary Ring arrived in Plymouth in 1629/1630, she was already a widow; her husband, William, had died in Leiden, in the Netherlands. Fully literate—she could read and write and owned several books—Mary must have been adept in managing her money because she was owed debts at the time of her death. Her 1633 probate inventory reveals that Separatists did wear elegant and colorful garments and that they may have adopted some forms of Dutch dress. Among her belongings were a stuff gown; a black say kirtle; three petticoats, one red, one violet, and one "mingled"; a Dutch "yoke" (possibly a type of collar or partlet); a pair of sleeves "called a buffe"; one white, two violet, and one "mingled coloured" waistcoats; four stomachers; a black say, three blue, and two white aprons; two hats; three linen caps; seven shifts; six ruffs; three fine and one coarse kerchiefs; two pairs of stockings, one white and one blue; and two pairs of shoes (Inventory of . . . Mary Ring).

In 1644, the inventory of widow Margery Wathin was brought to the Salem, Massachusetts, court for the settlement of debts. Her extensive clothing list contains some high-status goods as well as garments that at the time of her death were out-of-date or very worn. The appraisers noted these latter items as "old:" a mixed-color wool gown, a purple petticoat and matching waistcoat, four coifs, and a pair of shoes. Her main garments included a purple cloth gown lined with green say and a purple waistcoat with lace; a red petticoat and waistcoat; one russet cloth gown, "ripped open"; three white wrought stomachers; a tawny-colored woolen cloak; and a pair of perpetuana hoods. She owned eight aprons. Three were likely for formal wear—one holland, one "fleecy" holland, and one white. The remaining five were for work and of wool, two identified as russet-colored and one blue. Her undergarments included five shifts and a pair of whalebone bodies. Margery's small linen was extensive: nine neck handkerchiefs, four with lace edging; three coifs, two of holland and a white one that was embroidered; two plain crosscloths; and three pocket handkerchiefs. To cope with the cold climate of New England, she had, for added warmth, one white holland and one wool waistcoat, four white woolen coifs, three white woolen stomachers, and a flannel neckcloth. Accessories included a pair of white linen knitted gloves, a pair of wrist ruffs, and two girdles (probably sashes for gowns), one of silk and one embroidered (Dow 1911, 1:71–72).

In 1666, Sarah and William Cottle had packed their belongings on board a vessel to move from Newbury, Massachusetts, to New Jersey. Unfortunately, the goods were never delivered to their destination so the couple brought suit against the ship owner in 1668. Among the goods lost in the many packed trunks and chests was most of Sarah's wardrobe. Enumerated were three holland, three dowlas, and four cotton shifts; four holland aprons; a taffeta gown and blue taffeta petticoat; a hair prunella gown; two serge gowns, a scarlet cloth petticoat; two serge petticoats; three cloth petticoats (likely under-petticoats); a pair of blue satin bodies; a green apron; and a white hood and matching scarf (Dow 1916, 4:20–21).

The 1668 will of Dorchester, Massachusetts, resident Jane Humphrey both illustrates the language some New England women used in disposing of their personal effects and reflects the two general categories that many New England appraisers used to describe women's wardrobes: "woolen clothing and linen clothing." Among the goods Jane bequeathed to family members and friends were five petticoats of woolen or mixed fabrics—serge, kersey, and linsey-woolsey—of which two were red, one was "blackish" and one green (the "best" was of red kersey). She left five waistcoats, one of sad gray-colored kersey, one of green serge, one murry (mulberry colored), one blue, and one of white fustian. Among her six aprons, three were probably for formal wear: her white holland with a "small lace at the bottom," a white holland "with two breadths in it," and her "best" white. The one green and two blue aprons were likely work aprons made of woolen fabric. She bequeathed only her "best" shifts as well as jumps and a green under-petticoat. Her small linen included two pocket handkerchiefs, three coifs (two plain, one of which was black, and her "best," which has decorated with "a lace"), and seven neckcloths or neckhandkerchiefs. These latter consisted of one of black silk, one of black wool, a calico "vnder neck cloath," a square neckcloth "with a little lace on it," and "one of my best Neck-Cloaths, . . . My fine thine [i.e., thin] Neck Cloath, [and] My next best Neck Cloath." Miscellaneous effects included "my best hat," a hood and muff, a fringed whittle, a cloak, "my blew Short Coate . . . [and] Staning Kersey Coate" (quoted in Earle 1893). These two latter coats may have been short jackets or gowns.

In 1686, during a trip to New England to sell a "venture of books," Englishman John Dunton had the opportunity to attend an "Indian Lecture" preached to a group of "converted Natives" in Natick, some 20 miles away from Boston (Dunton 1818, 1:115). In attendance were the local sachem and his wife. Dunton described her attire, which included trade as well as indigenous elements: "her dress [was] peculiar, she had sleeves of mooseskin, very finely dressed, and drawn with lines of various colours, in Asiatic work, and her buskins were of the same sort; her mantle was of fine blue cloth, but very short, and tied about her shoulders, and at the middle with a zone curiously wrought with white and blue beads into pretty figures.

Her bracelets and her necklace were of the same sort of beads; and she had a little tablet upon her breast, very finely decked with jewels and precious stones. Her hair was combed back, and tied up with a border, which was nearly worked both with gold and silver" (116).

Although many of the women of New England's middling to upper ranks owned and wore colorful clothing of fine woolen or worsted fabrics with delicate linen and silk accessories, the wardrobes of many of their southern counterparts reflect the luxury fabrics and trims that were available through London factors. Anthony Haviland and his wife, whose name is unknown, lived in Surry County, Virginia, near the James River. She predeceased him, and, although some of her clothing was likely given away or bequeathed before her death, the clothing that was enumerated in Anthony's 1688 probate inventory indicates that she had cut a fine figure. Her remaining wardrobe included a black ferrandine (silk) gown and matching petticoat; a flowered silk gown with matching petticoat, both trimmed with silver and gold lace; a watered tabby silk petticoat; one blue silk and one red serge petticoat, both trimmed with silver and gold lace; a flowered satin riding hood and a silk cloak; and two pairs of stays, one of them old (Surry County, Virginia, 44a).

Very few 17th-century inventories have survived for the early Jewish residents of New York City, so the probate record of prosperous flour merchant Asser Levy, who was also a kosher butcher and real estate investor, is a window on the formative Jewish community there. The clothing of his widow, Miriam, was enumerated in his inventory. She owned a "Suite with a redd petticoate" and five additional petticoats, of which one was blue, one scarlet, and one silk. She owned two loose-fitting gowns—called a "casjack" in the inventory—one "Coloured" and one of velvet. Her undergarments included 16 smocks, six pairs of linen drawers, and a pair of bodies. Headgear comprised 25 hoods, a dozen of them of white linen, another dozen of "Santeen," and a dozen caps with lace embellishment. Accessories included three pairs of red worsted and two pairs of silk stockings; a black silk and six white aprons; a muff; 20 neckcloths "with Lace & without"; a dozen handkerchiefs; two silver girdles, one "with hanging keys" and one with three chains and hooks for small objects; three hair bodkins, one gold and two silver; and two pairs of gold pendants (quoted in Hershkowitz 2002, 258–60).

In 1710, John Bonner placed a notice in the *Boston News-Letter* asking for the return of his wife's wearing apparel, which he thought had been stolen from his house during his wife's last illness. The thief had made off with three silk gowns (striped, flowered, and changeable); two double (i.e., reversible or fully lined) gowns, one of silk and russel, the other of two silks with a matching petticoat; a black crepe gown and petticoat; three silk petticoats, one of black, one black flowered, and one changeable; a flowered serge petticoat (perhaps a brocaded Norwich woolen); a hood and scarf of lustring; three headdresses with lace and one without; three each of caps and undercaps with lace; two handkerchiefs with lace; three pairs of sleeves with lace; three white aprons; two white muslin hoods; a muff; an amber necklace; two gold rings and two gold buttons. From the size of her wardrobe, it may be assumed that Mrs. Bonner had shifts, stockings, and shoes of the same quality, but the thief likely stole the most valuable and accessible of her garments (February 12, 1710).

1715–1785

THE EVOLUTION OF CUT, CONSTRUCTION, AND SILHOUETTE, 1715–1785

During the 18th century, colonial women had three basic choices of dress, depending on their wealth and status. The first was the gown, or closed robe, made of an attached bodice and skirt. The skirt was not open so a petticoat was not required. The second option was the open robe, a gown whose skirt was open at the front and worn with a petticoat. Filling the open bodice was the stomacher; this could be embroidered, covered with ribbons or the bodice could lace across the top of it. The third alternative was the bodice and skirt. This pairing could take the form of a jacket and matching petticoat, a loose-backed jacket called a *pet-en-l'air* with matching or contrasting petticoat, or a fitted riding jacket and skirt. Philadelphia antiquarian John Fanning Watson (1779–1860) noted that before the American Revolution, colonial women of status were discriminating of appropriate dress: "Ladies never wore the same dresses at work and on visits; they sat at home, or went out in the morning, in chints; brocades, satins and mantuas were reserved for evening or dinner parties. Robes . . . were always worn in full dress. . . . Worsted was then thought dress enough for common days" (Watson 1830, 177).

The wives and daughters of the wealthiest colonists could obtain bespoke garments from London tailors and skilled colonial manuta makers. The wardrobes of women from the middling ranks likely contained some bespoke articles as well as items constructed at home. Many articles of women's clothing, however, were imported ready-made and of materials to suit almost all purses.

Main Garments, 1715–1750

"To be seen at Mrs. Hannah Teatts Mantua Maker at the Head of Summer Street Boston a Baby [i.e., fashion doll] drest after the Newest Fashion of Mantuas and Night Gowns & everything belonging to a dress" (*New England Weekly Journal*, July 2, 1733). While many colonial women aspired to attire themselves "after the Newest Fashion," the increasing "love of dress" was of concern to colonial Quakers. At the Friends of Philadelphia Yearly Meeting for 1726, held in Burlington, New Jersey, the women Friends issued a letter to other Friends, "Tenderly to Caution & Advise" them about immodest fashions, which they felt sprang from the "Corrupt root of Pride." Among their admonishments were the wearing of hooped petticoats, or any imitation that caused gown skirts to be fuller "than is Necessary"; gowns should be "plain and Decent," without superfluous folds in back. Women were never to be seen without an apron, "nor to wear Superfluous Gathers or Pleats in their Capps or Pinners, Nor to wear their heads drest high behind, Neither to Cut or Lay their hair on ye fforehead or Temples," nor to go about with "bare Breasts or bare Necks." Footwear did not go unnoticed: Friends were to avoid wearing striped shoes, "Red or White heel'd Shoos, or Clogs, or Shoos trimmed wh. Gawdy Colours." Finally, Friends were to avoid the unnecessary use of fans in Meetings "least it Divert ye mind from ye more Inward & Spiritual Exercise wch. all ought to be Concern'd in" (quoted in Gummere 1901, 152–53).

Gown

Gown styles were distinguished by details of cut. The first distinction was whether the gown skirt was open in the front, requiring a separate petticoat to complete the outfit, or whether the gown skirt was closed and made a complete dress with the attached bodice. The second distinction was in the cut of the back of the gown. The sack, or *sacque*, style (robe *à la Française*) had fullness across the back that was pleated in at the neckline and shoulders. The pleats were stabilized by a flat neckband, and sometimes also stitched down for a few inches, then released. Alternatively, the back tucks or pleats were stitched down to the waistline, fitting the upper body, and then released (robe *à l'Anglaise*). The term night gown refers, not to a garment for sleep, but to an unboned, one-piece gown for informal wear. For all gowns and petticoats the side seams of the skirt were unstitched a hand's breadth so the wearer had access to the pockets worn underneath.

In the 1710s, bodices were conical, with relatively high square necklines in the front and a pointed front waistline. Sleeves were shaped and were of elbow length, but not tightly fitted, and ended in a cuff that was either round or pleated at the inner elbow and allowed to open into a wide wing at the back. The shape of the skirt in the early 1700s continued to be the modified A-shape seen at the end of the 17th century. In the 1720s, the A-shape of the skirt was replaced by either a dome or, for formal wear, a flattened oval shape held out by side hoops. Colonial portraits suggest that these latter side hoops were less common in this country than in Britain. Still conical, the gown's bodice now had a lower neckline, which was still relatively square.

It is unfortunate that although fabrics and colors were often given, the details of construction were almost always omitted from descriptions of gowns in inventories and advertisements. For example, an anonymous advertiser in New York City announced the loss/theft of a brocade gown, the fabric of red and green flowers on a white ground (*New-York Journal*, April 11, 1737). In June of 1747, Charlestonian Hannah Proctor advertised the theft of her personal clothing, which included 16 gowns: one brocade, two of striped lustring, one red taffeta, two of green India damask, two of brown silk, one chintz, one gingham, three of calico, one linen damask, one striped garlick, and one coarse white linen (*South-Carolina Gazette*, June 29).

Loose wrapped or wrapping gowns became fashionable in the second quarter of the century. The bodice fronts were crossed over a stomacher or decorative stays and fastened with a sash or pin and a petticoat was worn. The wrapper might be faced with a contrasting fabric or pattern or it might be fully lined, or reversible. The latter wrapping was called in contemporary sources a double gown. Because woolen fabrics were not always used, warmth may not have been the primary reason to wear a double gown. Mary Barnes, an indentured servant in Virginia, ran away from her master with a green silk-poplin gown, faced with yellow (*Virginia Gazette*, October 22, 1736). In New York City a "Servant Maid" took a "Calico Wraper, and a striped Calamanco Wrapper" (*New-York Weekly Journal*, January 22, 1739). In 1741, William Harbert reported the theft of a "loose double Gown one side light colour'd Calimanco, the other side an olive colour'd Serge" and a "coarse holland loose Gown with blue and white stripes, lined with Ozenbrigs" (*Pennsylvania Gazette*, July 9, 1741). A 20-year-old Irish servant left her master in Chester County, Pennsylvania, in 1745 wearing "an old striped gown faced with old stamped Callicoe" (*Pennsylvania Gazette*, March 26).

Short Gown and Jacket

Used by the upper sorts informally or at home, and by working women most of the time, both the short gown and the fitted jacket were worn with an outer petticoat. The jacket, or waistcoat, was a fitted garment with set-in sleeves. Women with the financial means would have worn a jacket known as a *pet-en-l'air*. Styled like a sack gown, it reached to the knee in the early 18th century, but by the 1750s, fell about a foot or so below the waist.

Contemporary records, however, are unclear concerning distinctions between the short gown and the bed gown, and they were likely synonymous (to confuse matters, in some records jackets were also referred to as short gowns). Both were slightly longer than hip-length and open down the front, with long or short sleeves that were cut from one piece with the rest of the body. Some surviving examples exhibit piecing that extended the body or sleeve length.

References to bed and short gowns appear frequently in runaway advertisements, indications of their use by the working sorts: Sarah Butler wore a homespun yellowish petticoat and short stuff bed gown; Margaret Brown ran away in a dark linsey bed gown with a quilted petticoat—half yellow and half checked; Elizabeth Cowren owned a shalloon bed gown and linsey petticoat, both brown; Mary Porter escaped from jail wearing a short calico bed gown lined with linen over a blue stuff petticoat (*Pennsylvania Gazette*, January 15, 1745; January 21, 1746; December 10, 1747; July 3, 1746).

Petticoat

Petticoats, also referred to simply as coats or quilts in contemporary records, changed little from the 17th century. They were made of breadths of fabric seamed together and either pleated at the top into a waistband or gathered with a casing and drawstring. The band was most commonly split at a side seam and was fastened there with ties. The split also served as an opening to access a tied-on pocket. The petticoat might match or contrast with the gown or jacket. Elegant ladies wore petticoats of silk fabrics or fine imported cottons from India; often these were quilted. Plain and quilted petticoats of woolen fabrics or osnaburg and mixed cloths such as linsey-woolsey commonly were worn by working women, indentured servants, and slaves. As discussed in Chapter 2, petticoats could be bespoke, ready-made, or products of a household.

A style of linen petticoat made in the colonies and worn from the 1740s through the American Revolution features a wide border of crewel (worsted wool) embroidery at the bottom hem. The petticoat material was usually a plain-weave homespun linen (and uncommonly twill-weave); the border usually was embroidered just on the bottom front of the garment, where it would be seen with an open gown. Designed and executed by colonial embroiderers, the border designs consisted of meandering vines of flowers, fruit, and foliage, or, more rarely, scenes with fauna and people. Although crewel-embroidered petticoats may have been made throughout the colonies, extant examples are from New England.

Peppering the notices of colonial merchants were imported ready-made petticoats of all qualities, plain and quilted, and made of plain and satin-weave silk, wool and worsted, flannel, stamped linen, dimity, and calico. In Charleston, James Reid advertised "silk, callimanco and stuff [i.e., woolen] quilted and border'd petticoats" (*South-Carolina Gazette*, January 5, 1740). Captain Bogg imported a cargo of textiles from London to Charleston in 1748 for public auction, which included persian, satin, and calico quilted petticoats and figured dimity petticoats with fringe (*South-Carolina Gazette*, October 17).

Stomacher

The shape and size of the stomacher conformed to the needs of the bodice style as the latter changed over time. It could be boned to accentuate a flat front or merely padded. The obverse side of the stomacher was often ornamented with embroidery, metallic cord and braid, and/or ribbons; the lining usually was linen. Surviving English stomachers dating between 1700 and 1720 are relatively long and narrow, the point extending just below the natural waistline. Sometime in the 1720s the stomacher shape shortened and widened. A set of tabs was sometimes added to the point—a survival from late-17th-century stomachers—or the point might be rounded. Between about 1730 and the 1760s, imported stomachers of quilted and embroidered whitework, called Marseilles embroidery, were worn with a day ensemble (Hart and North 1998, 200–01). Other examples have crisscross lacing—a decorative anchor for the ends of a neck handkerchief.

Outer Garments, 1715–1750

The long cloak, which reached midcalf or longer, barely changed in style from its 17th-century antecedent. The cardinal was a cloak that usually reached below the knee. Both styles buttoned or tied at the front; they might have an attached collar or hood or an attached cape covering the shoulders and upper arms. The capuchin, a short cloak with an attached hood, had front edges that met in long points. The term "mantle" likely referred to a large square or rectangle of fabric worn over the shoulders. Imported ready-made cloaks, cardinals, and capuchins of silk, wool, and worsted were available in hues of red, black, and cloth color.

A cloak with an attached head covering was called a riding hood; ready-made versions were available of plain-weave silk, napped woolens and worsted, or velvets. In 1730, an Irish servant named Jenny ran away from her Boston master wearing "a Homespun Cinnamon Colour'd Druget Riding Hood" over a striped woolen gown "cuf'd and fac'd with Red, and a Yellow and Red Quilted Petticoat" (*Boston Gazette*, April 27, 1730). That same year Jane Braiser left her Philadelphia master wearing a red-and-white-striped calimanco gown and a yellow quilted petticoat; she took with her a white fustian gown "the Sleeves turn'd up with an Indian Chintz" and a "Blue Camblet Riding-Hood" (*American Weekly Mercury*, July 23, 1730).

Safeguards were still in use, but more fashionable ladies' equestrian attire—bespoke and ready-made—was now advertised. In 1729, Mrs. E. Atkinson notified Boston patrons that she designed and made riding dresses "after the newest fashion" (*Boston News-Letter*, March 27). In 1737, *South-Carolina Gazette* subscribers could go to Charleston's Elizabeth Cooper for bespoke riding habits or to Thomas Crawford for bespoke riding habits and dust gowns; the latter possibly were wrap-around coverings for travel (*Boston News-Letter*, March 26, April 16). Tailor William Valance, who was trained in London, made all sorts of riding habits for Charleston ladies, "all after the newest Fashion, and at the cheapest Rates" (*South-Carolina Gazette*, May 1, 1742). Philadelphia tailor John Johnson assured his patrons that he made ladies riding dresses "after the newest mode" (*Pennsylvania Gazette*, Mary 24, 1747). Trowell's store sold ladies "New-Market riding Caps made of the best Velvet and interlined with Leather" (*South-Carolina Gazette*, November 2, 1747).

Undergarments, 1715–1750

Shift or Smock

Because of changes in the cut and fit of main garments, the cut of the 18th-century shift was generally less full in both the body and the sleeves than in the 1600s, and the sleeves were now of elbow length. The linen fabrics used to make shifts varied greatly from coarse brown or unbleached osnaburg and dowlas to homespun and to fine holland. As status garments, those of finer linens were generally bleached after laundering and then starched before pressing. The edge of the neckline of the shift was seen as an edging above the bodice neckline; the ends of the sleeves were exposed below the bodice. In about 1740 bell-shaped bodice sleeves came into fashion and the shift sleeves were no longer exposed.

In the 18th century, enslaved women might own one or two shifts, depending on their duties as household or field workers; indentured servants and working women might own two shifts, one for work and one for attending church; and the well-to-do might have five or more. Period advertisements rarely describe shifts. In 1746, an English indentured convict, Mary Porter, stole a woman's shift with silver buttons on the sleeves (*Pennsylvania Gazette*, April 24, 1746).

Stays and Jumps

The 18th century brought newspaper advertisements for a variety of both bespoke and ready-made stays. These could be constructed of narrow or wider channels and fashioned with stiffer whalebone (baleen) or more flexible packthread. Staymaker John Frost, "lately from London" advertised stays for "Gentlewomen and others . . . after the best and newest Fashion. . . . He can make Stays without Padding, shall make Women look strait that are not so. Likewise Customers may be furnished with very good Whale bone, and all Sorts of Stay trimming cheap" if they wished to make or repair their own stays (*Pennsylvania Gazette*, August 27, 1730). More comfortable jumps, either unboned or stiffened only with packthread, were suitable for both women and young girls. In the 1730s and 1740s, baleen was advertised by a number of Philadelphia merchants, such as John Breinthal (or Breintnal), George Brownell, and Peter Braynton, suggesting that there was a healthy market for stays and other support garments, such as hooped petticoats (see below).

Under-Petticoat

Under-petticoats supported the shape of the gown and provided warmth. They might be made of linen or woolen flannel. They were frequently imported as ready-mades to the colonies. In 1732, John Jones, on the Bay in Charleston, offered ready-made under-petticoats as well as other clothing (*South-Carolina Gazette*, December 16).

A hooped petticoat of cane, wood, or baleen splints connected and shaped with cloth tapes was worn to create the fashionable rounded skirt silhouette during this period. Unlike 19th-century hoops, which were usually ankle length, 18th-century hoops, whether rounded or oblong, were usually only hip length.

The fan hoop was fashionable in the 1740s and 1750s, pulled by internal tapes to form a fan shape. This form developed into the oblong hoop worn primarily in the middle decades of the century. In its extreme form, this petticoat, with its cane or baleen framework, gave a grossly exaggerated width to the hipline. Side pieces were often hinged to turn upward so that the wearer could negotiate narrow spaces.

Women who wore hooped petticoats were not without their detractors. In 1726, the *New England Weekly Journal* editorialized that although hoops had been fashionable for many years, "For my part I was always willing to indulge it under some restriction: that is to say if 'tis not a rival to the dome of St. Paul's to incumber the way, or the tub for the residence of a new Diogenes" (quoted in Holliday 1922, 161).

Small Linen, Bonnets, and Hats, 1715–1750

In the 18th century, a woman who was without a cap during the day was considered to be in a state of undress. Early in the century, the ruffled cap with lappets—a holdover from the starched linen caps that formed the foundation of the fontange—were worn by most women during the day; the lappets, or streamers, might hang down the back or be pinned up atop the cap. These caps and their lappets were called pinners. The full ruffled cap went out of fashion in the 1720s, replaced by a smaller pinner, ruffled at the front but not the back, with or without lappets. In 1737, a servant woman fleeing her master wore plain muslin pinners (*Pennsylvania Gazette,* May 19, 1737).

Round-eared caps covered more of the head than a pinner; they had a slightly gathered crown and ruffled front and were worn with or without lappets. Female servants sometimes wore round-eared caps that completely covered the hair. Everyday caps and working caps were usually plain white linen. Fancy caps of gauze, lace, or silk fabrics usually were also elaborately trimmed with ribbon, lace, feathers, artificial flowers, or other millinery goods. Another style of cap featured a gathered crown and frill that fitted tightly around the head with a drawstring tied at the back. Called a mob cap, this style of headgear changed in volume and shape with changing fashions in hair dress.

Indentured servants and the enslaved sometimes used a neck handkerchief as a head covering. In Boston, Janto ran away from a new master in 1740, within seven days of her purchase, wearing a "speckled Handkerchief" on her head (*Boston Weekly News-Letter,* May 8). Margaret Brown, an indentured servant, left with a checked cotton handkerchief tied on her head (*Pennsylvania Gazette,* January 21, 1746).

Hoods were worn over caps throughout this period. Unstructured hoods without shoulder capes usually were tied on under the chin. The front edge might be turned back to reveal a lining of contrasting color. Those that fitted the head more closely also extended to cover the neck and ears; they were sometimes quilted and might provide more warmth under a more decorative hood. Hoods were made of a variety of fabrics, from silk or wool to cambric or muslin. When riding a horse, a lady might wear a velvet cap or hood.

The neckline of a gown or jacket was usually filled in with a neck handkerchief. These ranged from coarse to very fine linen or cotton, according to status of the wearer and the occasion. Under a handkerchief a woman of means might wear a ruffle or band of lace or linen that either edged the stomacher or the entire neckline.

Advertisements illustrate the variety of imported ready-made small linen that was available to colonists. In 1734, Charleston merchant William Lasserre advertised tabby stomachers, suits of pinners, quilted caps, spotted cambric and muslin hoods, and embroidered aprons (*South-Carolina Gazette*, November 30). Goods sold by Bostonian Thomas Fleet included "fine flower'd Muslin handkerchiefs; rich Gawze Handkerchiefs Embroider'd with Gold and Silver; Likewise Pinners or [head-]Dresses just arrived from London, and set in the Pink of the Mode" (*Boston News-Letter*, May 19, 1737). Merchant John Bell, of Philadelphia, offered a variety of women's flowered ruffles; these likely were of fine muslin or linen and embroidered with white silk or linen thread (*Pennsylvania Gazette*, September 27, 1750). Shopkeeper Joseph Stevens sold sets of neck and wrist-wear that included fine linen in a checked pattern, fine white lace with or without colored ribbons of blue or purple, and French gauze (*Pennsylvania Gazette*, September 5, 1754).

As in the 17th century, women usually wore a hat, also called a bonnet, over the cap when out-of-doors. The most common hats were of woven straw and usually described only as "plaited." For example, an enslaved girl living in New Castle County, Pennsylvania, owned a plaited bonnet lined with light red silk (*Pennsylvania Gazette*, January 29, 1740). Leghorn hats of straw and horsehair hats appeared in colonial advertisements in the 1740s. Both of these woven hats had a low round crown and a flat brim of varying width; they were fastened under the chin with a ribbon tie. This style sometimes was called a shepherdess or milkmaid. Bonnets were also made of fabrics; usually silk but also calico. A paduasoy bonnet lined with black silk was stolen in Philadelphia in 1741 (*Pennsylvania Gazette*, April 16). In Philadelphia, women Friends sometimes wore white hats of felted beaver; these had a very low crown and wide brim; they were tied under the chin with silk cords (Watson 1830, 177).

Footwear, 1715–1750

Besides noting the fiber and sometimes color, detailed descriptions of women's stockings are uncommon in 18th-century records. A parcel of women's blue stockings with clocks "some of the Clocks Silk and some Worsted" was stolen from a Connecticut shop in 1735 (*Pennsylvania Gazette,* March 4). In 1736, a 20-year-old runaway servant wore blue stockings with white clocks (*Pennsylvania Gazette,* May 27, 1736). In 1746, another runaway servant also wore blue stockings, but hers were recognizable as having been "new footed with blue," suggesting they were two different shades of blue after the repair was made (*Pennsylvania Gazette,* January 21, 1746).

As in the previous century, in the 1700s women's shoes were not shaped for the right and left foot, but were cut as straights. Fashionable shoes were made with thin leather soles and curved heels between one and a quarter and three and a half inches high. Toes were generally pointed, or very slightly rounded at the tip. The vamps, latchets, and quarters of fashionable shoes were made of thin leather—calf skin or the sumac-dyed goatskin called red morocco—as well as fabrics such as silk, calamanco, or worsted brocade. These uppers were bound with silk, wool, or linen tapes. The latchets were fastened with buckles of base metal, brass, or silver, which were sometimes ornamented with paste. If present, the rand, a thin cording between the sole and upper, usually contrasted with the color of the upper. The tongue of the shoe came well up on the front of the foot early in the century, but shortened and narrowed as the century progressed, as did the latchets. Slippers, open-backed shoes with high heels but without a heel quarter, were worn indoors.

Working women's shoes were of sturdy leather, with thick, rather stiff leather soles and low, wide heels. Toes were rounder than for fashionable shoes, and the latchets across the front were likely fastened with a cord or a tape rather than a buckle. Descriptions in runaway notices indicate that some indentured servants went without footwear. For example, Irish servant Mary Brown ran from her Philadelphia master "with no shoes nor stockings" and Irish maid Katherine Anderson left wearing "no shoes or stockings that is known of" (*Pennsylvania Gazette,* September 18, 1746; July 7, 1748).

Pattens were made to match fashionable shoes made of fragile materials, and worn over them out of doors. The shoe slipped into a sturdy leather oversole that tied over the top of the foot. Iron pattens strapped onto their shoes and elevated them several inches above the ground.

Hairstyles and Grooming, 1715–1750

The most fashionable levels of colonial society followed English styles. The curls and twists of hair piled high at the forehead and worn with the fontange cap became old fashioned in about 1710, replaced with a lower and less elaborate dressing of the front hair, with the back hair divided between a bun and a few long curls. Most women continued to wear their hair more simply, pulled away from the face and pinned under a cap, with perhaps small curls or tendrils at the sides and nape of the neck. The description of an attractive, young Philadelphia woman, Hettie Levy, in 1744 indicates that to enhance her "Beautiful head of Hair, Coal Black," she wore false hair: "A Wigg, waving in wanting curling Ringletts in her Neck" (quoted in Wharton 1893, 211). In about 1715, following men's fashions, elite women in Britain began to powder their hair for formal occasions. It was likely, however, that colonial women only occasionally powdered their hair until mid-century.

Accessories, 1715–1750

All respectable and workingwomen wore aprons. Most work aprons were made of a woolen or worsted fabric, but some were of a sturdy linen like osnaburg, coarse tow linen, or a finer linen like lawn or holland— striped, checked, or bleached white. Advertisements from this period mention aprons dyed blue or green, speckled, and woven in checks or stripes. Aprons might be marked in silk thread with the owner's initials as was the fine linen apron, "mark'd AA" stolen by a convict servant woman Catherine McClue in 1749 (*Pennsylvania Gazette*, August 10).

Elegant ready-made aprons for formal wear were sold in urban areas. Surviving examples indicate that these were short, just to the knee or higher. John Inglis offered embroidered silk aprons (*Pennsylvania Gazette*, September 9, 1731). John Watsone of Charleston and William Dames of Philadelphia both advertised short aprons wrought with gold and silver (*South-Carolina Gazette*, December 6, 1735; *Pennsylvania Gazette*, November 18, 1742). Hutchinson and Grimké in Charleston offered embroidered short silk aprons (*South-Carolina Gazette*, September 27, 1735).

Ribbons and tapes used for gartering stockings were generally the same for men and women, excepting perhaps the color. It is uncommon to find descriptions of garters specifically for women. A Mrs. Hogg, however, advertised in the *New-York Weekly Post-Boy* that she had lost a black silk garter, lined with red, "with a Stone Buckle set in Silver" (February 22, 1748).

The fan became a popular accessory for almost all ranks of women in the 18th century. Fan sticks and guards were made of a variety of materials: painted or japanned wood, tortoise shell, ivory, bone, brass, and silver. The curved mount was usually painted or printed paper or silk and might be edged with lace. Mourning fans had mounts of black crepe or gauze. Both fans and fan mounts were imported. In 1739, a Williamsburg resident lost "a large Ivory Stick Fan, mounted with Leather, neatly guilded, the two out Sticks [i.e., guard sticks] handsomely carved, the rest all plain" (*Virginia Gazette*, June 8). John Seymour advertised ivory fans with paper and leather mountings, and William Crofthwaite offered "duke's carved ivory, black and sundry other fans" (*Pennsylvania Gazette*, April 24, 1740; March 24, 1747). Ann Willson advertised to Charleston patrons that she mended and mounted fans, and William Stone sold "rich leather mounted and other Fans" (*South-Carolina Gazette*, May 18, 1738; November 13, 1740).

For those who could afford them, close-fitting necklaces of pearls were popular as well as finger rings with garnets or other gems, and gold and silver pendants and ear rings. Less expensive rings for fingers and ears made of base metals were also offered. In Charleston, Elizabeth Scoulie reported the theft of two gold rings, one each engraved "the Poises are these, Remember me when I am at Sea" and "No Recompence but Love" (*South-Carolina Gazette*, May 3, 1740). In 1743, Charleston jeweler John Paul Grimké offered his patronesses diamond finger and ear rings; garnet, crystal, and composition ear rings; girdle hooks set with stones; fingers rings set with garnet, emerald, sapphire, amethyst, or topaz; composition and amber necklaces "with Arm Strings"; as well as pinchbeck and gilt equipages—small cases for sewing or writing tools that hung from the waist by a chain and hook (*South-Carolina Gazette*, January 24).

In 1741, an elaborate set of "Breast Jewels for a Stomacher," with mounts of gilded silver, was stolen from Shepard Kollack, in Lewistown, Pennsylvania. The collection consisted of six pieces: the largest was set with a large crystal surrounded by smaller crystals; four were set with a central moss agate surrounded with "small Stones of different colors"; the last was a girdle hook set with emeralds and a pearl from which hung silver chains for a scissors and other accessories (*Pennsylvania Gazette*, August 27).

Masks were worn out of doors in cold weather to protect the complexion. Watson (1830, 180) noted that to keep it on, the mask had a silver mouthpiece that the wearer held in her mouth. Patches, fashionable in European high society, were small shapes that could be affixed on the face to cover a spot or call attention to a pretty feature, such as a dimple.

As in the 17th century, robings were a stylish trimming for gowns. On closed gowns the robings went around the neck and down both sides of the bodice. On open gowns, they decorated the front edges from skirt hem to around the neck. After joining the fabric strips at their short edges, the long edges of the robing strips might be cut to make scallops or another decorative pattern; the strips then were pulled into ruffles or ruching with gathering stitches worked down the center of each strip. An alternative was to gather both of the long edges of joined strips and draw the fabric up into small puffs. Robings might match the gown fabric or be of a contrasting color. For example, in 1741 Philadelphian William Harbert reported the theft of a "callico Gown robed with blue silk, and a linen border round the bottom" (*Pennsylvania Gazette,* July 9).

Breast and sleeve knots of ribbon bows and loops and sashes and girdles of both ribbon and fabrics were fashionable; milliners sold them ready-made as well as the materials to make them. Bostonian shopkeeper Catherine Marriott sold a stock of "Laces, Edgings, Fringes, Fanns, Masks, Patches, Silver Ribbons and Girdles, Tossels for Hoods and Mantels" in 1737 (*Boston News-Letter,* November 24). Other imported notions included French stay cord (lacing cord), gartering, gold and silver laces, and lace from Flanders.

Main Garments, 1751–1785

Fashionable women had a wide choice of imported and domestically produced clothing in this period. Anything that was up-to-date and available in Britain could be obtained in the colonies. For example, two Irish mantua makers, in partnership in New York in 1757, advertised their readiness to make "sacks, negligees, negligee night gowns, plain night gowns, pattanliers [*pet en l'air*], shepherdesses, roman cloaks, cardinals, capuchins, dauphinesses, shades, lorrains, bonnets, and hives" (*New-York Mercury,* January 3, 1757).

Gown

Just as in the first half of the century, gown styling can be divided between open and closed fronts and *sacque* and English backs. Sack-back gowns usually had an inner bodice or panels of linen that laced close, allowing for the gown to be controlled on the body while still allowing the

The silk for this gown was woven in Spitalfields, outside London. The gown itself was probably made-to-measure in 1752 by a Boston dressmaker; it was remodeled in the 1770s. (Museum of Fine Arts, Boston, Massachusetts, USA/Gift of Miss Anne Winslow/The Bridgeman Art Library)

pleats to fall free. Open gowns might have an open front bodice as well, which displayed a separate stomacher or had a false front stitched in that buttoned close or the bodice might be cut to close by lacings, hooks and eyes, or buttons. Through the 1750s and 1760s, bodices were shaped like truncated cones and dipped below the waist in front with a rounded point. Necklines were low and square; sleeves were fitted and generally elbow length. In the 1750s, sleeve hems for formal gowns transitioned from cuffs to a shaped circular flounce that matched the gown. The full skirts were held out by under-petticoats and possibly a hooped petticoat.

In the 1770s, the bodice took on more of a curve along the sides, and the bodice fronts met edge to edge and were squared off at the bottom, below the waist. Skirts remained full all around and were worn with side hoops. In the 1780s, the most fashionable bodice had a rounded waistline at the natural waist; skirts were fuller at the back than across the front and sides. Necklines were also more rounded, but still low. By the 1780s, long sleeves were more fashionable than elbow length, and the flounce or tiered flounce that lasted through the 1770s was replaced by a fitted cuff in the 1780s.

The polonaise gown, introduced in about 1775, had skirts that were drawn up, or kilted, by two cords at the sides to create a festooned draping or puff-balls at the sides and back. These could be arranged to suit the taste of the wearer. This style complemented the light silk taffetas fashionable in the 1770s and the layers of silk gauze and cotton muslin of the 1780s. The sleeves could be three-quarter length or longer.

The newspaper report of a theft from Benjamin Franklin's house in Philadelphia in 1750 included "a woman's gown, of printed cotton, of the sort called brocade print, very remarkable, the ground dark, with large red roses, and other large and yellow flowers, with blue in some of the flowers, and smaller blue and white flowers, with many green leaves" (*Pennsylvania Gazette*, November 1). During Benjamin Franklin's many years in London and Paris, he often sent fabric and accessories home for his wife, Deborah, daughter, Sally, and other female relatives. In February 1758, he sent Deborah two lengths for gowns: seven yards of a blue-ground printed cotton, which he "bought by Candlelight, and lik'd it then, but not so well afterwards" and 16 yards of "flower'd tissue" that cost nine guineas and which Franklin thought "a great beauty" (Franklin 1905, 3:433).

Franklin had supported the patriotic ban on imports and the encouragement of home manufacture during the Stamp Act crisis, however, in April 1766 he wrote to Deborah: "As the Stamp Act is at length repeal'd, I am willing you should have a new Gown, which you may suppose I did not send sooner, as I knew you would not like to be finer than your Neighbours, unless in a Gown of your own Spinning. Had the Trade between the two Countries totally ceas'd, it was a Comfort to me to recollect, that I had once been cloth'd from Head to Foot in Woolen and Linnen of my Wife's Manufacture, that I never was prouder of any Dress in my Life, and that she and her Daughter might do it again if it was necessary. . . . Joking apart, I have sent you a fine piece of Pompadour Sattin, 14 yards, cost 11 shillings a Yard; a silk *Negligee* and Petticoat of brocaded Lutestring for my dear Sally, with two dozen gloves" (Franklin 1906, 4:449).

Night Gown

The term "night gown" or "negligee" referred to a sack-back dress worn for formal and informal occasions at any time of day and not to a garment for sleeping. Anna Winslow described the dress worn by Miss Suky Pierce at her wedding to Samuel Jarvis in August 1772 as a "white satin night gound" (Winslow 1974, 67).

Double Gown

Loose wrappers and double gowns were still popular at the close of the colonial period. In 1766, a woman stole clothing and textiles that included a long calico double gown, "purple and white, the Figure on one Side much smaller than the other" (*Pennsylvania Gazette*, June 5). Crossing the ocean to be with her husband in France in 1784, Abigail Adams wrote to her sister Mary that, "Whilst you, I imagine, are scorching under the midsummer heat, we can comfortably bear our double calico gowns, our baize ones upon them, and a cloth cloak in addition to all these" (Adams 1841, 2:7).

Short Gown, Jacket, and Bed Gown

The loosely fitting short gowns and bed gowns were still informal wear for the upper classes and working wear for many women and girls. There are also extant short gowns from the last quarter of the 18th century with a T-shaped cut and side godets—long, wedge-shaped pieces of fabric set into the garment to give it more volume. Jackets, more fitted in the body and sleeves, with skirts or peplums, were still worn by all classes. For the upper ranks these gowns remained proper for informal or day wear. Styles followed fashionable gowns and bodices. By the 1780s, the *pet en l'air,* a short version of the *sacque* or robe *à la Française,* was no longer fashionable.

Hot weather was one reason to wear a short gown. Janet Shaw, a Scottish visitor to the colonies, was staying in Point Pleasant, North Carolina, during a heat wave in June of 1775 and noted the irritating increase of "the Musquetoes, the bugs and the ticks." To make themselves more comfortable, she and her hostess, Fanny Rutherfurd, lay on settees canopied over with green mosquito netting, "panting for breath and air, dressed in a single muslin petticoat and short gown" (Schaw 2009, 182–83). In 1786, Ann Head Warder (1758–1829), an English Quaker who visited New York and Philadelphia, noted that the women of New York "all wear short gowns." Ann found them an ugly style but was told that she would soon be wearing them "on account of the heat" (quoted in Gummere 1901, 139).

Sarah Wister was caught in informal attire when some Continental army (American) officers arrived unexpectedly in 1777. She recorded: "Several officers call'd to get some refreshment, but none of consequence till the afternoon. Cousin Prissa and myself were sitting at the door; I in a green skirt, dark short gown, &c. Two genteel men of the military order rode up to the door: 'Your servant, ladies,' &c; ask'd if they cou'd have quarters for Genl. Smallwood" (Wister 1902, 75–76).

John Watson reported that in the decades before the American Revolution, working women in Philadelphia all wore short gowns and petticoats of domestically produced fabric and "could be instantly known as such whenever seen abroad" (Watson 1830, 177). A convict servant who ran away from her Maryland master in 1750 owned a black and white striped bed gown.

A version of the short gown called a wrapper was worn by some enslaved women in South Carolina, as the following runaway advertisements from the *South-Carolina Gazette* indicate. A slave named Daphney ran away wearing a check wrapper, green "Negro cloth" petticoat, and a white handkerchief around her head (May 17, 1760). An Angola-born slave, Flora, left her master carrying a calico wrapper, two osnaburg petticoats and short gowns, and a white shift (May 23, 1761). In 1763, a girl just brought to Charleston from Angola was brought to the city's workhouse wearing an osnaburg shift and a white "negro cloth" petticoat and wrapper (November 19).

Petticoat or Skirt

Among quilted petticoats of colonial make are examples with face fabrics of plain silk or glazed woolen fabrics such as calamanco and with the lining fabrics of coarser linens or woolens, often striped (Rowe 1976, 161–71). Hannah MacSparran of Narragansett, Rhode Island, with the help of her niece, "put her red durance petticoat in the frame," which was probably a quilting frame (quoted in Woodward 1971, 86). Durance, or durant, was a fine plain weave of worsted yarns, with a glazed finish, like calamanco. The fabric name evoked one of its most important properties: it was hard wearing, or enduring, and therefore a suitable choice for a quilted petticoat.

The word skirt was occasionally used in that period, somewhat more often after 1770. In 1779, a reward was offered for a stolen striped cotton skirt and three yards of matching fabric stolen from a Pennsylvania tavern (*Pennsylvania Gazette*, October 6, 1779). In 1785, runaway Nancy Robertson was described as having taken a variety of garments, including two striped linsey petticoats in brown, blue, and white, and a light blue moreen skirt (*Pennsylvania Gazette*, November 9, 1785). This may indicate that the word petticoat was beginning to be used for under-petticoats and skirt for the petticoat that was worn as the outermost layer.

In 1756, Charleston merchants Archibald and Richard Park Stobo imported from London "womens stuff, callimanco, russel, worsted damask, and silk Quilted petticoats," and in 1764 shopkeeper Sarah Swallow advertised "pucker'd [likely quilted] silk petticoats" (*South-Carolina Gazette*, October 7, 1756; November 26, 1764). It is notable, however, that although South Carolina joined the boycott British goods in reaction to the Townsend Acts, beginning in 1767, Charleston continued to import British luxury textile goods, which included petticoats. In 1772 alone 14 different merchants and shopkeepers advertised petticoats for sale in the *South Carolina Gazette*. For example, William Valentine and Simeon Theus advertised "black, blue, Pink, and green Calamanco Petticoats" (December 10, 1772). William Doughty had "A few Ladies SATIN PETTICOATS, Pink, Blue, and white, beautifully flowered" (August 10, 1772). And Roberts and Taylor offered "yard wide figured and bordered and callimanco petticoats" (January 25, 1772).

Stomacher

Stomachers could match or contrast with the gown. A woolen gown in a British collection dated 1755–1775 has two matching stomachers; one with several rows of pleated pinked silk stitched vertically up the center, the other with the pleated silk stitched in a curvilinear design. Stomachers were also purchased separately and worn with different gowns. From the 1750s through the 1770s the stomacher bottom was rounded rather than pointed.

Outer Garments, 1751–1785

In 1772, shopkeeper Ann Thornton sold, fresh from London, "broadcloth and duffil cardinals, of scarlet, white, and cloth colours, trimmed with skin, snail and cord; mode ditto, lined with stuff and silk . . . also plain and spotted satin ditto, laced" (*Pennsylvania Gazette*, January 23, 1772). A woman's long scarlet cloak, almost new and with a double cape, was stolen from Benjamin Franklin's house in Philadelphia in 1750 (*Pennsylvania Gazette*, November 1). In the late 1750s Franklin sent fashionable cloaks to his wife and daughter from France: crimson satin for his wife and white for his daughter (Franklin 1905, 3:419, 431).

A cardinal was not always a red cloak. A "black silk cardinal" was stolen from the Philadelphia home of Elizabeth Reynolds by a runaway servant, and in 1774 another runaway servant girl took a "black silk cardinal, diced, not trimmed save the cap" (*Pennsylvania Gazette*, January 30, 1766; February 23, 1774).

Colonial advertisements for ladies' equestrian dress were numerous in the second half of the 18th century. Nesbett Deane opened a shop in New York City where he made "black or white, plain or furr'd, riding hats for ladies" (*New-York Mercury*, October 21, 1765). In Pennsylvania, however, Quaker women opted for the traditional outerwear hood while riding on horseback, especially to meeting—a cape or riding hood and a safeguard to protect their skirts. In 1786, Ann Head Warder noted in her journal: "They ride by themselves with a safeguard, which, when done with, is tied to the saddle, and the horse hooked to a rail, standing all meeting time as still as their riders sit" (quoted in Gummere 1901, 155).

Undergarments, 1751–1785

After 1750, newspaper notices for female runaways—especially in the *Pennsylvania Gazette*—sometimes note the quality of their linen shifts, including the color and coarseness. Shifts might be noted as made of brown or natural color unbleached linen or they may have been bleached white. Servant Lucy Granger owned a "tow bodied shirt, with flax linen sleeves" (*Pennsylvania Gazette*, April 17, 1755). Servant Margaret Rogers owned a shift, the body of which was osnaburg but "with good homespun sleeves" (*Pennsylvania Gazette*, October 26, 1752).

Stays and jumps continued to be important support garments through the end of the colonial period. (The term "corset," as a substitute for "stays," did not come into the English language until 1785, in *The Ladies Magazine*, where it described a quilted waistcoat, called in French *un corset*.) In 1766, John M'Queen advertised that he had imported from London a "neat Assortment of Wom-

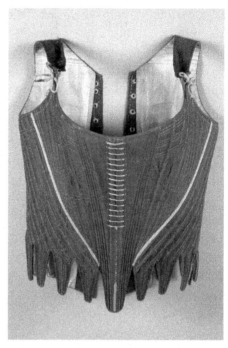

Pair of stays, c. 1775, linen face and lining with boning of baleen. (Fashion Museum, Bath and North East Somerset Council/The Bridgeman Art Library)

en and Maid's Stays . . . Women Packthread Jumps . . . Misses neat thin bound Stays of different Sorts and Sizes . . . [and] Misses and Childrens Packthread Stays from one Month to seven Years old" (*New-York Gazette*, February 24). A "pair of women's stays covered with white tabby before, and dove colour'd tabby behind" was among the items stolen from Benjamin Franklin's house in 1750; the description indicates that the stays were covered with a fashionable fabric on the front, and may have been worn without a separate stomacher (*Pennsylvania Gazette*, November 1). Two runaway advertisements in the *Pennsylvania Gazette* noted that the indentured servants, both of them Dutch, wore jumps, one of blue cloth and the other of a striped fabric (June 10 and July 8, 1756).

Under-petticoats were usually plain and most often simply described as linen, and therefore probably white. As in previous periods, they helped keep the fashionable skirt shape and also may have been worn for warmth.

Hooped petticoats, or hoops, were worn to present the most fashionable appearance, and are mentioned most often in relation to balls and parties. Court hoops were very wide and flattened front and back, giving an almost rectangular shape to the skirt. Otherwise, rounded hoops continued to be worn through the 1750s, as oval hoops begin to come into fashion.

In the midcentury panniers, or false hips, were added to hooped petticoats. These bag-like constructions of sturdy linen lied flat against the hips and extended out at the sides with semicircular canes. Both the hooped petticoat and panniers had openings in the canvas for access to the pockets. Contemporary descriptions of the ambulations of women wearing these supports were not often flattering. Of the recollections of a Philadelphian octogenarian, John Watson (1779–1860) recorded that before the American Revolution women wore hoops "from six inches to two feet on each side, so that a full dressed lady entered a door like a crab, pointing her obtruding flanks end foremost" (Watson 1830, 173).

By about 1775, fullness had moved to the back of the gown and hoops were no longer fashionable. Instead, a false rump or bum roll—a revival from the 17th century—was tied on to hold the skirt out at the back. This was a large rolled pad, tapering at the ends and tied around the waist and usually stuffed with cork.

Small Linen, Bonnets, and Hats, 1751–1785

Women of every class wore handkerchiefs around their necks to fill in the necks of their gowns or jackets. Plain, striped, or spotted silks, or linen cambric and lawn, plain, edged with ruffles or a narrow lace, embroidered or tamboured, printed with flowers or edged with decorative tapes, served upper class women and the higher tiers of the middle classes for daywear. Gauze, silk lace, and other semi-sheer fabrics such as cyprus served for evening wear. Servant women wore handkerchiefs of plain green or blue silk, white, striped or checked cotton or linen, but also mentioned in runaway notices are handkerchiefs of dark striped silk, blue and white and yellow and red spotted silk, and plain or flowered lawn.

Worn by women and girls almost at all times, caps changed in shape, in the degree to which it covered the hair and head, and in ornamentation with changes in hairstyles. In the 1770s, when the hairdress became fashionably high, hoods could no longer accommodate the hairstyle and caps were made more voluminous and wider. One type rose to a high point in front, fitted closely around the face, and tied under the chin; the front edge might have a fine full ruching or narrow lace gathers. As the hair grew higher, the cap no longer tied under the chin but just perched on top of the hair. The mob cap now had a full crown gathered into a shaped band with a ruffled front and covered the top and back of the head.

Merchants and shopkeepers advertised hats with wired frames covered in fashionable fabrics, "chip" hats of thin woven strips of wood, Dunstable and Leghorn hats and bonnets, and riding hats and bonnets. Hats were often trimmed with artificial flowers and fruit, plumes and feathers, or ribbons and laces. A runaway Philadelphia servant in 1750 had a "permeto [likely plaited palmetto] hat lined with yellowish silk" (*Pennsylvania Gazette*, July 19, 1750).

Bonnets were popular and they appear often in descriptions of stolen goods or runaway servants. They are described as of white silk, changeable silk, worsted, linen, and, most often, simply black. A black silk satin bonnet stolen in 1768 had "whalebone all round" (*Pennsylvania Gazette*, February 25, 1768). This headcovering was likely what Philadelphian John Watson called a "mush-mellon" bonnet, which was stiffened with pieces of baleen "set at an inch apart in parallel lines and presenting ridges to the eye" (Watson 1830, 176). A runaway wore a "cloth coloured pelong [a silk satin] bonnet, lined with pale blue mantua" (*Pennsylvania Gazette*, April 3, 1776). James Stevenson of Philadelphia advertised "mantua flounced bonnets" and colored satin bonnets, colored satin hats, and figured silk hats (*Pennsylvania Gazette*, May 4, 1758). To protect the high hairstyles of the 1770s and 1780s when out-of-doors, ladies wore a calash, a collapsible bonnet with ribs of wire or reed. John Watson noted that to keep the bonnet over the head, it was drawn up by a cord held in the hand of the wearer. When indoors, she released the cord and the bonnet fell back in folds "like the springs of a calash or gig top" (Watson 1830, 176). Surviving examples were made of both silk and cotton fabrics, in green, blue, brown, and black.

Footwear, 1751–1785

Imported stockings of superfine, fine, mid-fine, and common varieties in linen thread, cotton, and worsted were available, as were silk hose in superfine and fine qualities. Scotch knit silk, linen, and worsted hose came in plain and ribbed styles. Colors included blue, white, striped, and moss. To hold up the stockings, knee garters of silk as well as tapes, ferret, and ribbons of silk and wool that could be used for garters were widely advertised.

Fashionable shoes continued to have relatively pointed toes and high heels, but the heels were thinner and the curves were more pronounced than earlier. Pointed or curved rather than squared off, the tongue was shorter, no longer reaching high up on the front of the foot. Latchets were narrower and shorter, buckles smaller. Patterned silks, white and red leather, black leather, and woolen fabrics were all commonly used for fashionable shoes. Clogs and pattens were still used for protection. Benjamin Kendall, of Philadelphia, sold women's "silk and velvet tie clogs, morocco and common ditto" (*Pennsylvania Gazette*, September 20, 1752).

Working women wore much rougher shoes or none at all. Martha James, an indentured servant, wore old shoes that had been resoled, with nails in the heels and copper buckles; a Dutch servant, Catherine Plimlen, had calf skin pumps with large buckles (*Pennsylvania Gazette*, October 25, 1753; June 30, 1757). Irish servant Sarah McLaughlin ran away without shoes or stockings, and Irish servant Rose Crawford owned a pair of flat-heeled pumps with leather strings in them, "not half worn" (*Pennsylvania Gazette*, November 2, 1758; October 25, 1759).

Women as well as men sometimes donned Indian-style moccasins, also called shoe packs (see also Chapter 5). In 1769, Virginian Martha Jacquelin complained of corns on her feet and took to wearing "Mockasins" to relieve the pain (Norton 1937, 103).

Hairstyles and Grooming, 1751–1785

Beginning in the 1750s, colonial women of status began powdering their hair for formal occasions.

In the 1760s, ladies began having their hair dressed high off the forehead, the hair being supported underneath with a roll or pad. The sides of the hair might be dressed in arrangements of curls with one or two curls from the back of the head draped onto the neck or over the shoulders. This style also required the use of false hair. It was reported in a letter to the editor of the *New-York Journal* or the *General Advertiser* that the human hair used to make the artificial pads or rolls over which women combed their hair to heighten the hairdressing came from deceased hospital patients: "in the Hospitals, whatever Patients died, their Hair became the perquisite of the Nurses, who carefully sheared them. . . . That both the Small Pox, and a Distemper still more disagreeable, supplied the greatest part" (November 26, 1767).

In the 1770s, the hairdress of the English and French elite grew more exotic; colonial women likely followed rather than copied these towering and extravagant styles. During the British occupation of Philadelphia, Loyalist Rebecca Franks wrote to a friend describing a ball she attended there: "The Dress is more ridiculous and pretty than any thing I ever saw—great quantity of different colored feathers on the head at a time . . . [t]he hair dress'd very high" (quoted in Wharton 1893, 218). In 1772, young Anna Green Winslow wrote to her mother, describing distress and discomfort of having one's hair so dressed:

> I had my HEDDUS roll on, aunt Storer said it ought to be made less, Aunt Deming said it ought not to be made at all. It makes my head itch, & ach, & burn like anything Mamma. This famous roll is not made wholly of a red Cow Tail, but is a mixture of that, & horsehair (very course) & a little human hair of yellow hue, that I suppose was taken out of the back part of an old wig. But D made it (our head) all carded together and twisted up. When it first came home, aunt put it on, & my new cap on it, she then took up her apron & mesur'd me, & from the roots of my hair on my forehead to the top of my notions, I mesur'd above an inch longer than I did downwards from the roots of my hair to the end of my chin. Nothing renders a young person more amiable than virtue & modesty without the help of fals hair, red Cow tail, or D (the barber). (Winslow 1974, 71)

Accessories, 1751–1785

Pockets of various shapes, sizes, and fabrics can be found in many museum collections. Some were pieced from scraps and some were cut from single pieces of cloth. Solid colors, white, and printed cottons were used. Some were embellished with embroidery. They were most often shaped to be narrower at the top and wider at the bottom, the latter of which usually had rounded corners. Sizes vary considerably: small pockets might hold a pocket handkerchief and a pocketbook, others were large enough to hold a knitting or embroidery project or a baby's cap and bib.

Tiny purses called "guinea purses" were looped over the wrist by a silk cord. Somewhat larger beaded purses were also known, the beads worked in floral or figural designs. Long netted purses with beads worked into the net were popular toward the end of the period.

Aprons of checked and stamped linen or cotton, low-grade linen tow-cloth, and coarse osnaburg were worn to protect the gown or petticoat while doing everyday chores. These generally covered most of the front of the skirt. John Watson noted that in Philadelphia "decent women" went out and to church wearing checked aprons (Watson 1830, 177). Finer quality, decorative aprons of silk or linen, ornamented with lace or embroidery, were worn for dress occasions. John Jamieson sold a "great variety" of "gause spotted, sprig'd strip'd and flowered lawn aprons and ruffles . . . all newest and most fashionable patterns" in his Charleston shop (*South-Carolina Gazette*, April 10, 1755). Bernard Gratz sold "muslin aprons with borders" (*Pennsylvania Gazette*, August 2, 1759). In 1762, Thomas Fitzsimons of Philadelphia offered "green and black flowered short aprons" (*Philadelphia Gazette*, August 12). William Fair and Company of Charleston offered stamped linen handkerchiefs and aprons in 1763 (*South-Carolina Gazette*, November 19).

Muffs were stuffed tubes of cloth used to keep the hands warm in cold weather. Plain, ornamented, or made of fur, they hung from the wrist, the waist, or around the neck by a ribbon. A tippet was a long narrow scarf, usually of fur but sometimes lace or fabric, which was worn around the neck and twisted or tied at the front. Ben Franklin sent his daughter Sally "a scarlet feather, muff, and tippet" in 1757 (Franklin 1905, 3:419).

Advertisements in this period offer more details about the fans being sold: paper and gauze fans; India fans; bone, boxwood, and ivory sticks; leather; and crape fans for mourning. Both finished fans and fan mounts were offered for sale. Fan mounts were printed or painted with romantic or classical scenes, or with floral ornament. Plain silk satin fans might be decorated with metal spangles stitched in a variety of linear patterns. In 1751, the *South-Carolina Gazette* reported that Parliament proposed a tax "to be put upon plain and printed fan mounts. Painted ones (not coloured) to pass free as before. A six penny stamp to be afixed in the midst of a plain, or printed fan mount, and a shilling stamp on a leather one" (June 10).

Metal buckles to fasten shoes came in many sizes and styles. In Philadelphia, Rivington and Brown offered silver buckles "of the most beautiful new invented Patterns," with and without matching knee buckles, as well as buckles with paste stones (*Pennsylvania Gazette*, August 26, 1762). Benjamin Franklin sent buckles with "French Paste Stones, which are next in luster to Diamonds" to his family in Philadelphia (Franklin 1905, 3:438).

Jewelers advertised heavily until the mid-1700s, offering garnet necklaces, ear rings, and rings; hair pins, sprigs, and jeweled and tortoise shell combs for ladies' hair; diamond, ruby, emerald, sapphire, amethyst, and topaz rings, jewelry mounts for hair; and sewing tools and small cases of tools called etuis to hang from the waist. Among the items stolen from Benjamin Franklin's house in 1750 was a double necklace of gold beads (*Pennsylvania Gazette*, November 1). Servant girls might wear a ribbon around their neck, tied in the back; this was often black, but sometimes striped or another color.

Trimmings and Ornaments

In the last decades of the colonial period the designs for lace trimmings were less dense, with more open ground and lighter, asymmetrical motifs. James Wallace of New York advertised in 1775 that he made lace in both black and white silk to trim ladies' aprons and handkerchiefs and white linen lace for men's and ladies' sleeve ruffles and ladies' hoods, aprons, and tippets (*New-York Journal or the General Advertiser*, July 6). Philadelphia milliner Mary Symonds offered a fashionable range of laces in 1767: expensive bobbin laces from Brussels, Bath, and Mechlin along with "minionet, trawley, Hanover, blond, and silver blond" laces (*Pennsylvania Gazette*, May 14, 1767). This assortment gave Philadelphia's well-to-do women a selection that would have been respectable in London. By the 1780s lace was becoming unfashionable.

CLOTHING IN PORTRAITURE, 1715–1785

This bodice ornament of rock crystals and paste (glass) with foiled settings in a silver mount was worn on a stomacher. Made in about 1760 in England, it is an example of the more elaborate ornaments that colonial jewelers imported during the 18th century. (Victoria and Albert Museum, London)

The full-length portrait of Ariaantje Coeymans Verplanck (1672–1743), painted in about 1723 by Nehemiah Partridge (1683–c. 1737), depicts the 51-year-old resident of Albany, New York, and recent bride of 28-year-old David Verplanck, dressed in a dark closed gown with flat robings on the bodice, a black stomacher, a chemise with puffed sleeves that show under the turned-back cuffs of her gown, lace sleeve ruffles, fine linen ruffles at the bodice neckline, and a wide band of decorative trimming at the hem of her skirt. The ankle-length skirt reveals high-heeled shoes with elongated toes. In addition to earrings, Ariaantje wears a necklace of corn kernal beads.

In 1729–1730, Scottish artist John Smibert (1688–1751) painted a group portrait of Dean George Berkeley and the entourage Berkeley brought with him to the American colonies, hoping to start a college in Bermuda. Smibert, who had accompanied the group as a potential art instructor, completed the work while the group waited in Newport, Rhode Island, for the next phase of their journey. The project failed, and Smibert remained in New England. In this portrait, the two women—Berkeley's wife, Anne, and her female companion, Miss Handcock—are shown in what might be wrap-front gowns, or wrappers, of silk. These have wide oval necklines and elbow-length sleeves with ruffle-hemmed white chemise sleeves underneath; the skirts are not visible. The chemise necklines of both women are almost identical and oddly cut.

Joseph Badger's 1750s painting of Mrs. John Edwards (Abigail Fowle) shows her in a simple, brown closed gown. The fitted elbow-length sleeves have shaped cuffs, and the bodice front appears to close across a stom-

Dean Berkeley and His Entourage (The Bermuda Group) by John Smibert, 1729–1730. Yale University Art Gallery, Gift of Isaac Lothrop, 1808.1. (Yale University Art Gallery/Art Resource, NY)

acher. Robings edge the bodice fronts and a single horizontal band of the same fabric curves across the top of the bodice. The ends of her white linen neck-handkerchief, finished with ruffles of finer linen, are tucked under the band. Her sleeve ruffles and close-fitting cap are also of white linen, and plain. The cap frames her face and ties under chin with a brown silk bow.

In contrast, the c. 1762 portrait by William Johnston of Mrs. Jacob Hurd features much more elaborate and costly gown and trimmings. Her soft green open gown has white lace or embroidery on the flat robings and lace ruching above the sleeve hems. Lace ruffles finish the neckline, and triple lace ruffles terminate the sleeves. The bodice appears to be held by beads or a chain across a white lace stomacher. Her unpowdered hair is drawn up and back into a puffed style. Around her neck is an elaborate necklace incorporating three strands of beads, a black ribbon, and a filigree pendant.

Charles Willson Peale painted Mrs. Samuel Miflin in about 1780; she wears an open gown of a dull-finished, light gray-brown silk over a blue satin quilted petticoat. Draped around her neck is a sheer white, lace-edged handkerchief, which has been folded in half; an apron of similar material covers the front of her petticoat. A cloak of white silk patterned with small dots and edged with lace (coarser than the neckcloth edging) is draped loosely around her arms; the long tying ribbons are clearly visible. A close-fitting cap with ruchings around the face and a lace and blue silk bow at the top ties under her chin and obscures her hairdress.

CLOTHING FOR THE ENSLAVED, 1715–1785

Runaway advertisements suggest that in the 18th century there was no standard clothing for female slaves belonging to northern masters. African and African American women who were household or personal servants might be provided with less expensive versions of fashionable dress—especially if they were visible at social gatherings. Those who worked primarily outside or at a trade would have received plain and more serviceable garments, often of homespun. In 1734, an enslaved girl of about 16 or 18 ran away from her shoemaker master in Philadelphia wearing a seersucker jacket and a checked cotton petticoat (*Pennsylvania Gazette*, June 27). She likely was born in Africa because she had country markings—"mark'd around the neck with three rows like beads." But she also had endured being marked by her colonial master; she was "branded upon the breast N.R." Mimbo left her Boston master in 1737 wearing a dark-colored baise gown over a red petticoat, with a blue and white striped holland petticoat over the dress (*Boston News-Letter*, April 21, 1737). An Indian slave fled her Roxbury master in 1738 carrying a blue and grey striped homespun gown and a white, green, and red striped woolen gown of English-made cloth (*Pennsylvania Gazette*, January 26, 1738). Thirty-year-old Mary, an enslaved woman of "pale complexion," ran away from her Boston master in 1740 carrying with her a variety of clothing including some that may not have belonged to her: two gowns, one of blue and white Holland and one "a paned callico"; striped homespun and Holland jackets; two linen shifts and two cotton and linen shifts; several caps; and a pair of blue stockings, plus "sundry things yet unknown" (*Boston News-Letter*, August 18, 1740). She may have taken some of this clothing to change into, knowing her own clothing would be described by her owner, or she may have intended to sell or barter items for money, food, or other necessities during her escape.

In southern colonies the culture of the plantation and the culture of the town dictated clothing requirements and opportunities. Plantation owners usually provided female workers with either one set of clothing (a jacket and petticoat), two sets of clothing (coarse linen for summer and wool for winter), or yardage to make clothing. Instead of a jacket, a woman might be allowed only her shift as an upper garment. Sarah left her master's plantation to "conceal herself about *Charles-Town*" wearing an osnaburg shift and a blue petticoat (August 13, 1750). Slave owner James Habersham wrote to his London agent, William Knox, from Savannah, Georgia, in 1764 to order slave clothing: "I am told, what are called short gowns or wrappers with petticoats are best for women" (Habersham 1904, 15–17).

In areas of concentrated population, however, enslaved women were given or acquired a wider variety and amount of clothing, a situation that is reflected in newspaper notices for runaways. Sabina left her Charleston master wearing a plaid gown and blue quilted petticoat; she had wrapped blue and white handkerchiefs "about her Head and Neck" (*South-Carolina Gazette*, April 29, 1745). Flore ran away from her Charleston master wearing a checked jacket and petticoat, "but has [a] variety of other cloaths" (*South-Carolina Gazette*, September 13, 1751).

CLOTHING OF AMERICAN INDIANS, 1715–1785

Traveling between Albany and Saratoga, New York, in June of 1749, Peter Kalm (1716–1779), a Finnish visitor to the colonies, encountered a group of Indian women, probably Iroquois, sewing porcupine quills in decorative patterns on deer skins. His description of their dress reflects the kinds of merchandise that appealed to Native women in the 18th century: "The women wear no head-dress, and have black hair. They have a short blue petticoat, which reaches to their knees, and the brim of which is bordered with red or other ribbands. They wear their shifts over their petticoats. They have large ear-rings: and their hair is tied behind, and wrapped in ribbands. Their Wampum, or Pearls, and their money, which is made of shells, are tied round the neck, and hang down on the breast" (Kalm 1771, 281).

COMPOSITION OF A WARDROBE, 1715–1785

In 1722, an irate resident of Boston posted a letter to the editor of the *New-England Courant* complaining of a brothel "not an Hundred Doors from the old South Church, said to be kept by a very remarkable British woman." He reported that in "the Summer Season" she sometimes made her "Public Appearance" in clothing too outrageous for the local citizenry—especially its male constituents—adding that she wore a "handsome Jacket, edg'd with a fashionable Gold Lace, wearing a monstrous hoop'd Petticoat and a black Hat with a Gold Edging" (February 26).

According to runaway notices, many masters provided their female indentured servants who worked in the house rather than the field with respectable work clothing. In 1728, Bostonian John Menzies described what was likely the entire wardrobe—lacking the shoes—of his indentured Indian servant: a narrow striped gown of cherryderry (a fabric of mixed silk and cotton) faced with "a little flowered red and white calico," a striped homespun quilted petticoat, a plain muslin apron, "a suit of plain pinners," white cotton stockings, a red and white flowered knot, and a pair of green stone earrings (*Boston Weekly News-Letter*, August 15). In 1737, an English indentured servant who left her Philadelphia master owned less expensive but equally decent clothing: a yellow and red striped homespun gown with a blue quilted petticoat, blue stockings, black shoes, an osnaburg apron, muslin pinners, and a silk neck-handkerchief (*Pennsylvania Gazette*, May 19). When 20-year-old Irish servant Catherine Dunn ran away from her Baltimore, Maryland, master in 1747, she carried off an impressive number and variety of garments, which the runaway advertisement did not indicate were stolen. Enumerated were: two gowns, one of striped cotton and the other of blue and white birdseye linen; two quilted petticoats, one of striped silk and the other of red calimanco; several holland shifts and one of osnaburg; holland aprons; cambric caps and handkerchiefs; a pair of stays; a short red cloak; two pair of shoes; one leather and one calimanco; and straw hat (*Pennsylvania Gazette,* June 11).

Servants also suffered the opposite circumstances. In February of 1749 Dr. Alexander Reade was brought to the Middlesex County, Virginia, court to answer a complaint that he did not sufficiently provide for Jane Conran, his indentured servant, who likely worked out-of-doors as well as in the house. Ruling in favor of the servant, the court ordered that "for the future" Jane receive both winter and summer clothing. The winter wardrobe was to consist of two shifts, a "good" woolen waistcoat and petticoat, and new stockings and a pair of shoes; for summer she was to receive two shifts and a linen waistcoat and petticoat (Middlesex County, Virginia).

The probate inventory of James and Anne Pollard, Tyrrell County, North Carolina, was submitted in June, 1750 (Grimes 1912, 529–31). The couple held two women and three children as slaves. Although James's clothing was omitted from the inventory, a considerable quantity of women's clothing, presumably Anne's, was listed. Her undergarments, small linen, and accessories consisted of 12 shirts (likely shifts), two under-petticoats, two pairs of pockets, nine aprons, seven handkerchiefs, two pairs each of silk and linen stockings, one pair of everlasting shoes, five caps trimmed with lace, a pair of ruffles with lace probably meant for sleeves, three "workt knotts" for dress trimmings, a pocket book, two fans, some brass sleeve buttons, silver buckles, a gold ring, and several "eadgins" (probably narrow lace or linen ruffles to edge necklines)—three with lace and eleven plain. Her outer garments were also considerable: two cloaks, one of scarlett (either the hue or the cloth of that name); a velvet hood and bonnet; three plain hoods; two quilted petticoats, one of dimity and one of silk; four gowns, one chintz, one calico, one quilted, and one unspecified; and a "bed gown." The assessors listed a "Flowrd Gown Coat," which might refer to a gown and petticoat of flower-patterned silk or a petticoat that may once have matched a gown.

Elizabeth Thomas Lawson (c. 1688–1766) was the wife of a prosperous Prince Georges County, Maryland, planter, Thomas Lawson (c. 1684–1761). At the time of Elizabeth's death, the plantation supported diversified crops of wheat, corn, beans, cotton, and tobacco and a number of head of livestock—horses, cattle, sheep, and hogs. The field and husbandry work was accomplished with the labor of 12 slaves. Her probate inventory includes a mixture of old (likely worn) clothes, work garments, apparel for formal occasions and travel, and needles, pins, thread, bindings, and fabrics suitable for clothing—calico, striped holland, stamped linen, shalloon, stamped cotton, chintz, and taffeta. The inventory includes welch cotton (a napped wool fabric) and osnaburg—both used to clothe slaves—indigo for dyeing fabrics or clothing especially for the enslaved, and two pairs of "Negro Shoes." Among Elizabeth's worn clothing were gowns and short gowns, under-petticoats, aprons, handkerchiefs, caps, a striped and a black silk bonnet, a shift, a short cloak, linen stockings and a pair of pumps. Her everyday and formal attire included five short gowns, one of them not made up; six gowns, one each of fine India dimity, India persian, striped holland, black bombazine, printed linen, and stamped cotton; one paid double gown; a black taffeta gown and petticoat, likely worn after Thomas died; two quilted petticoats, one of silk, the other shalloon; and two petticoats for travel, one a "camblet riding skirt" and the other of "Life everlasting," a stout worsted fabric. Her undergarments consisted of six new shifts; five petticoats, two of brown sheeting (a furnishing linen), one of white sheeting, and two of "country cotton," either cotton or woolen. She owned one pocket made of sheeting, a pair of pockets made of ticking, and two small pocket handkerchiefs. Five aprons were for work, two of them described as coarse, but she owned one fine apron for formal occasions. For neckwear, she could choose from among 10 handkerchiefs—cotton, linen, lawn, check, and a fancy one of black gauze. Headwear included two new caps and two hoods, one of velvet and one alamode. Footwear consisted of linen, worsted, and calimanco hose, three pairs of leather pumps, and two pairs of calimanco shoes. For travel Elizabeth had a black velvet short cloak, one pair of black gloves, and two pairs of lamb gloves ("Inventory of . . . Mrs. Elizabeth Lawson").

The wardrobe of runaway Eleanor Armstrong details the repairs, patching, and reappropriation of clothing and accessories that marked much of the garb of indentured servants. Her three shifts were homespun with fine sleeves, oznaburg, and tow—this last with "broken ruffles." She had one pair of blue yarn stockings and one of white; and wore men's shoes with two different buckles, one brass and one pierced steel. Her headgear included a "clean cap" with a black satin ribbon that tied under her chin and a changeable silk bonnet lined with blue silk that tied with a white ribbon. She had a good checked apron and two handkerchiefs, one green silk and one with a large blue and white check. Two skirts, one old and one new, were of light blue and dark blue camblet. To wear over these she had the choice of a short gown of "with some red and stripes and sprigs . . . pieced under the arms with check linen," or a "long chits [i.e., chintz] wrapper" with a pattern of "large red and brown sunflowers" on a yellow ground, the lower sleeves repaired with "red and brown spotted calico" (*Pennsylvania Gazette*, April 2, 1772).

The 1778 inventory of Virginian Thomas Cooper, a cooper, included his wife Sarah's wardrobe. Her wearing apparel reflected the status of the wife of a successful artisan in a southern colony, with articles made of imported fabrics, ready-mades, and garments made from homespun. She owned seven gowns, among them a riding gown, two gowns made of homespun, or "Cuntry Cloth," three that were not described, and an old or out-of-fashion gown; five petticoats, one of them "old"; two short gowns; a cardinal; two hats, eight caps, and a black hood; five aprons and two handkerchiefs; two shifts; a pair of silver buttons; one pair of mitts; two pairs of gloves, one of them leather; and a three pairs of shoes (Fairfax County, Virginia, 69).

The letters of New Englander Abigail Adams, wife of John Adams, provide snapshots of sartorial trends from England and Europe at the end of the colonial period. When Abigail Adams joined her husband John, who was serving as ambassador in Europe in 1784, her family asked her to shop for them in London. In a reply to her sister Mary Cranch, she countered that fabrics were much cheaper in Boston because of the drawbacks on imports. "I have not found any thing, except shoes, that are lower; such a satin as my black, you must give as much as sterling for a yard, as I gave lawful money" (Adams 1841, 39).

Not only were fabrics more expensive, but London ladies dressed much more plainly than their colonial counterparts: "'Tis true, you must put a hoop on and have your hair dressed, but a common straw hat, no cap, with only a ribbon upon the crown, is thought dress sufficient to go into company" (27). "No silks but lutestring, and those which are thinner, are worn at this season;—mode cloaks, muslin and sarsnet,—gauze hats, bonnets, and ribbons,—every thing as light and thin as possible,—different gowns and skirts,—muslin skirts, flounced chintz, with borders white, with a trimming that looks like gartering." Abigail also sent her sister a silk pattern called "new mown hay" and "a specimen of the newest fashioned hats" from London (39).

In a long letter from France to a wealthy friend in Boston in January 1785, Abigail described the manners, modes, and amusements of French women of the upper levels of society. At the close of the letter, she got down to the business of imparting fashion trends:

The fashionable shape of the ladies here is, to be very small at the bottom of the waist, and very large round the shoulders,—a wasp's. . . . You and I, Madam, must despair of being in the mode.

I enclose to you the pattern of a stomacher, cape, and forebody of a gown; different petticoats are much worn, and then the stomacher must be of the petticoat color, and the cape of the gown, as well as the sleeves. Sometimes a false sleeve is made use of to draw over the other, and, in that case, the cape is like the gown. Gowns and petticoats are worn without any trimming of any kind. That is reserved for full dress only, when very large hoops and negligees, with trains three yards long, are worn. But these are not used, except at Court, and then only upon public occasions; the Queen herself, and the ladies of honor, dressing very plain upon other days. Abby has made you a miniature handkerchief, just to show you one mode; but caps, hats, and handkerchiefs are as various as ladies' and milliners' fancies can devise. (77)

REFERENCES

Adams, Abigail. 1841. *Letters of Mrs. Adams, the Wife of John Adams*, 3rd ed. Vol. 2. Boston: Little, Brown.

Arnold, Janet. 1988. *Queen Elizabeth's Wardrobe Unlock'd*. Leeds: W. S. Maney and Son.

Arnold, Janet. 2008. *Patterns of Fashion 4: The Cut and Construction of Linen Shirts, Smocks, Neckwear, Headwear and Accessories for Men and Women, c. 1540–1660*. London: Macmillan.

Bates, Susan Baldwin and Harriott Cheves Leland, eds. 2005. *Proprietary Records of South Carolina, 1675–1695*. Vol. 1. Charleston, SC: History Press.

Browne, William Hand, ed. 1887. *Archives of Maryland: Judicial and Testamentary Business of the Provincial Court, 1637–1650*. Vol. 4. Baltimore: Maryland Historical Society.

Bulwer, John. 1650. *Anthropometamorphosis: Man Transform'd, or the Artificial Changeling*, quoted in www.pepysdiary.com/archive/1660/11/21/.

Cornelius, Charles O. 1926. "Early American Jewelry." *Metropolitan Museum of Art Bulletin*: 99–101. www.metmuseum.org/pubs/bulletins/1/pdf/3254683.pdf.bannered.pdf.

Dow, George Francis, ed. 1911. *Records and Files of the Quarterly Courts of Essex County, Massachusetts, 1636–1691*. Vol. 1, 1636–1656. Salem, MA: Essex Institute.

Dow, George Francis, ed. 1912. *Records and Files of the Quarterly Courts of Essex County, Massachusetts, 1636–1691*. Vol. 2, 1656–1662. Salem, MA: Essex Institute.

Dow, George Francis, ed. 1913. *Records and Files of the Quarterly Courts of Essex County, Massachusetts, 1636–1691*. Vol. 3, 1662–1667. Salem, MA: Essex Institute.

Dow, George Francis, ed. 1914. *Records and Files of the Quarterly Courts of Essex County, Massachusetts, 1636–1691.* Vol. 4, 1668–1671. Salem, MA: Essex Institute.

Dow, George Francis, ed. 1916. *Records and Files of the Quarterly Courts of Essex County, Massachusetts, 1636–1691.* Vol. 5, 1672–1674. Salem, MA: Essex Institute.

Dow, George Francis, ed. 1917. *Records and Files of the Quarterly Courts of Essex County, Massachusetts, 1636–1691.* Vol. 6, 1675–1678. Salem, MA: Essex Institute.

Dow, George Francis, ed. 1920. *The Probate Records of Essex County, Massachusetts, 1635–1664.* Vol. 3. Salem, MA: Essex Institute.

Dunton, John. 1818. *The Life and Errors of John Dunton.* Vol. 1. London: J. Nichols, Son, and Bentley.

Earle, Alice Morse. 1893. *Customs and Fashions in Old New England.* New York: Charles Scribner's Sons. archive.org/stream/customsandfashio24159gut/pg24159.txt.

Earle, Alice Morse. 1895. *Margaret Winthrop.* New York: Charles Scribner's Sons.

Earle, Alice Morse. 1903. *Two Centuries of Costume in America,* 2 vols. New York: Macmillan.

Fairfax County, Virginia. 1775–1782. *Will Book D-1,* 1775–82. Microfilm.

Franklin, Benjamin. 1905. *The Writings of Benjamin Franklin,* edited by Albert Henry Smyth. Vol. 3. New York: Macmillan.

Franklin, Benjamin. 1906. *The Writings of Benjamin Franklin,* edited by Albert Henry Smyth. Vol. 4. New York: Macmillan.

Gallay, Alan. 2002. *The Indian Slave Trade: The Rise of the English Empire in the American South, 1670–1717.* New Haven: Yale University.

Goodfriend, Joyce D. 1992. *Before the Melting Pot: Society and Culture in Colonial New York City, 1664–1730.* Princeton, NJ: Princeton University.

Grimes, J. Bryan, ed. 1912. *North Carolina Wills and Inventories.* Raleigh: Trustees of the Public Libraries.

Gummere, Anelia Mott. 1901. *The Quaker: A Study in Costume.* Philadelphia: Ferris and Leach.

Habersham, James. 1904. "The Letters of Hon. James Habersham, 1756–1775." In *Collections of the Georgia Historical Society.* Vol. 6. Savannah: Georgia Historical Society.

Hart, Avril and Susan North. 1998. *Historical Fashion in Detail: The Seventeenth and Eighteenth Centuries.* London: V&A Publications.

Hershkowitz, Leo. 2002. "Original Inventories of Early New York Jews (1682–1763)." *American Jewish History* vol. 90, no. 3 (September): 239–321. www.newamsterdamhistorycenter.org/media/files/Inventory_Article_90_3hershkowitz.pdf.

Holliday, Carl. 1922. *Woman's Life in Colonial Days.* Boston: Cornhill Publishing.

Inventory of . . . Godbert Godbertson. www.histarch.uiuc.edu/plymouth/Godbert.html.

Inventory of . . . Mrs. Elizabeth Lawson. chnm.gmu.edu/probateinventory/pdfs/lawson66.pdf.

Inventory of . . . Mary Ring. www.histarch.uiuc.edu/plymouth/Pring.html.

Kalm, Peter. 1771. *Travels into North America*, trans. John Reinhold Forster. London: T. Lowndes.

Knight, Sarah Kemble. 1992. *The Journal of Madam Knight*, reprint of 1825 ed. Carlisle, MA: Applewood Books.

Mather, Cotton. 1676. *An Exhortation to the Inhabitants of New-England.* Boston. digitalcommons.unl.edu/cgi/viewcontent.cgi?article=1031&context=etas.

Merritt, Elizabeth, ed. 1956. *Archives of Maryland: Proceedings of the Provincial Court of Maryland, 1677–1678.* Vol. 67. Baltimore: Maryland Historical Society.

Middlesex County, Virginia, *Orders 1745–52.* Microfilm.

Mikhaila, Ninya and Jane Malcolm-Davies. 2006. *The Tudor Tailor: Reconstructing Sixteenth-Century Dress.* Hollywood, CA: Costume and Fashion Press.

Morton, Thomas. 1883. *The New English Canaan of Thomas Morton*, reprint of 1637 ed. Boston: Prince Society.

Northampton County, *Virginia Deeds, Wills, &c.*, Nos. 7 & 8, 1655–1668. Microfilm.

Norton, John. 1937. *John Norton and Sons, Merchants of London and Virginia, Being the Papers from Their Counting House of the Years 1750 to 1795*, edited by Frances Norton Mason. Richmond: Dietz.

Pory, John. 1907. "Letter of John Pory, 1629." In *Narratives of Early Virginia, 1606–1625*, edited by Lyon Gardiner Tyler, 282–87. New York: Charles Scribner's Sons.

"Proceedings of the Virginia Assembly, 1619." etext.lib.virginia.edu/etcbin/jamestown-browse?id=J1036.

Ransome, David. 1991. "Wives for Virginia, 1621." *William and Mary Quarterly* 3rd ser., vol. 48, no. 1 (January): 3–18.

"A Relation of Maryland." 1910. In *Narratives of Early Maryland*, reprint of 1635 ed., edited by Clayton Colman Hall, 63–112. New York: Charles Scribner's Sons.

Rogers, Horatio, George Moulton Carpenter, and Edward Field, eds. 1894. *The Early Records of the Town of Providence*. Vol. 6. Providence: City Council of Providence.

Rowe, Ann Pollard. 1976. "American Quilted Petticoats." In *Imported and Domestic Textiles in Eighteenth-Century America: Irene Emery Roundtable on Museum Textiles, 1975 Proceedings*, edited by Patricia L. Fiske. Washington, DC: The Textile Museum.

Schaw, Janet. 2009. *Journal of a Lady of Quality, Being the Narrative of a Journey from Scotland to the West Indies, North Carolina, and Portugal, in the Years 1774 to 1776*, edited by Evangeline Walker Andrews, reprint of 1921 ed. Bedford, MA: Applewood Books.

Smith, John. 1907. "Smith's Description of Virginia and Proceedings of the Colonie." In *Narratives of Early Virginia, 1606–1625*, reprint of 1612, edited by Lyon Gardiner Tyler, 76–204. New York: Charles Scribner's Sons.

Strachey, William. 1849. *The Historie of Travaile into Virginia Britannia*, reprint of the 1612 ed. London: Hakluyt Society.

Surry County, Virginia. *Deeds, Wills, &c. No. 3, 1687–1694*. Microfilm.

Watson, John Fanning. 1830. *Annals of Philadelphia, Being a Collection of Memoirs, Anecdotes, and incidents of the City and Its Inhabitants from the Days of the Pilgrim Founders*. Philadelphia: E. L. Carey and A. Hart.

Waugh, Norah. 1968. *The Cut of Women's Clothes, 1600–1930*. New York: Theatre Arts Books.

Wharton, Anne Hollingsworth. 1893. *Through Colonial Doorways*, 12th ed. Philadelphia: J. B. Lippincott.

Williams, Neville. 1964. "The Tribulations of John Bland, Merchant, London, Seville, Jamestown, Tangier, 1643–1680." *Virginia Magazine of History and Biography* vol. 72, no. 1, part one (January): 19–41.

Williams, Roger. 1827. *A Key into the Language of America*, reprint of 1643 ed. Providence: Rhode-Island Historical Society.

Winslow, Anna Green. 1974. *Diary of Anna Green Winslow*, edited by Alice Morse Earle. Williamstown, MA: Corner House.

Wister, Sarah. 1902. *Sally Wister's Journal: A True Narrative Being a Quaker Maiden's Account of Her Experiences with Officers of the Continental Army, 1777–1778*, edited by Albert Cook Myers. Philadelphia: Ferris and Leach.

Wood, William. 1865. *New-England's Prospect*, reprint of 1634 ed. Boston: Prince Society.

Woodward, Carl R. 1971. *Plantation in Yankeeland: The Story of Cocumscussoc, Mirror of Colonial Rhode Island.* Chester, CT: Pequot Press.

York County Deeds, Orders, and Wills Book 6. www.virtualjamestown.org/york%20runaways/york%20runaways—book%206.txt.

Men's Clothing

As with women's clothing, men's fashions were born at the English Court and trickled down through the social and economic ranks according to means, needs, social position, religious affiliation, and availability of materials and skilled labor. For the most part, the stylistic differences between clothing worn everyday and that worn for special occasions were minimal. Choices of fabrics and trimmings, the complexity of the cut and construction methods, and the selection of accessories all determined the quality of clothing and the appropriateness of appearance to activity. Of course, other national groups brought distinctive garments with them when they emigrated—for example, the wooden shoes of some German Pietist groups. When religious convictions did not guide the choice of dress, traditional garments generally gave way to versions of current fashions.

As discussed in Chapter 3, colonial men had increasingly more access to a wider variety of goods in a range of qualities and prices and more up-to-date style information as the colonies grew more settled and commerce expanded. Even in the early days of settlement, colonists were aware of dress as a factor in social prestige, and fashionable goods were desired and acquired throughout the colonial era. For most of the 17th century, almost all men's clothing was imported from England or Europe. As the number of surviving garments that were actually worn in colonial America is slight, the following discussions are based on evidence from English sources as well as descriptions from colonial documents. Armor and other military dress are outside the scope of this study.

1607–1714

THE EVOLUTION OF CUT, CONSTRUCTION, AND SILHOUETTE, 1607–1714

The 17th century saw a major shift in men's sartorial styles. For about the first two-thirds of the century, the main garments were the doublet for the upper body and breeches or hose for the lower body. In 1666, Charles II adopted what was known as "Persian" dress, consisting of a long vest and coat with breeches. A somewhat similar long coat had appeared in France a few years earlier. This new style became the standard for the ensuing century. Dress accessories changed at the same time to accord with the incoming fashion.

In the late 17th century, colonies began to legislate on slave clothing in an attempt to differentiate visually slaves from indentured servants and apprentices. In 1672, the Virginia General Assembly ordered that masters clothe their slaves in a coarse linen, preferably blue in color: "noe negro shall be allowed to weare any white Linninge, but shall weare blew shirts and shifts that they may be herby discovered if they steale or weare other Linninge" (quoted in Brown 1996, 154).

Main Garments, 1607–1670

Doublet

A garment whose origin dates to at least the 15th century, the doublet was a waist-length, fitted jacket with a high collar. The garment buttoned down the front and had a short attached skirt, or peplum (also called a *basque*). The doublet body commonly was cut in four pieces. Two front pieces extended around the body to a side back seam and were joined to two back pieces seamed together along the center back.

The doublet generally was worn with sleeves. These could be close fitting or tapering from a fuller sleeve at the shoulder to a snug band at the wrist. The sleeves were usually separate and tied to the armholes of the doublet with metal-tipped points, which laced through small eyelets. Flat crescent-shaped epaulets, called wings, or stuffed shoulder rolls covered the joint of the sleeves and the doublet body.

Virginia's earliest settlers wore a version of the doublet that was rigid and tight fitting, with a high tight collar. The front pieces were stiffened with buckram or padded out—bombasted—to form a ridge down the front center of the garment, ending in a point below the waist. The doublet also might be fitted inside with vertical strips of whalebone to hold the form. This padded form was a less exaggerated style of the fantastical peascod-belly shape popular in the last two decades of the reign of Elizabeth I (reigned 1558–1603). The doublet skirt, or peplum, consisted of a series of shaped tabs that were stitched to the waist seam. The doublet body could be left plain or decorated in front and back with vertical strips of fabric or ribbon.

By the time English Separatists (they were not referred to as Pilgrims until the end of the 18th century) landed in 1620 at what would be the settlement of Plymouth, the rigid outline of the doublet had begun to soften; much of the stiffening and padding was discarded. The front of the garment either closed with buttons or was held by clasps. The doublet waistline, while still pointed in the front, had begun to rise above the natural waist. The skirt tabs were lengthened and pointed at center front. Fashion-conscious colonists in the southern colonies might add decorative bow-knots or points at the waist. The doublet body sometimes was slashed at intervals across the chest, leaving vertical openings through which the shirt could be seen. Sleeves were cut in two pieces, with curved seams along the front and back of the arm, and they were relatively close fitting. These, too, might be slashed, or paned, to reveal the sleeves of the shirt. Wings at the shoulders were still common.

There were marked distinctions between the doublets worn by Virginia gentlemen and Massachusetts adventurers on the one hand and those of the English Separatists, on the other. While the basic cut and construction of the doublet were the same for both of the groups, those who had fled religious persecution would have shunned expensive fabrics and most types of ornamentation and slashing. Furthermore, the Company of Merchant Adventurers, who by contract supplied the Separatists with clothing, was unlikely to have provided more than basic garments. It was suggested that free men sailing for New England in 1629 bring several leather doublets lined with thinner

Man's doublet, 1620–1625, with high collar, short peplum, attached sleeves, and wings to hide the join of the sleeves to the body of the garment. (Victoria and Albert Museum, London

oiled skin, probably for work, and a doublet of woolen kersey lined with linen, likely for wear to religious services (Dow 1935, 61). Poorer settlers and indentured servants in the Virginia Colony likely wore a version of the doublet that, while shaped and having full skirts, was restrained and was of inexpensive wool or coarse linen.

By the 1630s doublets became even higher waisted; the waist, while still pointed, had straightened. It might be ornamented with points or bow-knots or left plain. The skirt now reached hip level, with two or three wider tabs on each side. The sleeves were cut fuller from the shoulder to the elbow and then tapered to the wrist. The sleeves might be paned or the front seam left completely open from shoulder to wrist. A high, standing collar finished the neck. Well-dressed Virginians and Marylanders as well as wealthy New England Puritans would have taken advantage of the extra ornamentation as a public sign of status. Working men, the elderly, and those whose financial status did not meet the requirements laid out by sumptuary legislation might wear plainer versions of the new fashion or continue to wear older styles.

By the early 1640s the doublet had changed significantly. The skirt generally was cut in one with the upper body although two long tabs stitched front and back to the doublet body gave an alternate styling. This cut eliminated both the distinct waistline and points and bow-knots. The garment still buttoned down the center front; but certain styles fastened only to mid-chest, leaving a wide inverted V of shirt exposed beneath. A new style sleeve still had curved seams but the paned sleeve went out of fashion. It might be open along the front seam, to allow the shirt to be seen, or the seam might have a button closure. Sleeves were sometimes cut long and turned back to form a cuff.

From the mid-1640s into the 1660s the doublet became shorter and less fitted. By about 1660 the length did not reach the waist, and it now resembled a short jacket. The doublet buttoned at the neck and down only a few inches. This opening allowed most of the front of the shirt to be seen. As the doublet body straightened and shortened, so did the sleeves. In the 1660s, one style of sleeve reached the elbow and turned back to form a small cuff. A second style, also elbow length, was bell shaped. The front seam of this latter sleeve might be closed or slit with the option of being buttoned or left open. These shorter doublet sleeves allowed much of the shirt sleeves to billow out, with the fabric being tied with ribbons in one or more places along the arm.

As reflected in estate inventories, colonial men continued to wear doublets for some time after the introduction, in the mid-1660s, of the coat and waistcoat.

Jerkin

The jerkin was a short, close-fitting jacket worn over the doublet, either for protection or warmth. Sometimes padded, the jerkin was usually sleeveless but the top of the armholes often had wings (in England styles with longer open or hanging sleeves were worn). The center front opening was either buttoned or laced with points. A less common closure method was lacing under the arms, along what would have been the side seams. The cut of the jerkin generally followed that of the doublet. Earlier versions were fitted with waist seams and separate skirts. Following fashion, later styles were looser and longer, with skirts that were cut in one with the body. When the doublet was cut short and straight, in the 1640s, the jerkin followed suit, falling at about waist level.

Sometimes jerkins were made to match a doublet and hose, both in fabric and trimmings. It was sometimes made of a different fabric from the doublet but of the same color. For example, in about 1610, Virginia gentleman George Percy received a bespoke jerkin, cloak, and breeches made from the same piece of broadcloth (Shirley 1949, 238).

Jerkins made of leather, also called buff coats, were worn by all but the poorest ranks in all the colonies during this period. The leather was sometimes oiled to make it more water repellent. With a thickness as much as an eighth of an inch, the leather provided protection against natural elements as well as knives and arrows.

Breeches

At the beginning of English colonization, two different silhouettes were fashionable for the garment men wore on the lower body The first was a full, padded breeches called trunk hose, which were cut full, spreading out from the waist and gathered above the knee into a band. Trunk hose were sometimes constructed of vertical strips of fabric attached at the waist and knee band only, allowing the lining, usually of a contrasting color to show. Stockings, also called nether hose or stocks, were usually fastened to the trunk hose with points. The second style, which had become popular in England in about 1575, was called venetians. These breeches fitted snugly at the waist, full over the hips, and tapered to below the knees, where they were tied or buttoned. Venetians could be padded or stuffed. In all cases, breeches were fastened to doublets by means of points tied through pairs of eyelets, or by hooks fixed through eyelets or loops.

Some breeches were constructed with canions, or wide fitted knee bands, sometimes of a contrasting color or ornamented. Knitted stocking generally were worn with canions. If the canions were snug, the stockings were pulled up over them and held up with garters tied just below the knee. If the canions were loose, the stockings were pulled up under them and tied.

In the colonies, trunk hose with canions may have been worn into the 1620s, but they gave way to full breeches that were cut on the pattern of venetians, but not padded and stuffed. Certainly popular by about 1625, these new-style breeches were not quite as full at the waist and were gathered above the knee into narrow bands. Those who wished to emulate the latest fashion might ornament the knee bands with points, loops, or ribbons.

Two other styles of breeches—less full around the waist and the thigh—came into fashion in the 1630s. The first was cut the same width down the leg and ended several inches below the knee; the legs were not gathered up or fastened at the hemline but allowed to hang loose. The second type was bellows shaped, the legs tapering below the knees. Well-to-do gentlemen might order either of these styles with trimmings of braid, loops of ribbon, bow-knots, or rosettes stitched down the sides or at the waistline and/or mid-thigh. The lower edges of the latter style usually covered either by the stocking tied with a wide ribbon garter or by boot tops.

In the late 1650s, petticoat, or pantaloon, breeches came into fashion, introduced from western Europe, where they had been in fashion since about 1655. Gathered at the waist and very full with shorter legs, this exaggerated style was likely adopted in the southern colonies by wealthy southern planters and those in high political positions. Even with the introduction of the tailored coat at the end of the 1660s, petticoat breeches continued to be in fashion in the colonies until the late 1670s.

Outer Garments, 1607–1670

Cloaks

Men's cloaks were generally cut on the same pattern as women's. However, men wore or carried their cloaks in different ways: draped over the shoulders, wrapped around the waist, or thrown over one shoulder and arm. Cloaks were held in place with a band or cord. Although usually of cloth, some colonists wore versions made of furs from colonial trappers or procured through the Indian trade. Cloaks also might be lined with a woolen fabric or fur.

The early male settlers of Massachusetts Bay Colony were provided with mandilions. The mandilion was a loose hip-length cloak that first had been fashionable in the later 16th century. The version worn by colonists was lined with wool and probably had loose long sleeves that could be unbuttoned along their length to allow more freedom of movement. The mandilion was constructed in several ways: to be a pullover garment or to fasten down the front with either hooks and eyes or buttons. The falling band was worn over the top of the garment.

Cassock or Casaque

An A-shape sleeved but collarless coat, the cassock had evolved from the military coat. Loose enough to fit over a doublet and jerkin, the cassock buttoned down the front and fell below the knees. The sleeves might be very short and open along the front seam or reach the forearm to end in a turned-back cuff. In 1620, settlers of Berkeley's Hundred in Virginia were provided with cassocks of broadcloth (Kingsbury 1933, 3:385). The 1647 inventory of a Connecticut trapper and Indian trader contained two coats made of raccoon skins and one made of cat, possibly lynx (Manwaring 1904, 10). These coats were likely made in the style of the cassock. This garment became more popular in the 1660s, at which time it ended above the knee or at mid-thigh.

Gown

The man's gown was a calf-length or longer garment that might have been worn over or instead of a doublet, depending on individual preference. Gowns could be fairly smoothly fitted over the shoulders and upper body and hang loose to the hem, or they might be gathered or pleated at the neck and shoulders to create a fuller effect. Sleeves could be fitted and seamed closed or button from shoulder to hem. In the latter case, they were usually worn open as hanging sleeves. Neckwear was brought on top of the gown. The Geneva gown, a style of academic robe, was adopted by many Protestant-reform clerics in the 17th century to symbolize both their rejection of the highly embellished Roman Catholic and Anglican vestments, and their academic training and achievements. The Geneva gown was full through the body, with pleats or gathers from the shoulders and wide sleeves. The gown was also worn by political officials. Thomas Willett, the first mayor of New York City, possessed three gowns at his death (An Inventory of . . . Capt Thomas Willett).

Frock or Smock

A frock was an overshirt of rough wool or coarse linen that reached to mid-thigh or knee and was belted as needed. Throughout the colonial period farmers and tradesmen wore frocks to protect clothing when working and/or the wearer from cold weather. A frock might slip over the head or be open down the front and close with buttons. The neckline style varied as well. The side seams of the frock were slit up several inches from the bottom to allow for ease of movement. Variations in style in colonial garments likely reflected regional differences in their respective English and European antecedents.

Undergarments, 1607–1670

All men wore some form of undergarments. Undergarments provided additional protection from the cold, and in an era when physical cleanliness was not as important as it is today, underclothing protected the valuable textiles of the outer attire from body oils and perspiration. For the working sorts and the poor, undergarments often doubled as outer garments. The primary undergarments for men were the shirt, drawers, and under-waistcoat. Separate attire for sleeping was reserved for those who could afford it.

Shirt

In the 17th century, the man's shirt, a pullover garment, was full and usually fell to about the knee. Depending upon the wearer's means, a shirt could be made of fine holland or cambric or coarse linen like lockram or osnaburg. The garment was cut from straight rectangles of linen and gathered at the neckline into a narrow band collar that stood up against the neck. Full sleeves were gathered into wristbands. The center front opening ended at mid-chest and a single button or pair of ties at the neck was sufficient to keep it closed. Probate inventories and other documents indicate that even the wealthiest colonists did not own a great number of shirts at any particular time. For example, Virginia merchant Henry James owned four shirts and two half shirts at his death in 1665 (*Accomack County Deeds and Wills, 1664–1671*, 9).

Examples from English contexts show that fine shirts were often embroidered in narrow patterns of black, red, or yellow silk along the seam lines, at the hem, and the front opening (Arnold 2008, 22–26). Among the religious conservatives of New England, a narrow linen or lace ruffle might edge the neck opening and wrist or unornamented neckwear might be added. New Englanders of rank and the fashionable of Virginia and Maryland, however, added accessories at the neck and wrist as described below. A working man's shirt generally had no ornamentation.

As the doublet lost its firm look and tight fit in the 1620s, the shirt was made fuller in the body and sleeves. When sleeves and doublet bodies were slashed, or paned, the added fullness of the shirt was meant to show through the slits. In the 1640s, fashion dictated that the doublet and its sleeves were shortened; thus, the lower sleeves and almost the whole body of the shirt were visible.

The half shirt was a warm-weather alternative to the full shirt. Hip length and made of the same materials as the long shirt, the half shirt was less bulky. It, too, could be enriched with embroidery, lace, or ruffles.

Night shirts were made for those men who could afford to shed their day shirts for clean linen. As long and full in the body and sleeves as their daytime counterparts, night shirts could be as elaborately ornamented as day wear—with lace insertions or embroidery at the shoulders and down the sides of the sleeves and ruffles at the wrist. The neck opening was probably deeper than that of the day shirt and the collar lied flat. Common folk, servants, and the enslaved simply wore their day undergarments to bed. English sources mention nightshirts of black silk that were worn by men of the upper ranks who were in mourning.

Drawers

Drawers, also called under-trousers, were of two styles. One was knee or ankle length and made of linen or woolen fabric that was cut on the bias to give a close fit. Long drawers usually were made with stirrups, a band that passed under the instep, to keep the garment from sliding up the wearer's leg. They were probably tied in front at the waist with strings. The second style was short trunks, cut full and square with a slit behind and tied at the waist. Short trunks were probably made of linen although English sources describe the nobility donning trunks of silk. Colonial sources do not provide enough information to determine the prevalence of long drawers and trunks. Many men likely used the long shirt tail for the same purpose.

Under-Waistcoat

Waist-length under-vests or waistcoats were worn under the doublet, perhaps for warmth. Sleeved and sleeveless versions were known, and they were often bombasted, that is, either padded or quilted. In cut and shape they resembled the doublet. Some versions were slipped over the head rather than buttoned in front.

Neck- and Wrist-Wear, 1607–1670

For the first half of the 17th century, gentlemen wore some type of detachable neck collar. Artisans, farmers, and servants would not wear a collar while working but might own a plain-style collar to wear when attending religious services. At the time of the Jamestown settlement and until about 1620, both the flared standing band, supported by a rigid frame, and the ruff were popular among the elite. These were the same types of collars worn by high-status women although for men, the standing band usually fitted closely to the neck and met in front to tie under the chin with strings. Sixteenth-century English chronicler John Stow (c. 1525–1605) tossed invectives at ruffs, opining that "a man's head looked like a head on a platter" (quoted in Raleigh 1916, 26). English commentator Philip Stubbes (c. 1555–c. 1610) warned that a fierce wind could set ruffs "like rags flying about," sitting on the wearer's shoulders "like the dish-clout of a slut" (quoted in Raleigh 1916, 27).

After about 1620, these platter-like ruffs went out of fashion and were replaced by falling, or limp, ruffs. Still constructed of gathered linen, the ruffs draped softly onto the shoulders of the doublet rather than stood out stiffly from the neck. Falling ruffs might be of plain linen or lace trimmed.

From the 1630s until the end of this period men wore a falling band: a wide, flat collar darted to shape it around the neck, and usually starched. Made of linen, the falling band turned down over the doublet's standing collar and spread stiffly over the shoulders. Well-to-do wearers might trim the outer edge of the band with lace. The band was kept

John Winthrop, after a painting by an unknown artist, c. 1630. Winthrop wears a version of the softer, falling ruff, which while heavily gathered, drapes onto the upper shoulders rather than standing out from the neck. (Library of Congress)

closed at the center front by bandstrings. The ends of these ties might be embellished with silk tassels or small tufts of ribbons. The width of the falling band expanded over time until it entirely covered the shoulders. Plain linen bands were the norm for everyday wear, but they could be edged with lace made in scallops or points.

Beginning in the 1640s, the falling band, also called a fall, decreased in size, was less heavily starched, and was worn without the lace edging. In the 1660s, the shape of the falling band changed again, narrowing into a deep and oblong collar whose points fell over the chest. The finest falls were made of sheer linen or entirely of lace.

The cravat, also called a neckcloth, was introduced in England in the 1650s and began to appear in colonial records in the 1660s. It was worn contemporaneously with the falling band until sometime in the late 1670s when it became the main neckwear accessory. A square or rectangular piece of linen finished along opposite edges with narrow hems, the cravat was folded and wrapped around the throat According to paintings and engravings of the period, the ends were often caught at the neck with a narrow ribbon bow. But if edged with a wide lace, the ends were allowed to fall over the chest.

Linen cuffs or sleeve ruffles that matched in fabric and trim a man's neckwear were usually worn by the upper ranks. Until about the midcentury, the cuffs or ruffles were turned back over the sleeves of the doublet and were sometimes starched to keep their shape. As fashion changed, cuffs were worn ruffled but limp. In the 1660s, the wrist ruffles expanded, according to fashion, to fall onto the hands. Cuffs or ruffles might be attached to the sleeve bands of the shirt, but if they were of wide lace, they would be detachable so that they could be laundered separately.

Headwear, 1607–1670

Hats

At the end of the 16th century, the most fashionable hat for men had a tall—perhaps six to eight inches—straight-sided or slightly tapering crown (that portion actually covering the top of the head) with a narrow brim of one-and-a-half to three inches. The early 17th century saw more variety, and this would have been reflected in the headgear of the first inhabitants of Jamestown. Now the crown could be tall, short, rounded, peaked, or a truncated cone shape. The brim could be narrow or wide and might be flat or turned up at one side (cocked). The hat might be decorated with an ostrich feather, plume, ribbons, or band or left plain. Ostrich feathers might also be added as a flat fringe around the upper edge of the hat brim. Hats were made of thick felted wool or fur (especially beaver), leather, or linen-covered wire frames, and lined with a suitable fabric. Felt and wire-frame hats might be covered with fancier fabrics like brocade or velvet, cut and seamed, gathered, or pleated to fit.

Until about midcentury, New England's religious conservatives—women as well as men—wore hats of felted wool, with high crowns and plain bands. Two styles were popular, the capotain and the sugar-loaf. By law, only men of rank and/or wealth were allowed to wear hats of expensive felted beaver fur or add a feather to the hatband. But this legislation was generally ineffective, and any man who was able to obtain a beaver hat wore one.

In the 1620s, a hat with a lower, rounded crown and a wider brim (four to six inches) came into fashion. The brim was often turned up at one side, and the hat was usually ornamented with a ribbon, ostrich plume, or ornamental hatband. Felted beaver was the preferred fiber although camel hair and less expensive wool were available.

Caps

Closely fitting the skull, caps served for both work and leisure. Worn by all ranks of men, the Monmouth cap was ubiquitous during the entire colonial period. The area of Monmouth, in southeast Wales had been known for the production of high-quality wool since the 14th century. A thriving cottage industry of cap making by hand knitters—primarily men—developed in the 15th century. Knitted in the round, Monmouth caps had a brim that could be turned up; they were fulled and shaped and fitted with a button or tassel on top of the crown. By the 16th century the Monmouth cap was essential headgear for soldiers, sailors, servants, and laborers; but the better sorts wore them as well because they were long wearing and provided protection against damp and cold. In the 17th century, all male immigrants who were supplied by English merchant companies received a Monmouth cap.

In a time when central heating did not exist and the interior of a house—except near the fireplace—was the same temperature as outside, men wore night caps to help prevent the loss of body heat from an unprotected head. This was especially true for men who shaved their heads because they wore wigs. The night cap was donned in the day as well as night, outdoors as well as in, as a more convenient alternative to the hat. Night caps were available in a range of prices and materials. Knitted caps might be of wool or silk. Fabric caps, dome shaped and constructed of several shaped pieces and with a turned-up brim, ranged from linen to fur to silk damask; they could be plain or trimmed with lace, quilted or heavily embroidered in silk and metallic threads. Some caps pulled down onto the head with no fastening; others were tied on under the chin.

Footwear, 1607–1670

Stockings or Hose

Both knitted-to-shape and tailored woven cloth stockings were used to cover the lower legs. Prosperous farmers and artisans as well as gentlemen and high-ranking officials wore knitted stockings of thread (i.e., linen) and silk. In portraits, knitted stockings are often depicted as form fitting, although there are occasional wrinkles up the leg, as if the knitted shape were more tubular than curved. Like fine women's stockings, men's hose could be ornamented with knitted patterns or clocks.

Coarser plain linen and woolen stockings served servants and laborers; these could be knitted or cut and sewn from woven cloth. The latter were cut on the bias, or diagonal, of the cloth in order to take advantage of the fabric's diagonal stretch in fitting the shape of the legs. Many farmers and laborers, however, wore only shoes or went barefoot.

When men wore boots, they were generally wore boothose, strong woven or knitted stockings, generally of linen, that protected the regular stocking from wear. The tops of the hose were sometimes embroidered or ornamented with lace and/or ribbons. Boot hose were attached to the breeches at the waist and front opening with points or buttons and buttonholes. When riding, additional protection was provided by long stirrup hose, sometimes of thick knitted wool, which were worn over all other hose. Instead of a sole, the hose had a strap under the instep.

Shoes

At the beginning of this period, latchet shoes worn by the better sorts had curved heels and wide gaps between the quarters and the vamp. These openings allowed elegant knitted stockings to show to effect. Sometimes trimmed with lace and spangles, elaborate confections of silk ribbons called shoe roses hid the latchet closure. Alternatively, the wearer could use ties of multiple ribbons. Practical versions of these shoes were made in leather, but the vamp, quarter, and latchets also could be made of fabrics such as brocade, damask, taffeta, and velvet. For protection when out of doors, wooden clogs with short vamps and quarters were worn over the shoes.

Following the fashion of the doublet, by the 1620s the upper portion of an open latchet shoe also might be slashed and the tongue was shortened. In the 1630s, fashion dictated shoes with squared rather than rounded toes. The vamp was elongated and the heel was made slightly higher. This shape remained popular until the end of the century. By the 1640s shoe roses were replaced by ribbon bows or loops that either hung limp down the sides of the shoes or were stiffened to stand out. In the 1660s, latchets were also closed with buckles rather than ties or ribbons.

The workers' version of the latchet shoe was made of heavy leather, with or without a low heel. The narrow-to-no gap between the quarters and the vamp completely enclosed and protected the foot. The latchets tied together at the top of the foot with points. The soles of these heavier shoes might be made of wood instead of leather; nails or narrow strips of metal were sometimes driven into the soles to help protect them from wear.

Boots

Men wore boots both indoors and out. At the time of the Jamestown settlement, gentlemen wore boots of soft leather with heels, rounded toes, and well-fitted tops that reached the thigh. By the mid-1620s, the boot tops were wide and cup shaped, ending just above the knees. The tops could be cuffed over or pushed down to wrinkle at the top of the calf. In either case, this allowed the ornamented tops of the boot hose to show. Bucket-top boots were in vogue by the early 1630s. These could be pushed down to below the calf. Bucket tops generally had a square toe and shorter and thicker heels. In the 1660s, fashion dictated that boots should not be seen with fashionable dress although men still wore them for everyday activities and for riding. The boot legs reached the thigh and fit the leg more closely than previous styles. One type laced down the outside of the calf; the tops sometimes turned down to below the knee.

Boot spurs were held in place by an oblong piece of leather worn over the top of the boot instep, with one strap under the foot and the other around the back of the heel. The oblong part of the spur leather developed early in the century into a large butterfly or quatrefoil shape, which covered most of the top of the foot. Spur leathers continued to be worn over boots throughout the period.

Hairstyles and Grooming, 1607–1670

In the colonial period, men's hair received considerable attention. During the first two decades of the 17th century, men wore their hair either cut quite short and close to the head or in a style that was cut full at ear level but closer at the nape of the neck. In both cases the hair was usually brushed back from the face. This short length accommodated the fashionable standing bands and wide ruffs. By 1620, the change in neck fashions brought longer, chin-length hair, styled in curls. The hair was parted in the center or at one side and locks fell onto the forehead.

Flowing hair was adopted by the elite in the 1630s. A section of hair on one side was allowed to grow longer— shoulder length or below—and brought forward over the shoulder. Called a lovelock, the section was sometimes tied with a ribbon. The hair on the forehead could be cut into a straight or lightly curled fringe, but not formally arranged—or the forehead could be left bare. The hair might be parted in the center or on one side.

Sir Alexander Carew, 2nd Baronet, c. 1630. Carew sports the bucket-top boots fashionable among gentlemen beginning in the 1630s. The boot tops have been pushed down to the top of the calves. (Antony House, Cornwall, UK/ National Trust Photographic Library/John Hammond/The Bridgeman Art Library)

The uneven curled locks of the 1620s and 1630s gave way to a looser and longer style in the 1640s and 1650s. Hair was cut to one length all the way around and often reached below the shoulder. It was parted in the center and left to hang more naturally around the face. The forehead was usually kept clear. In the 1660s, however, the fashion for long, full, tightly and elaborately curled hair came back in a more exaggerated form. Men with thick, well-growing hair could engage someone to dress their hair in this style. However, many men who wished to keep up with the mode found that the only way to do so was to shave or crop off what natural hair they had and wear a wig.

At the same time when hairstyles were changing among the well-to-do, men of Puritan persuasion, the elderly, and those below the rank of gentleman generally kept their hair closely cropped, bobbed, or of medium length. Of note is the fact that Puritans were called "roundheads" because of this hairstyle. Short hair was likely common among servants, farmers, and artisans because they had neither the time nor the resources to maintain elaborate hairdressing.

Young men might be clean shaven but facial hair was common. Beards were individual in shape, but a trimmed chin beard or lip tuft was most common among fashionable men. Men might wear a moustache as well—from pencil-thin to brush-like—which either blended into the beard on the lower cheeks or was worn separately from the chin beard. The moustache remained an important grooming detail among many in the higher ranks. Beginning in the mid-1630s, a moustache worn alone was the choice for some; from the mid-1650s until the end of this period, it was trimmed to a fine line and drooped to the corners of the mouth. Over the course of this period, beards became smaller; by 1630, the most common form was a small pointed beard covering the chin and perhaps blending with the moustache at the sides of the mouth. In the 1640s and 1650s they retreated to a strip down the center of the chin, a style called the imperial. Although some soldiers and clergymen continued to sport a small chin beard into the 1680s, both moustaches and beards went out of fashion with the adoption of the great wig.

Periwig

The wig, or periwig, had entered the fashion world in England and France in the 1660s. By the end of the 1660s, "false curls" were worn in the colonies. The first periwigs had little shape; the hair was crimped to fall in soft waves to the shoulders from a center part and divided so that one section hung down the back and one section each was brought forward over the shoulders. The front sections might be tied at their ends with bows. In the 1670s, the periwig assumed larger, more artificial proportions. The hair was set in thick curls that clustered on the crown and nestled in horizontal rows along the sides of the face and back of the head. The remaining hair was curled to lie on the shoulders in loose ringlets. A third style was the large, full-bottomed wig. Masses of haphazard curls were drawn forward over one shoulder while only a few curls showed on the other; the remaining ringlets cascaded down the back. As the periwig grew larger, it also was heavier to wear, more expensive to own, and more difficult to maintain.

Accessories, 1607–1670

Although many sartorial accessories of this period were purely status definers, three were of practical use: aprons, baldrics, and garters. For all of the colonial period the working dress of artisans, smiths, and other workmen included an apron to protect the front of their clothing. Aprons were a length or shape of cloth or leather tied at the waist or a piece that spread up over the chest. In England barbers and tradesmen often wore checked-patterned aprons (Cumming, Cunnington, and Cunnington 2010, 7). It is not known, however, whether this practice extended to the colonies.

The baldric was a belt worn crosswise over the right shoulder to opposite hip, usually used to carry a sword. Although obsolete today, baldrics were important accessories in a period when foreign invaders and unfriendly Indians posed intermittent threats. The baldric was usually of plain leather, although fancier versions were ornamented, or faced with silk and embroidered. For the well-to-do, a sash, of silk and often with fringed ends, sometimes served as a baldric. (When fashion introduced the high-waisted doublet in the 1650s, the sash was wrapped around the midsection, over the doublet, and tied at one side, toward the back.) The belts listed in the requirements for early settlers were likely used in place of baldrics.

Garters were tapes or ribbons of wool, silk, or metallic threads (depending on the status of the wearer) that tied around the leg just above or below the knee to hold up knitted or cloth stockings. Elaborate garters had fringed ends and tied in a bow at the outside of the knee or were bands with ornamental buckles placed below the knee.

Those who wished to announce their status visually, however, wore or carried accessories that were not merely functional. The most characteristic ornaments of the period for men were ribbons and lace: sleeves, collars, shoes, and hair were tied with them; hats, doublets, breeches, and shoes were trimmed with them. Men of rank accessorized with gloves, a handkerchief, a cane, and jewelry.

Made of leather, silk velvet, linen fabric, and knitted silk and worsted wool, ornamented gloves might be worn or carried. Some versions just covered the hand, ending at the wrist; others were fitted with cuffs, or gauntlets, that spread up the wrist and lower arm. Until midcentury, gauntlets were often heavily embroidered and embellished with fringe. Gloves of plain leather were generally for work or comfort.

Canes, made of any plant similar to bamboo or palm, were carried under the arm. Some canes were outfitted with an ornate head; others with a loop of ribbons or a tassel.

For most of the 17th century, the word handkerchief was used to describe a neckcloth. Handkerchiefs as we know them were called muckenders until the early 1700s. Pocket handkerchiefs were made of fine linen or silk and often edged with lace. These might be used to wipe the nose or face, but more elegant versions, with embroidery in silk and gold, were only for show.

Handkerchiefs were a must for those who took snuff, made from pulverized tobacco leaves. Snuff was inhaled through the nose and often caused the user to sneeze. In the 17th century, the taking of snuff was an activity that separated the upper ranks from the lower—the latter generally smoked tobacco. Snuff was carried on the person in small boxes made of common materials like wood and horn and brass as well as ornamented versions of silver and gold, mounted with precious stones.

A variety of jewelry options was available to men in this period. In England, even those from the middle of the social spectrum were known to have worn a single earring, rings, and jeweled hat ornaments, which might have been of precious or base metals, depending upon what the wearer could afford.

Main Garments, 1671–1714

As noted at the beginning of this chapter, the 1670s saw a major shift in men's fashion with the adoption of the coat, waistcoat, and breeches. The style was the same regardless of rank; only the fabrics and details distinguished the wearer. In July 1679, Jasper Danckaerts (1639–c. 1702), a native of the Netherlands, boarded a vessel with a companion in Falmouth, England, bound for America. They had purchased goods on speculation, including cloth, and intended to sell them at a profit in New York. By April of 1680, Danckaerts still had not disposed of a small length of very fine brown serge, for which he had paid too much. They sought out a tailor, who "cut up [the piece] for a coat, waistcoat, and breeches for both of us, with fur in front" (Danckaerts 1913, 187).

From its roots in the cassock of the previous period and encouraged by Charles II's foray into adopting the Persian-style long vest and coat in 1666, the coat replaced the doublet in the 1670s. It probably was worn in the colonies first by those in political and economic power. Collarless and with a round neckline, the coat was cut with a straight front closure that buttoned from neck to hem. The fitted body fell just to or below the knees, extending down into coat skirts that flared out slightly at the sides. The side seams reached slightly to the back of the body. These and the center back seams were left open from about waist level down to allow for ease in walking, mounting a horse, and carrying a sword. The coat could be worn completely buttoned, or left open to allow the vest to show. In the 1690s, more flare was added to the side seams of the coat skirts, which fell in unpressed pleats that radiated from a button on the hips. By 1700, the front of the coat was cut with some shaping over the chest and waist although both the center front and center back were still set primarily along the straight grain of the cloth.

The sleeve was cut in two pieces, curved to fit the arm. In the early 1670s, the sleeve had a turn-back cuff cut in one with each piece. Sleeve lengths ranged from extremely short—bicep level—in ultrafashionable coats of the 1670s and early 1680s to the much more standard forearm length. By the 1680s sleeve cuffs were often cut separately and attached, and cuffs became wider and deeper toward 1700.

John Freake (1635–1675), by unidentified artist, Boston, Massachusetts, c. 1671 and 1674. Freake wears a collarless coat left open to reveal his vest, a shirt with ruffled sleeves, and bib-style falling band of needle lace. (Worcester Art Museum, Massachusetts, USA/The Bridgeman Art Library)

Pockets, without flaps, were placed low down on the skirt fronts. The first coats had pockets with vertical openings, but these were replaced with horizontal openings and large flaps were added. Pockets held handkerchiefs, snuff boxes, and other small accessories.

The vest followed the general lines of the coat throughout this period. In general, it was slightly shorter than the coat and the skirt was flared but not pleated at the sides. If it was a sleeved vest, the sleeves were narrower and longer than those of the coat. The vest fronts and backs were the same length. In the later years of this period the waistcoat might be left unbuttoned for several inches from the top down, to show off a linen cravat. If a vest was for dress use, the front might be made of a more costly fabric than the back—for example, a silk damask front with a linen back. As according to rules of civility, a gentleman never removed his coat in company, only the front of the vest would show. A vest that was made of the same fabric throughout could serve as a jacket either for undress for the upper classes or in place of a coat for the lower classes. In the early 18th century, men sometimes wore a coat without a vest.

The jacket, which had evolved from the doublet, appears to have been worn in this period primarily by boys, but also by men and boys of any status when engaged in physical labor. In England, the jacket was a garment of "country people."

Full breeches, gathered or pleated into bands at the waist and knees in continuation of the fashion of the 1660s, were worn with the early coats. In the later 1670s, however, the fashion for knee breeches became entrenched. Knee breeches were similar to the older venetians: gathered into a waistband and tapering to the knee. The new-style breeches were narrower around the hips and ended just below the knee. The lower leg edge was cut in a modified S-curve—lower in the front to cover the kneecap but higher in back to reduce bulk behind the knee joint. At first knee breeches were gathered into a knee band and bloused slightly above the band, but by 1700 a more smoothly fitted style was common. The front opening of the breeches was fitted with a buttoned flap.

By the second half of the century, trousers had evolved as a garment for laborers. With straight, loose legs that reached mid-calf or ankle, trousers were usually made of rugged fabrics. Although common among field workers and sailors, trousers also could be found in the wardrobes of gentlemen, probably worn by themselves as undress or as a protective covering over breeches.

Outer Garments, 1671–1714

In the second half of the 17th century, the circular or semicircular cloak, either knee or calf length, continued to be worn for traveling and as protection against inclement weather. It was no longer draped but worn over the shoulders. The loose gown could still be seen in court, school, and church. The working man's frock, or overshirt, of rough linen or wool continued in use. In 1678, Salem merchant Edward Wharton had in his inventory a ready-made frock of green say (Dow 1935, 262). In 1696, a Philadelphia merchant sold a man's dimity frock (Account Book of a Philadelphia Merchant, 1694–1698).

An alternative to the cloak, the greatcoat, or surtout—pronounced "sirtoo"—coat, became common in the 1670s. Cut along the lines of the cassock, the greatcoat was loosely fitted with long sleeves. It buttoned down the front and the skirt reached to the calf; the center back seam was left open from the waist down. The front was constructed as single or double breasted. Collar types included flat, standing, or a cape.

Undergarments and Undress Wear, 1671–1714

The full shirt continued unchanged in shape into the 18th century. The bottom was squared, the sides vented; and the back flap was slightly longer than the front. Shirt sleeves were cut wide and gathered to a wristband, with ruffles below the band; several inches of shirt were revealed below the coat cuff. Shirt sleeves might be pressed into pleats to control the fullness. The sleeve ruffles tended to be longer in the 1600s and shorter in the 1700s. In the early 18th century, the neckband of the shirt became higher and the border of shirt opening gained a frill, or jabot, that was not detachable. Half shirts were not mentioned in the 18th century.

Linen or woolen drawers, with stirrups passing under the foot, continued to be worn. The inventory of Patrick Ewing, of Rowley, Massachusetts, taken in 1679 contained a pair of "old silke drawers" valued at three shillings (Dow 1921, 8:77).

In the colonial period the term "nightgown" referred to a loose, unstructured robe worn at home on top of a shirt and breeches for undress or in warm weather (the sleeping gown was called a night rail). In the early 18th century a garment similar in form was introduced to colonies from England. Called the banyan (derived from Portuguese and Arabic words), it was influenced by Persian and Asian clothing. Usually constructed with the sleeves and body cut as one piece, the garment could either be wrapped or buttoned in front and reached the knee or ankle. Period documents identify banyan fabrics: printed Indian cottons; plain, striped, and plaid linens; plain and striped thin silks; and wool or silk damasks. Expensive banyans were ordered bespoke from England or from local tailors. They were also available less expensively as ready-made garments. Records indicate that during the summer, men wore banyans outdoors to coffeehouses; in southern colonies they were likely worn more often in social situations or when conducting business.

Neckwear, 1671–1714

As noted above, from the 1660s onward the cravat, or neckcloth, was the most common neckwear for men. In the 1680s, it was no longer in vogue to use ribbon bows to fasten the cravat ends at the throat. Now lengthened and narrowed, the neckcloth was either tied or knotted. In the 1690s, it was fashionable to have a very long neckcloth and leave the ends free to tuck through a buttonhole. Thomas Smith, a successful New England mariner and artist, painted a self-portrait in 1680 showing himself wearing a neck-cloth with a wide bobbin lace border.

In about 1710, with the front opening of the shirt now more elaborate and with an attached frill, the cravat no longer hung down over the front of the chest but was folded around the neck. This allowed the frill to be exposed to view if the waistcoat was unbuttoned.

Headwear, 1671–1714

By the 1670s hat brim widths had greatly increased—to as much as six to eight inches. To prevent the brim from falling, one, two, or three sides were rolled up, or cocked. A plume might be attached around the crown. By the 1690s, the three-cornered hat—called today a tricorne—which sat low on the forehead, with a rounded or flat crown and the brim turned up in three sections, became fashionable. Plumes gave way to brim edges trimmed with braid, lace, or ostrich feather fringe. The large wigs worn by some men made it almost impossible for them to wear a hat at the same time. Rules of civility dictated, however, that the hat, if not worn, should be carried under the arm. So for men of quality, the cocked hat was likely more often carried than worn.

During this same period, Quaker men in Pennsylvania wore broad-brimmed hats as well. The brim might have a slight upturn, but it was not cocked. As a rule, they wore their hats most of the time—indoors as well as outside—which was a simpler matter because they generally did not wear periwigs.

Footwear, 1671–1714

Regardless of their station, in this period and in the 18th century most men wore knitted stockings, the exception being enslaved and indentured fieldworkers, who might wear woven hose or go bare legged. Hose were usually worn drawn up over the knee of the breeches and then turned down to hide the garter under the knee. Until about the time of the American Revolution, different hues were popular, especially blue, russet, and green.

Stylish shoes kept the squared toes, shaped heel, and high tongue seen earlier, but in a more exaggerated form: toes were elongated and wider, heels higher, and tongues longer—extending well up the front of the ankle—and wider at the top. The sides were cut high over the foot, and the toe might be cut square or shaped with a kind of forked tip. Buckles were introduced in England in the 1660s. By the 1680s buckles replaced all other forms of fastening. This style lasted into the first quarter of the 18th century. Although shoes were imported from England, colonial shoe makers and cordwainers were successful competitors by the end of the 17th century (see Chapter 3).

For indoor wear, well-to-do man might don slippers. Similar to a lady's slipper of the same period, it had a vamp that covered the top of the instep, but no quarters or latchets. The heels were lower than those for women.

By about 1675, boot shafts were made of stiffer leather, and they no longer wrinkled around the leg. Some had tops that turned up over the knee, with a split in the center back to allow for bending the knee. Boot heels were thick, but could be of any height. Particularly heavy types were called jackboots; they had bucket tops above the knees and square heels. Half jackboots were shorter and lighter. Spur leathers were still worn over the instep.

At the beginning of the 18th century, leggings of leather or heavy canvas called spatterdashes were worn for horseback. These covered the shoes and had a stirrup for the instep. They buttoned and/or buckled down the outside of the leg, reaching from the top of the foot to above the knee.

Hairstyles and Grooming, 1671–1714

In about 1685 an alternative to the cumbersome periwig was introduced: the peruke. The peruke (from an Old French word meaning a head of hair) was worn for less formal occasions—for riding, traveling, or everyday use. Instead of a mass of curls hanging about the face, the fullness was brought away from the face to the back, where clusters of curls were turned up on themselves and tied with ribbons.

The Ramillies wig, a plaited queue peruke, was introduced to the colonies in the early 18th century. A powdered affair appropriate only for informal use, the Ramillies wig was dressed with the hair puffed out at the sides. The hair at the top and back was pulled back and tied with a black ribbon at the nape of the neck and then plaited and tied with another ribbon.

In 1679, Mr. Daniel King, Nicholas Maning, and Edmond Bridges were presented to the Essex County, Massachusetts, Court for wearing periwigs. After determining that the men's estates were not worth the two hundred pounds sterling required to be able to wear wigs, the court found the men guilty and admonished them (Dow 1919, 7: 315).

Accessories, 1671–1714

Exotic garters made their way to the colonies as gifts from English travelers who had purchased them in the Holy Land. In 1688, Samuel Sewall was given a pair of Jerusalem garters in gratitude for money he had sent to aid colonial Americans being held prisoner by pirates in Algeria. He noted in his diary that the garters "cost above 2 pieces 8/8 [Spanish dollars] in Algier; were made by a Jew" (Sewall 1973, 1:158). Sewall's garters may have featured a woven Arabic inscription for "Jerusalem" as well as decorative floral and bird motifs. Such a pair is in the collections of the Victoria and Albert Museum. By the 18th century, merchants advertised garters with different words and phrases woven into them; these were called "lettered garters."

CLOTHING FOR THE ENSLAVED, 1620–1714

Very little has been recorded concerning the Western-style garments provided for the earliest Africans who were brought to North America; however, they were likely the same kinds of clothes worn by indentured servants: simple versions of the shirt, doublet, or jacket, breeches, hose, and shoes, all made of serviceable materials. The most fruitful 17th-century sources for slave clothing are county court records. The following are examples from York County, Virginia. In 1681 a runaway named Detro left his master wearing "sad Colord broad cloathes" (*York County Deeds*, 6:57). In 1686, Frank ran from Thomas Mitton of Jamestown clothed in a "Redd Cotton waistcoate Canvis Drawers, broad Brimed black hatt" (*York County Deeds*, 7:230). In 1689, Daniel Park of York County, willed one of his slaves, named Virginia Will, his freedom at Parke's death. He further bound his executors to furnish Will with "one Kersey Coat and Britches and hatt two pair of shoes, tow pair of yarne Stockens, two white or blew shirts, one pair of blew Drawers" as well as food provisions and tools (*York County Deeds*, 8:239).

CLOTHING OF AMERICAN INDIANS, 1607–1714

As discussed in Chapter 2, clothing was critical to Native/European commerce—Indians talked about it, traded for it, and used it to create social, economic, and political bonds. In acquiring new forms of dress, American Indians acquired the materials to create and transform a new "vocabulary of materials" with colonists. The speaker or headman of a group could signal his identity in diplomatic situations by wearing a laced coat; an interpreter might don European clothing but wear an Indian hairstyle. Thus, European cloth and clothing were more than replacements for indigenous garments of skins and furs.

Main Garments

The first English settlers noted that Indian men wore two garments: the breechcloth and the mantle, or matchcoat. As with indigenous women's clothing, men's garments originally were made of animal skins—beaver, moose, elk, deer, raccoon, bear, otter—but over time many Native men chose to substitute trade cloth for these traditional materials. In 1607, John Smith observed a hierarchy of dress among the Indians of the Powhatan Chiefdom. "The better sort" had breechcloths and mantles made of skins. However, "the common sort" had to make do "with grasse, the leaves of trees, or such like" (Smith 1907, 100). In about 1634, Thomas Morton recorded that men of the Algonquian-speaking tribes in Plymouth Colony wore the "hairy side" of the skins next to their bodies in cold weather and the "haire outwardes" in summer (Morton 1883, 142). Writing of the Aberginians in 1634, New Englander William Wood described "Indian Breeches" made of cloth instead of skins: "a yard and a halfe long, put betweene their groinings, tied with a snakes skinne about their middles, one end hanging downe with a flap before, the other like a taile behinde" (Wood 1865, 73–74). In 1670, colonist Daniel Denton (c. 1626–1703) observed that the American Indian communities living on Long Island had incorporated trade textiles into their daily dress. Concerning male apparel,

> Their Cloathing is a yard and an half of broad Cloth, which is made for the Indian Trade, which they hang upon their shoulders; and half a yard of the same cloth, which being put betwixt their legs, and brought up before and behinde, and tied with a Girdle about their middle, hangs with a flap on each side: They wear no Hats, but commonly wear about their Heads a Snake's skin, or a Belt of their money [i.e., *wampum*], or a kind of Ruff made with Deers hair, and died of a scarlet colour, which they esteem very rich. (Denton 1902, 52)

The mantle, or matchcoat, was fastened at one shoulder and wrapped around the body according to the wearer's custom and/or his community affiliation. The word matchcoat, which is found in contemporary documents, is probably a corruption of the Odjibua word *matchigod*, meaning petticoat. Smith recorded that members of the Powhatan Chiefdom had mantles of skin for the summer and fur for the winter; "the better sort" wore mantles of deer skins that were patterned with white beads or copper or painted (Smith 1907, 99).

Morton described several different kinds of mantles. Mantles of bear skins were the "usuall wearinge" for Indians who hunted bear. Moose skin was dressed with the hair removed; the Indians "make them wonderous white, and stripe them . . . around the borders, . . . like lace set on by a Taylor." The finest mantles were of turkey feathers, which they twined together, and to Morton's eye looked like knitting (Morton 1883, 142). Roger Williams reported that the Narragansett men of Rhode Island made turkey feather mantles that were as prized among the Indians as velvet fabric was among the English (Williams 1827, 107).

Wood noted that Aberginian mantles were made of bear, moose, beaver, otter, or raccoon skins; in the winter a "deepe firr'd Cat skinne, like a long large muffe" was worn on the arm that "lieth most exposed to the winde." The Aberginian fabric mantle consisted of "a good course blanket, through which they cannot see" or a piece of broadcloth, which doubled as covering for sleep (Wood 1865, 73).

Roger Williams, who studied the Narragansett closely enough to learn and record their language, concluded that English clothing was strange to the Indians: "I have seen them rather expose their skins to the wet, than their cloathes [i.e., presents and purchases of English clothing], and therefore pull them off, and keep them drie." He also noted that Indians who had English apparel wore it only when they visited English settlements (Williams 1827, 108).

Most Indians on the Eastern seaboard wore skin moccasins and leggings only in cooler weather or to protect the legs and feet when hunting. The skins most often used were deer, elk, and moose. Depending upon the tribal affiliation and the wearer, these skins might be decorated with paint and/or porcupine quills. The Algonquian of New England wore deerskin leggings that fit inside the moccasin "like a stirrop stockinge" and reached the waist, where they were tied to the breechcloth belt with leather cords (Morton 1883, 142).

Hairstyles and Grooming

All contemporary observers noted the attention American Indians paid to styling and adorning their hair. It is little wonder that almost immediately after contact with Europeans looking glasses became popular trade goods. Wood commented that Aberginian men sometimes wore their hair very long, "hanging down in a loose dishevel'd womanish manner" and others tied their hair "up hard and short like a horse taile, bound close with a fillet, which they say makes it grow the faster" (Wood 1865, 71). Writing in 1612 of the tribes of the Powhatan Chiefdom, William Strachey explained that the men had the hair on the right side of their heads shaved quite close to the skull, "keeping a ridge comonly on the toppe or crowne like a coxcomb" (this likely was to keep the hair on that side from tangling in the bowstring). The hair on the left side was kept long, with a lock "an ell long" that was treated with walnut oil to make it shine. Sometimes this lock of hair was tied up and "stuck with many coulored gew-gawes," like an antler; pieces of copper; "the hand of their enemie dryed;" "the whole skin of a hauke stuffed with the wings abrouad;" or the tail of rattlesnake, which as the wearer moved, made "a certaine murmuring or whisteling noise" (Strachey 1849, 67).]

As a rule, Indian men did not wear facial hair. Strachey noted that in the Powhatan Chiefdom women would shave the men with two mussel shells (1849, 66).

Adornments

Body adornment—jewelry, paint, and permanent body modifications—took many forms. In Virginia, Indian men had large holes in their ears through which they hung chains of pearls, hollow copper beads, the legs of birds, or mammal claws. A few hung a "small greene and yellow-coloured live snake" (Strachey 1849, 67). Aberginians wore ear pendants in the form of birds, fish, or mammals, caved of bone, shells, or stone. They also wore necklaces, bracelets, and belts of wampam (Wood 1865, 74). At about the same time as William Wood was recording Indian practices in New England, Father Andrew White was doing the same for the Pescatoway of Maryland. White (1910, 43) recorded that around their

Native American Indian, or A Twenty-Three-Year-Old Virginian Algonquian, by Wenceslaus Hollar, London, 1645. The hairstyle of this Algonquian warrior shows that the upper right and left sides of the head have been shaved, leaving a ridge of hair on the crown. The hair around the ears and in back has been allowed to grow. (Library of Congress)

necks the Pescatoway wore beads, a hawk's bill, eagle's talons, animal teeth, "or sometime a pare of great eagles wings linked together."

Pescatoway men generally painted their faces dark red—red ochre— "which they doe to keep away the gnats." Alternatively, some men might use blue "from the nose downeward" and red upward "and sometimes contrary wise" (White 1910, 42–43). When the red mineral pigment vermilion (also known as cinnabar) was added to the list of trade goods, it quickly replaced the traditional red ochre. The application of vermilion as face and body paint had tragic consequences, however; the compound contains mercury and is toxic.

Strachey described a practice among warriors of the Powhatan tribes in which the men would paint their bodies with colored oils—black or yellow—and then apply the down "of sundry couloured birdes" such as blue birds, herons, and cardinals "as if so many variety of laces were stitched to their skinns" (Strachey 1849, 66).

Many Indians practiced some form of scarification or tattooing. According to Wood, the Aberginians practiced both. He described the "better sorts" of men having permanent raised tattoos "upon their cheekes"; "pourtraitures of beasts, as Beares, Deares, Mooses, Wolves, . . . Eagles, Hawkes." Others bore impressions resembling fish and spur rowls "downe the outside of their armes and brests," which they made with hot irons (Wood 1864, 74).

COMPOSITION OF A WARDROBE, 1607–1714

Initial Settlements

What did the first male colonists actually wear? In 1629 explorer John Smith advised those contemplating resettlement in Virginia, whom Smith called "private persons" as opposed to servants, to provide themselves with three suits (each comprising a doublet and breeches, or trunk hose)— one each of hardwearing canvas, a coarse napped woolen frieze, and a finer wool broadcloth,—a waistcoat, three shirts, three falling bands, a Monmouth cap, four pairs of shoes, three pairs of linen stockings (these may have been knitted or made of linen cloth cut on the bias), a pair of garters, and a dozen points, which were used to tied the hose to the breeches and the doublet sleeves to the doublet body (Smith 2006, 315). In contrast, the fashionable and extensive wardrobe of gentleman George Percy, one of Jamestown's first settlers, suggests the luxury clothing that Gentlemen Adventurers brought with them or sent for in the first years of settlement. By 1611, Percy's wardrobe included six suits of various fabrics including worsted, silk, and broadcloth—all with trimmings; 18 shirts of fine holland linen; multiple pairs of shoes and boots; a pair of slippers; knitted worsted and silk hose; multiple pairs of garters and gloves; six night caps, a dozen handkerchiefs, a Monmouth cap, three hats with silk and gold bands, and a Dutch-style beaver hat with ornaments (the complete description of his clothing is given in Chapter 3).

In 1635, an anonymous author recommended for immigrants to Maryland a set of clothing similar to that of Virginians. His list included three suits of the same three fabrics, three shirts with falling bands, a waistcoat, a coarse wool coat for outerwear, six pairs of shoes and three pairs of stockings, two caps or hats, a dozen points, and broad tape for garters ("A Relation of Maryland" 1910, 93). Wealthier immigrants likely dressed similarly to gentleman Thomas Egerton of St. Mary's, who died in 1639. He owned one old and two new suits of wool, a woolen coat lined with plush, a shirt, two plain bands and a third with lace, three pairs of cuffs, an embroidered belt, a pair each of worsted and silk stockings, a pair of shoes, a gold hatband and feather, and a pair of silk garters (Browne 1887, 4:89).

In 1623, the financial backers of a fishing village at Cape Ann, Massachusetts, provided Puritan settlers with garments that bespeak a very different climate and set of social and economic expectations. The men were given two suits (doublet and trunk hose) of leather lined with oil skin, a woolen suit lined with leather, and an extra pair of breeches. For extra protection against the damp and cold, each man was allotted a green cotton—probably napped wool—waistcoat and a mandilion lined with wool. Accessories included four pairs of shoes and stockings, two handkerchiefs, four bands, a leather belt probably to hold a sword, one woolen and two red knit caps, a black hat, two pairs of gloves and a pair of Norwich (wool) garters (McClellan 1904, 84). These were workmen's clothes, appropriate for cold, wet weather, and harsh working conditions.

Among the first settlers to the newly established colony of Carolina were Irish servants who had been unable to furnish themselves with enough clothing for the journey and settlement. In 1670, Captain Joseph West wrote the Proprietors requesting clothing for these men: "espetially shoes and stockings, and shirts, coarse Kersys, Bays and blew linnin." West noted that he preferred yardage rather than "cloths ready made which doe little or noe service" (Cheves 2000, 246).

Sample Wardrobes through Time

Probate inventories from the Plymouth Colony suggest that at least for the middling sort of New England's male colonists, the first 50 years of settlement were not spent in luxury. Will Wright of the town of Plymouth, who died in 1633, had a two-room house, well but modestly furnished. His wardrobe included some older garments; all of his apparel was linen or wool except for two "wrought [i.e., embroidered] silke caps." His main garments included a doublet and breeches with matching cloak all of sad, or dull, color, another suit with unlined breeches, two pairs of boot breeches, and a doublet of black stuff, this last accounted an old one. Perhaps the doublet was once part of a matching suit of doublet and breeches, but the breeches had become too worn to continue to wear. He also owned four waistcoats—two red, one white cotton wool, and one of dimity. His undergarments included seven shirts, three pairs of linen drawers, and an old pair of cotton wool, and three bands. His collection of stockings represents some of the many common types available at the time: four pairs of linen and two pairs of cloth (these may have been of fabric cut on the bias rather than knitted), one pair of "wadmore," and three old pairs—two Irish and two knitted. Wright also owned two pairs of boothose although no boots or shoes were listed in the inventory. Headgear included a black hat, a white hat, a white holland cap, and the two silk caps mentioned above. For outerwear, besides the cloak that matched his suit, there were two old coats, one black and one blue (Inventory of . . . Will Wright).

Thomas Fenner, of Hartford, Connecticut, was a trapper and Indian trader who carried on some of his business by boat from a landing in Totoket. At his death in 1647 his estate totaled over £60, with most of his assets in furs and trade goods. His personal clothing consisted only of a jacket and pair of breeches; a "weareing Coate;" a short coat of darnex, a heavy cloth with a linen warp and woolen weft; an old hat, shoes and stockings; a pair of "Indean stockins," protective leather leggings of the type worn by Native hunters; and an unlined "Portingale," or Portuguese-style, stocking cap (Manwaring 1904, 10–11).

Richard Sawyer, a resident of Windsor, Connecticut—located in the Connecticut River Valley—likely had numerous opportunities to encounter Indians as well. The settlement at Windsor was connected by a road to Hartford in the south and Springfield in the south, a route that brought Indian trading goods as well as supplies for the settlers. Sawyer, who died in 1648, was probably a successful tradesman, which is reflected in his clothing inventory. His main garments included three suits of matching color and textiles: one "musck-colour'd" woolen doublet and breeches; a "liver-colour'd" doublet, jacket, and breeches; and a "haire-colour'd" doublet, jacket, and breeches. He also owned a buckskin and calf skin doublet, a woolen jacket, an old pair of gray-colored breeches, a pair of canvas drawers—which were likely breeches rather than an undergarment—and an old coat. The rest of the sartorial inventory included three shirts, 10 bands, an old and a new hat of unnamed colors, a pair of knitted green hose and a pair of old knitted cotton (probably wool) hose, a pair of cloth buskins, and a pair each of old shoes and old boots (Earle 1894, 22–23).

When John Winthrop, governor of the Massachusetts Bay Colony, died in 1649, his wardrobe was probably more impressive than many of his Boston neighbors'. According to the probate inventory, his main garments consisted of two satin doublets; a serge doublet and breeches; one old black and three cloth suits, two cloth waistcoats, and a pair of "old ship breeches." Undergarments and accessories included three shirts, five caps, 14 pairs of cuffs and 18 bands, nine pairs of gloves, several pairs of old stockings of silk or wool, one pair of worsted stockings and four pair of "wash stockings," a pair of silk garters, two belts (probably sword belts), and a "cloth of gold scarf." Winthrop possessed a number of articles of outerwear: five cloaks, three of them old; three coats, one of them "stuffed" (perhaps quilted); two wraps, one of which was velvet, a shawl; and two velvet jerkins, one tufted and one embellished. Of note is the valuation of the two jerkins at one pound and 15 shillings; this was the same value given for a set of six chairs and a cupboard (Earle 1895, 174–77).

Further south, in Accomack County, Virginia, merchant Henry James had cut a fine figure. His 1665 estate inventory listed six suits (doublet and breeches) in some detail: three were of wool, two were of worsted, and one was of silk drugget (probably a silk weft and worsted warp). His outdoor activities and travel were hinted at by a leather waistcoat trimmed with silver lace, a "closs bodyed" coat, two woolen riding coats, and a buff coat. Undergarments and accessories consisted of four dowlas shirts, two half shirts, four pairs of linen drawers, six bands and four neck cloths, five pairs of cuffs, seven handkerchiefs, three pairs of stockings, three pairs of shoes—one old and two new—and two hats (*Accomack County Deeds and Wills, 1664–1671*, 9). At the other end of the economic scale, Francis Sherwood, a wheelwright who died in 1666, left only a doublet, breeches, riding coat, two shirts, a pair of drawers, a pair of stockings, and an old hat (*Accomack County*, 41).

The 1673 inventory of Scituate resident John Howland shows a mixture of clothing of imported fabrics and garments of local homespun. Howland owned four "suites" of clothes; the word "suite" might refer to a doublet and breeches or the newer fashion of coat and breeches. Two of Howland's suits were of imported wool (cloth and serge); a third was of homespun wool or linen, and the last of an unspecified fabric. He possessed three waistcoats, or vests. Two of these were identified as red and one as of homespun. His three great coats and one jacket were valued less than his cloth suit, suggesting that the suit was of fine-quality wool. Of his five shirts, one was of holland linen. Instead of bands, Howland owned two silk neckcloths, suggesting that he was conscious of current fashion. Other accessories included a pair of boots and two pairs of shoes; 12 caps, some fine and some coarse linen; six pairs of stockings, and a pair of mittens, which may have been of fabric or knitted (A trew Inventory of Mr John howland).

Thomas Willett (1605–1674) was a Plymouth merchant, Indian trader, and sea captain. He held important political positions, including commissioner of New Netherland and magistrate of Plymouth Colony; he was also the first mayor of New York City (in 1665). Willett died a year after the aforementioned John Howland, in 1674. With a total estate that was valued at more than 10 times that of Howland's, Willett left an extensive and expensive wardrobe that reflected his wealth, rank, and elder position. Among the status items his estate appraisers noted were two cloaks and a doublet and breeches of camlet; one of the cloaks had gold buttons. In the 17th century, camlet was an elegant dyed-in-the-yarn fabric of wool or a silk-and-wool blend that was often figured or calendered (Montgomery 1984, 188). Willett possessed three gowns, which he likely wore when conducting official colony business; one of these had silver clasps. His three beaver hats were valued at the same amount as his gowns. The rest of his apparel represented a mix of older styles and newer fashions. He had one suit consisting of a doublet, coat, and breeches and another with serge breeches and a jacket. Other main garments included four doublets, three waistcoats, two coats, a pair of trousers, and four cloaks (one of black wool). Completing the wardrobe were three shirts, two pairs of drawers, a hood, a scarf, a pair of white linen gloves (possibly knitted), five pairs of knitted silk stockings, "a parsell of old stockens," three belts, a pair of boothose tops, one pair of boots, and two pairs of shoes (An Inventory of . . . Thomas Willett).

The 1682 estate inventory of Bostonian Colonel Thomas Richbell suggests the sartorial richness of urbanites from the middle to upper ranks. The Colonel, who was likely a member of the Boston Militia, dressed at the height of fashion, in the modern style suit of coat and breeches. He owned seven suits: a satin coat with gold flowers and blue breeches; a scarlet coat and breeches with silver buttons; a suit of silk crape; a woolen suit with silk buttons; one of black wool; and one of "stuffe" (wool) with metallic woven trimming. Additional main garments included a camlett coat with frog closures, a pair of white damask breeches, and seven white waistcoats. His undergarments consisted of 12 shirts and three pairs of holland drawers. Footwear amounted to 12 pairs of stockings—seven of white linen, one of scarlet worsted, and four of silk—and a pair of boots. The estate assessors were careful in noting Richbell's sartorial accessories: 11 handkerchiefs; three caps; seven cravats with the same number of pairs of ruffles and ribbons for the sleeves; three hats with hatbands; three small periwigs, one diamond ring and a mourning ring, a silver-headed cane, and two rapiers with silver hilts and a sword belt (Earle 1894, 18–19).

1715–1785

THE EVOLUTION OF CUT, CONSTRUCTION, AND SILHOUETTE, 1715–1785

According to merchants' advertisements, reports of theft, and other period documents, men's suits—coat, vest, and breeches—all might be constructed from the same fabrics or they might be of contrasting materials and/or colors. In 1736, Thomas Booth, an Irish servant of about 21, ran away wearing a suit of homespun linen—shirt, breeches, and waistcoat—as well as a good pair of shoes and an old felt hat with a cocked brim (*Pennsylvania Gazette*, September 9, 1736). In 1745, Benjamin Harvey of Bucks County, Pennsylvania, reported the theft of a suit and great coat: "Stole . . . a Coat and Vest of Woollen Drugget, lightish Colour; a Worsted Drugget Coat, of two Colours, blue and Sassafrass; a brownish Great coat . . . with Brass Buttons, . . . and a Pair of Buckskin Breeches, with Brass Buttons" (*Pennsylvania Gazette*, August 1, 1745). George Wells of York County, Virginia, had at his death in 1754 two suits: one consisting of a blue coat and silk waistcoat and breeches; the other a gray coat, scarlet waistcoat, and fustian breeches (Inventory of . . . George Wells). In 1773, Massachusetts governor Thomass Hutchinson (1711–1780) ordered from his London tailor, Peter Leitch, "a suit of scarlet broad-cloth, full trimmed but with few folds" (quoted in Earle 1903, 2:406).

Increasingly after 1750, contemporary documents—especially from northern colonies—record men's garments and accessories that were manufactured in the colonies rather than imported. For example, Adam Colson of Boston crafted jackets of moose skin "fit for Apprentices" and boasted that his garments would outlast "at least seven" jackets made of English broadcloth (*Boston Gazette*, October 1, 1764). In 1770, Bostonian gentleman Henry Lloyd set out to visit New York, Philadelphia, "and the Southern Colonies." Although a gentleman, his entire apparel was of New England manufacture: clothing, personal linen, shoes, stockings, boots, gloves, hat, and wig (*New-York Gazette and the Weekly Mercury*, April 2, 1770).

Main Garments, 1715–1750

Coat

The basic coat that had evolved from the 1670s was worn throughout this period, with certain changes in how the garment was cut. By 1715, the back sections of the coat were placed with the center back seam almost on the bias (diagonal) of the cloth. This allowed for some stretch across the back and made the coat fit the small of the back more snugly. A pleat or two was added to the center back coat skirts. The front pieces were still cut on the straight grain, but there was a more pronounced curve down the front over the chest, and the side pleats of the skirt now encompassed about a half circle of cloth on each side. The skirts were reinforced with firm interlining to keep the pleats in shape. Sleeves were cut in two curved pieces, with separate, very wide cuffs that allowed the lower part of the shirt sleeve to protrude. There was still no collar, but the shoulder seam and the side seam had both been moved further toward the back of the coat. Pockets had moved up on the body, near the waistline, from their previous position near the hem, and were most often covered with flaps.

In the 1730s, the coat front was also cut with the front edges tilted off the straight, although not on the true diagonal. Sleeves began to be more fitted on the upper arm, and wider at the hem. The cuffs, which had reached the elbow in the 1720s, diminished slightly to fall at the mid-forearm, but were still as wide as before. Open cuffs or open sleeves were not seamed completely up the back; round cuffs were closed all the way up. Coat skirts continued to be full, with pleats at the center back and each side. Generally, cut long enough to cover the knee caps, the coat buttoned from neck to hem or from neck to hip, but usually only a few buttons at the waist were actually fastened.

In order to whet the sartorial appetites of southern elites who followed English fashion, the *Virginia Gazette* occasionally reported on trends at Court. In its February 25, 1737, edition, the editor gave an account of a ball held at St. James's Palace the previous November, and commented on the latest change in fashion: "The Nobility and Gentlement were dress'd either in Flower'd Velvets of various Colours, of dark colour'd Cloth laced with Gold or Silver, the Breeches were either the Colour of the Coat or black Velvet, and all in general very rich Waistcoats . . . and some had the Sleeves of their Coats, the same as their Waistcoats; their Cloaths were much longer waisted than formerly; the Coat Sleeves much longer, and in general open; the Plaits on the Sides, were wadded to stick out . . . white Stockings the general Wear; and several had laced Neckcloths and Ruffles."

Vest or Waistcoat

The waistcoat or vest—documentary sources use the words interchangeably—changed as little as the coat did during this period. Only a few inches shorter than the coat and collarless, it was cut on the same lines except that the sides and back of the skirts were flared out without pleats. There were sleeved and sleeveless versions; some were lined with a pile fabric such as shag for warmth. Two short rows of eyelets were sometimes worked vertically down the center back to about waist level; these could be laced to adjust the fit. Following the practice of the 17th century, sometimes the upper back of a fashionable vest would be cut from plain linen or another plain fabric that was less expensive than the face fabric. As gentlemen did not remove their coats in company, this savings would not be remarked upon by others. Waistcoats worn by the working classes may have been the same length as the shorter jacket rather than nearly coat length.

The 1720s through the 1750s saw the importation of elegant waistcoats of white linen embellished with Dresden embroidery (see Chapter 3), which had been executed by professionals in Europe and Britain. Although worn throughout the colonies, extant examples confirm that these lightweight garments were especially popular in the southern colonies. Other specialty embellishments included bobbin lace plaited with metallic threads and embroidery in silk and metallic threads.

Jacket

For men and boys, the jacket was a hip- or thigh-length outer garment, probably worn most often by artisans, farmers, laborers, and sailors. Jackets may have been cut along the same lines as fashionable coats, but probably had a looser fit. They likely had fewer or no pleats at the sides and back, but were constructed with a simple vent or overlapping flaps. Both sleeved and sleeveless versions are mentioned in documentary sources. Jackets usually buttoned—single or double-breasted—but on occasion they were laced. Probate inventories sometimes listed a suit as comprising a coat, jacket, and breeches; here the jacket is likely a waistcoat, perhaps with sleeves. Just as in the second half of the 17th century, a vest made up of a single fabric for the fronts and back might substitute as a jacket (vests in which the fronts were of a fashionable fabric and the backs of a thin linen or other less expensive cloth were meant for show and not worn without a coat). Two indentured men-servants described as "Carolina Indians" ran away from their Boston masters in 1716; one wore a double-breasted jacket and leather breeches, the other a leather jacket and black stockings

(*Boston News-Letter*, September 17, 1716). An indentured servant living in New York ran from his master wearing a scarlet jacket with green velvet lapels and a striped flannel jacket beneath it (*New-York Gazette Revived in the Weekly Post-Boy*, February 17, 1752).

Underjackets are mentioned in advertisements for runaway servants. It is difficult to determine if the term is synonymous with waistcoat, or if the garment represents yet another layer of clothing between the waistcoat and shirt underneath and the jacket or the coat above.

Frock

By about 1700, the frock referred to two different but related garments. The first was the working man's protective overshirt of coarse material that had been worn in the 1600s. Versions of this garment were likely seen more frequently in the 18th century as country wear for farmers, carters, and waggoners. In the early 1720s, Scots-Irish Presbyterian immigrants who had settled in Londonderry, New Hampshire, began weaving for resale a striped fabric made of locally processed fibers: tow linen for the warp with a weft of alternating indigo and white stripes of white wool or tow linen. This coarse fabric was made into shirts and skilts, or loose trousers, for men. The fabric also was used to make a long, loose pullover jacket or frock named for the fabric: striped frocking. Many New England farmers and laborers wore striped frocking into the 19th century. The Boston servant who fled from his sea captain master in 1737 with a frock and trousers (in addition to a pea jacket, speckled shirt, fly coat, and sleeveless jacket) wore a pullover type of frock (*Boston News-Letter*, December 22).

The other garment called a frock was styled like a coat but was looser and with lapels and a turnover flat collar. Donned for undress or informal/everyday wear, this type of frock was not in common use until the mid-18th century. Writing to the Trustees of the Georgia colony on December 10, 1735, James Oglethorpe complained about the condition of some of the clothing provided for the settlers: "Robinson's coats shrink intollerably. Some of them that touched the Men's heels do not now touch the bottoms of their coats" (Candler 1910, 21:53–54). It is likely that the coats under discussion were not dress coats but loose-fitting collared frock coats for everyday wear.

Breeches

In the 18th century, breeches were more fitted in the leg. The waistband was now usually wider across the back than in the front, with the fullness of the breeches concentrated across the back. This allowed for ease when sitting. The fit of the breeches around the waist could be adjusted by means of lacing at the center back on the waistband. The legs were fitted enough to require the outside seam to be open for a few inches above the knee in order to be pulled on. It was closed with buttons while a buckle fastened the flat, narrow knee band. Due to wear, breeches were often relined or even reseated.

Breeches could be made of almost any fabric. As discussed in Chapter 3, leather breeches were worn not only by laborers, servants and apprentices, and artisans but by merchants and gentlemen. William Keith, of Williamsburg, Virginia, advertised that he could supply gentlemen, as well as others, with buck-skin breeches "made after the neatest Fashion" (*Virginia Gazette,* June 17, 1737). Fabric breeches usually wore out faster than coats. In January 1733, Massachusetts governor Jonathan Belcher (1682–1757) ordered two suits from his London tailor, a Mr. Tullit, one of grogram and one of "very good" silk—"a handsome compleat suit"—and "two pair of breeches to each suit" (Earle 1903, 2:402–03).

Trousers and Overalls

Following the styling of the previous century, trousers had loose straight legs reaching to the calf or ankle, rather than gathered in at the knee. Otherwise, they seem to have followed the pattern of breeches in the waistband and closure. Trousers were sometimes worn by working men and boys in preference to breeches, and also were worn by upper-class men in hot weather. A Spanish Indian servant ran away from a Newbury, Massachusetts, master wearing a pair of long trousers over his leather breeches (*Boston News-Letter,* March 2, 1732). Welsh servant Lewis Williams wore old and patched linen trousers with a checked cotton shirt and blue vest when he left his Boston master in 1738 (*Boston News-Letter,* June 1, 1738). An Irish servant who worked sometimes on the water owned a pair of "petticoat Trowsers" (*New-York Gazette Revived in the New-York Weekly Post-Boy,* September 11, 1749). Runaways were sometimes described as wearing trousers over their breeches, likely because trousers acted as a protective covering: an Irish servant of about 22 wore short trousers over a pair of linen breeches when he left his master (*Pennsylvania Gazette,* January 29, 1729).

The southern climate forced its own wardrobe needs. Thomas Causton, who had been a calico printer before immigrating with James Oglethorpe to Georgia in 1732, found that the colonists had suitable clothing neither for the climate nor the insects. He wrote to England requesting "some good chequed Linnen of a dark blue and strong Linnen for Waistcoats and Trowsers" (Temple and Coleman 2010, 16).

Overalls were a type of loose trouser worn over breeches or regular trousers to protect them while working. They are mentioned most frequently with regard to laborers, farmers, soldiers, and sailors.

Outer Garments, 1715–1750

Cloaks

Ready-made as well as bespoke cloaks were regularly imported from Britain throughout this period. Although not as fashionable in the 18th century, they were still worn, especially when traveling. For warmth, some had one or more attached shoulder capes and a heavy lining. Cloaks might also have an attached standing or turndown collar. In the 1730s, the gathers at the neck, which had made the cloak bulky, were eliminated. Now a tailored garment, the cloak was made in four pieces and shaped to the neck with a vent in back for riding. This style was known variously as a roquelaure, roguelo, or roculo. The front of cloak might be fastened with frogs, hooks and eyes, ties, or buttons.

Governor Belcher ordered from London the full, lined and trimmed cloak called a roquelaure in 1739 (Earle 1903, 2:404). A blue broadcloth cloak stolen from a New York City residence in 1746 was described as having "light blue silk Frogs [for closures] . . . with a double Cape, and Silver Hooks & Eyes" (*New-York Weekly Post-Boy*, December 29).

Overcoat

Overcoats replaced cloaks in the 18th century. They were called by many names and made of a range of materials to fit function and pocketbook. The surtout (from the 17th century) and the great coat were quite common although today it is difficult to distinguish what the differences between the two might have been. Both featured wide cuffs that turned back and one or more collars. If the latter, the topmost collar could be pulled up around the head and face and buttoned to give protection. Surtouts and great coats were sometimes worn belted at the waist.

Apprentices, slaves working in urban areas, farmers, and other working sorts as well as gentlemen wore surtouts and great coats. They differed only in details of construction and materials. James Mitchel, a servant, ran from his master near Skuylkill, Pennsylvania, taking with him an old great coat made of black kersey (*Pennsylvania Gazette,* November 19, 1730). In Charleston, Peter Horry sold ready-made "blew & red scarlet whitney great coats" (*South-Carolina Gazette,* December 13, 1735). In New York, John Croker reported the theft of his great coat: "a light coloured Cloth great Coat with Button Holes in the Inside under a Flap" (*New-York Weekly Journal,* December 3, 1739). An enslaved servant taken up in Bucks County, Pennsylvania, wore a light-colored broadcloth surtout (*Pennsylvania Gazette,* October 29, 1747).

The pea coat, or pea jacket, was generally worn by laborers and artisans as well as sailors and others who made their livings in maritime trades. It is likely that the form was similar to the modern version: a button front, fitted jacket of woolen cloth, probably falling to hip length, with a collar and long fitted sleeves. Pea jackets appeared in the records as early as the 1730s and were distinguished from the common jacket in runaway advertisements. For example, in 1730 Robert Naylor, indentured servant to a joiner, ran wearing a brown pea jacket with brass buttons (*Pennsylvania Gazette,* March 19). In 1737, a runaway sailor stole two pea jackets from his mates on board a sloop; one was a long jacket of rateen and the other a "new blue Rug Pea Jacket shorter" (*Pennsylvania Gazette,* October 7, 1737). Nineteen-year-old Joseph Cristophers, indentured to a Boston sail maker, ran away in 1742 dressed in a pea jacket with large plate buttons as well as a blue great coat and a black wig (*Boston News-Letter,* February 18, 1742).

A garment called a fly (fly-fronted) coat is mentioned in merchant advertisements and runaway notices. Most often it was worn with a jacket, but not always. In 1733, Peter Horry offered ready-made fly coats to his Charleston customers (*South-Carolina Gazette,* January 20). The first appearance of the term in the *Pennsylvania Gazette* was in 1734; a servant, a potter by trade, left his master wearing "a reddish colour'd Kersey Coat new made, Fly fashion" (June 27).

Other types of outerwear included frock, watch, and riding coats; these were not well described in contemporary records. Frock coats commonly had turn-down collars and were slightly looser fitting than the regular suit coat although they could be made as an overcoat or a suit coat. Fabrics for frock coats ranged from heavy woolen bearskin (a thick heavily napped woolen fabric) and plain woolen cloth to medium-weight cotton and linen fustian. The servant to a tavern keeper ran away wearing a bearskin coat "made Frock Fashion" (*The New-York Gazette Revived in the Weekly Post-Boy,* February 17, 1752). Watch coats were red or blue, sometimes made of duffel, with or without a cape. Imported ready-made riding coats were advertised from the 1730s on. Charleston merchant James Crokatt offered riding coats of cloth, drugget, and duroy for winter use (*South-Carolina Gazette,*

September 21, 1734). Stolen in Boston in 1742 was a man's riding coat of blue cloth with a red velvet cape (*Boston News-Letter,* June 24, 1742).

Gown

In the 15th century, the gown appears to have been worn only by academics and the clergy, its style fossilized from its 16th-century roots. Academic and clerical gowns were most often of woolen fabric, but sometimes of silk and always black. Colonial custom, however, from the 17th century into the 18th, was also to simply wear a good black suit of clothes with a clerical collar known as the Geneva tabs or Geneva band. This distinctive collar is seen in the painting of the Massachusetts Puritan cleric Cotton Mather (1663–1728) done in 1727 by Peter Pelham, and New England evangelical minister Jonathan Edwards (1703–1758) by Joseph Badger.

Undergarments, 1715–1750

The shirt changed little during the century. Whether plain or frilled, it was still made in the same pattern as the 17th-century shirt, wasting very little material in the cutting. Plain shirts had a neckband or higher collar, and perhaps an attached turnover collar; the sleeves ended in narrow cuffs or wristbands. The jabot, or frill, became more prominent by midcentury and showed to advantage if the waistcoat was left unbuttoned. In consequence, men of fashion needed to own a larger number of shirts in order to show a clean shirt at all times. The band collar became wider and was generally concealed by a neckcloth if one was worn.

The voluminous shirt sleeves were gathered at the wrist and closed by a narrow wristband with buttons. For the upper classes, shirt sleeves were carefully pleated and pressed to reduce bulk under the coat sleeves. Shirts of linen and holland were common, but checked, striped, and flannel shirts in both fine and coarse qualities were also worn.

In the 18th century, nightshirts—for those who owned them—were cut more generously than shirts for day. Although primarily made of linen, some mentions of flannel nightshirts can be found; perhaps these latter were worn primarily in cold weather.

In this period drawers seem to have been most commonly made of linen, of the same shape and fit as breeches. With a wide waistband and fly front, knee bands, and a full seat, they tied closed at the waist. Breeches sometimes had detachable, washable linings that likely substituted for drawers. Benjamin Franklin noted in his *Autobiography* that on a hot Sunday in June of 1750, "I sat in my chamber with no other clothes on than a shirt and a pair of long linen drawers."

The banyan, or nightgown, maintained its loose silhouette and unstructured appearance throughout the 18th century. Many upper-class men wore them at home or in situations in which a coat was not necessary—perhaps when women would not be present. Light linen or cotton banyans were worn in hot weather throughout the colonies. Banyans were also commonly made of silk damask, printed cottons, and plain woolens. William Lasserre offered his Charleston customers ready-made banyans and bed gowns (*South-Carolina Gazette*, April 26, 1735). James Crokatt imported ready-made silk night gowns (*South-Carolina Gazette*, May 26, 1733). A "Plad Night Gown lin'd with blue satin" was lost from a boat in 1735 (*Pennsylvania Gazette*, May 1). William Sorsby, a Pennsylvania school master reported the theft of "a grey flower'd Damask Banyan lin'd with Tammy, made to wear either Side outwards" (*Pennsylvania Gazette*, December 8, 1737). Governor Belcher ordered a "night gown of the best Geneva damask" in deep crimson in 1734 (quoted in Earle 1903, 2:404).

Banyans, or nightgowns, of silk damask, such as this example from 1715, were made in England and exported to the colonies either as bespoke garments or ready-mades. (Fashion Museum, Bath and North East Somerset Council/ Acquired with the assistance of The Art Fund and V&A/Purchase Grant Fund/The Bridgeman Art Library)

Neck- and Wrist-Wear, 1715–1750

The cravat, or neckcloth—sometimes trimmed with lace—survived as a fashionable accessory and was worn until the 1780s. Fashion rivals were the jabot, which was attached to the shirt, and detachable ruffles, the latter being used especially for formal wear. The turn-down collar, which might be sewn onto the shirt or detachable, was worn by the conservative dresser and those who did not follow fashion. In the absence of a neckcloth, a ribbon might be threaded through two holes in the neckband and loosely tied.

The stock was introduced by 1730. A band of pleated linen stitched to a base and fastening at the back of the neck with ties or buckled straps, the stock was a gentleman's formal neckwear. A black ribbon tie brought around the stock from the back of the neck to tie in a bow at the front was known as a solitaire. In 1747, a runaway manservant had two cambric stocks and two muslin cravats with him—to go with his holland and osnaburg shirts—when he left Baltimore County, Maryland (*Pennsylvania Gazette,* June 11, 1747). An enslaved man identified as a fiddler owned a black stock with a silver clasp (*New-York Weekly Journal,* September 7, 1741).

Imported, resist-dyed red or yellow silk handkerchiefs with white or yellow spots called bandanas (from the Hindu *bandhnu*) came into fashion as neckcloths in this period.

The social function of detachable wrist ruffles was to indicate that the wearer did not work with his hands—and could afford to do so. Often made of fine linen, more decorative versions could be had of imported Dresden work and bobbin laces—Brussels, Mechlin, and Flanders.

Headwear, 1715–1750

The three-cornered, or tricorne, hat of felted beaver was the most fashionable headgear; less expensive versions were made of felted wool. Fashionable tricornes were decorated with trim such as a flat braid or gold or silver lace, ribbon cockades, and buttons and loops. Or a feather fringe was applied to the outer edge of the turned-up brim. Indian trader John Musgrove (c. 1695–1735) had established a trading post in Georgia along the Savannah River in order to capitalize on the deerskin trade. In the year of his death, the Trustees of the Georgia Colony sent him a gift of a silver-laced hat along with scarlet camlet, blue silk, and silver trimmings for a suit (Egmont 1735). The tricorne was worn with a peak at the front.

The rounded crown hat called a wideawake, with a broad brim that was not cocked, was still worn. Older men, the clergy, and especially Quakers continued to prefer this style. Others might wear a version of this hat with a softer brim.

Many varieties of caps were available throughout the colonies, both knitted and cut and sewn from woven fabrics. In addition to sailors, those servants—indentured and enslaved—who did not wear a wig, likely wore some kind of cap or hat. In Andover, Massachusetts, a young enslaved man ran away with one felt and two worsted caps (*Boston News-Letter,* October

20, 1737). An indentured servant who left his ship-joiner master had a cap of white linen (*New-York Weekly Journal*, July 6, 1741). An enslaved servant owned a striped woolen cap (*New-York Weekly Journal*, September 7, 1741). More upscale than knitted caps were jockey, or jocky, caps, made for both sexes, often of velvet. These had round crowns and short flat brims in front.

Men who wore wigs donned fitted caps or turbans over their bare heads to keep warm when they were at home. Shop clerk Thomas Jones, one of the first colonists in Savannah, Georgia, decided it was too hot to wear his wig and appeared at militia practice in his velvet cap, for which offense an officer, Colonel James Cochrane, called him impudent (Temple 2010, 174–75).

Nightcaps, bed caps, or undress caps—worn instead of wigs—came in several styles: round crowns with turned up bottoms; round crowns with a turned up brim that stood slightly away from the crown; and a cone or truncated cone crown with a rolled brim and a floppy top. These might be knitted of silk yarn or cut and sewn. The latter were constructed of luxury fabrics like velvet or brocade or of embroidered linen, and embellished with a tassel or other ornament.

Footwear, 1715–1750

Colored silk stockings were elegant for daytime wear; however, the style set at Court was to use black or white silk stockings for formal occasions. In Pennsylvania, servants' stockings were often knitted of gray worsted. John Lee imported scarlet stockings with clocks for men in the early 1730s (e.g., *Pennsylvania Gazette*, March 19).

The square-toed shoe remained fashionable into the 1720s, but the exaggerations of the previous period gave way to lower, blockier heels, shorter and narrower tongues, and a length more nearly approximating the actual foot contained within. The small buckle-and-strap closure was replaced by a much larger buckle, sized to catch wider tabs from each side of the shoe. Shoes were still cut as straights. In the 1730s, the toe shape changed to an oval or rounded point. Very fashionable shoes curved up at the toes in this decade. In the 1740s the shape was more in line with the foot. The low-heeled shoes with pliable soles called pumps were originally worn in Britain by footmen who ran alongside a carriage. In the 1730s, gentlemen adopted them for wear in fine weather and indoors.

Shoes for laborers and the enslaved might have wooden rather than leather heels. Reverend John Wise of Chebacco, Massachusetts, provided his servants with wooden-heel shoes in 1713 (*Boston News-Letter*, January

26). In 1726, Jack, absented himself from his master in Dartmouth, Massachusetts, wearing a new pair of square-toed, wooden heeled shoes (*Boston Gazette*, June 27).

Although it is not known how widespread the practice was, men also adopted wearing Indian moccasins; the colonist-made version of this foot covering was called shoe packs. Men often wore moccasins when traveling or hunting. On December 12, 1749, Virginia physician and surveyor Thomas Walker (1715–1794) led an expedition of six men west from Albemarle County to survey land in what is now southeastern Kentucky. Although on horseback, the group must have trekked some on foot because on the following April 16 Walker noted that he "made a pair of Indian Shoes, those I brought out being bad." These shoes must have been a temporary solution because on May 10, the group began to dress an elk skin to make Indian shoes, "ours being quite worn out." Four days later the skin was put in order and the moccasins made (Walker 1750). Toward the end of this period, evidence from runaway notices indicates that servants and laborers wore shoe packs as everyday wear. In 1743, John Hacket, a runaway servant, had both shoes and a pair of shoe packs (*Pennsylvania Gazette*, August 18, 1743).

Not a part of fashionable everyday wear in the 18th century, boots were worn primarily for riding, traveling, and hunting. Jackboots, introduced in the late 17th century, were still heavy and had high tops. In about 1720, a lighter, more flexible boot that fit more to the shape of the leg began to be worn. These were so supple that a small strap was sometimes buckled around the boot, just under the knee, to hold it more securely to the leg. Spur leather, introduced in the early 17th century, was still in use.

Hairstyles and Grooming, 1715–1750

While even servants, artisans, and laborers wore wigs in this period, men might go without. This was especially true after about 1765 for younger men. Some wore their hair cropped, while others styled their own hair in less elaborate versions of the peruke. William Coleman, a servant gardener in Rhode Island, had his head completely shaved; a fellow servant, George Blackmore, wore his dark hair short and curled (*Boston Gazette*, October 17, 1737).

In his journal, Dr. Alexander Hamilton noted the embarrassment that could arise if one were unfamiliar with local fashion or custom: "I dined with Mr. Fletcher in the company of two Philadelphians, who could not be easy because forsooth they were in their night-caps seeing every body else in full dress with powdered wigs; it not being customary in Boston to go to dine or appear upon Change in caps as they do in other parts of America" (Hamilton 1948, 134).

Facial hair was not worn. Philadelphia's Printing Office advertised imported "superfine Crown Soap" whose "Sweetness of the Flavor and the fine Lather it immediately produces, renders it pleasant for the Use of Barbers." The notice explains that the soap is excellent for cleaning fine linens, lace, and colored fabrics "that are apt to change by the Use of common Soap" (*Pennsylvania Gazette*, November 22, 1733).

Periwig and Peruke

The heavily curled full-bottomed periwig introduced in the 1670s went out of fashion during the 1720s, but it was still worn by elderly men and those in professions. By the 1730s, following British fashion, smaller and neatly styled peruke wigs were in vogue. The queue wig usually had only one plaited "tail" at the back. The hair of the tie, or tye, wig was drawn back to the nape of the neck and tied with a ribbon bow. The arrangement of hair in queue and tye wigs allowed a puff of hair to rise up from the hairline at the front. Similar puffs of hair around the ears were sometimes called pigeon wings. A rolled curl could be substituted for the puff at the sides of the head. The pigtail wig consisted of one or two pigtails made of the back hair, which were tightly wrapped from the hair ends to the base of the neck in a spiral manner with black silk ribbons and tied at the top with a ribbon bow.

The bag wig became popular at this time. The front and sides of the hair would be puffed or curled but the back hair was gathered up in a square or rectangular bag at the neck. The bag was tied with a drawstring and a black bow tied around the gathers. Not just for decoration, the bag also served to protect an expensive coat from the wig powder and grease. Reporting on the latest trends in wigs at a Court ball, in 1737, the *Virginia Gazette* offered that "tye Wiggs were pretty generally wore, with rising Foretops, with both Tyes behind, and tyed long and fuller; there were some Bag Wiggs" (February 25). In the 1740s, a bag wig might be large enough to cover most of the wearer's shoulders.

The wig of a well-to-do gentleman demanded care. It had to be sent to the barber or peruke maker to be brushed out and the curls rerolled onto heated clay rollers. A more destructive method was to curl the hair with cold rollers and then heat the entire wig. For formal occasions, the freshly cleaned and curled wig was donned by the fully clothed wearer—whose clothing was covered with a large cloth—and the wig was then powdered.

It is important to note that all ranks of men, even the enslaved, had access to and wore wigs. A peruke for the poorer sorts may have been made of animal instead of human hair or of tow (flax) fibers and sold cheaply, given by a master to a servant when it was outdated or heavily used, purchased as second-hand goods, or even won in a lottery. In Charleston, William Lasserre offered inexpensive imported wigs (*South-Carolina Gazette*, January 27, 1733). Shoemaker's apprentice Timothy Million, about 18, had a wig made of his own hair (*South-Carolina Gazette*, August 14, 1736). Two "Irish Servant Boys" aged 19 and 20, were described as wearing wigs when they deserted from the ship *Molly* in 1743 (*Boston News-Letter*, November 25, 1743).

Accessories, 1715–1750

The following examples, from the *Pennsylvania Gazette*, illustrate the variety of garters seen in the colonies. In 1737, John Crues, who passed himself off as a Quaker preacher, broke out of a New Jersey jail; among his clothing accessories was a pair of garters with "his name wove at full length" (August 18, 1737). John McColbem, and Irish indentured servant, had garters flowered green and yellow "and wears them commonly below his Knees" (June 7, 1744). Isaac Jones imported "broad, narrow, plain, letter'd and scarlet garters" (June 21, 1750).

Leather gloves of all kinds were available in wrist lengths or with high tops. Gentlemen could choose gloves of kid, dyed and white "shammie," glazed lamb, knitted silk, and buck skin. Heavier leather gloves were worn by working men to protect their hands.

Pocket handkerchiefs were worn and used by working sorts as well as gentlemen, as indicated by notices for runaway servants. Imported varieties during this period included silk in white, colors, and striped; muslin and calico; and linen. For formal occasions, a handkerchief might be edged with bobbin lace. In Pennsylvania a runaway servant made off with "two muslin Handkerchiefs, and a red silk One striped round the Edges" (*Pennsylvania Gazette*, July 11, 1734). In Pennsylvania an Irish servant wore a bandana—"a red spotted Silk Handkerchief"—around his neck when he ran away (*Pennsylvania Gazette*, July 6, 1739).

Walking canes were popular with gentlemen. The wooden staffs might be topped with carved wooden, bone, or ivory heads or with worked metal or stone heads, depending on the status and wealth of the owner. In New York, a Mrs. Balthaser Sommer fitted spy glasses on the tops of walking canes (*New-York Gazette or the Weekly Post-Boy*, May 21, 1753).

For the elite, gold and silver coat and waistcoat buttons, either dome shaped or flat, were the most fashionable. Wooden buttons covered with fabric or embroidery in silk or metal threads were also known. Throughout the century coat buttons were larger in diameter than waistcoat buttons. Lower class men and boys wore buttons of brass, white metal, pewter and other base metals. Jonas Osborn, a Dublin tape weaver, sold wove buttons of horsehair and gold, silver, silk, and linen frog closures (*Pennsylvania Gazette*, May 5, 1743).

Fashionable men carried hand muffs, which were made in a range of sizes and materials—fur, cloth, and cloth edged with fur. Williamsburg furrier Edward Morris dressed "all Sorts of Fur-Skins, for Muffs" (*Virginia Gazette*, June 22, 1739). In 1742, furrier Peter Ruston advertised that he made muffs for men or women (*New-York Weekly Journal*, November 22).

During the 1740s it became popular for men to carry a watch with a fob attached to it. The fob ribbon or chain hung out of the pocket in which the watch was kept. Attached to end of the ribbon or chain were one or more seals, often capped with deftly cut stones or steel to impress into sealing wax.

Main Garments, 1751–1785

In the final decades of the colonial period, a suit of clothes consisted of a coat, waistcoat, and breeches of matching or harmonizing fabrics.

Coat

By mid century, two kinds of coats were common: the close-fitting dress coat, collarless or with a stand collar, and the more relaxed frock coat, looser and with a turn-down collar. (The full-skirted style, with many pleats at the side and back, began to go out of fashion after 1750.) No longer buttoning all the way down, the coat fronts were curved from neck to hem. Two narrow pleats at each side seam (which moved further around the body toward the back) and at the center back reduced the width of the coat skirts and let the coat hang almost straight at the sides. Sleeves were wrist length and more closely fitted. Separate cuffs were still attached, but in the 1760s the cuffs became narrower and shorter. A narrow stand collar was added to the coat neckline in the 1760s. Peter Marsh, an indentured servant, ran away from his master in Trenton, New Jersey, wearing "a Half worn blue Broadcloth Coat, with short close Cuffs, long Waiste, and short Skirts" (*New-York Gazette or the Weekly Post-Boy*, April 5, 1764).

After 1770 the dress coat became even more trimly cut. No pleats were added at the center back, but two narrow pleats were at each side seam; these still fell toward the back of the coat. The back piece was once again cut closer to the straight grain of the cloth. The standing collar was higher, and cuffs were only four to five inches deep and might again be cut in one with the coat sleeve and turned up. Philadelphian Patrick Ternon offered 20 dollars reward in 1778 for the return of a "suit of brown cloth" stolen from him. The design was highly unusual for colonial clothing: "the coat remarkable by having embroidered flowers upon the breast, skirts and hips, with silver spangle buttons" (*Pennsylvania Packet*, November 28, 1778). This was most certainly a dress coat with a stand collar.

Frock coats with a turnover collar became the standard for everyday wear; later in the period, a higher collar that fell from a separate standing band replaced the turnover. Period descriptions of these garments suggest that they were available in a variety of weights, such as plain wool or worsted cloth, fustian, and bearskin.

Vest or Waistcoat

Vests changed significantly during this period. By 1760 the vest reached just below the hips. The front skirt was cut back sharply from the waist, and the buttons ended at the waist. The vest back was often made of an inexpensive fabric, such as holland or fustian. By 1770 the vest reached only a few inches below the waist and had a small stand collar. Since the skirt was so short, pocket flaps also became smaller. Vest backs might be only waist length. For cold weather, vests were lined in shag or another pile or napped fabric. In 1771, apprentice William Marshall owned two red broadcloth vests: one "almost new" with long skirts, mohair buttons, and no sleeves; the other short skirted and lapelled, with gilt buttons and new sleeves (*Pennsylvania Gazette*, June 13, 1771).

Among the more affluent, imported vests or vest shapes with embroidery in tambour work or colored silks and metallic threads were popular. In 1774, Boston tailor Benjamin Goldthwait announced the receipt of tambour-worked shapes for waistcoats (*Boston News-Letter*, May 19). In Philadelphia, James Wallace offered shapes of embroidered silk for waistcoats (*Pennsylvania Gazette*, June 21, 1750). Deware and Bacot offered two "handsome waistcoats," one embroidered with gold, the other with silver, to their Charleston customers (*South-Carolina Gazette*, June 18, 1763).

Jacket

In this period jackets were still worn by farmers, laborers, apprentices, the enslaved, seafarers, sportsmen, and others. They might be tied shut with worsted tapes or fastened with buttons. Occasionally, a jacket was described as being "without skirts." The term is also often used in a context that suggests a waistcoat. An indentured servant in New York City stole from his master "a silk Jacket of orange and purple Colour, with the back Parts of light colour'd Fustian" (*New-York Gazette Revived in the Weekly Post-Boy*, August 19, 1751). An Irish servant absented himself from his mistress, wearing a light-colored wool jacket with "home made pewter buttons" (*New-York Gazette and the Weekly Mercury*, July 2, 1770).

Underjacket

The cut, construction, fit, and use of an underjacket—apart from warmth—is not known. The terms underjacket and waistcoat or vest may have been used interchangeably. Governor Hutchinson of Massachusetts owned two sleeveless underwaistcoats, or camisols, of warm swansdown, a napped cloth made variously of wool and silk, wool and cotton or all cotton (Earle 1903, 2:405; Montgomery 1984, 354–55). These were faced with some "cheap silk or shag" suggesting they were not for show. In December 1774, a runaway apprentice wore a double-breasted white flannel underjacket with metal buttons (*Pennsylvania Gazette*, December 28).

Breeches or Small Clothes

In the 18th century the term "small clothes" was sometimes used in lieu of breeches, the former expression being considered more genteel. Breeches became progressively slimmer in the leg and seat during this period. In 1750, the seat was still quite full and there was room around the hips, but by 1785 the cut had been modified to make a more fitted garment. Breeches still had a waistband that narrowed from the front to the back and a fall front opening. The waistband split in the back and may have had a gusset inserted for adjustment with laces or a buttoned band. A watch pocket with a welt finish was sometimes stitched into the waistband above the level of the fall. Very fashionable men wore their breeches above the knee cap. In German-settled districts, breeches and trousers were often called *hosen*.

Leather breeches were everyday wear for a large portion of the male population in the colonies, from slaves, indentured servants, and apprentices to farmers and artisans and gentlemen. Cut in the same manner as cloth breeches, they were especially durable and could be cleaned and redyed for several years of use until they finally wore out. Leather breeches in brown, black, blue, and many other colors are mentioned in advertisements for the trades and runaways. A New York runaway servant was described as wearing "blue Plush Breeches pieced behind with Buck-Skin" (*New-York Journal or the General Advertiser*, April 15, 1773).

Trousers

As in the previous period, trousers were cut with a standard fall or fly front, laced or buckled back waistband; the straight legs reached to lower calf or ankle length. Trousers were made of coarser fabrics such as osnaburg, hempen linen, coarse country linen, ticking, and tow. The fabric was usually of one color, but checked and striped trousers appear in advertisements. At the occasion of the launch of a new brig in Halifax, Nova Scota, the carpenters who built the ship attended the event wearing "clean white Frocks and Trowsers, Clean ruffle Shirts, and Gold-laced Hats" (*Boston Gazette*, July 2, 1751). David Kelly, an apprentice, ran from his Long Island master wearing striped coarse linen trousers (*New-York Journal or the General Advertiser*, August 6, 1767).

Outer Breeches, Slops, and Overalls

Outer breeches, slops, and overalls were all protective garments used by sailors, farmers, and laborers. A looser fitting version of breeches or trousers (without a fall front or fly opening with placket), overalls opened down the center front and had slits in the seams to allow the wearer to reach the pockets of the garment underneath. Sherryvallies were a type of outer breeches or trousers that buttoned all the way up the outer leg and protected a man's good clothing from the mud and dust kicked up when he rode.

Outer Garments, 1751–1785

Cloaks, overcoats, pea coats, and fly coats—all are represented in merchants' and shopkeepers' notices in the last decades of the colonial period. Although men continued to wear cloaks at this time, most of the ready-made cloaks advertised for sale in the colonies were for women. In the early 1750s, tailors produced overcoats with double or triple capes. These were also double-breasted and had large lapels that were turned back on each shoulder. No longer belted, they still had a back vent for riding. The pea coat continued to be a preferred outerwear garment for those in the maritime trades as well as for servants and the enslaved. No single color or type of cloth characterized fly coats at this time. Nor were details of cut and construction mentioned. In the newspapers, they were described variously as lead colored; black and white homespun; light-colored country cloth lined with linsey; brown fustian; and white Wilton. A fly coat sometimes was worn over a jacket. In 1753, John Maylam, who served a peruke maker in Boston, ran away wearing "a Fly Cloth colour'd Coat and Breeches, a blew Jacket and grey rib'd Stockings" (*Boston Gazette*, February 20, 1753).

Frock, Hunting Frock, Hunting Shirt

The frock remained a protective overshirt for working men. In New England, striped frocking was still popular among farmers. Rev. Joseph Kidder, who preached in Dunstable, Massachusetts, beginning in 1767, recalled that when he opened a town meeting with prayer, "a half an acre of striped frocking rose up before him" (Goodale).

Similar to a frock but buttoning down the front, the hunting shirt was also common among farmers and servants; it became an important garment for patriot soldiers during the American Revolution. In 1768, George Wilkinson, an English convict banished to Virginia, ran away wearing a hunting shirt, buckskin breeches, and a calico waistcoat (*Virginia Gazette*, June 30). Thomas Welsh absented himself from his master clad in a "hunting shirt filled with wool, buckskin breeches, linsey leggings, a wool hat, and his shoes nailed all round, both heels and soles" (*Virginia Gazette*, June 30, 1775). In his general orders to headquarters in New York, in 1776, George Washington expressed his reluctance to recommend any kind of uniform for his troops due to the difficulty and expense of providing such garments. To his mind, a decent alternative was "the use of Hunting Shirts, with long Breeches, made of the same Cloth, Gaiter fashion about the Legs. . . . No Dress can be had cheaper, nor more convenient, as the Wearer may be cool in warm weather, and warm in cool weather by putting on under Cloaths which will not change the outward dress. . . . Besides which it is a dress justly supposed to carry no small terror to the enemy, who think every such person a complete Marksman" (Washington 1776).

During the American Revolution, Colonel John Trumbull (1756–1843), an artist who served under George Washington and Horatio Gates, wrote a letter in which he clarified the difference between a frock and a hunting shirt:

You expressed an apprehension, that the rifle-dress of General Morgan [Daniel Morgan, 1736–1802] may be mistaken hereafter for a wagoner's frock, which he, perhaps, wore when on the expedition with General Braddock; there is no more resemblance between the two dresses, than between a cloak and a coat; the wagoner's frock was intended, as the present cartman's, to cover and protect their other clothes, and is merely a long coarse shirt reaching below the knee; the dress of the Virginia rifle-men who came to Cambridge in 1775 . . . was an elegant loose dress reaching to the middle of the thigh, ornamented with fringes in various parts, and meeting the pantaloons of the same material and color, fringed and ornamented in a corresponding style. The officers wore the usual crimson sash over this, and around the waist. . . . It cost a trifle; the soldier could wash it at any brook he passed; and however worn and ragged and dirty his other clothing might be, when this was thrown over it, he was in elegant uniform. (quoted in Longacre and Herring 1836, 3:18)

Undergarments, 1751–1785

Shirts were still cut along the same lines as in the first half of the century although they may have been cut with less fullness through the body and in the sleeves to accommodate the now more closely fitting coats and breeches. High turndown collars and wristbands with sleeve ruffles and shirt front ruffles were still in vogue for the best linen shirts, but plain shirts were often mentioned. In some cases the ruffles were made of a much finer linen than the body of the shirt and were sometimes detachable. Two buttons at the neck and one each at the wrist held the shirt closed. These buttons were made of bone, shell, glass, or linen thread wrapped and interlaced over a stiff flat core. Wristbands or longer turn-back cuffs might also be held closed with a pair of cuff buttons made of metal and sometimes embellished with gemstones. Checked, striped, and colored shirts of linen and woolen fabrics without any ornamentation were worn by those engaged in physical labor.

In 1769, Boston goldsmith Benjamin Tappan (1747–1831) moved to North Hampton, Massachusetts and attended a church meeting there for the first time; he was surprised to find that all the men but four or five wore checked shirts. He remarked that men from Worcester County, however, always wore white shirts and considered a checked shirt the mark "of a Connecticut River man" (quoted in Earle 1989, 238). Complaining of the cold during a raw New England June in 1771, John Adams recorded in his diary that he had ridden to Boston in a cloth coat and waistcoat, but had put on a thick flannel shirt once he arrived (Adams 1771).

Common in the colonies during this period, linen drawers were made either knee length to wear under breeches, or longer, perhaps to wear under trousers or as undress. Silk drawers are also mentioned in inventories and correspondence. Savannah merchant James Habersham (1712–1775) gave instructions to the London agent whose tailor was making Habersham some new clothes in 1767: "I need not mention, as we all wear Drawers here, that the breeches are not to be lined, and care will be taken to line the seams with something strong" (Habersham 1904, 62).

The long and loose-fitting banyan continued to be worn in every season as an undress garment over a shirt and breeches. They were offered in linen, cotton, wool, or silk fabrics, from plain colored cloths to printed, striped, or plaid material. Banyans for cooler weather were lined. Horse thief Neal McMullen of Londonderry, New Hampshire, sometimes wore "a banyan and ruffles" (*Pennsylvania Gazette*, May 16, 1751). A runaway indentured servant took with him a "shalloon banyan, striped red and yellow, lined thro' with gingham" (*Pennsylvania Gazette*, May 24, 1753). A "striped Damascus night gown" was stolen from Levi Hollingsworth's stores in 1778 (*Pennsylvania Packet*, December 10, 1778). In 1756, 29-year-old Ezra Stiles, the Newport cleric who later moved to Yale College, was painted by Smibert in a yellow damask banyan, possibly the one given to him by his Newport parishioners.

Neck- and Wrist-Wear, 1751–1785

The high collar of the formal shirt was concealed by either the wrapped and tied cravat or by a stock.

Enslaved workers and tradesmen often wore over or under the turned-down collars of their shirts a square of cloth called a neck handkerchief. (The neck handkerchief was also worn informally by gentlemen.) Usually of linen but sometimes cotton or silk, this square was folded diagonally, wrapped from the back of the neck to the front, and tied in a double knot. The ends were left hanging down the outside of the shirt front. Neckerchiefs of all colors and fabrics were used. Plain white, black, striped and plaid cottons and linens; spotted calicos from India; printed cottons from England; and black, white, or colored silks from China—all figure in inventories and advertisements. Neckerchiefs usually ran between 23 and 30 inches square, or very close to square. Selvages were used as finished edges, but cut ends were finished with narrow hems. Thomas Willing sold "figured and spotted bandanoe and Barcelona" handkerchiefs (*Pennsylvania Gazette*, January 1, 1756). In 1756, a convict servant, Benjamin Hensly, wore a lungi (a lightweight silk or cotton fabric) handkerchief about his neck and carried with him several muslin cravats (*Pennsylvania Gazette*, January 29). An English convict servant in Virginia, a barber by trade, absented himself from his master wearing a red and white handkerchief "with a hunting Song [printed] round the Borders of it" (*Virginia Gazette*, March 19, 1772).

Attached ruffles of linen for daywear and detachable ruffles of lace for formal occasions were still in fashion among gentlemen but disappeared in the 1780s. The working sorts generally wore their shirts with plain wristbands.

Headwear, 1751–1785

The tricorne continued to be popular until the end of the 18th century among all men who could afford to purchase one. Typically, the hat was worn with a point facing forward although soldiers might adjust the hat so that when they leaned a rifle or musket on the shoulder, the gun would clear the hat.

As part of gentleman's informal dress, caps were made of silk—plain, embroidered, or lace embellished—velvet, calico, worsted wool, and linen. Furrier Alexander Solomons made caps of fur and cloth caps lined with fur (*New-York Gazette*, October 26, 1761). The cap of a working man, whether free or enslaved, might be of knitted wool, worsted, or cut and sewn from cotton or linen cloth. An enslaved field worker ran away from the plantation he was working on with "an indico bag for a cap" (*South-Carolina Gazette*, September 24, 1753). Irish servant John Galohown ran from his master carrying several linen caps marked IG (*Pennsylvania Gazette*, September 19, 1754). William Wilson sold "mens red and blue and Germantown pattern worsted caps" (*Pennsylvania Gazette*, October 16, 1760). An enslaved boy, about 14 years of age, ran away from his Virginia master, taking a leather cap (*Virginia Gazette*, February 11, 1775). Hugh Rennals, who had been confined for stealing, broke out of jail wearing an old fur cap (*Pennsylvania Gazette*, October 14, 1756).

When skirmishes increased between colonists and Indians and the French, merchants begin to advertise clothing accessories for those settlers joining in the fight. Leather caps, "very convenient for Soldiers" were offered at auction in Boston in 1757 (*Boston Gazette*, March 14). During the French and Indian Wars, reports of the fighting in newspapers often noted that the soldiers wore red caps. In 1756, a small party of Indians masqueraded as soldiers, "dressed in red Caps" attacked a small town in Maryland at the mouth of the Conococheague Creek (*Pennsylvania Gazette*, August 12, 1756).

Footwear, 1751–1785

By the 1750s, shopkeepers were advertising stockings using an array of bewildering descriptive terms. In 1762, one assortment of men's stockings were described as "plain, mixt, motled, diced and peck'd" (*Boston Gazette*, January 25).The practice of ornamenting stockings with clocks continued. In 1764, Mr. Beall's Stocking Manufactory, in Annapolis, Maryland, made and sold knitted linen stockings with "AMERICA" worked vertically in stacked letters instead of patterned clocks (*New-York Gazette or the Weekly Post-Boy*, August 30, 1764). Well-to-do artisans and those traveling in the country might wish to wear leather stockings to protect the legs. Philip Freeman of Boston advertised leather stockings of different colors, including black, buff, and yellow in 1754 (*Boston Gazette*, June 25).

By the last decades of the colonial period, shoes and pumps had a much more rounded and natural shape in the toe. In addition to the heavier jackboots, at about midcentury, the elegant top boot became popular. The lower part of the boot, which fitted tightly over the leg, was constructed of black leather, which was usually polished. The top part of the boot—from the middle of the calf to just below the knee—was either brown or white leather. Spatterdashes were leggings of canvas or leather worn to protect stockings and breeches from mud.

The account book kept by Deerfield, Massachusetts, resident Ebenezer Arms recorded his transactions for making and repairing footwear for his neighbors. His handiwork included shoes, pumps, hightop shoes and boots, sandals, child's stitchdowns, and girl's red shoes. He also soled shoes, including slave shoes. A snapshot of these transactions reveals the balance among these tasks: in January 1751, he made 24 pairs of shoes, mended 19 pair, and soled 15 (Arms).

Moccasins and shoe packs became more common footwear in the second half of the 18th century. In Pennsylvania, indentured runaways were reported wearing or carrying shoe packs in 1751, 1768, and 1778 (*Pennsylvania Gazette*, August 1, 1751; June 23, 1768; *Pennsylvania Packet*, October 22, 1778). In Williamsburg, an Irish indentured servant, Andrew Kelly, wore "buckskin mockasons" when he ran away to enlist with British troops (*Virginia Gazette*, September 20). An enslaved servant involved in a theft in Charleston in 1760 had on a pair of Indian boots, which were likely moccasins and leggings (*South-Carolina Gazette*, February 16, 1760).

In 1777, a deserter from the continental regulars in Washington County, Virginia, dressed in a white hunting shirt, leather leggings, and moccasins (*Virginia Gazette*, July 3). During the French and Indian Wars, Adam Stephen reported to George Washington on Fort Cumberland, Maryland "The Indians discover our Parties by the Track of their Shoes, It would be a good thing to have Shoe-packs or Moccosons for the Scouts" (Stephen 1755). In 1775, Englishman Nicholas Cresswell (1750–1804), sailed to America and traveled for the next three years throughout Virginia, Pennsylvania, and Maryland. The rigors of traveling in the interior had worn out his shoes, and his clothing had been reduced to "three ragged shirts, two pair linen breeches in the same condition, a hunting shirt and jacket, with one pair of stockings." Encountering a small group of Indians, he "Employed an Indian woman to make me a pair of Mocheysons and Leggings" (Cresswell 2007, 97, 102).

Hairstyles and Grooming, 1751–1785

Although endless variations of queue and bag wigs were in style at the beginning of this period, in the 1770s many men began to wear their own hair. The exceptions to this were men in the professions and perhaps the elderly. Those who could afford to do so had their hair dressed in the style of the peruke—with puffs, rolls, queues, bags, and pigtails. And for formal occasions the hair was still powdered (this practice did not cease until a tax was levied on hair powder in England in 1795). In 1771, William Marshall, an apprentice to the trade of chaise and chair making in Pennsylvania, wore his own brown hair straight, "tied or cued [i.e., queued] behind" (*Pennsylvania Gazette*, June 13). In 1775, William Bateman, an indentured servant skilled in jewelry making and lapidary work, wore his own brown hair tied back (*New-York Gazette and the Weekly Mercury*, March 6).

A study of Georgia probate inventories between 1754 and 1778 found that by the beginning of the American Revolution wigs commonly were no longer worn by Georgia men. Of 39 inventories entered between 1754 and 1759, only 11 listed wigs. In the 1760s, when Georgia's population began to swell, of 148 inventories only 10 listed wigs. No wigs were at all found in 62 inventories dating from 1776 to 1778 (Davis 1976, 65–66).

Accessories, 1751–1785

Leather aprons are most commonly found in advertisements and inventories, although coarse linen fabrics such as osnaburg or duck also appear.

For example, Michael McGuire, a servant living near York, Pennsylvania, left his master wearing a half-worn leather apron that was scalloped around the edge (*Pennsylvania Gazette*, March 19, 1751). In 1752, Jacob Stroud jumped bail in Philadelphia wearing worn clothing that included a calf skin apron and old leather breeches (*Pennsylvania Gazette*, February 11). William Smith, an indentured servant living in Chester County, Pennsylvania, ran off wearing a new deerskin apron over his patched breeches (*Pennsylvania Gazette*, April 7, 1763).

"Lettered, striped, and scarlet" knee garters were still fashionable at the close of the colonial period (*Pennsylvania Gazette*, August 14, 1760). Stolen from Ellis Davies in Chester County, Pennsylvania, was a pair of "new red and blue Garters, with the Subscriber Name at large Wove in them" (*Pennsylvania Gazette*, February 11, 1762). An Irish servant to a Maryland shoemaker ran off with "Plaid Garters tying them at the Knees" (*Pennsylvania Gazette*, May 13, 1762). Mary Perrey advertised in Charleston that she wove garters for ladies and gentlemen, "with their names, or any posy on them" (*South-Carolina Gazette*, January 22, 1763).

Leather gloves and mittens, often of lambskin, were offered by merchants and shopkeepers. Robert Levers of Philadelphia imported "black, white and cloth coloured silk mittens figured and plain" (*Pennsylvania Gazette*, May 22, 1760). John Morrison, a runaway weaver from Chester County, Pennsylvania, owned a pair of blue and red mittens, "knit in diamonds, with his name near the fringe" (*Pennsylvania Gazette*, November 29, 1770). An enslaved man working in Virginia absented himself wearing "a pair of red flannel muffs;" these were likely muffatees, or fingerless mittens (*Virginia Gazette*, April 19, 1770). In 1774, an apprentice cooper named John Marks ran away from his master taking a pair of knitted mittens with the letters C:NE and the figures 1771 knitted into them (*Pennsylvania Gazette*, December 28, 1774). Muffs continued to be an accessory for fashionable men. Alexander Solomons advertised to his New York customers that he made fur trimmings for cloaks to match the muff (*New-York Gazette*, October 26, 1761).

John Morton Jordan of Annapolis, Maryland left "goods and chattels" worth more than £1820 in 1771. His jewelry and accessories were valued at more than £32: a silver mounted sword and silk belt and a mourning sword with a red leather belt; a gold watch with two seals and a steel chain; a gold stock buckle, two pair of shoe buckles, one silver and one brass, a pair of silver knee buckles set with stones; a pair of gold sleeve buttons; and a gold brooch (Inventory of . . . John Morton Jordan). Six robbers broke into the house of John Morton of Baskenridge, New Jersey, in 1782, taking, among many other things, five pairs of buckles, described as large square silver, round silver, paste, and two pairs of plated square; two gold rings and a gold locket; and a gold watchcase with a London maker's mark (*Pennsylvania Gazette*, May 1, 1782).

During the last decades of the colonial period, buttons were primarily flat and not domed. Metal buttons might be base metal (white metal), brass, gilt metal, or silver. Embroidered buttons might be made to match a dress suit, or have basket-weave or knot-patterned surfaces. The firm of Rhea and Wikoff offered "silk and hair death head buttons" and buttons of black horn (*Pennsylvania Gazette*, June 5, 1755). John Bayly sold "chrystal stone sleeve buttons" (*Pennsylvania Gazette*, December 11, 1755). John Edwards, a "well made Englishman" in the maritime trades, jumped bail wearing a "brown broadcloth coat with large wood or horn buttons set in the center with moth-apearl or silver" (*Pennsylvania Gazette*, February 16, 1780).

CLOTHING IN PORTRAITURE, 1751–1785

John Greenwood was a Boston portrait painter who lived in Surinam, in Dutch Guiana, an important port for the coastal trading vessels that transported goods between New England and Caribbean ports. In the 1750s, a group of Rhode Island ship captains, all from the upper levels of Rhode Island society, commissioned a group portrait of themselves. Greenwood painted the men not as if they were at home in formal dress, but in a satirical scene depicting them in various degrees of intoxication, carousing in a tavern. The sitters wear clothing of differing degrees of formality. In the rear of the scene a man dressed in a printed calico banyan tied with a cord at the waist, with his own hair hanging loosely down his back, receives a drinking bowl from a serving man behind the bar. The men at the tables in the foreground all wear knee breeches over white stockings and black shoes with buckles. Their white shirts have ruffled fronts and sleeve hems; most of them wear a cravat tied around their necks. Some wear coats with wide cuffs and pleated skirts just above knee-length over their waistcoats; others wear shorter coats—which could be considered jackets—that reach below the hips, also over waistcoats. Black tricorne hats are hung on the walls and on many heads, but one man wears a light-colored hat with a wide flat brim, and another wears an undress cap. Some wear their own hair tied back in a queue, others wear wigs (white or powdered). Their clothes are shades of brown, blue, gray, and a light tan, with some red and black. The shirts and stockings are uniformly white; the shoes are black.

Other portraits of upper-class men at home give a more sedate view of fashionable dress. A drawing by George Roupell, dating to about 1760, of

South Carolina planter Peter Manigault and his male friends at a drinking party, shows them in dress clothing: coats with pleated skirts and full cuffs, waistcoats, and breeches, shirts with sleeve ruffles, white stockings and black shoes, and hair dressed in rolls and queues. An enslaved servant boy dressed in livery dozes on a window seat.

New Yorker Cadwallader Colden was painted by Matthew Pratt in about 1772, seated at a table with his grandson, Warren De Lancey, by his side. In this informal pose Colden wears a double (reversible) banyan—the interior appears to be of blue silk damask, and a pinkish-plum figured cloth that may be a woolen is on the exterior. His breeches are covered by the banyan, but his white shirt with ruffled sleeve hems and white cravat at the neck create a foil for the bright orange-red of his waistcoat, which is a plain duff-surfaced fabric, probably broadcloth, with small gold metal buttons. His hair may be his own, brushed back from his face and ending below the ears in a single loose roll.

Two portraits by Charles Willson Peale illustrate the typical everyday suit of the professional, landed, and merchant classes. John Beale Bordley of Maryland was painted in 1770 wearing a rich brown coat, waistcoat, and breeches. His waistcoat is buttoned up to his throat; only a white stock and short sleeve ruffles show of his linen. White silk stockings and low-heeled black shoes with metal buckles complete his outfit. His hair is of its natural color, cut short in front and brushed back in waves over his collar. Samuel Mifflin of Philadelphia sat for his portrait between 1777 and 1780. His gray-brown suit bespeaks a wartime plainness of dress: a coat with a narrow stand collar and narrow cuffs, a waistcoat, and breeches. Although his breeches fasten at the knees with silver buckles, the breeches' buttons as well as those of coat and waistcoat all appear to be covered with cloth or thread to match the cloth. Aside from the silver buckles, the only evidences of wealth are his very fine linen shirtfront and sleeve ruffles and his white silk stockings. Miflin, too, wears his own hair, cut short on his forehead and brushed back over his ears to fall at the nape of his neck.

In contrast, John Singleton Copley's 1778 narrative painting *Watson and the Shark* illustrates a number of variations for workingmen's dress. The two men leaning over the edge of the boat to haul the hapless Watson out of the water wear white shirts, clearly of different fabrics, with full sleeves and colored neckcloths or bandannas, as does a boy at the oars. An older man wears what appears to be an overcoat above an open shirt, and two men in jackets and breeches man the oars. Two men stand: one is dressed in the sailor's garb of white canvas slops over full breeches, a short jacket over a shirt, and the low-cut shoes called pumps; the other wear trousers

Watson and the Shark by John Singleton Copley, 1778. Museum of Fine Arts Boston, 89.481. (Corbis)

and a shirt with a flowing neckcloth. All of these men wear their own hair, short in the front and longer at the back.

CLOTHING FOR THE ENSLAVED, 1715–1785

The best 18th-century sources for what enslaved individuals—American Indian as well as African—wore are newspaper advertisements, because notices for runaways almost always describe their clothing. This statement must be qualified, however. Unless a notice is explicit, it cannot be determined whether what the individual wore was all he owned; in other words, was his flight so unplanned that there was no time for packing. If a runaway did manage to carry away additional attire, did these garments belong to him or had he absconded with clothing from the household.

As with clothing for enslaved females, there seems to have been no uniform slave clothing among runaways belonging to northern masters, and at least some of them were decently dressed. This was due to the conditions under which they lived and worked. In the north, many slaves lived in more populated areas and probably worked in the artisan trades if not in households. A mulatto man servant who left his master in Scituate, Massachusetts, in 1739 wore a blue broadcloth coat with a black and white flannel jacket, a white flannel shirt, a pair of trousers, old stockings and shoes, a felt hat, and a worsted cap (*Boston News-Letter*, November 22, 1739). When he left Springfield, Massachusetts, in May of the same year, another enslaved male had on a faded gray drugget coat, striped calamanco waistcoat, "fine" shirt, stockings, good leather breeches and shoes, and a felt hat; by the following March, his master, still advertising for his return, thought that his clothes would be "most of them worn out" (*Boston News-Letter*, March 6, 1740). An Indian servant had not fared as well with clothing distribution. He owned a felt hat, orange-colored jacket, thick leather breeches with a patch in the crotch of shoe leather, a checkered shirt of wool, "pretty good" shoes, and light gray stockings whose tops had been grafted with the tops from another pair (*Boston News-Letter*, October 21, 1735).

A Boston shipwright's servant named Jack, a "Spanish Negro," wore a blue cloth jacket with red buttonholes and brass buttons, a homespun jacket, black breeches, a checked wool shirt, light blue stockings, a beaver hat, and "double channel pumps with large brass buckles" (*Boston News-Letter*, July 17, 1740) Sampson, aged 23, left Sudbury wearing a cap and a castor hat, a dark wool coat with plain white metal buttons, a blue cloth jacket with brass and wood buttons, a cotton and linen shirt, white cotton stockings, leather breeches, and "a pair of double sol'd turn'd pumps" (*Boston News-Letter*, June 23, 1743). An unnamed slave, trained as a cooper, ran away from a Newbury, Massachusetts, master wearing a cotton and linen shirt, black jacket, and white bays breeches. He, however, must have been an intrepid runner because he had been branded with the letters I.G. by one master and the shape of a crow's foot by a second; his third master had placed "four Chains of a Scale Beam lock'd about his neck" (*Boston News-Letter*, March 5, 1730).

In September 1764, a 19-year-old enslaved man, "this country born" named Abraham, ran away, supposedly in the company of a deserter from the army. This likely was not Abraham's first attempt at finding freedom; the first item mentioned in his description is an "Iron Collar," which was usually fastened on as a punishment for attempted escapes. He also wore buckskin breeches, stockings, shoes with white metal buckles, and a blanket coat. The suspicion of the deserter came from the theft from a tailor's shop in Philadelphia of a number of garments, not suspiciously new, but old and worn. These included a blue coat lined with white, a scarlet jacket, black cloth and nankeen breeches, and a light-colored coat with horn buttons. A soldier's coat was found abandoned on the outskirts of the town (*Pennsylvania Gazette,* October 11, 1764).

In southern colonies the clothing allotments for those in rural conditions were limited but standardized in terms of fabric. Some masters provided fieldworkers with two sets of clothes—or the fabric to make clothes— coarse linen for summer and wool for winter; others provided one set or none. In 1742, Pastor John Martin Boltzius (1703–1765), who was living in Ebenezer, Georgia, traveled to Charleston. In his diary he observed that many plantation slaves in the Lowcountry "receive no clothes from their master but must work on Sunday too, and afterwards they turn their crops into money and buy themselves some old rags" (Bolzius 1981, 104). In a recorded interview, however, Bolzius noted that enslaved men in the Lowcountry received five yards of white or blue "Negro cloth"—enough to make a coat and trousers—and a pair of shoes. In summer, they might receive another pair of trousers and a cap (Bolzius 1957, 256).

In 1764, John Habersham wrote his agent and friend William Knox from Savannah to order slave clothing. Noting that the governor of the colony and others wished to "cloth our Negroes a little better than common," Habersham proposed to have the clothing made up in London rather than cut and sewn in the colony. He ordered "120 mens Jackets and Breeches . . . of which at least 1/2 for middle sized or fourth for the larger, the remaining fourth for the smaller size." He hoped that the London fabric would be "at least stronger and more durable and consequently warmer and more comfortable" (Habersham 1904, 16).

Charleston merchant and planter—and later President of the Continental Congress—Henry Laurens (1724–1792) owned a considerable number of plantation slaves. In 1778, he had on hand 734 yards of imported coarse linen cloth and homespun for clothing for these people. His close friend and business associate John Lewis Gervais suggested that the men's jackets should be made "like Sailor Jackets which saved about half Yard to each," which suggests that the jackets were to pull over the head rather than button down the front (quoted in Starr 1965, 33).

Those who placed runaway notices for enslaved field workers sometimes commented on the condition of slaves' clothing. For example, Pompey, who had been in South Carolina only about seven months, left wearing "a white Negro Cloth Jacket and Breeches, but almost worn out, and a blue and white Negro Cloth Cap" (*South Carolina Gazette,* June 30, 1733). In 1735, four enslaved workers ran away from their master's plantation and all "had on new Jackets and Breeches made of Negro cloath" (*South-Carolina Gazette,* February 22, 1735). An enslaved runaway named July was captured and brought to the Charleston work house wearing white "Negro Cloth" jacket and breeches, "very ragged" (*South-Carolina Gazette,* October 9, 1740).

In southern colonial towns, however, like Norfolk, Charleston, and Savannah, opportunities for the enslaved were wider and as a result, individuals accumulated a greater variety of clothing. This resulted in the motley appearance demonstrated in so many descriptions in runaway notices of the 18th century. Primus absented himself from his master in Charleston clad in a "speckled shirt, and strip'd shirt, and strip'd Linnen Jacket and Breeches" (*South-Carolina Gazette,* January 20, 1733). In 1767, Peter ran away from his master in Virginia to see his wife and children in North Carolina wearing a "Newmarket bearskin coat, and blue and red waistcoats, osnabrugs breeches, country made shoes, white stockings, and generally wore a cocked hat" (*Virginia Gazette,* January 8). A mulatto slave named David Gratenread, who "plays the fiddle extremely well," left his master carrying "a new brown cloth waistcoat, lappelled, lined with white taminy, and yellow gilt buttons, a new pair of buckskin breeches, gold laced hat, a fine Holland shirt, brown cut wig, and several old clothes that I cannot remember, except an old lappelled kersey waistcoat" (*Virginia Gazette,* May 7, 1767). One of the most distinctive coats was worn by James, who left his master in Albemarle County, Virginia, wearing an osnaburg shirt, cotton jacket and breeches, and a coat with "Hearts on the Hips behind, and on the Shoulders, doubled and quilted, with horn Buttons" (*Virginia Gazette,* April 18, 1771).

Some enslaved were bequeathed clothing in their master's wills. In 1769, George Seaman of Charleston owned over 221 slaves. Nineteen of these lived with him in his house in Charleston; the remainder worked on one of four plantations which he owned. In his will he stipulated that £100 should be spent "by my executors in London to buy coarse Linnens, Checks, large Coarse Hatts, Oxnabrigs, Thread, Needles, Pipes, Coarse Handerchiefs, &c. which with remaining part of my apparel, I desire to be divided among such of my negroes as are deserving" (Withington 1907, 8:216).

Livery, a special category of slave clothing, was a uniform worn by household slaves whose occupations made them highly visible. The three-piece livery suit, usually constructed of broadcloth, shag, or velvet, often featured collar, cuffs, and sometimes the waistcoat of a contrasting color. The clothes were often embellished with elaborate woven tapes called livery lace and brass buttons. In 1773, James Minzies wrote London merchant John Norton to order livery for Governor Lord Dunmore's servants. With the letter Minzies enclosed samples of the colors of cloth and sizes; "I hope you will if possible send them in time that we may not be under the Necessity of buying their winter Cloathing here." The order was as follows:

> 60 Yds. Silver lace
> 30 Yrds. Blue Cloath for foot-Men
> 30 Do. [i.e., ditto] Brown do. for do.
> 6 Pieces of Brown Jeans for do.
> 1 Piece of Green Shag for do. 1 do.
> Blue do. for do.
> 30 Yds. Strip'd flannel for Grooms Waistcoats
> Lining Buttons &c for the liverys. (Norton 1937, 330)

CLOTHING OF AMERICAN INDIANS, 1715–1785

"Any Person inclinable to go out with an Indian trading Cargo, shall be furnished with an Assortment of very good Goods and at a reasonable Rate" (Joseph Dowding, *South-Carolina Gazette*, July 30, 1737).

As noted in Chapter 2, as the Indian trade expanded, trade goods were available on a more regular basis. By the late 17th century, Native Americans could also acquire ready-made woolen coats with seams and sleeves, linen shirts, worsted caps, stockings, and shoes. To trim and ornament this apparel, they purchased yards of colorful silk ribbons, laces and tapes, bells, buttons, and beads. Advertisements in Pennsylvania and South Carolina newspapers confirm the central place of textiles in the Indian trade in the 1700s. Between 1740 and 1775, the *Pennsylvania Gazette* carried notices for Indian blanketing—both striped and plain—red and blue shags, blue strouds, and striped duffels. In 1760, William West enumerated a variety of goods he carried: "A LARGE assortment of fine, super and superfine broadcloths, low priced scarlet, blue and cloth coloured cloths, strouds, match coats, vermilion, bed lace, gartering, ribbons, 3 qr. and 7 8ths garlix, and other sorts of Indian goods" (June 26). Mease and Miller offered at "exceeding low" prices "best French matchcoats, blue, red and black strouds, purple and white napt halfthicks, scarlet, rose, star and striped gartering, bed lace, [and] taffety ribbons" (January 22, 1767). Francis and Tilghman included "twilled blanketing, rings, jews harps, and Morrice bells" in their stock of trade goods (September 22, 1768). Philip Wilson carried ribbons, lace, beads by the pound, linens, and cottons by the piece, and Yorkshire woolens for the trade (May 16, 1771). From 1732 to 1765, the *South-Carolina Gazette*'s advertisements for Indian trade goods featured strouds; white, blue, green, and striped plains; striped, red, and blue duffels; shags; belts and girdles; looking glasses; narrow and broad caddice; and checked and white shirts. Merchant Peter Horry advertised "strip'd & blew duffils, blew & red strouds, vermillion, bowdy cadiz, Indian belts, stockings, knives, handkerchiefs, glasses & bead of various sorts, blew green brown & scarlet knapp'd witneys" (December 13, 1735). The firm of Macartan and Campbell also specialized in goods for the Indian trade, noting in their advertisements "They take in payment DEER and BEAVER SKINS . . . and will purchase any quantity of DEER and BEAVER SKINS with cash" (June 17, 1756). Jeweler John Paul Grimké carried "Silver Indian ear rings"; and "Arm and wrist bands, or breast plates for Indians" (February 5, 1753; April 14, 1757).

In 1732, South Carolina traders were exchanging a yard of strouds for five doe skins or a buckskin weighing the equivalent and a yard of woolen plains for one buckskin weighing "1 lb. 3 qrs. or Doe-skins answerable [i.e., the number of doe skins equal to a buck skin in weight]," the "Doe-skins not to weigh under 1 lb." (reported in the *Pennsylvania Gazette*, July 31, 1732). An examination of the prices for goods used in the Cherokee deer skin trade in South Carolina, drawn up in 1751, reveals the variety of textiles available to the Cherokee in exchange for buck and doe skins, the quantities strictly regulated by the colony's Commissioner for the Indian Trade (McDowell 1958, 166):

A Blanket	3 Bucks or 6 Does
2 Yards Strouds	3 Bucks or 6 Does
A Garlix Shirt	2 Do. or 4 Does
Osnbrigs, 1 Yard	1 Doe Skin
1 Pr. of Hose	1 Buck and one Doe, or 3 Does, &c.
Handkerchiefs of India	2 Bucks
Ditto, common	Ditto
2 yrds stript Flannen [i.e., flannel]	2 Bucks or 4 Does
Fine Rufel Shirts	4 Bucks or 8 Does
Callicoes	2 Bucks or 4 Does
Callicoes	Ditto, 1 Buck and 1 Doe, or 3 Does
Fine Ribands	1 Buck 2 Yards, or 4 Does
Gartring	2 Bucks per piece or 4 Does
Caddice Ditto	2 Bucks or 4 Does per piece
2 Yards stompt [i.e., stamped] Flanen	2 Bucks or 4 Does
Worsted Caps	1 Buck and 1 Doe or 3 Does

About two yards of strouds were required for a matchcoat, one quarter yard for a flap, or men's breechcloth (Braund 1993, 123). Stroud yardage was also fashioned into men's leggings. Three yards of the sturdy linen called osnaburg made a plain shirt. Calicoes, of cotton, could be made into shirts and waistcoats. Ribbons, gartering, and caddice tape all were used for bindings and hair ornaments. Handkerchiefs, also called neck handkerchiefs, could be used as shawls and to bind around the head for a turban-like effect. On average, a Cherokee could kill about 30 white-tailed deer per year (Reid 1976, 85). Thus, a Native hunter might spend much of what he earned in a year to clothe himself and his wife.

The Englishman Nicholas Cresswell was briefly involved in the deerskin trade in 1775. He was informed by his guide, John Anderson, that he could not venture into Indian territory wearing a hunting shirt, so he procured "a Calico shirt made in the Indian fashion, trimmed up with Silver Brooches and Armplates so that I scarcely know myself" as well as a "Calico short Breechclout, leggings, and Mockesons" (Cresswell 2007, 103, 109).

Discussions in Chapter 2 emphasized the importance of sartorial gifts in treaty negotiations between American Indians and the British government. In 1762, Cunne Shote (also known as Cumnacatogue or Stalking Turkey), an important headman among the Cherokee, traveled from South Carolina with two other headmen to the court of George III to reaffirm a peace treaty between the British and the Cherokee that previously had been agreed to in Williamsburg, Virginia. While in London, Cunne Shote sat for a portrait by artist Francis Parsons. The sitter's wearing apparel and personal accessories include important presentation goods such as the ostrich feather, pleated linen shirt, trimmed woven mantle, medallion engraved with the heads of George III and Queen Charlotte, and a gorget marked GR III. Other details of dress, however, were visual markers of Cunne Shote's Cherokee identity: the shaved head and hairstyle, his neck tattoo and slit ear lobe, and his hunting knife.

Cunne-Shote (c. 1715–1810) painted in London in 1762 by Francis Parsons (fl.1760–1780). (Private Collection/Peter Newark American Pictures/The Bridgeman Art Library)

COMPOSITION OF A WARDROBE, 1715–1785

Middling sort Captain John Jenckes of Providence, Rhode Island, was an apothecary and possibly a physician; he also managed a small shop. After his death, in March 1721, his assessors valued his estate at over £544. His personal wearing apparel consisted of a broadcloth suit (coat and breeches), a waistcoat and breeches; nine shirts and three pairs of stockings; seven neckcloths, including one of silk; a silk cap and three other caps; and a pair of shoes and one pair of silver buckles. Other clothing was listed in another section of the inventory: five waistcoats, five pair of breeches and a coat, a suit made of duroy, a greatcoat and hat, and a pair of gloves. It is possible that this clothing belonged to his shop inventory, but given the size of his estate and his role in the community, it is likely that these were his clothes (Rogers and Field 1901, 16:180–85).

A white servant of Boston gentleman William Stoddard owned an extensive wardrobe, all of which was stolen in January of 1731. Among the garments taken were a drab-colored coat with white metal buttons decorated with stars; a light-colored coat with brass buttons; a light gray duroy coat trimmed with black tape and gray duroy breeches; an untrimmed black broadcloth coat and breeches; a jacket and breeches of osnaburg; one blue-striped holland and one seersucker waistcoat; two pairs of white cotton and one pair of blue worsted hose; a garlix shirt; a pair of striped cotton bootlashes, and a new hat with a mourning band (*Boston Gazette*, January 18). In contrast, in 1737, a 20-year-old English runaway indentured servant named William White took what might have been his entire wardrobe with him. He wore a suit—coat, jacket, and breeches—of a dark color homespun with metal buttons; a loose red greatcoat with brass buttons; one "garlick" and one "cotton and linen" shirt; one pair of gray yarn and one pair of dark worsted stockings; a small brimmed castor hat and a silk handkerchief around his neck (*Boston News-Letter*, December 30).

At the other end of the sartorial spectrum, in 1739, while serving as governor of Massachusetts, Jonathan Belcher wrote to London to order some new clothing. In addition to the order for a new suit consisting of a "fine cloth jockey coat, waistcoat, and breeches lined with shalloon" and another suit of "three pile black velvet . . . lined with double shagreen of dark gold," Belcher wanted a nightgown, or banyan, of crimson silk damask. The remainder of his order comprised two pair of worsted hose to match the jockey coat, a hat, and two sets of knee and shoe buckles, one silver and one pinchbeck. He also sent his son a leather waistcoat and a pair of leather breeches that he already owned, in order to have them "laced with gold"—to have a woven gold trimming applied in the currently fashionable manner (Earle 1903, 2:404).

English Anglican priest George Whitefield (1714–1770), one of the founders of Methodism, went out to Georgia in 1737. In the event he petitioned the Georgia Board of Trustees to provide him with clothing for the journey: six shirts, four pairs of stockings, two pairs of breeches, a waistcoat, a close coat, a greatcoat, one night gown, a wig, a hat, six handkerchiefs, four pairs of shoes, and six pairs of socks, and a watch (Candler 1910, 21:396).

In 1742, a "negro Man-Servant, indented for 7 years named Pompey York" ran away from his master in Woburn, Massachusetts. He took with him two "much patch'd" cotton and linen shirts, a grey broadcloth greatcoat faced with yellow, a blue camblet coat "full trim's," a blue jacket "made up of divers pieces," breeches of light cloth but patched across the seat with brown, two pair of gray yarn stockings, and a patched pair of shoes and hat. His clothing is remarkable for the number and extent of the repairs mentioned (*Boston News-Letter*, April 9, 1742). A year later, Pompey ran away again from the same master. This time he wore and carried a turned and pieced grey homespun coat with flat metal buttons, a blue jacket with metal buttons, a sleeveless camblet jacket, an "old blew shag loose coat" and another of brown Holland, two good shirts of linen and cotton, leather breeches, gray stockings, one old and one new Castor hats, a striped cap, and "sundry wigs" (*Boston News-Letter*, March 31, 1743).

The probate inventory of Daniel Dulany (1685–1753), a well-to-do shopkeeper in Annapolis, Maryland, was taken on May 21, 1754. His estate, including the contents of his shop and the value of three indentured servants, one of them a tailor, and 13 slaves, came to more than three thousand pounds. Found in the "Parlour Chamber" was Daniel's wearing apparel: a blue cloak; three cloth coats (eight colored, brown, dark) and a bearskin coat; 12 waistcoats (black cotton velvet, black, cloth colored, and nine of dimothy or linen); three morning gowns, or banyans (India stuff, Callico, old Plaid); three pairs of breeches (black velvet, two of them old or out-of-date); three pairs of shoes, one of spatterdashes, and one of half jack boots with spurs; three pairs of linen leggings; 16 cambric stocks; eight damask and six linen night caps; four silk and six linen handkerchiefs, nine plain and 13 ruffled shirts, both old and new; three old and two new wigs; a hat and case; six pairs of new gloves; 31 pairs of yarn, worsted thread, cotton, and silk stockings; one pair of linen stockings; and an assortment of silver and gold jewelry and accessories such as buckles, stock buckles, mourning buckles, a watch and seals, buttons, a ring and mourning rings, spectacles, and a wig clamp. From the quantity of shirts, stocks, stockings, and gloves it is clear that Daniel was a well-dressed man. His coats, morning gowns, and waistcoats confirm his status. It seems likely, however, that a few pair of breeches were overlooked (Inventory of . . . Daniel Dulany). Daniel's shop inventory indicates that he sold quantities of cloth ranging from very coarse to very fine, for all uses, clothing and furnishing, along with household, farm, and craft tools and equipment. The only male clothing in the shop inventory consisted of a few boy's castor hats and felt ones for men; sole leather for shoe making or repair; and some watch keys and seals.

Ezekial Bascom (1700–1746), probably a weaver and clothier, lived and worked in Deerfield, Massachusetts. He owned textile-working equipment that included a loom, a tape loom, and three wheels. At his death, his estate was valued at over £1,739, of which £1,323 was in land. With such a valuable estate, it is curious that his surviving wardrobe was so limited: a jacket, breeches, leather jacket, coat, suit of clothes, greatcoat, three shirts, and two neckcloths (Inventory of Ezekiel Bascom). The 1754 probate inventory of Deerfield, Massachusetts, resident Nathaniel Hawks—also of the middling sort—is unusual in that it details the fabrics and sometimes the colors of his garments (Inventory of Nathaniel Hawks). Hanks owned three coats—one Spanish drugget, one brown, and one "duffold" (duffels). He had a vest to match the brown coat and another of calimanco; a leather jacket and breeches; an old leather jacket and a cloth jacket; linen breeches; a striped "gillet," which may have been another vest or undervest; four shirts, two checked and two checked linen; a beaver hat, an old hat, and a wig; a silk handkerchief; white gloves; a pair of worsted stockings and two other pairs; two pairs of shoes and a pair of old boots. Knitted boots were also listed.

A thief stole a significant portion of Samuel Pritchard's wardrobe from his Frederick County, Virginia, home in 1756. Samuel's new blue broadcloth coat with yellow pinchbeck buttons had been made "very fashionable." He also lost a sleeveless jacket of black broadcloth with glass buttons; another broadcloth coat and jacket with flat white metal buttons (the jacket lined in red), that he considered "half worn;" two other coats (half worn serge and an old blue one with white facings on the collar, lapels, and sleeves); blue cloth breeches; two pair of linen drawers; three pairs of homemade woolen stockings; new shoes; and five homespun shirts (*Pennsylvania Gazette*, October 21, 1756).

The climate dictated the kinds of fabrics that the better sorts demanded for their bespoke clothing. In November 1767, James Habersham ordered new clothing from London: "I want a *dress*, plain and grave Coloured Silk Coat—A black silk Waistcoat without sleeves, one pair of fine black frame knit silk stocking Breeches, and two pair of the finest frame knit black worsted stocking Breeches, as the best are the cheapest for common use—I chuse black Breeches as they suit my coloured Coat, and I want the black silk Waistcoat to attend funerals in Summer." Habersham noted that except for solemn occasions like funerals, he always wore jackets of light-weight linen holland in the summer. He also emphasized that the coat was to be lined "with something strong, and as light as possible, and the Taylor should particularly notice, that Cloaths cannot *possibly be made too light and airy for Summer* wear here" (Habersham 1904, 61).

Massachusetts Governor Hutchinson ordered many of his clothes from London. Between 1769 and 1773 he purchased a blue cloth waistcoat trimmed in blue and lined; 2 underwaistcoats of swansdown; a suit with embroidered buttonholes; a scarlet broadcloth suit lined with shalloon, the waistcoat backed with linen and the breeches lined with leather; two pair of breeches also lined with leather, of which one of worsted matched a coat he already owned and one pair of black velvet; a waistcoat of green corded silk backed and sleeved in thin silk, the body lined in linen and the skirts in silk—the one for comfort and the other for show; a wool frock coat, waist-coat, and breeches "not in a pure white but next to it;" and a surtout of light shag or beaver with a velvet cape (Earle 1903, 2:405–06).

William Graeme was an important man in the colony of Georgia, serving in the lower house of the Georgia legislature and as Attorney General and Advocate General of the Court of the Vice Admiralty in Savannah. Not a plantation owner or a businessman, but a professional man, Graeme owned little land and only six slaves, three of them children. At his death in 1770, his estate was valued at £772. The inventory reveals a large wardrobe that reflected his political and social position in the colony. The most formal occasions required his "suit scarlet regimentals, laced" and an officer's silk sash. He owned eight coats, five with waistcoats: one full-trimmed black coat and waistcoat; one sky blue coat and waistcoat, laced; one blue coat and one laced scarlet waistcoat; one black coat and waistcoat; one red coat and black cloth waistcoat; and three other coats. The "flowered gown" was probably a banyan either of a printed chintz or a flowered damask; it was paired with a blue waistcoat. Completing the wardrobe were eighteen miscellaneous waistcoats and jackets; ten white shirts; ten cravats and stocks; five night caps and two hats; an old wig; and a set of stone and silver knee buckles. It is odd that the listing did not include breeches (Davis 1976, 156–57).

William Reyn, a Pennsylvania schoolmaster who died in 1775, owned no land but had a horse and trappings, a walnut chest, and some assorted property related to his profession. His estate was valued at over £70; well over £14 was in clothing. His great coat passed without comment, as did his brown and white suits of clothes, his three pairs of shoes and one pair of boots, two pairs of stockings, three handkerchiefs, and his set of shoe and knee buckles. These must have been unremarkable garments—perhaps not brand new but not too worn. The remainder of Reyn's clothing consisted of a "new" suit of clothes; an "old" slip coat, drawers and jacket; two pair of old trousers; five old and two "waring" (i.e., perhaps meaning respectable) shirts; a "fine" shirt and hat, an "old" hat, and four pair of "old" stockings. Clearly Reyn's wardrobe was suitable for his middling but professional status in the community (Hersh and Hersh 1995, 202–03).

The apparel inventories for two Rhode Island soldiers who were killed in action at Fort Mercer, New Jersey, in October 1777 illustrate just how much of a soldier's uniform was in reality not uniform at all. Sergeant George Babcock owned two checked linen shirts, a pair of striped linen overalls, three sleeveless jackets (one striped cotton and linen mix, one flannel, and one homespun woolen), a linen and worsted mix "cotee" (probably a jacket with sleeves), a kersey "outside jacket" lined with flannel, a beaver hat, a pair of shoes, three pairs of stockings (blue worsted, thread, blue yarn), a linen handkerchief, and a knapsack. William Hicks, whose rank was not indicated, possessed a uniform coat, a blue "outside" coat, a wool double-breasted jacket (perhaps a pea jacket?), a black worsted waistcoat, one plain coarse linen shirt and another with ruffles, two pairs of linen overalls, one pair of coarse worsted stockings, a red broadcloth sleeveless jacket, and two knapsacks (Fort Mercer Clothing returns 1777).

In south-central Pennsylvania, west of the Susquehanna River in Cumberland County, Charles Stewart and his wife were "well above average" in wealth and property when he died in 1784. His clothing inventory attests to this although as is the case with other inventories the assessors did not list essentials such as shirts and stockings and outer garments such as a cloak or great coat. Stewart did own several sets of coats, jackets, and breeches: a blue cloth coat and jacket and brown cloth breeches; a blue cloth coat with a scarlet-colored jacket and green breeches; a regimental coat with a blue cloth jacket and black corded breeches; and a white coat and jacket with breeches. The other garments enumerated included a striped cotton coat, a linen coat and jacket, a linen jacket and a flowered silk jacket, a black velvet jacket and a knitted breeches pattern, two additional jackets, and a pair of drawers. His accessories included boots and silver-plated spurs, two pair of shoes, silver shoe buckles and sleeve buttons, a silver stock buckle, and a silver watch and silver mounted cutlass. The total value of these goods was almost £20 (Hersh and Hersh, 1995).

Rhode Island minister Samuel F. Fayerweather, a clergyman with the Newport Congregational church, left his parishioners to study again in England. He returned in 1760, ordained as a clergyman in the Church of

England, to minister at St. Paul's Church in Narragansett. He died in 1781, and his will and probate inventory must be taken together to give a clearer picture of his wardrobe. In his will he left bequests to two other clergymen: a suit of black paduasoy to the Rev. Mr. Bass of Newburyport, Massachusetts, and a black coat to the Rev. Mather Byles of Boston. Neither of these garments were listed in Fayerweather's inventory, nor do shirts, bands, shoes, stockings, drawers, or hats. The inventory enumerates suits of velvet and broadcloth, two morning gowns (one of red and blue damask, possibly reversible), a "motheaten" blue broadcloth cloak, linen and silk handkerchiefs, a wig case, green spectacles, slippers, a pocket book, rings and seals, and some textiles including gold thread, lawn, blue silk, and blue worsted damask—perhaps a remnant of the cloth used for one of his morning gowns (Carpenter 1924, 122–27).

REFERENCES

Accomack County Deeds and Wills, 1664–1671. Microfilm.

Account Book of a Philadelphia Merchant, 1694–1698, (Phi)108; Historical Society of Pennsylvania.

Adams, John. 1771. Diary of John Adams, June 17. Adams Family Papers: An Electronic Archive. masshist.org/digitaladams/aea/diary/.

Arms, Ebenezer, account book 14087, December 10, 1750–November 22, 1768, Pocumtuck Valley Memorial Association (PVMA), Deerfield, MA.

Arnold, Janet. 2008. *Patterns of Fashion 4: The Cut and Construction of Linen Shirts, Smocks, Neckwear, Headwear and Accessories for Men and Women, c. 1540–1660.* London: Macmillan.

Bolzius, John Martin. 1957. "John Martin Bolzius Answers a Questionnaire on Carolina and Georgia." *William and Mary Quarterly* 3rd. ser., no. 14 (April): 218–61.

Bolzius, John Martin. 1981. "John Martin Bolzius' Trip to Charleston, October 1742." *South Carolina Historical Magazine* vol. 82, no. 2 (April): 87–110.

Braund, Kathryn E. Holland. 1993. *Deerskins and Duffels: Creek Indian Trade with Anglo-America, 1685–1815.* Lincoln: University of Nebraska.

Brown, Kathleen M. 1996. *Good Wives, Nasty Wenches, and Anxious Patriarchs: Gender Race, and Power in Colonial Virginia.* Chapel Hill: University of North Carolina.

Browne, William Hand, ed. 1887. *Archives of Maryland: Judicial and Testamentary Business of the Provincial Court, 1637–1650.* Vol. 4. Baltimore: Maryland Historical Society.

Candler, Allen D., ed. 1910. *Colonial Records of the State of Georgia, 1735–1737.* Vol. 21. Atlanta: State of Georgia.

Carpenter, Esther Bernon. 1924. *South County Studies: Of Some Eighteenth-Century Persons, Places and Conditions in That Portion of Rhode Island Called Narragansett.* Boston: printed for subscribers.

Cheves, Langdon, ed. 2000. *The Shaftesbury Papers*, reprint. Charleston: South Carolina Historical Society.

Cresswell, Nicholas. 2007. *The Journal of Nicholas Cresswell, 1774–1777*, reprint. Carlisle, MA: Applewood Books.

Cumming, Valerie, C. W. Cunnington, and P. E. Cunnington. 2010. *The Dictionary of Fashion History.* Oxford: Berg.

Danckaerts, Jasper. 1913. *Journal of Jasper Danckaerts, 1679–1680,* edited by Bartlett Burleigh James and J. Franklin Hameson. New York: Charles Scribner's Sons.

Davis, Harold E. 1976. *The Fledgling Province: Social and Cultural Life in Colonial Georgia, 1733–1776.* Chapel Hill: University of North Carolina.

Denton, Daniel. 1902. *A Brief Description of New York, Formerly Called New Netherlands,* reprint of 1670 ed. Cleveland: Burrows Brothers.

Dow, George Francis, ed. 1921. *Records and Files of the Quarterly Courts of Essex County, Massachusetts, 1636–1691.* Vol. 8, 1680–1683. Salem, MA: Essex Institute.

Dow, George Francis. 1935. *Everyday Life in the Massachusetts Bay Colony.* New York: Benjamin Blom.

Earle, Alice Morse. 1894. *Costume of Colonial Times.* New York: Charles Scribner's Sons.

Earle, Alice Morse. 1895. *Margaret Winthrop.* New York: Charles Scribner's Sons.

Earle, Alice Morse. 1903. *Two Centuries of Costume in America,* 2 vols. New York: Macmillan.

Earle, Alice Morse. 1989. *Home Life in Colonial Days,* reprint of 1898 ed. Williamstown, MA: Corner House.

Egmont, John Percival. 1735. Letter from Mr. Verelst to Mr. Thomas Causton, May 15. Egmont Papers, typescript of vol. 14207, letters to Georgia, June 1732–1735. Hargrett Rare Book Collection, University of Georgia. fax.libs.uga.edu/egmont/epmenu.html.

Fort Mercer Clothing returns, October 1777. MSS 536 Box #1, Folder #13, Rhode Island Historical Society, Providence, Rhode Island.

Goodale, John H. A History of Nashua, New Hampshire. www.nh.sea rchroots.com/documents/Hillsborough/History_Nashua_NH_4.txt Hurd, History of Hillsborough, NH.

Habersham, James. 1904. "The Letters of Hon. James Habersham, 1756–1775." In *Collections of the Georgia Historical Society.* Vol. 6. Savannah: Georgia Historical Society.

Hamilton, Alexander. 1948. *Gentleman's Progress: The Itinerarium of Dr. Alexander Hamilton, 1744,* ed. Carl Bridenbaugh. Chapel Hill: University of North Carolina.

Hersh, Tandy and Charles Hersh. 1995. *Cloth and Costume, 1750–1800, Cumberland County, Pennsylvania.* Carlisle, PA: Cumberland County Historical Society.

Inventory of . . . Daniel Dulany. www.gunstonhall.org/library/probate/ DULANY54.PDF.

Inventory of Ezekiel Bascom. www.historic-deerfield.org/files/hd/docs/ EZEKIEL-BASCOM-1700–1746.pdf.

Inventory of Nathaniel Hawks. www.historic-deerfield.org/files/hd/ docs/hawks_nathaniel_1699–1754.pdf.

Inventory of . . . John Morton Jordan. www.gunstonhall.org/library/pro bate/JORDAN71.PDF.

Inventory of . . . George Wells. www.gunstonhall.org/library/probate/ WELLS54.PDF.

An Inventory of . . . Thomas Willett. Plymouth Colony Archive Project. www.histarch.uiuc.edu/plymouth/P231.htm.

An Inventory of . . . Will Wright. Plymouth Colony Archive Project. www. histarch.uiuc.edu/plymouth/WRIGHT.htm.

Kingsbury, Susan Myra, ed. 1933. *The Records of the Virginia Company of London.* Vol. 3. Washington, DC: United States Government Printing Office.

Longacre, James B., and James Herring, eds. 1836. *National Portrait Gallery of Distinguished Americans.* Vol. 3. Philadelphia: Henry Perkins.

McClellan, Elisabeth. 1904. *Historic Dress in America, 1607–1800.* Philadelphia: George W. Jacobs.

McDowell, William L., Jr., ed. 1958. *Colonial Records of South Carolina: Documents Relating to Indian Affairs, May 21, 1750–August 7, 1754,* edited by William L. McDowell, Jr. Columbia: South Carolina Archives Department.

Manwaring, Charles William. 1904. *A Digest of the Early Connecticut Probate Records: Hartford District.* Hartford, CT: self-published.

Montgomery, Florence. 1984. *Textiles in America, 1650–1870*. New York: W. W. Norton.

Morton, Thomas. 1883. *The New English Canaan of Thomas Morton*, reprint of 1637 ed. Boston: Prince Society.

Norton, John. 1937. *John Norton and Sons, Merchants of London and Virginia, Being the Papers from Their Counting House of the Years 1750 to 1795*, edited by Frances Norton Mason. Richmond: Dietz.

Raleigh, Walter. 1916. "The Ages of Elizabeth," *Shakespeare's England: An Account of the Life and Manners of his Age*. Vol. 1, 1–47. Oxford: Clarendon.

Reid, John Phillip. 1976. *A Better Kind of Hatchet: Law, Trade, and Diplomacy in the Cherokee Nation during the Early Years of European Contact*. University Park, PA: Pennsylvania State University.

"A Relation of Maryland." 1910. In *Narratives of Early Maryland*, reprint of 1635 ed., edited by Clayton Colman Hall, 63–112. New York: Charles Scribner's Sons.

Rogers, Horatio, and Edward Field, eds. 1901. *Early Records of the Town of Providence*. Vol. 16. Providence: City Council of Providence.

Sewall, Samuel. 1973. *The Diary of Samuel Sewall, 1674–1729*, edited by M. Halsey Thomas, 2 vols. New York: Farrar, Straus and Giroux.

Shirley, John W. 1949. "George Percy at Jamestown, 1607–1612." *Virginia Magazine of History and Biography* vol. 57, no. 3 (July): 227–43.

Smith, John. 1907. "Smith's Description of Virginia and Proceedings of the Colonie." In *Narratives of Early Virginia, 1606–1625*, reprint of 1612, edited by Lyon Gardiner Tyler, 76–204. New York: Charles Scribner's Sons.

Smith, John. 2006. *The Generall Historie of Virginia*, reprint of 1629 ed. Bedford, MA: Applewood Books.

Starr, Raymond. 1965. "Letters from John Lewis Gervais to Henry Laurens, 1777–1778." *South Carolina Historical Magazine* vol. 66, no. 1 (January): 15–37.

Stephen, Adam. 1755. Letter from Adam Stephen to George Washington, September 27. Report on Fort Cumberland, Maryland. The George Washington Papers at the Library of Congress, 1741–1799. memory.loc.gov/ammem/mgwquery.html.

Strachey, William. 1849. *The Historie of Travaile into Virginia Britannia*, reprint of the 1612 ed. London: Hakluyt Society.

Temple, Sarah Gober and Kenneth L. Coleman. 2010. *Georgia Journeys: Being an Account of the Lives of Georgia's Original Settlers and Many Other Early Settlers*. Athens: University of Georgia.

A trew Inventory of . . . Mr. John howland. Plymouth Colony Archive Project. www.histarch.uiuc.edu/plymouth/P204.htm.

Walker, Thomas. 1750. Dr. Thomas Walker's Journal. www.tngenweb.org/tnland/squabble/walker.html.

Washington, George. 1776. General Orders to Head Quarters, New York, July 24. In *The Writings of George Washington from the Original Manuscript Sources,* edited by John C. Fitzpatrick. Electronic Text Center, University of Virginia Library. etext.virginia.edu/toc/modeng/public/WasFi05. html.

White, Andrew. 1910. "A Briefe Relation of the Voyage unto Maryland." In *Narratives of Early Maryland,* reprint of 1634 ed., edited by Clayton Colman Hall, 25–45. New York: Charles Scribner's Sons.

Williams, Roger. 1827. *A Key into the Language of America,* reprint of 1643 ed. Providence: Rhode-Island Historical Society.

Withington, Lothrop, ed. 1907. "South Carolina Gleanings in England." *South Carolina Historical and Genealogical Magazine* vol. 8, no. 4 (October): 211–19.

Wood, William. 1865. *New-England's Prospect,* reprint of 1634 ed. Boston: Prince Society.

York County Deeds, Orders, and Wills Book 6. www.virtualjamestown.org/york%20runaways/york%20runaways—book%206.txt.

York County Deeds, Orders, and Wills Book 7. www.virtualjamestown.org/york%20runaways/york%20runaways—book%207.txt.

York County Deeds, Orders, and Wills Book 8. www.virtualjamestown.org/yorkfreedomsuits1685_1715.html.

6

Children's Fashions

Apart from certain details of dress that were differentiated by cut or construction, there is very little in regard to children's clothing that distinguishes it from adult dress during the 17th and 18th centuries. This chapter, therefore, offers abbreviated discussions of children's garments excepting how children under the age of three were dressed. In the colonial period, children were clothed in only two basic forms of dress: one was the knee breeches, the other ankle-length petticoats. These two forms, however, were not necessarily gender specific but depended on the age of the wearer. All girls wore gowns (or petticoats and bodices) and a cap. Boys under the age of six or seven also were dressed in a gown, or petticoats, and a cap. Both young boys and girls wore a shirt or shift next to the skin, over which might be worn padded stays. Once a boy was put in breeches, he entered the world of older boys and men, which generally was a public world. At this age, he was considered old enough to work in a shop, in the fields, or at school; in other words, he was old enough to venture out into the world and begin to make his own way. Breeches allowed for more physical activity and freedom. In contrast, women, girls, and young children remained in the private world of the home. It is important to note that little boys still in petticoats were not viewed as feminine; they simply were not old enough to enter the world of adult men and of more independence.

Unfortunately, few pieces of infants' and children's clothing from the 17th and 18th centuries have survived. Probate inventories are of little help in this category although shop inventories sometimes include goods for children. Most of the available evidence for what they wore comes from manuscript sources such as letters and diaries, prints and paintings, and advertisements of various kinds. By the middle of the 18th century, merchants' advertisements distinguished among goods for babies, children, boys, girls, youths, and maids.

Seventeenth- and 18th-century portraits of children must be examined with the same reservations as those of adults: was the clothing illustrated actually worn by the child or was it copied from a print to establish for the viewer the child's family status? In about 1755, painter John Wollaston depicted young Elizabeth Randolph (c. 1750–before 1773) of Virginia in a gold satin gown with short scalloped sleeves over a white chemise with elbow length sleeves. Her sleeve ruffles and neckline are finished with lace. It is a charming portrait—the child holds a fashionably dressed lady doll—however, the costume is very similar to the gown worn by the Duchess of Hamilton in a portrait that was published as a print in 1752. Charleston artist Jeremiah Theus used this same dress (in blue or golden brown) in several 1750s portraits of Charleston-area girls as well as adult women.

CONCEPTS OF CHILDHOOD IN COLONIAL AMERICA

In order to understand why children were dressed as they were during the colonial period, it is essential to be aware of the evolving concepts of childhood at the time. Although differences between infants, youths, and adults were acknowledged, for most of the period discussed here the notion of childhood did not include a period reserved solely for play and learning by the innocent young. Until the theories espoused by John Locke (1632–1704) and Jean-Jacques Rousseau (1712–1778) concerning childhood development began to filter into colonial society, in the mid-18th century, children were expected to grow up and assume a degree of personal and family responsibility at a much earlier age than is common today. Largely agricultural, colonial society relied on children to provide labor on family farms. Even in an urban setting, most children were expected contribute at an early age to family maintenance either in the home or at some useful work-related activity under the guidance of a parent or other adult. For example, in 1641 the colony of New Plymouth enacted a law to require townships to make adequate provision for the poor of each town; however, any poor whose children were not engaged in some useful employment "shalbe put to worke in fitting ymployment according to their strength and abilities" or placed somewhere to do so by the town (Plymouth Colony Laws, Appendix 1). On January 18, 1644, William Hoskine of Plymouth, gave his six-year-old daughter Sarah to Thomas and Winefride Whitney, "to dwell wth them vntill shee shall accomplish the age of twenty yeares, . . . vseing her as their child, and being vnto her as father and mother, and to instruct her in learneing and soweing in reasonable manner, fynding vnto her meate, drink, and apparell [and] lodging during the said terme"

(Plymouth Colony Records and Court Orders, Appendix 2). Seven-year-old Elizabeth Billington was made an apprentice on April 18, 1642, by her parents "to John Barnes and Mary, his wyfe, to dwell wth them and do their service vntill shee shall accomplish the age of twenty yeares, . . . the said John Barnes . . . finding her meate, drink, [and] cloathes during the said term" (Plymouth Colony Records and Court Orders, Appendix 2). Historians have theorized that these actions, if not necessary for economic reasons, may have been taken to help parents keep their emotional distance from their young, who were subject to a fairly high mortality rate (Smith 1982, 12). It may also have been an effort to ensure that children learned manners and correct behavior in an environment other than their own home.

The Stages of Childhood

Childhood covered the years from birth to roughly 14 years of age. There is much evidence to support that parents were not only tender and loving toward their children but that they also were aware of and interested in the stages of their development. Babyhood or infancy lasted from birth to two or three years (at this time, the term infant also referred to anyone who was still legally a minor). A child was weaned (fed solid food instead of breast milk) anywhere between the latter months of its first year of life and about two years of age, by which time he or she had learned to walk. For all of the 17th and much of the 18th centuries, crawling was not viewed as a stage in the process of learning to walk but rather as a demeaning habit that resembled the walk of animals. Thus, at least among the middling and upper ranks of society, most babies did not learn to crawl before they walked (Calvert 1992, 32–33). To encourage early standing or walking, a child just finding its feet might use a standing stool, a short stool with a hole in the seat into which the child would be placed. Some stools were equipped with wheels and were called walking stools. These devices allowed a child only to stand or walk; he or she could not get out of the stool nor sit down in it. The standing stool had the advantage of keeping a child off of dirty floors and away from hazards like fireplaces and stairs.

Colonial children received an education suited to their station, which might be practical or academic or both. The age at which any formal training began varied not only from family to family but even within families. As a basic education, both boys and girls were taught to read beginning at about age four, but generally only boys were taught to write and keep accounts, beginning at about age eight. After being taught to read, girls were taught sewing and other housewifery activities. They were also expected to begin learning the skills and chores suitable to their station in life either from older family members or by serving in another household.

In northern colonies, where colonists clustered in villages and towns, dame schools run by women who took in local children often provided a basic education if children were not taught at home. Boys could go on to town schools if family circumstances permitted. In the South and in the backcountry, where distances between families were often great, affluent colonists often hired private tutors. These teachers lived in the family and taught whatever academic subjects were required.

As noted above, colonial children of European heritage might be bound as apprentices as early as age six in the 1600s; however, the more common age for beginning an apprenticeship was between 10 and 12 (Beales 1975, 393). As discussed in Chapter 2, apprenticeship was a common method of educating children of the artisan and farming sorts as well as the poor. Boys were apprenticed to learn a trade or farming; girls generally learned the skills to run a house, although in the 18th century a girl was occasionally apprenticed to a mantua maker or milliner. Apprenticeship contracts, like indentures, usually required that the master provide at least one suit of clothes for the apprentice at the end of the term of service. Apprentices were sometimes taught to read, and for boys, to write and do simple arithmetic.

Enslaved African and Native American children might be brought up with Euro-American children in a well-to-do family, to be groomed as life-long personal servants for the children of their masters. Alternatively, they could grow up with their biological family and continue to serve at the master's pleasure as adults or be sold away from their families as young as four or five. In May of 1733, for example, an anonymous master offered for sale in Philadelphia "a very likely Negro Woman aged about Thirty Years who has lived in this City, from her Childhood. . . . She has a Boy of about Two Years old, which is to go with her. . . . And also another very likely Boy aged about Six Years, who is Son of the Abovesaid Woman. He will be sold with his Mother, or by himself, as the Buyer pleases" (*Pennsylvania Gazette,* May 10, 1733).

During the 1700s the concepts of refinement, gentility, and dressing according to one's station in life, which were so important among the well-to-do, were taught to "youths" and "maids"—those between the ages of about 12 and their mid-teens—in fashionable schools. Some teachers advertised a single activity or diversion such as dancing, painting, or fencing. Others offered a range of subjects geared to just one sex or the other, such as navigation and mathematics or drawing and embroidery. In 1732, Alice Christie Colden and her husband Cadwallader Colden sent their son

Sandie and daughter Bettie to New York City to board for three months at a fashionable school, and Alice tried to allay her mother-in-law Elizabeth Hill's displeasure at the decision in a letter.

> We found him & his Sister both desirous of haveing some improvement in their writeing & as we are not capable of teaching that so well as others we indulged them in that for one quarter. Danceing is taught in the same house with writeing & but 10 shilings a quarter more if they are taught both so we have allowed them a litle of that likeways pewrly to make them know how to cary their body in company and to rubb off some of the countrey air which they have a good deal of in their cariage. It will be some expenc to us but we will be as saveing as posible. (Colden 1937, 391)

In 1771, at the age of 10, Anna Green Winslow was sent from Halifax, Nova Scotia, to Boston to attend school; she lived with a maternal aunt—both sides of her family came from Massachusetts and she had many relatives in town. Most of Anna's schooling was in the nature of accomplishments and domestic skills rather than in academic subjects. Her journal of the experience reveals that she attended two "schools" on a weekly basis. To learn to write a fine hand, she studied with a well-known writing master, Samuel Holbrook. She attended a separate sewing school where she learned needlework and embroidery with an unnamed teacher.

The boundary between youths and maids and adults was a fluid one. Depending on the geographic location and time period, a girl attained her majority generally between the ages of 12 and 18; for a boy the age range was 14 to 21. At the age of majority, young people could inherit; if orphaned, select their own guardian; make a will; testify in court; or bind themselves out as apprentices. In 1645, orphan Priscila Browne went to the Plymouth Court to select a new guardian—her uncle—who was to invest her inheritance portion "into a breeding stock" until "the Court shall judg it meete for her to haue it at her owne disposeing" (Plymouth Colony Records and Court Orders, Appendix 2). In the 17th-century Massachusetts Bay Colony, 14 was the legal age of discretion for the prosecution of certain crimes (slander) while in Plymouth Colony the age of discretion was 16. The preferred age for receiving boys into the church as members in their own right, apart from their parents, also seems to have been between 14 and 16 in Puritan New England. While certain rights, such as inheritance and—if property requirements were met—voting, were not granted young men until the age of 20 or 21; boys of 16 could serve in the militia and could be executed for certain offenses. The all-male students at Yale and Harvard

Colleges did not necessarily enter all at the same age; members of a class might range in age from fourteen to 24 (Beales 1975, 384, 390–92).

Attitudes toward Children

In England, 17th-century parents of the upper ranks—those whose religious leanings were not Puritan—were often accused of being too lenient with their children. This approach to child rearing, in which a modicum of discipline and control was exercised over a child's actions and words, was adopted among the planter elite in colonial Maryland and Virginia (Stannard 1974, 459). In contrast, New England's Puritans stressed that even the youngest child was capable of the worst behavior unless constantly corrected and disciplined and given the right sort of religious training. Weak in intellect and lacking in judgment, children had to be broken to civilization and instilled with the rules of civilized behavior, moral principles, and religious discipline that governed the lives of adults. A parent's love for a child should not interfere with its willingness to correct that child: part of the parents' job was to ensure the child's salvation, and that could only be done through careful attention to its behavior and education (Stannard 1974, 461–62).

Puritan authoritarian attitudes toward children were common throughout the 17th century, and continued into the 18th. It is apparent, however, that the prescriptive literature on child rearing suggested modes of behavior for parents that were stricter and more severe than most parents actually adopted. Toward the beginning of the 18th century, for example, the Reverend Cotton Mather of Boston suggested that children should be shamed, not beaten, when they do wrong. As Puritan religious beliefs became less widespread and less intensely followed during the 18th century in New England, parents became even more moderate in their attitudes. Diaries and letters, from both the 17th and 18th centuries, indicate that most parent-child relationships were more affectionate and less rigid than the Puritan ideal. Quaker and Puritan parents regarded child rearing as important duties: the Quaker to develop a more nurturing relationship and encourage the child's loving relationship with God; the Puritan to break the child's will to God's will and ensure his or her salvation, but both groups of parents were focused on their children. Well-to-do southern families, perhaps because of plantation isolation, higher child mortality, and smaller families, exhibited a child-centered but less restrictive upbringing in the 18th century (Smith 1982, 13).

Physical discipline was somewhat more relaxed in the 18th century than in the 17th. Controlling behavior through rewards and instilling a sense of the honor of doing right was preferred to doing so through fear and corporal punishment, but parents were told that it was just as bad for a child to be too lenient as it was to be too strict (Sidwell 1968, 281). Child-rearing literature was widely available, appearing in newspapers and magazines and as pamphlets and tracts available at booksellers. Mothers were responsible for raising boys and girls to the age of six or seven and continued to be responsible for female children after that age (Norton 1984, 606).

By the late 17th century, educators and philosophers began to reconsider the standard precepts regarding how children should be brought up and educated, and clothing was one area in which reforms were suggested. John Locke (*Some Thoughts Concerning Education*, 1693) and Jean Jacques Rousseau (*Emile*, 1762) suggested loose, light clothing that would not constrict the growing body but would allow freedom of movement and vigorous exercise. They also felt that children would be healthier if they were not kept too warm, and their bodies would naturally become hardened to colder temperatures. It took the better part of a century for these ideas to be generally accepted. South Carolina's Eliza Pinckney (1722–1793), for example, asked a friend to send a specific toy that she could use to teach her son, then only four months old, "according to Mr. Locke's method . . . to play himself into learning. Mr. Pinckney, himself, has been contriving a sett of toys to teach him his letters by the time he can speak" (Ravenel 1896, 113).

By the 1770s clothing styles meant specifically for children were being developed, although these new fashions were not common until the mid-1780s, after the scope of this book. Even before the American Revolution, however, the influence of Locke's and Rousseau's theories on childhood development began to be felt in America. A pamphlet written in England by Dr. William Cadogan (1711–1797) for the care of children "from their Birth to three Years of Age" was reprinted in part in the *Pennsylvania Gazette* in 1749 (March 21). Cadogan was clearly influenced by Locke's precepts, although he did not adopt them all. In the physician's view, children of the "industrious poor" (i.e., those who were not destitute but had no money for anything beyond the basic necessities) were likelier to be healthy during infancy and childhood (specifically between birth and three years of age), than the offspring of wealthy parents. Children of the well-to-do, he wrote, were overfed and kept too warm until they were old enough to be sent to a wet-nurse of a lower economic status, and then they were too weakened to withstand the new and much less luxurious environment.

Similarly, in Rousseau's view, the natural development of a child was too often constrained and even warped by too much discipline and too many restrictions. He suggested that children be dressed in a manner that allowed free movement and a wide range of activity. Rather than breaking a child's will, the purpose of education was to teach him to control it, by learning from experience (Rousseau 1979). In practice, it seems that few of Rousseau's ideas affected the upbringing of colonial children until after the Revolution. Letters between parents and children, both boys and girls, show that regular habits of mind and body, moderation in food and drink, the discipline of work and study, were all still preached to children by their parents in the later 18th century.

Some communities experimented with altering the family structure and child-rearing rules. Moravian religious settlements, such as that in Bethlehem, Pennsylvania, created a family surrogate, which "explicitly subordinated a Moravian's familial obligations to his religious duties" (Gollin 1969, 651). This resulted in the communal sharing of labor and products and communal living arrangements in which sexes were segregated into "choirs." When a baby was weaned—between 12 and 18 months—it was given to the care of the nursery. At the age of five or six, boys and girls were segregated into childhood choirs, until the age of 12, where they were educated to a degree uncommon in colonial society, learning languages, mathematics, history, geography, art, and music. From ages 12 to 17, boys and girls, still separated, were apprenticed to learn a trade or skill. This system died out among the Moravians in the 1760s, when family units became the norm (Gollin 1969, 653–55).

INFANTS: BIRTH TO THREE MONTHS

> Beds, shirts, biggins, wastcoats, head-bands, swadlebands, . . . bibs, tail-clouts, mantles, hose, shooes, coats, petticoats.
> —*Thomas Deloney*, The Gentle Craft,
> *1648* (Deloney 1903, 49)

To the 17th-century mind, a newborn baby—boy or girl—literally had to be molded by the midwife into human form. After the umbilical cord was cut, the midwife rubbed, pulled, and shaped the baby's limbs to their full extension. She smoothed the baby's head to reshape it from the trauma of birth and carefully pushed together the bones of the skull toward the soft spot on the top of the head. To preserve what she considered a correct shape, the midwife firmly wrapped her charge in yards of long narrow linen bands, called swathing or swaddling (Calvert 1992, 19–20). Various methods of swaddling were practiced, but most involved three procedures. In the first, a long band was wound securely around the baby's feet, extended legs, and torso, stopping under the arms; a piece of fabric padding might be placed between the legs before wrapping to prevent chafing. A second band was wrapped around the infant's arms, from fingertips to the shoulders, pinning the arms to its body. A third piece of cloth, the stay- or headband, was secured at the forehead and shoulders with an additional strip of linen. The infant might then be wrapped in a blanket; the result resembled a small mummy bundle. Physicians cautioned that swaddling bands should be changed every 12 to 24 hours.

All of these bands were fastened together with straight pins (the safety pin was a 19th-century invention) and pincushions were common gifts for new mothers. In the 18th century, Anna Green Winslow described the "white sattan pincushin" her aunt "stuck" for a friend: "On one side, is a planthorn with flowers, on the reverse, just under the border are, on one side stuck these words, Josiah Waters, then follows on the end Decr 1771, on the next side & end are the words, Welcome little Stranger" (Winslow 1974, 12). Many of these pincushions were of satin-weave silk and imported readymade to be decorated. That many of these special gifts were never used is evinced by the number that have survived today with all of the designs-in-pins intact.

In addition to the swathing bands, the constellation of swaddling clothes could include a close-fitting cap, or biggin; forehead cloth; belly band; whittles, or blankets; bibs; padded stays; and clouts, or diapers. Period discussions on the use of clouts, including how many were considered necessary and how they were folded on the infant, are lacking, likely because it was such a mundane activity. It was the custom, however, that if the clout were only wet rather than soiled, it was hung outside or by the fire to dry and then reused without washing. It is also unclear when clouts were discarded; generally only nonambulatory children wore clouts. Some researchers suggest that once a child was able to stand and walk, clouts were no longer used as the toddler could relieve itself anywhere, by itself. To keep the infant's spine straight some mothers also put their babies in stays, with stiffening ribs of twine or other padding. Discomfort or injury could result, however, if the tightness of the stays forced the pins of the swaddling and bands and clouts to press into the baby.

Swaddling clothes are enumerated in 17th-century inventories, an indication that they were valued. For example, in Massachusetts, the inventory of John Lowle, recorded in 1647, included "a parcell of childbed Linnin, Headbands [staybands], &c." worth £1 and "swathing bands" worth 2 shillings (Dow 1916, 5:328–29). The inventory of John Cogswell, recorded in 1653, listed "10 diaper duble clouts"; "childs bearing cloth"; "one sucking bottle"; and "a swathe and pin cushen," the total value was £3 (Dow 1917, 6:69). The large estate of Salem merchant Edward Wharton, taken in 1677, included three sets of "childs swathes," each valued at eight pence (Dow

1935, 266). Baby's clothing also appears in court documents. For example, in 1682, in a paternity suit, it was revealed that the mother Sarah Stickny "told her [i.e. the witness] Samuel Lowel was the father, and when he went away he said he would bring her whittles and clouts" (Dow 1921, 8:262).

Among the poorer sorts and the enslaved, complete swaddling and all that it required was probably not an option. Although some mothers might have been able to afford to purchase used swathing from a shop or estate sale, others probably appropriated what was handy—scraps of cloth, worn clothing, and/or blankets. In March of 1756, for example, the wardens of St. Philip's church in Charleston advertised for a wet nurse for "A New born living Infant, wrap'd in an old oznabrugs [coarse linen] shirt"; the infant had been found in the cellar of an empty house (*South-Carolina Gazette*, March 11).

Babies were generally completely swaddled for the first three months of life. After that, a mother might shirt her baby and swaddle only the legs and torso, leaving the arms, hands, and head free to move. Toward the end of the 17th century, a mother usually swaddled her infant completely for only a few weeks and then wrapped only the legs and lower torso. Until about 1750, however, some form and length of swaddling was considered by most authorities essential for the health and development of a baby. By this time physicians also recommended that all the baby's garments should be changed daily, a nod to hygiene and cleanliness practices that were not apparently standard at the time.

In the colonies, most parents had given up the practice of swaddling by 1770 although among some ethnic groups such as the Germans and the Dutch swaddling persisted into the 1800s. This change indicates that adults had begun to modify the assumptions they made about the nature of very young children as they recognized the value of physical freedom and exercise. This new way of thinking, espoused first by Locke, was reflected in the literature of the period. Samuel Richardson's fictional heroine, Pamela, bemoaned the practice of swaddling as she defended Locke's system of raising children:

> How has my Heart ached, many and many a time, when I have seen poor Babies roll'd and swath'd, then or a dozen times round; then Blanket upon Blanket, Mantle upon that; its little Neck pinn'd down to one Posture; its Head, more than it frequently needs, triple-crown'd like a young Pope, with Covering upon Covering; its Legs and Arms, as if to prevent that kindly Stretching, which we rather ought to promote, when it is in Health, and which is only aiming at Growth and Enlargement, the former bundled up, the latter pinn'd down; and

how the poor Thing lies on the Nurse's Lap, a miserable little pinion'd Captive, goggling and staring with it Eyes, the only Organs it has at Liberty. (Richardson 1776, 286)

First published in 1740 and a best seller in England, *Pamela or Virtue Rewarded*, was exported for sale in colonial shops. In Philadelphia, Benjamin Franklin reprinted the volume for sale in 1742; Boston and New York issued their own editions in 1744.

INFANTS AND TODDLERS: THREE MONTHS TO THREE YEARS

The clothing of babies and toddlers was not distinguished by gender. Apart from swaddling, the clothing of very young children actually changed only slightly until early in the 20th century. Differences in cut and construction are difficult to detect when so few reliably dated examples of everyday baby clothing have survived.

Main Garments

When an infant was free from swaddling bands, it was usually clothed in a simply cut gown with a fitted bodice and gathered or flared skirts, which was worn over a shirt and one or more petticoats. Infants' gowns usually fastened in the back and could extend well past the legs. For colder weather, a jacket might be added.

A portrait of Mrs. Elizabeth Freake and her daughter Mary, painted in Boston by an unidentified artist, shows baby Mary (1674–1752) at six months of age. (The portrait was originally painted in 1671; Mary's figure was added in 1674.) Mary is depicted in a long yellow silk gown with elbow-length sleeves, which echoes the fashionable dress of her mother. The hem edges of the sleeves are folded back to reveal the sleeves of a white linen shift or possibly detached sleeves. These undersleeves are tied with yellow ribbons to create a puffed effect. Her stiff pose is likely the result of her wearing stays under her gown or being partially swaddled—or both.

In about 1679, the figure of Ann Patteshall (born 1678) was painted seated on the lap of her mother, Martha Woody Patteshall. About a year old at the time, Ann is dressed in a long black silk gown with short sleeves that appear to have been rolled back to reveal more of the undersleeve. The diaphanous linen bodice or bib covering her gown is ornamented with embroidered or bobbin lace inserts and may be detached from the

Elizabeth Freake and Baby Mary, unknown artist. (Burstein Collection/Corbis)

gathered apron. The same wide lace that edges her detached falling collar ornaments her cap, to which is fixed a knot of narrow ribbons. Ann likely wears stays under her gown.

The practice of dressing nonambulatory infants in gowns continued into the 18th century. In Pennsylvania, a two-month-old child taken by her mother when she ran away from an indenture was clothed in a "striped gown" and a five-month-old wore a "striped linsey gown" (*Pennsylvania Gazette*, October 25, 1750; August 27, 1752). (It is notable that in newspaper advertisements the gender of babies under about 18 months of age usually is not mentioned.) The Connecticut Historical Society possesses in its collection a printed cotton short gown or jacket, sized for a young baby. It has a straight cut body, open center front, with triangular gores at the side seams, a square neckline, and straight elbow-length sleeves, and appears to have been pieced from scraps. Written sources also occasionally mention double gowns: a reversible gown made of two different fabrics, which may have been worn primarily for warmth.

In the 18th century an alternative to the gown was a wrapper—a long open gown that folded across the child's torso in the front and was held in place by pins or ties. This might also be called a bed gown or night gown. In 1778, Daniel Fullan advertised that a woman who had been hired as a nurse for his wife, who had been "lately brought to bed" had taken the child, a two-week-old boy, and disappeared. The child was dressed in "nothing but an old chintz rapper" (*Pennsylvania Packet*, September 12, 1778).

Except for the length of the gown and petticoats, sartorial styles did not change for children who had learned to walk, nor were they differentiated by gender. In about 1670, 18-month-old Henry Gibbs (1668–1723) was depicted in a black gown. The gown's full elbow-length sleeves have a horizontal pattern likely made of applied metallic tape or lace and a single pane, or slash, as permitted by a Massachusetts sumptuary law of 1634. His hanging sleeves are trimmed with a tape woven in a pattern of scarlet, yellow, and white. A close-fitting bib, which looks stiffened, covers the front of the gown's bodice, and a gathered linen apron (which may be attached to the bib) ties at his waist. Over his bib is a plain square collar, and he wears a strand of coral beads around his neck. His reddish cap with wide white lace band fits so that the top of his hairline can be seen. Henry holds a bird to indicate his gender.

Nearly a century later, the child in William Johnston's portrait of Mrs. Jacob Hurd (Elizabeth Mason), wife of a Boston silversmith, exemplifies the change in children's fashions by about 1762. The child wears a white square-necked gown with a fitted bodice that closes in the back, and a full skirt. The elbow length sleeves have a ruched, or gathered, band above the hem and are finished with a sheer ruffle, as is the neckline. The bodice appears to be stiffened, and is conical in shape, but the dress fabric is probably a fine linen or cotton. This somewhat simpler style for children would evolve over the next decades into a much more relaxed set of garments.

Newspaper advertisements hint at the clothing worn by toddlers of the working poor in the 1700s. A two-year-old girl taken by her runaway servant parents in 1756 wore a brown woolen frock (*Pennsylvania Gazette*, August 12, 1756). Frocks and gowns in the context of babies and very young children most likely have the same meaning. (For older children, a frock also may have been more like a man's or boy's hunting or work frock—a long loose overshirt—or it may have been a button-front gown resembling the then-fashionable man's frock coat.) That same year a runaway couple took with them a 14-month-old child, dressed in a blue stuff gown and boned stays. When she ran away from her master in 1757, a single woman took her daughter, aged about 22 months, who was clad in an unnamed garment of black and white striped linsey (*Pennsylvania Gazette*, October 25, 1750; August 27, 1752; February 5, 1756; August 12, 1756; November 3, 1757).

Documents concerning baby clothing for the enslaved are uncommon. However, a book of accounts kept for the estate of Savannah resident Benjamin Farley between July 1766 and October 1769 contains five entries for the making of a total of 20 "Sutes of Negro baby Cloths" for enslaved mothers. Although no fabrics are identified and the ages of the infants are not indicated, the cost of labor for each "sute" was about eight pence (Gibbons).

Undergarments

Under all the rest of its garments, an infant wore a short linen shirt. Baby shirts had straight sleeves, which were sometimes cuffed, and a low neckline, either rounded or squared. They were open down the center front and reached to below the waist. By the mid-18th century a loosely cut, thick flannel shirt was being recommended for night wear for newborns.

Slips are sometimes mentioned: a long, sleeveless gown or shift, with the skirt gathered on to the bodice at or just above the waistline (like their 19th-century namesake). In the 18th century, the aforementioned Dr. Cadogan suggested that newborns should be dressed in a back-opening wool flannel gown (slip) made with a straight, sleeveless bodice and attached skirt about of ankle length, under a similar gown, made a few inches longer—whether this overgown should have sleeves was not specified, but is likely (*Pennsylvania Gazette*, March 21, 1749).

Children's petticoats (the word was also shortened to "coats") had a relatively wide waistband and a long gathered skirt. Petticoats worn by non-ambulatory children were of the wrap-around variety: open all the way from the waist to the hem, wrapped around the baby's torso, and fastened with pins or ties. In her diary, Salem, Massachusetts, resident Mary Vial Holyoke (1737–1802) noted the birth of her daughter Peggy, on March 4, 1763; about a month later, on April 11, she dressed Peggy in petticoats for the first time (Holyoke 1911, 58).

Many babies and toddlers were dressed in short straight-cut stays stiffened with packthread or whalebone (baleen). Packthread stays were corded with a thick twine between two layers of fabric. In her diary entry for March 23, 1762, Mary Holyoke noted that her daughter Mary, who was then 18 months old, first began to wear stays and shoes (Holyoke 1911, 55). Jumps is a term used for an unboned but still supportive bodice, something like a waistcoat without sleeves. A 1763 advertisement for a little boy's clothing stolen or accidentally taken in a trunk listed "Shirts, Stockings, and Petticoats, also one pair of jumps" (*Pennsylvania Gazette*, March 24, 1763). Physicians writing in the mid-18th century about child-rearing practices protested the practice of putting children into stays at any age.

Outerwear and Accessories

For the baby of a well-to-do couple, a bearing cloth made of a fine silk or wool fabric, embellished with lace or embroidery, might be part of a christening outfit and then used for the first few months of life. In general, blankets, quilts, and mantles were used to regulate warmth for nonambulatory children. Once children began to walk, they might wear simplified versions of hooded and plain cloaks and mantles; these are mentioned by various names in 18th-century merchants' notices.

Babies' heads were usually covered by caps. Many styles existed: some with straight bands of cloth gathered to flat round crowns; others with side pieces cut and sewn to pull a straight center band into shape.

Variations were worked with fancy needlework, lace, and ruffling. In the 17th century, infants' caps were usually tied under the chin. One style of cap was called a biggin or biggins. Seventeenth-century Massachusetts Bay colonist Mary Winthrop asked a family member who lived closer to the shops in town for "3 or 4 yards of fine buckrom and an ell of fine Holland for begins [biggins] for my child . . . Dwelling so far from the baye makes me oftener troublesome to you" (quoted in Earle 1895, 237). Square or triangular pieces of linen called forehead cloths were used to cover the baby's forehead, and held in place by the cap and either by ties or pins. More common in the 17th century, these were sometimes embellished with embroidery or lace.

Eighteenth-century caps were not always tied on. A plain linen undercap might be worn under a more ornate cap. By the mid-18th century proponents of the idea of hardening a baby to cold weather suggested that only one thin cap should protect the head, but it should not be tight or too thick. A ruffled white cap with pink and white ribbons added a touch of color to the white outfit worn by Mrs. Hurd's baby in 1762. The color pink was not yet conventional for wear by girls, so it cannot be considered a clue to the gender of the child in this portrait.

To protect the arms, a baby or small child might wear long detachable sleeves. Mitts were small fingerless gloves that slid on over the hand and around the thumb. A triangular flap attached to the top at the base of the fingers was brought over the fingers. Mitts could be cut of woven fabric or knitted. They were meant to keep babies—at least those out of swaddling wraps—from scratching themselves.

Since a baby's feet were completely covered by swaddling, a blanket, or long gown until it began to walk, it is most likely that stockings were introduced when the child was put into shorter clothes and began to need both warmth and protection for its feet. Dr. Cadogan remarked that shoes and stockings were useless until a child began to walk and play outdoors. Ribbon or ferret (a narrow woolen tape) garters probably held stockings in place below the knee for children as they did for adults. Paintings of babies with their feet showing are rare, as the long skirts of their petticoats and gowns cover their feet. However, flat soled, soft leather shoes that tie around the ankle are visible in some 17th-century paintings of children, and flat shoes with rounded toes appear in the portrait of Henry Gibbs. (The extended toe fashionable for older children and adults at this time would have made walking too difficult for toddlers.) During a visit to New York in 1697, Benjamin Bullivant, a Boston physician, noted, "The children of rich parents are usually without shoes or stockings, and young maids (especially Dutch) wear morning gowns all day Long and bare footed" (Bullivant 1697).

Babies in well-to-do families might be dressed with the same kinds of lace ruffles, aprons, bowknots, and ribbon sashes that ornamented the garments of their elders. Mary Freake and Ann Patteshall were depicted wearing the accessories fashionable for adult women in the 1670s: a white linen apron; lace-trimmed cap and falling band, or collar; and decorative bowknots on their sleeves. In variations to adult fashion, Mary's apron is tied or fastened at the neck rather than the waist; and her cap, probably of the same material as her gown, is fitted close to the head. Mary also wears either a decorative forehead cloth or a small undercap, the edge of which is barely visible at her hairline. Mrs. Hurd's child displays the accessories popular for children in the 1760s. A green sash, probably silk, circles the waist of the white gown. The linen ruffles on cap, neckline, and sleeve may be edged with lace or embroidered. A pair of green mittens dangles from the end of her silk sash. The child's mother holds a silver rattle with a coral teething stick at the tip. The portrait is of half-length, and we cannot see the length of the child's dress nor its shoes.

For toddlers just learning to walk a parent might also employ leading strings, which acted as reins to guide the child. Leading strings could be as simple as a rope or cord wound about the child's waist or as elaborate as strips of fabric that coordinated with the gown fabric and were sewn or fastened onto the gown at the shoulders. These latter were also called hanging sleeves. French engraver Abraham Bosse (1602–1676) illustrated a young child with leading strings in a standing stool. Samuel Sewell recalled to a friend that as a youth in Newbury, Massachusetts, he "met your sisters Martha and Mary in Hanging Sleeves, coming home from their school in Chandlers Lane" (quoted in Earle 1989b, 44).

A complement to leading strings, a pudding cap might also be worn to protect young skulls from the bumps and bruises of learning to walk. John Thomas Smith (1766–1833) described one that he wore when a boy, in the late 1760s: "This pudding consisted of a broad, black silk band, padded with wadding, which went round the middle of the head, joined to two pieces of ribband crossing on the top of the head and then tied under the chin" (Smith 1917, 196–97).

One universal accessory for babies and very small children was the rattle. This small toy, which could be made out of something as simple as a dried gourd whose seeds made a sound when shaken to expensive shapes of silver or gold with a whistle or little bells, was used to distract or entertain a young child. Although it is uncommon to find examples of meaner sorts of rattles from the colonial period, "coral and bells" have survived.

The Four Ages of Man, plate 1, engraving by Abraham Bosse, published 1636. The child at center left is in a standing stool. (Valabregue, Antony. *Abraham Brosse*, 1892)

Consisting of a stick of red coral set into a handle of silver or gold and usually mounted with several small bells, this object was at the same time a rattle, a coral teether, and an amulet to protect the child against evil and illness. Rattles with coral first appeared in European children's portraits in the early 16th century and later little bells were added; these elaborated forms are depicted in colonial children's portraits. Such a rattle is depicted in the portrait of Mrs. Hurd and her child. In 1733, a reward was offered for "a Child's Silver Whistle and Bells (the Coral lost)" (*Pennsylvania Gazette*, November 22). In Charleston, Roger Moore announced the theft of "a silver Coral with 8 bells quite new" (*South-Carolina Gazette*, May 1, 1736). Goldsmith John Leacock offered both "chased Silver Corals and Bells" and "curious Coral for Whistles and Bells" (*Pennsylvania Gazette*, May 25, 1758). The report of a birthday celebration for the Prince of Wales held in Boston included the observation that "little children who could not speak, laughed, clapped their hands, blew their whistles, and rung their coral bells" (*Pennsylvania Gazette*, September 5, 1765). Not everyone, however, favored the luxury versions of rattles. Noting that they introduce children to opulence at an early age, Rousseau counted that a twig, a stick of liquorice, or a poppy head was just as effective when entertaining a child (1979).

Hairstyles

As a child's hair began to grow in, it appears generally to have been combed simply and arranged away from the face, or as the painting of Ann Patteshall indicates, parted in the middle and allowed to fall to either side. Once a child reached the age of being dressed in clothing that reflected adult styles, hairstyles usually followed adult fashions.

Composition of a Wardrobe

The extensive estate inventory of Margrieta van Varick (1649–1695), who was born in the Netherlands and eventually settled with her family in Flat-bush, New York, details a generous supply of clothing for babies and very young children, all of it stored in a basket. At the time of her death, Margrieta had four children: Johanna, about thirteen years old; Marinus, about nine; Rudolphus, about five; and Cornelia, between two and three. Given the ages of the two youngest children, it is likely that some of this clothing was still in use. The baby's clothing included 12 diaper clouts, a pair of baby's sleeves; two baby's handkerchiefs; 23 navel bands; 14 baby's shirts; "one babyes quilt one pin kussion two pair babyes "; "six babyes capps"; and six cradle sheets, three with embroidered or laced borders. Among the clothing for young children were two woolen mantles, eight caps, six frocks, 14 "treckmutsies [a child's cap that tied under the chin]," 12 "forry Cloats [i.e., furry coats]," nine waistcoats, and 20 caps (Krohn and Miller 2009, 345–546).

In 1773, diarist Elizabeth Drinker enumerated the following belong-ings of her young son Henry, who was about three years old: "16 clouts, 3 frocks, 4 day caps, 4 arm cloaths, 2 night gowns [probably the afore-mentioned wrapper], 5 shirts, 4 night caps, 3 dimothy petticoats, 2 flannel petticoats, 1 long double gown, his jockey cap, 1 pair worsted stockings" (Drinker 1991, 1:187). The types and quantities of garments used by both these women likely represent the standard wardrobe for a child of the middling sort for each of the centuries of the colonial period. Poorer and wealthier families added or subtracted in quantity as well as the quality of the fabrics used.

GIRLS: THREE TO ELEVEN YEARS, 17TH CENTURY

Once little girls began to walk on their own, they were clothed in scaled-down versions of the same styles as their female elders. Because images of colonial children from the 1600s are so rare, two paintings by an unknown limner in Massachusetts, both dating to about 1670, serve as examples for the 17th century. Three of the five children of Arthur and Joanna Mason of Boston posed for a group portrait in clothing that suggests their position as children of wealthy parents. Joanna, aged six (born 1664), and Abigail, four (baptized in 1666), each wears a dark-colored gown (or skirt and bodice) with barrel-shaped gown sleeves. The sleeves have a single slash in the front. (A painting of their younger sister, Alice, at about two years of age, in the collection at Adams National Historic Park, shows her similarly dressed.)

The second example, is a portrait of seven-year-old Margaret Gibbs (born 1663), whose father, Robert, was a Boston merchant. Margaret is expensively attired in a salmon pink gown, with false hanging sleeves at the back. Her sleeves also have a single slash.

The Mason girls and Margaret Gibbs all wear a fine linen shifts, or chemises, with ruffled sleeves that show below the sleeves of their gowns. The ruffles of Margaret's chemise have a narrow lace edging. The girls were likely wearing boned or padded stays under their gowns.

In their portrait, both Joanna and Abigail Mason wear long white aprons with a lace-edged pinafore top over their gowns. The apron bodice is fitted, with a round neck and cap sleeves edged with lace. The bodice ends in a V at the center front waist, and a short peplum covers the join of the ankle-length apron skirt. The apron skirt covers only the front of the gown, while the bodice appears to close in the back. The girls' hair, which is pulled back from the face, is covered by three layers of textiles. The first is a forehead cloth, edged in lace, which is fitted to the head and can be seen at the hairline. Over the forehead cloth is a loose cap, also edged with lace. The final covering is a white hood, knotted under the chin. Bowknots of red ribbon hold the edge of slashed sleeves together at the elbow. Johanna carries a fan and a string of coral beads. Abigail holds a rose. The girls' shoes are fashionably shaped with low heels and extended square toes; the shoes fasten with large red ribbon bows over the instep.

Margaret Gibbs's apron may be of two-piece construction. A tucked white linen bodice, which stops before the neckline, comes to a point at center front waist and is cut high up to the armseye. The linen apron skirt, which may or may not be attached to the bodice, is either gathered into a narrow band or gathered tightly up on a drawstring. Both the bodice and skirt are bound or edged with a figured blue and white tape or trim. Margaret's collar is a wide flat length of needle lace stitched to a sheer linen yoke. She wears a necklace and carries a folding fan; a knot of narrow ribbons is fixed to the back of her head. Her shoes, also with elongated square toes, are white, the lighter color complimenting her light-colored gown. Like the Mason girls' shoes, these also have red ribbon ties.

Johanna and Abigail Mason's hairstyles are mostly hidden under the hoods they wear, but the visible front hair is dressed fashionably high and back from the forehead. Following contemporary fashion for women's hairstyles, Margaret Gibbs's hair has been pulled back from the forehead to form a small chignon about halfway down the back of the head. In front, side partings form spiral curls that frame her face.

BOYS: THREE TO ELEVEN YEARS, 17TH CENTURY

Portraits of children in the Mason and Gibbs families of Massachusetts illustrate the contrast in attire, in the 17th century, for boys under and over the age of six or seven. Robert Gibbs (1665–1702) was aged four and a half when he posed for his portrait in 1670. Like his younger brother, Henry, who is discussed above, Robert was too young to put off petticoats. For his portrait he was clad similarly to Henry, in a black gown with elbow-length slashed sleeves and false hanging sleeves. Although Robert's sleeve trimmings are not as extensive, the sleeves are finished at the hem with a band of red ribbon or fabric and his gown has been trimmed with fur at the hem.

Posing with his sisters Johanna and Abigail, who were discussed above, David Mason (1661–1724), aged eight, had likely been breeched at least a year before this portrait was painted. Instead of a gown, he donned an extremely fashionable black suit consisting of a short straight jacket—also called a doublet—with full single-slash sleeves and wide-legged breeches.

Robert Gibbs wears a shirt with full sleeves that end in a cuff with a ruffle. The sleeves puff through and below the slashed sleeve of his gown. In contrast, David Mason wears a shirt with full sleeves that end in a band cuff but without a ruffle. The full shirt is also visible at the breeches waist, peeking out below the edge of the doublet. Gathered white under-breeches show below his breeches and cover his knees.

Like his brother Henry, Robert Gibbs wears a bodice, or bibb, and gathered apron, which may be attached. His stiffened collar is a falling band style without lace trim, which fastens at the back. As befitting an older youngster, instead of wearing a cap Robert is bareheaded and his hair is fashionably long. His shoes have extended toes, and he carries a pair of leather gloves to denote his sex.

Completing David Mason's outfit is a high square-cut falling collar, edged with narrow lace, and fastened at the front of the neck. Gray stockings covering his lower legs and his square-toed leather shoes have heels and are tied with ribbons. Brushed off his forehead at the front, his fashionably long hair reaches his shoulders and hangs in loose curls and waves.

This eight-year-old dandy carries gloves in one hand and a silver-headed walking stick in the other.

GIRLS: THREE TO ELEVEN YEARS, 18TH CENTURY

The portraits of Jane Bonner, Martha Parke Custis, and Rebecca Mifflin Francis, from the late 17th/early 18th century, mid-1700s, and toward the end of the colonial period, respectively, illustrate some of the general changes in girls' fashions at that time.

Daughter of Connecticut captain, navigator, and shipwright John Bonner, Jane Bonner (1691–1739) posed for her portrait by an unknown artist between 1698 and 1700. Despite her youth (aged seven to nine), she is dressed in the fashionable attire of an adult woman. Her loose gown of pinked fabric has three-quarter-length sleeves that are set low on the shoulder and a neckline that is low and oval in shape. The stiff bodice tapers to a V point below the waist and has been ornamented with bobbin lace, possibly metallic; five rounded lace tabs ornament the taper.

In the joint portrait with her brother John, painted possibly by Matthew Pratt in about 1760, Martha "Patsy" Parke Custis (1756–1773) wears a pink and white gown of flower-patterned silk, with a wide, low, round neckline, that probably laces closed at the back (not visible in the portrait). Stiff and wrinkle free, the bodice reaches her waist.

The portrait of Philadelphian Rebecca Mifflin Francis (1775–1792) and her grandmother by Charles Willson Peale, completed between 1777 and 1780, illustrates the beginnings of the softer clothing that came into fashion for young children just about the time of the American Revolution. Rebecca is shown in a pink and white gown patterned with small flowers. It has a low square neckline trimmed with a lace ruffle. The bodice does not appear to be boned, although there are vertical seamlines at the side fronts. The elbow length sleeves are relatively loose fitting, and have a wide ruched band as trim.

Mrs. Mifflin and Rebecca Mifflin Francis, by Charles Willson Peale, 1777–1780. (Image copyright © The Metropolitan Museum of Art. Image source: Art Resource, NY)

The main undergarment for all of the girls discussed above is the simple linen shift, or chemise. In her portrait, the ruffled sleeves of Martha Parke Custis's white linen chemise extend a bit down her forearm from under the short sleeve of the gown. Packthread or whalebone (baleen) stays would have been worn over the shift. In the 18th century, the full-skirted fashionable dome-shaped silhouette as worn even by young girls required at least an under-petticoat, if not some kind of hoop.

In 1737, Thomas Mallabe, a Philadelphia stay maker, advertised that he "maketh Steel Stays for the Help of Children that are growing out of Shape; likewise Backboards and Collars, for Children of ill Carriage, such as are used in Boarding Schools in England" (*Pennsylvania Gazette*, April 14, 1737).

Jane Bonner's portrait includes a number of personal accessories. She wears stone ear bobs and a double string of beads—possibly crystal— around her throat. The sleeves of her gown are turned up at the ends to show off a wide band of delicate bobbin lace, which was probably pinned to the edge of the chemise sleeve. The edge of the gown's neckline displays a ruffle of lace that was probably starched to stand up off her décolletage. Jane holds a spray of roses in her left hand and in her right a closed fan with red guard sticks.

Martha Parke Custis's accessories, from about 1760, include a wide pink silk sash around her waist, a set of lace ruffles visible around the neck of her gown, and two tiers—one straight, one shaped—of ruffles on the gown sleeves. She holds a basket of flowers on her lap. A different style of ribbon sash was worn by Rebecca Miflin Francis in the late 1770s. A wide silk ribbon drapes from the waistline at one side around the body and dips down to hip level at the opposite side.

Jane Bonner's hair has been pulled away from her forehead and is dressed fashionably high. She may be wearing a hairpiece of curls that cascades down her back to below her shoulders. The hairstyle worn by Martha Parke Custis is very like her brother's: a short fringe at front and natural waves brushed back from the face, curling at the nape of the neck. Rebecca Francis's hair is also cut short at the front and sides, with longer tendrils at the back.

BOYS: THREE TO ELEVEN YEARS, 18TH CENTURY

Main Garments

Before a boy was breeched, he wore a gown that buttoned up the front. The skirts of the gown may not have been gathered into the bodice but rather gored to flare out over the petticoat. Three portraits illustrate the range of styles for a boy's gown after mid-century. In a Joseph Badger portrait of 1760, three-year-old James Badger (1757–1817) of Boston wears a long dark gown of a dull silk or silk and wool fabric with a pointed front buttoning bodice and a flared, but not gathered, skirt that is split at the front waist. The tight-fitting sleeves end at the forearm in a wide cuff. John Singleton Copley painted four-year-old Thomas Aston Coffin (1754–1810), son of a prominent Boston merchant, in 1758 in a gown of blue satin with silver buttons and frogging that is open under the buttons to reveal a white satin petticoat.

The portrait of the Custis children discussed above shows John "Jacky" Parke Custis (1754–1781), who was about six, in a dark green full-length silk gown with short sleeves. The open front gown is attached to a front-buttoned bodice with a short peplum and a matching petticoat. The garment is modeled after a waistcoat and coat: the sleeves are short and cuffed, with a button visible at the inner elbow; and the gown fronts do not meet at the center, but are set back to allow the under-bodice, or pseudo-waistcoat, with its peplum and pocket flaps at the waist, to be seen. The gown fronts also have buttons on the bodice; and just as in men's clothing, the buttons of the pseudo-waistcoat are smaller than those on the gown.

After breeching, boys' wardrobes contained the same types of clothing as their fathers. Alice and Cadwallader Colden's son Sandie was sent to school in New York City for three months with only one new suit of drugget to complement his existing clothing. The boy's best suit was of "brown linen of my Mother in laws huswifery which I keept unwhitened [i.e., unbleached] for his Father & him" (Colden 1937, 8:201–02). George Washington ordered clothing for his stepson, John (Jacky), several times over the course of his childhood and youth. In August 1764, Washington requested his London agent to supply "A suit of fashionable cloth cloaths . . . A Suit of thin summer Do, and . . . 3 pr. Nankeen breeches. Note that these are to be for a boy of Eleven years of age; those sent last year to him were rather too large but you are to consider he is growing" (Washington 1764). A boy's banyan, "one side plad, the other side strip'd callamanco" was lost in Boston in 1742 (*Boston News-Letter*, June 3, 1742).

Another three portraits illustrate how youths from well-to-do families who had been breeched presented themselves in the 18th century. A portrait of young Warren De Lancey (born 1761), painted by Matthew Pratt and completed about 1772, shows him standing at the side of his grandfather, Cadwallader Colden (see Chapter 5). Raised in an elite New York family, 11-year-old Warren wears a green frock coat, probably of wool broadcloth, with a collar, narrow sleeves, and wide cuffs; gold metal coat buttons stop at hip level. His white satin waistcoat fits almost too snugly and buttons to

Cadwallader Colden and Warren De Lancey, c. 1772, by Matthew Pratt. (Image copyright © The Metropolitan Museum of Art. Image source: Art Resource, NY)

the waist. Fitted breeches of a deeper shade of green have gold buttons and buckles at the knees.

Francis (1759–1809) and Saunders Malbone (1764–1831), from Newport, Rhode Island, sat for painter Gilbert Stuart in about 1774. The brothers wear well-tailored coats, waistcoats, and breeches of unadorned wool broadcloth. Both coats are frocks with turned down collars, tight sleeves, narrow cuffs, and silk buttons.

The portrait of an unidentified boy of the Crossfield family of Connecticut, painted by William Williams between 1770 and 1775, shows a youth of unknown age in a green coat, waistcoat, and breeches. The knee length, collarless coat has curved fronts with large ornamented silver metal buttons. The horizontally striped waistcoat, which ends below the hip, angles back sharply from the bottom button to the hem, and the pocket flaps are placed just below the button level as well. It appears to strain across the boy's torso, giving the effect of horizontal ridges from the buttoned front.

Undergarments

The shirts of the younger boys are of various styles. James Badger's shirt or shift has full sleeves with ruffles that are visible below the gown cuffs and at the wide round neckline. Thomas Coffin's shirt is not visible at the neckline of his gown; the full shirt sleeves are cuffed and have attached ruffles. The plain linen shirt worn by John Custis under his gown has a low round neckline, only the edge of which can be seen above his gown neckline; the shirt's elbow-length sleeves have been turned up to the edge of the gown cuff.

All of the older boys wear a shirt with a turndown collar. Warren De Lancey's shirt has narrow sleeve ruffles. A close look at the left shirt sleeve reveals that the sleeve ruffle is stitched onto a narrow band cuff with buttons. The sleeve may have been pressed above the cuff into pleats to make it easier to slip the voluminous fabric into the narrow coat sleeve. Francis Saunders wears a pleated stock over his shirt collar, and the ruffles of his white shirtfront protrude through his open waistcoat. The ruffles are caught by a heart-shaped brooch set with stones, probably paste. The boy from the Crossfield family wears a white shirt with a turndown collar; vertical shirtfront ruffles show above his waistcoat and narrow sleeve ruffles extend from the coat's sleeve cuffs.

Accessories

Around his waist, James Badger wears a sash that is heavily embroidered at each end and around his neck a black ribbon bow, or solitaire. White stockings and low-heeled black leather shoes with buckles complete his look. Wearing a bowed ribbon at his waist, Thomas Coffin is portrayed with a racket and shuttlecock. He holds two cherries in his right hand and ribbons tethered to doves in his left. Thomas's shoes and stockings are not visible.

Warren Delancey wears a black solitaire neck ribbon, tied under the shirt collar; white knitted silk stockings complete the ensemble (his shoes are not visible). Saunders Malbone wears a black ribbon solitaire. Both Malbone boys are portrayed with the accoutrements that advertise their potential as successful merchants: an elaborate inkwell, paper, quill pen, and several books. The Crossfield boy sports a wide black bow under his shirt collar, which is tied at the neck. White knitted silk stockings and heeled black shoes with buckles complete his outfit. Holding a racket and shuttlecock, he is accompanied by a dog.

Hairstyles

Thomas Coffin's hair has been brushed away from his forehead and falls in soft curls to the sides and the base of the neck. John Custis wears his hair cut in a very short fringe at the front and brushed back away from his face; the hair falls naturally below chin level. Despite being the youngest of the three gowned boys discussed here, James Badger sports the fashionable hairstyle of an adult man. The sides of his hair have been curled in a single roll above each ear; the back of the hair has been pulled down to the nape of the neck in a curled ponytail, or queue. The queue may be James's own hair or it may be a hairpiece that was tied on his head with a string.

Warren De Lancey's brown hair is fringed short on his forehead, but falls over his ears to his coat collar. The hair of the Malbone brothers has been pulled back away from the face and may be caught in a queue at the back of the neck. The Crossfield boy may be wearing a full wig, which has a single roll above each ear. The hair appears to have been powdered to make it fashionably white.

Even young boys were fitted for a wig. In 1750, a Mr. Freeman of Portland, Maine, paid to have the heads of his three sons, Samuel, James, and William—aged eleven, nine, and seven—shaved in preparation for wearing wigs. The cost of the wigs for his two older sons was £9 each (Earle 1989a, 51).

CHILDREN OVER TWELVE

As they entered their teens, girls and boys set aside all of the details of dress that indicated childhood and adopted fully adult dress, including hairstyles, especially when in company, paying calls, or attending social events.

Mary Mason (c. 1657–1740), the eldest sister of the Mason children discussed above, posed for an unknown artist in Boston in about 1670. Her portrait shows a teenaged girl in a dark bodice that laces across a matching stomacher, with wide elbow-length sleeves that are not slashed and a low round neckline. Her skirt, barely visible at one side of her white apron, appears to be of a patterned fabric (perhaps blue with white floral patterning). She wears no lace, but a broad sheer linen collar covers her shoulders and sheer cuffs accentuate the gown sleeves. Mary's white linen chemise has full sleeves with single puffs ending in a ruffle caught with narrow red ribbon bows. Red ribbons also ornament her hair, which is pulled back from her face and cascades into ringlets at the sides. She carries a closed folding fan.

Girls' gowns were as varied as their adult counterparts. When upper-crust New Yorker Alice Chrystie Colden sent her daughter off to school in New York City in 1732, she wrote, "Bettie is to have a plain blew silk gown and no other cloaths save ordinary calligoes she wore at home. I've made up my seersucker gown for her which is the best she has at present" (Colden 1937, 8:201–02). It is interesting to note here that Bettie's mother selected one of her own gowns to remake for her daughter as a best dress for country wear, but it was not considered good enough for town. On a different social scale, a 1741 advertisement offered a reward for "a fine holland Gown with blue and white stripes, fit for a Girl of about 9 Years old" stolen from one William Herbert (*Pennsylvania Gazette*, July 9, 1741).

One of the most fashionable gown styles of the mid-18th century is illustrated in the double portrait of Mary (1744–1786) and Elizabeth (1747–1775) Royall, daughters of wealthy Medford, Massachusetts, merchant and slave holder Isaac Royall Jr., painted by John Singleton Copley in 1758. Mary, in blue silk satin, is about 14; Elizabeth, in white silk satin, about 11. Mary's gown skirt is trimmed with a self-fabric ruching called robings, which may indicate that it is actually an open robe with a matching petticoat. The white gown appears to be a matching bodice and skirt seamed together, called a round or closed gown. Elizabeth's sleeves are the elbow-length style with bow trim and a shaped ruffle that were newly fashionable. Mary's gown sleeves, however, have short ruched tabs at the armseye instead of sleeves, so that the chemise sleeves and their fine ruffle are visible for the length of the upper arm. This sleeve style may have been adopted from a portrait of an English noblewoman, rather than reproducing a garment that Mary owned. In fact, in this case the costume of each girl may have been derived from a print source, just as in many portraits of adult sitters by New England's John Singleton Copley and Charleston, South Carolina's Jeremiah Theus.

Additional gown styles for girls, just as worn by adult women, were the short gown and the double gown. Sally Cary Fairfax (c. 1730–1811) mentioned in her diary in 1772 that, "On friday, the 3d of Janna, came here Granny Carty, she cut me out a short gown, & stayed all night" (Fairfax 1903, 213). A child's "double short gown and petticoat" were among the clothing stolen from a Philadelphia house in 1780 (*Pennsylvania Gazette,* July 26, 1780).

Philip Vickers Fithian, tutoring on a Virginia plantation, described the clothing of three of a group of teenaged girls during a visit they paid to the house in June 1774. Seventeen-year-old Jenny Washington wore a cotton chintz gown "with an elegant blue stamp" over a light blue silk quilted petticoat. A spotted apron, probably a sheer white cotton with a small figure such as were imported from India, finished the gown. Her hair was dressed up, "with two rolls at each side" a cap of gauze, lace, and artificial flowers perched on top. Fourteen-year-old Priscilla Hale had on a white Holland gown, a "cotton diaper quilt very fine," which was probably a white cotton Marseilles quilted petticoat, and a lawn apron. Her hair also was dressed up and her cap was made of ribbon. The youngest, 13-year-old Betsy Lee, wore a "neat shell callico gown" and a feather in her hair. There was little to distinguish between the youngest and the eldest, all dressed for paying a call (Fithian 1968, 123–25).

Sarah Wister (born 1761) kept a diary when her Pennsylvania family moved from Germantown, Pennsylvania, to near Valley Forge in 1776. At 15, Sarah was aware of the young officers nearby and tried to make a good impression. Before they removed from Germantown she was caught sitting in her doorway wearing a green skirt and a dark short gown—informal dress suitable for chores about the house. In June 1778, she was again caught unawares, wearing the same green skirt and dark short gown. In other entries Sarah mentioned a chintz gown, a muslin petticoat, a silk and cotton gown "made without an apron" that made her feel awkward, a bonnet and a white "whim," a purple and white striped gown of Persian worn with a white petticoat, muslin apron, gauze cap, and neckcloth (quoted in Evans 1975, 116, 118, 122, 125, 140).

When George Washington's stepson was 15 years old, in 1768, George made another purchase of clothing for him from London: "A handsome suit of fashionable cloth. Also a riding dress of green Cloth, and two suits of fine Jean's; the cloaths you sent him last year fit very well except the sleeves wh'ch are 4 inches at least too short; but you must make allowance for his growth . . . Let the jean suits be made without linings . . . and get him a pair of leather breches as you can direct the size" (Washington 1768). In an addendum to an order of his own, in 1772, he also asked for a dress suit of superior broadcloth, a second handsome and fashionable suit but for summer wear and only lined in the "foreskins" (a full lining would be too hot), a riding coat and buff waistcoat with gold lace, a pair of silk knit breeches, a pair of very fine black everlasting breeches, and finally, a "waistcoat of Superfine Scarlet Cloth with a neat light gold Embroidery (if embroidery is in fashion[,] if not to have gold lace on it)." In short he wants "a [fashionable] Winter Waistcoat which you will please to let this be" (Washington 1772).

ENSLAVED, APPRENTICED, AND INDENTURED CHILDREN

Images of enslaved, apprenticed, and indentured children in the colonial period are rare. The earliest known portrait of an African American in colonial painting is a young enslaved attendant to Henry Darnall III (c. 1702–1787), the son of one of Maryland's wealthiest families, painted by Justus Engelhardt Kühn in about 1710. In contrast to his master's finery, the unnamed slave wears an unadorned salmon-colored buttoned coat with contrasting blue lining. His cuffed shirt is closed at the neck but open down the chest. The silver collar around his neck indicates his status as property. About 50 years later, in 1761, John Hesselius portrayed another Maryland boy, Charles Calvert (1756–1777), and his young slave. Charles is dressed in fanciful military regalia; his African American attendant is dressed in livery—a yellow coat with matching waistcoat and breeches. The coat has a turndown collar and wide cuffs of black fabric. The front edges of the coat and waistcoat and the cuff edges are finished with ornamental tape. The boy's shirt has a small front ruffle. His black neck stock resembles a metal collar.

Enslaved children living in an urban context usually are not described as wearing the standard plantation or field hand outfits of blue linsey and white osnaburg. A 12-year-old enslaved African boy who was newly arrived in Boston disappeared in 1737 wearing an outer jacket of brown shag, striped under jacket and breeches, linen shirt, striped woolen cap, and black yarn stockings (*Boston News-Letter*, November 10). Another runaway notice described a "negro man-servant about 16," who took with him a patched gray broadcloth coat faced with yellow and a blue camblet coat, a pieced blue jacket, light cloth breeches with a brown patch on the seat, two cotton and linen shirts, two pair of gray yarn stockings, old patched shoes, and a patched hat (*Boston News-Letter*, April 9, 1742). An Indian boy runaway in Rhode Island (whether apprentice, indentured servant, or slave is not clear), aged 17, wore a thick kersey cinnamon colored jacket, black and white striped breeches, a flannel shirt, new shoes, yarn stockings, and a felt hat (*Boston News-Letter*, December 9, 1742). A mulatto woman ran away in 1778 taking her six-year-old son, who was wearing a brown cloth coat, osnaburg overalls, shoes, and a hat with a gold band. With the possible exception of the gold hat band, this was standard clothing for the laboring poor and indentured servants (*Pennsylvania Gazette*, October 15, 1778).

Young Negro, engraving by Wenceslaus Hollar, 1645. The enslaved boy wears a shirt with darted falling band. The sleeveless jerkin buttons up the front. (The Thomas Fisher Rare Book Library, University of Toronto)

Advertisements show that indentured or apprenticed teenaged girls and boys of European descent were dressed similarly to older adults of the same social and economic status, but might have owned (or stolen) a few pieces of finery. In 1743, a three-year-old girl went missing from her home in Lancaster County, Pennsylvania, dressed only in a pair of stays (almost certainly worn over a shift) and a quilted blue petticoat. With the addition of a jacket or short gown, this outfit would have been working dress for the average woman (*Pennsylvania Gazette*, February 10, 1743). A runaway servant girl aged about 14 or 15, wore a brown and blue flannel short gown with a patched brown wool petticoat, a tow shift, blue linen stockings, high heeled shoes, a linen apron, black mittens, and a black bonnet (*Pennsylvania Gazette*, June 4, 1772). Another runaway, about 16 years old, owned a long calico gown and a linsey short gown, a green striped petticoat and another of tow-striped linsey, a lawn apron, one silk and three lawn handkerchiefs, cotton mittens, shoes, two pair of white stockings (one worsted and one cotton), and a black bonnet lined in blue (*Pennsylvania Gazette*, February 5, 1777). Margaret Morison, a Scottish indentured servant who ran away from John Pinkerton of Philadelphia when she was 14, had two short gowns—one striped linen and one just "light coloured"—two linsey petticoats, olive and brown; two handkerchiefs, white and blue and white; a white apron, thread stockings, and low heeled shoes (*Pennsylvania Gazette*, October 17, 1778).

A 16-year-old Maryland runaway servant named John Sherlock left his master in 1746 wearing rather good clothes: a blue broadcloth coat, brown holland jacket, brown broadcloth breeches, a fine holland shirt, grey worsted stockings, "strong country shoes," a linen cap, and a felt hat (*Pennsylvania Gazette*, May 29, 1746). Seventeen-year-old George Parks ran away from his Philadelphia indenture in 1747 wearing wide trousers, a snuff-colored jacket, a homespun shirt, good shoes with large brass buckles, and a brown "bob wig" (*Pennsylvania Gazette*, August 6, 1747). James Logan, who left his Philadelphia master in 1769 with an older indentured servant, wore a snuff-colored cloth coat with yellow metal buttons, a white linen jacket, leather breeches, a checked shirt, blue and white cotton stockings, and shoes with pinchbeck buckles. His castor hat "much worn, but lately dressed, and cocked smart" with the broadest turnup worn at the front, was also much in fashion, while he wore his own "ill grown" hair sometimes loose and sometimes tied back (*Pennsylvania Gazette*, August 3, 1769). Two apprentices to gunsmith Michael Withir of Strasburgh Township, Pennsylvania, ran away in 1777. Philip Lowman, aged 16 or 17 wore a hunting frock over a shirt and trousers; and Andrew Fogle, 14 or 15 years old, wore a shirt and trousers of hemp cloth, a new felt hat, and shoes of neats leather, which tied rather than buckled (*Pennsylvania Gazette*, August 20, 1777). Carpenter's apprentice Carson Dickeson, aged 15, left Wilmington, Delaware, with a lead colored coat with pockets in the skirts, a blue and white linsey jacket and a white linen sleeved jacket, two Russia linen shirts, two pair of old trousers, a pair of buckskin breeches and a pair of fustian breeches, one pair each of yarn (wool) and thread (linen) stockings, neats leather shoes with copper buckles, and a felt hat (*Pennsylvania Gazette*, September 4, 1782).

AMERICAN INDIAN CHILDREN

Indian children were important during the colonial period for a number of reasons. Many Native communities persisted in educating their children in long-standing cultural and religious practices even as they were forced to adapt to Anglo-American society. In contrast, for English colonists, Indian children were often the focus of "civilizing efforts" which included religious conversion and apprenticeship or indentured servitude, especially in the northern colonies. Those children who were swept up into Christianity and/or servitude certainly would have adopted Western dress. For example, John Pitteme, an Indian servant, ran away twice—first at about 16, in 1737, and again in 1739. The first notice described his clothing as a gray coat, dark gray jacket with brass buttons, white linen breeches, no stockings, old shoes and a felt hat; in his second escape he wore a gray coat with pewter buttons, leather breeches, a tow shirt, gray stockings, shoes, and a felt hat (*Boston News-Letter*, September 15, 1737; October 4, 1739).

There are only a few first-hand accounts of how Native Americans dressed their infants, and these pertain to tribes in southern New England. Thomas Morton recorded in about 1634 that Ninnimissinuok "infants are carried at their mothers backs by the help of a cradle made of a board forket at both ends, whereon the childe is fast bound and wrapped in furres; his knees thrust up towards his bellie" (Morton 1883, 147). Many reports of the indigenous peoples encountered throughout the 13 colonies noted that young boys who had not yet attained puberty usually went naked, even in winter. Morton and Rhode Islander Roger Williams both observed that among the Ninnimissinuok tribes they encountered young girls wore a small skin apron. Writing in 1612 of the Powhatan tribes in Virginia, William Stachey reported that until the age of 11 or 12, young girls wore nothing and kept only to their own company. These practices slowly changed for Indians who were in closer and more frequent contact with settlers and who, in the late 18th century, abandoned their traditional ways of living and took up farming. For example, as early as 1635, the tribal leaders, or weroances, of the Patuxent and Portoback in Maryland desired that some of their children be brought up among the English settlers ("A Relation of Maryland" 1910, 88).

Well connected and successful in the Indian trade, William Byrd I (1652–1704) was doing business in the frontier area of what is today Richmond, Virginia. In 1686, he sent Yorkshire cleric John Clayton, who recently had visited Virginia and talked with Byrd: "an Indian Habitt for your Boy, the best I could procure amongst our Neighbour Indians, there is a flap or Belly clout 1 pr Stockings [likely leather leggings] & 1 pr Mocosins or Indian shoes also Some shells to put about his necke & a Cap of Wampum . . . these things are put up in an Indian Baskett, . . . there are a Bow & arrows tyed to itt" (Byrd 1917, 129). Byrd's gift reflected the attire of an Indian boy who had reached puberty. The age at which boys would begin to wear a skin breechcloth, or breechclout—generally 10 to 12 years of age—varied from tribe to tribe. The breechcloth did not change in style throughout the colonial period: every male "wereth a belt about his middell, and a broad peece of lether that goeth betweene his leggs and is tuckt up both before and behinde under the belt" (Morton 1883, 142). The belt could be made of leather, a snake's skin, or twisted cordage. (The leggings and moccasins Byrd sent Clayton would have been worn only while hunting or traveling; the cap of wampum was a status object.)

Among most tribes, puberty marked a change in hairstyle for men. William Wood (1865, 72) wrote of the Aberginians, a tribe living to the north of Massachusetts, that boys were not permitted to wear their hair long until the age of 16—and then by degrees: "some being cut with a long foretop, a long locke on the crowne, one on each side of his head, the rest of his haire being cut even with the scalpe."

Among the Ninnimissinuok, young women who had reached puberty and were ready to bear children, "weare a red capp made of lether, in forme like to our flat caps, and this they weare for the space of 12 moneths, for all men to take notice of them that have any minde to a wife" (Morton 1883, 145).

COMPOSITION OF A WARDROBE

Both girls and boys were dressed as fashionably as their social and economic circumstances allowed. In about 1636 Sara Dillingham was left an orphan. Her parents' estate was sufficient for her to be sent to school and supplied with a wardrobe: "a stuffe petticoat & waskote"; four "shifts with shewes"; and a gown that cost over £2 (quoted in Dow 1935, 35). The clothes sent with 10-year-old John Livingstone, of an elite New York family, when he went to a New England school in the second half of the 17th century were fairly extensive. His wardrobe included both warm and cold weather clothing. His main garments were two coats, one of stuff (with black buttons) and one of cloth (both generic names for woolen fabrics); one pair each of serge and blue plush breeches and four pair of new osnaburg breeches; five waistcoats, four striped with black buttons and one flowered; linen that comprised eleven new shirts, four pair of sleeves with lace, eight plain cravats and four cravats with lace, four white hand-kerchiefs and two "speckled;" two gray hats, one with a blue and one a black ribbon; three pair of fine stockings, one red and two blue; one new pair of shoes; five pair of gloves; two combs; and several sets of buttons: a dozen black, a dozen colored, three pair of gold, and three pair of silver. The family also sent along "Silk & Thred to mend his Cloathes," but it is unclear whether John was supposed to use them himself or turn them over to the schoolmaster's wife or housekeeper (Earle, 1989a, 288–89).

The 1737, wardrobe of a young Virginia schoolgirl was purchased in London and sent to her guardian, Colonel John Lewis. It included a lace cap ruffle and tucker, a pair of white stays, ten pairs of kid gloves (two colored and eight white), five pairs of hose (two worsted and three thread), eight pairs of shoes (one silk, one morocco, four plain Spanish, and two calf), a "hoop coat" (hooped petticoat or underskirt), a mantua (open gown) and coat (matching petticoat) of silk lustring, plus a hat, a mask, a fan, a neck-lace, a girdle and buckle, and four yards of ribbon for decorative breast and sleeve knots. Lewis also ordered a piece of fashionable calico, which would have most likely been made up into another gown, or perhaps a short gown and petticoat, and one and half yards of cambric, the fine linen fabric used to make the ruffles added to the sleeve hems and neck edges of shifts (Earle 1989a, 290). At the age of four, Nelly Custis, George Washington's stepdaughter, also was presented with a variety of fashionable clothing sent from England: packthread stays, silk petticoats, masks, caps, bonnets, ruffles and bibs, fans and necklaces, mitts and white kid gloves, "egrettes" (i.e., egret feathers) for her hair, and shoes of silk, calamanco, and leather (Earle 1989a, 291).

While Anna Green Winslow attended school in Boston, between 1770 and 1772, she wrote her parents of her activities and also kept a journal. In describing some of her clothing and also her textile and clothing activities, she left us verbal snapshots of her wardrobe. In November 1771, Anna's mother sent her some broadcloth, ribbon, a hat, and bags (for storage or show is unclear) just in time for Anna's 12th birthday (Winslow 1974, 5–6). The broadcloth may have been for a cloak, to be trimmed in ermine bought by her aunt. When faced with the possibility that her aunt would make her wear her new black hat with her old "red Dominie," Anna appealed to her mother: "Dear mamma, you don't know the fation here—I beg to look like other folk," adding that the old cloak and bonnet cut up and remade would make a good new bonnet for everyday use (7–8). At the end of December she made herself a new shift (she had previously made shirts for her uncle and shifts for her mother), and in the early spring of 1772 ten more shifts were added to her stock.

To pay a New Year's call in January 1772, Anna dressed herself in her best clothing: a yellow coat, a black bib and apron, pompedore shoes and gloves, a cap with blue ribbons, a heart-shaped locket and a paste pin, and her new cloak and bonnet. The word coat usually indicates a petticoat meant to be seen—perhaps of quilted silk. In this case, however, Anna did not describe an overgown or bodice, so her whole dress may have been yellow. She told her parents "for the first time, they all lik'd my dress very much . . . I have got one covering, by the cost, that is genteel, & I like it much myself" (13–14). To make a "setting up visit" to her aunt Suky, who had recently given birth, she dressed "just as I was to go to a ball" (15). Her finery came out again for a girls' evening party of dancing and other amusements; "I was dress'd in my yellow coat, black bib & apron, black feathers on my head, my past [i.e., paste] comb, & all my past garnett marquesett & jet pins, together with my silver plume—my loket, rings, black collar round my neck, black mitts & two or three yards of blue ribbin, (black & blue is high tast) striped tucker and ruffels (not my best) & my silk shoes compleated my dress" (17). In February she purchased with her aunt's permission and with money she had saved up "a very beautiful white feather hat" that was actually made of holland with white feathers sewn in place "in a most curious manner" (31). Another piece of headwear was made by a friend, called a "queen's night cap" and made of gauze (52). Anna also traded a piece of patchwork she was hoping to make into a bedcover for "a pair of curious lace mitts with a blue flap" owned by a school friend (62).

AVAILABILITY OF CHILDREN'S READY-MADE CLOTHING

As discussed in Chapter 3, there were several sources for children's clothing. The simpler garments that were generally made at home for adults, such as shirts and shifts, had their counterparts in garments for infants and children and were also made within the family. More fashionable garments could be made at home or ordered from seamstresses, mantua makers, or tailors. As early as the mid-1600s, however, children's readymade clothing and accessories in a range of qualities from fine to coarse were available from merchants and shopkeepers. Probate inventories of shops from the second half of the century list cloaks and coats, waistcoats, petticoats, shoes, stockings, and gloves.

In the 18th century merchants' advertisements generally distinguished between clothing for children, boys and girls, and, beginning in the 1760s, for youths and maids. In the 1720s and 1730s children's ready-made goods consisted of primarily stockings of cotton, worsted wool, linen (thread) and silk; gloves and mittens; and stays. Notices in the 1740s list clouting diaper, children's petticoats (coats), waistcoats, girls' stays and busks, jumps, bodices, pumps for boys and girls, castor and felt hats, jocky caps, gloves and mittens, stockings, and cane hoops. Every decade added more variety and more qualities to the types of goods previously sold. In the 1750s, gloves and mittens were designated as of "shammy" (chamois leather), lamb, or leather. Boys could find fine and coarse qualities of felt, castor, and beaver hats. Stockings for both sexes came in plain and ribbed, spotted, fine cotton, brown, and marbled. New items for children were red morocco leather shoes; damask shoes for girls; capuchins (a hood or hooded cape); black gauze handkerchiefs; and shoe and knee buckles for boys.

In spite of Britain's nonimportation agreements, luxury goods still entered the colonies in the 1760s. The finer items for children were often sold by milliners. Children's spotted hose came in four sizes; to go with them, children's morocco leather shoes came in randed (finished with an inserted leather strip) and stitched bottoms. In the late 1760s Philadelphia milliner Ann Pearson advertised an enormous variety of luxury goods for children: "black, white, and colored French and English silk gloves and mitts, with all kinds of furred and plain leather ditto"; "black and coloured silk Dunstable and chip hats and bonnets"; children's garland plumes and egrets; half-bone turned and packthread stays; and black and morocco leather pumps and shoes (*Pennsylvania Gazette*, August 28, 1766; May 14, 1767). For older children, boys' ribbed and plain worsted hose and girls clocked hose now came in all sizes; white, brown, and checkered thread (linen) hose as well as cotton hose came in best, fine, and middling qualities and plain and chevron worsted hose, "from the best to the lowest quality." Boys' new goods included worsted caps; black and blue velvet and satin caps (and black and white ostrich feathers to trim the latter); and silk hats and caps of many colors with gold or silver hat bands and with or without ostrich feather plumes.

From 1770 through 1785, beside all of the previously mentioned goods, more ornaments joined the list: French and Italian flowers and egrets; Bath, white metal, steel, block, tin and pinchbeck shoe and knee buckles; and, in 1785, boys "ruff caps." The continual increase in the types of goods imported or made specifically for the young, and the fact that several qualities and price ranges were offered to consumers, suggests that for status-conscious colonial parents, keeping their children dressed in a manner that reflected well on the family was an important part of family life. The fact that staples such as knitted stockings and caps were available ready-made in such variety also suggests that the traditional domestic employment of hand-knitting may have been superseded in some regions either by more elemental tasks in frontier areas or more elegant ones in urban centers.

REFERENCES

Beales, Jr. Ross W. 1975. "In Search of the Historical Child: Miniature Adulthood and Youth." *Colonial New England American Quarterly* vol. 27, no. 4 (October): 379–98.

Bullivant, Benjamin. 1697. *A Journal with Observations on my Travel from Boston in N.E. to N.Y., New-Jersies & Philadelphia in Pennsylvania*, excerpts. nationalhumanitiescenter.org/pds/becomingamer/growth/text2/newyorkdescriptions.pdf.

Byrd, William I. 1917. "Letters of William Byrd, First." *Virginia Magazine of History and Biography* vol. 25, no. 2 (April): 128–38.

Calvert, Karen. 1992. *Children in the House: The Material Culture of Early Childhood, 1600–1900*. Boston: Northeastern University.

Colden, Cadwallader. 1937. *Letters and Papers of Cadwallader Colden, Volume 8: 1715–1748*. New York: New York Historical Society.

Deloney, Thomas. 1903. *The Gentle Craft*, reprint of 1648 ed. and edited by Alexis F. Lange. Berlin: Mayer and Müller.

Dow, George Francis, ed. 1916. *Records and Files of the Quarterly Courts of Essex County, 1672–1674*. Vol. 5. Salem, MA: Essex Institute.

Dow, George Francis, ed. 1917. *Records and Files of the Quarterly Courts of Essex County, 1675–1678*. Vol. 6. Salem, MA: Essex Institute.

Dow, George Francis, ed. 1921. *Records and Files of the Quarterly Courts of Essex County, 1680–1683*. Vol. 8. Salem, MA: Essex Institute.

Dow, George Francis. 1935. *Everyday Life in the Massachusetts Bay Colony*. New York: Benjamin Blom.

Drinker, Elizabeth. 1991. *The Diary of Elizabeth Drinker*, edited by Elaine Forman Crane. Vol. 1, 1758–1795. Boston: Northeastern University.

Earle, Alice Morse. 1895. *Margaret Winthrop*. New York: Charles Scribner's Sons.

Earle, Alice Morse. 1989a. *Child Life in Colonial Days*, reprint of 1899 ed. Williamstown, MA: Corner House.

Earle, Alice Morse. 1989b. *Home Life in Colonial Days*, reprint of 1898 ed. Williamstown, MA: Corner House.

Evans, Elizabeth. 1975. *Weathering the Storm: Women of the American Revolution*. New York: Charles Scribner's Sons.

Fairfax, Sally Cary. 1903. "Diary of a Little Colonial Girl." *Virginia Magazine of History and Biography* Vol. 11: 212–14.

Fithian, Philip Vickers. 1968. *Journal and Letters of Philip Vickers Fithian 1773–1774: A Plantation Tutor of the Old Dominion*, edited by Hunter Dickinson Farish. Charlottesville: University of Virginia.

Gibbons, William. William Gibbons's Book of Accmpts for the Estate of Bejn Farley deceasd, Telfair family papers. Collection 793, box 13, folder 106, item 433. Georgia Historical Society.

Gollin, Gillian Lindt. 1969. "Family Surrogates in Colonial America: The Moravian Experiment." *Journal of Marriage and the Family* vol. 31, no. 4 (November): 650–58.

Holyoke, Mary Vial. 1911. "Diary of Mary Vial Holyoke." In *The Holyoke Diaries, 1709–1865,* edited by George Francis Dow, 47–138. Salem, MA: Essex Institute.

Krohn, Deborah H. and Peter N. Miller, eds. 2009. "The Inventory of Margrieta van Varick." In *Dutch New York between East and West: The World of Margrieta van Varick.* New York: Bard Graduate Center and New-York Historical Society.

Locke, John. 1693. *Some Thoughts Concerning Education.* London: A. and F. Churchill.

Morton, Thomas. 1883. *The New English Canaan of Thomas Morton,* reprint of 1637 ed. Boston: Prince Society.

Norton, Mary Beth. 1984. "The Evolution of White Women's Experience in Early America." *American Historical Review* vol. 89, no. 3 (June): 593–619.

Plymouth Colony Laws, Appendix 1. www.histarch.uiuc.edu/plymouth/Galleapp.html.

Plymouth Colony Records and Court Orders, Appendix 2. www.histarch.uiuc.edu/plymouth/Galleapp.html.

Ravenel, Harriott Horry. 1896. *Eliza Pinckney.* New York: Charles Scribner's Sons.

"A Relation of Maryland." 1910. In *Narratives of Early Maryland,* reprint of 1635 ed., edited by Clayton Colman Hall, 63–112. New York: Charles Scribner's Sons.

Richardson, Samuel. 1776. *Pamela or Virtue Rewarded: In a Series of Familiar Letters.* Vol. 4, 11th ed. London: printed for W. Strahan, et al.

Rousseau, John Jacques. 1979. *Emile, or on Education,* reprint of 1762 ed. and translated by Allan Bloom. New York: Basic Books

Sidwell, Robert T. 1968. " 'Writers, Thinkers and Fox Hunters': Educational Theory in the Almanacs of Eighteenth-Century Colonial America." *History of Education Quarterly* vol. 8, no. 3 (Autumn): 275–88.

Smith, Daniel Blake. 1982. "The Study of the Family in Early America: Trends, Problems, and Prospects." *William and Mary Quarterly* 3rd ser., vol. 39, no. 1 (January): 3–28.

Smith, John Thomas. 1917. *Nollekens and His Times*, edited by Wilfred Whitten. Vol. 1. London: John Lane.

Stannard, David E. 1974. "Death and the Puritan Child." *American Quarterly*, vol. 26, no. 5 (December): 456–76.

Washington, George. 1764. George Washington to Charles Lawrence, August 10, Series 5, Financial Papers, Account Book 1. The George Washington Papers at the Library of Congress, 1741–1799. memory.loc.gov/ammem/mgwquery.html.

Washington, George. 1768. George Washington to Charles Lawrence, June 20, Account Book 2. The George Washington Papers at the Library of Congress, 1741–1799. memory.loc.gov/ammem/mgwquery.html.

Washington, George. 1772. George Washington to Thomas Gibson, July 15, Series 5, Financial Papers, Account Book 2. The George Washington Papers at the Library of Congress, 1741–1799. memory.loc.gov/ammem/mgwquery.html.

Winslow, Anna Green. 1974. *Diary of Anna Green Winslow*, edited by Alice Morse Earle. Williamstown, MA: Corner House.

Wood, William. 1865. *New-England's Prospect*, reprint of 1634 ed. Boston: Prince Society.

Glossary: The Colonial Period

alamode: A thin plain weave silk used for hoods or scarves; also dyed black for mourning clothing.

baize: A heavy woolen cloth, usually heavily fulled and napped on both sides. Dyed brown or green, it was used especially for outerwear.

banyan: A loose gown worn by men for informal wear. Some banyans were T-shaped and others more closely tailored.

bay: A coarse woolen cloth, napped, lighter-weight than baize. It was used to line uniforms and to cover clothing.

bengal: Any of a variety of silk and cotton textiles made in and exported from Bengal, India, by the East India Company.

blanket: A white woolen cloth used for petticoats and heavy outer garments as well as bed covers. Blankets could be plain weave or twilled. Made in England, they were exported to America. Other varieties of blankets were part of the trade with Native Americans.

block printing: A method of printing fabric using blocks of wood that were carved to leave a pattern. To print polychrome designs, a block for each color was required. Registration of the colors was regulated by pins at the corners of the blocks. If finer details than could be carved in the block were required, metal strips and pins were inserted in the block to create them.

blond lace: An 18th-century term for a group of bobbin laces made of undyed silk thread. Blond lace was also made of white and black silk (black blonde).

blue resist (indigo resist):   The blue resist technique produced large effective designs in multiple shades of indigo blue at a low cost. The process was similar to the china blue technique.

bobbin lace: Also known as bone or pillow lace in the late 16th through 19th centuries. The design for a bobbin lace pattern is marked by a series of pricked holes on a parchment or card pattern that has been attached to a firm pillow or round or cylindrical shape. To make the lace, the worker plaits, twists, and/or interlaces together a number of threads wound on small bobbins. In the colonial period bobbin lace was made of linen or silk thread.

bodice: The upper part of a woman's dress.

bodies: A corset or pair of stays. The term was becoming obsolete in the 18th century.

bombazine: A twilled fabric with a silk warp and worsted weft that was dyed after it was taken off the loom. Black bombazine was used for mourning clothes.

bone lace: A 17th- through 19th-century term for bobbin lace.

breeches: Men's pants that ended either just above or just below the knee. In the 18th century, the leg portion was tapered and fastened around the leg with a band. These are in contrast to trousers.

broadcloth: A quality plain- or twill-weave fabric made of carded wool and fulled after weaving (see fulling). It was woven on a wide loom, hence the name. Made in England, broadcloths were known by a variety of names, including stroud and medley. Broadcloths were used for main garments.

brocade: In the 18th century, brocade was used in a strict technical sense for brocaded silk, a fabric in which the supplementary wefts making the pattern are carried only across the width of the motif, not from selvage to selvage.

buckram: A coarse, open weave, heavily sized linen fabric used as a stiffener in clothing as well as for wrapping merchandise for storage or travel.

buff coat: In the 17th century a jerkin or tunic of yellowish-brown leather, originally military wear.

buttonhole stitch: An embroidery stitch with a twisted edging along one side. Its original use was as a reinforcing stitch for the edges of buttonhole slits. The stitch, however, is also the mainstay of various embroidery cutwork techniques and needle lace.

calash: A collapsible bonnet usually made of silk with ribs of wire or reed; worn by women in the last decades of the colonial period.

calender: A machine used to press woolen, silk, and linen fabrics to make them smooth and glossy or to water them, that is, give them an indented wavy pattern.

calico: The term is derived from Calicut, a port on the west coast of Malabar, where Indian-made textiles were gathered for export by England's East India Company. In the colonial period, calico described Indian cotton cloth of several varieties, coarse or fine, plain or woven with colored stripes or checks, painted or printed.

calimanco: A plain weave glazed worsted fabric, either plain, striped, figured, spotted, or clouded (see clouds). Brilliantly colored, calimancoes were used for main garments.

cambric: A fine white plain-weave linen fabric. In the 18th century this bleached cloth was used for handkerchiefs, aprons, and caps.

camlet: A fine worsted plain-weave fabric, sometimes with the addition of mohair or silk, used for a wide variety of clothing and furnishings.

canvas: Various kinds of linen and hemp canvas were manufactured in the 18th centuries, including sails, toweling, and stiffenings for clothing. The term also referred to an open-weave, unbleached linen woven with regular squared holes (i.e., relatively equal numbers of warp and weft threads per square inch). This latter fabric was used for forms of counted embroidery, where the needle passes through the holes and does not pierce the threads of the fabric.

canvas work: In the 17th, 18th, and early 19th centuries, this term referred to any counted embroidery worked on canvas. The threads used included silk, crewel, and metallic.

capotain: A slightly conical hat with a tall crown and narrow brim, worn by both sexes.

castor hat: A felted hat for either sex made from the hair of the beaver, or castor.

chain stitch: An embroidery stitch that creates a series of linked loops. In the 18th century it was worked with a needle and, after midcentury, also with a tiny hook. When worked with the latter, the result was called tambour work.

changeable fabrics: Fabrics in which the warp and weft yarns are two different colors. Most often used in plain weave silks such as taffeta.

check: Plain-weave cloth with colored warp and weft stripes intersecting to form squares. Checks can be made of any fiber.

chenille: A kind of velvety thread made of short threads or fibers of silk standing out at right angles from a core of thread; from the French *chenille*, meaning hairy caterpillar. Chenille yarn was used to accent parts of brocaded dress silks and embroidery designs.

cherryderry: A cotton dress fabric from India.

chintz: The word chintz is derived from the Hindi word *chitta*, meaning "spotted cloth." In 17th-century India, chintz referred specifically to painted or printed cotton that was sometimes glazed. Demand for these imported textiles was so high that English dyers adapted the mordant technique for block printing on cloth about 1676. A wide variety of chintzes, from England as well as India, was imported to British North America. One appealing feature of the Indian versions of these gaily colored textiles was that they could withstand repeated washings without fading. Although they were used for clothing, chintzes were considered especially suitable for furnishings.

clothier: 1. In 17th-century colonial America, a weaver who was successful enough to employ apprentices and journeymen, with several looms at work. 2. In the 18th century, a man who oversaw all the finishing aspects of textile production, such as fulling, dyeing, and dressing fabrics.

clouds: Silks whose patterns were printed on the warp prior to weaving were called clouds in England and *chiné* in France. When woven, the color printed on the warp is muted by the uncolored or solid-colored weft. Clouds were especially fashionable in the second half of the 18th century for dress fabrics.

clouting, clouts: Linen fabric suitable for swaddling and diapering babies.

coat: 1. A body garment with sleeves, worn by men as the topmost layer of a three-piece suit. 2. In reference to women, a coat usually refers to a petticoat. 3. In reference to children (particularly boys before breeching) a coat probably refers to a frock made with sleeves and a front opening.

coif: A close fitting cap the covering the top, back, and sides of the head, sometimes tying under the chin. In the 17th and 18th centuries women wore a coif under a bonnet or hat when going outdoors; men wore a coif only as a nightcap.

copperplate printing: In copperplate printing, incised copper plates (up to 36 inches long) were used to print intricate and detailed images on washable cloth. This monochrome technique was confined to red, blue, purple, or sepia. Copperplate printing originated in Ireland and was brought to England after 1756. It was suitable for a variety of textiles, from handkerchief squares to large-scale furnishing fabrics. Narrative and figural scenes, historical subjects, and large-scale floral patterns were produced.

cotton: 1. The fibers that grow from the seed of the cotton plant. These fibers are called lint. The staple length of the fiber is important in determining how the fiber is handled in spinning. Longer cotton fibers are finer and make stronger yarn. Microscopically, cotton fibers are characterized by convolutions, or ribbon-like twists. 2. In the 15th through 18th centuries, cotton was also a term used to designate certain woolen cloths (the process of raising the nap of woolen cloth was called cottoning). In the 1700s, woolen cottons were used for slave clothing.

crape: In the 18th century, a lightweight crinkled fabric made of highly twisted yarns of silk, worsted, or a combination. Crape was often dyed black and used for mourning clothes.

crewel: A fine slack twist, two-ply worsted yarn especially suited to embroidery.

crewel work: In the 17th and 18th centuries this term referred to any embroidery done with crewel, or worsted, yarn. The work could be done on linen canvas or any fabric, such as wool, linen, linsey-woolsey, or fustian. The stitches could be counted into the canvas weave or worked without regard to weave structure.

crosscloth: Also called a forehead cloth, it was a triangular piece of fabric worn with the bias edge laid across the top of the forehead and the triangular point toward the back of the head. The crosscloth was worn under the coif.

cross stitch: A stitch unit composed of two crossed diagonal stitches of equal length. In historical examples, the cross stitch is worked as a counted technique; thus, the size of the stitch depends on the fineness of the fabric weave. Cross stitch was the most frequently used stitch on 18th-century girlhood samplers; it was also used to mark apparel, clothing accessories, and household linens. See marking stitch.

cutwork: A precursor to true needle lace, cutwork is any embroidery worked on a foundation fabric part of which has been cut away. It differs from needle lace in that the former depends upon a ground fabric, the latter does not. In the 17th and 18th centuries, cutwork was usually worked on linen fabric using linen thread.

damask: A reversible patterned fabric in which the design is formed by a contrast in the warp and weft float faces of a satin or twill weave. The patterns appear in relief against the ground. In the 18th century, damasks were made of linen, silk, and worsted, or a combination of fibers. The fabric had wide uses for clothing, furnishings, and table linens, depending on the fiber from which it was made.

darnex: A range of fabrics of various weaves with linen warp and woolen weft. Darnex was popular in the 17th century both as a coarse furnishing material and for coarse clothing.

darning stitch: Small evenly spaced stitches used to mend a hole or tear in fabric when worked in perpendicular sets of rows. The rows of stitches follow the weave structure of the fabric.

denim: A strong cotton or cotton and woolen cloth with a twill weave. The term probably derives from *Serge de Nîmes,* a twilled woolen cloth made in France. Denim is different from the fabric called jeans.

diaper: A twill weave fabric woven with lines crossing to form diamonds, the spaces variously filled with lines, a dot, or floral and leaf patterns. The fabric was usually of linen, but 18th-century linen/cotton examples have survived. Diaper was used for summer waistcoats, bodices, and petticoats as well as table linen and other furnishings.

dimity: A wide variety of fine cotton or linen fabrics with woven patterns. Dimities could be striped or corded, checked or figured, or tufted.

discharge: Printed on the cloth after dyeing or after mordanting, dischargers either bleached out sections of color or rendered affected areas of color soluble so that the color could be washed out.

doublet: 1. A waist-length, fitted jacket with a high collar worn by men in the 17th century. It buttoned down the front and generally was worn with sleeves. 2. A woman's version of the fitted jacket.

dowlas: A coarse linen first made in the 17th century in Brittany and then in Germany. It was used for rough shirts, sheets, and pillow cases. Dowlas could be plain, striped, or checked.

drawers: A term that in the 17th and 18th centuries could refer to either a man's undergarment or an outer garment. Knee-length linen or flannel underdrawers were worn under breeches. Evidence indicates that women sometimes wore drawers.

Dresden work: An elaborate form of white embroidery introduced in Europe in the 1720s for the commercial lace trade. Workers combined pulled thread embroidery with counted geometric patterns and surface stitches on very fine muslin to produce a fabric that was densely decorated and favorably compared to delicate Flemish bobbin lace. The best of this work was produced in the German kingdom of Saxony. It reached the rest of Europe and America through merchant wholesalers in the town of Dresden. In the 18th century, Dresden work was classified as a lace and was sold by lace dealers.

drugget: A light weight woolen fabric of narrow width, sometimes with a worsted warp, made in Wiltshire, England. In the 18th century, druggets were imported and sold for slave clothing. Druggets were also woven in colonial Massachusetts.

duffel: Heavy, napped woolen cloth that was woven in Witney, Oxfordshire. In the 18th century, blue, green, and red duffels were important goods in the trade with American Indians.

durance: Thick, heavily fulled woolen fabric.

egret: Tuft of feathers used as a hair or headdress ornament.

ell: Obsolete term of measurement for cloth. It varied according to the country of origin of the cloth. In 18th-century Britain, an ell equaled about 45 inches.

embossing: 1. The process of impressing patterns on worsted cloth to imitate expensive silk damask weaves (see calender and watering). 2. The process of printing colors with woodblocks on white serge or flannel.

everlasting: A heavy, closely woven worsted cloth, sometimes with weft patterned figures, dyed black and other colors.

falling band: Popular 17th-century collar with a wide, turned-down style; lace-edged for upper classes.

fearnought: A thick woolen cloth with a long pile. Sold both as yardage and readymade articles for slave and sailor's clothing in colonial America.

ferret silk: A poor grade raw silk that was used to make tapes. Ferret tape was used for binding shoe uppers, stays, or for ornamental purposes.

fichu: Neck handkerchief or scarf draped around the neck of a woman's bodice. It might be a square folded in half on the diagonal, a triangle or a shaped piece of fabric, usually semisheer linen or silk, often ornamented with embroidery or lace.

figured: Although the term is often used interchangeably with "patterned," it also refers to patterned with a small repeating motif.

flannel: A woolen cloth with a soft and spongy feel, napped on one or both sides. Usually sold white, flannels were also dyed. In colonial America, white flannel was used as shroud material.

flax: The plant from which linen and tow fibers and linseed oil are derived. Fibers from plant stems are called bast fibers. (Hemp is also a bast fiber.) Microscopically, flax fibers are characterized by crosswise markings called nodes or joints. The shorter, coarser flax fibers are called tow; long, combed, better quality fibers are called line.

fontange: High woman's headdress of pleated or gathered fabric, lace, or ribbons popular in the late 17th and early 18th centuries.

frieze: A coarse woolen pile cloth in which the fibers of the pile are twisted into each other to form a curly nap. This was done by hand or with a friezing machine. Woolen or mixed woolen and worsted fabrics could be friezed; however, worsted cloth was generally not woven with a pile so it was not friezed.

frock: 1. A button-front child's dress worn by boys until they were breeched. 2. A man's knee length coat with a collar. 3. An overshirt worn for hunting or outdoor work.

fulling: A process of scouring, shrinking, and pressing a woolen fabric to clean it of grease and thicken it. The surface of heavily fulled fabrics does not show the weave structure and has a napped texture.

fustian: 1. In the 17th century a plain-weave fabric with linen warps and woolen wefts. 2. In the 18th century fustian referred to plain-weave fabric with linen warps and cotton wefts. From 1736 to 1774, fustian was an important home product for British textile printers and dyers because during this time the importation of all-cotton cloth was banned in deference to the local silk and woolen industries. Some dyes took differently on the cotton and linen threads, creating a speckled effect.

galloon: Narrow trim, often woven of metallic threads.

garlick: A linen fabric first imported from Goerlitz, Silesia. Among the most commonly imported linen fabrics to the American colonies, it was used as for household textiles and for shirting.

garter: A band of ribbon, fabric, or specially woven tape worn around the leg, either above or below the knee, to keep the stocking from falling down. Lettered garters were tapes with a motto or phrase woven into them.

gauze: A semisheer or translucent weave with a crossed warp structure.

girdle: A woven belt or decorative cord that went around a woman's waist and was hung with small tools and accessories, such as keys, sewing implements, or a small purse. More expensive versions were woven of silk and metallic threads or decorated with embroidery or were constructed of intertwining metal links.

glazing: Application of a coating (such as a sugar solution) to a fabric to achieve a glossy surface. See calender.

gown: 1. A woman's dress. 2. An over-robe worn by academics or clerics.

great coat: An overcoat worn by men for warmth. Also called a surtout.

grosgrain: A plain weave textile in which the weft yarns are thicker than the warps, giving a rounded rib effect.

haberdasher: Originally a dealer in or maker of caps and hats, in the 18th century, the term denoted a dealer in small articles pertaining to dress, such as ribbons, tapes, buttons, thread, and dress accessories.

handkerchief: A large square or triangle of cloth worn about the neck by both men and women of all classes. In colonial America, slave women might use a handkerchief as a head wrap. Neck and head handkerchiefs were distinguished from pocket handkerchiefs.

head: 1. In the 18th century, women's powdered hair drawn up over a cushion or stuffing and dressed with gauze, ribbon, or lace. 2. A woman's headdress.

holland: Originally manufactured in the Netherlands, holland was a generic name for a variety of fine quality linen fabrics.

homespun: In colonial America, refers to any cloth of American manufacture as opposed to imported, whether of home or workshop production.

hood: Head covering that fits over the back and top of the head, close to the face. Cloaks often had attached hoods; separate hoods were worn for protection from bad weather or, in the 17th century, by fashionable women.

indienne: mordant-printed and -dyed cotton fabric from India, especially those having an exotic or particularly Indian design.

indigo: A powder used for dyeing cloth blue, manufactured from the decomposition of plants of the genus *Indigofera*.

inkle: 1. A variety of tapes or braids, usually of silk, used for trimming dresses, accessories, and furnishing fabrics. 2. The table loom used to make tapes or inkles.

irish stitch: An embroidery term in use from at least the 16th century to describe a counted thread technique in which vertical stitches of a predetermined length—usually over four threads of canvas—are worked in a stepped sequence in horizontal rows of polychrome colors. The resulting flame-like patterns are usually zigzag, but historical examples also feature scallops and other shapes. Irish stitch was used to embellish personal accessories as well as table carpets, cushion tops, book covers, fire screens, and chair seats.

jackboot: A heavy leather boot reaching above the knee.

jacket: 1. A woman's fitted bodice with long or three-quarter sleeves and a front closure. 2. A short coat with sleeves worn with breeches by men. Some men's jackets, however, were sleeveless. 3. In some contexts, the terms jacket and waistcoat were interchangeable.

jean: A sturdy twill-weave fabric, all cotton or cotton and wool, for working class wear.

jerkin: In the 17th century, a short, close-fitting jacket worn over the doublet, either for protection or warmth. It was sometimes padded and usually sleeveless.

jockey cap: A small cap with a round crown and long visor or bill.

kersey: A cheap, coarse woolen twill-weave cloth that was lightly fulled. It was used among the poorer classes, especially for great coats. Kersey also was used for slave clothing in colonial America.

kirtle: A fitted bodice with an attached floor-length skirt worn over the shift. The kirtle had detachable sleeves that laced to the armholes of the bodice. It was usually worn with an overgown.

knitting: In its simplest form it consists of successive vertical rows of encroached open loops. The work may progress either round and round or back and forth. All the loops in one row are maintained on needles or sticks and worked off one at a time as new loops are formed on other needles. Knitted fabrics are elastic.

knots: Fashionable dress trimmings worn on the sleeves and at the breast, made of ribbons or silk fabrics.

lace: 1. A term meaning a narrow woven or plaited tape or braid. 2. By the late 16th century it was used also as a generic term for all forms of bobbin- and needle-made open work. See also bobbin lace and needle lace.

lappet: Strips, or streamers, of lace or other trimming hanging from a woman's headdress or cap.

lawn: A delicate, semisheer linen fabric used for handkerchiefs, ruffles, caps, and aprons. Lawns could be plain, flowered, striped, or combinations of these. It was similar to cambric; the finest was woven in Flanders and France.

linen: Cloths of many grades and weaves made from fibers from the stem of the flax plant.

linsey-woolsey: A coarse cloth made of linen warp and woolen weft; solid-colored or striped. In addition to English manufacture, linsey-woolsey was woven in many of the northern American colonies.

lustring: A closely woven, lightweight plain weave silk with extra sheen imparted by a special process in which the warp was heated and stretched after being coated with syrupy gum. Produced from the late 17th to the early 19th century, lustrings could be plain, striped, changeable, or patterned. They were favorite exports to the North American colonies.

madder: A red vegetable dye derived from *Rubia tinctorum,* a plant native to Asia Minor. It was used for dyeing wool, silk, and cotton until the last quarter of the 19th century. In India, cotton cloths painted by hand with different mordants produced a range of fast colors when dipped in a madder bath. In the West, the mordants were printed on cotton with a series of woodblocks, one for each color. The fabric was then subjected to a madder bath. With different mordants, madder could produce a range of colors from pinks, reds, purples, tan, and brown to black.

Manchester velvets: By 1760, a variety of velvets made of cotton, manufactured in Manchester, England. They were dyed all colors except scarlet, which did not "take" on the cotton. The cotton fiber was imported from Jamaica or the French islands.

mantua: 1. An open gown worn by women in the 17th and 18th centuries. 2. In the 18th century, also a silk fabric suitable for use in gown making

mantua maker: In the 18th century, a gown maker, usually a woman. Mantua making involved draping the gown fabric on the customer to cut and fit the various parts, which were then sewn together. Some women were so successful in this business that they hired seamstresses to assist them.

marking stitch: In the 16th, 17th, and early 18th centuries, a form of cross stitch that was reversible, that is, identical on both sides of the fabric. It was used to mark the owner's initials on articles of clothing and accessories and household linens. The reversible form was replaced gradually by cross stitch in the 18th century. The practice of marking household linens and some articles of dress continued into the 19th century.

Marseilles quilting: 1. Professional handwork that began in the south of France, around Marseilles. The pieces were elaborately stuffed and corded, usually all white and made of silk or linen, although colors were used and sometimes made of cotton or wool. Marseilles (Marcella, Marsala, or Marsyle) quilting was imported into England and shipped to the colonies throughout the 18th century in the form of petticoats, vest and jacket patterns, stomachers, bed covers, and yard goods. 2. Loom-made goods that imitated hand-worked stuffing and cording, sold by the yard beginning in 1763.

matchcoat: Blanket or mantle worn by American Indians.

milliner: Originally, one who sold fancy wares and articles of apparel, especially articles of Milanese manufacture. In the 18th century milliners made up and/or sold articles of female dress, especially headgear, ribbons, and gloves.

mitt: A fingerless glove.

mob cap: Cap for girls and women with a high gathered crown and somewhat floppy brim.

Monmouth cap: A knitted wool cap with a brim, made in the area of Monmouth, England, and worn by working men in the 17th and 18th centuries.

mordant: A metallic oxide or mineral that bonds certain dyes to cloth so that they cannot be washed out. Each mordant, such as iron, tin, or alum, produces a different shade from a single dyebath.

moreen: A worsted fabric often with a waved or stamped finish.

morocco: Originally from Morocco, a goatskin leather treated to show the grain and often dyed red.

muff: Stuffed tube or sphere with an open interior used to warm the hands.

muslin: A fine cotton, considered the finest calico fabric, first made in India. Muslin was first imported to England in the 17th century. There it became so popular that it began to replace the fine imported linen fabrics woven in Flanders and Germany. As with other calicoes, muslin could be plain, striped, checked, printed, figured, and brocaded.

nankeen: A plain weave cotton cloth originally sold at Nankin in China and made from a yellow variety of cotton. By the mid-18th century it was being made in Manchester, England, of cotton dyed yellow.

needle lace: A lace technique that evolved from various forms of white-work, including cutwork, drawn-thread work, and pulled thread, practiced in Europe in the 15th and 16th centuries. It is constructed of row after row of detached buttonhole stitches, made with a needle and thread, and built up as filling patterns across outlines of thick threads that have been tacked down along design lines drawn on paper.

negro cloth: A coarse woolen fabric imported from England for winter clothing for slaves. It was probably synonymous with plains.

night gown: In the 18th century, a woman's dress, not a sleeping garment.

none-so-pretty: A generic term for tapes or ribbons.

organdy: A plain weave cotton semisheer or translucent fabric. It was sold plain or dyed or printed. See also muslin.

osnaburg: A coarse unbleached linen first made in Osnabrück, Germany, but later in Great Britain. In the 18th century, it was used in Europe for trousers, sacking and bagging. In the American colonies it was also used for slave clothing, especially shirts and trousers.

packthread: A sturdy twine or narrow cord used to stiffen stays, especially for children.

paduasoy: Possibly the heaviest silk plain weave available in the 18th century. A favorite silk for gowns and men's suits, it was usually brocaded. Paduasoy was expensive since it used much high-quality silk.

pannier: Side or bucket hoops worn over the hips to hold out the dress skirt.

partlet: A yoke-like garment that filled the open neckline of a gown or bodice.

paste: Fake gemstones of cut glass commonly used in buttons and buckles, other jewelry.

patchwork: A textile composed of cut pieces of different fabrics arranged to produce a decorative surface, all joined together with stitches.

patten: Protective shoe covering; most often a wooden or leather sole attached to an iron ring or wooden lifts to raise the foot above the mud or debris of the street.

pattern: 1. Pieces marked or shapes embroidered, knitted or woven into textile yardage for various articles of clothing, including waistcoats and breeches. 2. Lengths of fabric with patterns or designs suitable for use for a specific purpose, such as gown patterns. Both kinds of patterns were listed among the many items for sale by 18th-century merchants and differentiation is often difficult to distinguish.

penciling: The painting—or penciling—of indigo directly on a fabric with a small brush or reed. This produced a sometimes uneven and not always fast blue.

periwig: Introduced to England from France in the 1660s for men's wear, the periwig, or wig, had large clusters of curls that became more massive and cumbersome at the end of the century. In 1685, the peruke was introduced as a more comfortable alternative for informal wear.

perpetuana: Durable woolen fabric, possibly thinner and glossier than durance or everlasting.

persian: A thin plain-weave silk used in the 18th century as lining material for coats, petticoats, and gowns. It was imported from Persia beginning in the 17th century and later manufactured in Britain, India, and China.

peruke: A man's wig introduced in the late 17th century. Worn for informal occasions, the hair of the peruke was brought back away from the face and tied with ribbons. See periwig.

pet en l'air: A short version of the robe *à la Française*, with wide, loose pleats at the back, stitched down only at the neck, and a fitted front.

petticoat: A woman's skirt with fitted waist and full skirt of calf-length or longer. A petticoat was worn with a gown by the middle and upper ranks of women and sometimes by valued household servants or slaves. Or it was worn by working women with a jacket or waistcoat to form a suit. Expensive petticoats were made of silk fabrics to match a gown, or were quilted or embroidered.

piecing: The process of joining together the edges of cut shapes of fabric with stitches.

pillow lace: A 17th- through 19th-century term for bobbin lace.

pinner: 1. In the 17th century, a linen or lace edging that was pinned around the neck edge of a gown or bodice. 2. In the late 17th and 18th centuries, a woman's coif or cap with two long streamers or lappets hanging down, which could be pinned up on the cap.

plaid: 1. A twill or plain weave cloth usually having a check pattern or a pattern of intersecting stripes. Plaids can be made of any fiber. 2. A cheap woolen fabric, not necessarily with a pattern, used to make cloth hose for men and women (the fabric was cut on the bias for stretch) and for slave clothing in colonial America.

plains: Coarse woolen cloth, slightly napped, made in Wales and used for slaves' winter jackets, breeches, and petticoats. It was probably synonymous with negro cloth.

plain sewing: In the 18th and early 19th sources, this term referred to stitching seams on clothing and household linens, hemming, mending, and marking clothing and household fabrics. See marking stitch.

plain weave: The simplest interlacing of warp and weft threads. Each weft passes alternately over and under successive warps; the procedure is reversed for successive wefts. The warp and weft elements may be single or multiple threads.

pocket: A flat bag, usually made in pairs, and tied on under a woman's dress to hold everyday necessities.

pocketbook: A flat folding wallet used to hold papers or paper money.

pocket handkerchief: A square of fabric, usually linen, used for wiping the nose, face, or hands.

polonaise: A gown whose skirt is drawn up into three puffs over a petticoat.

plush: A fabric with a pile more than 1/8 inch long.

queen stitch: An embroidery stitch unit composed of four self-couched stitches that form a tiny diamond. Most surviving examples from the 17th and 18th centuries were worked in silk thread. Queen stitch can be found on historic samplers, pocketbooks, needle cases, and pin ball covers.

quilting: The decorative lines of stitches that join together the two or three layers of any quilted garment or furnishing accessory. The two stitches traditionally used were back and running. Among colonial quilted garments are petticoats, jackets, coifs and caps, stomachers, and waistcoats.

rail: A loose garment worn by both sexes for sleeping.

resist: In coloring fabric, resist is a preparation applied to those parts of the material that are not to be colored in order to prevent the dye from affecting them.

robe _à la Française:_   Also called the sack, or sacque, back, a gown with a bodice that was fitted to the body in front but in back the full fabric fell from wide loose pleats stitched only at the neck and shoulders.

robe _à l'Anglaise:_   A gown with a bodice that was fitted to the body in both the front and back. In back, the full fabric was made into tucks or pleats that were stitched down to the waistline and then released.

robing: Dress trimming of various kinds, whether flat, gathered or ruched, applied in bands down the front and around the neckline.

romal: A handkerchief imported from India and made either of cotton or silk.

round jacket: Short fitted jacket without tails or skirt worn by men.

ruff: Strips of lightweight linen gathered into cartridge pleats and attached to a neckband. They could be heavily starched to stand out from the neck or unstarched to fall onto the shoulders.

ruffle: A strip of lace or other fine material, gathered along one edge and used as an ornamental frill, especially at the wrist, neck, or breast. A deep ruffle on a skirt is often called a flounce.

running stitch: Small, evenly spaced stitches in a row. Running stitch is used in quilting and plain sewing.

russel: In the 18th century, a worsted damask fabric woven in solid colors, two colors, or brocaded. The fabrics were calendered to give a lustrous sheen. Russels were used in the American colonies for banyans, gowns, petticoats, and women's shoes.

safeguard: An outer skirt worn by women for riding horseback.

samare: A woman's loose jacket or overgown reaching between the hips and knees.

sarcenet: A thin silk used for petticoats, gowns, and accessories. Thicker than persian, it was produced as a twill as well as plain weave. Sarcenet was available in a variety of colors as well as checked, striped, and figured.

satin: A simple warp/weft float weave structure. The warp threads are ordinarily much finer than the weft and more numerous per square inch. Thus, they conceal the wefts and produce a smooth and apparently unbroken surface, which reflects light. This weave structure was especially suitable for silks, glazed worsteds, and some linens.

satin stitch: An embroidery stitch that imitates the reflective surface of satin weave. In working, there is as much thread on the reverse side as on the obverse side of the fabric.

seamstress: A woman whose occupation is plain sewing, as opposed, for example, to a mantua maker or embroiderer.

selvage: The self-finished edges of any fabric, created by the weft thread looping back at the end of each row in the weaving process.

serge: A smooth twilled cloth with worsted warp and woolen weft that was lighter and narrower than broadcloth. It was used for furnishings as well as clothing. In the 18th century serge was dyed rich, bright colors, embossed with patterns, or printed in colors with woodblocks.

shag: In the 18th century, a heavy worsted fabric with a long nap, related to duffel and blanket. Shag was used for coats, breeches, waistcoats, and petticoats.

shalloon: A lightweight twilled worsted fabric used in colonial America as a lining material.

shift: A woman's pullover undergarment, made of plain-weave linen and about knee-length whose shape changed somewhat in response to the changing silhouette of the outer garments. The shift was worn underneath a gown or two-piece suit. Female slaves who worked in the fields often wore only a shift and petticoat. In the 1600s and early 1700s a shift was called a smock. In the late 1800s, it was also called a chemise.

shirt: A man's pullover undergarment, made of plain-weave linen and about knee length. The fullness of the body and shape and length of the sleeves changed in response to changing sartorial styles.

short gown: A gown with a shortened skirt and cut looser than a long gown. The sleeves were sometimes cut in one with the bodice rather than being set it. A short gown was worn with a petticoat for working or informal attire.

silesia: A variety of inexpensive linens, unbleached or dyed, used primarily for household purposes and lining material. It was originally made in Silesia, near Hamburg. This cloth has given its name to the modern word *sleazy.*

silk: A fiber produced by the larvae of the silk moth, *Bombyx mandarina* (wild) or *Bombyx mori* (domesticated). Silk obtained from an unbroken cocoon is called filament. Silk from broken cocoons (from the inner portions of the cocoon) is called waste silk or fiber silk.

slop: 1. Any loose fitting outer garment, such as a loose jacket, tunic, or smock. 2. Slops (plural) are loose trousers or breeches such as those worn by sailors. A store in which these kinds of workman's clothing could be purchased was called a slop shop.

small clothes: In the later 18th century, synonymous with breeches.

small linen: In the 17th and early 18th centuries, a term for the fabric accessories—usually linen—that women wore at the neck and wrist on the head.

solitaire: An 18th-century term for a black ribbon worn around the neck or collar.

spangle: A small round thin piece of glittering metal—gilt brass or gilt silver—with a hole in the center to pass a thread through, used for the decoration of clothing and embroideries.

standing collar, or band: Worn in the early 17th century, a collar that spread out flat in a shape of fan around the head and held out by a shaped pasteboard or covered wire support.

stays, or pair of stays: A laced under-bodice (called a corset in the beginning of the late 18th century), stiffened by the insertion of strips of whale bone, metal, or wood and worn to give shape and support to the figure. Stays were made in two pieces and laced together.

stomacher: A roughly triangular ornamental covering for a woman's torso worn either under the lacing of the bodice or pinned or hooked to the edges of the bodice.

straw: Material from the stems or leaves of plants, processed into thin strips and plaited or woven to make hats. Popular types in the 18th century included Leghorn, Milan, and Sennit.

stroud: A fine broadcloth, usually dyed red, manufactured on the River Stroud in Gloucestershire. Strouds were used in the Indian fur and skin trade and were made to the Indians' exact specifications.

stuff: The general term for worsted cloth. Examples of stuff are calimanco, shalloon, moreen, and tammy.

sugar-loaf: A hat with a tall crown and a wide brim that could be worn flat, turned up in front, or turned down in both front and back; worn by both sexes.

swaddling: Cloth bands wrapped around a newborn to help straighten the limbs.

swanskin: A thick, soft woolen or mixed cotton and woolen fabric.

tabby: A plain weave silk, slightly heavier than lustring and stronger and thicker than taffeta. It was frequently calendered for a watered or waved finish.

taffeta: In Europe, this term referred to a plain weave silk whose weft threads were slightly thicker than the warp, creating a very fine ribbed effect. They were used for gowns as well as furnishings.

tailor: A man who made outer garments for men, and sometimes specialized garments for women, such as riding clothes and cloaks. In the 18th century, most women's clothing was made by the mantua maker.

tambour work: Embroidery designs executed in chain stitch, using a tiny hook instead of an embroidery needle. The technique was introduced to the West from India in about 1750. In France and Britain this embroidery was worked in a bent-wood frame, called a tambour because of its similarity to a round drum known as a *tambour* in French. The hook itself, made of steel, was known in English as well as French as a *crochet*.

tammy: A strong lightweight plain-weave worsted fabric with an open texture. It was often glazed. Available in a variety of colors, tammy was used for bed and window hangings, petticoats and gowns, coat linings, and sieves. Some late 18th- and early 19th-century samplers were worked on tammy.

ticking: A linen twill fabric used for work aprons, tents, mattresses, and pillow covers. Fine ticking was used to line garments. It was woven as a solid color or striped.

tiffany: 1. A thin silk used for gowns. Temporary accounts indicate that the fabric was often painted or embroidered, sometimes with spangles. Black tiffany was used for mourning clothing. 2. A fine open plain-weave linen produced in the 17th and 18th centuries that may have been used as an embroidery ground.

tippet: 1. A cape or short cloak, often with hanging ends. 2. A long narrow scarf or fur piece. In the South, the word is most often seen in women's inventories.

tissue: A thin, light, sheer fabric, sometimes woven with metal threads.

tobine: A warp-float pattern of small flowers or intermittent stripes and dots, often woven into silk, but sometimes worsted. The fabric may have additional weft effects such as float patterns or brocading.

trousers: Men's pants without a knee band. These were usually worn by workmen. The leg could be any length from knee to ankle. Trousers were sometimes worn over breeches to protect the latter.

tucker: Ruffle of lace or linen edging the neckline of a woman's gown or jacket.

twill: A weave that produces a diagonal effect in the finished cloth. The effect is created by a diagonal alignment of weft floats over groupings of warp threads. Each float is stepped up one warp thread in successive groupings.

velvet: A pile fabric made with an extra warp. Velvet pile could be cut or left uncut (looped) or a single fabric might exhibit both. Silk velvet was perhaps the most expensive fabric on the market, both because of the quantity of silk used and because of the technique. It was often used for men's suits.

waistcoat: 1. For women, a fitted bodice, often with sleeves, usually laced rather than buttoned up the front. It was worn with a petticoat to make a two-piece working suit. Also called a jacket. 2. Worn by middle- and upper-class men, the waistcoat was a vest (sleeved or sleeveless) worn as part of a three-piece suit. 3. The waistcoat of the working man was a short jacket, usually buttoned down the front.

warp: The threads secured on the loom before weaving.

watering: A technique used to finish plain-weave fabrics whose weft was heavier than the warp. The result was a watered or wavy effect on the surface of the fabric. See also embossing.

weft: The threads carried on bobbins/shuttles and passed across the warp or a section of the warp. In most 18th-century textiles the weft rather than the warp makes the pattern. Exceptions are damask, which relies on a contrast of light reflecting from warp and weft, and tobine, a purely warp effect. Wefts in patterned silks are thicker and glossier than the warp threads in the same material. The latter are more tightly twisted, for strength.

weld: A yellow dye derived from a flowering plant. When overprinted with indigo, the result was green. Weld was a fugitive, or nonfast, dye.

whalebone: Thin strips used for stiffening corsets, bonnets, or hooped skirts. Whalebone is not bone at all, but the flexible baleen from the mouths of baleen whales.

wood-block printing: The process of printing cloth by means of mordants, transferred to the cloth with carved wood blocks. When the printed cloth was dipped in a dye such as madder, a chemical reaction took place to fix the color to the cloth. A separate block was required for each color.

wool: Historically, refers to fibers obtained from sheep either by shearing or pulling the hair. Microscopically, wool fibers are characterized by scales. In the 17th and 18th centuries, there were two types of wool: woolen and worsted.

woolen: Cloth made of carded short-staple wool fibers. After weaving, the cloth was fulled or shrunk to make it denser and heavier. Broadcloth is an example of fine woolen manufacture. The fluffy fibers of carded wool were also suitable for knitting.

worsted: A smooth, tightly twisted yarn made of long-staple combed wool or the fabric made from worsted yarns. Often heavily glazed in the 18th and 19th centuries, it was used extensively in weaving for high-quality dress and furnishing fabrics (see embossing and stuff). The hard finish of worsted wool yarn made it suitable for embroidery (see crewel).

wrapper: In the 18th century, a woman's gown that wrapped closed across the front and was held by a sash.

Resource Guide: The Colonial Period

Print media and museum collections remain the best sources for accurate information about clothing and textiles in British colonial America.

PRINT RESOURCES

Arnold, Janet. 1977. *Patterns of Fashion I: Englishwomen's Dresses and Their Construction, c. 1660–1860*. New York: Drama Book.

Arnold, Janet. 1985. *Patterns of Fashion: The Cut and Construction of Clothes for Men and Women, c. 1560–1620*. New York: Drama Book.

Arnold, Janet. 1988. *Queen Elizabeth's Wardrobe Unlock'd*. Leeds: W. S. Maney and Son.

Arnold, Janet. 2008. *Patterns of Fashion 4: The Cut and Construction of Linen Shirts, Smocks, Neckwear, Headwear and Accessories for Men and Women, c. 1540–1660*. London: Macmillan.

Ashelford, Jane. 1996. *The Art of Dress: Clothes through History, 1500–1914*. London: The National Trust.

Baumgarten, Linda. 2002. *What Clothes Reveal: The Language of Clothing in Colonial and Federal America*. New Haven: Yale University Press.

Baumgarten, Linda, John Watson, and Florine Carr. 1999. *Costume Close-Up: Clothing Construction and Pattern, 1750–1790*. New York: Quite Specific Media Group.

Crill, Rosemary. 2008. *Chintz: Indian Textiles for the West*. London: V&A Publishing.

Cumming, Valerie. 1984. *A Visual History of Costume: The Seventeenth Century*. London: B. T. Batsford.

Gehret, 1976. Ellen J. *Rural Pennsylvania Clothing*. York, PA: George Shumway.

Gittinger, Mattiebelle. 1982. *Master Dyers to the World: Technique and Trade in Early Indian Dyed Cotton Textiles.* Washington, D.C.: The Textile Museum.

Hart, Avril and Susan North. 1998. *Historical Fashion in Detail: The Seventeenth and Eighteenth Centuries.* London: V&A Publications.

Hersh, Tandy and Charles Hersh. 1995. *Cloth and Costume, 1750–1800, Cumberland County, Pennsylvania.* Carlisle, PA: Cumberland County Historical Society.

Levey, Santina M. 1983. *Lace: A History.* Leeds: W.S. Maney and Son.

Maeder, Edward. 1983. *An Elegant Art: Fashion and Fantasy in the Eighteenth Century.* New York: Harry Abrams.

Mikhaila, Ninya and Jane Malcolm-Davies. 2006. *The Tudor Tailor: Reconstructing Sixteenth-Century Dress.* Hollywood, CA: Costume and Fashion Press.

Montgomery, Florence. 1970. *Printed Textiles: English and American Cottons and Linens, 1700–1850.* New York: Viking Press.

Montgomery, Florence. 1984. *Textiles in America, 1650–1870.* New York: W.W. Norton and Company.

Nylander, Jane C. 1993. *Our Own Snug Fireside: Images of the New England Home, 1760–1860.* New York: Alfred A. Knopf.

Pratt, Stephanie. 2005. *American Indians in British Art, 1700–1840.* Norman: University of Oklahoma.

Swan, Susan Burrows. 1995. *Plain and Fancy: American Women and Their Needlework, 1650–1850,* 2nd ed. Austin: Curious Works Press.

Styles, John. 2007. *The Dress of the People: Everyday Fashion in Eighteenth-Century England.* New Haven: Yale University Press.

MUSEUMS

The Charleston Museum
360 Meeting Street
Charleston, SC 29403
843-722-2996
www.charlestonmuseum.org

Founded in 1773, the Charleston Museum preserves and interprets the cultural heritage of Charleston and the Lowcountry and includes an historic textiles gallery with changing displays. Among the sartorial artifacts usually not on view are garments worn by men and women in colonial

South Carolina, which can be seen by contacting the curator of textiles for an appointment.

Chester County Historical Society
225 North High Street
West Chester, PA 19380
1-610-692-4800
www.chestercohistorical.org

Founded in 1893, this historical society has recently surveyed its clothing and textile holdings, which include 18th-century examples. Changing exhibitions highlight different aspects of the collections; permanent exhibitions may include rotating clothing and textile examples.

Connecticut Historical Society
1 Elizabeth Street
Hartford, CT 06105
1-860-236-5621
www.chs.org

The museum and library have many resources on colonial period clothing and textiles. The museum mounts regular changing exhibitions and some costume pieces are displayed in the permanent galleries.

Historic Deerfield
P.O. Box 321
84B Old Main Street
Deerfield, MA 01342
413-774-5581
www.historic-deerfield.org

While the historic area consists of 18th- and 19th-century houses on their original sites, the Flynt Center of Early New England Life, which showcases period objects, has a permanent textile gallery with rotating exhibitions. Costume and accessories from the colonial era are occasionally on display.

Colonial Williamsburg Foundation
P.O. Box 1776
Williamsburg, VA 23187-1776
1-757-229-1000
www.history.org

The collection is particularly strong in 18th-century fashion and accessories from Britain and Europe, with examples from colonial America. Some of these are periodically on public view in the DeWitt Wallace Decorative Arts Museum.

DAR Museum
1776 D Street
Washington, D.C. 20006
1-202-628-1776
www.dar.org/museum

Collections include clothing, accessories, and textiles imported into and made in Colonial America. Permanent display of period rooms with changing exhibitions. Virtual tours are on the website.

Metropolitan Museum of Art
1000 5th Avenue
New York, NY 10028
212-535-7710
www.metmuseum.org

The online database of the Costume Institute includes over one hundred colonial-period garments and accessories for both women and men, selected from the museum's comprehensive collection. Images of colonial paintings and sketches, jewelry, and needlework on the museum's website are also helpful for the study of colonial clothing.

Museum of Fine Arts Boston
465 Huntington Avenue
Boston, MA 02115
617-267-9300
www.mfa.org

Colonial-era garments from the museum are on view as part of special temporary exhibitions, but the museum's website offers images of period garments as well as portraits.

Nathalie P. and Alan M. Voorhees Archaearium
Preservation Virginia, Jamestown Rediscovery
1365 Colonial Parkway
Jamestown, VA 23081
757-229-4997

www.historicjamestowne.org

The Archaearium is the exhibition facility at Historic Jamestowne, the Jamestown archaeological project. Among the artifacts interpreted are the remains of armor, cloth seals, jewelry, and the small metal items used to secure or close garments, all associated with Jamestown's first settlers.

National Museum of American History
Smithsonian Institution
1400 Constitution Avenue NW
Washington, D.C. 20560
1-202-633-1000
www.americanhistory.si.edu

The NMAH displays some costume and textiles year round in its expansive galleries, but by far the larger portion of the collection is in storage. Some information is available in the online collections database, which is not comprehensive but is added to regularly.

National Museum of the American Indian (two locations):
Fourth Street & Independence Avenue, S.W.
Washington, D.C. 20560
202-633-6644
nmai.si.edu

Alexander Hamilton U.S. Custom House
One Bowling Green
New York, NY 10004
212-514-3700

A component of the Smithsonian Institution, the museum has one of the most extensive collections of Native American objects in the world, including ethnographic objects made by Native people living in North America during the British colonial period. Selections from the collection are on view at both locations and online.

National Society of the Colonial Dames of America
William Hickling Prescott House
55 Beacon Street
Boston, MA 02108
617-742-3190
www.nscda.org/ma/prescott_house

This is one of many properties owned around the country by various chapters of the NSCDA. The Federal-period house has a collection of colonial-period costume and accessories that may be seen by appointment.

New-York Historical Society
170 Central Park West
New York, NY 10024
1-212-595-5707
www.nyhistory.org

Collections are on view in temporary exhibitions and in the Luce Center. A searchable collections database is available on the website.

Pilgrim Hall Museum (The Pilgrim Society)
75 Court Street
Plymouth, MA 02360
1-508-746-1620
www.pilgrimhall.org

An excellent gallery display shows iconic paintings of the Pilgrims through time and explores the evolution of our understanding of how they actually dressed. The website also includes many virtual exhibitions exploring themes that relate to dress, status, and customs.

Index

Access to clothing, 69–73; economic factors, 72–73; effects of navigation laws on colonial textiles, 70; laws restricting manufactures, 70–71; legislation of encouragement by colonial governments, 71; local manufacture of wool and linen, 71–72; Navigation Acts, 70; Townsend Acts, 1767, 72

Account of Diseases Prevalent in America, 23–24

Act of Parliament, 1730, 28

African immigration and settlement, 12–16; black majority, 15; cash crops of tobacco, 13; market for slaves, 14–15; patterns of slaveholding, 15; ships, movement by, 12–13; West Indian plantations, 14

American Indian Children, 401–2; adopting Western dress, 401; infants dress, Native Americans, 401; Ninnimissinuok infants, 401; skin breechcloth, or breechclout for boys, 402

Animal (protein) fibers: wool and silk, 80–81; cultivating silkworms, 80–81; fiber's length, 80; wool, fiber's length, 80; worsted fibers, 80

Animal skins, 79, 104, 170, 249, 319; complements to clothing, 104; deer skins, 104; Hungary leather, 106; leather production, 104; Morocco leather, 106; oil- and alum-dressed skins, 105–6; tanner's work, 105; tannin, 105; trade in deer skins, late-17th- and 18th-century, 104–5

Bespoke clothing, 111–17, 205, 363; first recorded bespoke wardrobe, 112–13; mail orders, 111; Pringle's order, 113–15; quality of, 116; Washington, George, 115

Bleaching, 97–99, 138, 173; bleacher, 173; linens and cottons, 98; natural method, 98

Block-printing technique, 104

Boys: three to eleven years: accessories, 395; boys' wardrobes, 393; 18th century, 392–98; hairstyles, 395–96; main garments, 392–94; portraits, 390, 393–95; in 17th century, 390–91; undergarments, 394–95

Bribes of clothing and cloth, 56

British and European Settlement (1607–1714), 4–10; Chesapeake Region, 5–7; lowcountry, 10; middle colonies, 8–10; New England, 7–8

About the Authors

MADELYN SHAW is an independent curator and historian specializing in the exploration of American history and culture through textiles and dress. She has held curatorial and administrative positions at the New Bedford Whaling Museum, The RISD Museum, The Textile Museum (Washington, DC), and the Museum at FIT (New York). Other recent projects include a Civil War sesquicentennial book and traveling exhibition, *Homefront & Battlefield: Quilts & Context in the Civil War* (2012); "Silk in Georgia, 1732–1840: Sericulture to Status Symbol" in *Proceedings of the Third Biennial Henry D. Green Symposium* (2008); and "H. R. Mallinson & Company" in *American Silk: Entrepreneurs & Artifacts, 1830–1930* (2007), winner of the Millia Davenport Book Award.

KATHLEEN A. STAPLES is a textile historian and curator specializing in the cultural and technical histories of fabrics and embroidery in early modern England and colonial America. She holds an MA in anthropology from the University of Texas, Austin. She has served as curator and/or consultant for exhibitions at The Textile Museum (Washington, DC), Colonial Williamsburg, The Charleston Museum, New Bedford Whaling Museum, The Metropolitan Museum of Art, and the Museum of Southern Decorative Arts (MESDA). Recent scholarship includes "The Butler-Downer Coverlet: A Masterpiece of Embroidered Histories" in *Proceedings of the Fifth Biennial Henry D. Green Symposium* (forthcoming) and "Embroidered Furnishings: Questions of Production and Usage" in *English Embroidery from the Metropolitan Museum of Art, 1580–1700: 'Twixt Art and Nature* (2008).